'David Canter's 1977 *Psychology of Place* was one of the first comprehensive examinations of the psychological dimensions of places and place experiences. This new "re-thinking" of the original work is striking and valuable because Canter illustrates how a better understanding of place and placemaking can provide a physical bulwark against social media, virtual reality, community dissolution, and a smothering placelessness. After reviewing the wide-ranging interdisciplinary research on place, he examines placemaking via architecture, urban design, and landscape restoration. His in-depth discussion is an excellent distillation of the academic and professional progress that place researchers have made over the last fifty years. The book is a compelling contribution to the expanding work on place identity, place attachment, and placemaking. Canter makes a plea "in praise of actual, real presence and all it implies".'

David Seamon, *Professor Emeritus of Environment-Behavior and Place Studies, Department of Architecture, Kansas State University, Manhattan, Kansas, United States; Editor, Environmental & Architectural Phenomenology*

'Our thoughts, emotions, and social interactions are invariably influenced by the physical contexts in which they occur. What made David Canter's 1977 book so significant was its dual focus: while it aimed to identify the cognitive systems that enable individuals to interpret and navigate their surroundings, its deeper contribution lay in its exploration of the meaning of place—the idea that people and environments are inseparably connected. The unique value of environmental psychology lies in its effort to understand this dynamic relationship. This completely updated edition of the *Psychology of Place* incorporates five decades of research exploring how we understand different types of places from rooms and buildings through to the cities and landscapes, and considers the implications for both individuals and public policy. Today, we are better equipped than ever to understand why the psychology of place truly matters, and David's book continues to offer vital insights into this important field.'

David Uzzell, *Professor Emeritus of Environmental Psychology, University of Surrey, United Kingdom; Fellow of the British Psychological Society*

'In his latest book, David Canter reconstructs the "place", theme of his 1977 book, in a coverage now vastly broadened. He shows that while place operates as various parts of speech, principally as a noun, but also as a verb, it is most fruitfully considered as a powerful, all-embracing concept. This extraordinary book broadens our understanding of "place" much further than Canter´s earlier writings on the subject, transcending various disciplines and a lifetime's work. It represents many years of extensive, challenging research over more than half a century, drawing upon a vast realm of experience.'

David Stea, *Distinguished Professor, Universidad Nacional Autonoma de Mexico, and at University of Wisconsin, United States*

Rethinking the Psychology of Place

Rethinking the Psychology of Place presents a new approach to Professor David Canter's 1977 *Psychology of Place*. Providing a unified Theory of Place relevant to human transactions with buildings, cities, and nature, the book weaves together psychological, architectural, and social perspectives to demonstrate that place is a dynamic phenomenon emerging from embodied experience, memory, and social interactions. Central to this are 'place rules' and 'environmental roles' that mediate how individuals relate to and behave within locations, challenging deterministic notions that design directly causes place experiences.

Supported by over 160 illustrations, the book advances a nuanced, human-centred understanding of place as an evolving, dynamic nexus of action, meaning, and form by:

- Examining the home as an emotionally layered construct central to experiences of place.
- Positioning architecture as a filter of sensory input and a vehicle of symbolic meaning, shaped by cultural templates, architectural styles, and building types.
- Using techniques such as space syntax to illustrate how spatial arrangements facilitate human interactions at both the building and metropolitan scale.
- Critiquing modernist architecture's abstraction of meaning, highlighting streets as vital, participatory spaces, whilst considering how digital culture reshapes how we are present in these environments.
- Challenging dominant biocentric explanations for the restorative benefits of nature and related explorations of preferences for landscapes and place attachment, offering an alternative that emphasises human agency, culture, and context.

By integrating concepts such as place attachment, domocentricity, and environmental roles, this book will appeal to students and researchers in environmental psychology, architecture, landscape design, urban planning, and environmental sociology, as well as the general reader looking to understand our interactions with our surroundings. It is essential reading for anyone interested in the complex relationships between people and their built and natural environments.

David Canter, PhD (Psychology), PhD (Music Composition), Hon FBPs, FRSM, FAPA, is Emeritus Professor at the University of Liverpool, United Kingdom. He established the first graduate programme in Environmental Psychology at the University of Surrey, United Kingdom in 1973. He has published a number of related books, including *Psychology for Architects*, *Environmental Interaction*, *Architectural Psychology*, *Designing for Therapeutic Environments*, *Football in its Place*, and *Readings on the Psychology of Place*. The 1977 *Psychology of Place* continues to garner thousands of citations. He is also internationally acclaimed for his work in Criminal Psychology, creating the field of Investigative Psychology, the origin of which is described in his award-winning *Criminal Shadows*. The television series, combining his expertise in environmental psychology and investigative psychology, *Mapping Murder*, which he wrote and presented has been widely broadcast, giving rise to a popular book of the same name. In addition to his scholarly activities, radio and television broadcasts and popular blogs, he has consulted with major architectural firms and blue-chip companies and provided evidence in court and to government enquiries.

Rethinking the Psychology of Place

Being Here

David Canter

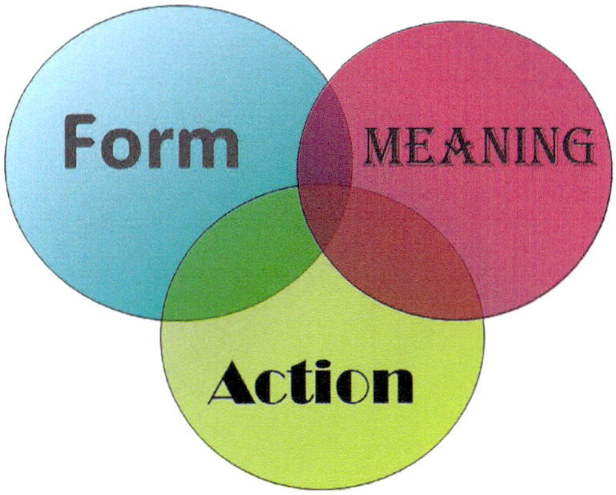

Routledge
Taylor & Francis Group
LONDON AND NEW YORK

Designed cover image: Olive Bancroft, "The Witness". Provided by Goldmark Gallery. Copyright Olive Bancroft 2024. Permission granted by Artist's Agent.

First published 2026
by Routledge
4 Park Square, Milton Park, Abingdon, Oxon OX14 4RN

and by Routledge
605 Third Avenue, New York, NY 10158

Routledge is an imprint of the Taylor & Francis Group, an informa business

British Library Cataloguing-in-Publication Data
A catalogue record for this book is available from the British Library

ISBN: 978-0-367-40712-4 (hbk)
ISBN: 978-0-367-40711-7 (pbk)
ISBN: 978-0-367-80865-5 (ebk)

DOI: 10.4324/9780367808655

Typeset in Sabon
by KnowledgeWorks Global Ltd.

For Sandra

Table of Contents

List of figures

Chapter 1

Chapter 2

Chapter 3

Chapter 7

Chapter 8

Chapter 9

Chapter 10

Chapter 11

Chapter 12

Chapter 13

Chapter 14

Chapter 19

Appendix A counterproductive approach

List of tables

Prologue

It is to be hoped that developing our understanding of the psychology of place will contribute to the driving force behind mankind's continued effort to understand itself and the universe, as well as the more pressing practical one of making places more fitting for those who live in them.

The Psychology of Place[1] *(1977). Last sentence.*

Rethinking the Psychology of Place seeks to enrich the understanding, experience, and use of places. My mission in writing it is to share my fascination with what the places we know, use, and hear of can reveal about what it means to be human. The many explorations of places throughout this book enhance insights into what it means to be present in the here and now, to be attached to places and identify with them.

For students, researchers, and practitioners accounts are provided of the psychological processes that give places meaning and facilitates their effective use. Comprehension of these productively contribute to the creation, modification, and use of places, generating more effective experiences and actions in place.

There is now a burgeoning scholarly literature studying many aspects of the meaning and implications of places. That is different from what was happening in the years before I wrote my 1977 book. There was little relevant research. Those academics involved in studies of places were typically lone individuals, scattered across different disciplines.

In addition to deciding what academic studies to include in this total revision, a further difficulty in writing, indeed completing, this total reworking of my 1977 *The Psychology of Place* was that every time I looked at a newspaper, listened to the radio, watched television, or explored any social media sources, I came across topics of relevance to the understanding and experience of places. New issues, or perspectives, features, or examples of, places, directly relevant to the experience of places, being in them and making sense of them, kept emerging. I had to decide which of these to draw in to develop further an understanding of the psychology of place. That was not an easy selection to make.

Beyond the scholarly and documentary explorations of place, there is widespread popular interest in many aspects of place experience. These include 'making a house into a home', exploring 'grand designs', discussing the charm of cities around the world, understanding why some people are determined to stay in places that continually suffer disasters and wars, or contrastingly, the assignment of outdoor experiences to increase mental health.

The mushrooming over the last half century of considerations of where we are and what that signifies has been supported by the manifold increase in the disciplines relevant to being here. Today, almost every area of academic research engages with the experience and significance of places. It is no longer the case, as it was in the early 1970s, that a few 'human geographers' or the then rare 'environmental psychologists', supported by rare historians, were the only ones who carried out studies of places, their significance and implications for people. Nowadays neuroscientists, and medical experts, anthropologists, archaeologists, sociologists, cognitive psychologists, and a host of different design professionals, as well as many others, publish increasingly innovative and sophisticated studies of human interactions with places.

These accounts, projects, and studies draw on many different conceptualisations, theories, perspective, and ideologies. Consequently, in settling down to revisit place psychology, I could see I would have to weave a path between many disciplines, whilst holding onto my central concern with psychological issues.

Writing this present consideration of places has been spurred on by the thousands of citations the original book has had and continues to garner. Very many of these citations reflect the power of the central proposal that places can be thought of as conceptual systems that emerge out of a mixture of physical form, meanings, and related actions. That tripartite model reflects much earlier explorations of places, especially in literature, as varied as A.A. Milne's 1926 account of Galleon's Lap in *Now We are Six*, or Albert Camus' description of Oran in his 1947 *The Plague*. Many academics and professionals around the world have found a tripartite model to be valuable, often creating their own versions. I've even met planners and architects who have told me the elaboration of such a model has contributed to how they have gone about creating their designs.

Beyond the academic and professional value of a completely updated, totally new version of *The Psychology of Place*, there have been significant changes in our relationships to places. Since I started Rethinking the psychology of place a number of books have been published that provide well-argued, serious concerns about the directions in which humanity is going. They sometimes remind me of the man standing on a street corner wearing a sandwich board declaring "The End Is Nigh!".

A recent widely read book is Jonathan Haidt's *The Anxious Generation*.[2] He argues that smartphones, social media, and overprotective parenting have led to a mental health crisis amongst young people. He campaigns for a return to real-world play and direct contact that actually engages, individually and socially with physical reality. This carries implications for how we understand what places are and how they are experienced. Another direct attack on how the experience of places is being denuded by involvement in technologies, notably 'smartphones', is the fascinating book by Christine Rosen, *The Extinction of Experience*.[3] She explores how digital technology erodes direct human experiences, replacing them with mediated interactions. She argues that weakening empathy and reduced real engagement with others, produced by reliance on screens, can be overridden by being in actual places with others.

Yet another essay that is decrying the destructive intrusiveness of screen-based technologies is Bruno Patino's *The Goldfish Civilization*.[4] Although the title of the book is somewhat insulting to goldfish, who have a rather longer attention span, memory, and capability for learning than the stereotype proposes,[5] the essence of the argument is that in a world where the screen has become a daily mirror, human attention is eroding. With notifications and social media everywhere, it is becoming increasingly difficult to maintain a sustained focus. The average attention span of modern humans is now estimated at… 9 seconds! Bruno Patino plunges us into the heart of this crisis of attention, as captivating as it is worrying.

The abandonment of direct engagement with actual places is being facilitated by many technological developments that are increasingly taken for granted. A visit to the shops is much more irksome than 'ordering online' with a delivery within a day or even a few hours. A journey to the cinema or theatre is replaced with screening on a domestic television. Working from home obviates the informal chat in the office or other workplace as well as the potential for informal interactions on daily commutes. The experience of the concert hall is replaced with a constant musical playlist delivered directly to the ears. Major sporting events are funded by payment for the broadcast rights, not by seats at the stadia.

Impresarios are fighting back against the withdrawal into digital, often just domestic, existence, with blockbuster films and striking stage performances. Musicians now earn what they can from elaborate, touring shows. The widespread flowering of 'festivals' that cover everything from early music to painting and trail running do bring people together in actual places. Football fans are notable for following their teams to distant locations in order to see the game in person. Yet, MySpace, which has been existing for over 20 years and is still striving to keep going, Fortnite, even social chess, and a myriad other online interactions, remove the significance of being somewhere specific. Virtual reality headsets and emerging glasses such as Apple Vision Pro that put you inside your computer, looking out on wherever you are, generate yet another leap into a cybernetic unreality.

The battle to keep the experience of being in real places, against their digital replacement is under threats beyond those currently concerning Haidt and Rosen. The emerging technologies have the possibility of going further and faster in removing us from direct contact with the here and now, than may be understood at the moment. This is shown in the disturbing account of *The Coming Wave*, by Mustafa Suleyman. As one of the founding developers of artificially intelligent systems, he sees those technologies combining with synthetic biology as full of potential for human good, as well, like all technologies, of being harnessed for evil.

Changing Relationships to Places

Understanding the importance of Places, as fundamental to being human, can provide a bulwark against all the impressive innovations that the 21st century has embraced. No robot, however much it pretends towards humanness, grew up within a place that supported its meaning and knowledge of self. Its identity and sense of self did not emerge out of opportunities for social interaction and achieving its self-determined purposes. For example, being in a hospital in contrast to an airport does not naturally evoke different emotions in an AI system, or algorithm, no matter how readily it could mimic those feelings by searching online accounts from human being. No synthetic systems have taken themselves off for a walk in the countryside to clear their head. Nor have they been disappointed by a theatre performance or let down because a friend failed to turn up for a meeting they had arranged.

In other words, the escalating developments in artificially intelligent systems, and the widespread existence people can have in the virtual reality of the world-wide-web, makes the power of place, for being human, increasingly important to understand. What is being emphasised here is that the rapidly evolving technologies that permeate the real and virtual world raise the growing question of what is, and will make us, different from, cyber bots, human-like robots and the fake creations that pretend to offer a vision of who we are. The answer is Places.

Each person is in, inhabits, gains meaning and significance from being in a Place. Algorithms, and all the unreal creatures they spawn, never have an existence that takes their identity or offers their relevance to a place. This is even true of simulated places. As Edward Relph pointed out[6] 20 years ago, "the most compelling virtual places might be regarded as continuously changing works of art that reflect the combined imaginations of those who are simultaneously participants and authors". They may ape actual locations. It would be difficult to make sense of and use virtual reality if it did not draw on some recognisable aspect of actual reality. But as they can never have the historical, social, and personal significance and layers of meaning that being in the world brings with it, they will always be works of imagination.

This difference from being in artificial spaces is causing it to be ever more important to understand the personal, social, and cultural significance of places. On the one hand, there are horrific, destructive wars over the control of places, on the other, many individuals are increasingly embedded into an existence in a virtual reality, where direct human interaction is becoming rare. Studying the importance of *being here*, in this place rather than another, the Psychology of Place, is a plea in praise of actual, real presence and all it implies. It explores how places gain their significance and what generates their meaning. This includes what underlies attachment to place, and how places can be enriching and health giving, or destructive.

To understand what is being lost by this move away from being present requires an exploration of our relationship with Places. The heads-down focus on our mobile devices removes us from the direct experience of where we are. With that, some of the significance of who we are is lost. The developers of Zoom and other video communication applications were aware of this when they included the option of blurring the background or even changing it totally. This removes the physical, environmental context of people who are engaged with discussions with others. A speaker is put into a limbo that removes the influence of the place where they are. But how do places take on that significance? What drives their meaning? How does this vary from the desk at which I am writing to the notion of a city or a landscape? Those are the questions that this book explores.

Rethinking the ***Psychology*** *of Place*

I recognise a requirement to defend the use of 'Psychology' in the title of my book. What may now be regarded as the essence of contemporary psychology is an insistence that for psychology to be a science it must be based on 'objective' measurements, especially those derived from biomedical recordings. I take a stance against that which raises questions about what my approach to Psychology is.

The fact is that the study of Place with all its nuances is now dominated by geographers and is frequently explored by sociologists, anthropologists, and archaeologists. It is also often a consideration for those in design and planning disciplines, as well as the arts, especially literature. I draw on scholarship from all of these areas in this book. My claim to the focus being Psychology is grounded in a very broad definition of that discipline, namely, the study of personal thoughts, feelings, and actions. This involves ignoring the silos which academic disciplines set up to artificially distinguish themselves from each other.

The recognition of the value of this academic miscegenation has made the current book very different from my 1977 *Psychology of Place*. Little attention is paid to the cognitive processes that are at the heart of that book. Instead, broader themes of the psychological nature of places and their significance in our experiences of the world are the emphasis. It concentrates on the experiences and actions of being in places. This requires a focus at times on the physical forms of places and how they contribute to the experience of them. Another emphasis is on the meanings assigned to places and how they develop their significance. Underlying both these are emerging and developing actions that characterise places. The different roles of people involved in those actions carry consequences for how places are used and understood. Those consequences are often reflected in explicit or implicit rules of place.

My 1977 book deliberately focused on urban settings. In fact, it was my awareness that my earlier focus on buildings – architectural psychology – had limited my exploration of places that led me to write a book requiring me to learn about larger scale environments. Rethinking this topic, I have taken the opportunity to broaden out my investigation of places. Starting with a careful examination of what Places are, moving on to examining the Home as an archetypal place, the basis is created for considering building, cities, and landscape. Unintentionally, that has made this a large book. I have therefore not shied away from repeating various themes and ideas in anticipation that some readers will dip into the book rather than steadily work through it. Generally, chapters should make sense on their own. Where cross-reference to other chapters is helpful that is indicated. Summaries and conclusions to chapters are also there to help the reader cope with the possibly daunting scale of this document.

References and endnotes

1 Canter, D. (1977) *The Psychology of Place*. Available on Kindle and as an Audiobook.
2 Haidt, J. (2024). *The anxious generation: How the great rewiring of childhood is causing an epidemic of mental illness*, Penguin.
3 Rosen, C. (2024) *The extinction of experience: Reclaiming our humanity in a digital world*, London: Bodley Head.
4 Patino, B. (2019) *The goldfish civilization*, Grasset.
5 Saito, K. & Watanabe, S. (2005) Experimental analysis of spatial learning in goldfish. *The Psychological Record*, 55, 647–662.
6 Relph, E. (2007) Spirit of place and sense of place in virtual realities. *Techne: Research in Philosophy & Technology*, 10(3), 24.

The book ahead

There are two organising principles to the following chapters. One is based on the central concepts and processes for understanding places. These include how ideas of home are central to place meanings, as well as mental representations of places and rules of place. In addition, how physical form takes on meaning, and the processes of place attachment. Attitudes to the environment and the mechanisms through which nature is beneficial are a further strand. A concluding chapter considers how new forms of places are emerging that happily reflect psychological processes. They illustrate the implications the psychology of place has for creating places. The inertia that characterises dealing with climate change is shown to be rooted in how the meaning of places is embedded in identity and place rules.

The second organising principle is the consideration of place psychology at different scales of places. The 1977 *Psychology of Place* focused on the large-scale environment, especially the urban environment. However, in the ensuing years it has become apparent that place psychology is relevant at every scale. An Introductory section explores the concept of Place. This is followed by consideration of how an understanding of the psychology of place is derived. The book then moves from understanding the body as a place and the implications that has for the home. Broader aspects of architecture are discussed and then the larger scale urban environment and onto the natural environment.

Introduction

The Introductory two chapters describe what is meant by Place and how Places are created through human endeavour. This establishes the concepts at the heart of the Psychology of Place. Places are not static; they emerge through use—whether by actions, perceptions, thoughts, or memories—and are inherently tied to human presence and embodiment. This presence, actual or imagined, implies relationships with others. Social interaction, either direct or implied, bring places to life, embedding within them identity and meaning. Thus, concepts like *social identity* and *self-categorisation* become relevant, with behaviour and role expectations shaping and being shaped by the place itself. This framework challenges the idea of *architectural determinism*—that buildings directly influence behaviour. Human agency and social processes mediate such effects, except under extreme physical conditions. Similarly, there is a critique of the idea of 'placelessness'. Even mundane locations hold distinct personal, social, and cultural meaning.

Section I: Exploring Places

The first section of the book reviews ways of exploring the psychologies of place. The three chapters in this section derived from the view that psychology as a systematic, many would claim, scientific, discipline, has required the development of a great number and variety of methods for exploring the interactions people have with places. These are fruitfully expanded by those which come from other research traditions, or from none. These latter – writers, poets, and painters – are usually dismissed by those who give pride of place to measurements. That is a mistake. It ignores the array of modes of interacting with and experiencing places. They open up a variety of ways of getting access to place-related feelings and activities. The strengths and weaknesses that different methods have are also explored.

Section II: Buildings

The second section discusses how architecture encapsulates meanings and place significance. As an illustration of this, the notion of *Home* is particularly rich, evoking emotional warmth and psychological comfort. Homes are made meaningful by the significance attached to objects and furniture, creating a mosaic of interconnected spaces. This fragmented, yet unified, concept of home offers insights into extreme conditions such as imprisonment, where the lack of such place assemblages leads to degradation and dehumanisation.

Similarly, for the homeless, the creation of makeshift homes reveals a powerful drive for belonging and identity. The improvised spaces people without buildings to live in mirror the personhood and resilience of their inhabitants, emphasising how place and identity are inseparable—even on the street.

Architectural design plays a key role in shaping Places. The process involves reconciling functional and aesthetic demands. Through professional education, planners, designers, and architects develop cognitive tools or heuristics, such as drawing upon architectural styles and building types, which provide templates for solving complex design problems. Architectural styles offer aesthetic consistency, whilst building types provide expectations about form and function. These types influence the layout and management of buildings, affecting how places are used and experienced.

Architecture is shown to serve three major functions: filtering experiences through form, facilitating activities, and symbolising meaning. These functions align with the Psychology of Place triad of form, action, and meaning. Additionally, *space syntax* is introduced as a method to mathematically model how spatial layouts influence human interactions. The ease or difficulty of movement between spaces, and the complex mixture of such networks of access shapes social contact, with profound implications for how Places are experienced and understood.

Section III: The City

At the urban level, the third section, reflects on how people make sense of the complexity of the city. That reveals the psychological limits on dealing with the urban environment. Out of this emerges forms of place attachment. That can be a powerful process that may be influenced by active engagement with places in the city, notably city streets.

Urban streets exemplify how physical forms and human activity co-create place meaning. This happens in what is fruitfully referred to as the *city at eye level.* Streets serve as the intersection of personal and public life, and their vitality depends on active social engagement. Streets document place meanings and local culture through art, names, and shared experiences. They host 'Third Places'—social venues distinct from home and work. However, streets face challenges from online shopping, malls, and digital communication, which reduce their social and commercial relevance. Revitalising them involves reimagining their roles beyond retail outlets, towards diverse, socially rich spaces.

People form mental maps of places based on their interactions, revealing personal and functional understandings of space. The concept of *domocentricity*—anchoring spatial understanding around home—illustrates how mental representations shape actions and experiences. These insights extend into practical domains like criminal geographical profiling and influence architectural design by considering role- and action-based building types.

Although *place attachment* has received growing attention, much research remains superficial, focusing on geographic rather than psychological mechanisms. Attachment is more effectively considered as an aspect of place *involvement*, which also includes identity, satisfaction, and commitment. This broader framework allows for a deeper understanding of how people relate to places emotionally and socially.

Section IV: Landscape

Once explorations go beyond the built environment to consider what is (often somewhat inappropriately) regarded as the 'natural' environment, the fourth section unpacks the many psychological processes that take on particular salience in the great outdoors. The roles people take in relation to the outdoors proves to be of profound importance. It lays the foundation for examining the power being in the landscape has for human well-being.

Natural landscapes are unique types of Place, important in the context of climate change. People relate to nature either as part of it (dwelling within) or as a resource (using it). These perspectives are a fundamental aspect of environmental attitudes. The benefits of nature—especially psychological restoration—are acknowledged, but explanations often suffer from over-reliance on simplistic evolutionary narratives.

Research demonstrates that well-being benefits of 'being in nature' vary depending on context, setting, and activity. Preferences for certain landscapes are shaped by roles and expectations rather than universal aesthetics. This complexity calls for a nuanced model of nature's restorative qualities grounded in the Psychology of Place.

Conclusions

Bringing an understanding of the types of place and the underlying psychological processes together is a central task for those seeking to shape our environments: designers, architects, planners and their financiers, and controlling authorities and their associates. However, although they are a necessary component for dealing with the environmental tasks the world faces, they are not sufficient to ensure that we do not leave it too late. For that we have to understand what it means to be here.

Why the Psychology of Place Matters

An understanding of the meaning of Place and the processes that create its significance can sometimes seem very abstract and removed from day-to-day matters. I challenge that perspective throughout this book. At its most elementary level, a vision of locations as preordained determinants of human actions and feelings regards people as malleable assets to be shaped to the whims of those who control the physical features of those locations. Therefore, a more nuanced understanding of how people make Places and Places make people gives rise to a more democratised and, indeed, civilised approach to the creation, use, and management of Places.

One consequence of understanding the nature of Place is the realisation that some schools of architecture are focused on the form of buildings and others on Place making. The psychology of Place explored in this book makes clear that these two aspects can never be separated, but nonetheless those who shape our surroundings may well seek to emphasise one aspect or the other.

These different emphases are not just stylistic practises. They carry implications for human well-being. Mental and physical health do derive from the experience of Places. Whether it be the curious phenomenon of 'sick building syndrome' or the increasing recognition of the benefits of being in natural settings, the understanding of the psychology of Place has a value far beyond its academic interest.

The most pressing consequence of understanding Places is for climate change and environmental degradation. Despite the massive amount of information which makes clear that human activity is destroying the Place we call Earth, the response to this is remarkably slow. That response parallels a recent railway accident in which it emerged that many trains had been, as matter of course, passing signals set at danger. It was the habitual activity, socially supported, which created the conditions for an accident waiting to happen. Similarly, it is the manifold ways in which our experience of Places is integrated with who we are, shaping our actions, which in turn change the nature of those Places. This is the complex process that is explored throughout this book, showing there will be no overarching response to climate change until we change who we think we are.

Reductionism

The spurious biophilia, and related biological explanations for complex human phenomena is part of a set of popular, reductionist theories that bedevil environmental psychology. They crop up in a number of chapters. Consequently, rather than interfering with the flow of the text in these chapters, to deal with criticism of them in detail, an appendix to the book provides a more detailed considerations of the weaknesses and dangers in these hypotheses and the methodologies they have spawned.

Distinguishing Place from place

As reviewed in Chapter 1, the term 'place' has a mixture of meanings. It can be a complex aspect of experience, which is what the psychology of Place deals with. Or it can mean just a location. For clarity, hopefully, I capitalise the word for the former meanings of Place but may use place when I am only referring to a location.

A Note on Citations

One huge difference from half a century ago, when *The Psychology of Place* was published, to writing a book today, is that so much of published academic and general literature is widely available online. Search engines of many sorts, including burgeoning artificially intelligent ways of seeking information, make finding original sources relatively easy. These also give access to material that may not have been formally published or exists in very limited documents. I have taken full advantage of this and deliberately cited sources whenever possible. This is a feature that makes this book itself a reference source for those wishing to engage with the wonderful world of studies and reports about Places.

One final point to mention. It surprises me how few books on the environment, especially Place, have many, or any, pictures in them. Like having an orchestra without a wind section. The ready availability of photographs makes this absence even more difficult to understand. I have therefore used the opportunity to provide many pictures. These have been selected to act not only as illustrations for the text but also as commentaries in their own right.

I have also provided a select bibliography of books on Place, most of which have been published this century.

Introduction

Being Here

Walking between the then and now,
Where shadows hide in trees and breath in stone.
Here every echo wears a furrowed brow,
A voice half-heard, a name long gone.
The air is rich with things unsaid, unsought,
Whispering about scarcely hidden bliss.
Briefly grasped like the passing thought
Of a half-remembered kiss.
The orchard through once we used to run
Out into open fields, now sadly overgrown.
The joy of seeking together for the sun.
A pulse that moves the earth that's never done.
To be is not to use, but to remain.
A silence shaped by pain and shaped again.

David Canter
August 2025

DOI: 10.4324/9780367808655-1

CHAPTER 1

What is a Place?

Being here?

Places exist independently of our being there, yet we become a part of them through our presence. Experiencing a Place means being engaged in that specific moment. Our perceptions, feelings, and actions shape how we define and connect with a Place, making us integral to its essence.

Some years ago, I visited Berlin. Like most tourists, I went with some friends to see the Memorial to the Murdered Jews of Europe near to the Reichstag and the Brandenburg Gate (Figure 1.1). The vast monument, designed by architect Peter Eisenman and engineer Buro Happold, is a remarkably simple, almost understated, set of grey, rectangular concrete slabs. They are of different heights from 20 centimetres to over 4 metres, arranged on a rectangular grid, covering 19,000 square metres. I have never found any artwork or monument so emotionally intense. There is an information centre to one side of the monument with a record of the murder of millions of Jews. But I had to leave my friends to visit that. All I could do was to sit on one of the low slabs and weep.

My father's immediate family had been murdered by the Nazis. Consequently, I never knew my father's sister or his parents. This meant I was brought up with very mixed feelings about the Germans and a sensitivity to anything to do with the Holocaust. I therefore set out to visit this memorial with mild anticipation. But when I was there, I found it difficult to understand why such a simple expansive area moved me so much. But as my tears eased, I began to appreciate that Place was so affecting because of the many layers of meaning and emotion it enshrined.

One aspect of its power was simply that it was there. That a country could so embrace the horrors of its history to build a major monument, covering such a large area, was heart-rending. To devote so much space to it in such a significant location, near the core of its government and country, added further to its emotional significance. Then there is the subtle imagery of the grey slabs. Was this an empty town? An array of gravestones? Coffins perhaps (denied holocaust victims)? A further power of the monument came from the way the aisles within slowly undulate. This means that at some points

DOI: 10.4324/9780367808655-2

Figure 1.1 Memorial to the murdered Jews of Europe, Berlin

the slabs are below the height of a person, at others way above. The consequence of this is that when children happily run along the paths within the monument, they disappear out of view. What could be a more apt reminder of how many people were never seen again because of the atrocities of the Nazi death camps?

Having written these paragraphs, about such a personal experience, I later came across references to it in the opening chapters of a number of books about Place.[1] As is so often the case, what seems to be profoundly personal resonates with many others. That is a salutary reminder that apparently idiosyncratic experiences of Places often capture moods, feelings, and meanings that transcend any one individual. Places are always both profoundly personal and at the same time richly social and cultural. With that come political, economic, and ideological implications.

The power of the Berlin monument reveals the richness of what Places can be. The poignant response everyone has to it illustrates the way even the simplest lumps of concrete carry history, meaning, culture, associations, and a host of psychological implications. There is a wonderful word used in the study of manuscripts *palimpsest.* That describes a document on which one text has been written over an earlier text without completely obscuring the earlier writing. Places are like that. They are created by layers of meaning and implications.

There is one other crucial feature of the Memorial to the Murdered Jews of Europe. The qualities I've described. The sense I've made of it. These are all an aspect of my experience of being there. Others will engage with it in different ways. As I mentioned my (non-Jewish) friends, impressed with the memorial as they were, were not as moved as I was. They were able to sombrely visit the information centre on its edge. For them it was a rather different Place to what it was for me. Furthermore, although I've had many other fascinating experiences in Berlin, that monument is now an integral part of my concept and understanding of Berlin as a Place, and indeed of Germany, and its people as a whole.

The Place conundrum

Here, then, is the conundrum that is the notion of a Place. Is it a physical location? The 2 hectares in central Berlin, which has a specified material existence. Is it a set of associations and meanings, with their emotional connotations, and cultural implications? Or is it a way of engaging with an area of activity? A Place for repose and contemplation, excitement, or study? A Place is always all of these. But is it also important to recognise it as an aspect of existence, such that each Place is unique to the person who is part of it? Is my Memorial Place being unique to me? Or is it a socio-physical entity that exists independently of any given person? The Place that got planning permission. These are the questions explored throughout this book.

It is important to emphasise that such questions are not just of academic interest. They are not only part of the burgeoning philosophical discussions that seem to be overtaking cultural geography, which are so apparent in the writings of authorities such as Casey,[2] Malpas,[3] Seamon,[4] and many others. They carry implications for how Places are created, used, and managed. This includes consideration of the purposes of Places that underlie how they are planned and developed, modified, and produced. At the heart of this is the point made by Karl Marx[5]:

> ...A bee puts to shame many an architect in the construction of her cells. But what distinguishes the worst architect from the best of bees is this, that the architect raises his structure in imagination before he erects it in reality. At the end of any labour-process we get the result that already existed in the imagination of the labourer at its commencement.
>
> *(p. 177)*

A crucial implication of this is that any Place has an existence independently of its physical form. It exists in the 'imagination'. That existence is an integral part of what it is.

The multifaceted nature of Places is interestingly captured when an attempt is made to translate the word into other languages. In Hebrew the usual translation is מקום (pronounced *makom*). But that takes on many nuances. It is used as one of the names of God as המקום (literally 'The Place'; the omnipresent). In Yiddish *makum* has taken on the association with 'safe haven'.

In Japanese there are two words, which make a clear distinction between location and Place, but both are often translated as Place. One is 所 (*tokoro*) which is close in meaning to the abstract idea of a position, spot, or site. The other is 場所 (pronounced *basho*, the same ideogram with the same meaning in Mandarin is pronounced chang suo). *Basho* has the more specific meaning of a physical location or a building. What is intriguing is that if you look closely at the ideograms, you can see that the second half of basho is the same character as for tokoro, the 所. (I won't bore you with an explanation of why and how Japanese ideograms can be pronounced in all sorts of different ways.) In other words, to make the general idea of a particular presence, tokoro, into a specific location basho, you need to add something to it. It needs to be nailed down. The combination of the ideograms makes clear that locations are a limited aspect of the much broader notion of a Place.

A range of other languages could be explored, but what typically arises is the problem of finding a word that goes beyond the idea of a location. This is because 'Place' has such a rich set of meanings in English, at least 24 from one dictionary I consulted. These many meanings have come a long way from the word's origins in the Ancient Greek πλατεία (*plateia*) meaning a 'broad way' but taking on the meaning in modern times of a Town Square, as in the Italian *piazza*. The rich associations and connotations of 'Place' are an elaboration of ways of experiencing being here. Existing in any particular socio-physical context.

Being in a Place is part of its significance. This implies that what happens there helps to define the Place and the experience. My sitting, weeping, in the Holocaust memorial, the children running through it, as well as my friends wandering off to the information centre, help to give the Place its layers of meaning and emotional power. If the memorial were hijacked, say, by a Nazi protest, it would become a very different Place. Another more benign example is when the streets of major cities are taken over by thousands of marathon runners. Those thoroughfares, thronged with crowds cheering on the determined joggers, become quite different Places from those of other days, when the streets are thick with cars and buses, and pedestrians take their life in their hands when they attempt to cross a road. Or the square in a small town (Figure 1.2) that is turned into a Place for communal singing at Christmas time.

Constructive seeing

The recognition that Places become different entities at different points in time assumes that we are making some sense of them. Constructing an understanding of what they are. Despite the sensation that no thought is needed to distinguish between the two Places in Figure 1.2 it is not a passive process. It is an active construction of what we are seeing. The idea that perception is constructed, informed by memory and related thoughts, could be regarded as one of the major insights, it could even be called a discovery, of modern psychology. The recognition that perception is a production, not just a reception, of stimuli laid the foundation for modern cognitive psychology.

The most readily identifiable starting point, heralding a new way of thinking about human interactions with the world grew out of studies of memory. The awareness that memory itself is not just an inert recording of experience can be traced to the book *Remembering,* published in 1932 by Frederick Bartlett.[6] Originally Bartlett was interested in perception as conventionally studied in his day, by for example, exploring optical illusions. He found that "an examination of normal perceptual process leads

Figure 1.2 St. Peter's Square Ruthin as two different Places

directly and inevitably to an investigation of related mental processes and, in particular, to a study of imagery and of recall".

To carry out these investigations he took the party game of pass the message and developed it into a fascinating scientific strategy. He would show someone a drawing, such as a simplified set of shapes that may resemble facial features, or tell them a story. This person would then be asked to reproduce it from memory. The reproduction would then be shown to a third person who would also be asked to reproduce it from memory, and so on over ten or more people. The resulting series of drawing, which I've repeated many times with students, gives rise to a finding common in Bartlett's investigations with both visual and verbal material:

> Whenever material visually presented purports to be representative of some common object, but contains certain features which are unfamiliar in the community to which the material is introduced, these features invariably suffer transformation in the direction of the familiar ... The whole series shows how speedily a pictorial representation may change all of its leading characteristics in the direction of some schematic form already current in the group of subjects who attempt its reproduction.
>
> *(Bartlett, 1932, pp. 175–176)*

Bartlett's central discovery was that there are internal representations which each individual draws upon, as a reference, when attempting to reconstruct a picture, or retell a story. It is this generally accepted set of expectations which enables people to produce a drawing and also contributes to its distortions.

> All the characteristics of the original which have any peculiarity are lost. A face is tilted upwards immediately, becomes oval and then round, acquires eyes, a nose and a mouth all of conventional form.

The explanation which Bartlett gave for these distortions was closely derived from the work of Sir Henry Head. As a neurologist, Head was concerned with how we are able to judge changes in bodily posture and movement in order to carry out effective motor actions. How we know where our limbs are. To explain our abilities Head proposed that we must carry in our brains a model of our body which is being continuously modified on the basis of information received about each action. The analogy was given of a taxi meter which accumulates the distance travelled and presents it to us "already transformed into shillings and pence" (as he said in the early part of the 20th century, before decimalisation).

From the foundations of these studies, and resulting theory of human agency, a century ago a blossoming of cognitive research has developed. This is based on studies of how we unconsciously fill in and elaborate what we think we see, hear, or remember. We give meaning even to the most ambiguous stimuli and experience. The liveliness of this aspect of psychology has been recently graced with a popular account[7] of the research, showing how many aspects of the understanding of psychology benefit from the awareness of this constructive process.

Acknowledging that Places are such mental constructions, filling in details based on previous experiences, understanding what is their nature, what is possible there, and what the experience of being there is likely to be, is the essence of The Psychology of Place.

A model of Place

In my 1977 book, as a way of trying to capture the fleeting, multiparous, luxuriant aspects of what creates a Place in our minds I offered a rather neat, but somewhat abstract Venn diagram (Figure 1.3). I suspect its simplicity and ambiguity has allowed

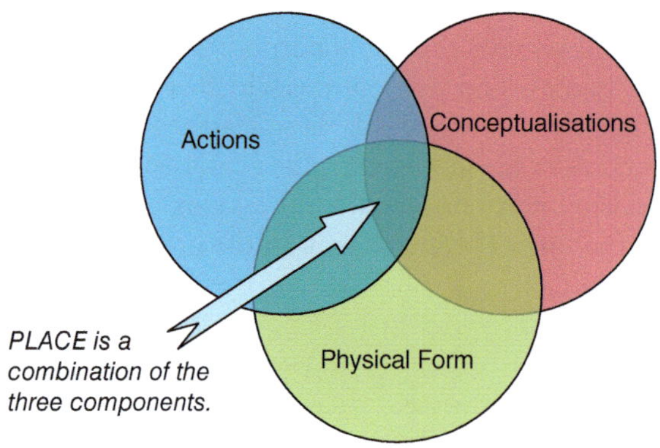

Figure 1.3 A model of Place

many people, in the subsequent 40 plus years, to make of it what they will, leading to it being cited thousands of times since. With at least 100 examples of it and variants of it in Google images (not counting the pictures of Mitsubishi trucks that for some reason they seem to have named 'Canter').

The challenge of this model is to develop a clear account of what the components actually are. Even more challenging is to explore how they relate to each other and together actually combine to create Places. These challenges are what I undertake in *Revisiting the Psychology of Place.*

Many explorations of the meaning of Place often develop this simple model. For example, it was helpful to read David Seamon's[8] considerations. He is a declared phenomenologist, focusing on subjective experiences of Places. Drawing on Bennett's[9] 'systematics', he identified "Three Impulses of Place". These provide a much richer account of Place constituents than my simple overlapping circles. Crucially, Seamon emphasises both the interconnectedness of these components and also their being part of a process that continually gives rise to the nature of any Place.

He elaborates the idea of the physical form of a Place, calling it the *Environmental Ensemble.* This provides the "material foundation for Place events, transactions, experiences and meanings". Every aspect of the physical components of the setting is included, natural and human-created, plants and animals, weather, and vista.

The feature of Places that I simply called, 'actions' are elaborated by Seamon to emphasise that "people actively manipulate and fabricate their worlds". They do this both conceptually, through their attitudes, perceptions, and understandings, as well as through their actions, habits, and routines. The creation of a Place by what people are able to do in any given location or may be unable or not allowed to do, is central to my arguments in this book.

Another important development of the model of Place, which Seamon provides, is the notion of the "character or presence" of a Place. This covers those emergent aspects of the relationships between the actions and the forms of a Place which give it its atmosphere, meaning, mood, and character. From a psychological perspective this aspect of a Place is an integral part of how people there relate to it and make sense of it, thereby creating its essence.

Kelly's personal constructs

A profound influence on regarding aspects of Places as a creation of how they are conceptualised, the meanings and associations that give them significance, are the writings of George Kelly, notably his *Psychology of Personal Constructs.*[10] Kelly developed the insights from cognitive psychology, which were foreshadowed in the research of Head and Bartlett, by applying them to personality theory. The essence of Kelly's theory of personality is that we naturally develop hypotheses about people and features of the world. These help us to navigate and make sense of our experiences. Such hypotheses are constructions built around personal ways of thinking about the world, what Kelly calls 'constructs'. A typical construct about people, for example may be 'friendly' or 'unfriendly', 'warm or cold', and so on.

The crucial aspect of constructs in Kelly's theory is that they relate to each other. He had been an engineer, so he was comfortable with the idea that constructs form a structure. It is the qualities and components of this structure that characterise an individual's personality. Kelly was providing a foundation for carrying out psychotherapy. He therefore focused on structures of constructs that relate to significant people in the life of a patient undergoing. Nonetheless, his model of human cognitions is applicable to any other entities with which a person may engage. It is not surprising therefore that it has been embraced, for example, by consumer researchers[11] studying products, as well as having a long history in psychological studies of architecture.[12]

What I take from Kelly's theory is that Places are in part construct systems, just as relevant people are in our life. They are a combined set of thought processes about being in Places. The constructs are as varied as the people who hold them. But those people live within a society and culture that shares constructs and the systems that give them structure. In part this sharing is brought about by recognition of what is possible where, physically, socially, legally, or culturally.

Rules of Place

The understanding of what is possible in a Place is one aspect that we will return to often. It relates to the question of how Places are recognised and what maintains them. If the actions that occur in a location are a crucial part of the existence of that Place, then there must be a process that manages those actions, usually to keep them appropriate to the conceptualisations and meanings of that Place.. I have rather loosely called these the 'rules of Place' I hasten to be clear that these are not fixed, strict rules like those in a game of football or canasta. They are better thought of as a rubric, or framework of the actions that are expected, tolerated, or encouraged in any given location. As we shall see, they are nonetheless quite robust and, although typically implicit, the great majority of people who experience Places follow them without question.

These rules are reflected in what David Seamon[13] calls a *Place-ballet* (which as we see in more detail in Chapter 13 derives from Jane Jacobs'[14] *street-ballet*. She, in turn, took the idea from the seminal work of Whyte[15]). Seamon characterises these as:

> an interaction of individual bodily routines rooted in a specific environment that often becomes an important Place of interpersonal and communal exchange, meaning and attachment.

Seamon's metaphor of a dance implies a recognisable pattern of activity, which is constrained by its physical and temporal location. It emphasises the role of actions in contributing to what Places are.The significance of Places in giving meaning to actions. These 'actions' also incorporate intentions. A person walking may be regarded as a 'behaviour', going to the shops is an 'action'. Place-ballets are the routine actions that enliven the experience of a Place. But they require an understanding of what is likely, or acceptable, where. These understandings are the rules that give shape to the meaning of a Place.

Behaviour settings

A helpful insight into the rules of Place is the work of Roger Barker and his colleagues.[16] He called his work 'ecological psychology', although rather confusingly other researchers,[17] notably in the area of visual perception, have appropriated this term. For Barker, the challenge was to understand what actual experiences shaped children's behaviour. He came out of the Skinnerian behaviourist tradition, in which what people do is seen as being shaped by the rewards and punishments ('reinforcements') they experience. Barker wished to establish what exactly were children's experiences. He went about determining this by the most rigorous and painstaking examination of the activities in a very small town in Kansas, Oskaloosa, which he called Midwest in his publications.

What Barker realised is that he had to specify the different settings in which people participated. He therefore identified what he called 'behaviour settings'. These were regular patterns of activity that had a distinct time and location. A formula was developed to specify the components that would add up to a value that enable a behaviour setting to be identified. Thus, a school band practice would be a behaviour setting, but a street corner where people sometimes stopped for a chat would not. The limitations of this rigid approach have meant that it now seems to be mainly of historical interest. However, the central concept that there exist location-specific forms of human actions is a rich one. Like Place-ballet, behaviour settings enrich our understanding of the implicit and explicit guidelines that shape what Places are – the rules of Place.

Places are not to be confused with behaviour settings. They are essentially social phenomena that reflect what Barker called 'standing patterns of behaviour'. A walk in the woods would be a part of that Place, but it would not be a behaviour setting. The physical context of an activity is not part of the conception of a behaviour setting. A French lesson in two different rooms would be recorded as the same behaviour setting in two different locations but would be manifestly two different Places. Another example, brought to my attention by a student of Barker's, was that an elaborate wedding, such as that which occurs over three days in India, would be regarded as one behaviour setting, although it occurs at a number of different Places, each of which has its own qualities and related expectations of actions.

Placelessness[18]

Around the same time as the original publication of *The Psychology of Place*, Edward Relph, a humanistic geographer, published his widely cited book *Place and Placelessness*.[19] He sets out a distinction between 'Place' and 'Placelessness'. He uses the term 'Place' in a rather different way to how it is used throughout the present book. He equates it to locations that have a distinct quality or character, a recognisable 'sense of Place', or *genius loci*.[20] His idea of 'Placelessness' is consequently, in effect, a criticism of all those anonymous, banal, indistinct locations that have been and are being created around the world. Those locations that Relph regards as 'inauthentic', or 'insincere'.

As Relph puts it "Placelessness- that is the casual eradication of distinctive Places and the making of standardised landscapes that results from an insensitivity to the significance of Place".[21] His mixing of description and value judgements is clear in his reference to 'pseudo-Places' that have been 'Disneyfied' and are 'kitsch'.[22] The followers of the notion of Placelessness are advocates of richer, more varied designs, preferably related to local traditions and culture. But that advocacy ignores the fact that there is some differentiation to be found everywhere, even between the most banal settings, whether you like it or not. Those differences can make anywhere that Relph considers to be placeless, as a significant Place for others.

An intriguing example, somewhat dated in the age of the internet, that Relph mentions are the shops that used to exist, selling pornography. Relph is very clear that these are 'Placeless' because they're the same everywhere. I am not sure what research he carried out to support this claim. I can certainly not present myself as an expert on these Places. However, I still remember the double-take my wife and I took when in Sweden in the late 1960s. We thought we had walked past a butcher's shop, but realised the body parts on display, in all their florid detail were actually close-ups of the private parts of naked people. This Place was so different, even from their window display, to what I have walked past in the Soho area of London. There the local laws and sensibilities were such that the shop may even have a sign declaring it was a purveyor of 'marital aids', with a blank, blacked out window. A peep inside the shop door revealed a dark interior typically with a curtain at the back, where I understand 'special collections' were kept. That contrasted with the clinical, almost medical, atmosphere of the Swedish shop. That again is a contrast with the virtually whimsical shop windows on New York's 42nd Street, that I walked past on my way to the Environmental Psychology Department. There the window displays emphasised equipment, including statuettes of the Virgin Mary that apparently could double as dildos. Even Places that Relph would declare as 'Placeless' take on a form that relates to local contexts, culture, and even legal constraints.

Objects and affordances

The focus on the conceptual structure of Places e does not mean that entities in a location are insignificant. Far from it. The patterns of activity and associated meanings, which include memories and possibilities for action, give many objects a particular salience that contribute to what a Place is. This is revealed quite engagingly in a BBC television series called *The Repair Shop*.[23] People bring objects that have been damaged, but which have special importance for them, to be repaired by exceptionally skilled craftsmen and women. What makes this, otherwise unremarkable, programme prime time viewing are the narratives enshrined in the objects, and the emotional reactions of the owners of the objects. A tearful response to seeing the restored object is not unusual. This is because the object cherishes a host of memories, usually related to a loved one, often a dead parent.

These become sacred objects, put in a location of honour in the home, helping to define that Place in relation to the person associated with it. The richness of how objects enhance the meaning of Places is illustrated by the way an army helmet that saved a grandfather's life, a music box which captivated reminiscence of a happy moment in a traumatised youth, or a dolls' house that was a gift from a father not long before he died, all contribute momentously to the experience of being in a particular room. They help to create the atmosphere of that Place, adding depth to what it means to be there.

The contribution of objects to domestic settings was thoroughly explored by Mihaly Csikszentmihalyi and Halton[24] over 40 years ago. The showed how objects in the home can be used "to express, or to explore, some of the purposes that animate their own individual lives as well as those that bond them to or divide them from each other" (p. 38). They can also have 'cosmic' significance that captures or boosts their owners' relationships to existence, nature, and the universe. In this way domestic objects can represent the self, involvement with significant others and a broader otherworldly relationship. An object can of course represent all three. One example that comes to mind is the *menorah*. This is the candelabra used by Jews for the ritual lighting of candles during the *Chanukah* festival. It can have a personal meaning as an indication of having achieved a particular personal status, as is the one I was given for my *Barmitzvah*. It defines a link to a religious community. It also can represent for some people a reaching out to millennia of existence. Like a crucifix, an antique teapot which was a gift from an aunt, or even a bicycle. Its presence in the room changes the nature of that Place.

Archaeology, of course, is obsessed with objects, trying to find the meaning of daily life, whether it be domestic or regal, in the objects that have survived hundreds or thousands of years. Apparently ignorant of Csikszentmihalyi and Halton's early work, the archaeologists Costall and Richards[25] explored the idea that the interpretation of the meaning of artefacts within archaeology assumes that these objects provide what they call 'canonical affordances'. This argument explores and develops Gibson's concept of *affordances*,[26] proposed over half a century ago.

Gibson's notion has found its way into many discussions of design and how we interact with our surroundings. In essence it is the claim that perception allows the understanding of objects in terms of the actions they make possible. The most obvious example is a chair. It is claimed that no mental processing is necessary to work out that it is an object for sitting on. This is an aspect of 'epistemic seeing'.[27] The idea that whenever we look at something it has some meaning to us. This is such a taken-for-granted idea that philosophers have exercised their intellectual muscles debating whether it is ever possible to look without some knowledge of what is being looked at – 'non-epistemic' seeing. But as Costall and Richards point out, when it comes the knowledge of what an object allows a person to do with it, its affordances, this can never be universal, independent of any cultural or idiosyncratic interpretations. The example of the chair illustrates this rather well. For those cultures in which chairs are not common, or people squatting on cushions is the norm, a chair may be looked at with some puzzlement. This is particularly apparent in cultural differences in toilet use, such that, in some places, special signs give guidance.

Physical form

The particular physical, spatial characteristics of a location are obviously relevant to defining a Place and contributing to its meaning. In his fascinating catalogue of architectural features Thomas Thiis-Evensen[28] discusses in great detail the salient features of the major components of buildings around three main categories: the floor, the wall, and the roof. He shows how subtle, and not so subtle, variations in how these are handled in a design carry many different implications for the experience and use of a building. But a challenging question remains how these components come to play a part in the nature of the Place they support.

Many years ago, I offered three processes as part of what I called 'the need for a theory of function in architecture',[29] although I now realise these processes are relevant to the natural landscape as much as to buildings. They are described in more detail in Chapter 8.

The most obvious function is as a *filter*. This keeps out the nasty things and allows in welcome aspects of the surroundings. When Neolithic people sheltered in caves, they were using these natural settings to keep off the rain or sun and to enable them to protect themselves from marauding animals. Caves allowed them to create a more comfortable environment by making fires. Buildings throughout the centuries have consistently used the available technology to increasingly control the experienced environment; glass in windows, thermal insulation, and acoustic separation. Ever more sophisticated designs have responded to the desire for particular spatial qualities, such as light in art galleries and acoustic management in concert halls. The ways in which these can be achieved are increasingly enhanced by modification of the actual fabric of the building, such as thermal insulation, window glass that reduces solar gain and solar panels to generate electricity or hot water.

All these contribute to other aspects, such as how public or private a Place is and whether its environmental qualities will support some activities but not others. An auditorium where people sit for a great length of time would usually need to be warmer than an art gallery that people walk through, for example.

A further limitation that any physical aspects of a Place impose and express are the *constraints* they impose on what can actually happen there. The number of people who can be accommodated in a space. What people are able to see from where. How they can move through a space and how that location relates to, or interacts with, other locations. These are all crucial aspects of the physical form of a Place. These may be designated or managed, consequently the import of significant physical aspects can never be isolated from Place rules and roles. The physical constituents of a country church carry quite different implications for patterns of use when that building is converted into a family home. The conversion of offices and light industrial buildings into churches is also not that rare, especially in the burgeoning growth of religion in the United States.[30]

A particularly novel reworking of a Place that shows how patterns of use of spaces can be repurposed is the conversion of a prison in Eindhoven into a luxury hotel (Figure 1.4). The central corridor allows for ready movement. Pairs of cells are interconnected to provide bedrooms and linked lounge and bathroom facilities. The management of the spaces revises the experience of them, although qualities of privacy and (in this case discrete) control are maintained.

Together the filtering and constraining processes that contribute to the nature of a Place, enhance its meaning, or *symbolic* qualities. The physical form of some Places is dominated by the symbol it represents, whether it is the enigmatic stone circle at Stonehenge, or Jørn Utzon's design for the Sidney Opera House. There are also landscapes that take on symbolic significance such as the desert in which Jesus spent 40 days in solitude. Exactly what is symbolised and how that meaning is created is a further central topic for this book.

The role of the physical components of Places is always a changing, often elusive one. They do not have fixed significance independently of their social and cultural context. This was highlighted in the influential book by the anthropologist Amos Rapoport.[31] When modernist architecture was the dominant approach, with the slogan of 'form following function', he astounded the architectural world by pointing out that even the most ubiquitous and commonplace of buildings, the house, took on a form that reflected its culture, not just the environmental demands on it. The interaction between

Figure 1.4 Hotel in a converted prison, Het Arresthuis, Eindhoven

culturally and personally embedded meanings with the qualities of physical forms is a crucial aspect of how Places exist.

No such thing as multi-purpose Places

The significance of human actions in shaping Places and their meanings has many important consequences. The expected and actual activities give an implicit or explicit purpose to a Place. Different actions or purposes generate different Places. That has the effect of forcing any Place whose character is ambiguous to quickly take on a specific definition. That undermines the ambiguity. This is most noticeable in any location that is naively defined as 'multipurpose'. Such locations naturally either divide up into a number of different Places or they are different Places at different points in time.

School halls are a common illustration of this process. At one time they may be a setting for a formal assembly or an examination room (Figure 1.5). At another time they might be turned into a dance venue, variously called a 'disco', 'prom', or in the distant past a 'hop'. When appropriate equipment is brought out, they can be converted into the school gymnasium. Each of these changes creates different Places for the time of the activity.

An ability to create different Places within one space requires the operation of social norms. Potential conflicts have to be resolved. An examination cannot be held in the

Figure 1.5 A school hall with indications that it can be used to create different places (*Facility hire at Trinity Primary School*)

school hall in Figure 1.5 at the same time as a band rehearsal. These requirements reflect socio-cultural expectations and traditions, which architects ignore at their peril.

One salutary example of disregarding the creation of Places in schools was the move in the 1970s to design 'open-plan schools'. This was heralded as part of the move to a more inclusive and 'open' approach to education. It's downfall was the result of taking no notice of the need to create different, distinct places for each activity in a school. An idea that is at the heart of behaviour setting theory, which took schools as its prime example.[32] Even at the most elementary level noise intrusion made aspects of these designs difficult to use.[33]

A contrast to the problems with open-plan schools is the requirement in many contemporary homes in Western society, for an 'open-plan kitchen dining room'. The earlier tradition of the kitchen being a separate Place from a dining room relied on their being very different roles for those in kitchens and those who ate formal dinners. In large country houses the men of the house, typically, would never enter the kitchen. That was the domain of the cook and her (almost always) assistants.

With the demise of servants and the emergence of women in a household to be a more integrated part of family activities there is the desire to recognise that cultural change by integrating the kitchen with Places where the family gather. The process of cooking is no longer regarded as some special activity that is essentially private, solely under the control of a woman. There are still distinct areas and different patterns of use in different parts of the open plan room, but it now reflects cultural changes.

Phenomenological geography

By the 1970s cultural geography and behavioural geography were becoming widespread. These focused on the significance and meaning of Places, drawing on theories in psychology and debates in philosophy. Since then there has been an outpouring of publications in this area, strongly influenced by the philosophy and methodology of phenomenology. This is not the place (no pun intended) for a detailed description of the many strands to this burgeoning area of scholarship. There are plenty of sources for that.[34] However, the central tenets of the phenomenological approach help to bring together the various strands of the psychology of Place explored so far and elaborated throughout this book.

One origin of phenomenology are some roots in German psychology of the early 20th century. At a time when the arts were in turmoil, with the emergence of cubism in painting, serialism in music and the early flowering of post-modernism in the writings of James Joyce and others, before and after the upheaval of the First World War, Max Wertheimer (1880–1943), Kurt Koffka (1886–1941), and Wolfgang Köhler (1887–1967) challenged the dominant mechanistic view of perception.

For psychologists such as Wilhelm Wundt (1832–1920), and Edward B. Titchener (1867–1927) perceptions could be built up from particular sensations; thought processes from the association of simpler ideas. This approach was inherently 'reductionist' in assuming that all higher processes could be reduced to their lower components. Their theories were atomistic and mechanical in regarding psychological processes as similar to the ways in which machines operate. This is a perspective that is still dominant in many areas of psychology, but instead of using engines for modelling how people perceive and think, they draw on parallels with computers.

Koffka and his colleagues challenged this. The slogan that summarises their view is that 'the sum is greater than the addition of the parts'. They proposed that perception was fashioned around what they called a *Gestalt*, meaning 'form' or 'shape'. A powerful example of this is the way a tune cannot really be explained in terms of individual notes or even notes and their relationships to each other. A tune is experienced as an entity. That is why it can be transposed into different keys, played at different speeds, and arranged for different instruments and still be recognised. They created many optical illusions to demonstrate that we perceive a whole even when presented with parts of it. Figure 1.6 is one I've created.

This idea, that perception, and related aspects of cognition, are experienced as holistic entities, did accord with a number of philosophical arguments. One philosopher in particular, Merleau-Ponty (1908–1961), embraced this idea and articulated a

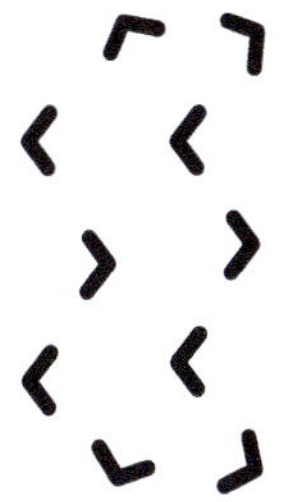

Figure 1.6 An illustration of Gestalt completion. Do you see a set of unconnected marks or a zigzag shape?

philosophy that has been very influential in the exploration of the nature and significance of Places. For my purposes in outlining a psychology of Place, the many debates around Merleau-Ponty's philosophy and those of the numerous other thinkers that relate to his work, are limited here to some key points. It will be appreciated that this brief summary is a gross oversimplification of the countless avenues that these debates have followed.

Merleau-Ponty argued for the central role of the human body as the basis for experience, rather than consciousness, as dominated Western thought from Descartes' "I think therefore I am". It is from this recognition of the essentially subjective nature of experience, which are *phenomena* characterising an individual's existence, thatputs Merleau-Ponty central to the phenomenology of Place.

It is the focus of experience in embodiment that gives rise to the holistic (Gestalt) structures discovered by Koffka and his colleagues. A body is always part of a location, which has its impact in relation to the body's physical presence. In this context all sensations combine to generate a particular experience. Even though attention can focus on particular aspects of that experience, experience is always multifaceted. As Seamon[35] puts it "In inhabiting Place, we automatically find ourselves present and engaged in a particular way that could not be otherwise". This viewpoint avoids the distinction between 'objective' and 'subjective', mind and body, person and location, by claiming that the person-in-Place is inevitably one entity. One holistic unit that can be examined from a variety of perspective whilst still maintaining its experiential unity.

Phenomenology may be considered a methodology as well a philosophy. It draws attention to the need to work with direct, untrammelled accounts of people's experiences. Indeed, those I think of as 'fundamentalist' phenomenologists take issue with any attempt to assign (they would say reduce to) quantities the experience of Places.

My brief account of my experience of the Memorial to the Murdered Jews of Europe is a step towards a phenomenological exploration of that Place. Although it is a memorial, rather than a lived-in location, nonetheless my experience of it was doubtless a total product of my sensations, memory, understanding of the physical, historical, cultural, and geographical context. The fact that I could sit on one of the concrete blocks, wander through the channels between them and watch others, all united to have the emotional impact it did.

The phenomenological viewpoint, then, emphasises that although Places have meanings, physical form and anticipated patterns of activity, these components are not distinct entities that influence each other. The whole point about the Venn diagram model of Place is that it shows these aspects are always present, interacting with each other to create the entity that is the Place. The focus on bodily experience, as the core of being in Place, draws attention to the coherent multi-faceted nature of that experience. Being here always involves the full mixture of aspects, senses, memories, understandings, significance, and actions. Although attention can be directed to any component, that aspect will always be influenced by all the others, as well as those contributions to the experience that are below the level of awareness. The whole being more than the sum of the parts, just as an optical illusion generates the perception of an image that goes beyond the individual blobs.

Place as an assemblage

There is one central challenge to making sense of the idea of Place as explored in this book. This is the challenge to the notion that Places are inherently fixed entities that have a distinct, clearly definable essence, intrinsic characteristics that define their identity.[36] As we have seen, not only are Places naturally dynamic, changing with use, history, and layered meanings. They take on different significances and use depending on who is present in them, the purposes a person has for being there and their expectations.

Dovey[37] proposes that any Place operates as a whole whose properties emerge from the interactions between its parts. He draws on the concept of an 'assemblage' to characterise this process. He derives this term from Delanda[38] who makes clear that in an assemblage "the parts that are fitted together are not uniform either in nature or origin, and that the assemblage actively links these parts together by establishing links between them". The fascinating insight this concept provides, when a Place is considered as assemblage, is that it is not necessary to assume that places are nested in any way. A room takes on its identity and meaning from the different furniture, activities and people who are present there. But any piece of furniture takes on its significance from being in that particular room and typically being used by a person at any point in time. Similarly, the meaning of the room draws on the meaning of the building that houses it, just as the building makes sense in terms of the rooms that it is composed of.

It is the relationships between the form, meanings, and uses of locations, their assemblage, that creates Places. One crucial aspect of this is the recognition that it is the interaction between Places that contribute to the meaning and experience of Places at every scale. The psychological consequence of this is that those processes that help us to understand what places are have relevance at whatever scale is being considered. How you make sense of a room or building is similar to how you make sense of a city, or importantly, planet Earth.

There are many examples in the following pages which assume that the Places being described derive their meaning and significance from Places that make them up and the Places they create. Those assemblages include past, present, and possible future Places within the culture, history, and social process that they create and are created by.

Conclusions

The idea of what a Place is, from a psychological perspective, has its origins in phenomenological, cognitive, and behavioural considerations. These all emphasise human agency. Actively making sense of the world, anticipating the social processes that help to give Places their meaning. These different aspects combine to create a rich concept. That elaborates the meaning of the physical, geographical location to which the term 'place' usually refers in daily discourse. This term adds "weight to the argument that we will only discern the role of our physical surroundings in the matrix of human experience and activity, by studying how we react to and cope with the complexity and variety of those surroundings".[39] The active practices this involves is the theme of Chapter 2.

References and endnotes

1 For example, in Ellard, C. (2015) *Places of the heart: The psychogeography of everyday life*, New York: Bellevue Literary Press, p. 23.

2 Casey, E. S. (2009) *Getting back into place: Toward a renewed understanding of the Place-World* (2nd ed.), Bloomington: Indiana University Press.

3 Malpas, J. (2018) *Place and experience: A philosophical topography* (2nd ed.), London: Routledge.

4 Seamon. D. (2018) *Life takes place: Phenomenology, lifeworlds, and place making*, New York: Routledge.

5 Marx, K. (1959) *Capital I*, Moscow: Foreign Languages Publishing House.

6 Bartlett, F. C. (1995) originally published in 1932. *Remembering: A study in experimental and social psychology*, Cambridge University Press.

7 Yon, D. (2025) *A trick of the mind: How the brain invents your reality*, London: Cornerstone.

8 Seamon. D. (2018) *Life takes place: Phenomenology, lifeworlds, and place making*, New York: Routledge, p. 83.

9 Bennett, J. G. (1963) Systematics and general systems theory. *Systematics* 1(2), 105–110.

10 Summarised in Kelly, G. A. (2003) A brief introduction to personal construct theory, in *International handbook of personal construct psychology*, pp. 3–20. But originally published in two volumes as Kelly, G. A. (1955). *The psychology of personal constructs: A theory of personality*, London: Routledge.

11 Catulli, M. & Reed, N. (2017) A personal construct psychology based investigation into a product service system for renting pushchairs to consumers. *Business Strategy and the Environment*, *26*(5), 656–671.

12 Honikman, B. (1973) Personal construct theory and environmental evaluation, in W. F. E. Preiser (Ed.) *Environmental design research*, London: Routledge, pp. 242–253.

13 Seamon. D. (2018) *Life takes place: Phenomenology, lifeworlds, and place making*, New York: Routledge, p. 15.

14 Jacobs, J. (1961) *The life and death of Great American Cities*, New York: Vintage.

15 Whyte, W. F. (1943) *Street corner society: The social structure of an Italian slum* (Doctoral dissertation, The University of Chicago).

16 An especially clear account is given by Schoggen, P. (1989) *Behavior settings: A revisions and extension of Roger G. Barker's ecological psychology*, Stanford: Stanford University Press.

17 Reviewed in Lobo, L. Heras-EScribano, M., & Travieso, D. (2018) The history and philosophy of ecological psychology, *Frontiers in Psychology*, 27 November 2018, https://doi.org/10.3389/fpsyg.2018.02228

18 Phillips, J., Walford, N., & Hockey, A. (2011) How do unfamiliar environments convey meaning to older people? Urban dimensions of placelessness and attachment. *International Journal of Ageing and Later Life*, 6(2), 73–102.

19 Relph, E. (1976) *Place and placelessness* (Vol. 67), London: Pion, p. 45.

20 In his erudite review of the concept of *Genius Loci*: *Essay on the meanings of place*, London: Reaktion Books; Hunt, J. D. (2022) reveals this is an ambiguous and contentious idea, which nonetheless "serves us well", p. 188.

21 Relph, E. (1976) *Place and placelessness*, London: Pion, p. ii.

22 Relph, E. (1976) *Place and placelessness*, London: Pion, p. 97.

23 *Farrington, Karen (5 November 2020)* The repair shop: Tales from the workshop of dreams, *BBC Books*. There are now also Australian and Dutch versions.

24 Csikszentmihalyi, M. & Halton, E. (1981) *The meaning of things: Domestic symbols and the self*, Cambridge: Cambridge University Press.

25 Costall, A. & Richards, A. (2013) Canonical affordances: The psychology of everyday things, in P. Graves-Brown, Rodney Harrison, & Angela Piccini (Eds.) *The Oxford handbook of the archaeology of the contemporary world*, Oxford: Oxford University Press, pp. 82–95.

26 Gibson, J. J. (1966) *The senses considered as perceptual systems*, London: George Allen and Unwin.

27 Demircioglu, E. (2017) *Dretske on non-epistemic seeing*, pp. 364–393, https://doi.org/10.1111/theo.12127

28 Thiis-Evensen, T. (1987) *Archetypes in architecture*, Oxford: Oxford University Press.

29 Canter, D. (1970) Need for a theory of function in architecture. *Architects' Journal*, 151, 299–302.
30 Retrofitting a Commercial Building into a Church - Religious Product News.
31 A review of Rapoport's work and its influence is given in Moore, K. (Ed.) (2000) *Culture-meaning-architecture,* London: Routledge, https://doi.org/10.4324/9781315200248
32 Barker, R. G., & Gump, P. V. (1964). *Big school, small school: High school size and student behavior*, Stanford, CA: Stanford University Press.
33 Shield, B., Greenland, E., & Dockrell, J. (2010). Noise in open plan classrooms in primary schools: A review. *Noise and Health*, 12(49), 225–234.
34 For widely quoted works, see Malpas, J. (2018) *Place and experience: A philosophical topography* (2nd ed.), London: Routledge; Casey, E. S. (2009) *Getting back into place: Towards a new understanding of the Place-World* (2nd ed.), Bloomington: Indiana University Press.
35 Seamon. D. (2018) *Life takes place: Phenomenology, lifeworlds, and place making,* New York: Routledge, p. 51.
36 This notion is known in philosophy as 'essentialism'. Sahin, M. (2018) Essentialism in philosophy, psychology, education, social and scientific scopes. *Online Submission*, *22*(2), 193–204.
37 Dovey, K. (2020) Place as assemblage, in *The Routledge handbook of place*,London: Routledge, pp. 21–31.

Elaborated a decade earlier in Dovey, K. (2010) *Becoming places: Urbanism/architecture/indemnity/power,* London: Routledge.

38 DeLanda, M. (2016) *Assemblage theory*, Edinburgh: Edinburgh University Press, p. 2.
39 Canter, D. (1977) *The psychology of place,* London: Architectural Press, p. 10.

CHAPTER 2

Making places happen

The body in space

The actions that underlie the meanings of places are profoundly influenced by the relationships our bodies to our surroundings, *embodiment*. That is the foundation of experiencing places. As touched on in Chapter 1, recognising the significance of our bodily experiences owes a lot to the writings of the French phenomenologist Maurice Merleau-Ponty.[1] He elaborated how the experience of being present, is integral to being a body in its physical context. His argument was that it is inappropriate to consider our bodies as just objects like other objects. They are central to how we see and make sense of the world. The body is the channel through which we engage with our environment. Our understanding of the world is shaped by our physical presence within it.

One consequence of this is that it creates an inherently two-dimensional perspective on the world around us, despite an awareness of the third, up/down aspect. Even an elementary consideration of how our body is organised shows that the positions of our eyes and other sense organs are arranged to relate to the world horizontally. Our sight is forward looking, as are our ears and nose. Merleau-Ponty's 'embodiment' draws attention to how the positioning of our body in space provides the foundation of all interactions with the world around us. Places are the experience of being here which is shaped by that inescapable bodily aspect of being human.

When astronauts, who had spent a lot of time on the International Space Station, were asked, what it was that was initially difficult to get used to, they replied it was the three-dimensional, gravitation-free existence (Figure 2.1). Their comments show that our daily activities, where we are anchored to the earth, are essentially two dimensional. Working out the implications of being able to move up and down as easily as front to back or side to side, took some learning. The placing of objects without awareness of how they could move in three dimensions also brought surprises in astronauts early days floating around the earth.

As Peled[2] pointed out, in his examination of people redesigning their homes, the physicality of our bodies is reflected in the how we make sense of buildings and other

DOI: 10.4324/9780367808655-3

Figure 2.1 The gravity-free experience

aspects of the physical environment. Front has its significance because that is the direction in which we look. It is also where we house the more sensitive parts of our bodies. Similarly, the back of a building is more hidden, containing aspects that may not be talked about. For a right-handed culture there are sometimes even differences between what the left of a building means compared with the right. The word 'sinister' comes from the Latin for left side *sinister* or *sinistra*. This contrasts with the idea of being dextrous, meaning skilful, which has its origins in the Latin for the right-hand side *dexter*. People tend to go round art-galleries and museums to the left (clockwise when seen from above). Many other manifestations of how we relate to the physical world are reflections of how our bodies are constructed.

I remember asking a student of mine, who was blind from birth, what he found most surprising about a person being sighted. He said, 'the fact that all parts of an object are not directly apparent'. He built up a mental image of his surroundings all the time, aided by sound, movement, and sometimes touch. This gave him a natural awareness of distance and depth.For sighted people the what exists behind something that is immediately visible, has to be constructed conceptually.

The horizontal, front-back, left-right, emphasis, that shapes human experience of places, influences the difficulty of building up a mental image of the world that takes account of vertical aspects. This was demonstrated with fatal effect in 1987, when there was a fire on the escalator of an underground station at London's Kings Cross. Police officers guided people up from the tube train platform to the ticket hall which led into the mainline station above. They did not appreciate that they were leading them into the area into which the smoke from the fire would pour. Sadly, that smoke killed 31 people. When I was asked to look into the actions in that evacuation, I had to study the plans for that complex set of subterranean passageways. This turned out to be rather difficult to make sense of. For the subsequent enquiry into the fire a three-dimensional model was built so that the enquiry team could properly understand what happened to the fire development and the movement of people. The truth is that many architects are surprised when they see the actual building, in all its solid existence, which they have been imagining and drawing.

Another example of how buildings can be produced without considering how people can make sense of them, with commercial consequences, is the St John's Shopping Centre in the centre of Liverpool. I was commissioned to advise on an issue they were aware of with the design of the precinct.

It is built on a number of levels down the side of a slope. This means you can enter at one level and move to another with the relationship to the outside changing at each level. To complicate matters further, the floor plan at each level is different. This means that it is easy to become disoriented as you change levels. One casualty of this is that those shops that are situated along corridors that lead nowhere or are not obvious as customers move from one level to another, do not attract the same footfall as others. People tend not to venture in that direction. Not being sure where they are in the precinct, they fear of getting lost. These shops were therefore rather difficult to let out for use. My advice was to have some central feature that would always allow people to orient themselves, as well as an improvement in signposting.

Some architects either ignore these issues of making sense of a building in three dimensions or deliberately challenge it. Figure 2.2 is a photograph I took of Reykjavik Concert Hall. I was trying to capture the dizzying incorporation of the vertical dimension with horizontal. This integration of the plan and elevation, I found very disturbing to engage with.[3] Working out where I was at any given level of the vast atrium was sometimes quite alarming, although it did engender excitement as well.

Even in imagination we relate to the world in the only way we can. When I dream of flying, I am still moving horizontally, connecting with the imagined world as a person with my eyes and ears facing forward. I may move between levels, as when I move up or down an escalator, but at any point in time my experience is embodied. This is surprisingly true for apparently disembodied experiences such as dreams. Although in a dream you may not be conscious of quite where you are, you are still somewhere. You move around that Place as you would when awake. You still have an awareness of your body, relating to the situation as your body allows you. The powerful visuals of today's computer games, still move the player forward and back, or side to side, even when they are jumping from an imaginary helicopter or running over a hill.

The body and social interaction

There is a simple but profound consequence of experiencing places essentially in two dimensions. The interactions with others and our surroundings are dominated by what is in front or behind us, to the left or the right. I still remember the guidance in a comic I read as a child about where to hide. It said, 'climb up a tree'. People rarely look up. Staying in places, where I could look out of a window on the street below, I've tested

Figure 2.2 Harpa Concert Hall and Conference Centre, Reykjavik, showing the dramatic way in which all three dimensions interact

this hypothesis many times. It is necessary to shout to draw attention to being in the third, up/down, dimension.

There is further consequence of embodiment being mainly on a plain, level surface. When looking at the use and experience of places it is productive to consider usage on a plan. Who and what is found where? How do people face each other? Who brushes shoulders with whom? Are there places in which being back-to-back with others is encouraged? In other words, embodiment shapes how we experience and interact with places by grounding our perceptions in bodily sensations, movements, and memories. Our physical presence in a space influences how we navigate, interpret, and emotionally connect with it.

The distinctiveness of the third dimension also helps to explain why height carries particular significance, as explored in Chapter 10. Being above other people and activities is to be superior, out of the ordinary, special. It also gives advantages. Castles or cathedrals, office for senior executives, even sculptures as major landmarks, are nearly always high above their surroundings. If not, like the Eifel Tower and church steeples, they reach aloft. People have to look up to them, physically and metaphorically.[4]

Environmental roles and place rules

Human embodiment also entails interactions with other humans. These interactions give rise to patterns of social structures. A key feature of these, directly pertinent to the nature and experience of Places, are the expectations people have of each other and of what is possible where. These are the *rules* that shape those expectations and the *roles* that people take in relation to those rules.

The concept of 'rules' here owes a lot to studies of disorder in classrooms and at football grounds.[5] However, they have their origins in the sociology of Durkheim[6] and the anthropology of Malinovsky.[7] It is important to be clear that, in relation to what may or may not happen in particular Places, rules are not the strict requirements as, for instance, in a game of chess. They are more closely related to the idea of 'guidelines', or even expected, or habitual patterns of activity. They help to maintain order, predictability, and social cohesion by indicating acceptable actions and interactions. Norms are an aspect of such rules. Unwritten expectations about behaviour, such as politeness, dress codes, or conversational etiquette. What is worn in a particular Place, for instance, is not usually specified, but may be in special circumstances, such as what is acceptable to wear in a church or on the beach.

An important aspect of the rules explored here is that they are specific to particular locations. They help to give those locations some meaning. This may be something as small scale as the habit I have of always making my wife's tea in the cup on my right. On a more draconian scale the rules associated with traffic lights, or speed limits, have legal force. Others are widely acted on, but typically implicit, such as sitting in an auditorium rather than on the stage of a theatre. Doffing a hat when a hearse drives past is more localised. The examples are legion because all Places take their meanings, in part, from the rules that shape what goes on there.

These examples make clear that a crucial aspect of social rules is that they are open to interpretation and elaboration. Different societies and cultures will support different patterns of activity for what might seem to people outside those cultures like similar situations. In many cases the physical setting will contribute cues to what rules are relevant. In turn the rules that are deemed appropriate for a setting help to define the sort of place it is. As a consequence, there are sets of rules specifically relevant to places – Rules of Place.

Rules vary in a number of ways. They may be what you can or should do. Or as in Figure 2.3 they may be a list of what you are not allowed to do. Interestingly, the notice in the Italian city of Verona is in English as well as Italian. It therefore makes clear the sort of shenanigans that the authorities are keen to outlaw, and who they think the most likely culprits are. However, by listing six different activities that are likely to take place in that area, they are (possibly inadvertently) indicating what others see as the nature of the place and the jolly times they expect to have there. The authorities in Verona assume different rules guide what goes on there from the roles that some English tourists perform.

Figure 2.3 A number of place rules in Verona

A detailed exploration of rules and roles within a domestic setting demonstrates how prevalent place rules are.[8] As illustration the rules that children had to abide by in the living room: "Don't touch, Be careful, That's fragile, Stay away from that table, Don't sit in that chair, That clock's not something to play with, NO RUNNING IN THE LIVING ROOM" (p. 5). These help to define the nature of the place, what the qualities of using it are intended to be.

One important aspect of place rules reflects what Goffman, over half a century ago, in his widely influential writings[9] called 'frontstage'. This draws on a dramaturgical model of human activity, that is often summarised using Jacques speech from Shakespeare's *As You Like it*:

> All the world's a stage,
> And all the men and women merely players;
> They have their exits and their entrances;
> And one man in his time plays many parts,

The perspective which proposes that much of human activity relates to how people present themselves to others, and want to see themselve,s is also found in many novels predating Goffman. In the charming but little known novel by Kate Chopin[10] the author comments that her protagonist was "casting aside that fictitious self which we assume like a garment with which to appear before the world". This reflects the fact that there are aspects of human activity which are influenced by some form of 'being on show'. The physical aspects of a place, in this context, act analogously to a stage set. These are places characterised by what Cooper Marcus[11] calls a reflection of a person's self-image. She develops this argument, with many illustrations, to cover many aspects of the house. How even the most private parts of a house take on a form, consciously or not, that relate to how a person sees themselves. The places in the home are thus imbued with the identity of those who create and use them.

Environmental roles

When I was about 12 years old, I was on a summer camp with other children. We were divided into pairs and given string and collected wood with the instruction to build some sort of windmill. I was put together with my friend Mike Leigh (who subsequently became an award-winning film director). We happily set about organising the material but soon got into a serious argument. I wanted the windmill to actually rotate, a challenging prospect for the material we had available. Mike was not interested in its functionality. He just wanted it to look good and interesting. We had taken on different roles for the project. He the nascent artist, me the unskilled engineer. We were approaching the experience at the edge of the wood, not far from our campsite, with different implicit rules in mind. We actually came to blows, which is I think one of the reasons I remember this event so clearly. In microcosm we reflected the common debate between architects and civil engineers. A debate now superseded by computer aided design with civil engineering capability, as illustrated in examples of contemporary architecture in Chapter 12.

Social roles are expectations tied to specific positions, like being a teacher, parent, or leader. These roles dictate behaviours based on societal or group standards. Roles are a negotiation of identity within social structures. It is important to be aware that very different role labels, or organisational roles, can have similar environmental roles, and vice versa. I became aware of this when exploring the evaluations of a new children's hospital by different groups.[12] To my surprise the senior management and the hospital cleaners had very similar views of the new building. Then I realised that they both related to it in similar ways, moving around the whole building. By contrast, the nurses tended to only experience the wards on which they worked giving them a very different environmental role.

Separate environmental roles lead to distinct differences in what places are for the people in those roles. This is most likely to be the case when the purpose they have for being in that location also differs. That *purposive* perspective is crucial to consider when examining how a person relates to a Place.[13] No understanding of the psychology of Place can make full sense without taking into account the Place-related roles people have that gives them a reason for being there.

One of the most interesting variations in environmental role is that of children of different ages. Once a child is able to walk and move around with a reasonable degree of physical agility, social processes come into play to manage and control interactions with the physical surroundings. The actual ability of the child to navigate and move around becomes circumscribed by what is permitted. This is the toddler environmental role. Yet this role is also defined by the young person's being in the world. The actual height above the ground and stability gives the toddler an experience of places that is different from the adult towering above. I was struck by this when being on a long boat journey with my very young daughter. We left our cabin to go for a stroll. On our return I could not remember which cabin it was. But my daughter, closer to the ground level than me, recognised the slight variation in the details of the threshold to each cabin and unthinkingly stepped into ours.

As children grow older their relationship to their surroundings evolves, both in terms of what they are physically and psychologically able (or allowed) to do.Also by where it is acceptable for them to be. Changing friendship patterns, emerging social norms and purposes for being in places, all mean that the environmental roles available, for example, to a five-year-old, are very different to those of an eleven-year-old, or a teenager. Just as the parts of a building frequented by a senior office manager are different to those of a receptionist. They experience the building very differently. It is a different Place for each of them.

It is worth noting that one of the origins of the psychological consideration of Places was the work of a psychiatrist informing architects that they needed to take account of how psychiatric patients experienced hospitals.[14] The point was that architects could not understand the experiences of those suffering from mental illness, because those patients relationship to the world (their environmental roles) were so different from the 'god-like' perspectives of architects.

Different environmental roles and associated Place rules relate to distinctions between the ways in which the conceptions, physical form, and patterns of activity interact. A person responsible for the maintenance of a park, for example, will react to graffiti and what needs to be done about them, as well as the implications for expected patterns of use, very differently to the person who sprayed the paint initially. In subsequent chapters these issues are unpacked to develop a rich understanding of the psychology of Place.

One all too frequent illustration of the power of these Environmental Roles is the common, photographic selfie. It is often a representation of the role of being in a place. Many years ago, a then student of mine, Haig Khachatoorian (now a distinguished industrial designer), called this 'role documentation'. That was before the word selfie existed and the smart phone made them ubiquitous. For example, being pictured as a tourist, friend, or occupant; this is me at the pyramids, or in a restaurant with friends. Here's what I look like in my new bedroom, running a marathon through London, or high on the hill I've just climbed. In contrast to the primitive belief that being photographed steals your soul, these selfies imply that you do not have an existence until you are present within some reality represented in what is, after all, a virtual image.

Social identity and the meaning of places

One further elaboration of the understanding of what Places are, can be derived from the emphasis that emerges when considering rules and roles. This is the social nature of Place experiences. It is noteworthy that in the earlier incarnation of *The Psychology of Place* I e made considerable reference to perceptual processes.. Although seeing and hearing physical forms of places are crucial for understanding what places are and their meaning, the way those features are relevant is modified by social processes. The essence of the experience of a location integrates with who is using them and why. Place rules and roles serve to stress the social psychological processes which contribute to what a Place is.

A general framework known as 'social identity theory', linked to 'self-categorisation theory',[15] is currently a dominant perspective within social psychology in many countries. When thinking about places a number of processes become clearer when it is appreciated that how we categorise ourselves interacts with our understanding of where we are. This is captured in the Churchillian quotation that is usually cited at the start of most environmental psychology textbooks: "We shape our buildings and afterwards they shape us". That statement is interpreted in the context of the rebuilding of the Houses of Parliament, after bomb damage during the Second World War. The statement is taken to imply the processes of Parliament required a particular physical layout. But in the light of Social Identity Theory the quotation can be understood as more profound than merely relating to parliamentary processes. It emphasises the meaning of parliamentary government. The identity of British democracy enshrined in the Palace of Westminster.

The key point here is that what we do where, is part of who we think we are; our identity. If I think of myself as an outdoor type, happy with my own company, then I will readily stroll across the hills. Of course, I may only become aware that this is what I think of myself when contemplating what I have been doing or might have done. Anyone who enjoys being on a beach, basking in the sun, surrounded by hundreds of other people is likely, at least implicitly, to see themselves as part of that beach crowd. This has been apparent in the vast crowds that descended on

Figure 2.4 A beach in Bournemouth during the COVID-19 lockdown showing people totally ignoring government regulation on social distancing

Bournemouth Beach during the lockdown because of the COVID-19 pandemic (Figure 2.4). The authorities were appalled that so many people would break 'social-distancing rules' against such gatherings. However, the communal support that came with many people being together on the beach, helped to define the identity of those who were there, producing a positive cycle of group identification This brought with it a related set of Place rules.

The study of crowds from the perspective of social Identity has been developed by Cliff Stott.[16] His intense, immersive studies of many different crowds, notably those attending football matches, and from the examination of riots, has shown how people within a crowd identify with those around them. These place-located interpretations can be converted into antagonism towards authority figures, notably the police, unless the police are understood to be legitimately on the side of the group.

This was clearly illustrated when Liverpool's football team won the League Cup for the first time in 30 years. Those who identified themselves as Liverpool supporters gathered together to celebrate the win. They acted as Liverpool fans rather than citizens obeying government social distancing restrictions. The Places where we do things are experienced as part of our identity, but that in turn is shaped by the various social groups with whom we identify. What we see and react to, is part of that process.

What is proposed here is that people actively shape how they see themselves, and how others see them by the nature of their actions in places. These ideas will be part of the exploration of many different Places in later chapters of this book. They reflect a cycle of self-definition and place definition that can be presented as a simplified cycle (Figure 2.5).

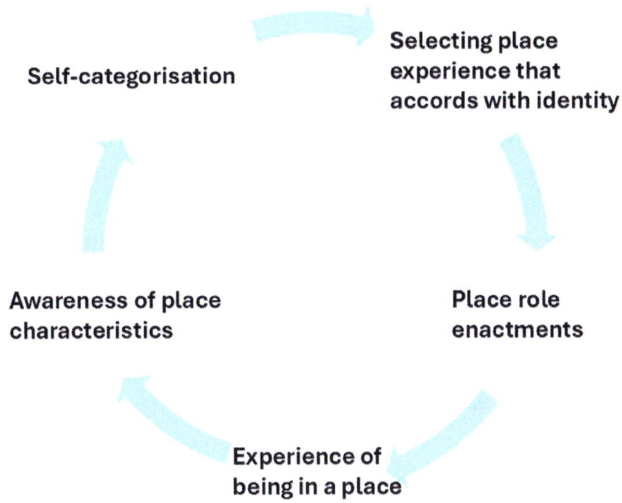

Figure 2.5 Simplified representation of how place experience and identity support each other

Creating places

The dynamic model of place

The active processes involved in creating places are reflected in refiguring the model of Place, as in Figure 2.6. This emphasises that places can emerge from any point in this cycle. A particular physical form may be interpreted as indicating certain actions. The meanings a person assigns to a form may suggest rules that generate appropriate actions. There could even be actions occurring in a location that supports the meanings of that Place and the appropriate roles to take there.

The dynamic nature of Place creating was illustrated in a rather amusing way by a study I carried out.[17] For that study I took advantage of having been asked to give a series of lectures at the Architectural Association in London. A radical School of Architecture, very much part of what we now think of as a 'new age', or even 'hippy' lifestyle associated with the 1970s, epitomised by the music festival at Woodstock in 1969. It was not the babies that students brought in with them to my lectures that were distracting, but rather the large wandering dogs.

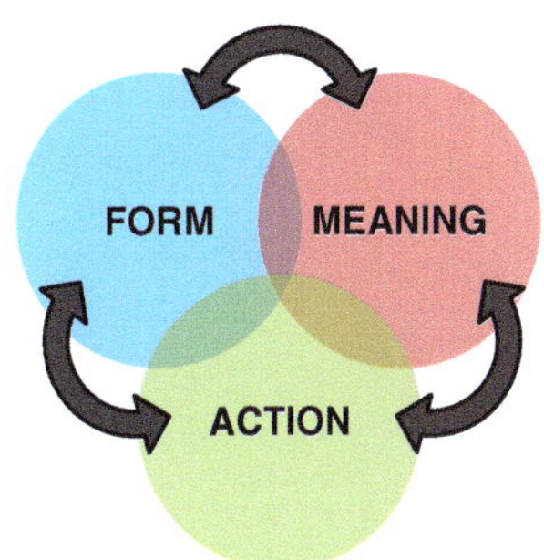

Figure 2.6 The dynamic model of place

I was giving a series of lectures on psychology and architecture over a number of weeks. Curious about student reactions to what I was doing, I decided to arrange the seating in the small hall where we met in various ways and to position myself at different locations s in relation to the seating, before the students entered the room. There were two seating arrangements. One in a semi-circular pattern, as for an informal seminar. The other in the rigid rows of a formal lecture. On some occasions I stood close to the front row of seats. In others I stood at some distance. This gave four experimental conditions, which I repeated over a number of days. In each I noted where the students sat as they came in to hear my talk.

The results were very clear (Figure 2.7). With the semi-circular layout the position in which I stood, as the students came in, made no differences at all. The main seat choices were towards the middle of the layout, favouring the second row. The results were very different for the formal seat arrangement. When I was positioned near the front, they tended to sit five rows back. When I stood far from the front row, they tended to sit in the first two rows of seats. How can these results be explained?

Any idea that students just take up seats to maximise their engagement with the lecture, simply being pushed by the layout to use it in a logical way, is not supported by this experiment and by the experience of lecturers around the world. Observation of the students coming into the room revealed that many would take one look at the seat arrangement and wander out again (with their dogs). Those that did decide to participate arranged themselves in relation to their interpretation of the nature of the event. The layout of the room was used to signify the sort of event they assumed would happen. When it was the informal, semi-circular arrangement those few who were intrigued by what this brash young psychologist had to say, would sit in the position where they could ask questions and actively participate in the talk. When the students

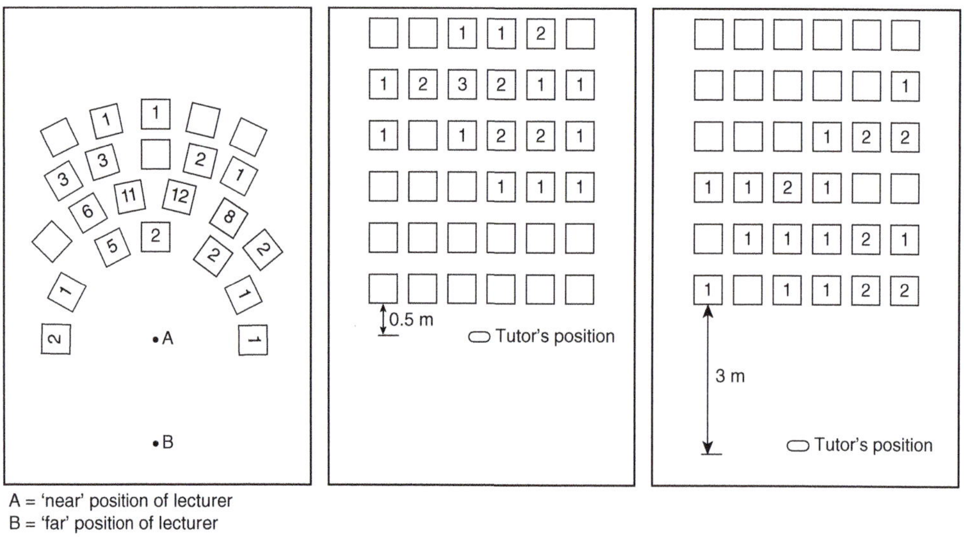

Figure 2.7 Comparison of seminar seat selection between two layout and two positions of the lecturer

assumed the event was a formal lecture, they selected seats that enabled them to be at a passive distance from the tutor, able to avoid too direct an interaction with him.

The frequency of such engagement will be recognised by lecturers around the world. Reported from the United States, for example, by Sommer in his seminal book.[18] In a large lecture theatre, questions most frequently come from those seated more or less in the middle of the first few rows. The students playing noughts and crosses or tapping away of their phones (although not in 1969!) will be on the back row, probably near the door.

A further example of this process can be drawn from the study that Dennis Wood carried out on a bus tour across Europe with a group of students. He categorised his students into three groups in terms of their approach to being tourists. *Rangers* were those who were highly motivated to explore, but in the bus such opportunities were limited. In that context they preferred social engagement. They therefore occupied a place at the back of the bus, where they can interact freely with their friends "prioritizing conversation over observing Europe" as it sped past.

A second group Wood called *Fixers*. They have, in general, low exploratory motivation and prefer familiarity. They take advantage of a Place in seats at the front of the bus, near adults, where they can avoid social interaction and passively observe Europe through the windows. The place in the middle is defined by *Mixers*, who balance exploration with social caution. They form small groups and create various spots that enable them to adapt to varying opportunities without fully committing to extremes. Although Wood's study was of a specific group on a particular tour, youngsters and adults who have been on similar bus journeys will recognise the behavioural pattern he found.

The seating arrangement gives rise to three distinct Places within the bus. Each has its own implicit rules of engagement, and interaction. It is no accident that the Rangers are at the back away from the adults, who tend to be towards the front. These Place-related role differences contribute to the definitions of the distinct Places on the bus. They are a consequence of how people define themselves in relation to others. As in many aspects of self-categorisation they may not be fully aware of how they regard themselves and are thought of by others. Nonetheless, those social-psychological processes contribute to the emergence of diverse Places with all the roles, rules, and experiences that implies.

Another more recent example illustrates the same challenge of seeking direct effects of physical environmental features. In a recent study the prolific criminological psychologist, David Farrington examined the impact of turning off street lighting on the frequency of violent crime.[19] Rather surprisingly it was found that there were fewer violent events when the streetlights were turned off. (A brave study this. I wonder what the ethical committee made of the research proposal?) The conclusion the researchers came to was that fewer people were abroad in the dark because of the fear of being more vulnerable. Once again illustrating that it was the interpretation people made of the situation and their consequent actions which gave the Place a particular character. This set in motion a process that reduced the opportunity for violent attacks.

In this framework, what a person brings to a setting is as much part of their experience and use of it as what that setting makes possible. Consequently, my modest experiment in a lecture hall illustrates a fundamental challenge to the idea that the environment determines in any simple way what people do.

Place attachment

There is a further consequence of Place experience relating to a person's self-categorisation. Being in Place supports a person's view of their identity. In many circumstances this support for a person's views of who they are is so important that attachment to that Place takes on great significance. The Place and the person help to define each other. Separating a person from the Place they identify with can be as painful as cutting off a *daemon* from its owner, which is the central trauma in Philip Pullman's *His Dark Materials* novels. The division of the person from their daemon leaves that person bereft and soulless

A powerful example of attachment to Place is given in the final volume of Hilary Mantel's[20] *magnum opus*. When she has her protagonist meditating on the comfort of getting back to his rooms within his home. He remembers a famous 15th-century event during the siege of Florence. This is well-known for the eloquent way Margherita Borgherinei declared her commitment to her bedroom, which was extravagantly furnished when she got married.

> Seven years back, when Florence was besieged by the Emperor and begging for French aid, the burgesses went to the merchant Borgherini's house: 'We want to buy your bedroom.' There were fine painted panels, rich hangings and other furnishing they thought might make a bribe for King François. But Margherita, the merchant's wife, stood her ground and threw their offer back in their faces. Not everything in life is for sale, she said. This room is my family's heart. Away with you! If you want to take my bedroom, you will have to carry your loot over my body.
>
> *(p. 64)*

Margherita's example is reflected in many, many other commitments to Places across all times and geographies. As we see in Chapter 15, there are very important consequences of Place attachment, especially when the Places take on a sacred meaning, or are embedded within the identification of cultures.[21] This gives the quality of those places a significance far beyond their particular physical form, just as Eisenman's Memorial, explored in Chapter1, has an impact that surpasses the simple grey blocks of which it is composed.

Approaches to being here

A central conundrum emerges when thinking about the psychological processes inherent in Places. From one perspective Places are distinct locations that carry significance and meaning. From another angle they are components of spatially related entities. My friends who visited Eisennman's Memorial with me, certainly experienced it as a powerful symbolic monument. But they did not react to it in quite the same way that I did. The question therefore emerges of how to relate these two sides of a coin to each other? I expressed this question in one of the first pieces I ever wrote in discussions in what was then called 'Architectural Psychology'. "Should we treat building users as Subjects or Objects?"[22]

I posed that question in 1969 at the first conference on Architectural Psychology. I had organised this at the country retreat of the University of Strathclyde, on the shores of Loch Lomond. It is a little daunting to realise that 50 years on that question still resonates with me. The privilege of longevity gives me the opportunity to consider what the origins and foundations were of that question. There were many sources both in psychology and architectural research. Some of these were summarised in Chapter 1. Further elaboration here provides additional clarification of how Places are dynamic entities.

Half a century ago in psychology, there was still a battle between those who regarded themselves as strict scientists, who could only study observable phenomena. Broadly referred to as 'behaviourists', they followed B.F. Skinner, focusing on what could be directly observed; actions not thoughts. Skinner's research favoured teaching pigeons to peck in response to specific stimuli. Within architectural research there was a burgeoning of observational studies of building users. They were regarded as objects that could be pushed around by aspects of design. This gave rise to initial ideas on the geometry of building plans which gained traction in Hillier's 'space syntax',[23] to which Chapter 9 is devoted.

The challenges to behaviourists have a long tradition in psychology, going back to one of the founders of modern psychology, William James (1842–1910). But in the 1960s this became encapsulated in what was known as a 'cognitive' perspective. The idea that people made sense of their world and acted on that interpretation. In 1969 I emphasised that the distinction between these two perspectives were actually differences in views of the nature of what it means to be human. As I put it then (at the naïve age of 25!):

> Some theoretical formulations seem to develop from the idea that people are motivated by forces either deep inside them or completely external to them but always pushing them around and difficult to control. Other theories see people trying to get to grips with their environments, trying to understand and organize them, pulling them into amenable shape.... The 'push' theorists look at their subjects from the outside, so much so that it would be more accurate to call their subjects objects.... The 'pull' theorists, on the other hand, use people very much as the subjects of their experiments. These subjects are often remarkably verbose and assumed to know more or less what they want of their environment.
>
> *(pp. 11 and 12)*

Places are created. People make sense of them. This may often be implicit rather than overtly expressed, unless that is part of a planning and design activity. Even then, what comes into existence relies on what those who use those locations make of them. The pushes and pulls are constantly interacting with each other. This is dialectic in the sense that actions and places interact to create the unfolding synthesis of a Place.[24]

Distinguishing places

One of the consequences of the existence of social expectations, rules, and roles that help to define any given Place is that the differences between the rules of different Places help to give rise to their differentiation.

This became very apparent when the UK government issued procedures for working safely because of the threat of COVID-19.[25] A dozen different settings were identified that each would benefit from focused guidelines. In doing this the government advisors were recognising that the patterns of activity in each of these types of employment are different enough to warrant different detailed instructions. These instructions are the more explicit type of rule that we've all came to know during the pandemic, most notably the rule of 'social distancing'. The different recommendations are identifying different types of Place, which have different frameworks for their activities. These patterns of activity are influenced in part by the physical nature of the situations in which they typically operate. They are also, importantly, shaped by the regime. That is the management of the activities that characterise their work. These are produced by the objectives and reasons for each setting.

The differences between the various locations of work may seem obvious, but a closer look at the guidelines do reveal the implicit rules that shape how those Places are experienced. The underlying intentionality of the Place, why people are there, is also highlighted by the government guidelines. It is therefore possible to get an understanding of variations in the nature of Places from the list of distinct government guidelines for setting, as listed in Table 2.1.

This only lists Places which house activities which have commercial implications. However, it does serve to emphasise that the nature of Places varies considerably. Exploring these variations enhances the understanding of what Places are and the psychological processes that maintain, develop, and create them. Subsequent chapters in this book therefore consider Places in relation to the variations in the features of their purposes and the related rule structures that characterise them.

I broadly distinguish those Places where the focus is close and personal, such as the home and other places in which people live, notably prisons. Beyond that are public buildings that encompass activities which are not highly specified, such as offices and shops. Those Places that house very specific activities, such as schools, hospitals, and highly regimented ones, notably airports, raise distinct issues about their nature and the experience of them. One crucial aspect of these is that in them people typically interact with others who are not close associates. There are also a fascinating

Table 2.1 List of places identified by the UK government as each needing specific guideline for managing the risk of COVID-19

- Shops running a pick-up or delivery service
- Working in people's homes as a tradesperson, cleaner, or nanny
- Construction
- Manufacturing and processing businesses
- Retail
- Logistics businesses
- Outdoor businesses
- Farming: visiting farms for animal health and welfare
- Fishing or other short-term offshore work
- Cargo-shipping or other long-term offshore work
- Transport businesses
- Waste management businesses

set of Places that emphasise a lack of activity: contemplation, and passivity. These include art galleries and churches. Then there are the naturally open Places ranging from streets to the countryside. All inviting further considerations of the psychological processes that generate the experience of them and elucidate their nature.

In urban planning, a "third place" refers to any informal, social space that exists outside of the home (the "first place") and the workplace (the "second place"). These are the Places where people gather, connect, and build community. Examples of third places include coffee shops, parks, community centres, libraries, and public squares.

The concept, introduced by sociologist Ray Oldenburg in his 1989 book "The Great Good Place", emphasises the importance of these spaces for fostering social interaction, community engagement, and a sense of belonging. Third places are often seen as vital for creating vibrant, liveable cities where residents can come together and form meaningful relationships.

Building types

The distinction between different Places is encapsulated in architectural education and design by the idea of building types. As Thomas Markus[26] makes clear buildings are social objects. They emerge in a particular time, when there is an existing pattern of both power and available technology. They are designed to achieve certain objectives, these include images of authority, opportunities for wealth and to house socio-cultural processes. These different processes enshrine different patterns of activity, each of which requires its own meaning and related building form, creating distinct Places.

As Markus points out this creation of different Places was particularly notable in the middle of the 19th century because of the rapid changes in society. These changes were brought about by a mixture of developments. They included new technology, notably the steam engine, the emergence of a powerful middle class associated with a burgeoning democracy, and an array of associated institutions. This had many related consequences. Perhaps a particularly intriguing one was the recognition of the importance of childhood, with the requirements for everyone to be educated, and the designation of 'play' grounds.

It therefore became necessary to house new objectives for buildings. The socio-technical developments were also reflected in advances in education, which required new forms for schools and universities; the evolution of municipal government required expanded town halls; inter-city transport needed railway stations. The flourishing middle-class wealth and education also gave rise to the need for art galleries and museums. Elaboration of institutional demarcations gave rise to prisons and hospitals.

Different types of buildings are another way of considering the different Places the UK government identified, which required specific guidelines for managing the risk of COVID-19. Their ostensible purposes, for education or looking after the sick, incarcerating the guilty or exhibiting cultural artefacts, carry with them a multitude of meanings and associations, anticipated activities, moods, and expectations. Each building type is therefore the basis of distinct sets of Places.. That will be explored in later chapters.

Conclusions

The dynamic interplay between physical forms, Place meanings and actions are emphasised in this chapter. Emerging out of these processes, attention is drawn to the need to consider rules of places and their associated environmental roles. It is argued that an understanding of this interactive relationship has its roots in the phenomenological emphasis on subjective, bodily experience. The consequent impact of being in place on personal identity and place attachment is noted, developed in subsequent chapters.

Environmental roles draw attention to the reasons people have for being in a Place – their purposes. This combines with the actions and meanings of Places to generate the great divergence of many different types of Place. Those differences are enshrined in the notion of building types to be explored in Chapter 7.

References and endnotes

1 Merleau-Ponty, M. (2002) *Phenomenology of perception*, London: Routledge, is a recent translation of his most cited work. It is dense, detailed, and lengthy. I am only drawing a sliver of the vast insights this work contains.

2 Arie Peled, sadly died in 2019, but his work is still available at www.livedplace.com where it was uploaded in 2008. I accessed it on 20th September 2020.

3 I did enjoy an excellent jazz concert there, though.

4 Further intriguing evidence for the commitment of humanity to being on the level is the frequency with which people, especially as they age, finding stairs a challenge. The single storey bungalow is consequently often desired retreat for those so afflicted. My Darwinian colleagues may well claim this is the price homo sapiens paid for coming down from the trees onto the African savannah.

5 Marsh, P., Rosser, E., & Harré, R. (2005) *The rules of disorder*. London Routledge.

6 Gofman, A. (2014) Durkheim's theory of social solidarity and social rules, in V. Jeffries (Eds.) *The Palgrave handbook of altruism, morality, and social solidarity*, New York: Palgrave Macmillan, https://doi.org/10.1057/9781137391865_3

7 Malinowski, B. (1932) *Crime and custom in savage society*, London: Routledge & Kegan.

8 Wood, D. & Beck, R. (1990) Do's and don'ts: Family rules, rooms, and their relationships. *Children's Environments Quarterly*, 7 (1), 2–14.

9 The original presentation of these ideas was in Goffman, E. (1956) *The presentation of self in everyday life*, New York: Doubleday, but there have been many elaborations since.

10 Chopin, K. (1993) *The awakening*, New York: Dover Publications – first published in 1899 (p. 57).

11 Cooper Marcus, C. (2006) *House as a mirror of self: Exploring the deeper meaning of home*, Berwick, Maine: Nicolas-Hays.

12 Canter, D. (1970) A psychological analysis of the Royal Hospital for sick children: Yorkhill, Glasgow. *Architects' Journal*, September 6, 525–564.

13 Canter, D. (2023) The purposive evaluation of places: A facet approach, in D.Canter (Ed.) *Readings on the psychology of place*, London: Routledge, pp. 79–104.

14 Osmond, H. (1957) Function as the basis of psychiatric ward design. *Psychiatric Services*, 8(4), 23–27.

15 Reicher, S., Spears, R., & Haslam, S. A. (2010) The social identity approach in social psychology, in M. S. Wetherell & C. T. Mohanty (Eds.) *Sage identities handbook*, London: Sage, pp. 45–62.

16 Stott, C., & Radburn, M. (2020) Understanding crowd conflict: Social context, psychology and policing. *Current Opinion in Psychology*, 35, 76–80.

17 Canter, D. (1969) Should we treat building users as subjects or objects, in D. Canter (Ed.) *Architectural psychology*, London: RIBA Publications, pp. 11–17.

18 Sommer, R. (1969) *Personal space: The behavioral basis for design*, Englewood Cliffs: Prentice Hall.

19 Davies, M. W., & Farrington, D. P. (2020) An examination of the effects on crime of switching off street lighting, *Criminology and Criminal Justice*, 20(3), 339–357.
20 Hilary Mantel (2020) *The mirror and the light*, London: 4th Estate.
21 Kimmerer, R. (2013) *Braiding sweetgrass: Indigenous wisdom, scientific knowledge and the teachings of plants*. Milkweed editions, is widely admired book that relates indigenous knowledge to current understanding of ecological systems reveals the depths of cultural identity that even small details of places can have.
22 Canter, D. (1970) Should we treat building users as subjects or objects?, in D. Canter (Ed.) *Architectural psychology*, London: RIBA Publications Ltd., pp. 11–18.
23 Hillier, B., & Hanson, J. (1984) *The social logic of space*, Cambridge: Cambridge University Press.
24 Canter, D. (2023) Action and place: An existential dialectic, in D.Canter (ED.)*Readings on the psychology of place*, London: Routledge, pp. 145–158.
25 https://www.gov.uk/guidance/working-safely-during-coronavirus-covid-19
26 Markus, T. A. (1993) *Buildings and power: Freedom and control in the origins of modern building types*, London: Routledge.

SECTION I

Exploring Places

1

DOI: 10.4324/9780367808655-4

CHAPTER 3

Studying the psychology of Places

My epiphany

In the mid-1960s I was engaged in studying "the Psychological Implications of Office Size" for my PhD in a Department of Building Science.[2] I had wanted to study psychological aspects of art but was encouraged to join a research team[3] commissioned to study offices. Modern office buildings were being built at a rapid rate, so it was deemed valuable to gain an understanding of their use and design in ways that could influence planning guidelines. One aspect of these developments was the production of vast open offices. There was an interest in the consequences for workers of being in these large open spaces, in some cases housing many hundreds of people without any divisions above seated eye-level.

Coming out of a strongly experimental psychology tradition I set about carrying out a 'field experiment'.[4] I therefore brought together a variety of tests for clerical workers to perform. In a tidy experimental tradition, I tested clerical workers who worked in offices of three different sizes; half a dozen people, 20 or 30 people and hundreds of people. In each these offices I got them to perform the tasks. Some where in offices of the size they were used to working in and some in offices of different sizes. Figure 3.1 summarises the results.

These results seriously puzzled me. When people were tested in a room of a different size to the one they normally worked in, there was no statistical difference in their scores. This meant, of course, that workers who normally worked in large offices were being tested in small- or medium-sized ones. People who normally worked in small offices were being tested in Places housing 20 or 30 people or hundreds of people. But the size of the offices they were tested in made virtually no difference to their performance. This suggested that my central hypothesis that the Place where a person was tested would have an impact on their performance was not supported at all.

By contrast, there was a strong relationship between the average score for each group and the size of office in which they typically worked. I was searching for the impact of office size on worker performance. So how could I make sense of these contradictory results? In the process of giving my first talk about this research I suddenly realised what

DOI: 10.4324/9780367808655-5

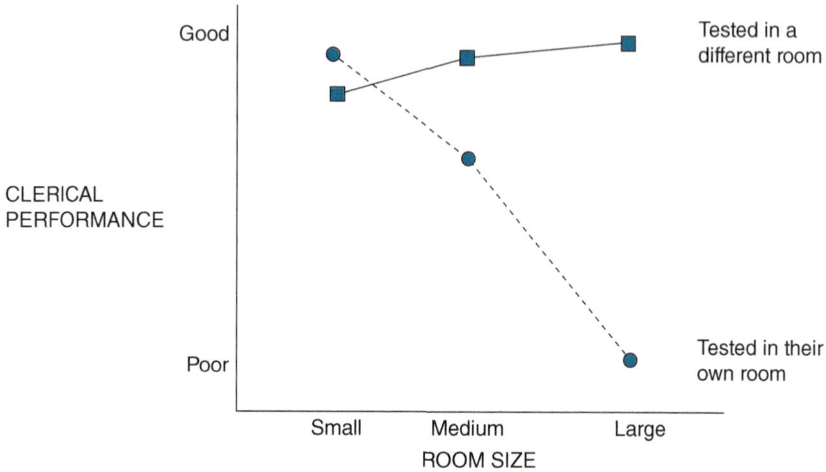

Figure 3.1 Summary of field experiment results, studying the effect of room size (number of people) on clerical performance, indicating average scores for each group

I had found. Now it is painfully obvious, but from my simple-minded perspective, looking for the influence of environmental design *on* human behaviour,[5] I struggled to see it.

Answering a question I was asked after I had presented these results to colleagues, I had an epiphany. It suddenly became clear to me that what the results were demonstrating was not the direct difference in the environments – the size of the offices – but the differences in clerical ability between people who worked in offices that housed different numbers of people! I tended to express this as preferences for working environments, indicating the agency of where people chose to work. But less optimistically it can be seen that the administrative and social structure of office work is such that the more senior people are the smaller the number of people they tended to share an office with. In the 1960s office workers had no computers. Much of their work was clerical in the sense of dealing with mundane, repetitive tasks. As those tasks became more demanding more intellectual skills were required. Selection for the more demanding jobs would be more stringent.

With hindsight I came to understand that what I was picking up with my battery of clerical tasks were aspects of the organisation and culture of the organisations in which I was working. It seems from my results that the physical form of the offices, summarised in the number of people working in them, reflected many aspects of how companies work. How they select their staff. The layout of offices in relation to the tasks that had to be performed. The variations in abilities and skills that were spatially distributed throughout their buildings.

The problem with this hindsight was that I had not collected the right sort of data to develop and elaborate that likely explanation of my results. I had not spoken to staff about how they came to be working where they were, about their qualifications and the nature of their work, or the selection processes the company used. I had not discussed with them their experiences of being in their particular working environment. In effect, I had treated them as robots carrying out tasks, not as people with emotions and aspirations, social relationships and organisational roles.

Figure 3.2 Room friendliness study

An experimental study

I had not fully learnt the lesson of my PhD study of office size when I took up a research post in Strathclyde School of Architecture in Glasgow. Still enamoured with the power of tidy experiments I worked with an architect on a set of studies of room 'friendliness'.[6] Excellently realistic scale models of rooms were built. They could be modified in various ways. The ceiling could be flat or sloping, the window large or small, the furniture formal or informal, and so on.

Each of the different combinations of these could be photographed and presented to respondents, who were asked to rate them on how friendly they thought the rooms were. Two examples are shown in Figure 3.2. The room in Figure 3.2a has a flat ceiling and informal furniture. That in Figure 3.2b has a sloping ceiling and formal furniture. Using conventional statistics for such experiments relatively clear results were found. Rooms with sloping ceiling and informal furniture were indeed rated as more friendly than other rooms.

The problem, though, that I soon became aware of was that the methodology was extremely limited. Once we tried to add further components it all became too complicated to run as an experiment. The interactions between independent variables became too difficult to make sense of. A research design that includes three variables, each at two levels, e.g., sloping/flat ceiling, formal/informal furniture, and small/large windows, generates 8 different room combinations. Add another variable, such as wall colour, then there are 16 rooms. Adding any more features and the number of examples become too large to manage. Not only are they difficult to deal with in practical terms of actually running an experiment, the complex interactions are difficult to make sense of. How does an orange colour when combined with informal furniture differ from its friendliness if it has a sloping ceiling?

Further, when the study was run in Easter Europe we got totally different results. Asking our colleagues why, they said 'The sloping roof reads to us like an attic, where we would keep an elderly relative!". Also, when running studies with videos rather than static photos, there were no clear results.

The importance of this insight into the problem of dealing with components of building in such a simplistic, determinist way is revealed in Figure 3.2c. This is a photograph from a Japanese magazine that claims the design of this storeroom was influenced by my room friendliness study. The extrapolation of a naïve experimental result to such a different context demonstrates the dangers of such research when the results are used by those who do not understand experimental procedures.

It was these considerations that made me alert to the idea that buildings are dealt with as Places. These are whole entities that are reacted to in relation to their meanings and why a person might be there. Dealing with components of a building, such as the curvature of a wall, proportions or degree of enclosure, in isolation of the nature of the Place they are part of can be very misleading. Consider, the admittedly extreme example, of a man in a cell weighting execution the next day. Will his stress levels be reduced by being in a round cell?

Archetypes in Architecture by Thomas Thiis-Evensen also points to the complexity of building components and the reactions people have to them,. It was published in 1987 by the Norwegian University Press, but I think it is still relevant, especially to any attempt to deconstruct architecture into distinct components. They will all interact with each other to create Places.

The lesson for studies of Places that I took from the insights my unexpected results gave me[7] are:

- The way the research is planned– the research design – makes assumptions about the processes that are being studied.
- The details of the measurements that are made carry implications for what can be explored about aspects of people, their actions and experiences.

These issues have consequences for understanding the psychology of Place. The methodology employed in any study shapes the sorts of models and theories that are likely to be supported by the results. In this chapter I therefore review the many ways in which Place experience has and is being studied, in order to bring to the surface, the implicit assumptions and crucial limitations the methodologies have.

Hurdles to studies of being in Place

Before examining how Place psychology is studied it is helpful to consider the challenges to carrying out research into being in Places and experiencing them.

We are always both in and part of a Place. In other words, not only is the experience of a Place one of a present existence in a particular location. Being there is also a contribution to the nature of that Place. In addition, our being in that Place carries implications for both us and the Place itself. These existential aspects create momentous hurdles to exploring the psychological implications of Places separately from who is there, why and where they are. People are always somewhere. You and I never have a presence as a disembodied entity, floating in some vacuum, devoid of physical existence. Even within 'virtual reality' simulations we still have our bodily existence. That can become obvious when we bump into something in the room we are actually in whilst wandering around a virtual Place. Where we actually are, comes with physical sensations, smells, and sounds. More importantly, we have a reason for being where we are, even if we do not want to be there, or we are there mainly to escape from being somewhere else. In online space some of those aspects are still present. Computer game players do not have eyes in the back of their heads. Shooting and moving is controlled as in a recognisable body. Even leaps into the air land on a notional ground. There are tasks to complete which influence actions and how they are performed.

Against the background of these challenges research has to focus on limited aspects of being in a Place. The full richness of thoughts, feelings, purposes, and actions cannot be amassed and analysed. Such a plethora of information would not usually be an objective for a research project anyway. Studies are shaped, implicitly or explicitly, by particular research questions and the assumptions that underly those questions. I gave people tests at desks because I had formulated a hypothesis that assumed people would be influenced in their performance on those tests by the room where those desks were. I gave them clerical tasks because I wanted to study issues that related to their day-to-day activities as office workers.

In the natural sciences the context of where a measurement is made can be removed by carrying out studies in the highly controlled, rarified context of the laboratory. The sources of all known forms of impurity, which may distort the results obtained, can be managed and removed as much as possible. Great expense, notably in elementary particle physics, goes into keeping any possible unwanted influences at bay. But even in less expensive sciences such as biology careful laboratory control is at the heart of research.

In psychology there is often a similar attempt to reduce, or even remove, 'unwanted variables', to 'control' for 'contaminating' or 'confounding' variables. I've put all these terms in quotation marks because they are used in a rather arcanely specialist way. They are drawn from physics and chemistry, where they make eminent sense. Consider, as a common example, judgements of photographs of landscapes. What aspects of those photographs would compromise, or contaminate, the results of judgements of them? The time of day when the photograph is taken? The season of the year? Whether it is a close up or panoramic? Whether it is familiar to respondents or not? The reason why a person may be in that particular landscape? All of these would probably influence responses. They are going to 'confound' the results? Any or all of them. What does it mean to select the crucial aspects of those photographs that are of value for testing specific hypotheses, carefully omitting any influence that may limit the validity of the test of the hypothesis.

The problem is that those aspects of the photographs that are considered to potentially 'contaminate' the results are thought of in that way because they are *relevant* to the experience of the Place. If they were not relevant there would be no need to control for them. To take just one potentially 'confounding' variable – time of day when the photograph was taken. If time of day were regarded as having an influence on reactions to the photograph, then making sure all the photographs in the study were taken at the same time of day would mean that the influence of time of day is being ignored. A study with a controlled selection of photographs, reducing unwanted variations, would not be without value, but its generalisability beyond the time of day the photographs were taken would be open to serious question.

The same issues emerge with a less artificial research design based on observing the use of Places. It is practically impossible, and often ethically undesirable, to record everything that goes on in a Place. There is also the difficult task of determining which of the many possible actions should be taken note of. This can be problems of scale. Should every gesture be logged or just the broad patterns of activity? What about the details of time and location? How precise should they be? Any answers to these questions shape the nature of the enquiry being carried out.

The choice of what information to collect is always significant when exploring aspects of naturally existing phenomena. Besides the entities to present, as in the photograph example, or the observations to be made, there is the selection of questions that may be asked in an interview or on a questionnaire, or the tasks that may be set, illustrated for example, by getting people to draw maps of an area they know. In all these cases the research question being answered is constrained by the selection of the data that is being used to answer that question. This is not to say research is impossible, but it is essential to emphasise that selection in studies of Place. This is not challenging in the same way in physics or chemistry because what is being studied, usually, does not take its meaning and significance from its context and human relationships to it. Therefore, Place studies require a special understanding of the research process. The conclusions drawn from the research always need to be carefully cautioned with reference to the details of how the study was set up, the data collected and the assumptions made.

Experimenter effects

A further aspect of how a study is set up, that is often ignored, is known as its 'demand characteristics'.[8] These are the beliefs that participants have about the study and what is expected of them (its 'demands') which are derived from cues present in the testing situation – its demand 'characteristics'. In many studies,[9] these beliefs have been shown to alter the outcomes of the study. The most obvious of these are those produced by participants wanting to present themselves in a good light. Or wishing to please the experimenter by giving the responses they think the experimenter wants, known as a *social desirability response bias*.[10] That can be a real challenge to overcome in interviews and questionnaire studies.

A more general feature of research beyond 'demand characteristics' are those influences on outcomes that are known more broadly as 'experimenter effects'.[11] Intriguingly one of the first studies to examine experimenter effects directly was also an early environmental psychology study. The implications on judgements of being in a particular Place[12]were studied Participants were asked to assess the amount of 'energy' and 'well-being' in pictures of faces. The pictures were somewhat ambiguous negatives of actual photographs of faces in which the person wore a small head covering to hide their hair. The judgements were made in different Places, some in a laboratory, others in a broom cupboard. Although in the research accounts these were referred to as 'beautiful' and 'ugly' rooms. The faces were judged to be less energetic, showing less well-being in the 'ugly' room.

Another widely cited study that is also an exploration of the power of Place are the famous (some would say notorious) Milgram Experiments. In these, peoplein an apparent laboratory situation, were asked to shock others they thought were being trained to respond. The results indicated that participants continued issuing 'shocks' that they thought were at an extremely dangerous level. This has become known as demonstrating the power of authority to influence people to break social norms.

The Milgram study has become extremely contentious. In a very detailed examination of the data from the study, Gina Perry and her colleagues[13] demonstrated that there were very powerful demand characteristics at work.W hat participants thought was really happening influenced what they did. If they believed they were actually shocking people, they were far less likely to 'give' severe shocks than those who did not believe this was actually happening.

Another important consequence of the Milgram experiment, and other similar experiments that try to mislead participants, is that there is widespread scepticism about what psychologists ask people to do. This can often add a layer of misapprehension to their involvement in psychological research. The wide range of unwanted influences on respondents from a combination of experimenter and demand characteristics is now even recognised as crucial in experimental economics.[14]

A framework for considering material collected to study Places

The distinction between a 'social' neighbourhood and one held in mind – cognitive – draws attention to productive differences between measurement. The example of studying the concept of neighbourhood also highlights the underlying assumptions about what is being studied by different forms of data collection.

As a more general framework for considering the implications of the forms of data being collected it is useful to be aware of two dimensions of what can be gathered about the use and experience of Places, as indicated in Figure 3.3.

The framework outlined in Figures 3.3 provides two facets of data sources. Combined they point to four broad types of material collected in studying Places. Each of these four types carries particular implications for the psychology of Place theories that are assumed when these methods are used. It is only a loose framework because the details of the way in which the material is collected, converted into data and analysed can all enable different sorts of hypotheses to be tested.

One generally crucial aspect of any data collection methods is whether they are highly structured or open. This really operates as a third face to the two in Figure 3.3.

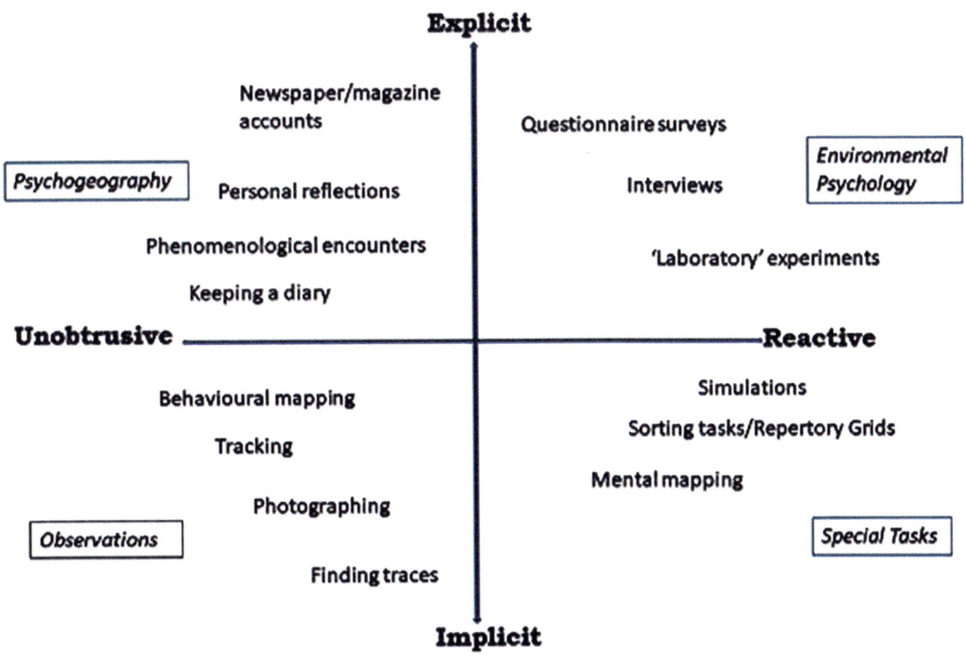

Figure 3.3 Examples of data sources in relation to their typical position on two dimensions

That is whether there are limited opportunities of what responses or observations can be made. This contrats with providing more open possibilities for what data is generated. For example, an observational study may just count the number of people in a particular location, or it can film what goes on there and seek to identify its dominant themes. Similarly, an interview or questionnaire can give people possible answers to choose from, or phrase questions in a way that allows respondents to determine what sort of information they will give. A closed question, such as "do you like it here?" implies a yes or no answer. The open question "tell me what it is like to live here" could generate a great variety of different answers. In closed questions researchers assume they know the answers that are relevant. With open questions they are giving respondents a much more participatory role in the research process. Allowing them to reveal what they consider the important issues to be.

Unobtrusive–reactive

The unobtrusive–reactive continuum reflects the degree to which the researcher needs to consider the impact of the study on what is being studied.[15] Some forms of data collection are referred to as 'nonreactive' measures. The proposal is that they can enhance the objectivity of any study because they reduce the possibility of the participant responding to the experience of the study, as well as what is being studied.

The crucial aspect of methods that are less obtrusive is that the source of the information is generated without any awareness that it is going to be a source of data for research. That does not imply that the material from which the data is derived is necessarily objective or complete. There may be an appreciation of public interest in the material being produced, as in a newspaper article or a book about experience of a Place. The potential bias in why the information has been made available will need to be considered when analysing any 'unobtrusive' material.

The irony is that although the nonreactive sources of information are not influenced by the researcher, precisely because they are not collected for research purposes, they are likely to have many flaws and biases. The people who do make this material available have their own purposes and agendas. Journalists want an interesting and exciting story, preferably with some 'human interest'. What they chose to report will therefore be biased towards those events and people that are particularly dramatic. Accounts by authors will also be written to engage. They will highlight features of Places which the author finds particularly interesting. Observations of what happens where can be very useful. But its significance and meaning to those being observed is not necessarily available.

At the other end of this continuum are those research interventions for which the participants, respondents (or as they are called in experimental studies – the subjects) are required to act on instructions given by the researcher. This may be responses to questions on a pro forma or in an interview, participation in an experiment or even acting out a role.

Another distinction in aspects of data collection runs from material that is publicly available, through to that which is essentially private. At the public end are reports in newspapers and other published accounts. Magazines and websites are a remarkable resource for researchers The photographs that people put on their Instagram and other social media feeds indicate what people think it is interesting to share. This is rather different from what people may reveal in private conversation.

Explicit–implicit

The explicit–implicit dimension is subtler. It draws attention to the extent to which the data recorded can be taken at face value or whether its implications need to be inferred. For example, the answer to a question or the account in a diary, in different ways, can be treated as a direct account of what the person generating that data is indicating. By contrast, the photographs of a scene or the map a person draws need to be interpreted. Some further analysis process needs to be carried out in order to make psychological sense of what the raw data indicates.

Taken together, these various facets can be combined to propose four broad themes inherent in data about Places and people's interactions with them. They loosely imply four different ways of thinking about research methods. Each of these carries assumptions about the sorts of theories or explanations of Place use and experience that are appropriate.

Observations

There are many observational sources of data available for studies of Places, from careful observations of locations in use and even traces that people have left, as illustrated in Figure 3.4. The implications of these data sources also have to be interpreted. They do not

Figure 3.4 Showing a trace left by an informal path cutting off the corner between two sets of steps, linking another path to the stairs. A simple (often found) example of how design may ignore people's desires to reduce effort. Some planners deliberately leave open spaces for the chosen, informal paths to emerge then pave those areas

directly indicate what their significance or meaning actually is. The crucial point about this material is that it is raw information that must be converted into data for analysis.

Observations of what happens where can be very useful. But the significance and meaning of the observations may be difficult to infer. Seeing someone walking may be regarded as a neutral observation, but it takes on a different meaning if it is known the person is walking to get lunch or to meet a lover. To take a more extreme example, when studying a murder scene, deriving the characteristics of the crime and criminal[16] will often be extremely speculative. The disarray at the murder scene could imply a young, haphazard criminal, who was extremely violent and impulsive. Or it could indicate a person desperately searching for something who killed when disturbed during the search.

However, even specific observations, such as the recording of what happens where, 'behavioural mapping' is not without its problems of intrusiveness. I remember well, an architecture student who had been carrying out observations in a children's hospital ward.[17] He returned from his study rather upset. He had been carefully following my instructions to carry out his observations without getting involved in any way with what was going on, just objectively recording. But when he left, one of the children he had been watching burst out crying! Obviously, being watched playing with toys had meant something to this lonely child waiting on a hospital ward. Observing what is going on is never entirely unobtrusive. In some cases, it may even be disturbing or illegal.

In a nutshell, despite the apparently objective nature of observing and collecting information that has not been generated for research purposes, there are two central challenges to its effective use. The first is the practical challenge of converting this material so that it can be carefully analysed, often requiring the time-consuming, and not always particularly objective, process of 'content analysis', usually considered as an aspect of 'qualitative research'.[18] The second is the theoretical demand of making sense of the results. Without direct contact with those who have generated the material that is being studied there is always the risk that the interpretation of the data is misleading. For example, even the example in Figure 3.4 may be the result of something other than students rushing to their lectures, urgently taking the shortest route. The informal path may have been produced by an animal such as a badger. More information is often required to make reasonable sense of the material collected.

Environmental psychology

The set of Explicit, Reactive data sources are the ones most commonly found in studies by Environmental Psychologists, although they may be as readily thought of as overt contact with people, typically focused around asking them questions. This does allow direct exploration of attitudes and emotions, which can only be inferred from the observations without direct interactions with people.

These more 'obtrusive' forms of data collection facilitate clear results that can, at least initially, be taken more or less at face value. They also lend themselves to ready analysis and usually quantitative data. However, as already noted, they are prone to experimenter demand influences. In other words, they may generate reactions to the whole process of being involved in the research.

The contrast with observational studies is that there is no necessary indication that the responses will be reflected in actions.[19] It is also worth noting that questionnaires can be rather crude affairs in which a set of questions are put together rather haphazardly on the assumption that they do relate to a particular topic. Or, they can be highly sophisticated, thoroughly developed to ensure they do adequately and clearly deal with the topic they purport to explore. There will be no mention of the former in this book.

Despite the problems of studying the use and actions in Place there has been a vast array of questionnaire studies of many aspects of Places. It has been said over a century ago that "because of its ease of use the questionnaire is the bane of modern society".[20] Putting together a set of questions and asking a selection of people to answer them has grown steadily easier with the growth of the internet and various forms of online interaction.

The value of questionnaire surveys in psychological research goes beyond the public opinion survey that present day politicians and newspapers thrive on. The possibility of measuring the vagaries of human experiences, emotions, attitudes, actions, and desire, as well as human characteristics, notably intelligence and personality, can be seen as the making of modern psychology. The realisation that people could be pinned down, and their features which cannot be seen, given some sort of number opened up a mountain of research possibilities. It also became a major industry that is thriving evermore so today.

An intriguing development of observational studies that I have called ***Place studies*** is a methodology that explores what happens where, with and by whom in a more holistic way than just observing what happens. This allows the build-up of a rich account of the nature of a Place akin to a case study of an individual. However, it requires insights from the more subjective experiences of those using a Place to garner a fuller picture of the meanings of Places.

A number of carefully prepared questionnaire-based studies are considered throughout this book. These include measurements of attitudes towards the environment, satisfaction with a building by its users, the meanings building forms carry, preferences for landscapes, the feeling of oneness with nature, and many more. Understanding the strengths and weaknesses of these, supports an evaluation of studies using them and their conclusions.

The thorough construction of questionnaires is time-consuming. It requires a precise identification of what is being studied and the initial exploration of what are the appropriate questions to ask. The questions need to be tested in pilot studies to establish if they make sense to the relevant population. An interesting challenge in making sense of these studies derives from the internationalisation of studies of Place. It is not at all unusual these days for studies to be published in English journals, but the original questionnaires are in Polish or Chinese. Unfortunately, any confusions that may be inherent in translating questions for an English audience are rarely discussed.

Studying attitudes

Attitudes are general dispositions towards something. Broadly characterised as being positive or negative, for or against, a person, thing, concept, or Place. They are regarded as precursors to, predictions of, and reason for, what people do. With the onslaught of climate change and associated requirement of changing how people relate to the environment, their actions and reactions to their natural surroundings, there has been an unleashing of studies of environmental attitudes. Googles Scholar found well over a 100,000 journal articles in a search for "environmental attitudes". These studies go back well into the 1990s and earlier.

Interestingly, many of the questions exploring 'environmental' attitudes ask directly about Nature. In this context the 'environment' tends to be equated with natural settings. Although there are certainly environmental campaigners protesting about pollution in cities. Recently, for example, traffic has been stopped in crucial locations around London by people drawing attention to the need to insulate British homes. Yet the dominant rhetoric is not about the 'Dark satanic mills' of William Blake and the Dicken's era. The appalling conditions still present in many cities, as well as the horrors of internment and refugee camps, are very different to those under the heading of environmental impacts. It is the damage to the 'Blue Planet' on which studies of environmental attitudes focus.

The typical approach to exploring these issues consists of getting people to complete questionnaires. Cruz and Manata[21] identified 26 such questionnaires. Although they all investigate attitudes, they use a host of different labels for what they claim to be examining. They may be called 'environmental concerns', 'ecological world view', 'ecological paradigm', 'value orientation', and a few more (all listed by Cruz and Manata).[1] This mixture indicates the variety of approaches to attitudes and how they are inevitably influenced by the theoretical stance of the researchers.

However, for our concerns with the meanings of the environment and how people relate to nature, questionnaire surveys reveal the roles that people take regarding the environment. These are well illustrated in one of the most comprehensive studies of many aspects of environmental attitudes by Milfont and Duckitt,[22] considered in more detail in Chapter 16. They had 455 undergraduates complete a 99 items questionnaire made up of questions used in many other studies of environmental attitudes, with results similar to those found by others.

Questionnaire surveys typically ask about the 'environment' and words that relate to that. The meanings of words relating to 'environment'raise questions about what is actually being explored in studies of attitudes towards the environment, landscape, and nature. There is a need for caution when making sense of questionnaire surveys about attitudes using these terms. The range of subtle meanings that these and related words have warns us that these surveys are explorations of the stereotypical sense of these terms, for any particular subgroup, rather than a reflection of their direct experience of outdoor Places.

The term 'environment' is probably the most slippery. Although it literally means that which surrounds, or more specifically "the aggregate of conditions in which a person or thing exists", it has come to mean the natural world, or even the Earth.

To be clear, I am not criticising these questionnaire surveys. My intention is to indicate something of the cultural background inherent in the terms used as a way of clarifying what is being studied. It is the meaning of these terms to the respondents, with all their associated connotations that is being explored in such surveys.

Milfont and Duckitt's questionnaire illustrates the range of issues that can be considered under the heading of environmental attitudes. Their questions were structured to ask respondents to indicate how strongly they agreed (from 1 'not all' to 7 'very much indeed') with statements such as:

- I think spending time in nature is boring.
- I would like to support an environmental organization.

- Humans are severely abusing the environment.
- Humans are no more important than any other species.
- Nature is valuable for its own sake.
- I could not be bothered to save water or other natural resources.

There are many ambiguities in using a questionnaire to explore such crucial and complex issues. For example, some of the questions have as their subject the respondent 'I', others are about 'humans' and others phrase the question's subject as 'nature'. Yet other questions deal with what industry should do, or governments, involvement or otherwise in environmental organisations, and so on. This questionnaire, therefore, illustrates the great range of topics that are encapsulated in the idea of 'environmental attitudes' across many different studies. Interestingly, in their 2004 study, Milfont and Duckitt do not ask questions directly about global warming or climate change as such. They focus on aspects of nature and more generally 'the environment'.[23]

Their results consequently rely heavily on how the questions are phrased and worded. This is not to castigate a very thorough and detailed analysis. That is helpful in pointing to the complexity of the concerns involved. Their sophisticated statistical analysis pointed, for example, to a distinction between 'the belief that nature is primarily for human use' and 'Support for conservation policies regarding industry and the use of raw materials'. These are different again from questions that reveal a belief that 'human ingenuity and science will solve environmental problems'. Aspects that I revisit in Chapter 16.

Summarising the assumptions inherent in data collection

A greatly simplified summary of the models which are generally implicit in different research strategies and tactics is offered here.[24]

- *Observations*, for example, even when part of a case study, tend to regard people as organisms – objects of study. Admittedly, usual human insights make it possible to infer some aspects of what the observed people are experiencing. Yet, in essence, the model of person-environment interaction that is at the base of making decisions on what can be observed happening, owes a lot to the idea of their being stimuli in a Place that generate or at least invite a response.
- *Questionnaires and surveys* emphasise the accounts given by people. They may not relate closely to what they actually do. If developed carefully they are derived from what people normally express about the topic being studied. However, the format still tends to explore what the researcher has in mind. Often this assumes that there is some definitive truth which is revealed in analyses of the answers.
- *Special tasks,* discussed in more detail in Chapter 5, such as asking people to draw sketch maps, or put photographs in piles according to some personal criteria, emphasise cognitive processes. They explore the internal representations people have of the world. They recognise that subjectivity is a significant part of being human. They may operate within the positivist tradition[25], expecting to find some reflection of reality in a person's cognitions. Or they may be more open to an acceptance that people construct meaning in their interactions.

Conclusions

As Italo Calvino elegantly states in his exploration of accounts of cities:

> ...the city must never be confused with the words that describe it.
>
> *Italo Calvino,* Invisible cities[26]

A city is always a complex mix of actions, meanings, and physical forms. Consequently, any studies of them, or any other Places, inevitably only capture a limited aspect of them and the experiences of them. Those limitations derive from the impact of the assumptions embedded in each approach to setting up a research project and deciding how to collect data. These are perspectives or theories about what shapes human activities and experiences. That is, appropriate ways to explain human behaviour, thoughts, and emotions.

This chapter has reviewed the methods available for the study of actions in and experiences of Places. The aim has been to draw attention to the embedding of psychological assumptions in the methods chosen. The major distinction is between methodologies that assume there is a direct influence of aspects of the physical environment on people. That is usually summarised as a determinist perspective. This contrast broadly with a framework that foregrounds human agency and purposes. This recognises the complexity and context specificity of human participation in Places.

Although ways of collecting data and its implications have been described in this chapter, I always like to point out that to understand research and how to do it is rather like learning to ride a bike. You cannot fully understand the process or how to do it by reading about it in a book. You have to get on doing it, possibly falling off once or twice, before you master it.

References and endnotes

1 A clerical worker being tested in a vast open plan office as part of my PhD work in 1965. The thumb with the stopwatch is mine (aged 21).

2 This was initially as a student within the Department of Building Science at The University of Liverpool, then eventually moved to the School of Architecture at Strathclyde University, following my supervisor Brian Wells, then joining The Building Performance Research Unit.

3 The Pilkington Research Unit.

4 The book by Campbell, D. T., & Stanley, J. C. (1963) *Experimental and quasi-experimental designs for research*, Chicago: Rand McNally, was contributing to the move to get psychological research out of laboratories and away from just studying students.

5 Often characterised as a 'determinist' theory. The environment (as a stimulus) influencing behaviour (as a response).

6 Canter, D., West, S., & Wools, R. (1974) Judgements of people and their rooms. *British Journal of Social and Clinical Psychology, 13*(2), 113–118. The study described was the basis of Roger Wool's PhD.

7 *A Lesson Ignored.*

I have to comment here that the limited experimental approach just described is now the principal methodology in what is called 'neuroarchitecture' But it uses clinical biosensors rather than questionnaire responses. How can it cope with the complexity of building forms and human experience? How can the meaning of Places be unravelled when considering simple components of buildings? This is a critique of many contemporary studies to which I will return.

8 Corneille, O., & Lush, P. (2023) Sixty years after Orne's American psychologist article: A conceptual framework for subjective experiences elicited by demand characteristics. *Personality and Social Psychology Review, 27*(1), 83–101.

9 Corneille, O., & Lush, P. (2023) Sixty years after Orne's American psychologist article: A conceptual framework for subjective experiences elicited by demand characteristics. *Personality and Social Psychology Review*, 27(1), 83–101.
10 Bernardi, R. A., & Nash, J. (2023) The importance and efficacy of controlling for social desirability response bias. *Ethics & Behavior*, *33*(5), 413–429.
11 First elaborated in details by Rosenthal, R. (1976) Experimenter effects in behavioral research.
12 Maslow, A. H., & Mintz, N. L. (1956) Effects of esthetic surroundings: I. Initial effects of three esthetic conditions upon perceiving "energy" and "well-being" in faces. *The Journal of Psychology*, *41*(2), 247–254.
13 Perry, G., Brannigan, A., Wanner, R. A., & Stam, H. (2020) Credibility and incredulity in Milgram's obedience experiments: A reanalysis of an unpublished test. *Social Psychology Quarterly*, *83*(1), 88–106. Also given in great detail in Perry, G. (2013) *Behind the shock machine: The untold story of the notorious Milgram psychology experiments*, New York: The New Press.
14 De Quidt, J., Vesterlund, L., & Wilson, A. J. (2019) Experimenter demand effects, in *Handbook of research methods and applications in experimental economics*, Cheltenham: Edward Elgar Publishing, pp. 384–400.
15 Webb, E. J., Campbell, D. T., Schwartz, R. D., & Sechrest, L. (2000) *Unobtrusive measures* (Rev. ed.), Thousand Oaks: Sage; later revised by Lee, R. M. (2005) *Unobtrusive methods*, London: Elsevier.
16 Canter, D., & Alison, L. J. (2003) Converting evidence into data: The use of law enforcement archives as unobtrusive measurement. *The Qualitative Report*, 8(2), 151–176, https://nsuworks.nova.edu/tqr/vol8/iss2/1
17 Canter, D. (1972) A psychological analysis of The Royal Hospital for sick children: Yorkhill, Glasgow. *Architects' Journal*, September 6, 525–564.
18 There is considerable literature and ideology around qualitative research and the process of content analysis with many different ways of approaching it. Silverman, D., & Marvasti, A. (2008) *Doing qualitative research: A comprehensive guide*, London: Sage, is one of a number of books overviewing these issues.
19 There is a significant literature exploring the relationships between expressed views, notably attitudes and behaviour, for example, Ajzen, I., Fishbein, M., Lohmann, S., & Albarracín, D. (2018) The influence of attitudes on behavior, in D.Albarracin & B.T. Johnson (eds.) *The handbook of attitudes, volume 1: Basic principles*, New York: Routledge, pp. 197–255.
20 I'm pretty sure it was William James the founder of modern psychology who said this, but a search using an AI algorithm says it was the satirical singer-songwriter and mathematician Tom Lehrer. He could have been quoting William James.
21 Cruz, S. M., & Manata, B. (2020) Measurement of environmental concern: A review and analysis. *Frontiers in Psychology*, *11*, 363.
22 Milfont, T. L., & Duckitt, J. (2010) The environmental attitudes inventory: A valid and reliable measure to assess the structure of environmental attitudes. *Journal of Environmental Psychology*, 30(1), 80–94, https://doi.org/10.1016/j.jenvp.2009.09.001
23 It is worth noting that this is a perennial problem of psychology and other social science research on issues of general significance. Research can take so long to conduct, analyse, and publish that it often is behind the curve of what is of public significance.
24 An overview of many different ways of studying Places is given in Gifford, R. (2016) *Research methods for environmental psychology*,London: John Wiley & Sons.
25 A rather abstract but thorough critique of positivism in psychology is given by Teo, T (2018) The consequences of "positivism" in psychology, in T. Teo, *Outline of theoretical psychology: Critical investigations*, LondonPalgrave Macmillan pp. 103–132.
26 Calvino, I. (1974) *Invisible cities*, London: Vintage Classics, p. 61.

CHAPTER 4

Active engagement with Places

Introduction

Chapter 3 considered formal, objective methodologies for exploring the uses and experiences of Places, as well as approaches to measuring aspects of their physical form. They are all part of environmental psychology and human geography research processes. Characteristically, they do not engage directly with Places. They draw on structured accounts that people give, or procedures that people go through to indicate their conceptualisations of, and reactions to Places. These methodologies have many similarities to those used in many other areas of research. There is little about most of them that takes special advantage of the nature of Places. The fact that Places have a here and now existence.

Places have a presence that can be explored directly. Human activity and related social processes are available to be observed and even interacted with. As a consequence, a variety of methodologies have been developed and explored which engage directly with Places in use. The disciplines of archaeology and anthropology[1] have long connected directly with actual Places. The only difference from those traditions for the psychology of Place is the search for overt indications of use and the social and psychological explanations of that use.

Observing Places in use and building up data on the patterns of use offers insights and enables the testing of hypotheses, providing a pathway to understanding that is not available to archaeologists. Human actions are sometimes the focus of anthropological research, but more usually aspects that relate to culture is what is emphasised, rather than psychology and social interactions.

Over the last half century subjective accounts have been given a strong framework within the tradition of phenomenology. That thoughtful approach to personal engagement with Places has garnered a huge following within geography, although many psychologists in their search for objective reality are disdainful of these fundamentally personal explorations. Those empirically minded social scientists who search for neutral, objective accounts of Places have tended to eschew these types of engagement with

DOI: 10.4324/9780367808655-6

Places. However, there is little doubt that they can provide rich insights. That has been demonstrated especially by geographers such as Relph[2] who has written for nearly half a century about the informal experiences of Places. Or Tuan[3] who is happy to call his exploration of Places 'philosophical musings'.

Beyond the formal observations of Places in use, or the somewhat structured musings of phenomenologists there is a long tradition, going back millennia, of informal, personal explorations of Places. As discussed later, over the last century these have become part of a melange of claims and ideas, emerging as a variegated movement. This has been given the rather confusing name *psychogeography*. For some it is a radical, rather anarchic challenge to the social order. For others it is a label that allows them to pontificate on their own engagement with Places. However, as with the more philosophically grounded phenomenology, the insights from psychogeographical meanderings can still be of value. At the very least, they help to illustrate aspects of engagements with Places that are studied by more formal means.

Studying public life

Unlike most other aspects of human actions and experiences, Places exist over time. They have a presence whether or not a researcher takes an interest in them. They are typically in use and often potentially available to access. It is therefore possible to engage directly with them as part of research into their use and influence.

The study of Places in use takes what I am calling the 'psychology' of Place into realms that others would more readily categorise as sociology, human geography, or more broadly just social science. It is even regarded by some as an aspect of architectural training. Jan Gehl[4] promoted, for many years, what he called the "study of public life" from The Royal Danish Academy of Fine Arts, School of Architecture. He elaborated many ways in which the use of Places in cities can be observed and recorded. He calls this an examination of the relationship between public space and public life. Yet, Gehl is curiously ignorant of a long tradition, known as 'behavioral mapping'[5] that has been used in many different types of Places.[6] Or the highly regarded studies of Barker[7] and his colleagues, which they called 'Ecological Psychology', introduced in Chapter 1 and discussed in more detail later in this chapter.

All these observational methods vary in focus and detail. Such variations relate to the objectives of the study and the assumptions about people underlying them. Gehl and his colleagues seem very ready to presume they know why people they observe are doing what they do. For example, in recording where people prefer to stand in a public square, seeing people stand in different locations is taken as unquestionably indicative of their preferences. The objective facts cannot be faulted, but the reasons why a person chose a particular location to stand may be complex and idiosyncratic: where they arranged to meet a friend, where they have a good view of passing pedestrians, keeping out of the sun or rain. Those reasons probably do not matter too much if the objective is focused on revisiting design decisions. However, if the desire is to understand how and why people make use of Places and the objectives that guide their actions, simple observations are not enough.

As Gehl elaborates, the sorts of purposes of his observational studies are rather practical. They may be a basis for planning decisions, or to generate before/after statistics to evaluate a project. They can also be the basis for developing a brief to provide guidance for a future design. More general research questions can also be answered by observational studies, such as gender differences in the use of Places. But understanding,for example different uses by men and women become problematic if purposes and habits as well as cultural codes and subjective experiences are relevant. They are not always apparent from just observing what can be seen.

Behavioural mapping

Behavioural mapping emphasises not just where people are but what they do there and how that is distributed in time and space.[8] In general terms it can emphasise either Places and their use, or individuals and what they do. Not that dissimilar from physicists studying either the movement of elementary particles or their location – doing both at the same time not being possible as Heisenberg pointed out.

Observing where people do what, as mentioned in reference to Gehl's work, can be systematically drawn on when making design recommendations. One clear example comes from study of children's use of outdoor space.[9] The researchers claim that results, such as those shown in Figure 4.1, reveal that "the method can be used to accurately link environmental components and affordances of behavior settings to children's activity".

This mapping of activities can take many forms. The rapid development of recording devices is also making the process much easier and richer. It is now possible to record people's movement in virtual reality.

From a theoretical perspective both Gehl's and behavioural mapping procedures are embedded in an emphasis on people as objects to be studied. Although the reasons for people being in a location may be inferred, there is still an implicit determinist view that their actions are shaped by the opportunities the physical environments provide. The

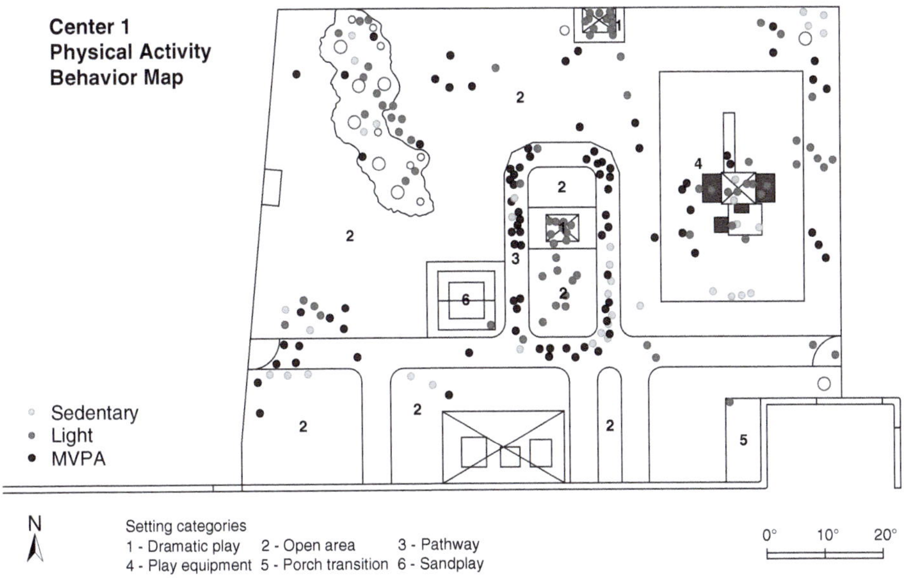

Figure 4.1 Example of behavioural mapping record of children's outdoor activity[10]

reasons why people choose to be in a particular location, or perhaps more interestingly, carefully avoid being there, are not always apparent from mapping who is, or goes, where.

Behaviour settings

The observations made under the umbrella term Ecological Psychology as derived from Barker's initial[11] description of that framework[12] derived from a Skinnerian learning theory perspective that human behaviour is shaped by patterns of reinforcement. Barker therefore claimed it was necessary to develop an account of the actual existence of reinforcements in daily life, especially for children. This gave rise to extremely detailed recording of what individuals did and said in different locations.

The central ideas were, firstly, that in any milieu there tend to be *standing patterns of behaviour*. These are recurring activities in which role relationships are usually the same. One example would be a French lesson for children in a specific school grade. Another would be a dentist's surgery with a patient undergoing treatment. For this to be recognised as a behaviour setting there needs to be some relationship between the form the activity takes and the physical context in which it happens, known as *synomorphy*. Barker and his colleagues developed various measures of what was observed in order to determine if any event could be labelled as a behaviour setting or not.

Behaviour settings[13] became the units of study allowing a more social perspective than simply looking at patterns of reinforcement. The roles that people had in those settings, most interestingly in studies of schools,[14] emerged as an important feature of any setting. This revealed how many more opportunities there were to take on different roles in small schools compared with big schools, even though there were far more behaviour settings in big schools. For example, a small school would still tend to have a football team and a school band. But would have so few pupils that some would have to participate in both. By contrast, a large school may have a number of football teams and a band, but students could only take part in one of them.

The notions of a behaviour setting, and standing patterns of behaviour, have been more influential than the detailed methodology developed to identify them and measure their occurrence and composition. They have highlighted the power and significance of recurring social processes that have distinct locations. However, although the concept of *synomorphy* implies a relationship between physical form and behaviour this has never been studied in detail in the Ecological Psychology tradition.

Ethnomethodology

An exploration of actual social interactions, that makes use of directly engaging with them, was developed by Garfinkel.[15] He called this *ethnomethodology*, deriving it from the idea that people are always engaged in some form of implicit or explicit strategising about what they are doing. In their day-to-day interactions with each other people reveal that they are following norms and rules of which they may not even be aware. The researcher can reveal these underlying expectations, for example, by asking a stranger "do you know the time". If the stranger tells the researcher what the time is that shows how the context has generated a response acceptable within that situation. If, on the other hand, the response is "Ghosh! Is it that time already. I'm late", a quite different context with different rules is revealed.

Ethnomethodology is regarded as a rich theoretical and methodological perspective within sociology. It has been particularly influential in related areas such as linguistics. However, like behavioural mapping it has ignored the significance of Place in contributing to the expectations associated with rule following and norm negotiation. I was stuck by this when playing with a musical ensemble in an art gallery. When we stopped playing it was clear that visitors to the gallery were unsure whether to applaud or not. The unwritten rule of galleries is to maintain quiet contemplation of the artwork. Our intervention raised questions about that strategy.

A weakness of both Barker's ecological psychology, and Garfinkel's ethnomethodology, from the perspective of Place studies, is not only the lack of consideration of the physical aspects of Places but, importantly, the cognitive, or experiential, features of being in a Place. This weakness contrasts with the emphasis that comes from the focus on personal experiences of Places within the framework of phenomenology.

Phenomenology

For over half a century David Seamon,[16] has made a prolific contribution to contemporary studies of Places, drawing directly on the philosophical tradition of phenomenology. The focus on lived experience in Place and the related awareness

> that through bodily encounters and actions, the person or group contributes to the constitution of a place as, at the same time, those encounters and actions contribute to the person or group's sense of lived involvement and identification with that place.[17]

That emphasis, on the holistic embodiment of person and Place, leads to methods that highlight accounts of personal experiences. This may be through first-person accounts of Place -related experiences in order to draw out crucial features. Or through third-person descriptions of experiences and the situations that they are part of. The overall aim is to find common underlying themes and processes in what are acknowledged as importantly subjective reflections on being in those Places.

Rather than a research strategy or even a tactic, phenomenological explorations are ways of doing research. Most studies can be carried out with the personal, subjective experience being taken as its essence.The more open-end the approach the more possible is it for those personal experiences to be revealed. The crucial point is that this perspective takes as its starting point that human beings have agency. They have objectives and goals, purposes and desires. People are not just reactive organisms, shaped by the external environment. They make sense of being in Places.

The subjective recounting of experiences is not limited to social scientists. For example, in her recent book, sub-titled *Travels in Search of the Emotions of Place*, Alice Maddicott[18] provides enthralling descriptions of Places she has visited, endeavouring to capture the 'atmosphere' of those Places. The difference from Seamon's phenomenological accounts is that she is seeking to depict the unique qualities of those Places as she experienced them. Although her vivid descriptions can be gleaned to reveal intriguing aspects of commonalities in Place experience. As an artist Maddicott does not have that objective. In this regard she is part of the multifarious, evolving tradition of 'psychogeography'.

Bringing psychogeography home

The silos of intellectual life can be quite remarkable. Scholars tend to interact and publish with people who share not only a common interest, but an ideology and ways of exploring their chosen subjects. They live in constrained worlds that symbiotically feed those within, whilst ignoring those outside. There is a reluctance to seek out new realms that might challenge their usual habits of thinking about and doing research.

Awareness of this divisive process was given impetus by C.P. Snow's unhelpful designation of 'two cultures'.[19] He claimed that the sciences and the humanities operated in such totally different ways that it was difficult for them to communicate with each other. Beyond the lack of transactions between the two realms of discourse, Snow insists they are ignorant of each other's contributions and disinterested in what the others have to offer.

In recent years, there have been critiques of this stance,[20] supported by many examples of interactions between these different 'cultures'. To take just one amusing example, elementary particle physicists decided to name a crucial new particle that had three states as a 'quark', drawing the term from the arcane novel by James Joyce.[21] However, Snow's distinction did, I think, contribute to most psychologists (me included) wanting to side totally with the scientific 'culture', eschewing any cross-reference or involvement with the humanities.

This could be regarded as rather ironic when considering, for instance, the theories of Freud and his followers. They have had far greater impact on the humanities, notably the visual arts, than they have had on scientific psychology. Significant movements in art, most obviously surrealism, have taken their impetus from psychoanalytic ideas of the subconscious and associated processes.

I am offering these considerations as a partial explanation why a whole area of intellectual discourse, and related modes of investigation, have been ignored in studies of Place, and more generally in environmental psychology. The term *psychogeography*[22] hints at this area of intellectual exploration. Although it is a term with some rather different meanings.

Without going into the detailed history and development of the use of this term it is important to mention that 'psychogeographers' also appear to be ignorant of social science studies of Place, and of environmental psychology. Although the two realms clearly draw on similar concepts, for instance 'sense of place', they do so unaware of each other's writings. This can be readily illustrated by examining the index of the massive 729 paged *Routledge Handbook of Place.*[23] There are brief mentions of how films can be a 'tool of placemaking'.[24] But only one contribution engages directly with psychogeography[25] as a contribution to an understanding of the experience of Places.

This extremely limited awareness by social scientists of psychogeography is particularly curious when the often-quoted definition of it, by the person who claims to have invented the term, Debord,[26] is considered. It is:

> the study of the precise laws and specific effects of the geographical environment, consciously organised or not, on the emotions and behavior of individuals.

Would that not be a, somewhat simplified, definition of environmental psychology? Also as made clear, for example, in the commentary on www.mookychick.co.uk "Debord was talking about the way humans shape their environment, but also how the environment shapes humans".[27] A statement that reflects Churchill's frequently cited comment which begins many environmental psychology textbooks.

Perhaps the clue to the disparity between the awareness of psychogeography and social science studies of Place is the fact that the mention of psychogeography in *The Routledge Handbook of Place* is in the last section on 'Creative Engagements with Place'. In other words, the editors of the Handbook see psychogeography as part of novel ways of understanding Places and their consequences. They do not reflect on it as part of any empirical scientific tradition.[28] This does accord with the way in which many of the over 200,000 online accounts of psychogeography are presented.[29] They typically refer to an exploration of Places, usually urban environments, with an emphasis on playfulness and the French notion of *dérive*, 'drifting'.

This playfulness is, in its turn, as aspect of another concept favoured by 19th-century French aesthetes, of the flâneur. The casual, possibly haphazard, but perceptive urban wanderer, whose drifting opened him (usually) up to aspects of the city that he would otherwise not have become aware of. Some contemporary writers, notably Wil Self, have raised this activity into a journalistic art-form, heralding it as an exciting way of engaging with Places.

In fact, such a way of being in Place has an even older French origin in Rousseau's promeneur solitaire,[30] published posthumously in 1782. His book is a set of meditations, or 'reveries', each resulting from a different walk. These are descriptions of the sights, especially plants, that Rousseau saw in his walks on the outskirts of Paris. These also gave him the opportunity to think about philosophical and political issues, stimulated by the sights and sounds of the city.

The idea of reflecting on the here and now situation, of being in a Place, re-emerged in a more political form over a century and a half later. That was part of a curious art/philosophy movement of the late 1950s and 1960s which called itself *situationism.* A sort of democratisation of phenomenology. The philosophical origins are usually linked to Marxism and a related anti-consumerist, anti-capitalist stance. But the writings of Debord and his *Situationist International* associates are so obscure, and led to so many break-ups and expulsions, that it is not surprising to find today most writings in the psychogeography tradition focus on an uninhibited openness to Places.

Psychogeography has thus become advocacy of walking around urban settings. Wandering around and recounting the affects the Places have on the wanderer. Most of the stories of these encounters with Places focus on the writers' subjective reactions to the process of walking with relatively little details of where they have walked or what they actually saw.

A slightly different example within the phenomenological traditions is the suggestion to monitor the ephemera in environments such as graffiti.[31] Discovering this, I realised I had unwittingly been a psychogeographer, fascinated by the history of a Place revealed in the layers of meaning encapsulated in ripped posters and overlayed comments, as in the examples from Krakow and Santiago de Compostela in Figures 4.2a and b. This, almost inevitably, was earlier an art movement – the *affichistes*[32] – who collected torn posters in the 1950s and 1960s and added to the rips as a commentary on art as a consumer product. But they were also very much aligned to the spirit of the *situationists*, even though in the spirit of French art and philosophy of the time they tended to ignore each other.

Figure 4.2 (a) Torn poster and graffiti, Krakow in 2017. (b) Torn poster, Santiago de Compostela in 2024. Both capturing a hidden mood of these cities.

I would claim that the rather different qualities revealed in these two photographs do capture interesting differences between the experience of the rather down-at-heal Kracow and the vibrant cultural life of Santiago de Compostela. But that is me imposing a researchers' mentality on some existing artefact, which is open to many other interpretations.

Treating this graffiti as indication of local Places and the cultures that characterise them move beyond the consideration of them as part of street art. However, the richness of this material is elegantly capture in a book published by the Istanbul Modern art gallery.[33]

This way of exploring Place experience may seem haphazard and unscientific, but as already noted, the phenomenological tradition that has taken over many areas of human geography has much in common with psychogeography. The key difference, I suppose, is the scientific search for generalisations – going beyond the data – as opposed to the uniquely enriched experience of the artwork. However, such a distinction loses its power when the implications of the activity are considered.

In a remarkably moving illustration of psychogeography Dyson[34] makes clear that it is essentially a methodology that she is using so that she can seek "to understand and more deeply connect with the place in which I live". She does this by using the 'drifting' process, akin to what the French identified almost as a profession, the *flaneur*, already mentioned The affluent individual who wandered the streets, an explorer of the urban, a connoisseur of the street. By being open to what is on view then relating that back to maps and historical documents, an intense understanding of what has been and how what remains, reflects the imposition of centuries of human activity. The proposal that wandering round the city is a worthy activity has origins that go back at least to John Gay's (best known for writing "The Beggars' Opera") 1716 lengthy poem *Trivia: The art of walking the streets of London*. This has an ironic tone, with warnings of what to wear and to be aware of. So, it does presage both Dyson's urban roaming and the French Parisian wanderers.

What emerges from Dyson's meandering Southwest of Melbourne, focusing on the River Yarra, is an intense criticism of what has been lost by ignoring the lives and Places of the First Nation peoples who had inhabited the area for millennia. Her output from this research is not an academic treatise but what she calls 'Song Maps' which are drawings that provide the basis for songs set to music, which she performs.[35] It seems to me that these songs, as so many other songs throughout history, may have more impact on decision makers than heavy tomes describing the activities she decries.

The methodological point is how explorations of Places, and how those explorations are summarised and presented for a wider audience, can have an impact. In my experience, although policy makers like to believe they are basing their recommendations and decisions on hard, systematic evidence. They are actually more directly influenced by newspaper headlines and strikingly illustrative case studies.

The other aspect of psychogeography, clearly revealed by the work of Dyson and many others, is that by drawing on maps and earlier accounts to "understand and more deeply connect" with a Place, a bridge is also being made from psychological insights to an historical perspective. This draws attention to the ways in which the history of a Place can have profound significance for a person. An issue rarely explored in psychological or geographical explorations of Place experience.

Conclusions

Whilst the processes of engaging with Places may not have the systematic, objective, or scientific credentials of the methods explored in Chapter 3 they do enrich our understanding of Places. They also provide illustrations of insights that are difficult to generate from questionnaires or interviews, distant observations or tests performed by respondents. In this book, therefore, my own engagements with Places, and the accounts from others are drawn on from time to time.

References and endnotes

1 A clear statement that anthropologists must take account of people being 'in place' is given by Weiner, J. (2002) Between a rock and a non-place: Towards a contemporary anthropology of place. *Reviews in Anthropology, 31*(1), 21–27.

2 This combines philosophical considerations with personal experiences. Relph, E. (2007) Spirit of Place and sense of Place in virtual realities. *Techne: Research in Philosophy & Technology, 10*(3), 17–25.

3 Tuan, Y. F. (2020) Time, space, and architecture: Some philosophical musings, inX.Ruan & P.Hogben (Eds.) *Topophilia and topophobia*, London: Routledge, pp. 22–30.

4 Gehl, J. & Svarre, B. (2013) *How to study public life*, Washington, DC: Island Press.

5 One example of such a study is Klein, C., Kuhnen, A., Felippe, M. L., & Silveira, B. B. (2018) Place-centered or person-centered? Considerations about the behavioral mapping approach. *Trends in Psychology, 26*, 593–616.
6 Behavioral Mapping achieves about 4,000 references in Google Scholar.
7 Barker, R. G. (1965) Explorations in ecological psychology. *American Psychologist, 20*(1), 1.
8 A very full account of environmental psychologists' use of such mapping is given by one of the pioneers of environmental psychology and his wife in Sommer, R., & Sommer, B. (2002) *Mapping and trace measures. A practical guide to behavioural research: Tools and techniques*, New York: Oxford University Press.
9 Cosco, N. G., Moore, R. C., & Islam, M. Z. (2010) Behavior mapping: A method for linking preschool physical activity and outdoor design. *Medicine & Science in Sports & Exercise, 42*(3), 513–519, p. 518.
10 Cosco, N. G., Moore, R. C., & Islam, M. Z. (2010) Behavior mapping: A method for linking preschool physical activity and outdoor design. *Medicine & Science in Sports & Exercise, 42*(3), 510.
11 Barker (1965) Explorations in ecological psychology. *American Psychologist, 20*(1), 1.
12 Barker's ecological psychology should not be confused with the use of the term by cognitive psychologists as discussed, for example, by Lobo, L., Heras-Escribano, M., & Travieso, D. (2018) The history and philosophy of ecological psychology. *Frontiers in Psychology, 9*, 2228.
13 Schoggen, P. (1989) *Behavior settings: A revision and extension of Roger G. Barker's "Ecological psychology"*, Redwood City,Ca.:Stanford University Press.
14 Barker, R. G. & Gump, P. V. (1964) *Big school, small school: High school size and student behavior*, Redwood City,Ca.:Stanford University Press.
15 A clear account of this is given in the discussion by Neyland, D. & Whittle, A. (2018) Garfinkel on strategy: Using ethnomethodology to make sense of "rubbish strategy". *Critical Perspectives on Accounting, 53*, 31–42.
16 Summarised in Seamon, D. (2018) *Life takes place: Phenomenology, lifeworlds and Place making*, London: Routledge.
17 Seamon, D. (2018) *Life takes place: Phenomenology, lifeworlds and Place making*, London: Routledge, p. 15.
18 Maddicott, A. (2023) *Tender maps: Travels in search of the emotions of place*, Lamberhurst: September Publishing.
19 Snow, C. P. (1961) *The two cultures and the scientific revolution. The Rede Lecture 1959*, New York: Cambridge University Press.
20 Massey, W. E. (2019). CP Snow and the two cultures, 60 years later. *EuropeanReview*, 27(1), February 2019, pp. 66–74, https://doi.org/10.1017/S1062798718000595
21 It was the quotation from Joyce's *Finnegan's Wake "Three quarks for Muster Mark!"*.
22 One of many books reviewing this endeavour is Coverley, M. (2018) *Psychogeography*, Harpenden: Oldcastle Books.
23 Edensor, T., Kalandides, A., & Kothari, U. (2020) *The Routledge handbook of place*, London: Routledge.
24 Roberts, L. (2020) Navigating cinematic geographies, in T. Edensor, Kalandides, & U. Kothari (Eds.) *The Routledge handbook of place*, London: Routledge, p. 661.
25 Dyson, M. (2020) Walking West: *Bewer volcanics* song project, in T. Edensor, Kalandides, & U. Kothari (Eds.) *The Routledge handbook of place*, London: Routledge, Chapter 61, pp. 692–706.
26 Debord, G. (1955) Introduction to a critique of urban geography. *Les Lèvres Nues #6*, in Ken Knabb (1981) (Ed. and Trans.) *Situationist international anthology*, Berkeley: Bureau of Public Secrets, p. 5.
27 See also Psychogeography: A way to delve into the soul of a city (theconversation.com).
28 The view that psychogeography is rather different from systematic, scientific studies within the rubric of environmental psychology is rather confused by the acclaimed cognitive neuroscientist Colin Ellard (2015) givingthe subtitle *The psychogeography of everyday life* to his review of neuroscience interpretations of environmental psychology that has the main ttile *Places of the Heart*, New York: Bellevue Literary Press. This shows how terms can lose their potency by overuse.

29 "Environmental Psychology" does get more than twice that number of mentions.
30 Published in 1782 ***The Reveries of the Solitary Walker*** (French: *Les Rêveries du promeneur solitaire*) is an unfinished book by Genevan philosopher Jean-Jacques Rousseau, written between 1776 and 1778.
31 https://tinyurl.com/yxe4eaef
32 See, for example, The affichistes - Artmarketinsight - Artprice.com.
33 Dogançay, A., Temel, B., & Dogançay, B. (2012) *Burhan Dogançay: Fifty years of urban walls*, London: Prestel Publishing.
34 Dyson, M. (2020) Walking West; new volcanics song project, in T. Edensor, Kalandides, & U. Kothari (Eds.) *The Routledge handbook of place*, London: Routledge, pp. 692–706.
35 https://tinyurl.com/5xnxbfwj19

CHAPTER 5

Expanding explorations of place experience

Taken together with the methodologies described in Chapters 3 and 4, a plethora of ways of recording reactions to and actions within Places are available. These are the tactics for chronicling behaviour and experience. However, there are also ways of working with that material, research strategies. This chapter therefore concludes with an account of the research strategies that can be harnessed to make use of that rich array of research tactics.

Special tasks

To get beyond overt statements that can be gathered through questionnaires and interviews, to explore more implicit aspects of how people think, and feel about Places, procedures have been developed that give respondents tasks to perform. The underlying processes revealed in how respondents deal with the tasks allow a subtler exploration of cognitive and emotional aspects of Place experience.

In the 1960s and early 1970s the Repertory Grid procedure,[1] which had its origins in psychotherapy, proved to be readily adaptable to studies of Places. The significant people in the respondent's life, which make the typical *elements* of the Grid in a therapeutic context, were replaced by Places.[2] The grid procedure requires people to characterise those different elements. The comparison of these ratings or ranking allows statistical analysis which generates information about the underlying structure in the assessment of those Places. The method can be used with individuals, or the results combined in various ways to give group aggregates.

The original Repertory Grid is time consuming and benefits from the application of specialist statistical analysis software. A simpler to use procedure was therefore developed that focused on the comparisons between elements, which is the essence of the repertory grid. These comparisons are made by asking respondents to assign entities, such as photographs of locations, to categories such that all those in one category are similar to each other and differ from those in other categories. It is therefore known as a form of 'sorting task'.[3]

DOI: 10.4324/9780367808655-7

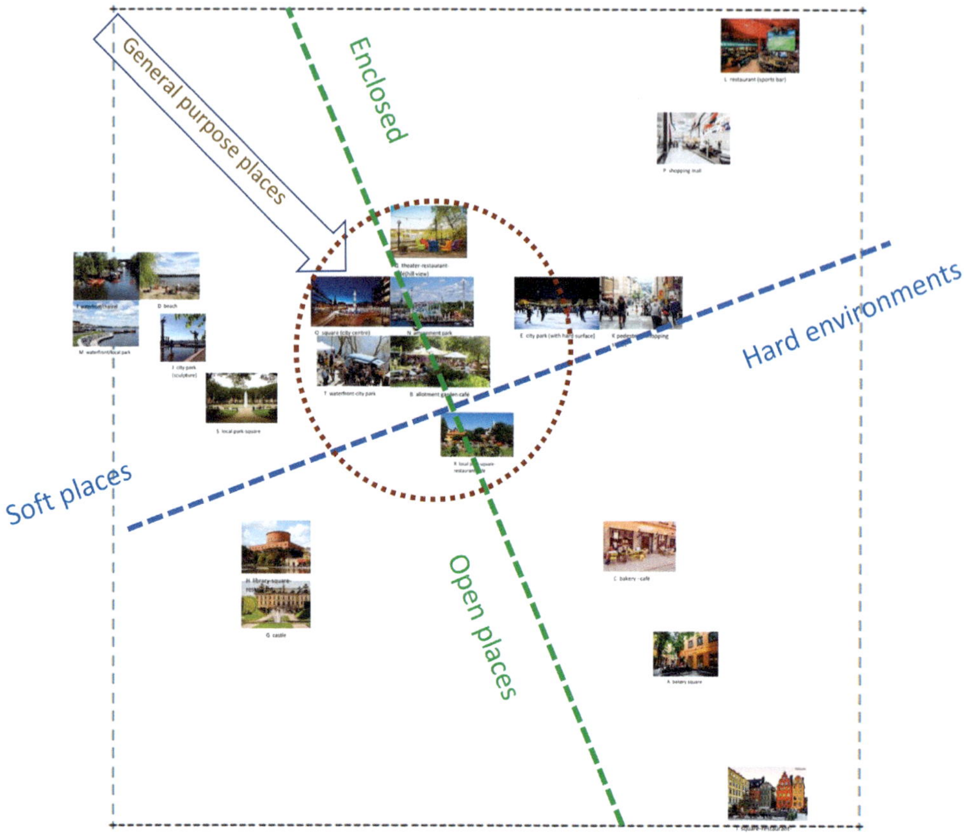

Figure 5.1 The MSA of overall structure of 20 participants' conceptions of 20 public spaces

As an example of this sorting methodology a recent study that focuses on role of public Places in relation to loneliness[4] produced the visual results given in Figure 5.1. For these results 20 people in Stockholm, were asked to sort photographs of 20 public Places, of which they had some experience. Respondents were allowed to use what ever criteria they wished, for the categories they used, provided they regarded those categories as significant. The responses were subjected to a form of multi-dimensional scaling know as multi-dimensional scalogram analysis.[5] This enables the photographs to be represented on a notional graph such that the greater the similarity in how the Places are regarded the closer together they are in the space.

The great advantage of this methodology is that there is no need to understand the clever statistics that generate the spatial configuration, illustrated in Figure 5.1. All that is needed is to be aware that the closer together any two items are, the more likely are they to be assigned to similar categories by respondents in general. For example, the pictures on the left show Places with expanses of water. Those opposite them on the right are built-up locations.

By considering the actual pictures and the comments of the respondents it is possible to interpret what the dominant characteristics are that distinguish these Places for the people involved in the study. In Figure 5.1, a summary is provided of the bases people used for assigning pictures to categories. Lines are drawn on the configuration to indicate a two-way classification on the basis of hard/soft and open/enclosed. This provides a basis for further in-depth examination of the concepts respondents offered, as discussed in more detail in the published study.

The sorting task is engaging and straightforward for people to complete.[6] It has the advantage of revealing underlying concepts that people may not be able easily to articulate in words. However, it is sensitive to the entities that are offered for sorting. If the mix is biased in some way, for example, in the present study by choosing a predominance of pictures of open spaces, then that will influence the categories that emerge. The instructions also have to be carefully framed to avoid demand characteristics, discussed in Chapter 2. Nonetheless the opportunity it provides for exploring the bases of conceptions of Places in a somewhat novel way has proven worthwhile.[7]

A step beyond sorting tasks and related explorations of conceptual systems are those methods that require respondents to perform a particular task. It may be asking them to estimate distances between locations in a city[8], or the more complex requirement of instructing someone to draw a sketch map of a city, or an area within it. This was given impetus by Kevin Lynch's widely cited book *The Image of the City.*[9] It has become such a significant part of the study of Places that Chapter 14 is devoted to what I called 'cognitive cartography' in *the original Psychology of Place.*

The crucial aspect of Lynch's book is there in the title – the 'image'. That derived from the earlier elegantly short book by Boulding[10] and other writers who had a growing interest in the way aspects of our lives take on significance. These aspects become abstractions that have their own coherence and related existence. As discussed in other chapters, this move towards a more cognitive framework for understanding human actions and experience was gaining ground in the 1950s although it had much earlier origins. The idea, therefore, that people would hold mental representations, or 'images' of a city, was latched onto by Lynch and given a form of apparently objective existence by asking people to draw sketch maps.

Lynch, a town planner, used these sketch maps to identify components of cities that he argued contributed to their image. In particular, he was interested in the influence of these components on how easily people could understand the layout of cities. As he put it how 'legible' they were.

Psychologists and geographers took this methodology further, as illustrated in Chapter 14, to consider what these sketch maps reveal about how people form experiences and interactions with cities. Instead of assuming they were reflections of maps produced by cartographers, the distortions and emphases in these maps became the aspects of interest. These studies allow more agency to respondents. Rather than regarding the city as a stimulus that influences a person's mental image, the ways in which people actively make sense of their surroundings is given priority.

As with all research methods, caution is need so that interpretation of the results does not ignore weaknesses in the procedure itself, especially biases produced by expectations introduced by the task participants are required to carry out.

An illustration of this influence of a data collection method on results within the study of place can be demonstrated from another very early psychological study of Places. In 1954, Terence Lee[11] completed his PhD at the University of Cambridge. It was an exploration of what people thought of as the neighbourhood in which they lived. This was a psychological consideration of the emerging planning concerns about building Places that would form socially supported neighbourhoods. This is perhaps even more relevant today with the proposal of 15-minute cities discussed in the final chapter of this book. The same topic of how a neighbourhood is conceptualised, has also recently been explored in the Japanese context[12] (in complete ignorance of Lee's study published over half a century earlier).

In both the Cambridge study and the Tokyo study the task given to participants was to offer them a map and ask them to "draw a line round the part which you consider acts as your neighbourhood". As an example, Figure 5.2 illustrates a response for a similar task in Guildford, a city about 40 kilometres South of London. It shows a clear line that is apparently demarcated mainly be roads. The Tokyo study, using very sophisticated mathematics, also concluded that the neighbourhood's people identified were defined by roads. These are intriguing results and certainly open up further consideration of the cognitive aspects of neighbourhoods. These could have planning implications when determining road layouts for new developments.

However, the power of the map as a starting point has the possibility of creating demand characteristics that have influenced the tidy, street bound result. In a further exploration of that possibility people were given a list of locations (names of shops, cinemas etc. in the area around their house) and were asked to say which of those were inside their 'neighbourhood' and which outside. They were also asked to draw a line on the map around their neighbourhood. Figure 5.3 shows a typical response with the answers to the two questions superimposed.

Although all the locations that were designated as 'outside' the neighbourhood line were actually outside, only three of them were indicated as 'inside', within the line drawn. In a study of 30 respondents, on average, only two-thirds of the locations

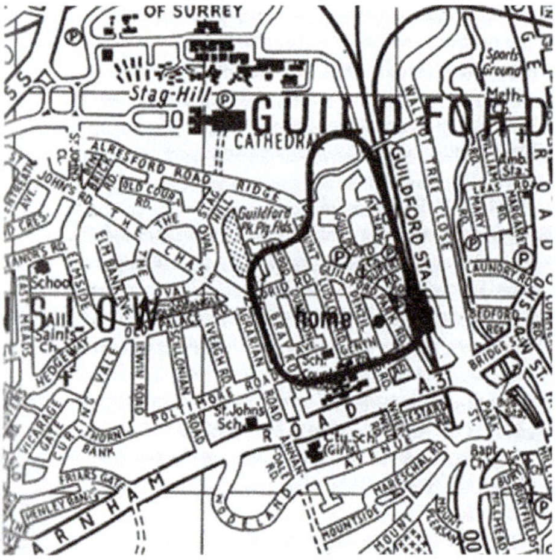

Figure 5.2 A response to the request "Please draw a line round that part which you consider acts as your neighbourhood"

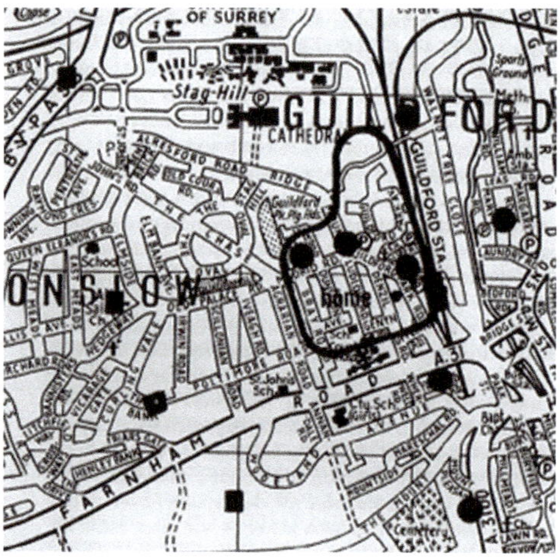

Figure 5.3 Places identified ● as 'inside' ■ or 'outside' a person's 'neighbourhood', compared with the line drawn round their neighbourhood

indicated as being in the neighbourhood were within the line drawn, although that varied from 9% to 100% between different people.

This example reveals that different aspects, of what a neighbourhood is thought to be, are revealed by the different tasks given to respondents. The comparison helps to elaborate the complexity of the concept of neighbourhood. A local shop you use regularly may seem to be part of your area of activity, or neighbourhood, as may be other Places, such as a friend's house. But drawing a line on a map is not about these activities and social processes. It is a more cognitive exploration of what the area you identify as yours may mean.

Recording and measuring physical features of Places

The many ways in which the use and experience of Places can be studied have been considered. That was in order to draw out the underlying theories that shape those methods. No attention has been paid to another crucial aspects of Places, their physical form. Just as the actions within, and subjective reactions to, Places are multifarious and multidimensional so too are the physical aspects. As any guidance on writing about Places makes clear, even though the visual features may be the most obvious to describe, should it be their colour, shape, form, how they catch the light, or their relationship to other features. Beyond the visual aspects there are thermal, acoustic and other aspects of sensation that can be mentioned. Determining what to record or measure of the physical features of a Place is therefore also very challenging.

The choice of any features, as with other aspects of research methods, carry implicit and explicit theories about what is relevant. That relevance will draw heavily on the context in which the study is being conducted. Different research questions draw attention to different aspects of the physical setting. For example, different local concerns about the possibility of wind turbines being built nearby may emphasise different features of the turbines. Some may consider their physical form is too industrial for the pastoral setting in which they are to be erected. Others may emphasise the noise they might make and how disturbing that may be. Ornithologists will stress the risk to local bird life of the rotating blades.

The point here is that it is often not possible to specify the features of the physical environment that are to be recorded or measured without identifying the reasons for making those recordings or measurements. Different reasons can lead the study into different conceptual bases, such as acoustic science or ornithology. In a more social science context, these may be concerns about the participation of those who experience the Places or the financial implications of for home owners.

As a consequence, no definitive set of physical features of a Place can be identified which are generally relevant to its psychology. As will become apparent in the following chapters, from time to time there are some features that emerge as particularly relevant for understanding particular aspects of Places. There is also the rich understanding of the relevance of how Places relate to each other. That is the grammar of Places explored in Chapter 9. These cautions have considerable relevance for evaluating studies of Places that claim general reactions to specific components of Places, such as curved walls, as discussed in later chapters.

Strategies for the war on ignorance implications for theories of place

So far, my focus has been on what may be measured in any study of Places. These are often thought of as the 'variables'. This has been used to indicate the psychological assumptions that underly the chosen measures. But they are only one aspect of how research is created and acted on. It is fruitful to consider two aspects of any piece of research,[13] both of which embed underlying assumptions. The variables may be considered the 'tactics'. In addition, there is the overall design of the research, which I regard as the 'strategies'.

The terms strategies and tactics are deliberately taken from military theory in which the overall plan of how to fight the war is a strategy. The particular weapons and personnel used in any given battle are the tactics. This distinction is necessary because the term 'methods' or 'methodology' can mean so many different things. Many books with one of those words in their title just describe statistical processes that can be applied to different types of data. Other books explore abstract notions of the nature of research or even philosophical meanderings as in the consideration of 'scientific' method. The distinction between strategies and tactics removes these confusions.

Consider the recent study that makes a very detailed comparison of the reactions of occupants in two different student residents.[14] This is presented as a type of scientific experiment, using the term 'quasi-experiment'. In reality it is a comparison of the experiences of students who inhabit two different graduate residences. The reason it is couched under the label 'quasi-experiment' is that the term 'experiment' implies, in essence, a research strategy in which the experimenter introduces some change into a situation – the 'experimental condition' for comparison with a very similar situation into which no change has been introduced – the 'control condition'. This is seen by many researchers as the golden standard for research because the introduction of the change, which is typically called 'the independent variable' can be regarded as the causal agent. This variable can be claimed as the primary agent that influences the measurements made. They are called the 'dependent' variables. Although what they 'depend' on is not always clear.

Unravelling what causes what is seen as the most sophisticated form of scientific study. When seeking the causes of a disease, being able to identify a particular causal agent is crucial for diagnosis and treatment. Finding the bacterium or virus in ill patients, but no other similar people,is a step forward in understanding the illness. Setting up a study that uses the experimental strategy assumes that an identifiable independent variable is causing changes in a measurable dependent variable. But such cause-and-effect processes do not make as much sense when studying Places.

In relation to the physical attributes of Places there is always a complex system of interactions. The same is true of the experiences that are being explored. This is nicely illustrated in the comparison of student residents mentioned earlier. The paper states as a major finding that "Significantly lower perceived mental well-being was found among students without bedroom windows". In the spirit of an experimental paradigm this draws attention to the causal influence of the absence of bedroom windows. However, unlike in a controlled laboratory experiment, the two buildings compared were not identical except for the absence of bedroom windows. Nor were the populations residing in the buildings, one was much older than the other, including families with babies.

In other words, the study was a rich and detailed exploration of the differences in experiences between the two buildings. There were many differences found in the well-being of the respondents. The buildings that had windowless bedrooms had limited social and other amenities, which may have encouraged people to spend more time in their bedrooms, making their windowless feature more distressing. As with my own implicitly deterministic study of the size of an office on worker performance described in Chapter 3, by starting with the idea that it is the effect of a building on well-being that is being tested, the study is structured in a way that can only consider cause-effect relationships rather than understanding the systematic processes of which the physical form is a part.

Because the comparison of the two residents is so detailed, providing analyses of qualitative questions about the experience of the windowless bedrooms, it is possible to unravel some of the processes involved. The detailed responses listed reveal a wide variety of experiential aspects of the windowless bedrooms. These cove a range of claims such that they are "dehumanising", make the room "feel like a prison cell", reducing the ability to know what time it is, and social tensions over who has a window and who has not. The supposedly 'experimental' control by comparing with another building does not add anything to these direct experiences of the students. The formulation of the study as a pseudo-experiment undermines the rich consideration of what students feel in a particular sort of bedroom. What they feel tells us all we need to know about the windowless bedrooms. The 'comparison' with the other residence adds nothing. Unfortunately, it was unlikely the study would have been published without the patina of the term 'experiment' to give it the gloss of scientific rigour.

The strategy of the case study, which allows detailed consideration of the rich processes involved in experiences of Places, presents different challenges from an experimental strategy. The very richness of the information collected requires time and imagination to reveal its inner patterns. Comparisons across case studies to find generalities also demand the systematic identification of themes. These themes themselves will also implicitly, or explicitly, be driven by prior theories or expectations. The widely utilised approach to qualitative material, known as 'grounded theory'[15] seeks to reveal underlying processes without the influence of prior assumptions. I remain to be convinced that, as valuable as this detailed approach is, its results are not influenced by the researcher's background and theoretical predilections. Indeed, in some areas of research, notably anthropology, the researcher's pre-existing biases have to be declared.

One other strategy, besides the experiment and the case study, should also be mentioned. That is what I am choosing to call a 'survey'. Whilst a questionnaire may be regarded as a tactic. The way of obtaining the crucial information for the research. The use of a questionnaire as the main framework for organising data collection and analysis, its strategy, is usefully called a survey. The study of student residences, already discussed, used questionnaires to assess some of the 'dependent' variables, but a survey can stand alone without the trappings of experimental design.

One thing that distinguishes this type of questionnaire study from an opinion survey is that it is not an attempt to assess the level of commitment to a topic for a particular population. That is the purpose of the 'public opinion poll'. These polls focus on obtaining a representative sample of respondents to indicate their reactions.

Typically, in an opinion poll a few questions are asked around the central topic, but in essence there is one key issue that is being explored, such as 'should abortion be allowed for non-medical reasons', 'who will you vote for in the next election', 'do you think drilling at the bottom of the ocean should be allowed'. The matter of who is to be asked is crucial because it is rarely the case that everyone in the population of interest can be questioned. Therefore, there is the need for a sample to be taken that is representative of the population that the results will be applied to. This may not be as easy to achieve as may be assumed. Many biases can creep into samples without them being obvious. In the past pollsters have got inaccurate results, for example, by using telephone surveys, when only a limited segment of the population had phones. Using the internet today adds similar biases. There are also, of course, people who are reluctant to answer survey questions, or they give answers they don't really believe in. Some years ago, I found it particularly problematic to get answers from an older generation in countries that had been under NAZI rule for some years. They felt any answers could put them in jeopardy. There are parallels today.

Questionnaire surveys differ from public opinion surveys in a number of ways. They are more detailed. They explore the underlying structure of reactions. Yet, although questionnaire surveys have been in use for over a century, they are certainly not without their challenges.[16] The key advantage of these surveys is that many questions can be asked around a topic. They are then open to detailed analysis of their inner relationships. This allows the structure and organisation of the topic being studied, in the experience of the respondents, to be revealed. These analysis systems have a long history in psychology, starting with the study of the nature or 'structure' of intelligence, moving onto many examinations of attitudes, values, and the dimensions of personality.[17] There are examples of the structures of experiences of aspects of Places such as place attachment in Chapter 15, and landscape preferences in chapter 17 of this book.

Conclusions

This chapter has reviewed extensive methods available for the study of actions in, and experiences of, Places. The aim has been to draw attention to the embedding of psychological assumptions in the methods chosen. In general terms, each approach to setting up a research project and deciding how to collect data carries assumptions. These are perspectives or theories about what shapes human activities and experiences. In other words, appropriate ways to explain human behaviour, thoughts, and emotions. The impact of these considerations is that all methodologies have strengths and weaknesses. Those need to be understood in order to evaluate the results of any research. Sadly, there are many rituals and habits in doing psychological research. They tend to undermine the generalisations of any results. The related caveats will be explored in later chapters.

There are many ways of studying and getting to understand Places. These methods have a history going back centuries as well as innovative approaches that are being developed today. All approaches to studying Places have their strengths and weaknesses. It is important to understand these in order to make sense of and evaluate the results of any study. There are, in addition, many questions to answer about how to describe and/or measure the physical components of Places.

References and endnotes

1 Fransella, F., Bell, R., & Bannister, D. (2004) *A manual for repertory grid technique.* John Wiley & Sons.
2 It is still widely used see Rahman, R., Bidoun, D., Agiel, A., & Albdour, A. (2022) Advancing the use of the repertory grid technique in the built environment: A systematic review. *Frontiers in Built Environment*, *8*, 1082149.
3 Canter, D. V., Brown, J., & Groat, L. (1985) A multiple sorting procedure for studying conceptual systems, in M. Brenner, J. Brown, & D. V. Canter (Eds.), *The research interview: Uses and approaches*, London: Academic Press, pp. 79–104.
4 Jing, J., Canter, D., & Haas, T. (2019) Conceptualizing public space using a multiple sorting task—Exploring the links between loneliness and public space. *Urban Science*, *3*(4), 107.
5 Lingoes, J. C. (1960) *Multiple scalogram analysis: A generalization of Guttman's scale analysis.* An Arbor, MI: M.A. Press Michigan State University.
6 An example of a further development of this method for use online is given in Jing, J., & Canter, D. (2023) Developing a mixed-methods digital Multiple Sorting Task procedure using Zoom and Miro. *Methodological Innovations*, *16*(2), 250–262.
7 Canter, D. (2016) Revealing the conceptual systems of Places, in R. Gifford (Ed.) *Research methods for environmental psychology*, Chichester: Wiley, pp. 137–159.
8 Canter, D. & Tagg, S. K. (1975) Distance estimation in cities. *Environment and Behavior*, *7*(1), 59–80.
9 Lynch, K. (1964) *The image of the city*,Cambridge, MA: MIT Press.
10 Boulding, D. (1956) *The image: Knowledge in life and society*, An Arbor: University of Michigan.
11 Published some years later as Lee, T. (1968) Urban neighbourhood as a socio-spatial schema. *Human Relations*, *21*(3), 241–267.
12 Oyama, Y. (2024) Spatial city image and its formative factors: A street-based neighborhood cognition analysis. *Cities*, 149, 104898, https://doi.org/10.1016/j.cities.2024.104898
13 Much more detailed elaborations of these ways of thinking about research, with examples of projects students can do to explore the various methods are given in my recent book Canter, D. (2024) *Criminal psychology in action: A project-based approach*, London: Routledge. Although this focuses on examples from crime psychology, they are all can be modified to be used in studying the psychology of place.
14 Myers, H. E., & Rollings, K. A. (2024) Perceived effects of residential design on mental well-being: A quasi-experimental study of the University of Michigan's Munger Graduate Residences. *Journal of Environmental Psychology*, 102408.
15 Birks, M., & Mills, J. (2022) *Grounded theory: A practical guide*, London: Sage.
16 Berinsky, Adam J. (2017) Measuring public opinion with surveys. *Annual Review of Political Science*, 20, 309–329.
17 I've avoided what would be a mammoth list of references to these topics. For those exploring them for the first time, they are usually considered in psychology under the general heading of 'individual differences'.

SECTION II

Buildings

Place is inextricably *connected to architecture—its very origins and substance—and therefore [is] as* inescapable *in architecture's mainstream practice as in its theorization.*[1]

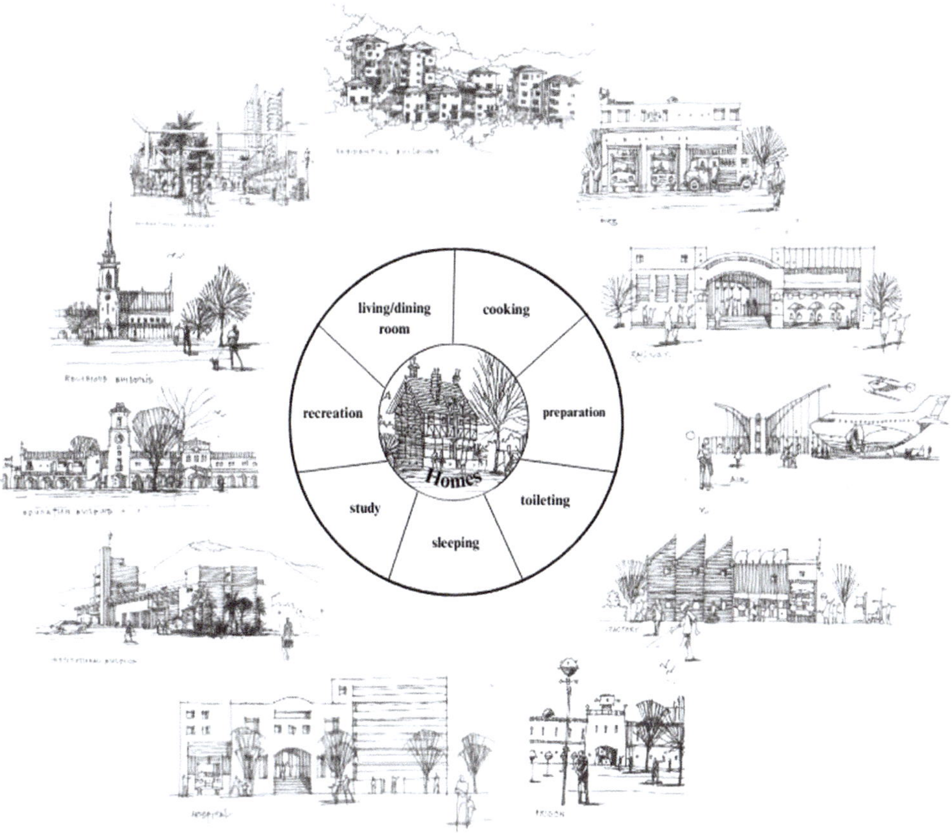

DOI: 10.4324/9780367808655-8

CHAPTER 6

Home as the archetypal place

Our house is our corner of our world.... It is our first universe, a real cosmos in every sense of the word.[2]

...is it not said of the jackal, the incarnation of all this is savage in nature, that it does not have a home?[3]

The insights provided by the components of a home elucidates the implications of conditions in of long-term imprisonment. This framework underscores how the experience of place within a prison can be profoundly inhumane and degrading. Those impoverished conditions illustrate the importance of being able to designate an assemblage of related places. Each of those places supporting a different aspect of being 'at home'.

For those who lack a traditional house, often labelled as homeless, the phenomenon of creating makeshift spaces, embodying the essence of 'home' highlights the resilience of human beings in their pursuit of place and belonging. Their created places on the street reflect their inhabitants' identities, character, and modes of existence, bringing into focus the profound implications for the personal and collective identities that homes are capable of representing.

The meaning of home

In their attempts to demonstrate the wide range of products they sell; Sainsbury's vast supermarket chain has drawn on emotional associations with ideas of what a home is. They promote the prospect that buying their goods a house will be converted into warm and friendly domestic bliss:

> A place that lifts the soul and the spirit, a place to call your own. If home is where the heart is, Sainsbury's Home is what brings it to life.

DOI: 10.4324/9780367808655-9

Figure 6.1 A Sainsbury's banner using the concept of *home* as a marketing tool

> From sturdy plates and weekend (or weekday) wine glasses to soft bedding, throws and bathroom bits – our in-house designers craft great value quality pieces, made for everyday living. Fill your home with people, laughter, memories and something from Sainsbury's Home.[4]

Marketing gurus have always tried to tie in emotions to particular products. To do that effectively they have to be alert to what sentiments are embedded in the *zeitgeist*. Those feelings must be widely recognisable across the society to whom they are selling. Therefore, the awareness of advertising executives of the power of the concept of 'home' is possibly a better indication of its social and psychological significance than the thousands of academic studies[5] that debate its meaning, whilst still emphasising its importance. Another obvious illustration of the importance of home as a topic and essential feature of existence is that there is actually in London a *Museum of the Home*.[6] I've not come across any other type of place that has a museum dedicated to it.

The potency of the meaning of home was brought to scholarly attention by the writings, over half a century ago, of Marc Fried with the elegant title of his work "Grieving for a Lost Home".[7] He showed that a home can operate as if it were a person such that moving from it may give rise to the sort of grief that is experienced on the death of a loved one. Such influence helps to distinguish a place where we live from the tab of a pull-down menu on a word processor "Home" that is the main hub for essential document formatting tools. The intuitions of software developers, in using this label, draw on the subtle associations inherent in language.

The widespread discussion of what home means provides further insight into the psychology of Place. The significance home has in people's lives, careful consideration of what homes are as places and how they are given meaning opens up the possibility that the home is the quintessential place. What makes homes important is how they embrace many aspects of being and consequently act as the foundation of the meaning and experience of places in general.

The mantlepiece

Objects in the home encapsulate identity and social significance. This is revealed through the intriguing explorations of sociologist Rachel Hurdley. She has demonstrated, in her detailed study of mantelpieces,[8] how the objects displayed on them and in other places in the home, such as a shelf or a windowsill, or even magnets on fridge doors, reflect how people view themselves and how they would like to be seen by others. It is both the objects selected for display and how they are organised that reveals the 'work' they are doing as social performances, bridging the personal and the public, capturing layers of meaning and identities.

As Hurdley points out Middle-class mantlepieces and other displays in the home will often tell stories about the inhabitants tastes and record their travels. These displays often subtly narrate stories about the provenance and meaning of objects, showcasing how individuals account for themselves through their possessions. Those with fewer resources may focus their objects as small-scale symmetrical exhibitions. Imposing a structure on the items as a way of making them abstract presentations. Symmetry in such displays can symbolize order, balance, and aesthetic harmony, which may reflect broader societal values or personal preferences. It also plays a role in how people organise and present their living spaces, creating a sense of structure and meaning.

A friend's mantelpiece in Figure 6.2, looks uneventful enough, but a quiet question of what was on it revealed that he did not really know, but his wife had arranged it. He 'didn't have the heart' to touch it since she died. Her conscious arrangement of it is clear in its almost symmetrical layout. Notably, however, there are some remote-control devices on the left-hand edge, that he was keen to remove before I took the photograph. In other words, he did not see these devices as part of the display but was nonetheless aware that it was indeed a display. The brass candlesticks also were made from some metal of personal significance, again adding to the nostalgic significance of what is on show.

Places in the home

Furniture in the home go a step further, beyond the sort of objects that night be found on a mantlepiece, in helping to define the places that make up a home. The open plan living preferred by many households today, when their resources allow that

Figure 6.2 A mantelpiece displays personal and social identity

possibility, is nonetheless one of a number of places that define a home. It usually itself an assemblage of places, defined by furniture, within that open space. Chairs, tables, beds, and desks provide an account of the expected activities in the different parts of a house.

The process of signifying place uses, and their related rules of action has a long history in archaeology. Even remnants of pot shards on Neolithic sites, when linked to the location of where the fire was,

> clearly indicated that an area to the West of the fireplace, between it and the huts, and including some of the huts, was a primary area of pot-using activity. This distribution would suggest the preparation and storage of food in this area.[9]

That may be extrapolated further to suggest where the women, children, and men typically would be. Just as archaeologists try to make sense of place use and related social norms, the presence of different piece of furniture in modern homes allows an examination of what makes up a home.

This exploration is particularly interesting in Japanese apartments because of the tradition of flexible room use. Sliding screens are present rather than doors. Bedding would typically be brought from a cupboard for use at nighttime, leaving the space available for other use during the day. As Nishihara[10] put it:

> The West operates on the idea that each function has its own space.... The Japanese house, however, names its rooms by their location...without direct reference to function...Japanese spaces, instead of having a fixed function, suit the function to the occasion and need. In other words, the use to which a space is put varies with the time of day. The size of a given space freely changes as we open or close the *fusuma (sliding screen)*.

Figure 6.3 shows a small room today that is part of a larger Japanese house. As can be seen everything is easily movable. The room could be quickly turned in a spare bedroom, but crucial small pieces of furniture are stored there. With its tatami floor covering the room could be part of many traditional Tokyo apartments such as those I was able to study.

The inherent flexibility of these spaces might lead to the expectation that there would be a highly variable and possibly idiosyncratic use of space in a Japanese home. A study of the location of furniture in a Japanese house therefore provides an interesting test of the hypothesis that this apparently flexible space will give rise to distinct Places. The places that emerge from this analysis help to indicate what the essence of a home is.

I was fortunate to able to study this possibility when I spent 12 months in Japan in 1970.

A group of architecture students at Tokyo University had been laboriously mapping the location of furniture in Japanese apartments,[11] as illustrated in Figure 6.4. This was to inform the design of future apartments. There were five different apartment types, varying in size from two rooms to five rooms. This provided a total of 16 spaces

Figure 6.3 A small room in a Japanese house

across the whole sample. The study recorded the locations on plans, in each the 16 spaces across all the building layouts studied. The furniture was first content analysed to produce 43 categories of furniture. A matrix was then produced that recorded the frequency of each of the types of furniture in each of the spaces.

When I returned from Japan, I was able to work with a Korean student, Kyung Hoi Lee, fluent in Japanese, who was studying with me at the time. Together we were able to analyse the patterns of furniture combinations[12] using a statistical visualisation procedure[13] that was rather unusual at the time but has since been widely applied in many different contexts.[14] The statistical process consisted of identifying 43[15] distinct furniture types that occurred across all the apartments. The matrix that lists the frequency of each of the 43 types of furniture across the 16 spaces provides the basis for a statistical procedure that starts by comparing the patterns of frequency of occurrence between every type of furniture and every other. An example of these correlations reveals, for example, that a tea-table very often is found in the same space as a Japanese style chair but is never found in the same space as an armchair.

The actual furniture found does indicate something of the culture of these apartments in late 1960s Japan. There is still a place for a small Buddhist or Shinto altar and the charcoal brazier, known as a hibachi (火鉢), as well as the Zabuton (座布団). This is the Japanese cushion nowadays associated with meditation. But contemporary equipment such as a television, stereo, and radio are all present as well.

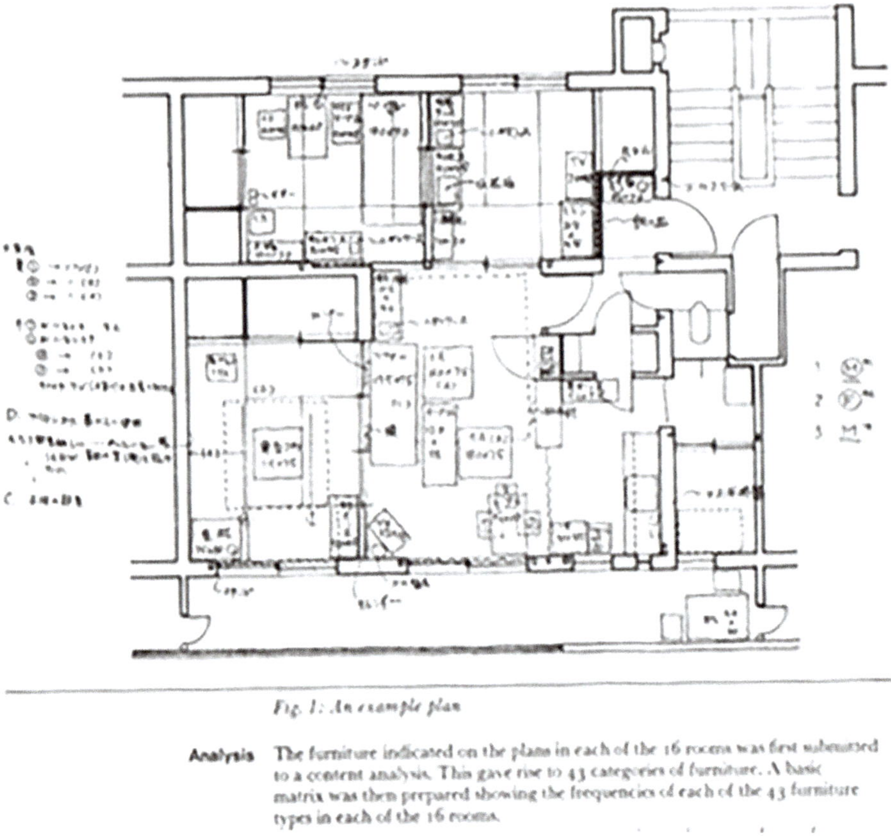

Figure 6.4 Example of a Japanese apartment with location of furniture indicated

In order to reveal the pattern (or 'structure' as I consider it) underlying the placement of furniture a statistical procedure is applied which represents each type of furniture as a point in a notional geometric configuration. The closer together any two points are the higher the likelihood is that the two types of furniture they represent will be found in the same space. The resulting configuration as shown in Figure 6.5 represents similarities in the use of places within homes as reflected in the furniture that tends to be in the same space. It could be regarded as analogous to an archaeological summary of the artefacts found in these Japanese apartments in the late 1960s. A summary based on the activities revealed by how different subsets of furniture tend to be found in the same space.

Figure 6.5 should not be confused with an actual plan of an average Japanese apartment. It indicates which items are most likely to be found in the same space. The statistical analysis is such that the closer together are any two pieces of furniture in the figure the more likely are they to be found in the same area of an apartment.

One consequence of the statistical analysis is that the closer to the centre any items are the more frequently will they be found in apartments and the larger the range of spaces they will exist in. The more likely it is to be found any space. The clearest example of this is the traditional Japanese cushion, known as a zabuton, or sitting futon (座布団). These can be found in most areas of Japanese residences. They have a high

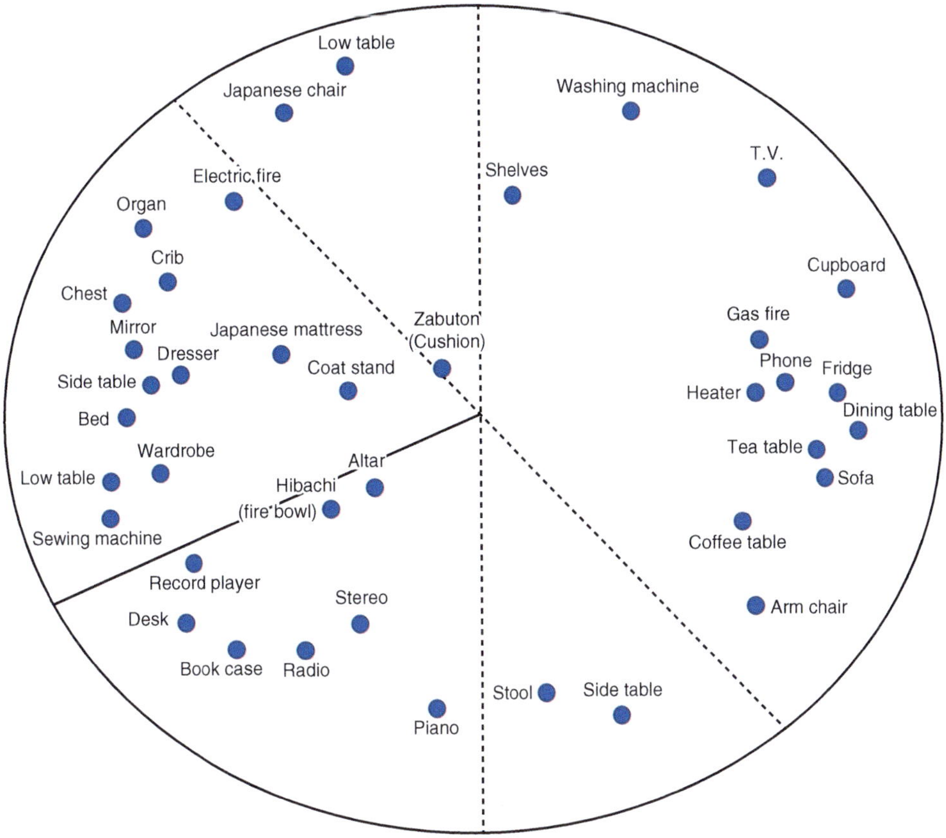

Figure 6.5 Representation of the co-occurrence of 40 types of furniture across 16 spaces in 5 types of 137 Japanese apartments. The closer together the points representing pieces of furniture the more frequently they are found in the same space

average relationship to most of the other pieces of furniture. Near it are the altar, mattress, and hibachi. A configuration for a traditional Japanese household in which there are few large pieces of furniture that are clumsy to move.

The centrality of the movable objects highlights the other significant property of the configuration. The further away a piece of furniture is from the central 'core' the more specific is its role. Moving around the figure, the fridge, washing machine, electric fire, sewing machine, and piano can all be seen as at the edges. They therefore provide a basis for identifying the activities, and the places they help shape, which characterise these homes.

For example, a piano or washing machine, were both relatively rare when this study was carried out. They were only located in particular areas, which leads the statistical procedure to indicate them at the edge of the diagram. Their position at opposite sides of Figure 6.5 shows that they are never found together in the same space.

Archaeological studies have also revealed how dwellings reveal structures to domestic activities that go back across many centuries and cultures.[16] Figure 6.6 shows the schematic layout of the use of space in an Evenk tent. The culture and traditions of the

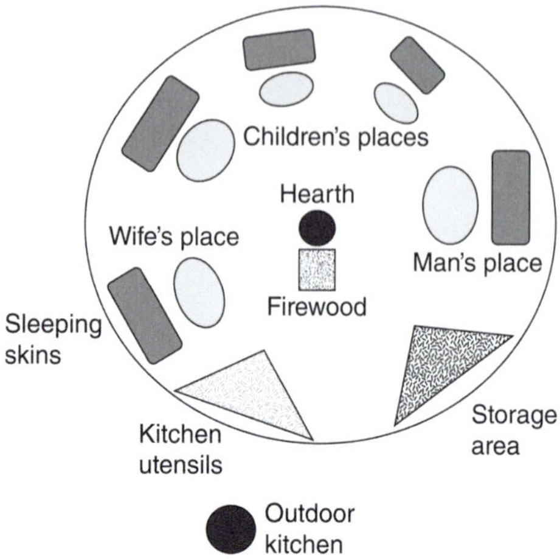

Figure 6.6 Grøn's[17] representation of the Evenk spatial code for the use of tent space in the day

Siberian Evenki, nomadic reindeer herders of Northern Russia are clearly reflected in this layout.

As Grøn explains this layout "displays surprising uniformity over an enormous area". According to the Evenk, this strict and uniform spatial code is necessary to avoid situations in which 'one makes a fool of one-self when visiting other Evenk'.[18] In other words, the layout instantiates expected rules of interaction. Because these wide-ranging nomads have different dialects that can make verbal interaction problematic, the uniform layouts provide an understanding of who and what is where, so avoiding social faux pas.

A distinction between places within these homes emerges, as represented in Figures 6.5 and 6.6. They are not necessarily totally distinct places. They may even take on apparently different uses, creating different sorts of places at different points in timeThat is reminiscent of Places as assemblages considered in Chapter 1.

To take one somewhat ironic examples, Bob Sommer found that many students tended to study on their beds and sleep at their desks. Examinations of use of spaces in Spanish homes have found that bedrooms are often used for meetings and other gatherings. In a recent television documentary[19] about the conversion of an old school building into living accommodation the new bathroom was furnished with a large ottoman couch and a fine drinks trolley. This indicated the room was to be used for more than ablutions.

Living universals[20]

As already noted, though, there are some common types of place found across most domestic settings This is indicated in Figure 6.5 by the dotted line down the middle of the plot. To the right are more formal or public places, with the dining table, sofa, armchair, and coffee table.

The use of space in the home is not solely a matter of function or even ritual.[21] Everyday experience supports the fascinating way in which rooms can be used and their meanings read.

The noted architect and anthropologist Rapoport[22] pointed out that in no society is the form of a house uniquely related to functional requirements or to particular climatic circumstances. He argues that there were always ritualistic and symbolic qualities that are represented in house form. The studies of archaeologists and anthropologists are replete with accounts of uses of space that relate to particular cultures. What is also remarkably the case is that the examination of space use in any modern, western culture, is amenable to similar analysis. The office of a company director has parallels to the space in a tent of a shaman priest. There will probably be space to move through before access to the significant individual is possible. Once there, there will be many symbols and other representations that indicate the importance of the individual. These symbols and indications are enshrined both in the location of the space, its shape and size and in the particular paraphernalia that are associated with it.

Such considerations of, say, a headmaster's office, of a hospital ward or of a prison cell, are not intended as an indication that these places can understood as merely reflections of primitive lives that are guided by the type of symbolic, superstitious ritual that are proposed by anthropological or archaeological studies. It is social patterning that derives from culturally specific knowledge of day-to-day space use. That is informed by traditions and symbols as well as the requirements for carrying out tasks in a socially acceptable way.

How rooms speak

Think of a room. It may be in a primitive hut in East Africa. It may in an old settlement on a Mediterranean island: it may be a room of a shaman priest in the far East; or it may be at the top of a tall office building in New York. Looking at this room reveals a number of conclusions about its use.

For example, it will be possible to formulate some idea of the status of the person whose room it is. This judgement may be inappropriate in some settings, but generally the larger the room the higher the status that will accrue to the person who is associated with that room. But even at a simpler level, the usage of the room may well be discernible, particularly if it has some artefacts in it. Some idea of whether it will be used for sleeping or for eating, whether it is a place in which people meet. Whether there will be many people who use that room. Whether there are rituals associated with the use of this place. All these different aspects of the use of the room are apparent despite the huge diversity in actual functions and environmental constraints.

In his intriguing book *Snoop* Gosling[23] reverses the idea of the physical context as a mirror of the self by exploring, as he puts it in his sub-title *What Your Stuff Says About You*. This is an ambitious and amusing foray into detecting a person's characteristics from the material artefacts that abound in their rooms. He illustrates what is about a person's personality that can be gleaned from whether they, for example, tidy their socks away, have inspirational posters on their walls or camping equipment in the corner. Gosling is very honest about the difficulty of generalising about personality from broad brush aspects of the 'stuff' found in student bedrooms, or academics offices. The bass clarinet, that you may stumble over when you come into my study at home, tells you more directly about me than the colour scheme and desk arrangement.

The power of a setting may therefore be more relevant when making judegements of people you do not know. I demonstrated this many years ago[24] by asking respondents to make judgements of a person when presented against different backgrounds. (A process that is readily manipulated these days by people changing their backgrounds when participating in a Zoom meeting.) Photographs of a person against a more informal background tended to give ratings of the person higher on friendliness than those against an anonymous, wide open office. This is a phenomena that politicians attempt to manipulate by creating 'photo opportunities' of talking to workers in a factory, whilst wearing workers' overauls and a hard-hat. Or in the days before the demands of social distancing, kissing babies. The context is intended to give the message rather than anything that is said.

Gosling's work was an interesting development of my earlier studies, which has been explored further by others. A particulalry interesting relatively recent consideration is the role of 'ethnic' objects in creating 'atmosphere' in a home.[25] In her sudy Olesen reveals, through conversations with women, how the concept of home and its related atmosphere of domesticity is deliberately enhanced by objects such as Bògòlan candles and cloth coverings. These help to distinguish their living rooms from neutral, anonymous institutions. These tokens of white, middle-class taste may be understood as symbols of the personas that the occupants wish to portray to themselves and any visitors.

Goffman's 'front-stage' therefore has to be considered as a complex mixture of aspects of self-presentation in everyday life. The contrasting left-hand side of the furniture in Figure 6.5 may be appropriately thought of as more 'back-stage', a more private area in which preparation and less social activities take place. Here we can see the bedroom with a study area near it and an area for musical activity. The objects here will also, of course, reflect the characteristics of the occupants, although possibly not in so overt a way as the living room. A baby's crib and an 'organ' are not likely to be present in every Japanese appartment. The crowded nature of these apartments is also indicated by the fact that the fridge is often found in the same space as a dining table as indicated in their close location in Figure 6.5. That analysis gives the basis for a general model of the places that create a home.

The assemblage of places that make up a home arerevealed by shops that sell furniture. For example, Ikea organises its furniture for sale in relation to rooms in the house as listed in Table 6.1. These reflect 13 distinct Places each with its own character and purpose. In each of these types of Places in the home there will be distinct rules of use and different patterns of role relationships, depending on family dynamics. Access to

Table 6.1 Rooms in Ikea's advertisement for furniture

Kitchen
Living room
Dining room
Children's room
Bathroom
Home office
Study room
Gaming room
Garden
Hallway
Laundry
Garage

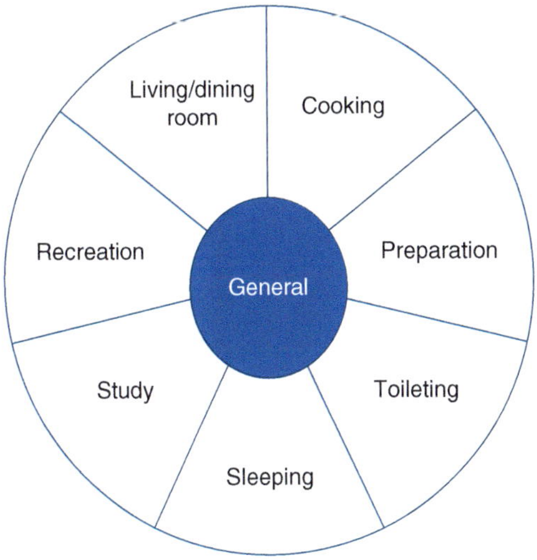

Figure 6.7 A generic model summarising the activities of a home and their relationships to each other

the bedroom, for isntance, will have rules that vary with the age of the occupants and how much control they are allowed to have over that space. The spatial relationship of any bathroom to other rooms is likely to influence who has access to it and when. Interestingly the 'Garage' is not presented as a place to keep a car. Rather it is illustrated as a workshop and store room. In my experience, when looking for a house to buy, I have yet to see a garage in which a car it is usually kept!

A generic model of the places that make up a home is offered in Figure 6.7. The relationship of places to each other draws on the implications of Figures 6.5 and 6.6. This not meant to imply any great discovery, rather as a summary of what a home usually has to provide for. This is the case if it is just one room or a mansion.

Figure 6.7 does not imply a totally distinct set of places, although walls will often be placed between the activities they house. Rather, as noted, they are more productively thought of as an assemblage of Places. This draws on the idea, considered in Chapter 1 that the home is a Place that emerges from the interactions between the Places that constitute it.[26] Nonetheless, it does draw attention to the dominant components of a home. This is amusingly illustrated by Bryson in his book[27] in which he explores his own house and its history. Importantly, the subtitle of the book 'a short history of private life', makes clear that the former Church of England rectory in which he lives enshrines the lifestyles, aspirations, and social interactions of its residents. Of particular interest in this account is that Bryson, like Ikea, chooses to organise the book around room names: hall, kitchen, larder, drawing room, dining room, cellar, study, garden bedroom, bathroom, attic, and so on. Each of these rooms in his house is a very particular Place, with its own expected uses, rules, and roles.

Bryson's former vicarage has a highly differentiated set of Places, but the study of Japanese apartments helps to reveal the natural process of the development of Place differentiation. In the smallest, one room apartment there is little possibility for distinct rooms for each Place. As the apartments become bigger, which in the Japanese context usually means job promotion and a move on in life-stage, notably marrige and children, rooms are given more distinct meanings. They become identifiable Places. This development in differentiation also occurs within a culture. The Japanese example is a particulalry interesting illustration of this.

Japanese furniture includes a mixture of the traditional highly portable, relatively small furniture as well as the much bulkier Western style pieces. The introduction of more Western style increases the total floor space used by the furniture.[28] This made me wonder if this Westernisation was reflected in the differentiation of Places in the home?

To study this I identified four stages in the Westernisation of furniture: (1) Japanese Style, (2) Western forms of Japanese Furniture, (3) Japanese forms of Western furniture, and (4) Western style furniture. The actual examples used are listed in Figure 6.8. The next stage was to determine how specialist the furniture was. You will remember that the further any item of funiture is from the notional centre of the configuration in Figure 6.5 the more differentiated is the Place that furniture helps to define. The computer software that generates Figure 6.5 provides a measure of how far an item is from the notional centre. This indicates how specific, or 'specialist' the item is. The higher the score the further it is from the centre of the configuraiton and thus the more specialst is the item. It was therefore possible to calculate the average specificty score for each of the four groups, as shown in Figure 6.8. The results are very clear. Western style furniture starts being used for very specific purposes. Over time aspects of that style become absorbed into the home.

A consequence of this development, as can be seen in Figure 6.5 is that Japanese apartments are now much more crowded than in my study from half a century ago. This is making space use less flexible. The Places in the home are more clearly defined than they originally were. Although traditional Japanese Inns (Ryokan) still reflect those earlier traditions, as can be seen in Figure 6.9. Even so, the room in Figure 6.9 shows some adjustments, especially for Western visitors who often find sitting on a zabuton without back support uncomfortable.

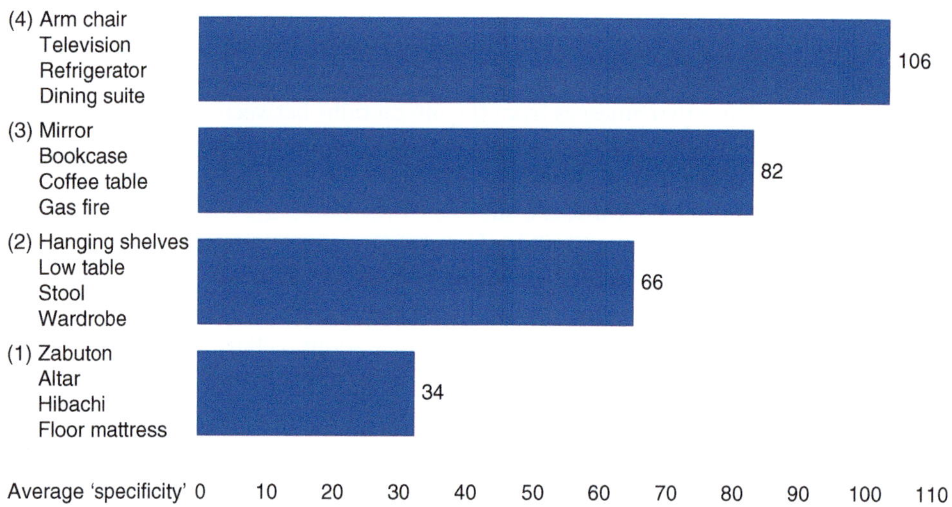

Figure 6.8 The increase in specificity of Western style furniture

Figure 6.9 A room a contemporary Japanese inn (Ryokan) illustrating a traditional approach to room use. The bedding is drawn out at night from one of the cupboards behind a screen

Changes in the definition of Places in modern Japanese apartments are one of many illustrations that Places evolve, or develop, over time. Two interacting processes can be identified, that generate these changes. One, an internal aspect of the activity, and the other the influence of external forces.

The internal development is likely to have its origins in the initial division between a Place that houses 'front stage' activities and one that is more private or preparatory. The bed area and kitchen are separated off from the more social, potentially public Places. Observe a group of people sleeping rough in a derelict area. There will probably be a Place that is communal, possibly around a fire. This will be distinct from the locations that people chose away from this, in which to sleep. If they sleep around the heat source, then there will be temporal controls rather than spatial ones that distinguish the different Places.

The sleeping location is particularly important. It is inevitably at the back, away from public view. Characteristically behind, or backstage. This is in part because of the need for darkness and quiet, but it is also because when asleep we are most vulnerable. This significance of the Place of the bed is brought into high relief in the remarkable artwork by Tracey Emin, 'My Bed'[29] (Figure 6.10). This pays homage to the significance of the private bedroom and how it cherishes the character of the person whose room it is. Emin has always treated her life and personhood as an artwork, revealing things about herself that others would keep private. As she pointed out about this artwork, she had to climb into the bed in the gallery and disturbe the bedclothes by her actual presence within it. Her body creates the character of the Place which the artwork

Figure 6.10 Tracy Emin's 'My bed', 1999, Tate Britain

portrays. She herself admits that the emotional state she was in is captured by the representation of her bedroom. In so doing it makes a comment not only on her particular self at that time, but on all bedrooms in art and in life.

As was clear in my study of Japanese apartments, when people had apartments with more rooms, then spaces became more functionally defined, more differentiated Places. This rather contrasts with Nishihara's[30] claim that Japanese homes have great flexibility of use. Indeed, one of the intriguing details available on the plans provided by Professor Suzuki was the location where people slept. These were distinct positions within the apartment, showing where the husband, wife, and children rolled out their mattresses, or climbed into their Western style beds.

The elaboration of different Places within the home continues as people have the resources for more subtle distinctions. The provision of servants' quarters in upper middle-class homes, gives rise to whole wings of mansions being designated for particular sub-groups, epitomised in the title of the well-loved 1970s British drama series about a rich household called *Upstairs, Downstairs*.

The other influence that encourages Place differentiation and development are external influences. The emergence of Primal Scream Therapy[31] gave rise to the need for Places in which this could be practiced, especially in the home. Subsequently, Places for Yoga or meditation are also available in many domestic settings (especially in California).

On a more mundane level the elaboration of kitchens and associated breakfasting activities, for example, are ways of helping Places to evolve. These can then house experiences, with their associated meanings and assumed activities, that would not have been recognise by an earlier generation. One aspect of these developments can be seen in the social implications of open-plan, kitchen/dining areas. When the chauvinist, male-dominated perspective was that the 'woman's place is in the home', this was associated with very distinct domains that distinguished male from female activity. The place for women was seen as the kitchen. This was a location into which the 'man of the house' would rarely enter. With the opening up of women's roles in society, even though they are still saddled with the majority of domestic chores, the kitchen becomes more a social hub for the home. That Place changes from a separate location for food preparation to reflecting the general activities supported by preparing and eating food, although still frequently dominated by women.

These two processes mean Places are always changing. In the home, which is the focus of this chapter, these may be changes as a direct consequence of changing activities, as when children emerge. Or they may be developing expectations due, for instance, to the desire to reflect a new status. Different conceptions of what a Place is for may also set in motion the evolution of a new Place. This can happen with many personal life changes. If the physical form of existing Places in the home do not allow these developments, then they are likely to be changed. These changes can be small scale, such as students putting posters on their bedroom walls, or they can be larger, with the purchase of new furniture or building an extension. If they will not support personal goals, then a whole new physical setting may be sought.

Telling illustrations of the way people interact with their physical setting are the ways people often modify new houses they buy. They develop them into Places that achieve their emotional and practical purposes, reflecting how they see themselves. A large proportion of home modifications occur soon after a property is purchased. This is often referred to as 'personalisation'. Omar et al.[32] studying this in Malaysia found that a common area of modification was the front of the house, either by the modification of gates, or the façade. This, after all, is where the 'front of house' is, both literally and metaphorically.

Human rights and prison conditions

What if any change to Place of living is fiercely constrained? This is the situation when a person is incarcerated. Furthermore, as my own studies of prisons demonstrated,[33] the cell in which a person may often spend the great majority of their waking and sleeping hours has to provide all the possibilities for Places that would be provided by a home: sleeping, recreation, possibly study, and even toilet activities. Thus, the significance of the components of Place, and the dehumanising consequences of not being able to articulate them, is highlighted by the consideration of imprisonment. This was drawn to my attention when I was asked to comment on the circumstances of being in a cell in the notorious Barlinnie prison in Glasgow (before these cells were upgraded). For although there are parallels between being in a prison cell and being in a confined space station rotating the Earth, the difference in the control over how and why you are there is crucial.

In countries that pride themselves on civil liberties there are laws that forbid certain forms of punishment. In Europe this law is the Convention on Human Rights.[34] Its Article 3 does not allow "inhuman or degrading" punishment. Article 8 enshrines a person's right to "respect for his personal and family life". In the United States the eighth amendment of the constitution, which deals with the rights of those convicted of crimes, outlaws "cruel or unusual" punishment. Prisoners in Barlinnie were therefore bringing cases against the Scottish state, which had responsibility for their imprisonment, on the grounds that their experience was against the requirements of the European Convention on Human Rights. The case of Mr Napier was the one on which I was asked for a professional opinion.

Napier spent most of his time in a small cell, designed for one person, which he shared with another prisoner (Figure 6.11). The latrine facility was a bucket kept behind the door (as illustrated in Figure 6.12), which he shared with the other resident of the cell. Although these conditions were not of the horrific kind that are found in many other countries, Napier's claim was that they were inhuman and degrading. This is quite a challenging claim because he did not suffer the sorts of brutalising experiences that happen in those countries where arbitrary beatings, very severe overcrowding, and

Figure 6.11 A typical cell for one-person, housing two

Figure 6.12 Toilet facilities, in a prison cell that has no integral sanitation

other forms of humiliating punishments are commonplace. My task was to provide an account of the Place he lived within in relation to what could be considered inhuman and disrespectful of his personal life.

Sadly, such impoverished conditions are not limited to old British prisons. Substandard rental accommodation in many countries but was especially noted in Britain with the death of two-year-old Awaab Ishak.[35] He died from the insanitary conditions his parents had to live in, with poisonous mould on the walls. Circumstances that are not that unusual even in a rich country like the United Kingdom.

To do this I took as a starting point the idea of what domestic places consists of, drawn from research described earlier in this chapter. My argument was that the inability of Mr Napier to create the range of Places within the confines of his cell reduced his possibility of existing as a full human being. For Mr Napier the conditions were made worse by his suffering from severe eczema. These conditions were therefore brutalising in the sense that they treated him as an animal or 'brute'.

Judge's comments

When the judge, Lord Bonomy,[36] gave the reasons why he found in favour of Mr Napier he quoted fully from my report especially my conclusions:

> .... although each of the major debilitating components of the conditions which Mr Napier suffered;
>
> (a) The small shared cell with its conflicting functions and the consequent lack of possibility for creating appropriate places within it,

(b) The institutional harshness and lack of any opportunities to develop effective coping mechanisms for 'escaping' from the ever-present experience of incarceration, and,
(c) His ability to deal with prison life and medical vulnerabilities that reduced further his ability to create a human context for himself,

in and of themselves might not be expected to be dehumanising and demeaning to a very large degree, taken together as the multiplicity of stresses, they create circumstances in which it would, in my opinion, be difficult for Mr Napier to hold onto any sense of self-worth or value as a human being.

In my opinion, that view is consistent with the impact that the conditions did in fact have upon the petitioner. He did manage to get through his period in C Hall without suffering mental illness, but was constantly made to feel small, inadequate and worthless by the combination of conditions in which he was detained, his perception of the threat these conditions posed to his vulnerable skin, and the stress which that combination of factors caused.

Lord Bonomy said "that view is consistent with the impact that the conditions did in fact have upon the petitioner". In other words, this distinguished judge accepted the relevance and importance of a conceptual analysis. That was derived directly from over a quarter of a century of the study of how people use and experience their surroundings. The Judge t acknowledged that the contribution of science is not solely a set of facts or finding, but a way of thinking about processes. This may seem very abstract but as Kurt Lewin said 'there is nothing as applicable as a good theory'.

In accepting the framework, I had emphasised three aspects of the nature of Places, especially a 'domestic' Place:

(1) The experience and related nature of a place is unique to the person experiencing it. Robert Napier suffered from a skin condition which made the confined, and inherently unhygienic nature of his cell, particularly uncomfortable and distressing.
(2) The management and social proscriptions of a place influence how it is experienced. In a prison the regime, which kept Robert in his cell for most of the day, greatly magnified the deleterious consequences the cell had for him.
(3) The context of a place in relation to other places also shapes the nature of that place. This is particularly apparent in a prison because some of the places available throughout the establishment, such as a gym or church, are very similar to those outside the prison. They therefore can provide a means of psychologically escaping from the experience of incarceration.

The Sou Fujimoto Challenge

One apparent challenge to the proposal that homes assemblages of Places, each Place with its own pattern of roles and rules, are the fascinating constructions of Japanese architect Sou Fujimoto. His mission is to break down the distinction between spaces, creating flexible surroundings that can be used in a variety of ways that are not

Figure 6.13 Fujimoto's design for House NA

predetermined.[37] One striking example of this is his *House NA* (Figure 6.13). As Fujimoto describes it, the design was for:

> a young couple in a quiet Tokyo neighbourhood, the 914 square-foot transparent house contrasts the typical concrete block walls seen in most of Japan's dense residential areas. Associated with the concept of living within a tree, the spacious interior is comprised of 21 individual floor plates, all situated at various heights, that satisfy the clients desire to live as nomads within their own home.[38]

This building can be regarded as a three-dimensional extension of the traditional flexible Japanese design. Instead of just being able to slide back screen to change the size of spaces, the half levels and overlapping areas mean that a location can be a seat for another area, a cupboard or part of a larger open space. The users of the space can constantly change what type of Place any area houses. Nomads living in a tree! The house clearly symbolises the residents' aspirations at a particular point in their life cycle. There is no acoustic separation between spaces. I wonder what a crawling child, or an arthritic person would make of it?

Although House NA reflects Fujimoto's search for a different way of conceptualising spaces and responds to a young couple who share his vision, the building does not undermine the notion of a house as an assemblage of Places. There is a car port and a bathroom, and the residents can set up a desk for study and computer use. Unusually for a famed piece of contemporary architecture, the photographs of the building actually show people in it, getting on with their lives. They are all youngsters, sitting reading, or looking over books in a well-stocked bookcase. What seems to emerge is that various spaces are treated as particular Places. The initial idea of flexibility would appear to be greatly reduced once people impose upon the house the Places they need to make it a home.

The house as a mirror of self

So far, I've mainly dealt with Places in the home in a more or less objective way. Identifying them from their furniture and the purposes they facilitate. But there is another important dimension to Places that is particularly powerful in the home. The emotional significance of the Place where you live. The power of feelings about the home was intriguingly documented by Clare Cooper Marcus in her book, *House as Mirror of Self,* first published in 1997.[39] She used novel ways of getting her respondents to comment on the significance of their homes. This enabled her to develop the argument that the houses people choose, decorate and furnish, typically reflect significant aspects of their unconscious.

The particular way of thinking about the unconscious that she embraced was that espoused by Carl Jung. As she makes clear, she sees Jung's 'unconscious' as very different from the atavistic, maelstrom of repressed desires that characterises Sigmund Freud's version. Instead she views the unconscious as drawing on both personal and collective processes of striving to what Jung called 'individuation' – and 'inner wholeness'. She takes this to imply that we selectively pay attention to the objects and Places within our lives by investing them.

> with emotion as it serves the deeper, largely unconscious process of individuation, or becoming who we truly are. Objects, like people, come in and out of our lives and awareness, not in some random, meaningless pattern ordained by fate, but in a clearly patterned framework that sets the stage for greater and greater self-understanding. We all play roles in each other's dramas: sometimes as lead, sometimes as supporting actor.
>
> *(p. 8)*

I have to be honest, here. I was brought up in a strict scientific psychology tradition. From my earliest years as a student I was taught that the unconscious is a slippery concept – difficult to define and impossible to measure or prove the existence of. Therefore my initial reaction to Marcus' book, when I first obtained a copy some years ago, was to dismiss it as anecdote and conjecture. However, with my mellowing maturity, I can now appreciate that much of what I have been arguing about the psychology of Place can be enriched by recognising that, with some change in vocabulary, there is much to learn from Marcus.

As I explored earlier, Places are in part defined by the purposes people have for being in particular locations. It is not a big step to see that a central aspect of these purposes can be regarded as 'becoming who we truly are'. For that 'becoming' to be meaningful it does not have to take on the profound life change that is central to intense therapeutic interventions. Or the processes that are present in so many novels. These include *The Awakening*[40], quoted from earlier, in which part of the central characters' finding of herself is to move from her husband's large mansion to a smaller house over which she has control. The search for something that helps the person to feel more comfortable with themselves could just be a desire replace the dining room furniture so that it creates an atmosphere that is appropriately calm.

Marcus also makes clear the house mirrors the self by the ways in which people interact with it. It is not a passive reflection, like a fixed backdrop to daily life. The selection of where to live, then all the details of embellishment and furniture choice, reflect what the residents are trying to achieve as echoes of themselves. This helps to elucidate the emotional elaborations that are inherent in the Japanese furniture study discussed earlier. It also develops the understanding of the significance of finding appropriate Places within a confined prison cell.

A further powerful insight in Marcus' book is that the active interactions with a home lead to an inevitable change over time in what those interactions seek to achieve. This is most clearly revealed when there is a conflict between people living together. Intriguingly, Peled[41] turned this on its head. In his family therapy work, he showed that the interpersonal conflict a couple was engaged in was reflected in disagreements over spatial organisation. Helping the couple to redesign their home contributed to resolving their conflict.

In studies I did of house buying activity I found that elderly people, now living in houses far too big for their needs, took many, many years to find a new Place more appropriate for their current life style. Finding the 'right Place' took so long because a crucial part of the search was the need to come to terms with the fact that their roles in society, and how they saw themselves, had changed. Their current house reflected years of creating a view of who they are, and their relationships. The wrench of changing significant aspects of that was something they had to find a way of dealing with.

When a house is not a home

The interviewees around which Marcus explored the significance of their houses were selected from a limited range of residential situations. Although they varied considerably in the types of Places in which they were living, they all had some choice over where to live. They all had the resources to act on their aspirations for Places in which to dwell. There are, unfortunately, many people who have far less control over their choices of Places and their experiences within them. Beyond the brutal conditions of incarceration discussed earlier, there may be aspects of the home which turn it into the antithesis of the supportive, nurturing environment that we all seek. Domestic violence can turn the experience of a home into a living nightmare. The fact that it is a Place normally associated with caring kindness aggravates the distress caused by the violence.

The house can come to symbolise the trauma that may dominate a person's life. This was illustrated in the use by Peled and Schwartz[42] of the design of an 'ideal house' as part of therapeutic interventions. The young woman, who had been raped, became better aware of how that was distorting her relationships when she proposed a highly defended structure for her home. That design was fashioned to stop any possibility of unwanted penetration.

The significance of the home, in housing so much of our being, helps to elucidate how the home has been such a powerful symbol of our selves over a long history. As Hanes (2019)[43] makes clear "the mythic and metaphoric meaning [of the home] permeates the language, art, poetry, and music of virtually all cultures". He illustrates this with how the ideal house and its various elements were created by a patient:

> ...presented as a symbol of her ego-self and reflected how she viewed herself both as an individual and in relation to the outside world. Her multilevel home represented two plans of consciousness. The entry floor consisted of a living room, kitchen and bathroom and represented the ordinary of everyday existence. Her

kitchen portrayed concerns with domesticity and the lack of social resources and supports to adequately address nurturance and domestic needs within the home. Latoya's well-equipped entertainment room provided her the opportunity to remove herself from the stressors of everyday life. Theclient's house and its various elementspresented as a symbol of her ego-self, and reflected how she viewed herself both as an individual and in relation to the outside world.

Homelessness

Sometimes the creation of a Place on the street is a direct reflection of the different purposes people have for being there. The street is a common location for them to create such Places, especially if hostels and other institutions are not available or attractive. The tent in Figure 6.14a is on the main thoroughfare of Tottenham Court Road in central London. A prime location for access to what that vibrant city has to offer.

The tent clearly has many qualities that declares its meaning to the public. The Saltire flag boasts the origin of the resident in Scotland. The waste bins next to the tent demonstrate the domestic nature of the habitation. It is located next to a tree to give it more stability and less intrusion from passersby. Of particular note is the QR code on the top of the tent. That is a 21st-century mechanism for inviting donations.

The Place here combines personal control and aspects of identity with a clear recognition that this is a public Place. That requires a certain degree of control and protection

Figure 6.14a Homeless residences in the centre of London

Figure 6.14b Sleeping in a street in the United Kingdom

whilst still offering opportunities. It is a striking example of how Places on the street combine public and private aspects.

The second person, in Figure 6.14b, with his dog, situated outside the National Portrait Gallery, in London, does not have a tent, but has nonetheless created a domestic setting. He even has a cupboard, created from a cardboard box. This is sheltered from the passing crowds. That allows him to role his cigarette in seclusion (when this picture was taken). The dog is on a bed with a blanket on top of a sheet of cardboard. Despite the busy street, a usable domestic setting has been constructed which contains enough possibilities for survival, no matter how uncomfortable.

The study by Fried and Gleicher (1961)[44] explores the sources of satisfaction in an urban slum. The point they make is that the middle-class professionals and politicians who look at a slum area may often feel it is bad and, therefore, that it should be removed. However, when careful interviews are carried out with the residents it may be found that their conceptions show a different picture. The picture was found to be far from entirely gloomy. There were a number of sources of satisfaction, not least being the various ways in which the residents felt that they belonged to the area and were a part of it.

The many ways in which a house reflects the person, and what they seek to mirror of themselves, make clear that when a person has no home that has many psychological consequences. These cause distress beyond the practical trials and tribulations the absence of a home creates. But even in this parlous situation people will attempt to create some semblance of a living Place. This can be seen whenever there is a person

Figure 6.15a Sleeping in a field in India

sleeping in public. They find a way of making it private and of defining, even in small gestures., See where this sleeping person in Figure 6.15a has positioned his footwear, drink, and belongings The sleeper on the street in Figure 6.15b has defined his Place to sleep with the cardboard bed and the raised paving for his head and belongings. His sandals can just be seen nearer the wall, away from possible theft.

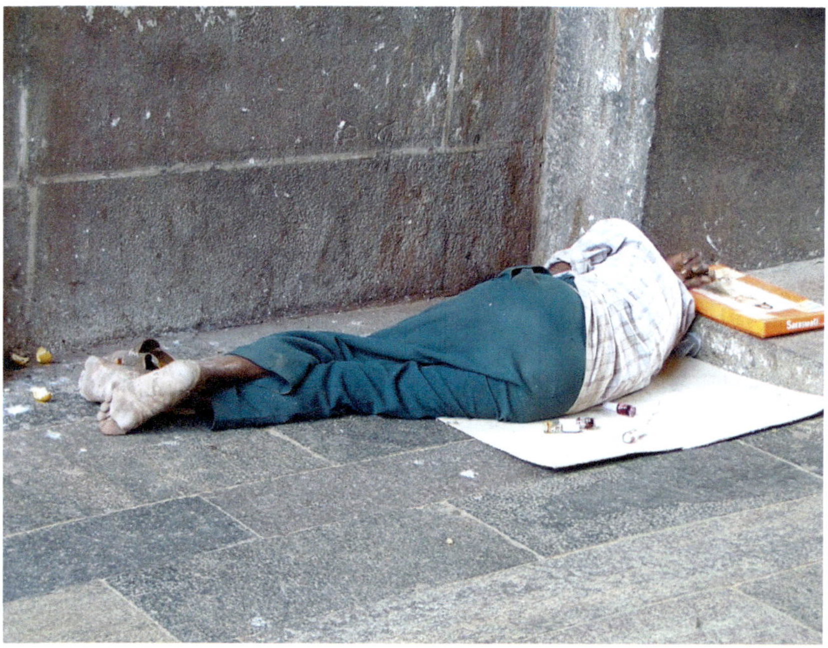

Figure 6.15b Sleeping in a street in India

The home as the essence of places

The range of Places which a house encompasses capture all but the most specialist Places that we ever experience. COVID-19 required home studying, reflecting the way schooling originated in people's living rooms. Working from home has been the usual practice for many different professions as varied as writers and clergymen. Even Places of worship started as a special adaptation of a room in a home. Shops were the front of homes in Roman times. Workplaces were often at the back of houses.

As the styles and types of Places became more specialised the domestic versions evolved into the building types that we can recognise today. But the components essential for a home are still often attached to the more specific features of a building. The most obvious are toilet and eating facilities.

When I explored with Sandra Canter[45] therapeutic institutions that housed people, often referred to as 'homes', as in for example a 'nursing home', one important question was what makes these Places feel more domestic and less institutionalised. We found it was access to the kitchen. The ability to prepare or make food distinguished institutions that were homes from those that were not. This is where the person interacts with and defines the mood and style of a Place in a way that relates directly to their own existence. In most homes the kitchen is a significant heart of the household. It was only in those highly segregated homes, in which people were specifically employed to cook, that the kitchen was a very distinct and different Place. In those cases, the rules of Place mark it off from the rest of the house, as do the defining environmental roles. As we proceed through this book the ways in which Place rules and roles help to distinguish Places from their domestic counterparts will be a theme to which we will often return.

Conclusions

The Home illustrates most profoundly the changing nature of domestic existence. The first draft of this chapter was written as COVID-19 brought the home into high relief. People all over the world were being required – usually legally forced – to isolate themselves, not go into their offices,to try and school their children themselves, avoid public entertainments, mainly by staying at home. As noted, this process pushed back into houses many of those processes that had their origins there.

But for the modern house the need to accommodate all those different activities and experiences created many challenges, most of which operate around the difficulty of identifying distinct Places to support the various activities, moods, and objectives that a home supports. If the kitchen table has to do service as a child's school and a parent's office, whilst still being available for family meals, a regime is needed that allows the inherent conflicts in these activities to be resolved through timetabling.

The impact of the COVID pandemic is only one powerful illustration of the inherent changes that characterise the Home. Technological innovations are having an influence here as they are everywhere else. Smart speakers increase the flexibility of room use just as individual entertainment devices (smart phones) can become Places within a home, turning a living room into a set of isolated Places. Kitchens, in those homes that can afford and embrace new technology no longer require the tradition of 'working over a hot stove'. The related open-plan, kitchen-dining room generates a context for ongoing social interaction that would have been considered unthinkable half a century ago.

This chapter, helps us to understand that the challenges and potential conflicts, and inevitable developments in Places in the home, come from how human beings i relate to the world around them. If we could float in our homes, like an astronaut in a space station, we may be able to use our spaces more effectively. Although that seems unlikely, given that our essential nature is built upon our rootedness to the ground. Homes reflect our social being, housing our relationships to ourselves as well as to others who live within, as well as those outside who may visit or know us. This makes the absence of a home or constraints on where, or how we live, far more distressing than just the physical inconvenience. As we see in chapter 15, this also provides the basis for our understanding of Place attachment and its implications.

References and endnotes

1 Randall S. Lindstrom (2024) *An architecture of place: Topology in practice*, London: Routledge. Reproduced with permission of the Licensor through PLSclear.
2 Bachelard, G. (1964) *The poetics of space,* New York: Penguin Books, p. 26.
3 Bourdieu, P. (1970) The Berber house or the world reversed. *Social science information*, *9*(2), 151–170, p. 160.
4 Sainsbury's Home I Sainsbury's.
5 For example, Mallett, S. (2004) Understanding home: A critical review of the literature. *The Sociological Review*, *52*(1), 62–89; Easthope, H. (2004) A place called home. *Housing, Theory and Society*, *21*(3), 128–138.
6 https://www.museumofthehome.org.uk/
7 Fried, M. (1963) Grieving for a lost home, in L. J. Duhl (Ed.) *The urban condition,* New York: Basic Books.
8 Hurdley, R. (2006) Dismantling mantelpieces: Narrating identities and materializing culture in the home. *Sociology*, *40*(4), 717–733. Also, in a BBC Radio 4 programme available online at BBC Radio 4 – The Hidden History of the Mantelpiece.
9 Madsen, T. & Jensen, H. J. (1982) Settlement and land use in early Neolithic Denmark, in *Analecta Praehistorica Leidendsia XV,* pp. 63–86, p. 69.
10 Nishihara, K. (1967) *Japanese house: Patterns for living,* Tokyo: Japan Publications, p. 49.
11 Suzuki, I. (1971) *Architectural planning 6: Planning of communal housing,* Tokyo: Tokyo University Press, pp. 49, 52.
12 The original paper describing this study is Canter, D. & Lee, K. H. (1974) A non-reactive study of room usage in Modern Japanese Apartments, in D. Canter & T. Lee (Eds.) *Psychology and the built environment,* London: Architectural Press, pp. 48–35.
13 A good starting point for understanding this approach is Shye, S., Elizur,D., & Hoffman, M. (1994) *Introduction to facet theory: Content design and intrinsic data analysis in behavioural research,* London: Sage.
14 An overview of the origins of this approach with many examples is brought together in Levy, S. (1994) (Ed.) *Louis Guttman on theory and methodology: Selected writings,* Aldershot: Dartmouth.
15 There were 43 different categories of furniture in the original study, but for clarity here I'm only considering 39.
16 Grøn, O. (2014) Human spatial behaviour in dwellings and social psychology. *Dwellings, Identities and Homes. European Housing Culture from the Viking Age to the Renaissance*, *84*, 29–38.
17 Grøn (2014). Human spatial behaviour in dwellings and social psychology, Figure 4.
18 Grøn (2014). Human spatial behaviour in dwellings and social psychology,, p. 33.
19 https://www.channel4.com/programmes/our-welsh-chapel-dream
20 Explored in more detail in Canter, D. (1991). Social past and social present: The archaeological dimensions to environmental psychology. *Odense University Studies in History and Social Sciences*, *147*, 10–16.
21 Martin Heidegger's Philosophical Insights on the Essence of Home: A Journey through Iraqi Kurdistan's Dwellings Sardar S. Shareef, Shajwan Nariman Fatah, Hozan Latif Rauf, & Atta

Abdalwahid Ahmed. To cite this article: Sardar S. Shareef, Shajwan Nariman Fatah, Hozan Latif Rauf, & Atta Abdalwahid Ahmed (22 April 2025): Martin Heidegger's Philosophical Insights on the Essence of Home: A Journey Through Iraqi Kurdistan's Dwellings, Housing, Theory and Society, https://doi.org/10.1080/14036096.2025.2496285

22 A more recent consideration of Rapoport's seminal book is Lawrence, R. J. (2019). House form and culture: What have we learnt in thirty years?, in K. D. Moore (Ed.) *Culture-meaning-architecture,* London: Rutledge, pp. 53–76.

23 Gosling, S. (2008) *Snoop: What your stuff says about you,* London: Profile Books.

24 Canter, D., West, S., & Wools, R. (1974) Judgements of people and their rooms. *British Journal of Social and Clinical Psychology*, 13, 113–118, https://doi.org/10.1111/j.2044-8260.1974.tb00097.x

25 Bodil Birkebæk Olesen (2010) Ethnic objects in domestic interiors: Space, atmosphere and the making of home, *Home Cultures*, 7, 1, 25–41, https://doi.org/10.2752/175174210X12572427063760

26 See Dovey, K. (2010) *Becoming places,* London: Routledge, for a detailed exploration of the idea of places as 'assemblages', especially his Chapter 2.

27 Bryson, B. (2010) *At home: A short history of private life,* New York: Doubleday.

28 This is explored by Suzuki, I. (1971) *Architectural planning 6: Planning of communal housing,* Tokyo: Tokyo University Press. He found a 10% increase in floor space taken up by furniture over a decade.

29 https://www.tate.org.uk/art/artworks/emin-my-bed-l03662/tracey-emin-my-bed

30 https://www.tate.org.uk/art/artworks/emin-my-bed-l03662/tracey-emin-my-bed

31 Janov, A. (2013) The origins of anxiety, panic and rage attacks. *Activitas Nervosa Superior,* 55 (1–2), 51–66.

32 Erdayu, O. O., Esmawee, E., & Masran, S. (2012) Personalisation of the home. *Procedia - Social and Behavioral Sciences*, 49, 328–340.

33 Canter, D. (1980) *Prison design and use study,* Department of Psychology, Unpublished, University of Surrey.

34 https://www.echr.coe.int/Documents/Convention_ENG.pdf

35 Iacobucci, G. (2024). MPs demand action to protect tenants from "catastrophic" health impacts of poor housing. *BMJ: British Medical Journal (Online)*, *384*, q146.

36 https://www.scotcourts.gov.uk/search-judgments/judgment?id=0f8387a6-8980-69d2-b500-ff0000d74aa7

37 A revealing talk by Fujimoto is available at https://www.youtube.com/watch?v=kWN2ab6Igps accessed 21 September 2020.

38 From https://www.archdaily.com/230533/house-na-sou-fujimoto-architects accessed 21 September 2020.

39 Marcus, C. C. (2006) *House as a mirror of self: Exploring the deeper meaning of home,* Berwick, Maine: Nicolas-Hays.

40 Marcus, C. C. (2006) *House as a mirror of self: Exploring the deeper meaning of home,* Berwick, Maine: Nicolas-Hays.

41 Peled, A., & Ayalon, O. (1988) The role of the spatial organization of the home in family therapy: A case study. *Journal of Environmental Psychology,* 8 (2), 87–106.

42 Peled, A. & Schwartz, H. (1999) Exploring the ideal home in psychotherapy: Two case studies. *Journal of Environmental Psychology,* 19, 87–94.

43 Hanes, M. J. (1999) House as a mirror of self: A case study of a twenty-one-year-old female in an inpatient psychiatric hospital. *The Arts in Psychotherapy*, 66, https://doi.org/10.1016/j.aip.2019.101601

44 Fried, M. & Gleicher, P. (1961) Some sources of residential satisfaction in an urban slum. *Journal of the American Institute of Planners*, 27, 305–315.

45 Canter, D. & Canter, S. (1979) *Designing for therapeutic environments: A review of research,* New York: Wiley.

CHAPTER 7

How architecture works

A major purpose of building design training is to provide routes into dealing with the complexity of the requirements for what is to be constructed. Two aspects of thishave notable consequences for the nature of the Places created. One is the influence of architectural styles. These provide a readymade set of solutions to draw on for dealing with design problems. They can be modified and elaborated as well as, from time to time, new templates being generated.

Beyond the dominant aspects of visual form, the other set of conceptual shortcuts that facilitate architectural decisions are building types. The type of a building draws on a composite of uses and structural as well as visual expectations. These two combine to provide a set of templates around which a design can be shaped. They are given life during the design process and on into management and regimes for making use of a building. They include an indication of a building's components and how they are likely to be arranged. The conventions of building types from earlier centuries are no longer so obviously drawn on. This is especially clear when developments in post-modernism and beyond are considered in Chapter 12.

Architecture as a unique profession

There are two forms of professional activities. Those that make life possible, notably doctors and the health professionals as well as aspects of engineering. There are others that make life worthwhile. This includes the arts and those who support social and meaningful experiences. Architecture is probably unique in being a profession that contributes to both.

Architecture's contribution to well-being and enjoyment is carried out by the creation of Places. But it would be simplistic to assume that a Place emerges from the straightforward putting together of materials into a physical form. No matter what inspiration or functional determination sets in motion the production of a building,

DOI: 10.4324/9780367808655-10

or the modification of an existing piece of architecture, the nature of the Place that emerges, and how it is experienced and used is created by complex forces.

The mixture of practical and aesthetic aspects of buildings adds considerable complexity to the consideration of the psychological components of building forms. It also complicates the understanding of the decision making of architects.

Whilst architectural designs relate to the intended use of the building, they are often influenced by stylistic considerations. Styles, such as modernism, brutalism, post-modernism and so on, can be thought of as summaries of a number of different features of a design. They reduce the complexity of the decision-making process by providing a limited selection of options to work from. These options are illustrated by famous architects, just as movements in painting or music composition provide templates from leading exponents of a particular style. Examples, such as Cézanne's *impressionism*, or Berg's *serialism,* have an analogous influence to *Corbusier's modernism*. That has generated offspring around the world.

Architectural education typically has the aim of weaning students from imitation on to some ability to work with the internal logic of their favoured architecture. To understand the principles underlying any particular design process and use them for their own creations. The analogy comes to mind of Berg understanding Schoenberg's serialism, but tweaking its rules somewhat, thereby composing music that outshines his master.

Socialisation in architectural concepts

Those styles and development of an internal logic by students are initially based on their preferences, and intentions for what they want to produce. Just as Berg sought emotional impact in his use of a 12-tone system, but his colleague Webern, also a student of Schoenberg, stuck rigorously Schoenberg's system, emphasising brevity, clarity, and mathematical precision. The parallel in architectural education is the development of ways of thinking about buildings by learning about approaches to architecture and developing preferences for different architects and their buildings.

Studies of architecture students' preferences elucidates some of the details of how this educational process takes Place. This was revealed, for example, over 35 years ago[1] in a detailed study by Margaret Wilson. She asked students in two different British Schools of architecture to organise pictures of buildings into groups that made sense to them. When first year students sorted the pictures they made a clear distinction between vernacular, modern, and postmodern styles. There was an indication of an awareness of a sub-set of postmodern buildings that could be called 'hi-tech'.

By their fifth-year students had a much richer set of concepts to draw on. They made distinctions between 'modern hi-tech', 'late modern', 'modern vernacular', 'traditional vernacular', 'classical vernacular', 'post-modern', 'post-modern hi-tech', and 'modern hi-tech' building forms. As Wilson[2] put it:

> results demonstrate the development of architectural concepts from concrete tangible concepts to more complex abstract ones. The students' evaluative judgements show both development with each year sampled, and school specific differences in the type of architecture preferred. Architectural evaluation is shown to be based upon architectural style.

Wilson also found that conceptualisation of differences between buildings was different from these student for those without that training. Further studies with other groups showed differences between architecture students and non-architects[3] in how they think of buildings. This extends to the aesthetic evaluation of buildings.[4]

The results demonstrate the development of architectural concepts from concrete, tangible ones to those that are more complex and abstract. The students' evaluative judgements show both development with each year sampled, and school-specific differences in the type of architecture preferred. The students' judgements of the buildings, combined with their architectural 'heroes', those leading architects they admired, demonstrates the power of stylistic orientation in architecture.

The point worth emphasising here is that architecture students learn to think in terms of styles of design rather than the more limited, overt concepts, such as shape and usage, that they come into the school of architecture with. This increase in the complexity of concepts about the nature of professional activity is not limited to architectural training. It has been demonstrated in many other professions.[5] As a person learns more about any area of activity, they develop richer ways of thinking about that activity and its components. This may be a wine connoisseur being able to distinguish between varieties of wine, that others cannot. Or an experienced entrepreneur who can spot important differences between apparently similar business opportunities.

The differences between architects and non-architects have been demonstrated in their architectural preferences. As is the way these days, such preferences have been supported by neurophysiological recordings. Apparently, when 21 design students and 21 non-design students had their brain activity recorded, whilst looking a virtual reality portrayal of rectangular, round or curved spaces, on average there was a difference between the groups. This related to 'subjective' judgements showing the design students preferred the rectangular spaces.[6] Such an artificial set up does not reveal as much as the presentation of drawings of actual buildings. It does nonetheless show that the validity of even rather crude neurological measures is supported by actual judgements people make.

A demonstration of how architecture is driven by fashions, styles, and 'movements', rather than only by matters of civil engineering and overt functions, is the comparison of the results from Wilson's studies with a similar, much smaller study carried out over 30 years later by Ebru Erdogan.[7] She selected photographs of 22 buildings by well-known architects who had won major architectural awards in the last 25 years. These were designed by 11 different architects, two separate building for each architect, as listed in Table 7.1.

This selection of buildings, all designed by award-winning architects, many of the buildings regarded highly enough to win awards, reveals how major architectural commissions no longer follow any obvious, or single movement. Looking at these buildings, you would be hard-pressed to say what sort of Places these buildings were there to help create. There are a majority of art galleries and museums, some city halls and foundations, two schools, the headquarters of a major industry, a library and an apartment building. Furthermore, not only are these building an eclectic mix of geometries, but many of the architects also have no style obviously recognisable to non-experts,

Table 7.1 List of 22 buildings that had won architectural awards in the previous 20 years, two for each architect

Buildings Used in Figure 7.1 (Architects)	
01	Moma Museum of Modern Art (Botta)
02	Himeji City Museum of Literature (Ando)
03	Fosun Foundation (Foster)
04	London City Hall (Foster)
05	Guggenheim Museum (Gehry)
06	Haydar Aliyev Cultural Center (Hadid)
07	Tsinghua Art Museum (Botta)
08	BIG Isenberg School (Ingels)
09	Hague City Hall (Meier)
10	Zollverein School (SANAA)
11	Poly Grand Theater (Ando)
12	VIA 57 West (Ingels)
13	Museum of Contemporary Art (SANAA)
14	Rock and Roll Hall of Fame (Pei)
15	Minneapolis Institute of Art (Graves)
16	Burda Museum (Meier)
17	BOC Headquarters (Pei)
18	International Design Museum (Siza)
19	Denver's Central Library (Graves)
20	Vitra Design Museum (Gehry)
21	Riverside Museum (Hadid)
22	Iberê Camargo Foundation (Siza)

The numbers refer to the pictures used in Erdogan's study's results in Figure 7.1

Figure 7.1 Fo Sun Foundation Shanghai, China (2017) Norman Foster Architects

Figure 7.2 London City Hall, United Kingdom (2002) Norman Foster Architects

as earlier generations of architects did. For example, Foster's building for the Fosun Foundation in Shanghai (03 in Table 7.1), Figure 7.1 and his London City Hall (04), Figure 7.2, have little in common (other than perhaps that they both look as if they are about to collapse?). Neither is there anything obvious about them that would indicate they are built for and exist on opposite sides of the world. Although Bjarke Ingels' Group Isenberg School (08) Figure 7.3, and VIA 57 West apartment building (012), Figure 7.4 are both on the East Coast of America they could not be more different in geometric form. Nor could the essential activities they are built to facilitate be readily identified from their physical structures.

All 22 buildings in Table 7.1 are famous buildings designed to make a 'statement'. They cannot be ignored. They utilise, mainly, new possibilities for producing designs by computer and new developments in materials and technology for building these exotic configurations. In most cases they are as much feats of engineering as they are illustrations of the architectural imagination. Unlike high fashion design, which eventually finds its way diluted into the design of clothes in shopping malls, there is little evidence of the inventions of award-winning architects influencing domestic housing or the architecture of local schools. There are other types of awards the highlight innovation in more day-to-day buildings, but the buildings listed in Table 7.1 can be regarded as some of those for which the overused word 'iconic' is appropriate.

Figure 7.3 BIG Isenberg School, Massachusetts, United States (2019) Bjarke Ingels Architects

Figure 7.4 VIA 57 Manhattan, United States (2016) Bjarke Ingels Architects

They reflect the epitome of what architecture students may aspire to. In revealing that, they demonstrate how far grand architecture has drifted from earlier attempts either at producing 'forms that follow function' or at giving rise to recognisable movements, such as the post-modernism, as discussed in Chapter 12. The curious paradox, though, is that just as Modernism was decried by many for ignoring local, cultural roots, living up to its description as an International Style, the buildings listed in Table 7.1 could be anywhere in the world. It is difficult to distinguish any aspect of them which would indicate where they are, or the types of Places they reflect.

From the point of view of student socialisation into the architectural profession it is interesting to determine what underlies their preferences for famous architects and the buildings they have created. As part of her study Erdogan asked 131 students in one school of architecture to indicate their preferences for the 22 buildings. These preferences were then subjected to a statistical procedure that helps to reveal the basis of those preferences.

The great advantage of this analytic process is that it create a picture that can be understood without any knowledge of the underlying matrix algebra that produces that picture (or even without any understanding of what matrix algebra actually is). The pattern of preferences for every picture across all 131 students is compared with the pattern for every other picture. A point, representing each picture, is then put in a notional square, such that the more similar the pattern (the higher the 'correlation') between any two pictures, the closer together are the points in the square that represents those pictures.[8] Of course, vice versa, if two points are far apart then those pictures are unlikely to share the same pattern of likes or dislikes.

In Figure 7.5 there are 22 points, each point representing one of the pictures in Table 7.1. The numbers next to each thumbnail image are the numbers for each building in Table 7.1. It can be seen that building 13, SANAA's New Museum of Contemporary Art in New York is very close to building 10, Zolverein School in Essen, by the same architects. That means those sudents who liked, or disliked the New Museum also liked or disliked the Zolverein School. By contrast Building 6, Hadid's Aliyev Cultural Center in Baku is on the opposite side of the configuration to building 18, Siza's International Design Museum in Hangzhou. That means that students who preferred Hadid's building disliked Siza's and vice versa. There was a negative correlation between the preferences for these buildings.

It can be a bit difficult to get your head around what Figure 7.5 represents. I will explain what its purpose is a little further. Because the analysis procedure is based on the amount of *similarity* in preferences between buildings, not how much they are liked or disliked, the spatial representation in Figure 7.5 can be examined to reveal the inherent basis of the judgements, in general, made by these 131 students.

There are a number of possibilities (hypotheses) that would explain the underlying reasons for the students' judgements. One is that that they all have their own personal preferences, each student indicating rather different likes and dislikes from the others. In that case the distribution of the buildings in Figure 7.5 would appear to be somewhat random. No sense could be made of it.

Another hypothesis is that students are basing their judgements on some idea of the styles of buildings they prefer, or do not. That would be revealed by buildings creating

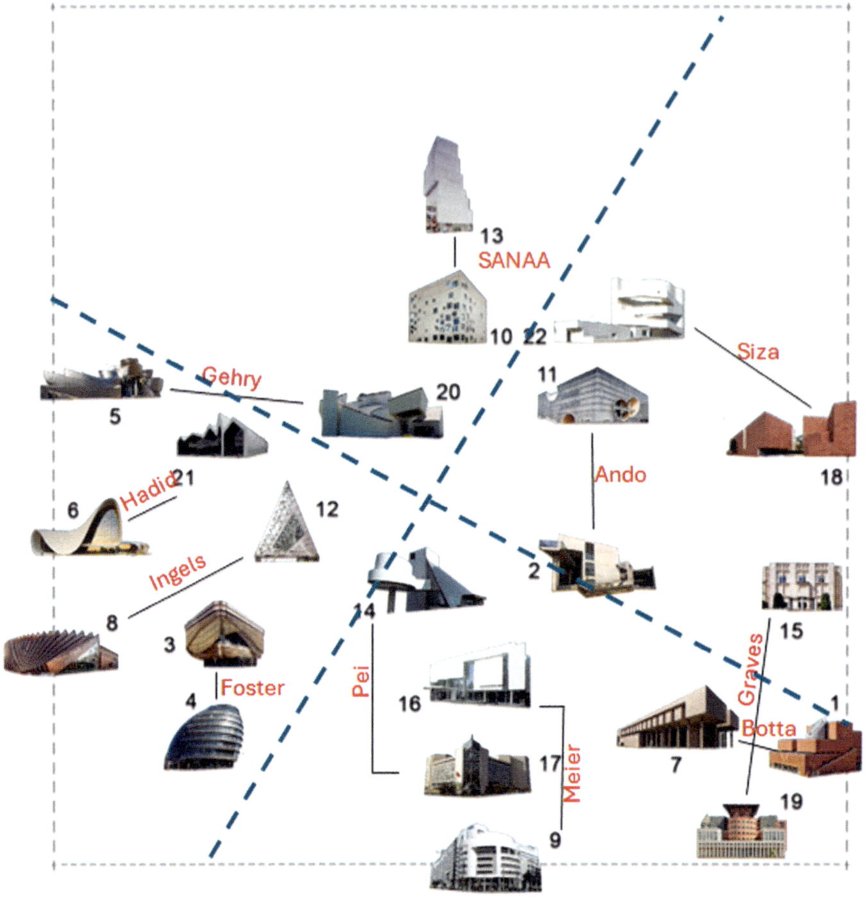

Figure 7.5 Results of statistical analysis that represents the similarities and differences between the preference judgements of 131 students in a British school of architecture. The closer together the points, the more similar the preferences for the pictures they represent. Numbers refer to the buildings in Figure 7.1. The main lines broadly demarcate different styles of building. Thin lines link buildings designed by the same architects

areas of similar styles next to each other. Examining the distribution of buildings for any stylistic differences would reveal that pattern.

A third possibility is that students' preferences relate to the architects' who designed the buildings. As already mentioned, the 11 pairs of buildings by the same architect in this set are not always obviously of the same geometrical form, or style. Therefore, there might be expected to be some mismatch between the position of the building pairs and the physical structure. To assist that examination lines have been drawn to link each of the 11 pairs to the architect who designed that pair of buildings.

If the building design has more influence on the students than the architect that would be revealed by the lines being long, crossing each other, across the configuration. In fact, as can be seen in Figure 7.5 all the lines are quite short. Even when they cross each other that is over a very short distance. The two SANAA buildings are next to each other as are those by Gehry, Hadid, Ingels, and Foster, on the left of Figure 7.5. Siza's and, Ando's buildings on the right are also adjacent. There is a little bit of confusion in the bottom right, Graves' building being slightly confused with those of Botta. Although the latter are very close together. Pei and Meier are another pair of architects whose buildings are mixed together. This could be because Pei's two buildings are very dissimilar in form.

This initial examination therefore strongly supports the hypothesis that students are basing their preference judgements on the architects who designed those buildings. That is a salutary finding when considering the contribution of a building to the creation of a Place. Of course, this is a rather artificial study in many ways. As detailed earlier, there are many influences on the production of built forms. There is no guarantee that once they are practicing architects students will wish to, or have the opportunity to, produce designs that emulate their preferences. Nonetheless, the evidence here is that one significant influence on their design decisions is likely to be the sorts of buildings created by the architects they admire.

The discovery here is that, although students may be aware of the innovative solutions that the architects have created for particular design problems, nonetheless their preferences lean towards those solutions that particular architects have generated. Further examination of the distribution of buildings in Figure 7.5 also enables views to be formed about the differences between students in their patterns of preferences. As indicated, the distinctions across the figure show differences in bases for preferences. Those who preferred the buildings on the left disliked those buildings on the right, and vice versa.

This shows that the second hypothesis of the influence of style on judgements, does have some support. The buildings on the left are those that are more complex, unconventional geometries, dominated by curves. Those on the right are rectangular, perhaps owing more to the older modernist tradition. The buildings in the middle are those that all students agree on, possibly moderately preferred. They are a more eclectic mix of architects and building forms.

A more in-depth examination of the judgements these students made, and their own accounts of why they made them, would enable a richer exploration of the influences that create architects' conceptualisations of the forms their designs can take. The difference between their views and those of non-architects is a burgeoning area of research,[9] but the essence of the argument here points to an issue that is not usually considered. There is a contribution to the experience of Places from particular building forms, especially for significant buildings. That contribution draws on innovations from established architects that influence students' thoughts about what it is possible to create. Although Places may get their meanings from use and traditions, in many cases there will be a creative, innovative influence on the physical form that cannot be ignored.

Those inherent influences on students, when they turn on their computer-aided design software, have parallels in influences on other designers. The local builder will know both what forms buildings can take, but also what it is easiest to sell. That knowledge derives from what others have produced.[10] That in turn is influenced by innovators like the buildings explored in Erdogan's studies.

The sources of architectural creations

The preferences for designers/architects in the Wilson and Erdogan studies indicate some of the foundations on which a creative process can be based. The differences in approaches to building that students imbibe during their education, is part of developing pathways to the process of design. Mark Gelernter helpfully summarises a complex and varied range of theories about how architectural design happens. He offers two distinct processes.[11] One is what he calls a passive discovery by the designer "in something external to designer, in something external to himself or herself, either in the material constraints of the design brief, or in the prevailing 'spirit of the times', or in the prevailing social and economic conditions".[12]

The second process is much more active. These designs are generated "within the designer's personal artistic resources, independent of – and even in advance of- outside influences".[13] This framework challenges a functionalist, scientific view. It questions whether the building should, or ever does emerge out of systematic, methodical, considerations. That foregrounds the idea of architecture being essentially a product of an artistic imagination. For although Gelernter claims these two routes to creating designs are 'diametrically opposed' only a little consideration reveals that they must both be present to some degree in all designs. In some cases, for example, a prison, the functional requirements may be so strong as to dominate. In others, the creative imagination of the architect (and her team) will provide the dominant design concept. This is most obvious, for instance, for many modern major art galleries, as is clear in Figures 7.5. Although even for those edifices some acknowledgement of functional requirements is essential.

A personal example of the range of people and organisations involved in creating buildings has recently been brought home to me when I heard of a person deciding to have his own house built. The first contact was to purchase the land and be clear on the regulations about what was permissible to build on it. He then found an architect to produce a design for a building following lengthy discussions with my son and his wife, taking account of the possibilities on the site available. That drew on opportunities for types of building, especially as the peson and his wife wanted to build an ecologically sound, environmentally sustainable house. Others, such as landscape experts and related consultants were therefore required to provide some input.

A builder needed to be found who was willing and able to act on the designs produced for the building. In addition, the local authority had planning guidelines and also building regulations that had to be dealt with. Two different parts of the local authority influenced what it was allowable to build. Then there was the mortgage company that would provide the funding for the building. That company required the builder to possess certain guarantees, which meant the builder needed to contact other insurance organizations. Which in turn had their own requirements.

All this was for a relatively small, family dwelling. For more complex buildings there will be other stakeholders who can, and usually want to, influence the design decisions. In those more complex situations the owners, managers, investors, and others who have an interest in the design, are typically quite different from those who will use the eventual building. Those users are also likely to be a heterogeneous mix. Think for instance of a school. Children of different ages, teachers of different kinds of subjects, head teachers, technicians, cleaners and maintenance people, will all have different experiences and expectations of the building. A hospital adds further dimensions of complexity to those inherent in designing a school.

Beyond cognitive architecture

The importance of understanding the elaborate, complex influences that produce a building, and the related experiences of it, is brought into high relief when evaluating the growing research tradition, designated as 'Cognitive Architecture', or 'Neuroarchitecture'. That research is founded on the premise that it is possible to reduce to a few key components the experiences of creating a building or utilising it. The weakness of this was illustrated in Chapter 3. There the difficulties of modelling the supposed psychological effects of even relatively simple components of a design, such as the ceiling angle or window size were elaborated. Even more bizarre are claims from cognitive psychologists that some personal foible, even mental disturbance are explanations for what architects have produced. The intricacies of the creation of buildings already illustrated have not stopped writers proposing *ad hominem* explanations of architectural design innovations. Such writers propose that it is oddities of the personality of an individual architect, such as their traumatic experiences, that caused themto create a particular building form.

When there are attempts to reduce the contribution of architects' creations to the influence of their own mental health problems, the naivety of such claims illustrates how egregious those arguments are. They oversimplify what is involved in creating and making a building. They ignore the fact that any architects, their associates, and assistants manage complex constraints set by budgets and regulations, site geometries, materials available, and many other limitations and opportunities. All those involved in this process are actually creating a Place that will have an existence beyond any personal inspiration or demons.

The many actors and shareholders contribute to a distributed cognitive activity in which architects and related designers, even engineers, as form givers, are only one set of influences on the resulting building. There are many examples of architectural teams being sacked because they have not responded to the brief provided by the clients.

One further limitation on the eventual form a piece of architecture takes is demonstrated by the studies of students' preference explored earlier. Design decisions are profoundly influenced by a variety of traditions. Any examination of contemporary housing being built in the United Kingdom reveals the heavy hand of convention. This contrasts with how similar housing is shaped in other countries. These norms, cultural traditions and expectations are drawn on by all those involved in producing buildings, not just an architect.

An illustration of the reduction of the design process to the influence of an architects' idiosyncratic predilections is the attempt by Sussman and Hollander[14] to reduce the design process to crude mental health issues. They claim that two of the most influential early 20th-century architects, Walter Gropius and Mies van der Rohe, produced their elegant designs because of the post-traumatic stress disorder they suffered as a result of their involvement in the First World War. This claim is based on an apparent similarity between their designs and those of bomb shelters. That included the careful Placement of windows to protect from views in, and rooms without any windows, apparently to provide protection. In so doing, Sussman and Hollander claim, this was an unconscious desire for the sort of security the architects had needed in the war.

The possibility is ignored that these architects may have been 'influenced' by the brutalist, functional designs of bomb shelters and look-out posts, because they inadvertently reflected a move towards the modernist aesthetic that was overtaking building designs at the time. An approach to a paired down, ornament-free conception of what was proper in design. Not least influenced by, and contributing to, other movements in the arts. This is epitomised by the rectangular paintings that Mondrian found his way towards. But even those paintings were influenced by Theosophy, rather than earlier trauma. He made clear he was searching for a representation of the spiritual harmony that could be found underlying the chaos of existence.

Attempts to explain a significant creative endeavour by reference to mental or biological failings in the artist is reminiscent of many examples in art criticism. Perhaps most notable are the claims that Cézanne was schizoid, suffered from agnosia, that is difficulty in processing sensory information, such as sights or sound, or that he was colour-blind.[15] None of these speculations advance the understanding of the enormous contribution he made to the development of painting and to ways of seeing.

Another example within the tradition that attempt to reduce the richness of human experience to some spurious biological mechanism is Sussman and Hollander's claim that because, for example, it is obviously of evolutionary benefit to be able to recognise a face, and faces can be found in many otherwise random images, then this should be the basis of design. Similarly, they insist symmetrical forms are typically preferred to others. A finding that is also proposed as indicative of what should be produced to 'design for human behaviour'.

A delightful challenge to these claims was offered to me by Reid Bishop who indicated his delight in the house illustrated in Figure 7.6. As he said, "I walk past this small house almost every day, and I notice that almost every time I do, I smile to myself — I feel a fraction better about life." The building is not symmetrical, nor is there any hint of the layout of a face in its façade. It breaks the recommendations of a 'design for human behaviour'. It can be argued that it is because it does not follow those overly naïve rules, whilst still being obviously a pleasant house that is part of its attractiveness.

Pierre Bloch, who designed the house illustrated in (Figure 7.6, claims it was inspired by pictures from Snow White & the Seven Dwarfs. It also has some reference to conventional Alpine chalet design. By having the main entrance to the right of the building rather the conventional centreadds what could be thought of as a whimsical innovation, in a small way that innovation reflects the power of the larger innovations in, for instance, the buildings in Figures 7.1, 7.2, 7.3 and 7.4. The Place becomes more distinct and has a clearer character because it plays with convention.

At the heart of the arguments, graced with the label 'Cognitive Architecture', is the proposition that likely benefits to the survival of the species have created *innate* ways for human beings to interact with their environment.[16] Throughout my considerations of being in Place I have drawn attention to social cultural, stylistic, habitual, and many other aspects, of being a member of society in a particular milieu. Although interesting aspects of perception can be identified in carefully selected examples of buildings, the claims of cognitive architecture, and even 'neuroarchitecture',[17] do, by their limited focus, ignore what it means to be a person in a civilisation that has been developing

Figure 7.6 *La Villa Shalom*, Carrouge, Switzerland, pleasant without being conventionally symmetrical

for over 10,000 years, with all that entails about language and culture, politics and economics.

The carefully selected examples of the designs of architects in support of the claims by Sussman and Hollander is, sadly, typical of those who seek to reduce human creativity and experiences to limited biological and 'innate' explanations. To examine one more illustration, Le Corbusier's massive simple block-like design for Tokyo's Museum of Modern Western Art is presented as an illustration of his autism. The reference this has to the simplicity of traditional Japanese architecture is ignored. More importantly, the elegantly curved forms of Le Corbusier's Ronchamp Catholic Church (Figure 7.7) challenge any such pseudo medicalisation of his creative insights. Rather than being an aberration brought on by some neurodivergent personality, the design followed the brief from the church reformists who commissioned it. In the early post-Second World War years these reformists wanted to get rid of what they saw as the decadence of the highly ornamental past. They regarded embracing modern art and architecture as a way of doing this.

The point here is that architecture reflects and helps create the artistic *zeitgeist*. In the early twentieth century, when Gropius, Mies van der Rohe and the other creators of what became known as Modernism, all of the arts were seeking new ways of expressing and exploring formal qualities. They wanted to shed the overly complex creations

Figure 7.7 Le Corbusier's Ronchamp Church, France, hardly minimal or even modernist

of the past. Of course, the traumas of the First World War contributed to the desire for change. But that desire had already been signalled earlier, notably by what was already emerging at the turn of the century, when Sullivan's framed the slogan, embodied in his designs for high rise buildings, that 'form should follow function'. The idea was that reference back to earlier approaches to design, especially classical components, embellishment and apparently unnecessary decoration, should be avoided. The limited number of artisans available to provide the embellishments, and the consequent increased expense of employing them, probably also contributed to design decisions.

Without reviewing all of the massive changes in society impelled by war and the developments in technology, it is informative to mention the composers embracing serialism, most closely associated with Schoenberg and his students Webern and Berg, but also apparent in the music of some 19th-century composer, notably Scriabin and even much earlier in some of the music of Mozart. Explored in different ways, they stripped-down music to its essence as a sequence of notes. This eschewed the rich overlay of harmonies that had emerged out of the previous 500 years. Painters also became more abstract. Notably, cubism reduced depictions to their elemental forms. Literature also shook off the complexities of earlier eras. This was even reflected in how they wrote. Hemmingway and Orwell espoused a direct, simple English style very different from that of the previous century, as did Kafka's German move away from the complexity of earlier writers such as Goethe.

The creative aspect of architecture thus draws on stylistic issues. They have their roots in trends within society, highlighted by contemporary fashions. For these reasons, many countries have detailed and complex sets of regulations for the design of each type of building. They attempt to limit the impact of fashion in favour of producing useable buildings. Although it has to be admitted, as in examples already mentioned, the legal constraints on what can be built are not totally divorced from the pressure of styles and fashions.

Given the weight of controls on what is allowed, the job of the architects, or building designers, is often to do little more than put these details into a feasible and cost-effective proposal. That would have to take account of the site and location of the building(s) as well as the finance available. Just to add one further control, which happens in cities, such as London. There is a limit on how high a building can be in certain locations. In London the building must not obscure the view of St Paul's Cathedral from various, specified directions.

What is implicit in all these influences on what is actually built is that architectural designs can be regarded as emerging out of a power struggle. Tom Markus's magnum opus *Buildings and Power*[18] explores the implications of these conflicts of interest. Providing many detailed illustrations, he argues that the emergence of the different types of building was a consequence of the battles over what buildings were for and what they represented. In other words, the commonly accepted idea of 'building types' is itself a representation of who has determined what should go on in any building.

Building types

The combination of functions that make up the types of Place that a building encapsulates are summarised in the notion of building type. Each type brings together a mixture of forms, assumed uses and related conceptualisations. As Tom Markus points out in his erudite exploration of the origin of building types[19], building type labels "were a shorthand for an immensely rich social description". He explored whether these labels are of real use in understanding the experience of buildings, in other words, the sorts of Places they are. As he writes:

> What beneath the experience described by such labels as 'museum' or 'office' do we really sense? ...Why is a 'factory' more like a barracks than a hostel, despite the fact that the sleeping accommodation of barracks and hostels is so similar?

It is apparent from Markus' questions that the differences between buildings, giving rise to their type being recognised, is not solely about the building's physical form. This is a difference in emphasis that distinguishes between essentially visual and aesthetic aspects, considered earlier in this chapter and buildings contributing to being a type of Place. As explored in Chapter 8, built form provides some clues of what is likely to go on there. These are derived in part from the shapes and structures needed to house various activities. Recognising what sort of Place the form of a building encapsulates is not the dominant aspect of a building type. Rather, the details of a building's form draws on use, personal experience and cultural context to give cues to the activities and experiences that it would be expected were facilitated there. The symbolic qualities of buildings also contribute to the nature of Places, as discussed in Chapter 10, when considering the examples of religious buildings and their particular liturgies. However, these details are not always unique to specific building types. A school can look more like an office, which a hospital can mirror, and so on.

In other words, as has been apparent throughout the consideration of Places there are no discrete, inevitable demarcations between building types and the Places. Each is a varying assemblage that defines and is defined by the Places it houses. Markus hinted at this when he questioned why a 'factory' is more like a barracks than a hostel. A building's context in time and culture contributes to an understanding of what sort of building it is. But there are inevitable overlaps in the Places associated with any dominant example. Hospitals have cafés, schools have medical offices, or wellness centres. Some large offices even have bowling alleys, or swimming pools. Airports include prayer rooms, as do prisons.

However, despite these overlapping, elisions between types of built Places there is still value in identifying prime examples. This is similar to the value of recognising the existence of primary colours. It is rare to find pure examples of red, blue, and yellow. But being aware of primary colours allows distinctions between purple and pink to be understood because the former has more 'blue in it' than the latter. Similarly, as a painter or interior designer it is essential to distinguish different shades of green in relation to the amount of yellow or blue they 'contain'. More yellow creates a lighter, warmer green, whilst more blue results in a deeper, cooler green.

It is, correspondingly, fruitful to consider the ways different building types relate to each other. This requires identifying some archetypal examples, indicating their relationship to each other. The model of types of built Places I propose is a first attempt at such a framework. There are empirical procedures available for testing this empirical structure such as that illustrated in Figure 7.5.[20]

Such a model recognises the distinctiveness of different building types whilst also being alert to their overlapping similarities. A fascinating benefit of this model is that it allows the identification of how Places can take on the meanings of different but similar Places. That facilitates insight into the subtleties of differences between similar Places. For example, how a prison can shed some of its punitive aspect by being designed more like a hotel. Or an airport be made to feel like a factory to be processed through. Such a framework draws attention to how the mixture of Place types may give rise to slight differences between building types.

Revisiting home as the archetypal Place

In Chapter 6 the types of Places that make up a home was explored. That illustrated the proposal that a Home typically houses the main activities that support typical domestic existence. That is the case even if the home is an area of pavement on a busy street. As mentioned in Chapter 6, dominant facets of this division reflect what can be thought of as 'frontstage', where residents expect to be 'on show' or at least have the opportunity of reflecting themselves in notional or explicit contact with others. By contrast 'backstage' Places combines Places that facilitate preparation for the frontstage or house more distinctly private activities.[21] Another facet distinguishes between social Places and those that a more closely related to being alone. Consideration of likely physical, psychological, and social similarities between Places gave rise to a circular model of Places in the home in Chapter 6. That circle is arranged around a notional general-purpose area.

Following from that conceptualisation of the Places in the home is the proposal that all Places that are shaped for human actions can be understood as derivatives, or elaborations of Places in the home. From this point of view building types can be seen as developments of those domestic Places. That model of the Places provides a framework for considering the different types of Places that distinguish building types and the relationships between them, as illustrated in Figure 7.8.

The gifted architect and published cartoonist, who signs his name Mikko, responded with the drawings in Figure 7.8 to my request for sketches to the list of a variety of types of buildings typical of different Places that I gave him. It was fascinating to see what he produced in response, for instance, to my label 'Hospital, or 'Airport'. As an experienced architect, all his drawings reveal buildings that have a similar feel to them, drawing on related stylistic decisions. They each are nonetheless distinct. They also help to capture the contribution of building forms to feelings of Place.

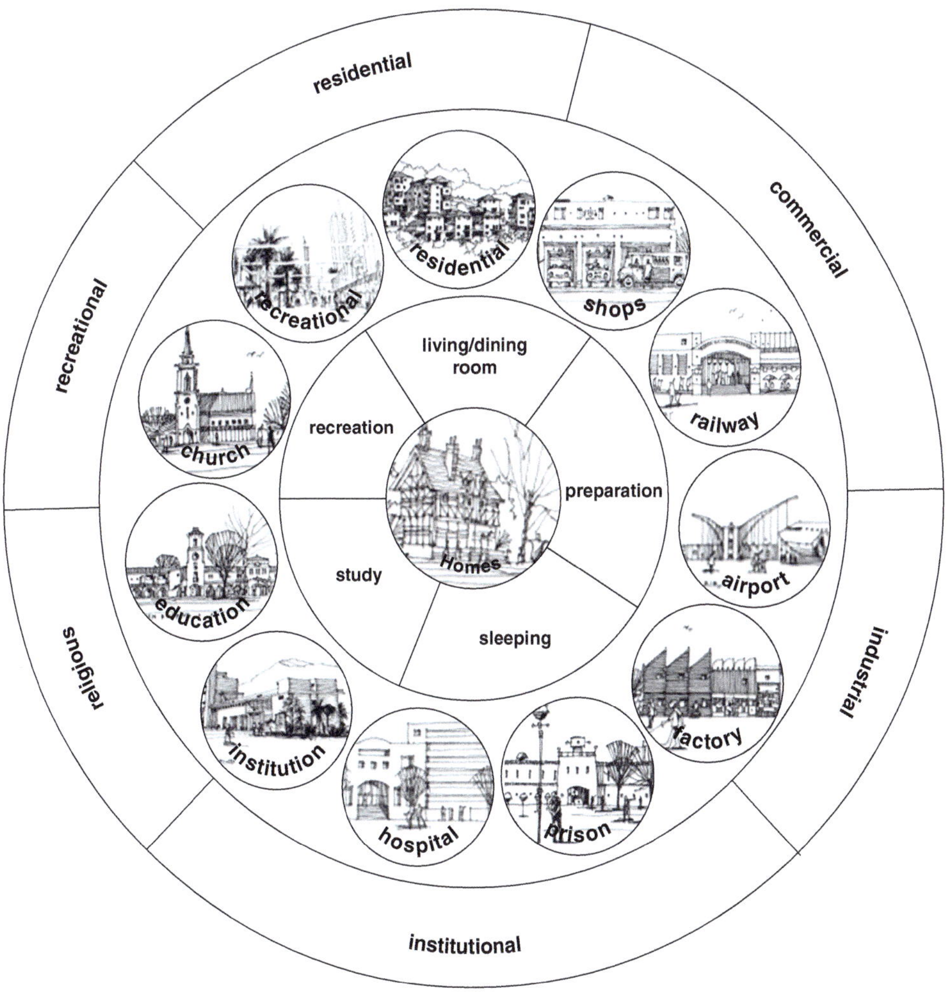

Figure 7.8 A conceptual circle of building/Place types

A notional single domestic dwelling is at the centre of the configuration in Figure 7.8. That reflects the hypothesis that a domestic dwelling is the generic foundation for the more specific Places around the circle. As mentioned, the spacing of the buildings around the circle derives from the model of Places in the home presented in Chapter 6, indicated there in Figure 6.7. There is not a perfect matching of building types to Places in the home, because some Places have emerged over recent times that are greatly elaborated aspects of what might be found in the home, notably airports. Those very private, backstage, aspects of the home, such as washing and toilet activities have also been left out, although public baths and toilets might have been included on the right with other public buildings.

The circular model allows many ways of building to be characterised. Broadly speaking, there are to the left those Places that are to do with personal development and sustenance. In the home these are areas for relaxation, being with the family, study and sleeping. Such 'backstage' Places emerge, for instance as hotels, libraries, colleges, and recreational facilities. Religious buildings have been put in that region, reflecting the role of a crucifix on the wall, a buddha, or small altar in the homes of many religious traditions. People play active roles in these 'backstage' Places. They have agency, mainly determining what they do there by their own volition to achieve their own personal goals.

To the right are the externally controlled, productive Places. This can include prisons as well as fire stations and factories, airports and railway stations. There is an important sense in which these can be regarded as 'frontstage'. People active there are typically on show. Their roles are shaped by the organisation they are part of. The agency of those active there is typically constrained by the requirements of what the organisation is trying to achieve.

The distinction between the Places at the top and those at the bottom in Figure 7.8 could be understood as differences in the sorts of institutional qualities that influence the activities and related roles in those Places. At the top, with the recreation facilities and apartment blocks, individuals are active in a range of different ways. They are acting on the personal concerns relating to those Places. At the bottom in large institutions like universities, and hotels, even prisons, there is a greater similarity in the roles people take on in those Places.

These are all speculations about the variations in Places as reflected in different building types. Variations that relate to differences in the roles and rules typical of each Place. Many more could, of course, have been added, such as department stores, barracks, and significant public Places like town halls, museums, and art galleries. They would fill what is already a crowded picture. Future studies could reveal locations in the model into which they would fit.

The point is to introduce they idea of range of types of Place, with typical, even stereotypical examples. These can be seen as operating as key pointers in understanding variations between Places. The analogy of colours, mentioned earlier, helps to clarify this..

An illustration of how variations across adjacent Place types can operate is when a railway station has apartments on top of it. That is not uncommon for many early railway stations in Britain. Some aspects of the experiences of those Places draw from the awareness of the accommodation. Many other examples of how Places draw on each other's qualities can be derived from this model.

The crucial point is that the built forms and nature of Places are only points on a continuous circle. Some prisons may be more like hotels. Indeed, as illustrated in Chapter 1 some prisons have actually been converted into high-class hotels. That mixture (like blue and yellow giving green) has an added piquancy to it because of the clash of Place types. Furthermore, many hotels, of course, operate as conference venues and support institutional processes. Factories can take many different forms, depending on what it is they are producing, or the image they wish to present. This is the same as the variations in domestic kitchens in relation to what sort of food is typically prepared there and how that relates to the nature of the family for whom the food is being prepared.

The main purpose of this hypothetical model is to indicate how the built form is a rich and often subtle part of the experience of Places. As Lindstrom[22] argues at length, architecture does not *create* Places. Rather it is an aspect of any location becoming a Place. The use and roles within a Place contribute to the Place it is. That may be reflected in the built form that houses it and therefore produces a positive cycle that supports the use and significance of that Place. Or the architecture may provide a contrast to the stereotype of where a Place is expected to be housed. In so doing, as when a prison is experienced as a hotel and vice versa, the contrast adds extra implications and meanings to the Place and how it is experienced. The model of built Place types proposed in Figure 7.4 is presented to open those considerations and to offer a set of hypotheses for future scientific test.

Conclusions

Reflecting how architecture works has supported a further understanding of the interactions between built forms and the nature and experience of Places. This is part of the process of encouraging more complex ways of thinking beyond merely what buildings can look like. That reveals the weaknesses of attempts to claim that building designs can be generated by or reduced to simplifications of cognitive processes. The proposal that simplistic issues such as edges, the delight in visual symmetry, and the power of recognising faces, can be the basis by "designing for how we respond to the built environment" [23] is undermined by the aspects of building design and development of architectural ways of thinking explored in this chapter.

This is a critique of explanations of human interactions with buildings that draw solely on neurobiological processes, referring to what the *brain* does. That is as if the 'brain' were operating without any person involved. A person who has an upbringing, history, memory, habits, personality, education, relationships with people and ideas. Whose experiences, delights and distastes cannot be reduced merely to generalities, reflected in superficial measures of brain activity. This critique helps to emphasise how understanding what it means to be in a Place requires consideration of very much more than can be revealed through simple perceptual phenomena such as preference for symmetry or awareness of edges.

The complexity of what is being sought in design demonstrates that the forms of buildings inevitably draw on many influences. These have contributed to the differentiation into different building types, which in turn elucidates the experience of the Places those buildings are part of. This perspective emphasises that a building is never ever just a set of geometries. It is a wholistic entity that contributes in various ways to human endeavours. A variety of functions characterise any piece of Architecture, as explored in Chapter 8.

References and endnotes

1 Wilson, M. A. & Canter, D. V. (1990) The development of central concepts during professional education: An example of a multivariate model of the concept of architectural style. *Applied Psychology*, *39*(4), 431–455.

2 Wilson, M. A. & Canter, D. V. (1990) The development of central concepts during professional education: An example of a multivariate model of the concept of architectural style. *Applied Psychology*, *39*(4), 431–455. This one part of her extensive PhD thesis, which is also available online: Wilson, M. A. (1989) *The development of architectural concepts: A comparative study of two schools of architecture*, PhD thesis, University of Surrey (United Kingdom).

3 Groat, L. (1982) Meaning in post-modern architecture: An examination using the multiple sorting task. *Journal of Environmental Psychology*, *2*(1), 3–22.

4 Šafárová, K., Pírko, M., Juřík, V., Pavlica, T., & Németh, O. (2019) Differences between young architects' and non-architects' aesthetic evaluation of buildings. *Frontiers of Architectural Research*, *8*(2), 229–237.

5 For example, Chief Executive Officers increase their cognitive complexity the longer they are in the job Graf-Vlachy, L., Bundy, J., & Hambrick, D. C. (2020) Effects of an advancing tenure on CEO cognitive complexity. *Organization Science*, *31*(4), 936–959.

6 Shemesh, A., Talmon, R., Karp, O., Amir, I., Bar, M., & Grobman, Y. J. (2017) Affective response to architecture—Investigating human reaction to spaces with different geometry. *Architectural Science Review*, 60(2), 116–125.

7 Erdogan, E. & Canter, D. (2020) *Conceptualisations of architecture: Aspects of student professional socialisation.* Final Report: International Post Doctoral Research Fellowship Programme.

8 This is the same statistical procedure as that illustrated in Chapter 5 when considering the similarities in room locations of furniture placement. It is part of the family of analysis tools known as multi-dimensional scaling (MDS). They represent measures of similarity as distances in a notional abstact space. A reasonably clear, brief technical explanation is given in the American Psychological Association online dictionary at APA Dictionary of Psychology.

9 For example, Gifford, R., Hine, D. W., Muller-Clemm, W., & Shaw, K. T. (2002) Why architects and laypersons judge buildings differently: Cognitive properties and physical bases. *Journal of architectural and Planning Research*, 19 (2) 131–148.

10 The concept of 'social representations', proposed by French sociologist Serge Moscovici is relevant here, not least because design innovators add to, or unsettle, commonly held conceptual systems. However, developing that here at would take us into abstract realms of French sociology and British social psychology. The following is a reasonable summary of that area of study. It is in English although published in a Russian language journal: Pascal, M. (2021) Introduction: The heuristic value of social representations theory. *Вестник Российского университета дружбы народов. Серия: Психология и педагогика*, *18*(2), 291–298.

11 Gelernter, M. (1995) *Sources of architectural form: A critical history of Western design theory.* Manchester University Press. A useful summary is available in Garlernter, M. (1993) The concept of design and its application to architecture, in B. Farner & H. Louw (Eds.) *Companion to architectural thought*, New York: Routledge, pp. 399–403.

12 Gelernter, M. (1995). *Sources of architectural form: A critical history of Western design theory.* Manchester University Press. A useful summary is available in Garlernter, M. (1993) The concept of design and its application to architecture, in B. Farner & H. Louw (Eds.) *Companion to architectural thought*, New York: Routledge, p. 399.

13 Gelernter (1995). *Sources of architectural form*, p. 399.

14 Sussman, A., & Hollander, J. (2021) *Cognitive architecture: Designing for how we respond to the built environment*, New York: Routledge.

15 Benvenuto, S. (2013). The gaze of the blind: Notes on Cézanne and cubism. *American Imago*, *70*(3), 385–406.

16 An excellent review of the many claims for Darwinian explanations of psychological phenomena is given in Rose, H. & Rose, S. (2000) (Eds.) *Alas, poor Darwin: Arguments against evolutionary psychology*, London: Jonathan Cape.
17 Discussed in more detail in Chapter 5.
18 Markus, T. A. (2013) *Buildings and power: Freedom and control in the origin of modern building types*. London: Routledge.
19 Markus (2013) *Buildings and power* p. 37..
20 I would happily guide anyone who wishes to undertake such a study via www.davidcanter.com
21 As a reminder from earlier chapters the terms 'front stage' and 'backstage' are drawn from consciously from Erving Goffman's 1959 dramaturgical theory of social behaviour, reviewed for example by Serpa, S. & Ferreira, C. M. (2018) Goffman's backstage revisited: Conceptual relevance in contemporary social interactions. *International Journal of Social Science Studies*, 6, 74.
22 As a reminder from earlier chapters the terms 'front stage' and 'backstage' are drawn from consciously from Erving Goffman's 1959 dramaturgical theory of social behaviour, reviewed, for example, by Serpa, S. & Ferreira, C. M. (2018). Goffman's backstage revisited: Conceptual relevance in contemporary social interactions. *International Journal of Social Science Studies*, 6, 74.
23 Sussman, A. & Hollander, J. (2021) *Cognitive architecture: Designing for how we respond to the built environment*, New York: Routledge..

CHAPTER 8

The functions of architecture

Are we determined by our built environment?

The debate about how/whether the physical surroundings manipulate what we do, feel, and think has been ongoing since human beings first became conscious of their selves. For centuries this debate was couched in beliefs about how various aspects of the environment directly influenced people's emotions and actions. Although recent studies do support some loose general relationships, particularly between ambient temperatures and wellbeing,[1] the view strongly held in the 19th century that climate was a major influence on culture, has been shown to be based on colonial and racist stereotypes. However, the simple stimulus-response belief of environmental characteristics (the stimulus) causing emotions and actions (the response) is hard to shake off.

Great cathedrals were built to cause people to revere God (and admire the people who built them). Fortunes have been made by claiming that a particular shade of pink will calm people down.[2] Many people put great effort into choosing the 'right' furniture for a living room. Campaigns are mounted to save an ancient tree or renovate an old building. At any given moment a noticeable proportion of television channels have a programme dealing with the selection, modification or creation of a building. They are all couched in terms of how the product will influence their user's activities and wellbeing. These all enshrine some simple, direct view of the impact of our surroundings on us.

There is one powerful explanation of this fond belief that creating or changing the built environment will have directly beneficial effects. Those who design buildings have to sell their wares. If the architecture has some grand sculptural claim to fame, its impact on the users may be considered less important. In the absence of such grandeur, architects and their colleagues must claim their design suggestions will have some psychological benefits.

A recent example of this view of the influence of the physical environment on actions and experience is given in Bernheimer's[3] well-informed exploration of the impact of our surroundings on us. She has no qualms in starting her book with a bold, unconstrained

DOI: 10.4324/9780367808655-11

statement "The spaces we live in shape our lives" (p. xi). The sub-title of her book shouts this claim out loud: "How everyday spaces structure our lives, behaviour, and well-being". This is just a more recent version of the claim central to Gallagher's earlier book,[4] which insists on its cover that it reveals "how our surroundings shape our thoughts, emotions and actions".

These daring statements capture a perspective often referred to as 'architectural determinism'. This viewpoint has its origins in 'environmental determinism'. These were the beliefs, noted earlier, about the impact of climate and the features of the large scale, geographical environment on the characters of peoples. Anthropological and geographical explorations that brought Western scientists into contact with societies they considered to be 'primitive' were combined with views drawn from a naïve interpretation of the Darwinian process by which evolution takes place, through organisms adapting to their physical surroundings.

To be clear, at the extremes of environments, such as heat and noise there are of course direct influences on how we can act. There are also spatial requirements for different activities. A lot of people crowded together in one room cannot do very much there. But beyond these extremes the sense people make of their surroundings, their own purposes and activities, limit any direct and simple determination of the environment on behaviour. Human agency requires people to make some sort of sense of what is possible in any location. That interpretation process will vary from person to person and culture to culture. Consequently, within the limits of physical tolerances the impact of where you are is always mediated by thoughts and feelings, purposes and active endeavours.

A well-known example of the indirect influence of the physical environment on human actions are the so-called Hawthorne studies. They were carried out at the Western Electric Company's Hawthorne plant in Chicago in the mid-1920s. They set out to explore the effects of physical conditions on employee productivity.[5] They changed various aspects of the working conditions, in different parts of the factory, and measured what the workers did. This included modifying the lighting levels. When the lighting was improved, as expected, performance improved. However, to the surprise of the researchers, when the lighting level was reduced performance also improved. This has always been interpreted as illustrating that social norms and expectations were more influential than the physical conditions. It was a time when employment opportunities were scarce so that people were keen to do well at their jobs in order to keep them. Being aware of being tested they tried to do well.

What is often ignored about this, and similar studies at the Hawthorne plant, is that actions did vary in relation to environmental changes. The impacts of these changes were not on the individual as an organism. The changes carried meaning. They were a sign for the workers that they were being watched and their performance assessed.

The workers' reactions to lighting levels are one of very many illustrations that our physical surroundings carry significance for our experiences and activities. They show that the processes involved are more complex than the crude ideas that architectural or environmental determinism promote. It is therefore to be expected that when considering the nature of Places, a range of psychological, social, and cultural issues emerge.

Pragmatic origins

The early studies of the social and psychological relevance of the built environment had the clear, objectives of providing design guidelines. The roots of this in the United Kingdom were surveys conducted after the Second World War as preparation for a massive house building programme. This was due to the necessity to rebuild the country after the devastation of aerial bombardment. It was also seen as an opportunity to get rid of the poor, squalid housing conditions in which many people had lived before the war.

In that post-war era there was an excitement about the application of science to all areas of life. The Festival of Britain in 1951 emphasised new materials and the contributions of technology to the possibilities for architecture. Psychology and the social sciences were in the ascendant. It was natural to start thinking about how people used space and the implications this had for a more systematic design process. This included early studies on noise annoyance[6] carried out by the first psychologist to be based at the Building Research Station, John Langdon, who had a conventional experimental psychology background. Prior to his studies most of this work had been carried out by engineers[7] with little awareness of the psychological issues involved.[8]

By the early 1960s there was a new excitement in the air, a positive exploration of new opportunities. Kennedy formed a rapprochement with Khrushchev that resolved the Cuban missile crisis in 1962. In 1963, Martin Luther King Jr. gave his 'I have a dream speech' opening the way for radical changes in society (still sadly greatly needed). In the same year The Beatles changed the nature of pop music for ever with "Please Please Me", and artists such as Andy Warhol, Peter Blake, Roy Lichtenstein, and Robert Rauschenberg created a new, much more democratic, approach to art, which embraced popular culture. In 1969 Americans landed on the moon.

Parker Morris guidelines

As part of the reduction of the impact of an upper class deciding for 'the people', governments set in motion the study of how people live[9] and what this implied for the design of the rash of new buildings that were being produced. A notable example of this in the United Kingdom was the Parker Morris report in 1961,[10] with the forward-looking title *Homes for Today and Tomorrow*. It was produced by a government committee chaired by Parker Morris, a civil servant, who had been a Town Clerk in London (not an architect or planner).

The main aim of the Parker Morris Committee was to set space standards for public housing. The committee did not consider the layouts of buildings. It regarded a minimum amount of space as important itself. It was innovative in considering the activities people want to carry out in their homes. One reason for this was an awareness of the need to explore the consequences of the changing nature of work and what they called the 'new affluence'. The report had an unusually behavioural science perspective on how to specify minimum space requirements:

> ...changes in the way in which people want to live, the things which they own and use, and in their general level of prosperity, and perhaps the greater informality of home life, make it timely to re-examine the kinds of homes that we ought to be building, to ensure that they will be adequate to meet the newly emerging needs of the future, as well as basic human needs which always stay the same.

Table 8.1 Summary of the 1961 Parker Morris report – *homes for today and tomorrow*

Ministry of Housing and Local Government, Great Britain

A report by a sub-committee of the Central Housing Advisory Committee, set up to consider the standards of design and equipment applicable to family dwellings and other forms of residential accommodation' in order to make recommendations.

The report includes the following Chapters and Appendices.

Chapter 1 NEW PATTERNS OF LIVING

Chapter 2 HOMES FOR FAMILY NEEDS:

The Requirements of Different Families
- A Families with children
- B Married couples
- C Persons living alone
- D Elderly people
- E Very small houses and bungalows.

Factors in Home Design
- A Heating the home
- B Kitchens
- C Storage
- D Electric socket outlets
- E Safety

Aspects of Living in Flats
- A Lifts
- B Private balconies
- C Sound insulation
- D Refuse disposal

Summary of Recommended Standards Relating to Floor Space

The contents of the Parker Morris report listed in Table 8.1 shows how remarkably thorough and prescient it was. It draws attention to the requirement for double-glazing, play space, and provision for cars. Remember, this is 1961, when the country had only come out of rationing a few years earlier. Only a little under one in three households had a car. Yet the committee saw the needs for all these features to be included as basic requirements for design.

Especially noteworthy was the fact that the report was based on studies of what people did in their homes. Information was given on the sizes and arrangements of furniture as well as other anthropometric details. They understood that patterns of space use were changing as household arrangements changed. Therefore, flexibility in design was encouraged as well as considerations of heating and acoustic conditions. Lighting was also explored, especially the assumed benefits of daylight.

The Parker Morris recommendations became part of building regulations in the United Kingdom until 1980, when a Conservative government reduced their mandatory nature. The claim was that it was making building of homes too expensive. There can be little doubt that the quality of mass housing reduced as a consequence.

Beyond 'needs'

The introduction of the idea of 'basic human needs' was a bold grasp at what is a somewhat controversial topic in psychology. Beyond the need for food, water and the ability to breathe, there is debate about what other 'needs' are 'basic'. Sexual activity is often offered as a possible candidate, but plenty of people survive without satisfying that need. Beyond these fundamental needs, many other requirements for a sane, productive life are debated. The various constitutions of many countries as well as the United Nations move away from satisfying 'needs' and treat people not as organisms to be fed and watered, but as citizens who have rights. For example, the U.S. Bill of Rights declares that inherent rights are:

> freedom of speech, freedom of religion, the right to keep and bear arms, the freedom of assembly and the freedom to petition. It also prohibits unreasonable search and seizure, cruel and unusual punishment and compelled self-incrimination.

None of these have immediately obvious implications for the shaping of buildings, except the consequences of the prohibition on cruel and unusual punishment for prison design, as discussed in Chapter 6.

The United Nations' *Universal Declaration of Human Rights* has 30 articles which go further than the U.S. Bill of Rights, but at its heart is the central promise to provide:

> ... all the economic, social, political, cultural and civic rights that underpin a life free from want and fear.
>
> *(article 3)*

I have elaborated these rights to contrast with the idea of the human needs that the Parker Morris report introduced into architectural discussions. With hindsight, no matter how well intentioned, there is still something rather patronising about thinking of people with 'needs' rather than seeing how designs may help people to be free from want and fear. This would open up considerations of support for a person's self-respect and effective social interactions.

A couple of years after Parker Morris there was a boom in office building. That led to a new law that specified minimum physical conditions for office spaces – The offices Shops and Railway Premises Act 1963. This was part a movement to get rid of the appalling workplace conditions that had remained since Victorian times. With the new democratic mood spearheaded by a Labour government it extended the Factories Act 1961, which was aimed at the protection of workplace health, safety and welfare of employees, to workers beyond factories.

Office design

In the 1960s office building design was influenced by ideas from architectural modernism, using steel and large glass windows. The main manufacturer of plate glass, Pilkington's, therefore set up research groups to advise architects on how to use Pilkington's products. Initially these were studies of daylight and how it entered the building, but the research broadened out with the establishment of the Pilkington Research Unit to consider a wide range of aspects of office design.[11] These, notably, started to include interviews with users of buildings and explorations of their experiences. It was this unit to which I was attached to carry out my PhD study of offices.[12]

The post-war mood challenged the idea of architecture being essentially an art form. Architecture was being opened up to influences beyond engineering by those who recognised that the users of buildings had not been seriously considered as part of the design process. This was especially recognised, where the experiences of building users were obviously distinctly different from those of architects. A strong case was made that architects needed to connect with the experience of those users whose experiences and lifestyles were radically different from those making design decisions. In the United States an early advocate of this was the psychiatrist Humphry Osmond.[13] He drew attention to how different were the worldviews of his patients from those of architects. His reference to 'function' as a basis for design, was still somewhat novel in the mid-1950s when he advocated concern for building users.

Of course, the client's requirements had always been part of the design process. However, as elaborated in Chapter 7 the many interests involved in producing buildings could ignore those who would live in them. The turn to emphasise users' experiences of buildings found their way into some areas of research in architecture in the 1960s by drawing on ideas from cybernetics.[14] This was the view that any system needed to have a 'feedback loop' to ensure it was effective. This was interpreted as the requirement to obtain users' reactions to the buildings they inhabited. This gave rise to a significant area of building evaluations research. This was often focused on 'user satisfaction surveys', or 'post-occupation evaluations'. Thus, my first study was surveying clerical workers' satisfaction with Pilkington's new head office building.[15] This was given further impetus by the establishment by Thomas Markus[16] of a unit with the clear aim of establishing methodologies for evaluating the performance of buildings.

Architectural psychology

An initial burgeoning of this area, that we called Architectural Psychology, is illustrated by the contents of the first book in this field, based on papers presented at a conference in 1969 which was held on the shore of Loch Lomond in Scotland in a building known as Dalandhui (Figure 8.1). The wooden doll in a building made of computer, punched cards, somewhat symbolises the mechanical orientation that was dominant in the early days of the psychological study of buildings.

The affiliations of the dozen contributors to the Dalandhui volume[17] shows how much this field was the child of developments in architectural thinking, rather than any particular interest from psychology. Gordon Best, Ivor Stilitz, and Peter Stringer were at the Bartlett School of Architecture and Bill Hillier was soon to take up a post there. David Walters was at Birmingham School of Architecture and Ifan Payne at the Welsh School of Architecture in Cardiff, from where Tom Markus had recently moved to take up the Chair in Building Science at Strathclyde University. He had come there after association with Peter Manning's Pilkington Research Unit, where he had worked on the building science and perceptual challenges of window design. Ian Griffiths, although an experimental psychologist, was also working in an engineering context at the Electricity Council's Research Centre, having started working with John Langdon at the Building Research Station. Except for Terence Lee, who was in a psychology department at University of Dundee, the other contributors, Jackie Lau (an architect),

Figure 8.1 Cover of the proceedings of the Dalandhui conference

Adrian Hill (an ophthalmologist), and me, were all in the school of Architecture at Strathclyde University in Glasgow.

The atomistic quality of the studies in the Dalandhui proceedings, dealing for example with thermal comfort, visibility and privacy, railway noise and room friendliness,[18] show the influence of the experimental, laboratory psychology tradition. The idea of a place being experienced as an entity was absent, although there clearly was a search for some sort of theoretical framework. However, any contribution from architects themselves, or even discussion of actual buildings was absent.[19]

It is worth remembering that 1969 was before President Nixon had declared the management of the environment as a major political issue and long before global warming was a widely debated topic. The 'green movement' had not been named, and young activists were far more concerned with nuclear disarmament and getting rid of United Kingdom's nuclear weapon, Trident, than the melting icecaps or the demise of whales. Indeed, I remember Ian Griffiths telling me that the Electricity Research Centre he joined was originally set up to help increase electricity usage because it was feared nuclear power stations would generate more electricity than they could get rid of! It was also still the days of high-rise, tower blocks that looked like up-ended match boxes, and rows of uninspiring urban sprawl.

It was claimed that more housing had to be built by the end of the 20th century than had ever been built throughout history. The same probably went for schools, hospitals, office blocks, airports and most other building types. There were therefore many agencies trying to work out how to guide the design and development of all these buildings. A small number of them and the people designing them did think that there could be some help in making the designs what might be called more 'user friendly'. It was into this framework that psychologists were being sucked.

Architectural education was also undergoing one of its perennial bouts of navel gazing. Bill Hillier, Tom Markus and Peter Manning, had all found their way to user-oriented studies as part of enhancing how architects were educated. By the mid-1970s most Schools of Architecture in the United Kingdom had a reasonable amount of psychology being taught by psychologists. I even wrote a book that summarised the teaching I gave when I was on the staff at the School of Architecture at Strathclyde University in the late 1960s. This moved from consideration of perception, through child psychology on to social and organisational psychology.[20] It is interesting that when I meet practicing architects today, who qualified during the 1970s, they speak of their awareness of a psychological perspective on architecture that they imbibed during their training. But on the rare occasions when architecture students contact me these days, they express surprise that there is actually a named field of scholarship that links psychology and architecture.[21]

Those psychological contributions to architectural training doubtless impacted the growing awareness that buildings were not just civil engineering projects that were given the patina of 'art' by an architect. Those students became more aware of the functions of buildings that went beyond the notional reflection of use that was part of the mantra of modernism. Even more, they realised that the paired back formalism of what became known as 'modern architecture' omitted many of the functions that buildings perform.

A theory of function in architecture

Osmond's[22] plea for considering the function of architecture, together with attention turning to users and what the purpose of a building was for them, encouraged reflection on what the function of a building actually is. I offered up an initial consideration of this, which seems to have stood the test of time.[23] Three aspects of buildings provide their role, reflecting as they do the three components that create places, physical form, cognitive/emotional aspects and the activities the places facilitate. As noted in earlier chapters, these all interact to create the nature and experience of any place. An architecture that creates Places therefore functions by facilitating these aspects. They are reflected in major features of any design.

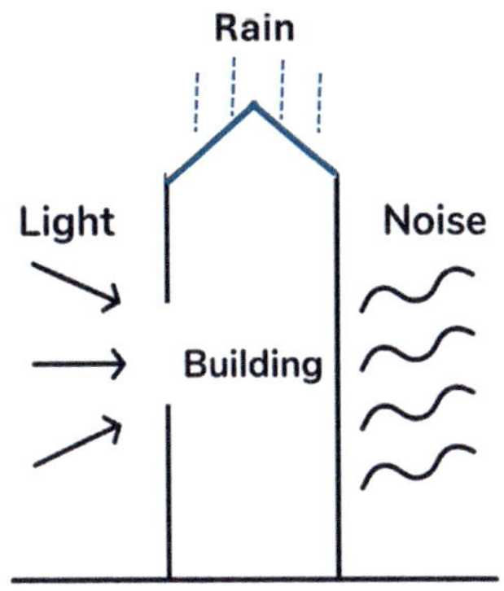

Figure 8.2a Sketch of buildings acting as a filter

Buildings as a *filter*

The form of a building, at its most basic level, reflects an aspect of the caves in which humans (and animals) first survived. They let in and keep those aspects of the environment that benefit humans. This includes lighting and heating. They keep out debilitating elements out such as noise and rain (Figure 8.2a).

The rather obvious idea that it is good to be able to see approaching threats, whether it is woolly mammoths, hurricanes or annoying neighbours, whilst still being safe to observe these, has been graced with the term prospect-refuge theory. The validity of this as a general theory of what makes a place comfortable is open to question.[24] An important reason for the variations in support for this proposal is the physical context. The idea of a filter helps to elaborate that.

Buildings can adjust what can be seen, heard or felt by their construction. From the earliest days of constructions of places to live, they did much more than allow refuge and prospect. They adjusted for the environment in which they were situated. The other functions of buildings interact with those that I've called filtering.

Buildings as a facilitator/inhibitor

The positioning of walls and doors (as discussed in Chapter 1) allows or limits particular activities and social interactions (Figure 8.2b). The size of a space is the most obvious feature that enables what can go on there. I remember visiting a Kibbutz in Israel that had built a school for its children. The classrooms were so designed that no more than 15 children could ever be in them.

That example of the influence on the nature of the places that size of spaces create goes beyond just how many people may be housed where. A central feature of behaviour setting theory (introduced in Chapter 1) draws attention to what, in the 1970s (before we were sensitive to the use of gender related terms) was called 'undermanning theory',[25] now called 'understaffing theory'. This theory had its origins in the comparison of the setting that occurred in big schools with those that took place in small schools.[26]

The general finding was that each school had a similar number of behaviour settings. They each had a school band, a football team, a French class, and so on. But when the engagement in these setting was examined, it was found that in the small school pupils were likely to have active, often leadership, roles in more than one setting. They could

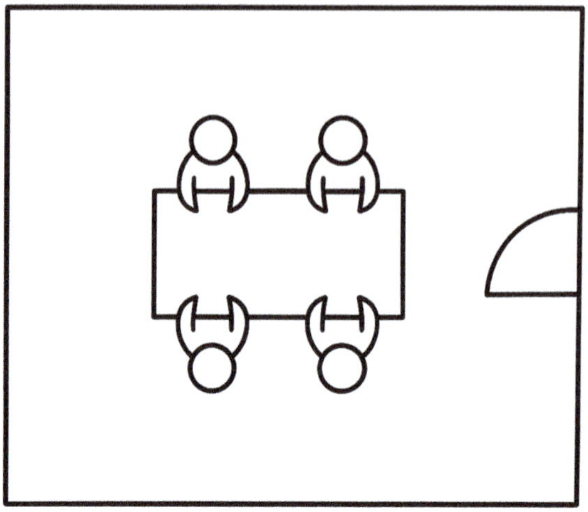

Figure 8.2b Sketch of a room facilitating 4 people in group work

be in the band and the football team. But in the large school students only had active, significant roles in one setting.

This led behaviour setting theorists to propose that understaffing was a good thing. That was against the trends in the late 1960s and early 1970s with moves towards ever bigger enterprises of every sort. Although a widely cited 1977 book by the economist E.F. Schumacher called *Small is Beautiful*[27] supported the benefits of keeping economic activity at the human level. An argument that still finds support today, but with a more balanced view on gender equality.[28]

The architectural implications of the behaviour setting perspective was clearly spelled out by Robert Bechtel, a great advocate of behaviour setting theory.[29]

> The general principle of undermanning would support the reducing the scale of any large project. For example, in a large housing project, the houses should be arranged in clusters to develop smaller units. In a large office building, the tendency to mass numbers of people in a large room should be avoided.
>
> *(p. 161)*

This is particularly interesting because it indicates the design implications for the roles people may play in any physical context. It also shows how a research framework inevitably carries ideological, or sometimes even political connotations. Bechtel and his colleagues placed involvement and opportunities over quality and achievement. A school football team that had players who may have to go off to band rehearsals and so miss practice sessions, is unlikely to be able to compete with a team that has selected players from a range of possible students who focus on that one particular activity. The latter is at variance with the slogan that it is not winning that matters but taking part.

However, the possibilities that spatial extension provides are not, as fixed as a belief in architectural determinism would imply. The flexibility of humans and their organisations can overcome such controls. For example, prison cells clearly designed for one inmate are sometimes doubled in capacity by putting in bunk beds. There are social and emotional consequences for such overloading. They are not necessarily all bad. As ever, it depends on the people involved and their relationships.

The prison example highlights the impact of the management, or regime that oversees use of space. Some intriguing examples are decisions about how open or enclosed will be spaces in a building. The move towards open-plan schools is a clear illustration of how design decisions were driven by views about society and the nature of education, not just functional requirements.[30] It was driven by an ideology that education should be less constrained, more uncluttered by arbitrary demarcations. However, practical experiences of such school designs were not always as utopian as their originators had intended.[31]

Buildings as a *symbol*, providing meaning and significance for places

Beyond the implications of the actions that are possible and what the forms of buildings communicate about what they house, there are many personal, social and cultural meanings that architecture instantiates Figure 8.2c. This has become such a major area of research that Chapter 10 is devoted to how places signify. Further aspects of this in relation to how building form contributes to the meaning of places are dealt with in Chapter 11 and the consequence of architectural movements, notably postmodernism and beyond, or styles in architecture are the focus of Chapter 12.

There are components of the *filter* function that carry psychological implications, influencing the experience of places. Poor conditions, for example, carry meanings about

Figure 8.2c Sketch of a column which provide a core structural function within buildings but have been used across cultures to symbolise support, qualities, and veneration, often through variation in stylisation, see Figure 11.3

the inhabitants, which in turn are likely to influence their sense of who they are. Bright, airy spaces, undisturbed by unwanted noises or intrusions, speak of privilege and significance. However, the dominant filtering considerations are aspects of building science that have established relationships to comfort levels. I therefore do not intend to explore them further here.

The *facilitator* and *symbolic* features combine in the physical component of places, their form. These are usefully distinguished typically by two aspects of a design, which can be loosely labelled 'plan' and 'elevation'. Plans deal with how the place will look from above (or below), the distribution of the components in two dimensions. The elevation characterises the third dimension, what you see when you look at the place. These create two very different ways of considering our relationships to Places. A plan is always an abstract approximation of the experience of being in or moving through a Place. It is an imagined representation of how different locations relate to each other. It is therefore perhaps not surprising that studies of movement around buildings and streets, tend to work with plans, with a bird's eye view of places. This view allows some interesting mathematics that helps to explain aspects of Place experience, especially at the level of large buildings, neighbourhoods and cities. This is investigated in Chapter 9, where 'space syntax' is illustrated.

By contrast the third (up/down) dimension, what you see when you look at a building or around a Place, is immediately perceived. It carries direct meaning and significance. Studies of aesthetics in architecture therefore focus almost entirely on facades and the direct experience of a building. The size and shape of a space may be part of that experience, with its visual, acoustic, and even thermal aspects. But how it relates to other spaces within the overall plan of a building will only be relevant when considering the relationships captured when moving from one to the other, looking, or listening from one to the other.

Summary and some conclusions

There is a long history to the debate on whether the built environment shapes human actions and experiences. At one extreme is the claim that form and qualities of physical spaces directly influence behaviour and emotions. This is reflected in present-day arguments under the heading of cognitive and neuroarchitecture, critiqued in other chapters. At the other extreme is the view that designs enable rather than direct behavioural impacts. Linked to this perspective is the emphasis on the symbolic power of built forms, embedded in personal and cultural histories and experiences.

Strongly held historical beliefs about the environment's influence on emotions, actions and even cultures were influential as 19th-century environmental determinism. Although aspects of this view still persist, in the main they have been debunked. Yet those who hold onto 'architectural determinism', derived from 'environmental determinism', are often ignorant of the geopolitical ideologies they imply. These experts assert that the nature and features of spaces shape lives, typically defending their assertions with reference to naïve consideration of Darwinian evolution without any genetic or other firm evidence of inherent processes.

The physical environment at its extremes does of course influence what people feel and can do. There are well-established connections between ambient temperatures and wellbeing. Intense heat and noise influence actions, individuals' interpretations of their surroundings limit their actions. The amount of space available controls who, what and how many activities can be in that space. However, the influence of extreme environmental levels has to be regarded with caution. The Hawthorne studies are the primary example that changes in lighting levels affected worker productivity through the meaning workers attributed to being observed, rather than as a direct consequence of the effects if the lighting conditions. These studies were the forerunners of many that illustrate the ways in which environmental consequences are mediated by the meanings aspects of those Places carry.

In contrast to seeking to determine human behaviour, early studies aimed at providing design guidelines for personal activities. This was in the wake of the destruction of the Second World War and the need to build many new homes. The decision to produce these guidelines was influenced by the scientific emphasis of the 1951 Festival of Britain, and rising interest in psychology and social sciences. That gave rise to the Parker Morris guidelines of the 1960s. Crucially these set space standards for public housing, considering the activities people wanted to do in their homes. These guidelines were couched in the notion of supporting the needs of families and individuals. They were not motivated by any overt objective of shaping human behaviour and experience. The aim was to provide for what people required for comfortable living.

That approach to the direct functional requirement for housing is rather different from concern for notable structures like cathedrals, and significant buildings like art galleries and parliaments, as well as efforts to preserve old buildings. The design of publicly significant Buildings underscore the commitments to the belief in the psychosocial relevance of the built environment. Those processes are somewhat different from the consideration of what building forms can facilitate. That includes the ways in which buildings carry meanings, explored in subsequent chapters.

References and endnotes

1 Wei, W., Lu, J. G., Galinsky, A. D., Wu, H., Gosling, S. D., Rentfrow, P. J., ... Wang, L. (2017) Regional ambient temperature is associated with human personality. *Nature Human Behaviour*, *1*(12), 890–895, https://doi.org/10.1038/s41562-017-0240-0

2 See, for example, the claims by Daniela Späth. https://www.colormotion.ch/download/cool-down-pink/Konferenz-Poster%20AIC.pdf. The problem with these studies is that they rarely take account of the effect of introducing any change into a challenging context. Any observed effect usually wears off very quickly, or cannot be replicated. There are also interesting discussions about the sexist implications of using pink as a possible environmental influence.

3 Bernheimer, L. (2017) *The shaping of us: How everyday spaces structure our lives, behaviour, and well-being*. London: Hachette UK.

4 Gallagher, W. (1994 – reissued 2007) *The power of place*, New York: Harper Perennial.

5 Gale, E. A. (2004) The Hawthorne studies—A fable for our times? *QJM*, *97*(7), 439–449.

6 Griffiths, I. D. & Langdon, F. J. (1968) Subjective response to road traffic noise. *Journal of Sound and Vibration*, *8*(91), 16–32.

7 Waldram, J. M. (1954) Studies in interior lighting. *Transactions of the Illuminating Engineering Society (London)*, *19*, 95.

8 Hopkinson, R. G. & Longmore, J. (1959) The permanent supplementary artificial lighting of interiors. *Transactions of the Illuminating Engineering Society (London)*, *24*, 121.

9 An amusing example of this was that the BBC, run up until the 1960s entirely by an elite with little contact with the populace at large, started doing surveys of how people organised their lives, with a view to scheduling programmes to reflect that. Apparently, to their surprise they discovered that the working class had their evening meals much earlier than the 8.00 pm typical of when the BBC schedulers ate their 'dinners'.

10 'Homes for Today and Tomorrow' report by Sir Parker Morris for the Ministry of Housing and Local Government, 1961. BADDA2543. Museum of Domestic Design & Architecture, Middlesex University. Accessed 3 November 2020. https://moda.mdx.ac.uk/object/badda2543/
11 Manning, P. (1965) *Office design: A study of environment*. Liverpool: Department of Building Science, University of Liverpool.
12 Canter, D. (1968) Office size: An example of psychological research in architecture. *The Architects' Journal Information Library*, 24 April, 881–888.
13 Osmond, H. (1957) Function as the basis of psychiatric ward design, Published Online: 1 April 2006, https://doi.org/10.1176/ps.8.4.23
14 The term is most closely associated with Norbert Wiener and his 1948 book *Cybernetics; or, control and communication in the animal and the machine*, Paris: Hermann & Cie; Cambridge, MA: MIT Press, ISBN 978-0-262-73009-9; 2nd revised ed. 1961.
15 Canter, D. (1968) Office size: An example of psychological research in architecture. *The Architects' Journal Information Library*, 24 April, 881–888.
16 The work of this unit was eventually published in a curious multi-disciplinary volume: Markus, T. A., Whyman, P., Morgan. J., Whitton, D., Maver, T., Canter, D., & Fleming, J. (1972) *Building performance, building performance research unit*, London: Applied Science Publishers.
17 The contents of this volume (which I note I edited at the tender age of 25) are a good illustration of the issues that were being studied around that time. There does seem to be pirated version of the volume online but my malware protection would not let me access it.
18 Described in Chapter 3.
19 An interesting overview of the rise and fall of 'Architectural Psychology' is given by Petrović, Emina, Brenda Vale and Bruno Marques (2015) On the rise and apparent fall of architectural psychology in the 1960s, 1970s and early 1980s, in Paul Hogben and Judith O'Callaghan (Eds.) *Proceedings of the Society of Architectural Historians, Australia and New Zealand, Vol. 32: Architecture, Institutions and Change*,. Sydney: Sahanz, pp. 480–487. Their historical analysis redresses my UK bias in this chapter by considering, albeit briefly developments in the United States and across Europe.
20 Canter, D. (1975) *Psychology for architects*. Chichester: Wiley.
21 Although the lack of interest in architectural psychology over recent decades is beginning to change with a conference on psychology of architecture in Austin, Texas, in 2016, https://www.psychologyofarchitecture.org/
22 Osmond, H. (1957) Function as the basis of psychiatric ward design, Published Online: 1 April 2006, https://doi.org/10.1176/ps.8.4.23
23 Canter, D. (1970) Need for a theory of function in architecture. *The Architects' Journal Information Library*, 4.2, 299–302.
24 Dosen, A. S. & Ostwald, M. J. (2016) Evidence for prospect-refuge theory: A meta-analysis of the findings of environmental preference research. *City Territ Archit* 3, 4, https://doi.org/10.1186/s40410-016-0033-1
25 Popov, L. & Chompalov, I. (2012) Crossing over: The interdisciplinary meaning of behavior setting theory. *International Journal of Humanities and Social Science*, 2(19), 18–27.
26 Barker, R. G. & Gump, P. V. (1964) Big school, small school: High school size and student behavior.Stanford: Stanford University Press
27 Schumacher, E. F. & Beautiful, S. I. (1977) *Economics as if people mattered*. London: Harper Colophone Books.
28 Varma, R. (2024) Commemorating 50 years of publication of *Small is beautiful* by E. F. Schumacher: Adding women to "Small = Beautiful". *Perspectives on Global Development and Technology*, 22(3–4), 149–170.
29 Bechtel, R. B. (1977) *Enclosing behavior*, Stroudsburg: Dowden, Hutchinson & Ross.
30 McLeod, J. & Rosén Rasmussen, L. (2021) Open-plan schooling and everyday utopias: Australia and Denmark in the 1970s. *Oxford Review of Education*, 47(5), 659–680, https://doi.org/10.1080/03054985.2021.1958771
31 Bennett, N., Andrae, J., Hegarty, P., & Wade, B. (1980) Open plan primary schools: Findings and implications of a national inquiry. *Education, 3–13*, 8(1), 45–50, DOI: 10.1177/1365480211434796

CHAPTER 9

The grammar of Places

Introduction

Put simply, if it is possible to move easily from one room to another the chances of contact between people in those adjacent rooms are much higher than if a circuitous route is necessary to get from one to another. Writ large, the arrangement of the network of links between Places carries consequences for social interactions and therefore influences both the meanings of those Places and the experiences of them.

The pathways which relate spaces to each other carry social significance. They manage the opportunities for encounters between people. They set up a framework for potential interpersonal interactions. That potential typically reflects the roles and related rules of engagement between people. Configurations of Places therefore are part of how the rules of Place are made physical.

An extreme example is the consideration of who has access to a prison cell. That is controlled by the prison authorities. But how readily they can exert that control is influenced by the layout of the prison. By contrast, the same general layout could reflect access to hotel rooms, as illustrated by reference to Het Arresthuis, Eindhoven luxury hotel from a converted prison, described in Chapter 1. In that case the control over access to the hotel rooms (prison cells) follows quite different rules to when it was a prison. However, how those controls operate still reflect aspects of the physical relationships between Places. Such patterns of role/rule relationships inherently carry implications of power structures. Explorations of the rules that govern spatial networks are therefore a rich way of understanding the particular contributions such networks make to the power of Places.

Some of these Place rules are clear and fixed, but when they are less controlled, they provide the opportunity for flexible use of Places and radical changes of function. That is another aspect of what characterises building types, elaborated in Chapter 7.

DOI: 10.4324/9780367808655-12

Does physical form define function?

It is no accident that, in the lockdowns brought on by attempts to control the spread of COVID-19, it is those Places specifically established to boost and assist social interaction – covered under the umbrella term 'hospitality industry' – which were the main target of controls. Attempts to modify the physical form of these Places by introducing screens and requiring people to keep a distance from each other, as well as wearing face-covering, are totally at variance with what these Places were created to support, namely people engaging with each other. This highlights how the layout of locations and boundaries between spaces can facilitate or inhibit interactions between people. This is the contribution physical forms make to enabling or limiting human encounters. Built and natural settings can encourage or discourage opportunities for who meets whom and under what conditions.

Essentially, those properties of buildings which influence the possibilities for movement and related social interaction help to create the sorts of Places they are. Movement patterns have consequences for person-to-person encounters. It follows that many aspects of how we live and what we do, flow from the patterns of contacts (or lack of them) with others. The configuration of spaces thus can be seen to be fundamental to our experience of spaces and buildings as Places.

A stark example of the power of space configurations is Frank Lloyd Wright's design for the Guggenheim Museum on New York. Heralded as one of the most significant buildings of 20th-century architecture, it takes to the ultimate degree the creating of physical form to reflect the nature of a Place. Wright produced a plan form that encapsulates, as he saw it, the central purpose of the building and the Place related rules which shape activity there. Uniquely for an art gallery, the building is, in effect, one space. The idea behind it is that viewing art works is a continuous process. Visitors, consequently, go straight to the 'elevator' and start their journey at the top floor, working their way round the spiral to view the exhibits against the external wall, as in tfigures 9.1a, amd 9.1b.

Many people explore galleries and museums in this way, travelling to the top first, then walking through the galleries, going down floor by floor. Wright's spiral embodies this totally. Visitors enjoy the ability to experience the gallery as one Place with a view of the whole exhibition from most locations (Figure 9.2), although side galleries do allow for a distinctly different subset of art works.

Because the Guggenheim Museum has such a distinct, some might even say Draconian, form it represents a powerful attempt to shape visitor's experience of a Place by the layout of the building. This Place apparently allows little alternatives for visitors. They are expected to follow what the architect wanted them to do. The assumed rules of Place and the physical form of the building map directly onto each other. It may be possible to break these rules, for example by walking up the spiral instead of getting the lift and walking down. But the management will strongly discourage that happening. The management have embraced the Place rules that Frank Lloyd Wright insisted on.

This fundamental quality is captured by shaping the building almost entirely through limiting the possible, or at least the most likely, sequence of human movement through the building. The building is defined by its axis. This building therefore illustrates most clearly Hillier's argument[1] that "The act of building is ... inevitably a social act" (p. 25). In other words, buildings are not neutral functional objects. The form of buildings reflects the aspirations and purposes of those who create them. This was the insight

Figure 9.1a External view of Solomon R (Guggenheim Museum in New York)

that Rapoport[2] introduced into architectural thinking, summarised in the elegant title of his book *House Form and Culture*, discussed in Chapter 11. His demonstration that even vernacular architecture did not simply serve functional needs but reflected many aspects of the social and cultural processes it housed. That, was a challenge to the domination of 'modernist' thinking, explored in Chapter 12.

Figure 9.1b Schematic layout of the Solomon R (Guggenheim Museum in New York)

Figure 9.2 The Guggenheim Gallery internally as one space

Configuring interactions

There was, however, one useful legacy of the modernist'functional' approach to building design. This was the awareness of the significance of what is often called the 'communication' between spaces. That draws attention to the relationships between spaces. How that influences the movement of people through buildings, with all the consequences for patterns of social interaction. Such social patterns have always been implicit in the creation of buildings, especially grand buildings. The need to move through various halls to get to the throne room represents a social construction of the pre-eminence of royalty. The choir at the end of a cathedral separated from the main body of the building designates its spiritual distinctness. The need to unlock many gates before a prison cell is reached is a very clear aspect of using the layout of the building for social control. The openness of supermarket shelves to customers reflects a very different view of the nature of customers' transactions with products than the traditional shop. Traditionally customers are expected to know what they want or take advice from the shopkeeper. Supermarkets put the customers in charge of the selection (and reduce the need for supportive shopkeepers).

I first became aware of the study of building layouts in 1965 when I was based in a Department of Building Science to work on my PhD. One of the other PhD students had the plan of a hospital stuck on a board. Each room on the plan had a nail hammered into it. He was then tying a piece of black string from one nail to another to reflect his observations of journeys individuals made between rooms. There was one board for doctors, another for nurses and so on, for each of the major roles in the hospital. As the journeys built up the thickness of the string became apparent, showing where the most frequent journeys occurred. These were the days when we still had mechanical calculators, and the university had one central computer that you had to book time on to run any computations. The string diagrams were therefore the starting point for working out which rooms should be next to each other in order to minimise the journey times across the hospital. This reflected the use of human patterns of movement to contribute to building design. Similar studies had been done, for instance in kitchens, observing them in use in order to work out which appliances should be next to each other. This remains an active area of design ergonomics, still often referred to as 'time and motion' study.[3]

What string diagram researchers ignored, though, was that the pattern of space use reflected the nature of the building and the sorts of Places of which it consisted. The configuration of these Places tells a story about the social processes that gave rise to the building and subsequently are housed there. For instance, the fact that the pattern of movement of surgeons is so different from nurses, tells us the sort of hospital department it is. These patterns will be very different for accident and emergency departments than for an orthopaedic ward. The patterns of movement are not just functions of activities. They reflect roles and the meaning of Places.

Space syntax

In earlier chapters it was argued that the rules which control social behaviour take some of their constraints from the physical forms they inhabit. They are 'rules of Place'. The corollary of this is that physical forms also have rules, essentially geometric principles, which underlie their plan forms. It is the interplay between the social rules and their geometric counterparts that helps to clarify Place use and meaning.

The consideration of ways in which relationships between Places enshrine their meanings draw attention to those aspects of the built environment that are reflected in what can be thought of as a 'bird's eye view'. That is looking down on the arrangements of spaces in relation to each other, the plan or layout of a building, a collection of buildings, or the streets of a city. Studies of these configurations have demonstrated how much of what is taken for granted in society is preserved in the arrangement of spaces. The examination of these arrangements reveals how environmental roles are often preserved in spatial configurations.

The awareness of the power of spatial configurations has benefited enormously from studies that emerged in the 1970s from the Unit for Architectural studies at the Bartlett School of Architecture in London. A research group was brought together there, led by Bill Hillier, who had studied English literature and the philosophy of science at Cambridge. His team came from a wide range of academic disciplines. He was joined early on by the geographer Adrian Leaman[4] and later by the architects Julienne Hanson[5] and John Peponis.[6] People from many other disciplines moved through the attached master's program and PhD activity, leading to an outpouring of research and applications that continue around the world to this day.

The multidisciplinary nature of the team introduced a radical and challenging perspective to architecture. At the heart of this work was an analogy between the grammar that structures language; the rules that shape how words go together to make sense, and the configuration of spaces that make up buildings, streets and cities. This powerful analogy was enshrined in a theory of architecture given the inviting name of 'Space Syntax'.[7]

Today a Google Scholar search for the term 'space syntax' gives nearly 40,000 hits, showing the scale of research this approach has generated. It is therefore rather difficult to briefly describe what Space Syntax theory is and all the findings and applications it has generated. But in a relatively recent review of the theory Bafna[8] has summarised its central premise as, "social structure is inherently spatial and inversely that the configuration of inhabited space has a fundamentally social logic" (p. 18). The relationships people have with each other, the roles they play in their interpersonal transactions, have an inevitably spatial aspect. Consequently, spatial relationships carry implications for the ways in which people can or cannot engage with each other.

The crucial concept here is 'configuration'. This is the examination of how locations relate to each other. In essence it is an exploration of the plans, or layouts, of buildings, streets, settlements, cities, or in some cases natural landscapes. What turns the not uncommon consideration of plans into a rich set of theories is the application of geometric measurements, and related graphs (link diagrams), to represent and measure crucial aspects of layouts.

Over the 35 years since the first detailed account of Space Syntax[9] a number of sophisticated measurements of spatial layouts have been developed. The basis of these is illustrated by considering a simple building as illustrated in Figure 9.3.[10]

Building A has a connection between rooms *a* and *b* as well as a direct connection to the outside, *c*. For building B only room *a* has a connection to *c*. It is necessary to go through room *a* to get to room *b*. If each of the rooms is regarded as a 'node' represented by a circle and the direct access between them indicated by a line, a graphic representation of the spatial configuration can be drawn. To clarify this graph a key location, in this case the outside *c* is selected as the starting point giving rise to what is known as a 'justified' graph. In Figure 9.3 the justified graphs for buildings A and B are given. It can be seen that even for these simplest of examples the graphs reveal clearly the very different nature of the two buildings.

This analysis also reveals a powerful feature of this form of analysis. The closing of the access point to room b in Building A, creating the configuration in Building B, changes the nature of the Places in Building B. From rooms a and b being part of a symmetrical framework, which gives them equal status in the building, as in A, an asymmetrical, inherently hierarchical, arrangement is created between the Places that inhabit the rooms. That small change gives rise to quite different prospects for rooms *a* and *b*. As summarised in Space Syntax vocabulary, relations between spaces take into account other relationships.

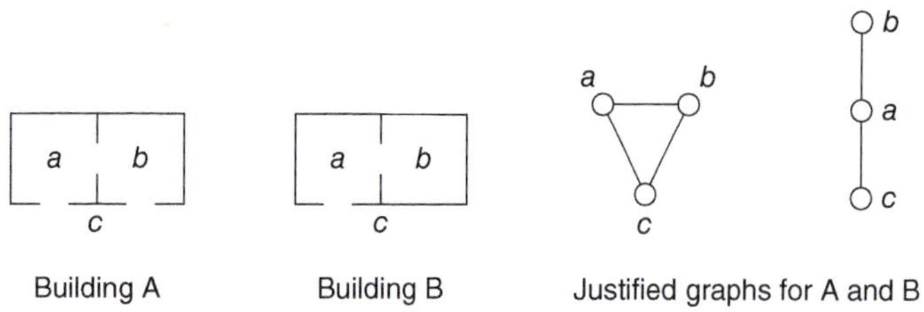

Figure 9.3 Illustration graphs derived from the connections between spaces[10]

In addition to the power of the visual representations of layout configurations, measurements can be calculated to reveal their implicit structures and consequences. One of the most fundamental of these is the 'depth' of a space. In the simple example in Figure 9.3, for building A each of rooms *a* and *b* are just one step from *c*. For building B *a* is one step, but *b* is two steps. This allows the 'depth' of *b* in the building to be given a value twice as much as the depth of *a*. Having established such measurements, more involved calculations can be carried out, such as the average depth of all spaces in a building or larger entity, in relation to each other. This is a measure of how 'integrated' a layout is. Or if the calculations are made for separate rooms in relation to all other rooms, the degree of integration of any one space can be compared with others. These calculations have been shown to have implications for the meaning of Places, as illustrated later in this chapter when particular examples are considered.

Important developments took a step beyond the movement potential revealed in plans, to consider what is visible from various locations. Such patterns of visibility are of some significance, to take just one example, for the design of parks.[11] By using space syntax measures to calculate the integration of what can be seen from where in a variety of arrangements of trees in a public park, Mahmoud and Omar[12] concluded that a curved free-form arrangement of trees generated relatively integrated and connected spaces within the park design. They claim that this helps to predict pedestrian movement and the social structure implicit in proposed planting scheme for a park. In other words, the patterns of possibilities of what can be seen through the trees contribute to the experience of the social nature of the park.

The awareness that the spatial configuration of Places closely reflects the contact people are likely to have with each other, when moving through an environment, has many consequences. For example, the distribution of pedestrian movement around an urban area can be predicted from Space Syntax measures.[13] Those measurements help to elaborate the effect of land use, providing a clearer picture of what gives rise to particular flows of people.[14] A development of this finding has been the correlation of Space Syntax measures with the prevalence of street level crimes.[15] Within buildings, a perhaps unexpected illustration of the power of Space Syntax formulations is the consequence that spatial layouts in laboratories have for informal contact and consequent innovations in research.[16] These and many other examples all draw attention to the importance of the spatial patterns of social encounters. These may be explicit occurrences of people coming into contact with each other. Or they could be the implicit opportunities for interactions provided by lines of sight.

Spatial roles and rules

Although there are many design implications derived from Space Syntax analyses,[17] they also contribute to understanding how Places take on their meanings and identities. The possibilities for encounters of different forms and frequency, revealed by Space Syntax analyses, indicate how spatial forms carry social consequences. The experience of a Place is in part a product of the human relationships it supports or inhibits. Crucially, interactions between people involve the roles that they are taking in those Places and the associated rules of engagement. The roles that people have in any location give meaning to that Place. At the same time the location of that Place helps to define the role of the people there.

From the many examples that could be chosen of this interaction between roles and positions in a spatial configuration, the study of factories by one of the initial developers of Space Syntax, John Peponis,[18] illustrates rather well how the role-related meanings of Places are a part of their spatial position.

Peponis examined the association between aspects of the spatial configuration and the status of the occupants of different spaces, as part of many detailed analyses of the configuration of spaces in six different factories. He specified three levels in a hierarchy of roles – 'Management', 'Foremen', and 'Shopfloor'. The spaces assigned to each of these groups were then measured using two of the more commonly used Space Syntax formulae, briefly mentioned earlier. One, referred to as 'depth', is essentially an indication of how many spaces, on average, it was necessary to go through from the nearest entrance to the building before you would reach the assigned space. As is a common experience of organisations, the management's offices were most deeply embedded in the sequence of routes into the building, despite often being on a side of the building facing out to the surrounding area. The foremen's offices were next in depth, and the spaces of the workforce were most readily available from the street.

A rather more complex measure was the integration of the spaces in the buildings in general. As noted, this is how readily any given space can be used to connect to other spaces in the building. The management tended to have offices in more segregated spaces than the foremen, whose offices in turn were less integrated into the building complex as a whole than the workforce.

These findings of course reflect some functional issues. These include the access the foremen readily need to the workforce and the need for privacy of the management as wella as the different forms of control exerted by management and foremen. Very different manufacturing processes were carried out in the six different factories in this study. Peponis therefore claimed that the consistent findings support the view that 'factory layouts have social functions over and above the purely technical ones' (p. 357). However, this is perhaps to undervalue the technical significance of the various roles in an organisation.

From the viewpoint of the experience of Places within factories, this claim can be taken a step further. The meaning of the Places which house each organisational role, interacts with the location of that Place within the spatial configuration of the building. A person's role within a factory is in part defined by where that individual typically is based.

I remember from my own studies of open-plan offices that the status of individuals was immediately apparent from how close their desk was to the window, as well as how far away it was from the entrance. The corollary of this was that people who aspired to move up through the organisation often expressed that desire as a wish to change the desk at which they worked to a higher status location. Considering the consequences of COVID lockdown, which has produced a move towards working from home, I wonder what new forms of status definition are emerging?

Configurations of knowledge

Museums are curious Places. They have their origins in the personal collections of amateur enthusiasts. When eventually offered/donated for public access they continued to have that quality of a fascinating enclave: an entry to the curious world of a private collector.

It has taken many years from museums around the world to evolve beyond those private origins. They still often are the sorts of Places that are typical of many people's garage. A storeroom for items that may be of interest to some or may one day be of value.

The researcher mentality, which imbued the original private collections, also has morphed into major museums being stores of artefacts that provide the basis for many different strands of study. Their maintenance of the artefacts provides a sanctuary for their safe keeping, in the anticipation that they will one day earn their position in the annals of scholarship.

When selected items are considered to be of public interest museums can become more like religious buildings. They present the hallowed objects to inspire awe, usually not even allowing the touch of the faithful, as would a reliquary. Attempts to turn museums beyond storerooms, sanctuaries or shrines necessitates a revision of the nature of knowledge that they reflect in their spatial organisation.

Museums are therefore intriguing illustrations of how locations within a configuration encapsulate ways of thinking about the nature of what goes on within those spaces. Place meanings emerge from the layout of spaces. This is powerfully illustrated in a widely cited, early Space Syntax comparison of two galleries in London's Natural History Museum by Peponis and Hedin.[19]

One part of the Natural History museum analysed by Peponis and Hedin is the Minerals Gallery, which has hardly changed since it was first created in 1881 (Figure 9.4). They compared this with the Human Biology Hall, a much more recent exhibition about human beings.[20]

Figure 9.4 The minerals gallery reflects an earlier approach to exhibitions. Its form has an historical as well as a scientific significance

When studied in the early 1980s the Minerals Gallery consisted of display cases off a central aisle along a lengthy corridor. It still does to this day, although the details of the design of the display cabinets themselves have been changed.

The Space Syntax version of those original string diagrams, ignoring the frequency of movement just focusing on the geometry, in which each space is treated as a node and the open links between nodes is represented as a line, generates a striking visualisation of the layout of that Minerals Gallery (Figure 9.5).

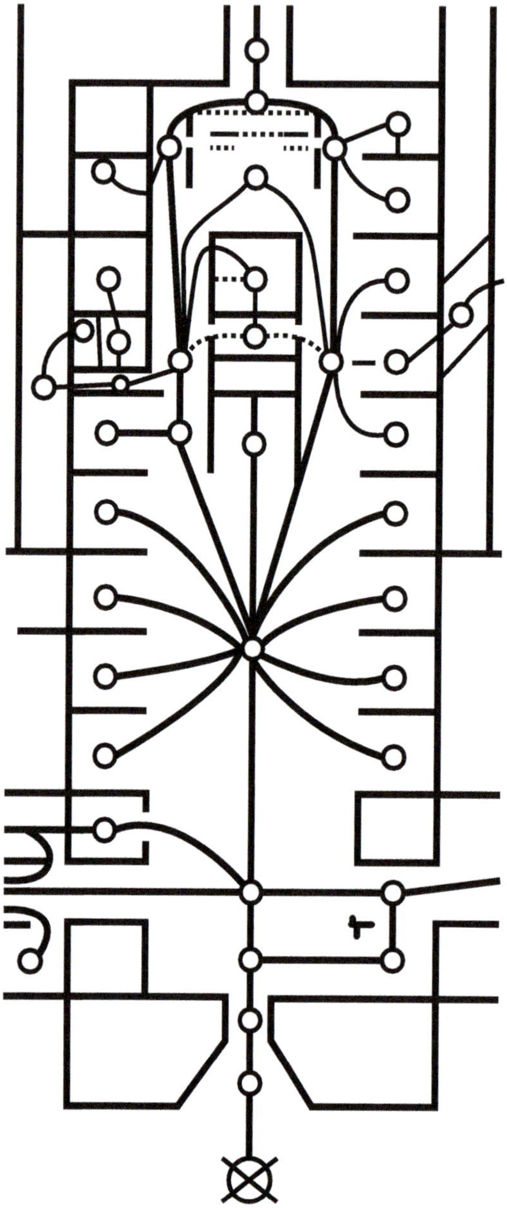

Figure 9.5 Space Syntaxsyntax diagram of the minerals gallery

Figure 9.6 Human biology hall

By contrast the Human Biology Hall (Figure 9.6) is a much more complex set of interrelated spaces. This provides the opportunity for a variety of ways of moving around and between the spaces as well as interacting with the exhibits. It is an organic response to the topic being exhibited. Developments in exhibition technology, has meant the details of the exhibition has changed over the years, although its open, inherently engaging layout is reflected in many recent exhibits.

Here a much more complex Space Syntax diagram reflects the rich possibilities for movement through the Human Biology Hall (Figure 9.7).

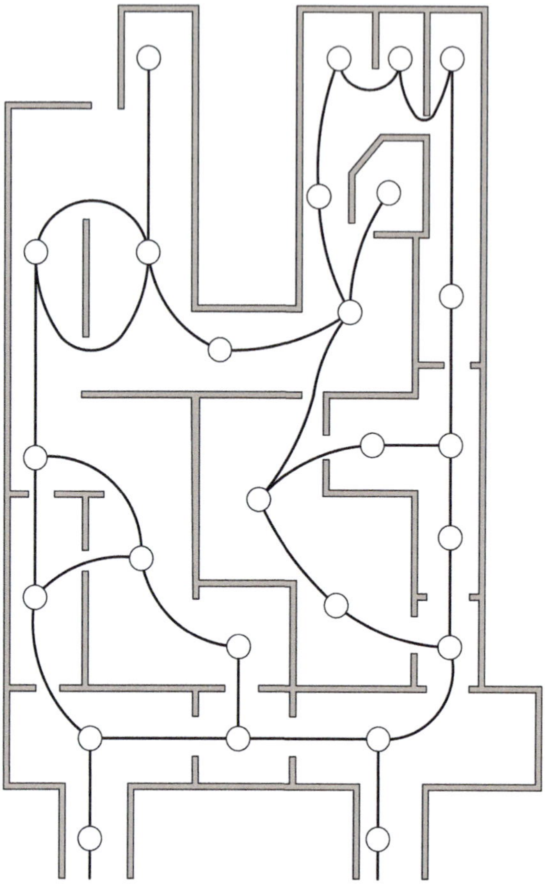

Figure 9.7 Space Syntax of the human biology hall

The very different layout configurations speak directly of the very different functions and associated meanings of the two exhibitions. The Space Syntax analysis of the different possibilities of movement around the galleries reveals distinctly different ways of thinking about the nature of scientific knowledge. In the 19th century knowledge was a matter of listing and classifying. The exhibition provided this knowledge by systematically arranging the exhibits in some logical order.

In the late 20th century knowledge had become something acquired through investigation and interaction with the relevant material. It is not regarded as having one inevitable structure. Its organisation varies depending on what you want to know and why. Gaining this knowledge informally and idiosyncratically, where visitors could find their own ways around the displays, in accord with their interests and predilections, is to be celebrated and encouraged. There is no longer a belief that the curator needs to impose a distinct perspective on how and when each exhibit should be examined. Knowledge is multifarious and there are many ways of embracing it. The Place for the exhibits is exciting and engrossing, quite different from the didactic, distancing experience of the Minerals Gallery.

Managing interfaces

What is particularly salient about these considerations is that what is being managed by the layout is how, and also when, visitors interact with the exhibits. The building influences the interface between the people who come into the gallery and the conceptions the curators have of their appropriate interactions. The curators' views of the how knowledge is gained, and the implications that has for the experience of the museum, and how the visitors should be allowed to interact with the displays, is enshrined in the layout of the galleries.

Galleries of various sorts, whether they are museums, art or craft galleries, or even shops, reflect an anticipated physical relationship between the various roles that are present. Usually these are the roles of visitors/customer in relation to those who curate or sell the art works or products. That management of relationships occurs in all buildings to a greater or lesser degree. Indeed, Hillier in the context of elaborating the themes of Space Syntax has claimed that the central purpose of a building is precisely to manage the interfaces between the different roles the building houses. He expresses this succinctly as "encounter being the spatial realisation of the social".[21]

The focus on 'encounters' leads to the powerful thesis that a major consequence for the configuration of spaces is to manage the interface between the different roles that inhabit those spaces. At the level of a space in a shop the counter is indeed there to manage the encounter between the customer and the salesperson. The example of the law court, illustrated in Figure 9.8, is a more extreme and detailed illustration of how the configuration of a Place focuses on the organisation of the possible interactions between the different roles people are playing there.

The jury would never sit in the spectator gallery, or the defendant stand in the witness box. Not only are the positions specified for the people playing each of the different roles but their routes into and out of the courtroom are controlled. The actions require a particular physical form, but the presence of the form shapes the possible actions, and their sequence. In the courtroom this reflects the nature of the legal process. It is therefore not surprising to find that different legal systems give rise to different courtroom layouts.

Even when a building is converted for use as a courtroom, the pattern of activity is still reflected directly in in the layout. The 1800 layout of Old Cahokia Courthouse, in Figure 9.9, which was earlier a domestic dwelling, is easy to relate to the contemporary US courtroom. There is no difficulty in determining where the judge would preside, where the clerk to the court would sit and the benches for the jury. The public seating is obviously behind that.

Forms of engagement

Any particular pattern of possibilities for encounters, the configuration of the spaces, is typical for any given type of building. The configuration not only influences the potential for people coming into contact with each other, it also provides guidance of the form those meetings are expected to take. This allows subtleties in the details of the configuration to reflect nuances in the expected actions and the consequent nature of the Place. A Quaker meeting house (Figure 9.10) is very different from a Catholic church (Figure 9.11), although the essential relationship between the person leading the ceremony and the congregation is maintained.

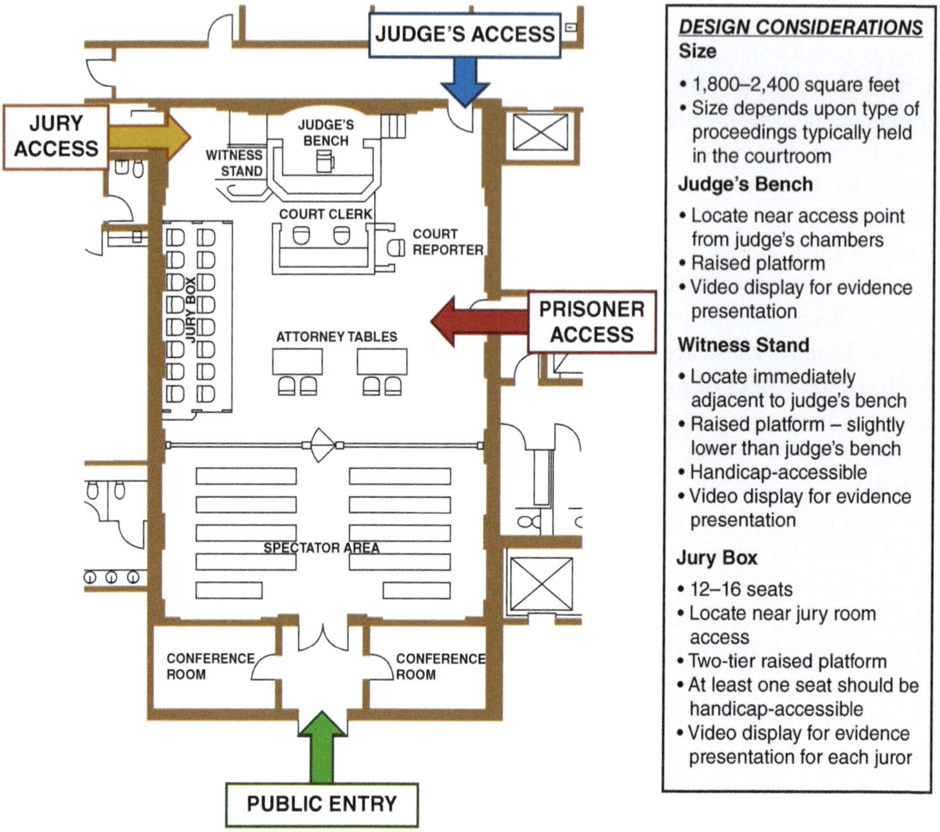

Figure 9.8 A typical court layout indicating the way the different roles are assigned different locations and the relationships between those locations and access to them

Figure 9.9 1800 layout of Old Cahokia Courthouse

Figure 9.10 A Quaker Meeting House

Figure 9.11 A Catholic church

Some major differences are in visual and related symbolic features of these spaces. There are also important differences in the implied message about the relationships between the different roles. The Catholic Church allows for a procession into the building and presents the priest as significantly distant leader of the religious ceremony. In the Meeting House the placing of the location of the leader of the ceremony close to and within the congregation implies a more equal relationship between the person who leads the ceremony and the other participants.

These examples of the interplay between the layout of a space, often reflected in how the furniture is arranged, and the ideology the activities the space supports, are everywhere to be seen. This can occur at the level of the single office[22] (Figure 9.12a). When the office chair is on the open side of the room between the door and the desk, it speaks of involvement and engagement with whoever comes into the room. If the desk is Placed between the office worker and the rest of the room Figure 9.12b, then an inherently confrontational approach is created. It would be no surprise to find that the majority of academic offices have the former layout, but that offices of senior management, especially within the civil service, have the latter.

A similar distinction can be found in parliament buildings (Figure 9.13). The inherently confrontational government of the British House of Commons reflects the firm principle of a party in power facing a 'loyal' opposition; the distance between the front rows traditionally being slightly longer than a sword can reach. This contrasts, as shown in Figure 9.14, with the recognition of gradations of political opinion that had its origins in the French Revolution. Originally those sitting to the right of the president supported the king. Those opposed sat on the left. From this originates the idea that

Figure 9.12a A welcoming office

Figure 9.12b A distancing office

political views have *wings*, left and right; Labour being left-wing and Conservative right-wing. This is different from the essentially elitist system of the Whigs and Tories embedded in the British system.

All these examples illustrate a commonly occurring aspect of physical from. It carries the meanings of a Place by indications of how people are expected to act there,

Figure 9.13 British Parliament

Figure 9.14 French National Assembly

especially how they are expected to act in relations to each other. This distinction could be thought of as hierarchical or democratic, coercive or open, inviting or distancing.

Such definitions of Places can be manifest at the scale of streets and cities as will be explored in later chapters. At the level of building configurations, as considered here, or at the level of rooms and arrangements within rooms, similar influences on the experience of Places exist. When studying room arrangements Robert Sommer's discussed in some detail their significance in his widely quoted book on *Personal Space*.[23] One distinction he made was between spaces that encourage interaction, which he called *socipetal*, as shown in Figure 9.15. This contrasts with those that discourage encounters between people; *sociofugal* arrangements (the term being derived from the idea of centrifugal forces that spin entities away from each other), as shown in Figure 9.16.

For present considerations, the important aspect of these differences is the atmosphere they create. The type of Place is implied by the forms of social interaction that is encouraged there. Places are partly a product of what people expect to happen there, especially the sort of person-to-person transaction that the Place supports.

Varieties of Place

Working from the viewpoint of what sort of computer algorithm would be needed to generate any given spatial layout, Hillier makes the interesting distinction between those plan forms that require very detailed sets of rules, which he calls 'long models', and those that need very few, 'short models'. The Place rules inherent in a courtroom are detailed and specific. There is a long list of them. Hence in Space Syntax terminology it requires

Figure 9.15 Seating to encourage interaction

Figure 9.16 Sociofugal seating

a 'long model'. This is a Place in which the interplay between the expected patterns of behaviour and the physical form is so closely aligned that it is difficult to separate them.

Many other Places also have a close alignment of spatial and social feature. Galleries and factories have inherently distinct relationships between different roles, such as visitor/curator, management/workforce. They are instances of a wide range of contexts in which roles are clearly structured and reflected in the organisation of spaces. Schools and hospitals, offices and railway stations, theatres and sports stadia, all typically have strong, often hierarchical, sets of interdependent social positions. These are inevitably mirrored in the configuration of their layouts.

For other Places the rules are less structured. In these locations there is only a loose connection between the spatial forms and the patterns of activity, having 'short models'. The significance of this binary framework is expressed directly by Hillier as:

> A key distinction is made between 'long and short models', that is, between cases where space is strongly governed by rules, and therefore acts to conserve given social statuses and relationships and cases where space acts to generate relations over and above those given by the social situation.
>
> *(p. 190)*

These differences between fixed and less distinct forms of social rule systems were proposed by Lévi-Strauss,[24] probably drawing on earlier ideas from Durkheim.[25] Lévi-Strauss claimed that there was an important distinction between social structures that were 'mechanical' and those that were 'statistical'. (Durkheim contrasted 'mechanical' with 'organic'.) The mechanical social structures are essentially clear and fixed. The statistical (or organic) have a much more probabilistic nature, growing out of particular manifestations of social processes. But as Ruijter[26] elegantly reveals, in Lévi-Strauss' writings the distinction between 'mechanical' and 'statistical' models is far from clear. Furthermore, in the sort of debate that theoretical sociologists are so good at, Thijssen[27] demonstrates that Durkheim's original distinction is also very ambiguous.

These ambiguities serve to undermine Hillier's example of a 'short model' and with it his claims that the dichotomy helps us to explain the relationship, or lack of it between behaviour and physical configurations. Hillier claims that "The concept of long and short models permits social relations and spatial configuration to be conceptualised in an analogous way" (p. 5). The example he gives of a 'short model' is a party event "since its object is to generate new relationships by shuffling them in space".

The suggestion that there are no Place related rules to a party ignores common experience. This is delightfully illustrated in Anthony Trollope's[28] description of The Warden's tea party:

> ...fat old gentlemen stood up with their backs to the empty fireplace, looking by no means so comfortable as they would have done in their own armchairs at home; and young gentlemen, rather stiff about the neck, clustered near the door, not as yet sufficiently in courage to attack the muslin frocks, who awaited the battle, drawn up in a semicircular array.
>
> *(p. 51)*

There are different roles, such as a host and invitees. The former take it on themselves (or are employed) to serve others. Invitees are likely to drift towards certain Places, meeting with specific others. The group who ends up in the kitchen, or on the terrace, are likely to be following slightly different rules from others. All of these different subgroups will move around the space in different ways. Hosts will welcome others as they enter. Guests will move into the space and seek Places in which they will feel comfortable. As discussed in Chapter 2, where people position themselves in a lecture theatre, gives rise to specific types of Places related to where people chose to sit. The physical configuration of these locations provides the opportunity for the different roles, and their related rules, to find spatial expression.

Ruijter's[29] unpacking of Lévi-Strauss' twofold distinction of social rules makes clear that amongst the many possible meanings it can have, the clearest is between formal and informal processes. These can be further elaborated by taking on board the much more strongly psychological proposal by Josselin de Jong[30] that the distinction is best thought of as that between participants and observers. All human activity occurs somewhere. It has a Place. Whether someone observing that activity can discern the rules that govern it (as in a courtroom) or it requires some perspective from those involved in the activity to indicate those rules, as at a party, does give rise to a distinction between how the relevance of the physical layout of a Place may be understood. In the former the layout speaks directly to the spatial configuration. For activities in which human agency and freedom to act is more feasible, the spatial configuration operates in the more subtle way of providing opportunities that may be acted on.

Two aspects of these differences between formal and informal rule/role systems are useful here. First, the distinction between the formal and the informal house as described in Mark Girouard's *Life in the English Country House*.[31] The informal house is definitely a shorter model than the formal house. However, the rule systems that guide these uses of Places do tend to be implicit rather than explicitly enacted. Thus, in the formal house rules are strong and explicit and as you adhere to them, you enact your role and reveal little about your person. In the informal house, rules are implicit. Actions are likely to reveal much about the nature of the actor. This shows the power of Place configurations. They influence not just who does what, but also how they are likely to feel about it.

Rather than a simple dichotomy between mechanical and organic social patterns it is more appropriate to recognise that there is a continuum. This runs from those social processes that are only loosely related to spatial configurations to the other extreme, where the significance of what happens is defined by and in turn help to designate the meaning of Places. Yet, all spatial forms are projections and reflections of some aspect of social processes. The consequence of this is that mental processes reflect spatial forms. Where there are clear rules then the configuration of Places will follow. Crucially, the interaction between the rules and the spatial configuration reflects a sense of Place.

The rules of change

When a building is created with some idea of how it will be used, the configuration of spaces are likely to reflect the role/rule relationships that are housed within that layout. What happens, then, when there is a radical change of use of a building? How does the meaning inherent in the original purpose of the building translate to the new use? What is left of the former idea, inherent in the design, that carries over to the new Place experience?

What are the consequences when a church is converted into a house, or a restaurant, or a school is transformed into a set of bijou apartments? Such as the school I went to, with the old, circular school hall being turned into a garden – after suffering an arson attach and being burnt down. Houses become shops. Cinemas become bookstores, or Indian restaurants.

The activity of a market cannot be more different from the solemn religious ceremonies in a cathedral. The informal, individual search around a bookstore implies a totally different use of space from the coherent collective activity of watching a film. What remains when a new use occupies the building, but the original intention of the creators of those Places has been ignored? What it is about the original Place, that carries on into the changed design and use, is fruitfully elucidated by considering the change in environmentally related roles and associated Place rules. The spatial configuration still houses the ghost of the original role structure. That adds some piquancy to the newly emerging Place.

This influence, of the spirit of past Places, overlays new Place meanings and anticipated actions. This is most commonly the additional division of spaces to support new interfaces, as discussed in Chapter 1 in reference to a primary school. It can also result from a reorientation of how the space is used. An interesting example of this is the Winter Arts Market introduced into Liverpool's Anglican Cathedral, shown ready for a service in Figure 9.17 and in use for the market in Figure 9.18.

Figure 9.17 Liverpool Anglican Cathedral

Figure 9.18 Cathedral in use as a market

The domination of the central axis provides the anticipated basis for the focus on the bishop leading the church service. By adding divisions parallel to this axis, this open space becomes a very different Place. The dominance of the open space to house a congregation typically has a very simple rule set to define its use. Many more person-to-person encounters are required for a market, but the dominant axis still exists, augmented with details for the interfaces between customers and stall holders.

One way to summarise this syntactically, is to distinguish between an axis that stretches between poles, from the profane at the entrance to the sacred at the altar. The market requires many interfaces at right angles to that central axis. This is a fundamental syntactic switch of interfaces. Such a change in how interfaces are organised within a space can be seen as a common basis for change of use, bringing with it rather different kinds of Place. Another example -of how role differences are related to change in spatial configurations, is when an old-fashioned shop, or market, consisting of contact between customer and seller across a counter, is changed to one in which the customer has direct access to products, as in a supermarket or department store.

The addition of divisions to spaces either as further walls or through furnishing, would seem to be the natural development of changes of use. In the studies of the use of school buildings[32] with which I was engaged, we found that there were many modifications to buildings. However, they nearly all consisted of making smaller, more distinct Places. This accords with the hypothesis that there is a natural drift from attempts at multifunctional spaces towards distinct Places. It is unusual, although not unknown, for organisations to take walls down and open up spaces. The change towards open-plan kitchen-dining rooms is one example of this. However, a more common process in many buildings is to introduce more segregation to manage encounters not currently catered for. The simpler (short) model of the open space has to be made more complex for the new use. This can be done by introducing new Place rules, but eventually those rules are supported by the introduction of spatial divisions.

The task of enabling Places to respond to changing use, and for patterns of activities to incorporate inevitable modifications of physical form, is a natural process that continues over time in most buildings. This reflects emerging variations and changes in forms of anticipated interactions between people. Therefore, the considerations here of the ways in which buildings manage the possibilities for interactions are only the first steps to understanding how Places become what people experience. Some of the different kinds of developments and changes that different Places undergo are considered in subsequent chapters.

Conclusions

The rules and roles that characterise the recognised functions of a building contribute to the sort of Place it is. This is supported by those specifics of its built form which make possible particular ways in which people can make contact with each other. The nature of the types of encounter which any Place supports contributes to the sort of Place it is.

The set of potential encounters helps to define the type of building. A school, for example, was traditionally created to allow one-to-many interactions between a teacher and students. With the advent of a more open approach to education, as happened with the Human Biology Hall at the Natural History Museum, schools required opportunity for individual study and small group activity. Developments in technology and equipment resources also put pressure on new forms of building. But the ancient relationship between a teacher and a class of children remains dominant.

Many other building types can also be defined in terms of the anticipated relationships between the different roles and the rule-governed patterns of activity that they facilitate. Theatres, hospitals, airport terminals, prisons, and offices, all can be readily specified in terms of the varieties of social interaction they support.

The variety and changes, with a related evolution of the designs of buildings over recent years, all can be seen as attempts to modify the forms of interaction between different roles in those buildings. In doing this they change the relationship of the building users to the Places they are part of. That raises the large issue of a person's Place related identity – a topic worthy that is dealt with in chapter 15..

One particular feature of Places has been the focus of this chapter. How they fit into the configuration of spaces. The ways in which spaces relate to each other carry significance for how people can engage with each other. This in turn carries implications for the nature and meaning of those Places. The modification of building forms deals directly with the facilitation or hindering of these interactions.

References and endnotes

1 Hillier, B. (1996) *Space is the Machine: A configurational theory of architecture*. London: UCL Space Syntax available to freely download at https://spaceisthemachine.com/
2 Rapoport, A. (1969) *House form and culture*, Englewood Cliffs, NJ: Prentice Hall, 150 pp. ISBN: 978-0133956733.
3 Magu, P., Khanna, K., & Seetharaman, P. (2015) Path process chart – A technique for conducting time and motion study. *Procedia Manufacturing*, *3*, 6475–6482.
4 Hillier, B. & Leaman, A. (1973) The man-environment paradigm and its paradoxes. *Architectural Design*, *78*, 507–511.
5 Hillier, B. & Hanson, J. (1984) *The social logic of space*, Cambridge: Cambridge University Press.
6 Peponis, J. (2018) What does the syntax of space say? Understanding and designing buildings as interfaces. *World Architecture*, *179*, 33–41.
7 Klarqvist, B. (2015) A space syntax glossary. *NA*, *6*(2), 722.
8 Bafna, S. (2003) Space syntax: A brief introduction to its logic and analytical techniques. *Environment and Behavior*, *35*(1), 17–29, https://doi.org/10.1177/0013916502238863
Gottdiener, M. (1993) A Marx for our time: Henri Lefebvre and the production of space. *Sociological Theory*, *11*(1), 129–134, https://www.jstor.org/stable/201984
9 Hillier, B. & Hanson, J. (1984) *The social logic of space*, Cambridge, UK: Cambridge University Press.
10 Hillier, B., Hanson, J., & Graham, H. (1987) Ideas are in things: An application of the space syntax method to discovering of housing genotypes. *Environment and Planning B – Planning and Design*, *14*, 363–385.
11 Mahmoud, A. H. & Omar, R. H. (2015) Planting design for urban parks: Space syntax as a landscape design assessment tool. *Frontiers of Architectural Research*, *4*(1), 35–45.
12 Mahmoud & Omar (2015) Planting design for urban parks.
13 Baran, P. K., Rodríguez, D. A., & Khattak, A. J. (2008) Space syntax and walking in a new urbanist and suburban neighbourhoods. *Journal of Urban Design*, *13*(1), 5–28, https://doi.org/10.1080/13574800701803498
14 Ozbil, A., Peponis, J., & Stone, B. (2011) Understanding the link between street connectivity, land use and pedestrian flows. *Urban Design International*, *16*, 125–141.
15 There are many studies showing how space syntax measures relate to the occurrence of crimes. Two readily available publications are:
Summers, L. & Johnson, S. (2017) Does the configuration of the street network influence where outdoor serious violence takes Place? Using Space Syntax to test crime pattern theory. *Journal of Quantitative Criminology*, *33*, 397–420, https://doi.org/10.1007/s10940-016-9306-9
Shu, S. C.-F. (1999) Housing layout and crime vulnerability. *Space Syntax Today Proceedings*, *I*, 01.1–01.12.
16 Penn, A., Desyllas, J., & Vaughan, L. (1999) The space of innovation: Interaction and communication in the work environment. *Environment and Planning B: Planning and Design*, *26*(2), 193–218.
17 A commercial company, Space Syntax Ltd., set up to provide consultancy to design projects has been very influential in a number of significant planning projects.
18 Peponis, J. (1985) The spatial culture of factories. *Human Relations*, *38*(4), 357–390.
19 Peponis, J. & Hedin, J. (1982) The layout of theories in the Natural History Museum. *9H*, *3*, 12–25.
20 A detailed account of this and subsequent research is given in Peponis, J. (2024). *Museum configurations. An inquiry into the design of spatial syntaxes*, London: Routledge.

21 Sadly, Bill Hillier died in 1999.
22 Duffy, F. (1974) Office design and organizations: 1. Theoretical basis. *Environment and Planning B: Planning and Design*, *1*(1), 105–118.
23 Sommer, R. (1969) *Personal space : The behavioral basis of design*, London: Pearson Education.
24 Lévi-Strauss, C. (1978) Scientific criteria in the social and human disciplines. *Structural Anthropology*, *2*, 288–311.
25 Durkheim, E. ([1893] 1969) *The division of labor in society*, trans. G Simpson, New York: Free Press.
26 wDe Ruijter, A. (1981) Ambiguities in Lévi-Strauss's distinction between mechanical and statistical models. *Bijdragen Tot De Taal-, Land- En Volkenkunde*, *137*(1), 126–144. Retrieved 1 November 2020, from https://www.jstor.org/stable/27863349
27 Thijssen, P. (2012) From mechanical to organic solidarity, and back: With Honneth beyond Durkheim. *European Journal of Social Theory*, *15*(4), 454–470, https://doi.org/10.1177/1368431011423589
28 Trollope, A. (1855) *The Warden* republished by Penguin Books in 2004.
29 De Ruijter, A. (1981) Ambiguities in Lévi-Strauss's distinction between mechanical and statistical models. *Bijdragen Tot De Taal-, Land- En Volkenkunde*, *137*(1), 126–144. Retrieved 1 November 2020, from https://www.jstor.org/stable/27863349
30 Josselin de Jong, P. E. (1977) The participants' view of their culture, in P. E. Josselin de Jong (Ed.) *Structural anthropology in the Netherlands, pp. 233–252*. Den Haag: Martinus Nijhoff (published originally in 1956).
31 Girouard, M. (1978*) Life in the English Country House*. New Haven: Yale University Press.
32 Building Performance Research Unit (1972) Building performance: Building Performance Research Unit. London: Applied Science Publishers Ltd.

CHAPTER 10

Signifying Places

Places as symbols

The rich mixture that creates a Place, embodying our interactions in particular locations, through the combination of its form, meaning and the actions it typically houses, give Places powerful symbolic qualities. This was most tragically illustrated on the 11 September 2001 when a group of Jihadi terrorists attacked the Twin Towers of the World Trade Center in New York, and The Pentagon at the same time, intending but failing to also attack the White House. Matusitz[1] elaborates, in his detailed exploration of terrorist use of symbols, that these buildings were chosen because they exemplified the Western way of life that the terrorists wished to subvert. As Matusitz puts it, "The World Trade Center was targeted by Al Qaeda because the Twin Towers epitomized Western civilization, US imperialism, financial success, modernity, and freedom". The Pentagon similarly symbolised US military domination and the White House (before Donald Trump took up residence) represented Western democracy.

These buildings had such power as symbols because of their iconic presence as distinct Places. The physical form of the Twin Towers of the World Trade Center (Figure 10.1), with such a simple and literally outstanding geometry, combines with its housing of the essence of World Trade and the connotations associated with that. It was not just the building, or only the organisations it housed that was the target. Rather it was the symbol that the Place encapsulated.

Similarly the Pentagon (Figure 10.2) is both the description of the physical geometry of a building and a form of synecdoche whereby the name of the building is used to designate the management of the US military. It is an image redolent with associations and meanings, an internationally recognised Place that embraces the idea of US martial leadership on the world stage. However, unlike the Twin Towers that, rather unexpectedly, proved extremely vulnerable to the airborne attack, the Pentagon, although seriously damaged, was much more resilient. This helps to indicate that the targets of these attacks were Places that had symbolic significance rather than being solely of military relevance.

DOI: 10.4324/9780367808655-13

Figure 10.1 The World Trade Center Suffering attack on 11 September 2001

Figure 10.2 The Pentagon under attack

Another, less dramatic, demonstration of the importance of the symbolic quality of a building for supporting the meaning of Places is given in the remarkable study by Marta Saniewska.[2] She interviewed people in three small Italian villages of the Marche region that had suffered a devastating earthquake. Even a few years later their villages were still unsafe to live in. They were therefore housed in temporary accommodation in a safer location a short distance away. It became clear to Saniewska quite early in her interviews that the villagers were determined to stay near their original homes. This was due in part to their identification with their village and region.

For the present consideration of symbolic aspects of buildings, a notable way in which the displaced people reflected on maintaining their Place identity was the building of a makeshift belltower a *Campanile*. The inhabitants of Amatrice, for example made it of scaffolding, as in Figure 10.3. This is one example illustrating that a number of villages with displaced people have, as Saniewska put it "are still holding onto the remnants of their local identity in the form of reconstructed campanili" (p. 78). This reflects a well-established aspect of pride in a very localised culture sometimes referred to by Italians as *Campanillismo*. That is using the height of the belltower as a sign of a village's dominance and achievement. It is tempting to find parallels in village churches across Britain, although they are fortunate not to have suffered destruction by earthquake.

The multifaceted nature of Places makes them extremely authoritative as symbols. What symbols are and how they have their significance has been explored within many different disciplines. Jung[3] in his final years brought together a book to introduce his

Figure 10.3 Campanile made of scaffolding, Amatrice

Analytic Psychology to a general audience. This book notably focused on the significance of symbols for understanding what it means to be human. His emphasis was on symbolic aspects of dreams and the ways in which cultures provide common referents upon which such symbols are built. But without the need to accept his views ofn the unconscious and the almost pagan, and highly contentious, idea of the 'collective unconscious',[4] his elaboration of the nature of symbols and their psychological significance is fruitful.

Jung makes clear that the human need for symbols and their power derives from their implying something broader than any obvious or direct meaning. This distinguishes them from 'signs' that denote a specific object or idea. Symbols can therefore be seen as a means of combining many different ideas and emotions. They are vehicles for managing important aspects of the complexity of daily life which are not immediately available to our awareness.

Anthropologists have elaborated this notion of the role of symbols within cultures, especially in the way they contribute to the meaning of rituals. Turner[5] supports Jung's view that the power of symbols comes from the way they condense multiple meanings. The most obvious of these is the crucifix which encompasses ideas of Jesus, crucifixion, and a religion as well as principles of a faith. It can be seen that such symbolism readily transfers to particular Places, notably both the location and institution of the Church. This illustrates how readily a church as a Place is both a symbol of a religion and The Church as a religious organisation.

Many features of Places can be seen to have symbolic implications in a variety of different contexts. They illustrate what Turner[6] calls 'condensation'. This is the way symbols simultaneously represent "many ideas, relations between things, actions, interactions and transactions" (p. 1100). Or as Jung argues "a symbol always implies something broader than the obvious direct meaning".[7] Turner draws his examples from the symbols used in rituals in rural African society, but the parallels in Western 'developed' society are easy to see. For example, in any company buildings the height above ground of an office carries implications of status.[8] The executive suite on the top floor brings together many concepts associated with the status of those who inhabit it, as well as their separateness and elevation above those employed.

The combination in a symbol of many different aspects gives rise to a further perspective on how they have their power. For Jung the richness of a symbol (especially in dreams) implies an attempt to resolve some equilibrium between conscious and unconscious thought processes. In a rather less mystical approach Turner enriches this understanding of how symbols have their significance by claiming that they inevitably unify apparently different ideas by analogy or association. These, he claims, tend to be contrasting components, some drawn from a moral and social order and others which simulate desires and feelings.

A powerful example of these contrasting components of the symbolic qualities of aspects of Places, returning to the significance of height in a building, was the location of the production and management offices in the original BBC Television Centre at White City in London. The lower floors, were a hive of activity, with many studios in which programmes were made, workshops and greenrooms for actors and other participants to prepare and wait. By contrast the top floor was a quietly carpeted, well-furnished oasis of calm. People who worked on the lower levels have reported[9] that being invited to the top floor always had an emotional component. It could be anxiety because of a potential rebuke or curiosity about how 'the suits' lived. The combination of the social aspects of the status hierarchy, and the emotional consequences of being given access to the hallowed upper floor, combined in the symbol the executive suite enshrines.

Now that television centre has been converted into apartments. It is no coincidence that the top floors have become a penthouse apartment with a swimming pool. The status symbolism, merging a reflection of the social order with pandering to sybarite sentiments, are still prevalent in choosing to put the penthouse suite on the top floor.

New freedoms

The symbolic power of Places reflects and enhances social and cultural processes. Many scholars emphasise, as explored in Chapter 9, that "space is socially constructed and the social is spatially constructed".[10] This carries across to considerations of Places in which the interaction between the social and the spatial generates a combination of meanings that are explored in this chapter as symbols.

Places make a crucial contribution to key life events such as birth, marriage and death. They elaborate the significance of these events and, reciprocally, those events help to add depth to the meaning of those Places.

Places may be chosen for key life events because of personal associations. The decision to use a particular Place may be based on some cultural significance or designation. The activities typically linked to particular locations also provide a basis for their importance. In keeping with the general model of Place, the meaning and activities as well as the physical form, all come together to create the circumstances that enhance the experience of an event. As discussed in earlier chapters, that comes about in part because of the rules that Place supports.In other words, action and Place interact with each other.

It is fruitful to refer back to Jung's analysis of symbols. He drew attention to two aspects. One was the idiosyncratic meaning that symbols have. They reflect the particular experiences, conscious and unconscious processes unique to each individual. But they are grounded in cultural traditions which provide implications shared between many people from similar cultures. It is not necessary to accept Jung's proposal that people inherit a 'collective unconscious' to accept that all cultures associate common meanings to many symbols. Indeed poetry, metaphor and analogy would be impossible if this were not the case. A consequence of this is that social changes will be reflected in the meaning and use of Places, with at the same time, the roles and rules that help to identify their character. One such social change can be seen, in some cases, in the changed symbols relating to the major life events of birth, marriage, and death. The move away from institutional settings and their related rituals, which can be seen in many aspects of daily life, are becoming apparent in the Places people choose to embody those rituals.

The Places people select relate to their power over the role relationships enshrined in those Places, and the related expectations (rules) of how people act. As Markus and Dovey, considered in earlier chapters, as well as many other commentators on social aspects of buildings and design, have emphasised, a major distinction in the roles embedded in Places relates to power variation. That is the distinction between those in charge and those who suffer the consequence of that difference in status and influence. The move away from formal involvement in institutions to more person-oriented control of who does what where is finding its way into the use of new and different Places for major life events.

Home birth

One emerging example of taking personal control over an event that has typically been institutionalised, by selecting a different Place, to that which has been the usual one for over a century, is the location in which to give birth. Some people in developed Western countries choose to give birth at home rather than in a maternity hospital. The proportions who choose to do so vary considerably between countries. For instance, in the technologically oriented United States only about 1% of women give birth at home. By contrast, for the independently minded Dutch it is around 30%. The differences relate, in part, to whether it is legally acceptable to have a home birth, as well as the nature of the health system and financing of birthing facilities. The prevalence of home birth in the Netherlands has led to it being a recognised part of the Dutch immaterial culture an aspect of its 'intangible heritage'.[11] Home birthing is seen as an indication of the importance of underlying Dutch values, namely: freedom of choice, autonomy, 'being at home' and not medicalising human experiences unnecessarily.

Why women select their home as a Place to deliver their babies, in those countries in which giving birth at home is an acceptable alternative to a hospital delivery, helps to clarify how particular Places enable distinct role-rule possibilities. Giving birth is both a highly significant personal occasion, whilst at the same time being of great social and cultural importance. It is therefore not surprising that all societies have rituals and traditions associated with giving birth.

In those countries in which medical effectiveness and procedures surrounding pregnancy and the delivery of babies have developed over the last two centuries it has become the norm for women to give birth in hospitals. In earlier times it was usual to deliver babies in the woman's own house. When women spent much of their fertile years either pregnant or nursing a baby, their home was a natural Place for childbirth, whether for royalty or peasants. In some senses, the process of giving birth was not regarded as a medical issue unless there were complications. It was the developments in medical technology that led to pregnant women, and the delivery of their children, becoming a focus for medical attention, supported by taking occurring in a special, technologically sophisticated Place, a hospital.

As a Place the hospital is defined by its specialisms, the highly differentiated roles, from porter, varieties of nurses and technicians, to house doctore, senior consultants and hospital management. They each have defined access to related physical locations, spatial and engineering requirements. Spaces are strongly demarcated by who has access and for what purpose. It is consequently a highly structured institution. From the point of view of pregnant women, it also has the important quality that the main focus of all activity in hospitals in general is on people who are ill. Distinct maternity hospitals, or wards within general hospitals, attempt to change this mind-set. But I do remember the director of one maternity hospital telling me that his main task was to ensure that his staff did not treat pregnant women as patients, recognising that they are not ill. But the medicalisation[12] of childbirth is a widely recognised aspect of maternity units, often having control of who can visit when, as well as such matters as food supplies and medical check-ups.

The structure of a medical maternity setting inevitably puts the women in an essentially passive role, reluctant to allow them much autonomy. This is one that many women welcome, of course, because of the security it provides for dealing with anything about which they may be anxious. It is therefore interesting that one of the reasons for selecting a home as the Place to give birth, revealed in Sjöblom et al.'s study in Sweden, is the confidence the woman has in her 'own competence'.[13] The home is the archetypical location for being in control. This is where 'they preserve authority and autonomy, whereby the women themselves ruled the situation'.[14]

When the women in Sjöblom et al.'s study described the key factors that influenced their desire for a home birth, it was clear that they wanted to optimise choice, comfort and control. All of the women felt that labouring at home gave them more choice of options to manage pain and ways of coping during labour. Specifically, some wanted a water birth, (Figure 10.4) an option only available at home. They articulated feeling freer to move and to eat and drink during labour in their home environment.

All of the women felt that they would be more comfortable giving birth in their home environment. They desired the privacy and intimacy of their home. Being relaxed at home was believed to facilitate the progress of their labour. The women also said they felt safer in a familiar and comforting space. Furthermore, they anticipated having an easier recovery at home.

Figure 10.4 A birthing bath used for a home birth

One woman reflected on her prior hospital birth:

> This is a funny thing, but I love having my own food. You know it's not something I had really thought about in the hospital until after I had given birth and I was voraciously hungry and they gave me a soggy tuna sandwich and a cup of tea.
>
> *(Irene)*

Murray-Davis and her colleagues in Canada[15] found essentially similar results. In addition to feeling at ease at home, their respondents indicated that they wanted a home birth as a means of having control over the birth experience;of being more involved in the related decision-making. Specifically, they wanted control over the birth environment, such as lighting, music, temperature of the room, but also who was going to be present with them. They wanted to have control over the pace of the labour:

> I didn't want people to make me feel weak and like I can't give birth. I didn't want people to be like, 'oh dear, we'll take care of you'. I really wanted to be in charge and do it my way.
>
> *(Danielle)*

They articulated being in control to avoid medications, C-section and the perceived cascade of intervention associated with hospital birth:

> To avoid intervention, I would say was my major motivator....I really trust in birth and I trust that midwives are well trained to know if something's going on and otherwise don't mess with it.
>
> *(Gail)*

The desire to have as many family and friends as they wanted present for the birth was also a strong reason.[16] Some women wanted to have a large group of support people with them throughout the labour. They knew this would not be possible with visitor restriction policies at the hospital. The home was also seen as a Place in which their partner and labour support people could become more involved. For many of the women home was thought to be helpful for their other children – either so the children could be directly involved in the birth or so they could meet the new baby sooner after the birth.

In an interview I carried out Lucia (in the Netherlands) explained in detail the relevance of being at home to give birth to her son:

> *As for me personally, I can say that it was not a huge issue to make the decision to have the baby at home as my pregnancy went smoothly and I was in rude health which meant the midwives in my practice saw that as a definite possibility. The general rule is that usually a medical indication leads to a hospital birth or when women do not want to have a home birth due to the fact that there is no possibility of sedation or are generally scared. I wasn't freaked out by the idea of not having painkillers and I felt I was strong enough mentally and physically to fulfil the task at home by myself. In general, I have a lot of faith in my body*

> *and the natural processes of life and knew instinctively that it can be done how it should be done and I was adamant in letting my body lead me.*
>
> *On a practical level, it was a nice idea to have your own bed, bath and shower for comfort and pain relief and go through the motions to fulfil such a grandiose task in your own bedroom! It was slightly surreal and fantastic. Also having your partner there at all times looking after you with food and drink and mental support the way you want it and need it.*
>
> *During the pushing out phase I remember vividly the sound of the children in the neighbourhood playing outside (it was a remarkably warm day – 24 °C – at the end of April) and thinking that although I was doing something very special, normal life just went on as usual. It gave the sacred act of birthing a mundane fringe and kept me slightly grounded as I was definitely floating in my own birthing bubble.*
>
> *Also, after it was all done and dusted and we were admiring our baby, we allowed our two curious cats to come into the bedroom (which had been a no-go area since the start of the pains) for a proper sniff about of the room and our newborn. Both were immediately aware of the big change in our household and it brought us all together at once. The cats were sweet and were eager to meet the new little one and be part of the joy. Later on, when we found out that I bloodstained the carpet, this became a fond reminder of the special and unique experience that we shared together in our own home. There was none of the clinical and unpersonal function that may have happened in a hospital ward.*

At the heart of the choice of their home as a Place to give birth was the desire to have a personalised birth experience, which they did not perceive to be available in an institutionalised setting. This desire goes beyond an avoidance of the implicit passivity of being in a hospital. 'Being at home' has symbolic significance as well.

> The experience embraced an earthly dimension, represented by reliance on inherent natural forces, and an existential, spiritual dimension, represented by faith in life itself, expressed in terms of the sacredness of giving birth, a heavenly experience, and wisdom about life itself.[17]

This illustrates that it is not only the opportunities provided by the domestic setting but what it implies about the meaning and significance of the event. The symbolism of giving birth at home has the qualities identified by Turner[18] of both social aspects and those relating to desires, feelings and even spiritual meanings – *the sacred act of birthing*. The home location carries with it memories and associations, meanings and habits, which give it a unique role in their lives. Its significance as a Place unique to them and their family provides a richness to the experience that could not be achieved in the anonymous institution of a hospital.

However, it is important to emphasise that the minority of women (and their families), who opt for home births seem to be distinct in their confidence in the naturalness of giving birth and their own competence in being able to carry it out. The choice of delivering at home can therefore also be seen as an aspect of the mothers' identity. The significance of the Place as interacting with a person's self-concept is also revealed by home birthing. As noted earlier, in the Netherlands home birth has been promoted as part of national identity, giving it a symbolic significance that goes beyond the individual.

A Place to get engaged or to marry

> I was taken to my favourite restaurant and was bought the most expensive bottle of champagne. We toasted after we ordered our meal and my boyfriend went on to say how he has had the best four years of his life, and that he wanted me soon to become his wife. He got down on one knee in the restaurant and asked me to marry him!
>
> *(Keeley Armer)*[19]

Marriage is another special life transition. But instead of drawing significance from an existing Place that already has meanings and associations, as with home birth, it is not unusual to select a Place specifically to create memories. Figure 10.5 shows a young couple towards the end of a Jewish Wedding ceremony in June 2025.

Figure 10.5 The 'breaking of the glass' at a modern Jewish wedding

They are under a contemporary version of the canopy, known as a *Chuppah*. That originally was a fabric canopy with open sides. Traditionally it was a prayer shawl supported on four sides with polls. The plastic version of the roof on plastic pillars, with open sides, is the creation of a Place with today's sensibility, whilst acknowledging the tradition it draws on. In essence, an allegory for the couple's future home together.

The location of the *Chuppah* in a large garden also gives a fresh openness to the ceremony, rather than the confines of a synagogue – a further selection of a Place that they have given meaning to. In that location the joyous 'breaking of the glass' adds a further significance to the event. That draws on an ancient tradition that has many layers of meaning when the act it is in that location on the wedding day. At the most obvious level it symbolises the delicate nature of relationships, warning that their bond should never be broken. At a more intense level the husband's breaking of the glass has been interpreted as representative of his breaking of the bride's hymen in the consummation of the marriage.

Figure 10.5 can therefore be regarded as another example of how significant events in life are often defined by the Places where they happen. That in turn gives special significance to what happens there. It sets in motion the cycle of actions and meanings facilitated by the properties of the physical location.

The wedding in Figure 10.5 takes happens in a location specifically set up to be a significant venue, in the south of England. Where it is permissible to get married has legal implications in most countries. Specific Places are designated and related ceremonies controlled to enshrine the importance of the ritual ceremony for both the individuals and their families as well as society at large. However, as with the selection of a Place of personal significance for childbirth, the developing move towards individual choices, breaking away from institutional settings, is leading to choosing Places to marry that carry special import for those involved. This has been recognised in the United Kingdom by a relaxing of the law about where marriages can take occurr. As the review by the Law commission reported:

> Our research shows that being married in a Place that has meaning is still important to couples and their families.

The desire to marry in a Place of special meaning is partly driven by the decline of religion and the resulting avoidance of getting married in a church. The consequent change in the location of marriages has been remarkable. In the United Kingdom in 1900, religious ceremonies accounted for 85% of all marriages; by the late 1970s this had fallen to less than half (49%) and then to 23% in 2017. Civil marriages have outnumbered religious marriages every year since 1992. In 2017, religious ceremonies accounted for less than one in four (23%) of marriages between opposite-sex couples (the lowest on record) and less than one in a hundred of marriages between same-sex couples. Only 43 same-sex couples married through religious ceremonies in 2017.[20]

It is tempting to see these changes as solely reflecting the decline in religion, but the choice of where to marry also enriches the meaning of the ceremony by the implications drawn from where it occurs. For those couples who regard a wedding as a more or less private establishing of a contract, with little significance in and of itself, beyond what they have already committed to each other, the location is likely to be a quiet registry office with a few friends.[21] But for others, who regard the ceremony as an important social event that epitomises 'the most important day' the location has special significance.

Many aspects of a wedding's significance are encapsulated in the importance of the records that are kept of it – the wedding photographs. For these, the meanings associated with the Place where they are taken illustrates an iconography. The personal and cultural associations with the locations of the wedding photographs are there to capture an image of "conjugal bliss" and the "the romance and splendour of the perfect wedding".[22] These photographs may focus on the couple and the stages of the wedding itself, but the choice of outside locations is often used to record the couple in an idealised romantic context. Of the first 100 photographs on Google images of a search for 'wedding photographs' 75 were in an open landscape settings. Most of those that were not, were in a church, or the celebration hall, except for one of a royal couple in a grand room.

Landscape has associated with it a long tradition of freedom and dreamy adventure. In the time of Henry VIIIth and his daughter Elizabeth Ist the countryside was a resource, owning land was the foundation of wealth. But as explored further in Chapter 16, 19th-century romantic poets, most notably Wordsworth, believed in the purity of nature as a spiritual source of renewal. Therefore, by the couple being photographed in a natural setting they are using the symbolism of Place to enhance the imagery for which they are reaching. Once again, we can discern the mixture of symbolic references. Partly the social aspects of freedom with the couple isolated together, away from others. The other aspect being the emotional associations and the spiritual excitement the natural context gives.

There is a sense in which the aspects of the Place where the wedding occurs, especially in photographs of the event, particularly in an open landscape, are appropriated to add another layer of meaning to the wedding. Because Places can have so many connotations, they are ripe for being plundered to provide a quixotic icing to 'the special day' itself. The symbolic qualities of where a wedding occurs, especially where the couple are photographed, illustrate the properties that activate symbolic meanings "condensation, unification of disparate referents and polarizations of meaning".

Where ashes are spread

Archaeologists and anthropologists agree that humanity's self-consciousness becomes apparent in the archaeological record when hominids obviously deal with their dead in some way, typically by burial:

> mortuary rituals carry an outsize importance in tracing the emergence of human uniqueness—especially the capacity to think symbolically.[23]

Carefully disposing of the body of a person indicates an ability to reflect on the past and imagine the future. Such practices can be traced back many millennia and even seem to have been carried out by modern human's near relatives the Neanderthals.[24] Associated with this practice the actual location of the disposed remains takes on social and cultural significance. Graveyards are rather special Places with many layers of meaning. But they are essentially institutional, defined legally and indeed spiritually

Figure 10.6 Scattering ashes at the sea's edge

as sacred Places. I will return to the consideration of sanctity of Place later, but there is an interesting process emerging that has parallels to the freedom of home births and landscapes for weddings. This comes about by the widespread use of cremation. This opens up the possibility of the ritual disposal of the ashes of a loved one (Figure 10.6) in a Place that may be chosen by their relatives, but more often indicated by the deceased, selecting 'their final resting Place'.

The conventional locations in the United Kingdom for the disposal of ashes were crematorium grounds, the cemetery or the churchyard. However, although in the 1970s as few as 1 in ten sets of ashes were removed from the crematorium, by the early 2000s more than half were.[25]

The symbolic aspects of scattering ashes have their roots in the weakening in the Christian belief in the resurrection of the material body. This has been furthered by the lack of any strong legislation in the United Kingdom, and some other countries, that would limit where ashes can be disposed of. As a consequence, the choice of location for scattering ashes contributes to an increased 'mobility' for the dead who are no longer 'pinned down as whole bodies in the sacred, regulated space of the burial ground'[26] (p. 883).

This mobility is facilitated by the rich symbolic meaning of the ashes which have "the formlessness and flow of a liquid" whilst having a "relationship with the materiality of the body" (p. 884). The ashes are "somehow, the body" of a loved one and at the same time they "transcend and condense the particularities of their previous bodily life" (p. 885).[27] The mixture of facets, so essential to give symbols power, opens the way for considerations of the ritual and Places where the ashes may be dispersed.

The Places offer a focus for remembrance that is established through the ritual of scattering ashes there. These Places are typically selected because of the significance they are believed to have for the deceased. Often the natural environment, as with weddings, provides an image of freedom that the deceased had enjoyed. Examples such as a favoured walking route, or on a mountain the deceased climbed, capture the significance of those Places as well as the emotions they evoke. Other rituals reflect Places the person most directly identified with, such as griding a small proportion of the ashes "into the soft furnishings of the deceased's favourite pubs"[28] (p. 885). So many people wished for their ashes to be scattered on the centre spot, or goal mouth of their favourite football pitch, that some football clubs banned the activity and set up gardens of remembrance near the football grounds.

In general, the selection of a Place for post-cremation ritualisation:

> needs to be understood within [a] broader context, as an aspect of disposal and memorialization strategies which not only creates greater scope for the imagination and the emotions, but also demonstrates resistance to the principles of modernist rationality.
>
> *(p. 887)*

Choosing Places that are not part of official, institutional settings, such as graveyards and crematoria grounds, symbolises a ritual of resistance. These avoid having their dead being absorbed into collective, depersonalised sites. There is a romantic aspect of this contrasting with scientific rationality.

The freedom given, in some countries at least, to the choice of location for disposal of the ashes, illustrates the profound significance that Place can have. This is especially true of the ability to utilise Places that have idiosyncratic importance for the dead or their loved ones. These Places provide unique possibilities for memorialisation, allowing the living and the dead to be together in a shared setting.

Garage or shrine

The memorialisation of objects takes on interesting features when considering museums. Art galleries and museums had their origins in private collections, brought together out of the interests of the collectors, or as mementos of their experiences, much as less wealthy people may keep an object on their mantlepiece to remind them of a happy holiday in Spain. Or they may be more personal objects that evoke memories of particular people or events, much as the hallowed objects that are brought for renovation in the UK popular television series, called *The Repair Shop* mentioned in an earlier chapter,

When a patron of the arts, or science, makes their collection available to the public and a specific Place to house them is created, there is the tendency to turn the objects into something sacred, or a process of "guarding them as private treasure".[29] When I gave a talk to the curators of the Victoria and Albert Museum in London, I somewhat teasingly called my talk "Garage or Shrine".

The garage reference comes from my observations, over many years looking for a house to buy, that it is very rare to find a car in a garage. As mentioned in Chapter 9 these Places usually function as out of the way, long-term storage spaces or workshops.

The car is parked outside. The garage space is too valuable, and useful, to house a vehicle. The only occasion on which this is not the case is when the owner has a special vehicle that is specially treasured; in this case the garage becomes less of a storage space and more of a shrine to the vehicle.

Major museums and art galleries do typically have vast storage spaces of artefacts that are not currently required for ongoing exhibitions – the equivalent of having them in a garage. The fact that they select exhibits from their stores gives those paintings, sculptures or other artefacts a particular cachet. How they are exhibited adds further to the creation of a revered Place. They are kept at a distance, often by some sort of barrier, to be viewed, not unusually, on a pedestal. This is amusingly, but profoundly, illustrated by Marcel Duchamp when he exhibited a bicycle wheel fixed into a stool (Figure 10.7). The everyday object is transformed both by being put on a support, as if in a plinth, and perhaps more importantly being exhibited in a gallery.

Duchamp is quoted as saying: "To see the wheel turning was very soothing, very comforting...I enjoyed looking at it, just as I enjoy looking at the flames dancing in a fireplace".[30]

However, the rules of Place imposed by a gallery meant that, when I came across this sculpture, I did indeed try to give the wheel a spin. I was instantly rebuked by the watching guardian of the esteemed artwork. Another experience I had that illustrates

Figure 10.7 Duchamp's bicycle wheel first exhibited in 1913. It takes its significance from where it is exhibited

the almost religious aura of a major art gallery was when a small musical group of which I was a part were allowed to play in one of the gallery spaces. When we finished any piece of music, those standing around us listening were clearly unsure as to whether they should applaud or not. The implicit rules of an art gallery are similar to those when visiting a cathedral. People talk in hushed voices and try not to disturb what is a quite unnatural calm.

The deferential quality of many galleries and museums is typically enhanced by a layout that implies a specific sequence or movement through the building. This may be the history of art or the biography of an artist. More recently art works are arranged around themes that the curator wishes visitors to recognise. This enhances the experience of the art works as something distinct and special. Seeing art in this way is very different from seeing a painting on a friend's wall, or a sculpture on someone's patio. Museum and gallery exhibits become the key representations of a particular aspect of the artefacts in question. They indicate, for example, a particular period in art, or crucial developments such as ofthe steam engine. The selection of the works interacts with the location to create a special Place which is both sacred in the sense of being revered, with the emotional qualities associated with that veneration, whilst at the same time inviting participation by being allowed access to view what is on display. The museum space becomes a multifaceted symbol of the nature of the meaning of the artefacts on display.

Stavroulaki and Peponis[31] help to elaborate the ways in which these symbolic aspects of museums are developed in their detailed study of Castelvecchio Museum. They demonstrate that the spatial construction of the museum and the location of its artefacts within the spaces do not introduce visitors to a story about art, but to the ways of seeing that are constitutive of the art being presented. Three aspects of the use of space shape these symbolic aspects: the actual layout of the building, the positioning of displays within that layout, and the structure of occupiable space. All of these contribute to what the visitors can see and where they can move.

In more rigid layouts in which the visitor is guided through a structured route, as was noted in Chapter 9 when considering the Minerals Gallery in London's Natural History Museum, the symbolic aspects of the Place take on formal properties. This is rather like those clever rides in Disneyland, on which the direction of gaze is controlled so that the visual illusions are most effective. This is achieved by trucking people in carriages on fixed routes, turning the carriage to face the view that will provide the best illusory effect.

Embodiment in the ride is further enhanced by allowing some degree of interaction with the exhibits, or a direct visceral experience in the swoop and fall of the carriage in which participants are strapped. An increasing number of museums are learning from Disney, making the Places in the building a more integral part of the visitors' experience by encouraging them to interact with what is on display. A more extreme example of this is when actors play roles within the replica of a given location. By having relevant participants, the exhibition Place takes on an even richer level of symbolisation.

Ballantyne an Uzzell have identified this change in the nature of museums as becoming more 'visitor-centred'.[32] This is a move away from 'the book on the wall', which keep visitors literally, as well metaphorically, at arm's length from the artefacts on display, to enabling and encouraging them to interact with objects being housed in the building. The Place takes on a more personal significance. The activities engaged

Figure 10.8 Vikings marching, Yorvik Viking Centre

in have their own particular spatial quality, as well as the bodily and psychological experience of participationThis isillustrated powerfully in the march through Yorvik museum's main street (Figure 10.8). This includes visitors and 'actors' bringing aspects of the historical context into being, changing the experience from one of passive looking to being an embodied part of the Place.

Interactive art changes the nature of Places

Many artists are aware of the importance of changing the experience of galleries as Places. The Dublin based artist, Rhona Byrne, has created both site-specific art for locations inside and outside conventional art galleries. She has also opened up visitors' involvement with artwork, thereby fundamentally changing their experience of the gallery. One notable example is her *Bolthole*, which has happaned in many galleries, including Tate Britain (Figure 10.9).

This invites visitors, notably often families with small children, to use the fabric and plastic panels provided to construct and reconstruct installations. This enables visitors to become participants in creating their own environments that can be entered and

Figure 10.9 Rhona Byrne's Bolthole, 2012
Fabric, plastic, carpet, and fasteners
Collection Irish Museum of Modern Art

explored, making shelters or dens that can be individual or part of a larger configuration. Visitors are thus contributing to and inhabiting an ever-changing installation. Typically, this involves families working together, changing the nature of the art gallery experience.

Here the interaction between actions and Places becomes very rich. What does it add to a landscape, or a building when a piece of art is introduced into it? Another of Byrne's artworks moves out of a museum to be part of a new building. She calls it *The Scribble* (Figure 10.10). By having such an abstract object moving right through the building this sculpture enhances the meaning of this as a Place of learning.

As she says:

> I love making art that considers the Place, context and the people who encounter it. I was really excited by the initial brief to respond to a building which houses four depts of education, a very creative Place where people are learning how to learn and teach learning methods and thinking processes. I wanted this energy to be translated into a sculpture that would bounce around a building with movement, flexibility and endurance. Something playful that is a continuous intrigue, a sculpture that you can't ever quite make sense of.[33]

What is particularly unusual about the sculpture is how it is present all over the building. This highlights the interconnectivity of the various Places that make the Education Hub. The sculpture emerges from the rear courtyard, where it is physically grounded

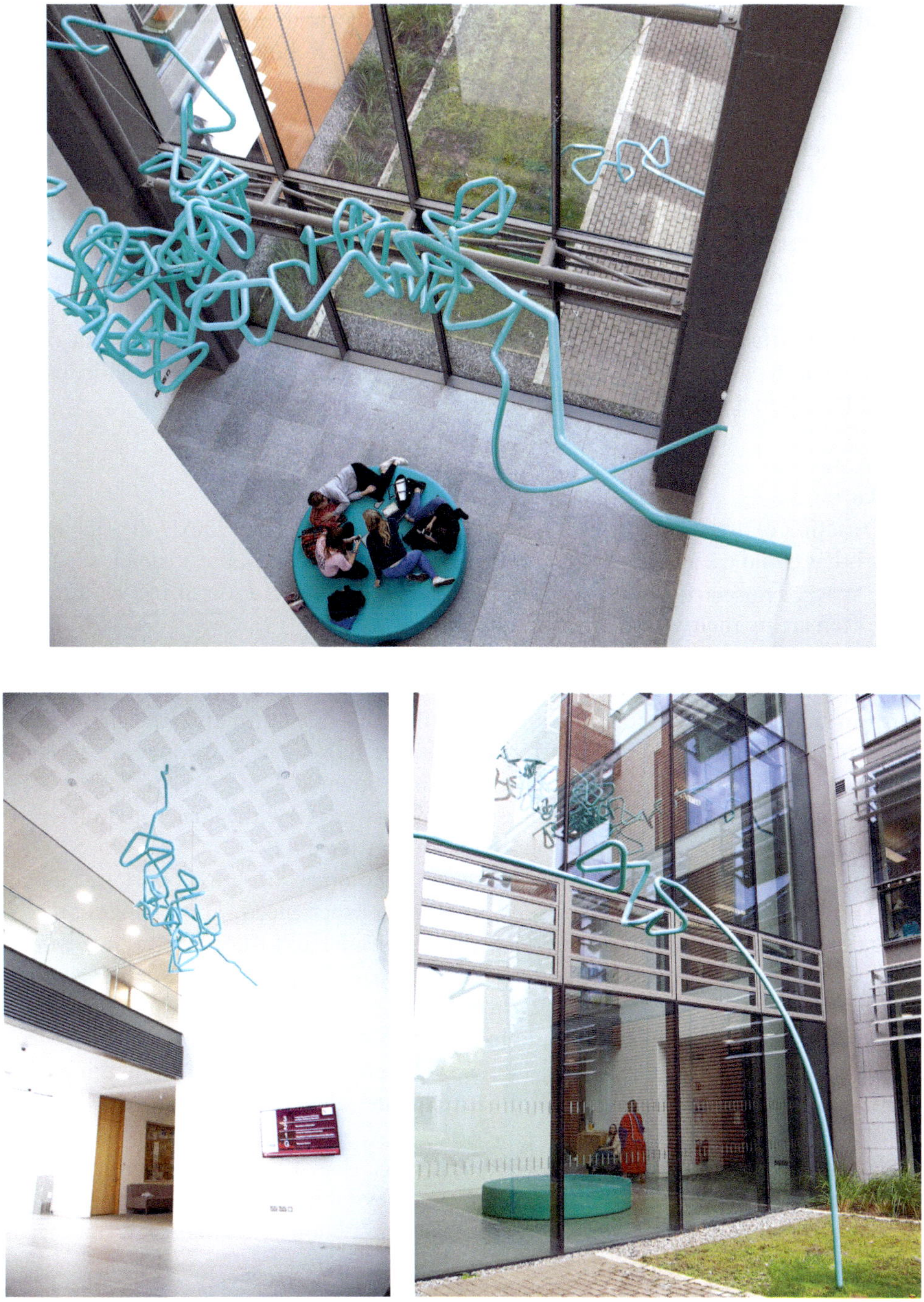

Figure 10.10 *The Scribble* (2019) by Rhona Byrne: per cent for art commission for a new major artwork for the education hub building in Maynooth University, Ireland

in nature. It passes into the glazed atrium space at the rear and disappears in the foyer. It then traverses energetically throughout the new Building. It is a continuous line that bends, loops, knots, clusters and apparently passes forcefully through walls. The coherence of the activities in the building is enhanced by this bright, turquoise painted steel, which is ever present. The nature of the Education Hub as a Place for learning is elaborated by the sculpture. Byrne claims it reflects and expresses: "The intricacies of neural networks and learning pathways, the journey of an internal thought process".[32] But its power is such that this interpretation is only one of many ways of understanding the relationship between the building and the sculpture, as symbols of aspects of learning. As with all symbols there is both a practical component of the interpenetration of the different Places within the Hub as well as the emotional component of the convoluted, dynamic reference to cognitions and feeling. It helps to enshrine the nature of the Place's focus on thought and learning.

Land art

One reaction of artists to the reverential aspect of galleries is that they will often create works that could never be exhibited anywhere except in an art gallery, or some similar large space. Those artists who want to break away from that form of institutionalisation often create their works in the landscape.

Place or site-specific art also elaborates our understanding of the symbolism inherent in locations when sculpture is put there. There is a long tradition of positioning sculptures in both cities and the landscape. Typically, this is to formalise the significance of both the sculpture and the location. But the art movement that focussed on natural materials, in natural settings, which became known as Land Art (or Earthworks, Environmental Art, Earth Art) changes the emphasis to how the structured materials give further meaning to the Places out of which they emerge.

This movement has its roots in a rejection of the commercialisation of art, eschewing the dominance of galleries shaping how art is to be experienced. This includes an ecological perspective on what might nowadays be considered 'carbon neutral' art works. Such works also incorporate a move away for urban living and an embracing of the natural landscape. They incorporate symbols that reach for some spiritual feelings for nature that the Romantic poets would have recognised.

Andy Goldsworthy is one of the leading proponents of this movement, making clear that although his focus is on the use of natural materials:

> My strongest work is now so rooted in Place that it cannot be separated from where it is made the work is the place .... Inevitably materials and places gather associations and meanings as my work develops, but in ways that draw me deeper into nature rather than distracting me from it.[34]
>
> *(p. 7)*

His works are usually impermanent. The round pebbles converted into the sculpture in Figure 10.11 kept collapsing. They only remained for a few weeks before high tides washed them away. Herein lies the paradox of most of Land Art, heightening its role as a symbol of Place. Its long-term existence is almost entirely in the photographs that are

Figure 10.11 Goldsworthy site-specific art, Kangaroo Island, South Australia, 27 February 1992

taken of it. These are usually taken by the artist, who chooses the time and perspective from which the photograph is taken. Goldsworthy claims that: "The photograph does not replace but comes out of the working process and can be as much part of an artist's vocabulary as recorded sound is of a musician's" (p. 120).[33] The photograph has a role similar to a religious icon. It captures the associations, qualities and emotions associated with a particular entity. In the case of land art that is a structure of natural, local materials which epitomise crucial aspects of a Place.

The transformation into Places of symbolic significance by art objects, goes back many centuries. One powerful example is the Uffington White Horse[35] in Oxfordshire (Figure 10.12). This is 110 m (370 ft) long, formed from deep trenches filled with crushed white chalk. Apparently, this may be as much as 3000 years old, demonstrating how Iron age inhabitants were aware of how to enhance the iconography of a Place. Its importance as a symbol of a Place is illustrated by the adoption of the image as an emblem, by the Vale of White Horse District Council and educational establishments including Faringdon Community College and The Ridgeway Primary School in Whitley, Berkshire. The image and the location give the Place its special qualities by

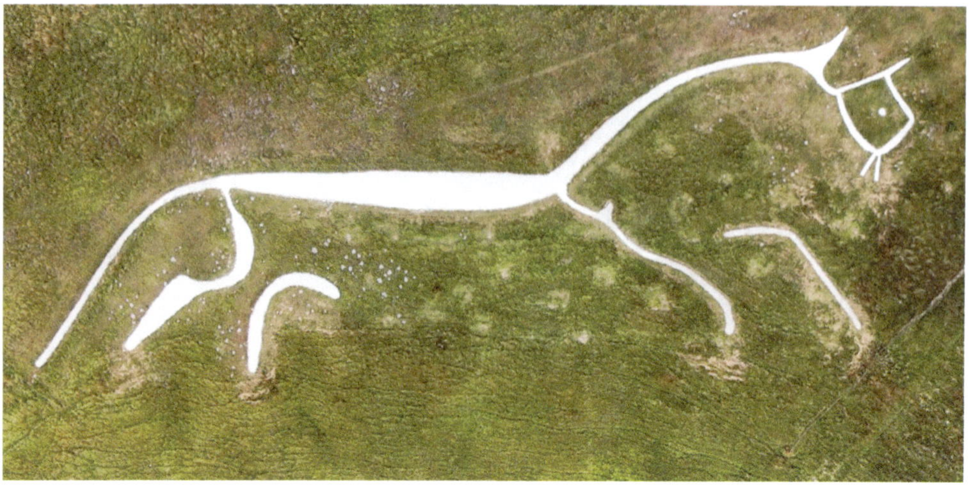

Figure 10.12 Uffington White Horse, Oxfordshire

drawing historical and folkloric references, as well as the simple power it captures of a moving animal.

Places can be given distinct and significant meaning, elaborating them as symbols by the intervention of rather more humble artefacts, most notably bronze age *menhirs*, 'standing stones', or monoliths (Figures 10.13a). These may just have been operating as boundary markers or as more significant indications of burial locations or other Places for rituals. They could be regarded as an early form of architecture, designating

Figure 10.13a Ancient monolith

Figure 10.13b Utah Desert Monolith

a location as a Place of note. Their enigmatic simplicity has led in recent times to the sighting of metal monoliths around the world (Figure 10.13b).

These are quintessentially abstract codes that symbolically designate a location. Their ambiguity and mysterious origins and meanings give them a power they would not have if they were just a signpost marking a footpath. Nor would they have any importance, nor would any notice be taken of them, if they were just one of many objects lying around a field. They epitomise how Places and the objects there can take on symbolic meanings be virtue of their combination and richness of possible meanings.

Differentiating Place symbols

These powerfully symbolic objects do draw attention to an aspect of architectural functions that are embedded in particular cultures. This was made clear in the groundbreaking 1969 book by the architects Amos Rapoport, that I have drawn on throughout this boook. Enshrined in its title was a challenge to the then current design maxim that 'form follows function'. He called his book *House, Form and Culture.*[36] To the surprise of many architects, it demonstrated that the forms of domestic buildings were not just a reflection of the activities they housed and the protective functions they provided. They carry meanings and significances. That work has generated a medley of explorations of the social and cultural concomitants of built forms.[37] It was one of the formative contributors to the area of research which can be summarised as meaning in architecture.

Rappoport developed a helpful elaboration of the meanings of architecture.[38] He proposed three levels of meaning. At the highest level of meanings, "are themes like cosmologies, cultural schemata, world views, reflections of philosophical systems". These are typically present in vernacular or traditional sacred architecture. They often have specific symbols such as the church steeple or the grand parliament building. These are the "symbols" usually discussed.

Secondly there are middle level meanings concerned with things like identity, power, status, wealth, etc.. Finally, there are low-level every day and instrumental meanings; these tell you where to walk in, where to sit down, etc. These two latter types are best studied using non-verbal communication models. Historically and culturally, these different types of meanings have differential importance. Their importance is partly related to the development of other symbolic systems like writing, printing, television, and social media. For instance, lately the high-level meanings in buildings have become less important because we can express them much more effectively through other symbolic systems. In pre-literate societies the only permanent Place for high level meanings was the built environment.

Conclusions

It is tempting to draw analogies between standing stones in a rural landscape and the twin towers of the World Trade Center in New York. They both bring together a variety associations and meanings as part of a designation of a location. There is a sense in which they both exhibit a form of designation of something sacred, explored by Kõiva and her colleagues[39] as the marking of a location that has symbolic significance with mythical and some form of religious associations. The Jihadi attack, with its religious background, recognised the Twin Towers as the symbol of what they saw as the worship of Mammon. The landscape chosen for the wedding photograph, as with the Places where ashes are disposed, are all actions that make those locations Places with a special meaning.

Museums, galleries, and the curators and artists who populate them, are increasingly breaking away from the definition of 'art' or 'significant artefact' that those Places encapsulate. By taking their art works to many other Places they both enrich the experience of where their work is as well as changing the way the art is engaged with. It is the combination of actions, associated meanings and the physical objects that designate those locations as significant, which mark them as special Places.

References and endnotes

1 Matusitz, J. (2014) *Symbolism in terrorism: Motivation, communication, and behavior*, Maryland, USA: Rowman & Littlefield.
2 Saniewska, M. (2024) Healing the landscape, healing the community: Exploring the relationship between Place attachment and post-earthquake recovery in Italy, MPhil thesis, The University of Cambridge, Unpublished.

3 Jung, C. G. (1974) *Man and his symbols*. New York: Doubleday (although there have been other more recent republications).
4 See, for example, Andrew Neher (1997) Jung's theory of archetypes. *A Critique Journal of Humanistic Psychology*, *37*(2), 71–91, https://doi.org/10.1177/00221678960362008
5 Turner, V. W. (1973) Symbols in African ritual. *Science*, March 17, *179*(4078), 1100–1105. [This is a paper readily available online, summarising some key aspects of Turner's (1977) book *The forest of symbols*, Ithaca: Cornell University Press.]
6 Turner, V. W. (1973) Symbols in African ritual. *Science*, March 17, *179*(4078), 1100–1105. [This is a paper readily available online, summarising some key aspects of Turner's (1977) book *The forest of symbols*, Ithaca: Cornell University Press.]
7 Quoted from Frarah, S. (2017) Man and his symbols in 2017: A current overview. Accessed 03/01/21. https://appliedjung.com/man-and-his-symbols-synopsis/
8 Rafaeli, A. and Worline, M. (2000) Symbols in organizational culture, in N.M. Ashkanasy, C.P.Wilderom, & M.F. Peterson (Eds.). *Handbook of organizational culture and climate*. London: Sage, pp. 71–84.
Schubert, T. W. (2005) Your highness: Vertical positions as perceptual symbols of power. *Journal of Personality and Social Psychology, 89*(1), 1–21, https://doi.org/10.1037/0022-3514.89.1.1
9 https://www.bbc.co.uk/programmes/b04d0k17
10 This phrase is from Dovey, K. (2010) *Becoming Places*. London: Routledge, who cites Massey, D. (1993) *Space, Place and gender*. Cambridge: Polity. But Bill Hillier, cited extensively in the previous chapter says something very similar.
11 Dutch add 'homebirth culture' to the list of intangible heritage – *DutchReview*. Accessed 20/01/21.
12 Johanson, R., Mary Newburn, M., and Macfarlane, A. (2002) Has the medicalisation of childbirth gone too far? *British Medical Journal* Apr 13; *324*(7342), 892–895, https://doi.org/10.1136/bmj.324.7342.892
13 Ingela Sjöblom, I., Berit Nordström, B., & Anna-Karin Edberg, A.-K. (2007) A qualitative study of women's experiences of home birth in Sweden. *Midwifery*, *22*(4), 348–355, https://doi.org/10.1017/j.midw.2005.11.004
14 Ingela Sjöblom, Berit Nordström, & Anna-Karin Edberg (2007), A qualitative study of women's experiences of home birth in Sweden
15 B. Murray-Davis, P. McNiven, H. McDonald, A. Malott, L. Elarar, & E. Hutton (2012) Why home birth? A qualitative study exploring women's decision making about Place of birth in two Canadian provinces. *Midwifery*, *28*(5), 577–581, https://doi.org/10.1016/j.midw.2012.01.013
16 Murray-Davis, McNiven, McDonald, Malott, Elarar, & Hutton (2012) Why home birth?
17 Murray-Davis, McNiven, McDonald, Malott, Elarar, & Hutton (2012) Why home birth?
18 Turner's (1977) book *The forest of symbols*, Ithaca: Cornell University Press.]
19 https://chillisauce.com/blog/post-8ddd70df400174b29fe5
20 https://www.ons.gov.uk/peoplepopulationandcommunity
21 For my marriage, over half a century ago, it was thus. On a wet Friday evening in November.
22 Bezner, L. C. (1997) "'Divine Detritus': An analysis of American wedding photography." *Studies in Popular Culture*, *18*(2), 19–33. Accessed 17 December 2020, http://www.jstor.org/stable/23413787.
23 https://www.sapiens.org/culture/hominin-burial/
24 https://www.sapiens.org/culture/hominin-burial/
25 Prendergast, D., Hockey, J., & Kellaher, L. (2007) Blowing in the wind? Identity, materiality, and the destinations of human ashes. *Journal of the Royal Anthropological Institute (N.S.)*, *12*, 881–898.
26 Prendergast, Hockey, & Kellaher (2007) Blowing in the wind?
27 Prendergast, Hockey, & Kellaher (2007) Blowing in the wind?
28 Prendergast, Hockey, & Kellaher (2007) Blowing in the wind?
29 Keene, S. (2007) All that is solid? Museums and the postmodern. *Public Archaeology*, *5*(3), 185–197, https://doi.org/10.1179/pua.2007.5.3.185
30 Quoted from https://www.moma.org/learn/moma_learning/marcel-duchamp-bicycle-wheel-new-york-1951-third-version-after-lost-original-of-1913/ accessed 12/01/2021.

31 Stavroulaki, G. & Peponis, J. (2003) The spatial construction of seeing at Castelvecchio 2003, Fourth International Space Syntax Symposium, University College London (Ed Julienne Hanson), London, UK, pp. 77.1–77.14.
32 Ballantyne, R. & Uzzell, D. (2011), Looking back and looking forward: The rise of the visitor-centred museum. *Curator: The Museum Journal*, *54*, 85–92, https://doi.org/10.1111/j.2151-7952.2010.00071.x
33 Personal communication January 2021.
34 Goldsworthy, A. (1994) *Stone*. London: Viking.
35 https://en.wikipedia.org/wiki/Uffington_White_Horse
36 Rapoport, A. (1969) House form and culture. Englewood Cliffs, NJ. Prentice-Hall.
37 Moore, K. D. (Ed.). (2019) *Culture-meaning-architecture: Critical reflections on the work of Amos Rapoport*. London: Routledge.
38 Rapoport, A. (1992) Interview with Amos Rapaport. Archictecture & Comportment (*Arch & Behavior)*, 8(1) pp.93-102
39 Kõiva, M., Jonuks, T., Kalda, M., Kuperjanov, A., & Hiiemäe, R. (2020) Marking of sacred Places. *Trames: Journal of the Humanities and Social Sciences*, *24*(74/79), 2, 129–144, https://doi.org/10.3176/tr.2020.2.01

CHAPTER 11

How buildings mean

It is the peculiar task of architecture to reach meaning: the human habitat is pivoted around meanings, not objects.[1]

Introduction

The title of this chapter reflects the title of an essay by Nelson Goodman[2] published almost half a century ago. That essay is part of philosophical explorations of how, or if, architecture could be considered as an art form. The exploration of meaning in architecture became a serious topic for discussion in the late 1960s,[3] spurred on by the opening up of architecture to richer and more varied form than the straitjacket of modernism. A lively debate ensued about whether architecture was some form of language. If so, what exactly does it communicate? In an engaging analysis of this conundrum Donougho[4] makes clear that, at best, language is a weak metaphor for architecture.

Such considerations, however, seem to have faded as various architectural theories and technical opportunities have emerged, as well as the demands of sustainability and related environmental concerns. However, there is an aspect of this discussion that has been lying dormant over recent years. This is how explorations of the meaning of buildings may contribute to the understanding of the nature of Places. The present chapter, therefore, sets out an initial exploration of how architectural features carry implications for the meaning of Places.

This can only be an introduction to a vast array of possibilities. It is nonetheless important because at its heart the study of built form and Place meaning is a consideration of how architecture goes beyond civil engineering. It also helps to explain the underlying processes that are influencing the changes in the sorts of buildings being created today, in contrast to Modernism and Post-modernism that dominated the 20th century. Atopic that is explored in more detail in the Chapter 12.

There is no doubt that the physical forms of buildings contribute to the meanings of Places. There would not be such a vast effort and cost into creating and modifying

DOI: 10.4324/9780367808655-14

buildings if they were merely ways of housing human activities. An issue I briefly explored, under the title 'Why Architecture is Necessary'.[5] This is now central to architectural training as articulated by the Royal Institute of British Architects declaration that it is important to recognise "Architecture for Social Purpose is about understanding the social value and economic and environmental benefits that architecture brings for individuals and communities".[6]

Ubiquitous places

Those features, of architecture that contribute to the nature of a Place, may be distinctive or generic aspects. They can carry idiosyncratic, personal, social, or cultural implications that help shape the meaning of a Place. Even ubiquitous 'everyplaces' often reveal features in their form, or use that expose distinct, usually context influenced, aspects of the nature of the Places they embody. The point that every place has some individuality needs to be addressed directly because of the pervasive opinion that some locations are 'placeless'. A claim spearheaded by Edward Relph,[7] discussed in Chapter 1.

In Chapter 1, reference was made to the sorts of downtrodden, apparently unremarkable Places that are found in city back streets or created by monotonous commercial developments. More salubrious examples can be shown in the buildings of the omnipresent McDonald's fast-food outlets. To take just two examples on opposite sides of the world, as in Figures 11.1 and 11.2, their local qualities are clear.

Figure 11.1 McDonald's Tokyo

Figure 11.2 Macdonald's São Paul

The Tokyo version, Figure 11.1 has illustrations, and plastic mock-ups of food, in the window. That shows what food is available, as do most restaurants in Japan. It also has the Japanese name "MacDonald's Hamburger" (in *katakana*, so phonetic rather than translated) to make clear, to anyone who still does not know, what sort of food is sold there. This contrasts with the restaurant in São Paul,[8] Figure 11.2, that celebrates being the 1000th Macdonald's store in Brazil, with the common Brazilian nickname for Macdonald's 'Méqui' emphasised over a grand, almost classical entrance. This is not only good marketing it also claims a very different experience, a different Place, from the Japanese example.

From the perspective of the Psychology of Place, Relph's 'placeless' Places are just one kind of Place. He is making an aesthetic or value judgement on locations that he does not like because he does not find a distinct character in them. There are indeed plenty of Places like this, although perhaps not as many as may be thought. I prefer to think of them as ubiquitous Places that may be found in many different locations. Their apparent lack of local identity and distinct character are part of their quality. Although that is a quality that may be decried by those who have a particular aesthetic sensibility, it may often have great value. There can be something comforting and undemanding in the banal, predictable and every day.

One clear example of this is Hilton Hotels. When asked whether a Hilton Hotel on the moon would be distinct from those on Earth,[9] the company made clear that the whole point of such a hotel would be to offer the predictability of Hilton Hotels everywhere. It is the ability for a guest to know what to expect that is one of the key features of their hotels. Many other hotel chains have embraced the same approach. This goes as far as making sure the same toiletries are available in the bathroom anywhere in the world. One consequence of this is that those hotels that want to compete with these global chains go to great pains to promote their uniqueness. They emphasise what makes the experience of staying there distinct.

The point here is that local sensitivities and tastes may be reflected in the physical form that Places take in different contexts. That is provided there are not pressures to override the influence of contexts, by making the ubiquitous qualities part of the design decisions. The denial of appropriate (and welcome) variation in built form also happens when particular architectural styles are imposed on design decisions, as explored in Chapter 12, when modernism and beyond are considered.

The power of archetypes

In 1978, David Young[10] carried out a small, but intriguing study. He asked his respondents to indicate which of a set of drawings, each a set of different sorts of building, best reflected that type of building. This might be expressed as the 'churchiest' church, the most obvious family dwelling, and so on. In other words, which was the most archetypal example of any type of building. He was exploring the idea that the form of a building indicated which of a variety of Places it represented. This relates to the idea that there are 'building types' considered in Chapter 7. In the present chapter we look a little more closely at how the forms of buildings contribute to the meaning of Places they are part of.

Although the concept of building type is not without its controversies, it is a useful summary of a set of uses, often dominated by a particular aspect of a building's physical form.[11] These are classifications of structures derived from an idea of the main activities the building is to house. In other words, the designation of a 'type' serves as a shorthand to indicate the components of the structure, what it is assumed the architect will be required to pull together to create the edifice. But it does more. Building types imply types of Places.

The studies by David Young, and many others, were looking at this idea of a 'type' from the point of view of non-specialists, ordinary people. An attempt to explore their ability to recognise what type of building a piece of architecture is, whether it is, for example, a church, an office block, a private residence, a stately home, a factory, a prison, and so on. However, this is not so much a test of the skills of non-specialists, but rather a study of how, or whether, particular building forms reveal their function; in other words, if or how the built environment enshrines meaning.

This consideration of the meaning of features of the built environment therefore operates in two directions. One is how these features help people to make sense of their surroundings. How they come to understand which buildings accommodate what. This is a crucial part of the Place cycle, as argued in earlier chapters, and central to the first outing of *The Psychology of Place*. Places take their meanings from what happens there, but what happens there also gives meanings to Places. This requires an informed interpretation of what sort of Place is indicated by that locations' physical form. To recall this central idea, it is helpful to quote Rapoport's[12] elaboration of the role of interpretations of the nature of Place:

> ...human behavior, including interaction and communication, is influenced by roles, contexts, and situations that, in turn, are frequently communicated by cues

in the setting making up the environment; the relationships among all these are learned...

Yet, Rapoport's concept of a Place is somewhat limited. As a creation of the constituents of form, meaning and action, the idea of a Place implies a more dynamic quality than the implicit determinism of an 'influence' communicated by cues, which Rapport provides. Being in a Place interacts with those cues. People bring their experiences, culture and predilections to assume the meaning of Places and act accordingly.

As noted, the other direction in which the meanings of built form have an influence, is how architects and other building designers determine the forms of their creations. They will approach design of a school differently from the design of a hospital in part because of the ideas they have associated with the different functions inherent in these different building types. Beyond the implications for the practical use of a building, they may be aware that their designs carry other implications. They may regard these as meanings they wish to express or ignore. Whatever they consider they will require some implicit or explicit understanding of how different building forms carry different meanings. An approach to how buildings exhibit meaning is often what is proposed as part of 'architectural theory'.

The oldest account of the qualities architecture should have, still widely quoted, is derived from Roman architect and engineer Vitruvius in his *De architectura*. He proposed that architecture should have *firmitas*, *utilitas*, and *venustas*. These are often translated as *firmness, commodity*, and *delight*. Architects have often left 'firmness' to structural engineering, but required that to be the literal and metaphorical underpinnings of what the architect wants to create. Engineering solutions are typically only the prime mover of designs when the task the construction is dealing with is a fundamentally engineering one, such as building a bridge. Although architects may still have an influence, such as what colour it should be?

Commodity is usually dealt with by relating to the assignment given by the client, the activities to be accommodated and facilitated. The plan of the building and the size of the spaces are normally the main response to this aspect of the design. Although the layout of a building does carry implications for the meaning of the building and Places within it, as mentioned in Chapter 9, the dominant stylistic issues may be interpreted as reflecting 'delight'. That is typically regard as the aesthetics of a building.

Vitruvius laid the groundwork for one particular way of considering delight in building form. The essence of this may be illustrated through his proposal about the significance of different forms of column. This idea is widely taught in schools of architecture, but is worth repeating here because of what it reveals about ways of thinking about the meaning encapsulated in architectural forms. It implies that building forms can take their meanings by analogy, even if that analogy may seem rather stretched for present day sensibilities.

At its simplest, Vitruvius, two millennia ago, acknowledged three 'orders', exhibited most strongly in types of columns (Figure 11.3). Their meaning was thought to derive from analogies to the human body:

Doric Order: The simplest of the orders, characterised by its sturdy, plain columns without bases and simple capitals. It is likened to the sturdiness and beauty if the

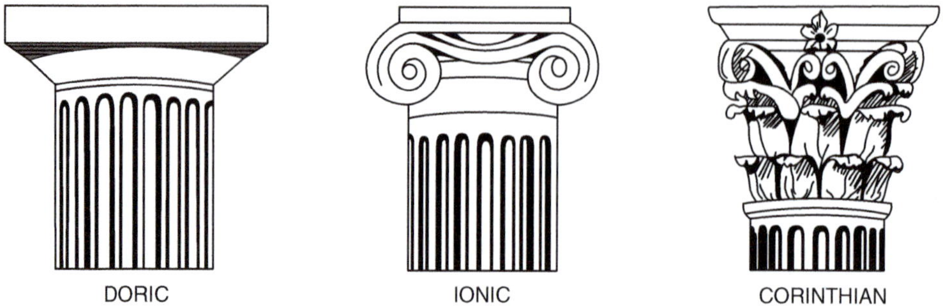

Figure 11.3 The three 'orders' of Greek columns

male body. The simplicity and sturdiness reflect the ideal masculine form, emphasizing strength and functionality.

Ionic Order: With slender and elegant columns, which have bases and capitals decorated with scroll-like ornaments, these are seen as displaying the elegance of a woman's body. They suggest a graceful and refined feminine figure. The base of the Ionic column can be seen as analogous to a woman's feet, providing a stable and attractive foundation.

Corinthian Order: Ornate but similar to the Ionic order with more elaborate capitals adorned with acanthus leaves. A young lady's body is thought of as the analogy here. Representing the beauty and delicacy of a young maiden. Its elaborate decorations evoke a sense of youth and ornamental elegance.

Putting the past in Place

Although these 'orders' are symbolised by types of columns, they epitomised the approach to the whole building and what it contained. A powerful instance in the 19th century, when reference to the much earlier Classical and Renaissance traditions were popular, were the many banks and other institutions that wanted to demonstrate their manly strength and trustworthiness. They therefore opted for Doric Columns at their entrances. The Second Bank of the United States in Philadelphia, built in 1824 is a classical (in many senses) example of this. It is fronted by Doric columns to denote the sturdy steadfastness of the Bank as an institution (Figure 11.4).

The sturdiness implied by the columns and pediment was a readily understood representation of established worthiness. It could be regarded as part of the set of features that carried meaning across many countries, a sort of 'international style' of its day. That is of particular note in the United States. There was no direct history of either a Roman invasion or of any archaeological sites showing evidence of classical Greek or Roman architecture. The reference back to those features of 'the old country' helped to suggest that the bank was a Place that enshrined the qualities linked to generations of trustworthy forebears.

In Britain, Ancient Rome is present in a way it is not in the United States. There are many Roman remains and Place names clearly derived from their original Roman form, such as the Caster ending in Lancaster, or Doncaster, or the name Chester. They are all derived from the Latin *castra*, indicating a fortified encampment for Roman

Figure 11.4 The second bank of the United States in Philadelphia, built 1824

legions. It might therefore be expected that people in the United Kingdom would have special regard for existing buildings in a Classical style. An intriguing exploration of this was carried out by Reid Bishop in a remarkably extensive study of the perception and importance of time in architecture.[13]

In reviewing architectural design concerns in the late 20th century, when he was writing, Bishop draws attention to "attempts on so many fronts at the moment to restore some of the missing, or at least weakened, links with historical and more immediate time".[14] He details many illustrations of this, including the evolution of post-modernisms. Quotations from criticism of the weaknesses in how history is absorbed into buildings are also used to question what aspects of historical links are really being used, as in:

> Architects may be rediscovering the past, but their knowledge of it is still so spotty, their enthusiasm so arbitrary and episodic, that a lot of what we are getting is do-it-yourself history.[15]

Exploring this, Bishop interviewed people in the market town of Guildford, about 30 miles Southwest of London. Their responses showed that most people are not only unaware of the factual historical details that make up their town, but that has little impact on their reactions to the town and its buildings. One prime example is

Figure 11.5 Tunsgate Shopping Centre, Guildford, United Kingdom; built 1818

the Portico of Tuscan columns that were originally built to front a corn exchange and Crown Courts, in 1818, Figure 11.5. Many were happy to assume it was the remains of a larger Roman building, although the discerning expert would recognise that the Tuscan columns were really a simplified version of the Doric order that owes more to the 16th-century Renaissance than ancient Rome. The edifice itself being an early 19th-century strategy to indicate the significance of the town as it grew in power.

Far more importantly, this building as well as many others that played with earlier building forms were all seen as providing the character of the town. They needed preserving because they indicated the sort of Place it was. A market town (although the main cattle markets had long since disappeared) with cobbled streets that exuded what many would regard as old-world, charm. The atmosphere and sense of Place were supported by its mock-Tudor facades and Roman-style portico. Despite the franchised shops found all over Britain, these architectural features support an identity that residents believe make them and their town distinct.

Building analogies

The analogy to the body was elaborated even further by the Renaissance architect and theorist, Palladio. He advocated architecture being based on the laws of nature, which he saw as being reflected in the mathematics of the human body. This meant that buildings should be:

- Symmetrical from the front with a central axis (spine)
- Most important elements in the middle (like the head, eyes, etc.)
- The proportions of parts to whole should reflect the mathematical proportions evident in the human body.
- Like the skin the building should be covered in elegant forms, most usually columns, pediments, and porticos.

Such analogies were dismissed in the bonfire of Classicism, as the 19th century turned into the twentieth. Yet many parallels in architectural designs can be found to this day. For example, the architect and sculpture Santiago Calatrava stated that his design for an apartment block in Malmö is based on his own sculpture of a twisted body (Figure 11.6). The intention was to sell apartments in the tower, but apparently

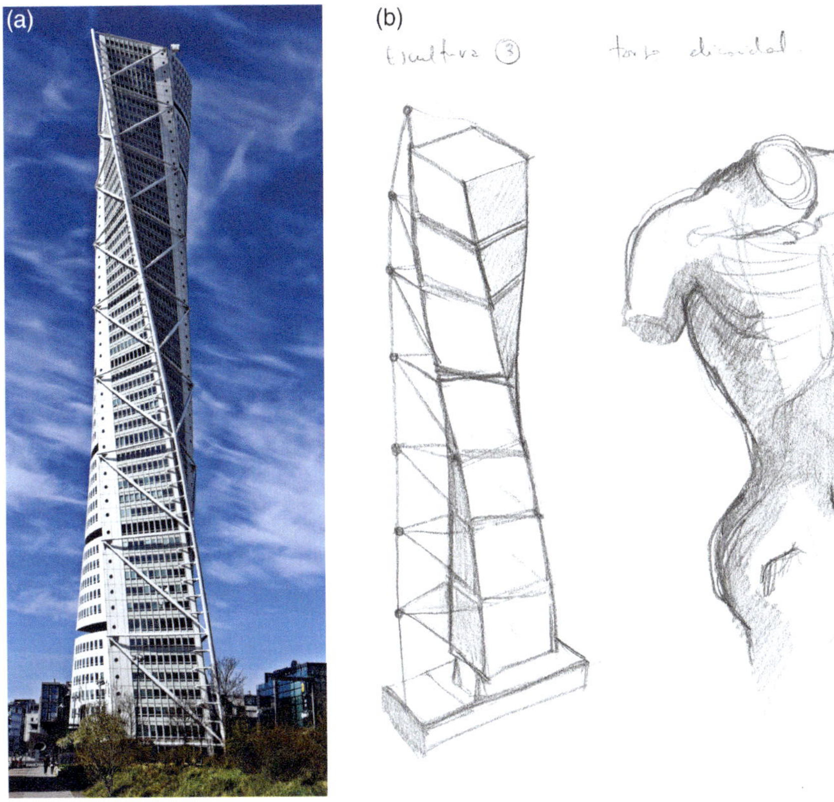

Figure 11.6 (a) Santiago Calatrava's turning torso in Malmö, Sweden. (b) Sketch of Santiago Calatrava's turning torso

there was so little interest in buying that they were eventually rented. The costs of building this vast sculpture are reported to have been twice what was originally estimated.

Although these analogies, whether for Roman columns or Swedish apartment blocks may be interpreted by analogy with the human body, and that may have been the initial design inspiration, it seems unlikely that non-specialist will recognise that. There is also an important question. Even when recognised will it seem relevant to what the building is intended to mean?

Distinguishing denotation and connotation

A second process that enables us to determine what a building houses are the physical requirements of its function. A small, detached, two-storey building with a clear entrance and a manicured garden at the front, is very likely to be a domestic dwelling – a house. Elaborations of this basic form may tell us something about the nature of the owners of the building. This can even be such a detail as to whether there are Christmas decorations on the door at Christmas time.[16]

At a more abstract level, following the seminal writings of Barthes,[17] the Christmas Decorations can be regarded as revealing not only 'denotations' that simply describe what they are, but also suggest 'connotations' that imply social involvement. This distinction is helpful by pointing to the layers of meaning inherent in physical objects. These can be small-scale such as the holly wreath on a domestic door suggesting a friendly Place. Or the large-scale iron tower designed by Gustave Eifel, representing human creativity and engineering prowess. As a consequence of that it became an emblem of the enduring appeal of Paris.

However, the distinction between denotated and connotative aspects of the meaning of buildings is an oversimplification of the complex and subtle processes involved. Unpacking the ways in which architectural form may signify something more than a civil engineering solution, providing appropriate spaces to contain equipment or activities, has generated heated debates. These draw on a variety of philosophical and social science frameworks.[18]

An early attempt to summarise the discourse on architectural meaning was Rapport's book on the *Meaning of the Built Environment.*[19] Rapoport decries the complexity of many of the approaches to explaining the meaning of buildings. He is particularly dismissive of the whole area that sits under the heading of 'semiotics'. Rapport happily quotes one of his students complaining that semiotic discussions have "very complex technical jargon" with "terminology so complicated it is totally beyond the grasp of the uninitiated". Instead Rapoport proposes that the built environment has meaning as a form of 'non-verbal' communication.

Yet this can be seen as another, admittedly more sophisticated, analogy, akin to the Greek view on the order of columns. He opens up the analogies between features of the built environment and the meanings they carry by simply suggesting these features carry personal or cultural significance in the same way that a non-verbal gesture can carry meaning. This generates a plethora of aspects that have particular significance. Intriguingly, a particular aspect of this significance implies the three-fold model of the psychology of Place.[20]

Rapoport makes clear, for example, that features in the built environment provide cues that are "meant to elicit appropriate emotions, interpretations, behaviors, and transactions by setting up the appropriate situations and contexts".[21] This is an elaboration of the proposal that aspects of a physical environment have cognitive components that relate to the actions that go on there. That elaboration draws attention to the cultural and personal contexts that inform the cyclical process explored in Chapter 1. Built form implies meaning, meaning suggest actions, those actions help to clarify the meaning of the Place. That, in turn, is part of the personal and cultural context that allows us to make sense of the sort of Place it is from the built form.

The actions themselves are carried out by various people who have different relationship to those Places. The student, the professor, the administrator, the cleaner, the maintenance engineer, all relate to Places in different ways. Consequently, the same physical form will carry different meanings for each of them. These may well influence the sense they make of a Place and the influence they will, or try to, have on its form.

But for Rapoport the dynamic, interactive quality that human agency brings to this cycle is rather undervalued. He also misses the point that this mixture creates Places, those conglomerations of experiences and actions in a physical context.

Examples of what might be considered non-verbal meanings of Places are noticeable everywhere. Gated communities carry implications beyond the control of access. They indicate the special nature of the people who live there. This contrasts in the United Kingdom with a recognisable 'council house look'. These are buildings put up by the local authority, typically on limited budgets with unimaginative, commonplace designs. In both cases the apparent consequences of wealth, or lack of it, are reflected in many aspects of the building forms. The difference, for instance, between the individualised properties typical of a gated-community and the uniformity of housing built by a local authority, carry meanings that are not entirely a product of the different financial inputs. They also reflect differences in attitudes of designers and builders about what these Places should look like.[22] Many recent examples of publicly funded low-income housing have demonstrated that the 'council house look' is not inevitable.

Another example of buildings indicating differences in the nature of the Places within them is the difference in the United Kingdom between those hospitals that are part of the National Health Service and those that are privately funded. Why do the latter tend to have carpets and carefully considered interior decor, whilst the latter typically are institutional grey? Funding availability is doubtless relevant, but once again, as with public housing, the consideration of what type of Place is being offered influences the aesthetic and implicit messages the design reflects.

The same processes are apparent in many other types of building such as office blocks and airports. One of my students was studying waiting areas in many types of office building. He declared that he could identify the whole quality of a building, the mood, and atmosphere it created, once he knew the sort of waste bins it had. When I studied safety in many factories, I found I could predict their accident rate once I saw how tidy the workspaces where.

These details in the design and organisation of Places reveal the meanings of those Places. Whether it be, for instance, decorations on the door or the presence of carpets. These aspects do spread to all the other aspects of the design of buildings. They all add up to give a sense of the use and experience of those Places.

Formal aesthetics

A reference to cultural and an experiential history of recognisable built forms does not totally satisfy a search for psychological explanations of how these forms take on their meaning in the first Place. Why does an increase in height add so much significance to the built environment? An aspect of design that, for example, is apparent in cathedrals as well as ancient pyramids in Egypt and Mexico. There are two approaches to explaining the power of particular built forms. One is the social implications of generating that form. The centuries-long efforts into building European cathedrals, or the actual political power needed to build a pyramid. A second are the influence of personal perceptual processes so thoroughly analysed, for example, by Ralf Weber.[23]

Weber draws on studies of people looking at various images and shapes, including tracking eye movements. From these he argues that there are natural fixation points when looking at any form. These tend to be the centre of complex images, or unusual aspects of those images. In addition, there is a tendency for the more detailed aspects of an image to be treated as the foreground with the less detailed becoming the background, so having a subsidiary role in perception.

All these ideas draw on the century-old writings of the Gestalt psychologists, notably Kurt Koffka,[24] also explored, amongst others, by the art critic and historian Rudolf Arnheim.[25] They emphasised the overall combination of components in the visual field, rather than dealing with one element at a time. Thus, a tower on a building stands out visually as well as physically. It becomes a dynamic centre, drawing attention to itself by its distinctness. The same element in a multitude of spires has consequently less significance. Another example is a repetitive façade in which the entrance breaks the pattern and therefore has a great impact. This is often enhanced by decoration of the entrance, the addition of awnings and other distinct features.

The power of these cognitive aspects of perception were demonstrated many years ago in studies asking people what features of a building, represented in pictures, enabled them to formulate a view on the nature of the Place it was.[26] The dominant influence is the coherent perception of the building as a whole. The façade adds to this, especially if it has identifiable features. Detailed elements of the building are then attended to more closely. The immediate environment adds further clarity to the judgements formed.

The aesthetic and perceptual influences are inevitably influenced by socio-cultural factors, as in the comparison of McDonald's outlets explored earlier. The different types of classical column also doubtless carried different meaning for 18th- and 19th-century observers, even if this were just from frequency of the experience of them in different settings. The combination of social expectations and perceptual dominance thus provides a basis for considering a number of aspects of building form which contribute to the identification and clarification of the nature of a Place.

Affordances

A perspective beyond the influence of perceptual patterns that has fascinated many of those considering how buildings become meaningful was the introduction of cognitive processes beyond the directly perceptual ones. This was led by Jame J. Gibson[27] with his notion of *affordances*. I introduced this theory in Chapter 1, but it is worth considering again here in relation to the meaning of buildings.

Gibson claimed that when we look at an object its potential uses and the activities is makes possible are immediately understood. They offer instantly detectable functions. A chair affords sitting on, stairs to walk up (or down), a room to allow a number of people to gather in. Although this idea can be readily challenged by providing examples that are specific to particular cultures, such as the side door to a building being for tradesmen and other servants, the front door consequently not 'affording' entrance to everyone, and the grass lawn of a Cambridge college not affording a short-cut across it to casual visitors. Such variations draw attention to the social and cultural meanings that indicate how things may be used. It is not simply their perceptual qualities.

Importantly, though, Gibson's claims draw attention away from the particular components of what is perceived, as emphasised by Weber,[28] to the sense given by a combination of textures, scales and forms. It is the entities in particular situations that provide an understanding of what may happen there. The built environment is not merely a form of large-scale sculpture that provides enough spaces in combination to meet the needs of the users. Beyond the chair for sitting and the stairs for climbing, affordances can be seen as a step towards the recognition of the nature of a Place with all that entails.

However, the concept of affordances seems to imply a fixed meaning to any physical configuration. Different people may determine that the same objects can be used in different ways. This is something that children demonstrate all the time. As illustrated in Figure 11.7. What to a passing adult is just a raised detail outside a car showroom. A young girl[29] sees it as a fun challenge that her brother is intrigued to follow. They've

Figure 11.7 Children reveal that a decorative detail 'affords' an interesting challenge

converted this architectural detail into a Place to play. A phenomenon that can be seen all over the world, as in recent images in Gaza of children using slabs of concrete from destroyed buildings as slides. These all illustrate that if the use of an object in a Place reveals the opportunity it 'affords' then the concept is circular. What is 'afforded' is shown by its use, which is what it 'affords'. What the concept adds is an emphasis on human agency, and sense making – the active engagement with Places that reflects their dynamic qualities.

Conclusions

In his widely cited book, now in its fifth edition, Ching[30] declares:

> Fundamentally, the physical manifestations of architecture accommodate human activity. However, the arrangement and ordering of forms and spaces also determine how architecture might promote endeavors, elicit responses, and communicate meaning.... Form and space are presented not as ends in themselves but as means to solve the problem in response to the conditions of function, purpose, and context – that is, architecturally.

However, except for a passing mention of a quote from Le Corbusier declaring that primary forms, such as cones, spheres and pyramids are "distinct and tangible within us and without ambiguity simple forms. It is for this reason that these are...the most beautiful forms", there is no indication throughout Ching's extensive listing of the geometrical constituents, which are combined to make architecture, of how those constituents "promote endeavours, elicit responses, and communicate meaning".

It is not surprising that Ching is reluctant to extend his cornucopia of geometries by indicating how they contribute to the experience of a Place, because, as he writes, they are used "in response to the conditions of function, purpose and context". The impacts of built forms are consequently a complex product of when, where and in what personal, socio-cultural, and historical context they are created and exist.

The way buildings contribute to the meanings of a Place are typically removed from the ideas which influenced the architects and builders who created them. Thus although, there are some insights into how buildings give Places meaning, which can be derived from psychological theories of perception and cognition, much of these are often masked by the knowledge and experience people have of built forms they've seen and lived in. These forms themselves draw on historical references. That interaction between what people know and expect of buildings and the reference, to historical examples, or deliberate lack of it, is even more obvious with the emergence of post-modern architecture. That is considered on the Chapter 12.

References and endnotes

1 Giurgola, R. (1965) Reflections on buildings and the city: The realism of the partial vision. *Perspecta*, 9/10, 107–130, 111.
2 Goodman, N. (1985) How buildings mean. *Critical Inquiry*, 11(4), 642–653.
3 Hershberger, R. G. (1970) Architecture and meaning. *Journal of Aesthetic Education*, 4(4), 37–55.

4 Donougho, M. (1987) The language of architecture. *The Journal of Aesthetic Education*, 21(3), 53–67. https://www.jstor.org/stable/3332870
5 Published in 1970 in the *RIBA* Journal.
6 The new topic mandatory for continuing professional development: What is architecture for social purpose, the new RIBA CPD topic?
7 Relph, E. (2016) The paradox of Place and the evolution of Placelessness, in *Place and Placelessness revisited*, London: Routledge, pp. 20–34.
8 There is a variety of pictures if McDonald's around the world on TikTok Part 2 | Most Beautiful McDonald's on Earth 🍔 🤩 #TikTokPromote #mcdon.. | TikTok.
9 Hilton's bizarre 1967 plan for a space hotel | CNN.
10 Young, D. W. (1978) *The interpretation of form: Meaning and ambiguities in contemporary architecture*. MSc Dissertation, The University of Surrey (unpublished).
11 Steadman, P. (2014) *Building types and built forms*, San Jose, CA: Matador, p. 68.
12 Rapoport, A. (1982) *The meaning of the built environment: A nonverbal communication approach*.
I can't resist pointing out that there is very much in this book that reflects details in my *The Psychology of Place* published five years earlier. Yet there is no reference to my book at all in Rapoport's. Whether he'd read it or not the encouraging aspect is that his arguments provide clear corroboration for my proposals developed independently.
13 Bishop, R. (1982) *The perception and importance of time in architecture*. PhD thesis, University of Surrey (United Kingdom) (unpublished). ProQuest Dissertations & Theses, 1982.27557816.
14 Bishop (1982) *The perception and importance of time in architecture*, p. 66.
15 Huxtable, L. (1981) The troubled state of modern architecture. *Architectural Design*, I/2, 13.
16 Brown, B. B., & Werner, C. M. (1985) Social cohesiveness, territoriality, and holiday decorations: The influence of cul-de-sacs. *Environment and Behavior*, 17(5), 539–565.
17 Notably Barthes (1957) *Mythologies*.
18 Elegantly explored in Heynen, Hilde, et al. *The figure of knowledge: Conditioning architectural theory, 1960s–1990s*, Leuven University Press, 2020. Project MUSE. https://dx.doi.org/10.1353/book.78083
19 Rapoport, A. (1982) *The meaning of the built environment: A nonverbal communication approach*, p. 37.
20 Although he never acknowledges that link.
21 Rapoport, A. (1982) *The meaning of the built environment: A nonverbal communication approach*, p. 107.
22 Thoburn, N. (2018) Concrete and council housing: The class architecture of Brutalism 'as found' at Robin Hood Gardens. *City*, 22(5–6), 612–632.
23 Weber, R. (1995 – reprinted 2025) *The aesthetics of architecture: A psychological approach to the structure and order pf perceived architectural space*, London: Routledge.
24 Koffka, K. (1935) *Principles of Gestalt psychology*, London: Lund Humphries
25 Arnheim, R. (1954) *Art and visual perception*, Oakland, CA: University of California Press
26 Quoted in Young, D. W. (1978) *The interpretation of form: Meaning and ambiguities in contemporary architecture*. MSc Dissertation, The University of Surrey (unpublished), pp. 86–87.
27 Gibson, J. J. (1977) The theory of affordances, in R. Shaw & J. Bransford (Eds.) *Perceiving, acting and knowing*, New York: Halsted. Also first proposed in Gibson, J. J. (1968) *The senses considered as conceptual systems*, London: Allen & Unwin.
28 Weber, R. (1995 – reprinted 2025) *The aesthetics of architecture: A psychological approach to the structure and order pf perceived architectural space*, London: Routledge.
29 My daughter many years ago, currently head of production for a Netflix company, with her brother.
30 Ching, F. D. (2023) *Architecture: Form, space, and order*, Hoboken, NJ: John Wiley & Sons, p. 9.

CHAPTER 12

Post-modernism and beyond

How modernism got it wrong

Many of the studies of the meanings of buildings had their impetus in the late 1970s and early 1980s. This was an era when the major, dominant approach to architectural design was demoted to a notion of its 'function'. Any more abstract meaning was regarded as unnecessary ornamentation or dissolute pandering to historical forms. This had all taken off after the First World War, when all art forms were consciously shaking off the legacies of the past. Music was being composed that deliberately eschewed the idea of scales and a movement towards a tonic chord, which had been the basis of composition for over three centuries. The much-vaunted Bauhaus school of architecture's leaders, such as Walter Gropius, even declared that students should not be taught about the history of architecture.

Architectural slogans ruled the day. Towards the end of the 19th century, the great architect of skyscrapers in the United States had claimed that a building's design should just reflect its function, with the often-repeated alliterative catchphrase "form follows function". Le Corbusier had enlarged on this in his requirement that a building should be "*une machine à vivre*". This is often translated as a 'machine for living in', but loses the subtlety of the French. In French a washing machine is "*une machine à laver*". That does not really translate as a machine for doing the washing in, but as a machine that washes. Similarly, Le Corbusier is pointing to building design being the creation of a machine in which one lives. He was building on the delirium about the new machine age. In which machines were regarded as totally a product of their purposes. Slim racing cars and elegant ships were being extolled as being beautiful because they responded so directly to the challenges of their use.

As many have pointed out, that was a remarkably naïve view of how industrial designers work. Even the great steam engines of the nineteenth century were designed to include the golden section that it was believed would make them more beautiful. Car and ship designers had an eye to the users and buyers of their products. The *art deco* of the 1920s and 1930s was a recognisable style all its own, not purely functional, even if

DOI: 10.4324/9780367808655-15

it was more elegant and simplified than the Arts and Crafts and Beaux Arts traditions that went before.

Most importantly, the idea that the only function of a building was to house particular activities in pleasant surroundings was a surprisingly oversimplified view of what the functions of architecture are. It also ignored how architects and others who design buildings actually go about their job, as discussed in Chapter 7. What is crucial about this oversimplification is that it attempted to ignore the meanings of buildings. It was these meanings and how they are carried by physical forms that generated a growing range of studies. They contributed to an emerging disillusion with modernism and the creation of, apparently, new approaches to creating buildings.

One particular curiosity of the movement that became known as *modernism* was that the same building form sprouted up everywhere. Where do you think the photograph in Figure 12.1 was taken? It could be New York or Tokyo, even Buenos Aires or possibly Baku. There is nothing that reaches for a meaning that might draw on locals' experience of places. This form of building was actually referred to as 'The International Style' of architecture because it undervalued even the differences in local

Figure 12.1 The view from the 23rd floor of the Hyatt Regency Hotel[2]

climates. Large plate glass windows cause problems of overheating in a subtropical city and run up great heating demands in Northern climates.

It really could be any of hundreds of cities around the world. Furthermore, there are a whole mixture of different activities going on in these different buildings. But there is no way of knowing which are offices, apartment blocks, churches, schools, museums or even factories. Idea of different places within the city has been homogenised out. An ironic way of illustrating this is shown in the humorous criticism of Modern architecture in Jacques Tati's film *Playtime* (1967). In one scene, in a travel agent's, the room is filled with posters advertising holidays in many places around the world. Yet every poster has the same high-rise modern building in it.

However, some historical leftovers perhaps indicate Figure 12.1 is in an older city? It is not entirely made up of the glass and steel that took over developments in other cities. The building in the centre of the picture, with its curved top-storey windows and other decorations on the roofline as well as lower down, point to an earlier era in architecture. This reveals how architecture, as with all arts and sciences, does build on what has gone before. The main point is that anything that is built inevitably, and often inadvertently, carries implications about what it means and the places it is part of, even when it attempts some form of neutrality.

Of course, this is not entirely the fault of building designers, whether trained as architects or not. There is a belief by those who commission buildings that there are simple commercial benefits by stacking floors on top of each other in upturned boxes. But a movement of 'Low-Rise High-Density' developments has shown that is not inevitable.[1]

Architectural modernism regarded ornamentation on and in buildings as an anathema. The rectangular boxes which characterised office blocks and housing, as well as many other types of buildings throughout the world, in the years after the Second World War, were claimed to reflect their functions. It took much of the late twentieth century to unravel the misleading implications of this as well as its inherent inconsistencies. The stripped back, glass and concrete boxes that 'modern architecture' generated were a style like any other. It was no more a machine than a Gothic church or the Houses of Parliament. As a style, it ignored the meanings buildings have for people. Often it did not even relate directly to the patterns of use.

The modernist style found an iconic nemesis when the Pruitt-Igoe housing estate in St Louis, built and given a design award in the 1950s was found to be so uninhabitable that it was very publicly blown up in 1972 and razed to the ground in the following years. The design had ignored the many subtle social processes it was supposed to support. The inability to manage the use of its spaces effectively. The opportunities the layout provided for criminal activity also contributed to its demise. The images of its death was widely heralded as sounding the knell for architects' love affair with 'modernism'.

Figure 12.2 is now an iconic image, widely published, because it represents so clearly the demise of a representation that was supposed to be the brave new world generated for mass housing in the clean, modernist, post-war world.

A further criticism of modernism, much to the chagrin of architects at the time, was the searing attack articulated by the then HRH the Prince of Wales. His fully illustrated 1989 book, A *Vision of Britain: A Personal View of Architecture,* even with overlays of views across the Thames at the time, to compare with Canaletto's painting of the same scene in 1750, decries the 'monotonous uniformity of housing

Figure 12.2 The death of architectural modernism with the destruction of the Pruit-Igoe housing estates in St Louis, Missouri

developments where every house has to have precisely the same amenities'. The prince inevitably conservative as a member of a millennium-old, unelected Monarchy, advocates the creation of developments "which echo the traditional, more intimate patterns of our villages and towns" (p. 15). He wanted "new buildings to look as though they belong and thereby enhance the natural surroundings" (p. 89). He goes further: "Many of our modern buildings are huge, blank and impersonal. We have created somewhat godforsaken cities from which nature, or indeed the spiritual side of life, has almost been erased" (p. 137).

The ugly monolith of Buckingham Palace, which is the Prince's, now of course as King Charles III, main residence, gets no mention in his tirade against modern architecture. But his opinions about architecture and what it should be and do resonated with many people. However, the emergence of post-modernism did not appeal at all to the Prince. As he said, "There is no longer a universal language of symbolism, and the gropings of some critics towards the imposition of 'meaning' on what they call post-modern architecture has been fairly unfruitful" (p. 90). In essence he advocates a return to what he regards as a meaningful tradition, somewhat ignorant of what inspires architects and those who commission them as indicated in Chapter 7. Nonetheless, Prince Charles' challenges to modernism were part of a groundswell of criticism that did change the approaches and actions of many designers, giving rise to a more clear-sighted view of how it is possible to contribute to the creation of places. It also has to be admitted that architects, as with any other artists, were fed up with the monotony of modernism and were looking for new ways of plying their trade.

Post-modernism and beyond

The growing challenges to the International Style, with its rigid simplicity and reference to industrial components such as steel and glass, led to a desire for something different. This was part of a search to give buildings meanings that were distinct. Although rarely articulated, this was a search that designated the qualities of places by utilisation of built forms that were different from anything that had gone before. This may be through the combination of components or the approach to the whole sculptural nature of the edifice. This required decoration and, in many cases, a reference back to historical models. The limits and possibilities of existing building technologies and builders, meant that there was not a wholehearted embracing of previous epochs of architecture. Although some references, for instance, to classical forms of the past were made from time to time as in the construction in the late 1970s and early 1980s of Espaces d'Abraxas complex in Marne-la-Vallée (Figure 12.3), with its columns and triumphal arch, as well as an overall crescent layout reminiscent of grand neoclassical developments in imposing cities such as Bath or even Paris.[3]

Notably, the meanings consciously built into this particular development derived from it being endorsed by the local communist mayoralty. The council wanted

Figure 12.3 Espaces d'Abraxas complex in Marne-la-Vallée, built around 1980

something that would enhance the spirit of the working class who lived there by giving them such imposing majesty. It is difficult, though, not to see this as totalitarian and patronising in equal measure.

It was Charles Jenks who promoted the term post-modern[4] to describe that architecture which began to emerge in the late 1960s and early 1970s. His inciteful, stimulating book being called *The Language of Post-Modern* Architecture, made clear that he saw the burgeoning developments in the buildings being produced as some form of communication. Rarely has the labelling of an artistic movement been more influential. The term was taken from literature, offering up linguistic models for describing architectural forms. Referring to a conscious break with the modernist past. Jenks makes clear that the need for the exploration of this 'language' was because of the then current state of the built environment:

> We see a babble of tongues. A free-for-all of personal idiolects, not the classical language of the Doric, Ionis and Corinthian Orders. Where once there were rules of architectural grammar, we now have a mutual diatribe between speculative builders; where once was a gentle discourse between Houses of Parliament and Westminster Abbey, there is now across the Thames the Shell building shouting at the Hayward Gallery, which grunts back at a stammering and giggling Festival Hall.[5]

Yet, Jencks claims, "this invective is still language even if it is not very comprehensible or persuasive". He goes on to draw on parallels to language as a way of understanding the breakaway from 'The international Style'. That, as already indicated, idolised the idea of simple forms, referencing the emerging technologies, built around the idea that the building was merely reflecting its function. Although the irony of the stated functional objective of modernism is that buildings for very different sorts of places, with distinctly different functions, were produced that often looked very similar to each other. Post-modern buildings, by contrast, were eclectic, acknowledging historical forms, as in the heroic arch in Figure 12.3, but also exhibiting a playfulness, and colour that would have been an anathema for international style.

Any direct denotation or meaning was abhorrent to modernist architects. By contrast, architects operating under the general umbrella of post-modernism offered meanings for the forms they built. Jenks offered a way into these 'communications'. This included metaphors drawn from critical and imaginative references to other forms that a building might remind people of. These could be egg boxes, a stack of washing machines, the unfolding petals of a flower and many more. Some of these draw directly on the requirements for accommodating particular functions. Jenks' main example is the jutting shape of an auditorium, but many of the examples explored in Chapter 7, when considering building types, can carry meanings too.

The question arises of how these contribute to the experience of Place. One broad way of answering this is from the theories and manifestos of architects themselves. Jencks and Kropf summarise these in a wide-ranging review.[6] They include advocates of continuity with historical forms, building types and traditional crafts, which they call 'Traditional'. They also recognise 'New Modern'. That is modernism in the new clothes of new materials, driven by digital tools and emerging technologies. Of particular note are the apparently different architectural pursuits of 'Complexity and Chaos Theory'. They claim an influence of exotic mathematical ideas such as fractals and nonlinear systems, apparent in some of the buildings illustrated in Chapter 7.

Much of these theories are opaque to most people walking past these buildings or seeing photographs of them. The differences between them may seem arbitrary. Non-specialists draw on their existing associations with recognisable forms in their search for meaning. That often leads to simple labels as illustrated in Figures 12a, b and c. Even the ambiguous communications that buildings offer when they do not clearly draw on recognisable historical and vernacular stereotypes are nonetheless interpreted from whatever associations can be drawn on.

One exception to the arbitrariness of post-modern designs was a group of architects that were given the label *Critical Regionalism* by Charles Frampton.[7] He set out to challenge the lack of individuality in the International Style, seeking to create a sense of place by drawing on the distinct characteristics of the locality and culture in which the building would sit. This approach to architecture did have origins before Frampton set out his manifesto. One notable example from the early 1950s is Alvar Aalto's Säynätsalo Town Hall (Figure 12.4).

Aalto's Town Hall integrates the elegant simplicity of the best modernist architecture with local Finnish architectural traditions. Aalto used brick, a conventional local material, rather than the concrete, glass and steel beloved of the International Style. It sits within its woodland context, with human-level entrances. There is a courtyard and tower as often found in European town squares. The Town Hall and all the facilities and offices it contains thus contribute to a place that is by, with, and for its local

Figure 12.4 Säynätsalo town hall designed by Alvar Aalto

community. It reflects a future-looking perspective whilst still being part of the here and now of local people's experiences. Although the somewhat austere internal brick-work has a feel that some may regard as rather institutional, the building's design now gives it historical significance that contributes to it being a cherished landmark in the community.[8]

A late 20th-century design movement that challenges the principles of *Critical Regionalism* is *Deconstructivism*, a facet of Complexity and Chaos Theory mentioned earlier. Made possible by developments in civil engineering and computer-aided design, the deconstructionist architects set out to challenge the shapes that architects had used before. They searched for the appearance of jumbled, unruly building forms, often seeming to be fragmented but having an organic quality to them as in Figure 12.5. This was a revised design by Randall Stout Architects.

The internal spaces provide plenty of opportunity for art galleries, but also provide sculptural experiences provided by the building forms themselves (Figure 12.6). The unexpected, rather exotic qualities of the design provide an intriguing place. This exudes the feelings of excitement and imagination that contemporary art embraces. Many visitors[9] found the building the most impressive part of their visit, but the friendliness of the staff was still mentioned more often.

The original building in Figure 12.7, designed by Donald G. Bittorf and B. James Wensle, was acknowledged as in the *Brutalist* style. That arose in the mid-20th century. It is known for its massive, monolithic forms typically using concrete slabs. As with

Figure 12.5 Art Gallery of Alberta, Edmonton

Figure 12.6 Inside the Art Gallery of Alberta, Edmonton

most of the other architectural styles following modernism in the second half of the 20th century, and into the present century a primary objective is to make bold statement in the urban landscape, to be noticed.

All these movements in architecture generated buildings that do, in general, respond to their brief. They provide more or less appropriate accommodation, but it is clear that they reflect a particular way of sculpting space. The change in the Art Gallery in Edmonton is a shining example of how architectural style is used to make daring statements about the building. It is no accident that many of the most startling examples are major art galleries and other public buildings associated with the arts, such as opera houses and theatres. The management of these places wants to draw attention to their building. They are also pleased to embrace the current styles and trends in the arts.

Those buildings emerging out of post-modernism can perhaps be best regarded in a similar way to many creations of modern art and contemporary music. Their enigmatic

Figure 12.7 The Edmonton Art Gallery (before its reconstruction as the Art Gallery of Alberta)

quality is an invitation for the observer and user to impose their own interpretation of what sort of meaning it may have. As aspects of Places, they offer the prospect of reading the opportunities the Place may provide. There is excitement in engaging with the potential meanings of the Places, as there is with a painting by Kandinsky or music by Webern.

The cathedrals and castles of the 21st century

The buildings illustrated, and many others that have shaken off the shackles of the Bauhaus and its followers, reveal an ostentatious demonstration of the significance of a building. Like the cathedrals and castles of earlier centuries, as well as the grand houses of rich landowners and the aristocracy they declare 'here we are'. 'We are this Place', join us if you wish. This has given rise (literally) to an even more brazen claiming of the ego of Place, with buildings that set out to be visible iconic landmarks.

As Jenks[10] declares they are:

> Driven by social and commercial forces and the demand for instant fame, it has to be both an amazing piece of surreal sculpture and an understated insertion into

> the urban fabric...[This is the creation] of a series of lively architectural icons that have courted publicity and controversy in equal measure. Some are successful creations that fulfil their contradictory requirements; others are Malapropistic metaphors that make the public wince.

Following his earlier foray into the 'language of post-modernism' Jenks offers provocative associations of the meanings these buildings, illustrated in Figure 12.8, might have. Often, however, public discourse encouraged by journalists' headlines has created these references before architectural commentators.

Beyond design agendas

As Lindstrom[11] argues the successors to modernism protested against "a universal design agenda", but "simply substituted and asserted their own design agendas". "Everything from Postmodernism...to Deconstructionism, and Biophilic Design..." provide an "alternative set of rules (including rules to challenge all rules) that supposedly lead to a superior outcome". The problem with this he states is that their rules, by their limited focus, and inherent selectivity restrict the aspects of Places that are considered. They advocate "agendas of various well-intentioned but always narrower movements".

Later architectural developments, inevitably influenced by the move away from such distinct references and ornamentation, eschewed obvious symbols and searched for a more welcoming and domestic style. A demonstration that the meaning imbued into architecture may have roots quite different from those of the heralded isms of the second half of the 20th century and beyond.

Although my comments have been cursory, attention has been paid to movements in architecture. This is because they illustrate the source of the rhetoric that elaborates the discussions of these styles. It offers perspectives on the significance of geometrical and sculptural forms. Whether the approach to design is framed as a desire to create a sense of Place, or to respond to urban and social needs, or any of the other patinas that are used to coat the architectural offering. Their mission is typically to tackle building forms in new and exciting ways. That architects can sell their ideas and vast sums of money are spent on them is testimony to architects' power and the obvious delight many have in their products.

Whose meaning?

The excitement, or dismay, generated by the examples of different movements in architecture over the last century or more, is less obvious when other than major buildings that shout for attention are the focus. Notable examples are those built by the Christian movement known as The Salvation Army. As made clear in the account of the history of its building in Britain, those buildings symbolised its mission "to save souls, grow saints and serve suffering humanity".[12] This Christian movement, being based on the structure and metaphor of an army, designated its early buildings as citadels and fortresses, incorporating "square towers at the corners, battlements and Crusader crosses"[13] (Figure 12.9).

Figure 12.8 Recently built 'architectural icons' in London: (a) 'the Gherkin', (b) 'the Shard', (c) 'Walkie Talkie Tower'

Figure 12.9 Salvation Army Citadel, Sheffield, United Kingdom

The Salvation Army Architecture Department is one example of a rather different approach to architecture from the much-proclaimed movements considered earlier. They illustrate other approaches that seek to give Places meaning beyond the rhetoric of architectural movements. Not surprisingly, these often relate to buildings that are not great exhibits of innovation and the eye-catching.

A rather different approach, from self-effacing Salvation Army architects, to what he calls 'humanising' buildings is the eclectic designer, Thomas Heatherwick.[14] He is a strong advocate for the much richer and more complex consideration of building designs. Reflecting some of the concerns of Prince Charles, considered earlier, the central feature of his polemic is the claim that architectural modernism is boring. In doing this he mainly ignores the outrages of many post-modern buildings, especially those in the 'deconstructionist' mode. Although he applauds the Burj Khalifa building in Dubai "because it's interesting enough from a city distance to create its own sense of place".[15] Heatherwick gives no indication what sort of Place this 830-metre-high spire gives a sense of. It is just a supreme example of what Jenks called an Iconic Landmark. That is not unlike the original such edifices, The Eiffel Tower and even the magnificent Taj Mahal. By its striking presence and the hub of activities it accommodates, such as galleries and restaurants, it becomes a vertical piazza that contributes to the identity of the city.

Heatherwick's main stance, though, focuses on adding details to designs in order to 'humanise' them. As an illustration, he offers the sort of complex highly patterned buildings of the Spanish maverick architect Antoni Guadi, as a model for Heatherwick of what architects should create. The emphasis is on the way people experience buildings, at least at a visual level. He elaborates this perspective by articulating the components of the built environment that contribute to those experiences. He does this by reference to the scales at which we experience buildings *in situ*, rather than as photographs in a magazine.

Three different levels of engagement with buildings are explored; distances of 40 metres, which Heatherwick calls the 'city level', closer around 20 metres – 'the street', and then in touching distance, 2 metres – 'the door'. As summarised in Table 12.1, this elaboration draws attention to the different scales at which buildings can contribute to the meaning of Places. That provides an important insight into the rich mixture of ways that buildings influence Place experience. It opens up a way of thinking about Places that is not often considered in the psychological or geographic literature. Throughout his advocacy Heatherwick emphasises the need for richness and complexity. There is no engagement with the Places being affected by the details of built form he discusses.

Heatherwick's proposals have been dismissed as being merely a plea for architectural populism,[16] with little conceptual or practical substance. This criticism reveals a paternalistic perspective that architecture that is 'popular' is somehow degraded. It has to have some theory that explains it, even if this is just as a response to practical challenges. Such an argument illustrates Heatherwick's claim that architects conceptualise buildings very differently from those without design training. Studies demonstrating this were reviewed in Chapter 7. Given that buildings are part of the life of people in so many other ways, architects completing their training with different ways of thinking about buildings from the rest of us, does support Heatherwick's argument that this gives rise to buildings that need 'humanising'.

Bottom-up design – building patterns

A different approach to generating designs, which carries implications for experiencing Places, is the proposal of components that can be drawn on, mix-and-match, for putting together buildings. This contrasts with what might be thought of as the top-down, grand theories of what buildings should be, whether driven, for instance, by the irony of post-modernism, or the search for the complexity of Humanising. The collections of components to draw upon are usually presented as Architectural Pattern books. These kits of parts have a long history in architecture. Drawing on Vitruvius' original proposals Renaissance architects, spearheaded by Andrea Palladio,

Table 12.1 Heatherwick's proposal for the way buildings "must be of interest" at different distances

Scale	*Distance*	*Interestingness*
City distance	over 40 metres	Sits in vision entirely. Has the power to make us feel something.
Street distance	around 20 metres	Texture and personality, celebrates its use.
Door distance	about 2 metres	Reveals any complexity in its details and materials

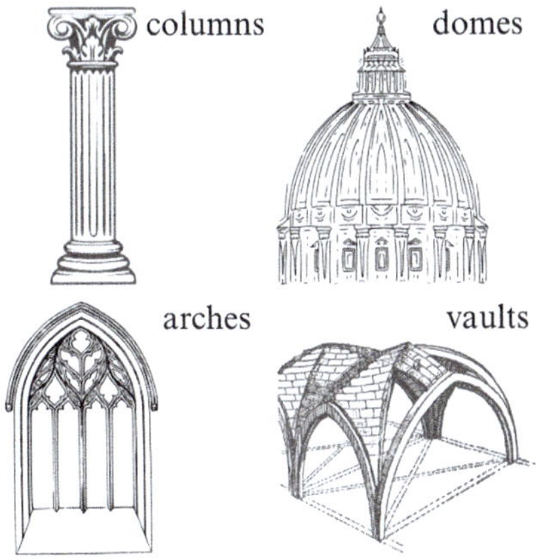

Figure 12.10 Examples of the components of buildings that Renaissance architects could work with

mentioned earlier, had a set of building components they could work with, as indicated in Figure 12.10. Although they had their origins in ancient Greece and Rome, they were drawn on across Europe from the 16th century right through to the end of the 19th century. There are even hints today in many aspects of post-modernism, as indicated earlier.

In the 19th century Architectural Pattern Books[17] became important resources, especially allowing middle-class clients to work with carpenters and builders. They had more to do with what was acceptable than the supposedly rational approach of Palladianism. They were crucial for Victorian house building, enabling the dissemination of good taste in housing. It is notable that such sets of elements to use were typically aimed at smaller scale, domestic places, as in Figure 12.11. They were not for the grand 'Iconic' buildings that aimed to be different and notable.[18] The houses illustrated indicated something of the owners' aesthetic choices. In so doing they indicated what might be expected about those who inhabited the house. The nature of the home within.

Christopher Alexander's pattern language

The complexities of architecture, and how the people who produce buildings create the foundations for Places, do pose great challenges for any attempt to provide clear guidelines for design that can go beyond any particular context. There has, however, been one brave attempt, widely cited, to surmount the challenges of the contextual influence and the difficulty of making sense of physical forms. These are the biblical-like tomes of Christopher Alexander's *A Pattern Language*,[20] and his earlier analysis of the design process under the heading *Notes on the Synthesis of Form*.[21] Where the Victorians were concerned with good taste and a shared aesthetic, a latter-day pattern book developed by Christopher Alexander and his colleagues claimed to be oriented more directly at human comforts and enjoyment of Places. It consequently comes closest to a set of prescriptions that are intended to generate meanings that characterise particular Place experiences.

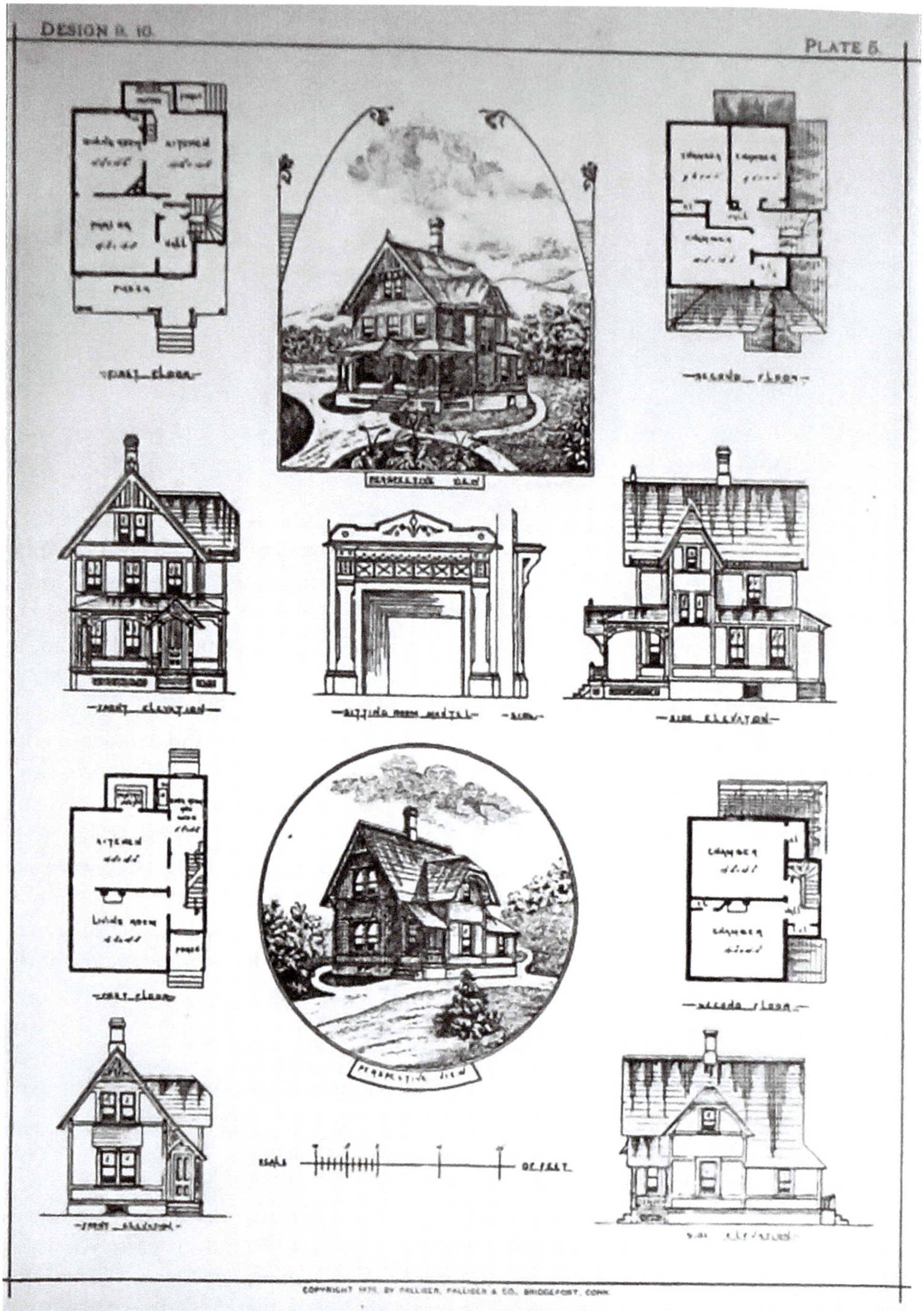

Figure 12.11 Example from a Victorian house pattern book[19]

At the heart of Alexander's argument is the proposal that all design aims to solve problems. In other words, it is a 1960s elaboration of the statement made in 1896 by the architect Louis Sullivan when proposing how tall office buildings should be designed, namely "form follows function". Sullivan was claiming that the outside of a skyscraper should reflect the functions of what goes on inside. However, Alexander's approach to the 'synthesis of form' takes this idea further in two ways. One is that design decisions are part of a hierarchy. He unpacks the ways in which the complex forms and structures that are the end result of design can be built up from simpler, basic, components. This is argued using a sophisticated mathematics to illustrate the essentially hierarchical nature of the designer's task.

Thie hierarchical model is a much more sophisticated way of considering the creation of Places than earlier pattern books or the more recent grand missions of architectural isms. An elaboration of this hierarchical framework is given by reference to the top of the hierarchy being wider-ranging decisions that cover overall aspects of a design, such as appropriate layout for a region or town. He then moves down through this to make decisions about a building and eventually a room. At any level of scale, Alexander urges the need for consideration of the interconnections between different scales. He introduces the idea of a search for 'wholeness' in which the parts and what they are part of are integrated into a successful entity. A perspective that would not be alien to Vitruvius or Palladio.

A second emphasis in Alexander's proposals for how design is to be carried out is to involve potential users in the design process. This is usually couched in reference to those who the city, building or room is intended to house. He advocates design decisions being built around the needs, experiences, and well-being of the people who will use the resulting design. He followed this up by the assertion that clearly identifying the purposes of a design, whether at the scale of a town, or a living room, should generate solutions. He and his colleagues identified 253 common purposes across cities, neighbourhoods, buildings and rooms. For each of these functions he proposed 'patterns' that dealt with the problems the functions enshrined.

A typical example is *Pattern 18: Network of Learning.* For this he maintains that education should be decentralised. Learning should happen through a network of small schools. These should be enhanced by informal settings that are integrated into the community. It is interesting to note that this proposal leans towards the polemical arguments of Ivan Illich, an Austrian priest, whose views many would regard as anarchist. He describes his views in detail in his 1971 book with the challenging title *Deschooling Society.* That connection helps to reveal that Alexander's pattern language examples are not devoid of ideological commitments.

Another example is *Pattern 181: The Fire.* This is based on the view that "There is no substitute for fire. Television often gives a focus to a room but is nothing but a feeble substitute for something which is actually alive and flickering in a room....". This idea is somewhat contested by a 1974 study of the focal point of a living room[22] carried out in Strathclyde School of Architecture. That concluded "focus is related to attention, which in turn is related to activity, so the focus may range from say the book while reading, through the occupants when conversing, to the room as a whole, and such things as fireplaces...adequate foci should be provided at all scales".[23]

If only it were that simple

Alexander's proposals are often cited and venerated. In his noble attempt to formulate distinct design solutions that are of general value, he reveals why that is not universally possible. Consideration of the contradictions within his writings serve to elaborate why no set of measurements of physical form can be provided independently of the whole social and psychological context in which they are to be used.

Alexander's insistence that users should be involved in design decisions ignores the great many different groups that 'use' a place. The owners, financiers, different professional groups and those who stay or move through a place all have some stake in what the place should be like. They will each have different degrees of influence over any design decisions. The suggestion (which I totally endorse) that design decisions should respond to the well-being and experiences, of those who will use a Place, is really a political, or even an ideological stance. It is not a neutral, solely objective decision. As noted in relation to pattern 18, Alexander's recommendation on schools is only a short step away from Illich's political activism.

There is also an inherent contradiction between the recommendation of user involvement in design and then producing 253 apparently generic design solutions. Pattern 181, on the value of having a fire in a room, whilst being one I personally have acted on, ignores climate and cultural traditions. It also has been superseded by laws banning open fires in houses because of climate degradation and their contribution to greenhouse gases.

The hierarchical perspective, whilst being apparently convincing, seems to be ignored by the pattern language. For example, pattern 180 *A window place* is based on the requirement "in every room where you spend any length of time during the day, make at least one window into a 'window place'" (p. 837). Yet the nature of windows in a building will often have been determined by overall design decisions. These may relate to what the view out would be, orientation of the building, or general stylistic requirements, which in their turn may be influenced by planning regulations or concerns to ensure the building is environmentally sustainable.

The distinct challenges of identifying those physical aspects of Places that can be generally specified is, perhaps ironically, illustrated by the fact that Alexander's writings have been taken up more assiduously by software developers than architects and other designers. I think this is mainly because they are the only creators that have common problems to solve that do not also draw readily on ideology, subjective judgements and embedded aesthetic influences.

The implications of human agency

The recognition that actions give Places meaning, with the physical form contributing to that, implies a dynamic process of constant interplay between actions and the Places they are part of. Although this dynamic process may stabilise from time to time, the general implication is that built form has to be responsive to the changes in the interactions between Places and actions. One intriguing study, carried out half a century ago, reflected the power of this.

The opportunity was provided in a study of 15 schools, which had recently been built, to examine what changes had been made in the use of space in the buildings since they were opened.[24] In a unique co-operation, an architect checked the current layout of the building against the original plans. By counting the number of modifications, he was able to give each school a score, such that the higher the score the more modifications that had been made. In addition, an environmental psychologist carried out a survey of the satisfaction of the staff with their new school building. An average score across all staff responses gave an overall indication of how satisfied they were with the building.

There are three possible hypotheses of what the relationships may be between the number of modifications and overall satisfaction with the building. One is that the building was so unsuitable that modifications were a way of coping with that. In which case a negative correlation may be predicted. It could be that modifications were of little significance producing a zero correlation. Or it could be that flexibility of the design was such that modifications allowed people to use the building in the way they wanted, giving rise to a positive correlation. What was found was a clear strong positive correlation as illustrated in Figure 12.12. Those buildings with few modifications only achieved low levels of satisfaction overall. Those with many modifications were those the teachers were most satisfied with. Consequently, the study of school buildings demonstrates the benefits of what people do to their buildings to create the sorts of Places they want. That value of that modification is powerful support for taking account of human agency in design.

A little more about the nature of the agency of the teachers and administrators can be gleaned from the three areas of the relationship shown in Figure 12.12. Area A shows a general low level of satisfaction with little modification of the building. This suggests either sluggish management or limited possibilities in the building. This latter may have been caused by overcrowding that did not allow any spare capacity for modification, or a design that did not allow modification. Area B shows a spread of moderate to higher satisfaction with a moderate level of modification. There are many

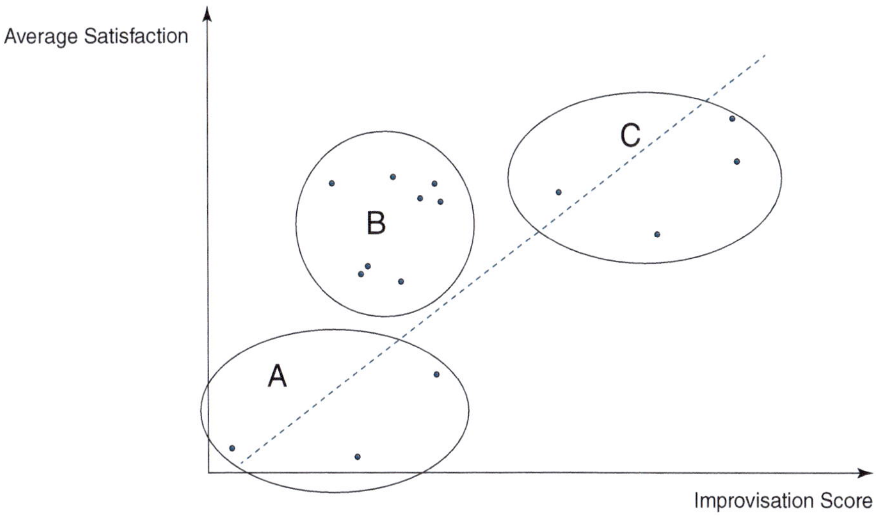

Figure 12.12 Relationship between satisfaction and amount of modification of a school building[25]

processes going on in these eight schools. That raises questions about the differences in the nature of the interactions between the users and the building form. Unfortunately, there is no data to clarify that. Area C shows an overall high relationship between improvisatory modification and satisfaction. These four schools were each able to make of their building what they wanted.

The demonstration that what people can do to their buildings to create the sorts of Places they want is powerful support for taking account of human agency in design. This is a finding that is often derided by purist architects and architectural critics. A fascinating example of this is the study[26] of Le Corbusier's housing development in Quartier Fruges in Pessac, France. The designs of the 70 houses there were developed from mathematical formulae of how spaces could be arranged into different house forms.

The architect, Philippe Boudon, closely studied the houses in Pessac to determine the changes that the occupants had made over time to Le Corbusier's modernist designs. He found almost all of them made changes to their houses. For instance, the colour was changed; the flat roof was remodelled to be pitched roof; the ribbon windows were changed to be narrow windows; the compartment wall was moved, and the passageways were changed visually or structurally. They had added new rooms and altered the terraces and roofs. This produced buildings very different from the geometric purity of Le Corbusier's original vision. These modifications reflected the background and lifestyles of the residents, which had been ignored in the original formulations.

Critics of Le Corbusier's decision to base the design of this worker's housing on his modernistic, geometric concepts[27] argue that the changes the inhabitants had made showed that Le Corbusier's sense of modern beauty did not always match up with the needs of the general public. Furthermore, the critics claimed that the users of the houses had rejected Le Corbusier's typology and consequently Le Corbusier's designs were a failure.[28] These designs are designated a failure because it is asserted that they ignore the dynamic nature of Places and the ways in which buildings evolve through their use by people. However, an alternative view is that the buildings were extremely successful. They facilitated so many different ways of in which people could modify them, interact with them to create the sorts of homes in which they wanted to live. That may not have been Le Corbusier's intention, but it is nonetheless a salutary indication of the power of users' interactions with built forms and the benefits the possibilities of that interaction can bring.

Some design considerations that influence the experience of places

The combination of potential affordances, cultural and personal meanings, drawing on Place experiences and known actions, has generated a number of Place-specific features of physical forms. These illustrate the subtle and varied ways in which aspects of design carry implications for being in Place. There are many relevant features of a design that allow these interactions. Some are more universal than others. Some are specific to particular cultures and times in history.[29] Or they may have very individual or personal implications. This all suggests that there may be other ways of considering the contribution of architecture to the meaning Places have. These could be attempts to avoid grand geometric or architectural theories or to provide patterns of built form from which people may choose. Instead, by considering the experience of Places and how built form interacts with that experience, other emphases emerge. The following list is not incompatible with many of the proposals explored earlier. Indeed, it reflects some of them. The main difference is that this is a list of Place relevant features and processes, rather than specific design recommendations.

Entrances

The initial indication of the nature of the Place you are entering is typically reflected in how the entrance is formed. This idea is inherent in Palladian design but does not require specific proposals of what entrances should look like. Rather, they can draw upon what is appropriate for any particular Place at any point in time.

What can you tell about Gwydir Castle from Figure 12.13a? It is not an exceptionally imposing entrance for a location with 'Castle' in its title. There is no door or other blockage apparent to actually close the entrance. A little ornamentation and decoration do imply an attempt to designate this entrance as somewhat special. The symbolic, functionally unnecessary shape on the top of the gate adds a further flourish to suggest some significance to the Place you are coming into. That is further enhanced by the vision through the gateway of the avenue of careful topiary seen through the gate.

Figure 12.13 (a and b) Front and back Entrances at Gwydir Castle LLanrhychwyn, North Wales

The entrance in Figure 12.13b is a simpler affair, although it still has a curved stone on the top. There is no difficulty in deciding which gateway implies an important way into the 'castle' and which is probably a back or side entrance of less importance.

These two examples have been chosen because of the relatively small differences in their details. Grand entrances to cathedrals, palaces or parliament buildings, for instance, all exude many features that declare the nature of the Places behind their grand doors. Those at Gwydir Castle reveal how even subtle aspects of entrances typically carry symbolic weight. A further point is that the lack of doors, or gates in Figures 12.13a and 12.13b is an indication that they are entrances to a Place open to the public. This is no longer a personal palace.

Height

Rapoport[30] notes the common experience that "height, in the sense above/below (in context), may be an important universal category for indicating the meaning of importance". He mentions cathedrals and churches, and how the throne is nearly always above those who must pay obeisance to whoever sits on it. The perceptual implications of this have already been noted earlier, but the symbolic, and in many cases functional, significance of being higher, 'above the masses' extends much further. I have yet to come across a Vice Chancellor, or President, of a university, whose office is not at the highest point of the campus. The Chief Executive Officers of most organisations choose to have their offices on the top floor. One unusual example I know of, was a company Director who chose to have his office on the ground floor near the front entrance. This was a determined statement to indicate his involvement with the workforce. A clear example of the exception proving the rule.

Of course, a tall entrance with great ornamentation, incorporating emblems, is only to be expected for Places of symbolic significance. This also means that when such entrances are created in contexts that seem inappropriate, they smack of falsification. Such as a highly decorated entrance with Corinthian columns to a small house.

Size

The physical size of a space, whether it is a Neolithic monument like Stonehenge, or the size of a person's living room, the expanse of the Grand Canyon, or the corner of a rose garden, deeply invests meaning derived from its scale. This will take on special significance when comparison is made with other locations. A crucial part of this are the resources needed to support, create or make use of it. This aspect goes to the heart of the meaning of Places. Size, or scale, on its own carries little significance. It is when there is consideration of the associated ideas and understanding of the human implications of the apparent magnitude of the Place, that its meaning unfolds. It is when who, are likely to do what, in a Place; the roles and rules that are, can or may be carried out there that the meanings of that being there emerges.

Seven aspects of buildings that reflect their roles in contributing to the nature of Places[31]:

Openness

Physical form does help to indicate the boundaries of a Place. But those boundaries may be permeable or impermeable to various degrees. The extent of possible interpenetration will influence the experience of the Place.

Context

Places derive part of their meanings from the relationships between them. The central issue explored in Chapter 9 when considering Space Syntax. That reflects the movement between Places and their context. This highlights the dynamic aspects of Places experienced. Places never exist for just one point in time. Following Heatherwick's three distances, Places are present from afar to close up. They also exist in representations, in the memory and conceptually. That is why dramatic and unusual building forms contribute to the meaning of a Place as much as memories of a childhood home.

Contextual fit[32]

Consideration of scale as well as size, height, distance from key locations, materials and form, as they relate to Places in the vicinity of any construction, all influence how a Place is understood and experienced. Effective architecture often starts from consideration of the location of the building. This may be orientation to the passage of the sun, sight lines in relation to neighbouring buildings, the shape of the site and the nature and qualities of buildings in the area. Relating to all of these, and many others, or ignoring them, will generate a physical form that contributes to the feeling of the Place it houses.

Materials

Different kinds of wood, steel, glass and concrete, bricks and stone, all carry meanings and associations. They imply, and often are experienced directly through, touch, acoustic and thermal qualities. Changing materials can change the nature of a Place.

Mass and form

Squares, circles, complex or simple, carry implications, but how they give meaning to a Place depends on what they are part of. Considering them as mere abstractions is doomed to failure because they will always mean something. Are circular windows a reference to portholes, or eyes, or a nudge towards modernism and all that entails.

Identifying places

As many of the illustrations in this chapter demonstrate, the experience and meaning of numerous Places is profoundly influenced by features that identify the significance and nature of that Place. This identity may be an indirect consequence of the built form or may be a conscious decision to proclaim what goes on there.

Conclusions

Although architectural design theories are typically reference styles or movements in architecture, the demise of modernism has generated a plethora of approaches which often deny simple classification. Modernism, with its emphasis on simplicity and function, often overlooked the human and cultural dimensions of architecture. This led to a backlash and the emergence of post-modernism, which sought to reintroduce historical references, ornamentation, and a sense of Place. The subsequent architectural movements, including Critical Regionalism and Deconstructivism, further challenged the rigid norms of the past, advocating for designs that respond to local contexts and human experiences. The ongoing dialogue between these styles underscores the importance of considering the diverse needs and interpretations of users, as well as the broader social and environmental implications of architectural design. Ultimately, the quest for meaningful and humane architecture continues to evolve, driven by the desire to create Places that resonate with people and their surroundings.

References and endnotes

1 Hanly, J. (20240The future of social housing: 7 low-rise, high-density developments. *Architizer Journal*, https://architizer.com/blog/inspiration/collections/low-rise-high-density accessed January 2026.
2 San Francisco in 2024.
3 Modern neoclassical architecture. *Apollo Magazine*, accessed January 2025.
4 Jencks, C. (1977) *The language of post-modern architecture*, New York: Rizzoli.
5 Jencks (1977) *The language of post-modern architecture*, p. 39.
6 Jencks, C., & Kropf, K. (2006)(Eds.) *Theories and manifestoes of contemporary architecture* (2nd ed.). New York: Wiley-Academy.
7 Frampton, K. (1983) Towards a critical regionalism: Six points for an architecture of resistance, in H. Foster (Ed.) *The anti-aesthetic: Essays on postmodern culture*, Port Townsend, WA: Bay Press, pp. 1–13.
8 Aalto, A. (2024). Säynätsalo Town Hall, 1949–1952. In *Great Windows in Modern Architecture* (pp. 86–97). London: Routledge.
9 www.tripadvisor.co.uk. Who needs user surveys when Trip Advisor has 334 reviews?
10 Jencks, C. (2005) *The iconic building*, London: Frances Lincoln.
11 Jencks (2005) *The iconic building*, p. 97.
12 Oakley, R. (2011) *To the glory of God*, Lemington Spa: Ray Oakley Publication, ISBN978 085412 827 3, p. 7.
13 Oakley, R. (2011) *To the glory of God*, Lemington Spa: Ray Oakley Publication, ISBN978 085412 827 3, p. 57.
14 Heatherwick, T. (2023) *Humanise: A maker's guide to building our world*. London: Random House.
15 Heatherwick (2023) *Humanise*, p. 404.
16 Bevan, R. (2024). Design for living? A manifesto for architectural populism. *Times Literary Supplement*, (6308), 7–8.
17 Long, H. (2002) *Victorian houses and their details: The role of publication in their building and decoration*, London: Architectural Press.
18 Exhibition on 19th-century DIY architecture manuals - Core77, accessed 5 February 2025.
19 From *Palliser's new cottage homes and details* from the 1880s. Published in 1975 by Da Capo Press.
20 Alexander, C. (2018). *A pattern language: Towns, buildings, construction*, London: Oxford University Press.
21 Alexander, C. (1964). *Notes on the synthesis of form* (Vol. 5), Cambridge, MA: Harvard University Press, p. 838.
22 Canter, D., Gilchrist, J., Miller, J., & Roberts, N. (1974) An empirical study of the focal point in the living room, in D. Canter & T. Lee (Eds.) *Psychology and the built environment*, London: Architectural Press, pp. 29–37.
23 Canter, Gilchrist, Miller, & Roberts (1974) An empirical study of the focal point in the living room, p. 37.
24 This study is described in Markus, T. (Ed.) (1972) *Building performance*, London: Wiley. The architect for the study was Peter Whyman. I was the psychologist.
25 Markus, T., Whyman, P., Morgan, J., Whitton, D., Maver, T., Canter, D., & Flemming, J. (1972) *Building performance*, London: Applied Science Publishers, p. 77.
26 Boudon, P. (1972) Lived-in architecture: Le Corbusier's Pessac revisited, Cambridge, MA: MIT Press.
27 Hsu, C. C. & Shih, C. M. (2006) A typological housing design: The case study of Quartier Fruges in Pessac by Le Corbusier. *Journal of Asian Architecture and Building Engineering*, 5(1), 75–82.

28 Wang, M. H. (1996) Typological specification as a housing design method. *Journal of Housing Studies*, 4 (Jan), 31–49.

29 The wonderful book, first published in 1856, reprinted as Jones, O. (2016) *The grammar of ornament: A visual reference of form and colour in architecture and the decorative arts—The complete and unabridged full-color edition*, Princeton University Press, is a delightful and fascinating exploration that even decorative features, typically considered as mere ornament, have deep cultural and historical significance.

30 Rapoport, A. (1990). *The meaning of the built environment: A nonverbal communication approach*. Tucson: University of Arizona Press. p. 80.

31 Canter, D. (1993) Chapter 81: Personal aspects of the architectural experience, in B. Farmer & H. Louw (Eds.) *Companion to contemporary architectural thought*,London: Routledge pp. 488–491.

32 Explored in detail in her PhD by Groat, L. N. (1985) *Psychological aspects of contextual compatibility in architecture: A study of environmental meaning*. PhD Dissertation, University of Surrey, United Kingdom (unpublished).

SECTION III

The City

DOI: 10.4324/9780367808655-16

CHAPTER 13

The city street

The character of a city is defined by its streets and public places. From squares and boulevards to neighbourhood gardens and children's playgrounds, public space frames the city image

Dr Joan Clos, Under-Secretary-General of the United Nations[1]

The street at eyelevel – the plinth

> The ground floor is where building and town meet, where we urbanites have our close encounters with buildings, where we can touch and be touched by them.[2]

A new movement of designers proclaims the importance of creating places for 'The city at eye level', summarised as reimagining the city's *Plinth* (Figure 13.1). Using this word draws attention to the idea that the plinth supports the city in the same way that a pedestal provides a firm foundation to define a sculpture, rather as a frame does on a picture. It also emphasises crucial aspects of cities that give them their unique identities. Just as little attention is typically paid to the pedestal a statue is standing on, planning processes that focus on commercial and overt functions often ignore the experiences generated by Places that city streets embrace.

What can be seen at eye level in a city reflects, in many different ways, what that city is taken to be. That is obviously the case for old cities in which tourists flock to the 'old quarters' to enjoy the ambiance and qualities of Places. But it is even the case for new cities, dominated by skyscrapers. The aerial view may be apparent from rooftop apartments, but it is still at ground level that the citizens share a similar experience of what the city is.

A significant aspect of the city plinth is that they are the Places where people experience the public realm. The ground floor is where building façades, shop fronts and cafés, street events, and many other interactions between personal or organisational concerns and public interests occur. It is no accident that a frequent reference drawn from Jane Jacobs' influential account of the demise of cities[4] is her reference to "eyes on

DOI: 10.4324/9780367808655-17

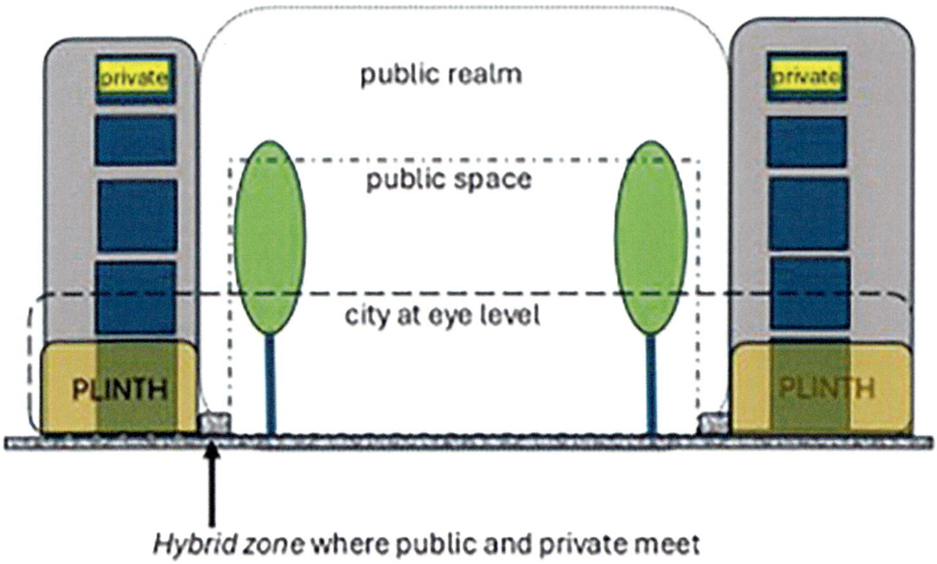

Figure 13.1 Illustrating the concept of the plinth on the street[3]

the street". This is the idea that streets are more secure and alive when residents and shopkeepers, as well as those who use the streets as pedestrians, or shoppers, are aware of what is going on there. She claimed that this provides an informal surveillance, which contributes to friendly social interaction and a sense of community. All generate the feelings of particular Places. This is an awareness that it is the reaching out from private realms to participate in communal experiences that creates the places that are experienced as the city at eye level.

There is such a rich panoply of Places and their features that streets encapsulate and generate that consequently this chapter, more than any others, is in part a photographic essay. I have to confess a delight in photographing the use of streets around the world. The invasion of personal or private activities into this public domain reveals a lot about the way people give a Place its special meaning. As will be demonstrated, the variations between the Places where people gather or pass through, linger or avoid, are indicative of the culture and history, values and habits that give the Places that make up streets their meanings.

Examining city streets and other public locations, which they link together as Places, provides insights into the complex interplay that creates the nature and experiences being there. The physical features, meanings and activities that are combined on the street elucidate what Places really are. This in turn influences what people expect to happen there, which produces a further cycle of meaning from what does go on..

Each facet of a Place interacts with the others to give rise to a Place's unique quality. The meaning and identity of a street corner are modified by painted walls. Street entertainers change what might be a pedestrian bridge into a concert hall. The history of a particular location changes how people may act there. Furthermore, by their very nature streets, squares and boulevards, as well as neighbourhood gardens and children's playgrounds are, dynamic Places. They change by the hour, day, season and over history.

Figure 13.2 A *thermopolium* in ancient Rome used to serve hot food and beverages to passersby, creating a special Place on the street

Public–private interaction

By their nature and presence within the city, streets have always been the source of transactions from private to public domains. Evidence for this is readily seen as far back as the 1st century. Figure 13.2, from Pompeii, shows what today would be recognised as a 'fast-food counter', known as a *thermopolium*. A barrier, containing the counter, is built between the residence and the street. Within the counter are places for cauldrons that would hold hot food so that a Roman version of McDonald's is created. A new Place on the street typical of the management of public and private domains.

The 1st-century Roman example is a powerful illustration of the way the High Street (or in the US, Main Street) evolved into a mixture of shopping areas and areas for meeting, inspired by people selling goods from their house.[5]They transformed from medieval marketplaces to modern shopping precincts. This had cultural and social significance, highlighting their role as community hubs. Shopping habits have changed rapidly, even during this century. Buying online, out-of-town retail parks, megabrands dominating high streets making them indistinguishable from each other, and working from home have all led to changes in what happens on urban streets. Yet they do survive and still house many different Places of importance for personal and civic endeavours.

The power of the prosaic

One of the reasons that streets are still so powerful for the study of the psychology of Place is that although they may seem like general amorphous locations that carry little personal importance, that has never been the whole story. The profound significance which even small aspects of streets may have was illustrated in Marcel Proust's major novel that explores memory in all its nuances. As he wrote:

> One of my feet stepped on a flagstone lower than the ones next to it ... and then, all at once, I recognised that Venice which my descriptive efforts and pretended snapshots of memory had failed to recall; the sensation I had once felt on two uneven slats in the Baptistry of St Mark had given back to me and was linked with all the other sensations of that and other days which had lingered expectant in their place among the series of forgotten years from which a sudden change had imperiously called them forth.
>
> *(Proust, 1957, pp. 210–211)*

Enjoying the details of city streets seems to be a particularly French pastime. The founder of surrealism André Breton[6] even declared that walking the streets was a form of poetry. Being a flaneur, mentioned in Chapter 3, is a way of being in an urban environment, wandering more or less aimlessly. The pleasure in these activities is surely to experience and be part of the many different Places that streets embrace.

Proust's account of details of a specific context triggering distant memories is a prescient forerunner to many psychological studies of the power of the physical context to reinstate long-forgotten memories.[7] Streets can consequently be seen as redolent with many meanings. I remember, as a lovelorn teenager, empathising with the love song 'On the Street Where You Live' written by Alan Jay Lerner for the 1956 Broadway musical *My Fair Lady*. The street in which the target of the singer's affections lives is lauded as having unique qualities. They are a consequence of the special inhabitant. That illustrates how Places can feel very different because of the private meanings of its inhabitant.

At a less personal level, it has been found the presence of Westerners in historic districts of Japan increased the positive evaluations of those locations by Japanese students'.[8] Aspects of Takayama City were seen as more active and unique with the obvious presence of tourists. This helps to explain that whenever I have been in tourist places in Japan, I have always been asked to pose for photographs with Japanese visitors. The mere presence of 外国人 (gaikokujin[9] – literally person from a foreign country, not only Westerners) adds to the meaning of a place..

Even for tourists, what may be regarded as prosaic aspects of cities, often give definition to Places as they are experienced. A number of studies have shown that "while the large-scale symbolic elements may draw tourists to a site, it is the everyday features ... that shape their impressions of the destination as a *place* once there".[10]

Interviewing tourists in Budapest it was found that:

> "Not a single reference was made to the Castle District, Heroes' Square, the Parliament or any other overtly symbolic sites in the city. Rather, the significant factors in shaping tourists' experience of the city as specifically Hungarian were its ensemble, the buildings and their varied architectural styles, the street signs

and shop names with indecipherable Hungarian words, the street layout and the cars, and of course the people and the food."[11]

Intriguingly, this study is titled "Background to the Fore". That is surely another way of drawing attention to the plinth rather than the monument that sits on it?

There are many examples of how particular features of streets act as a focus that draws in many other meanings. Foreign tourists are an example of how the experience of the Place may be powerfully influenced by particular details. This is an aspect of human cognition well established in studies of person perception.[12] First impressions of another person typically operate holistically. One characteristic may dominate and influence many others. To be aware that a person is 'warm' has been noted to relate to judgements of intelligence, honesty and other characteristics. But thinking a person is intelligent, for example, may not have such a wide-ranging influence. Anecdotal examples can be readily found of how particular features of public places colour all the thinking about those places. (Although I could not find any detailed studies of this.[13])

One prime example is the conceptualisation many hold of Amsterdam. This is highlighted by the tourist trinkets on sale, as illustrated in Figure 13.3(a), fridge magnets. Together with the distinctive windmill emblem for Holland, rather prettified images of the sex workers that ply their trade in the Red-Light District of Amsterdam, De Wallen, are take-home mementos that capture a way of thinking about the place.

Figure 13.3a Fridge magnets for sale in Amsterdam

This is another instance of how the activities that can be seen on streets give an identity to these Places. This may be threatening or salacious, enjoyable or disquieting. It can, however, be an aspect of the identity of a Place that is embraced by tourists, especially those who regard themselves as ironically witty.

The mixture of disgust and fascination provides a complex mixture of responses around the acceptance that this "is what Amsterdam is Famous for".[14] That provides an acceptance of the image of the city. This was consciously generated by the controlled area of 230 single-room cabins with windows on the street where women are allowed to promote their offerings.

Whilst the identity of De Wallen has a long history, the advent of easy, cheap mass tourism changed the nature of the street. The combination of gawking tourists and intent clientele, aggravated by acceptance of a cannabis culture, has led to questions about whether the De Wallen is sustainable in its present form. The local authority recognised that this particular type of Place is identified with Amsterdam. They are therefore proposing to create a distinct 'Erotic Center'[15] in a new location that will embrace many aspects beyond the sale of sexual gratification.

Figure 13.3b illustrates the tourist trinkets that are taken to epitomise the vast conurbation of metropolitan London. The red telephone box, designed in 1923 by the British architect Sir Giles Gilbert Scott, has become a readily recognised symbol of London and its benign cultureclosely followed by the red double-decker bus. The fact that the telephone boxes are rapidly disappearing or being repurposed to house defibrillators and wi-fi hubs because of their replacement by mobile phones has not diminished their encapsulation of things British.[16]

Studies of tourists show how important these quotidian uses of streets are. The contribution of the prosaic overshadows dominant icons that give cities their public identity. To take Paris, for example:

> While the Eiffel Tower and Notre Dame help give the city its characteristic identity, they are not what makes Paris *Paris*, rather it is the ensemble of cafés and boulangeries, the Seine and the chestnuts in blossom which contribute to the mis-en-scène which tourists seek in their validation of place.[17]

Figure 13.3b 'Iconic' images of London for sale as gewgaws

Life on the street

Urban streets are the quintessential examples of Places for which interactions between physical qualities, meanings and actions generate experience. These interactions are inherently dynamic. Their changes, whether through enhancements or destruction, cause streets to take on different meanings and significances from moment to moment, day to day and season to season. This relates to the climate and local culture as well as the economic circumstances, as can be seen in Figure 13.4. It is no surprise that the elegant street performers on a bridge in Figure 13.4a are in a very old university town. These street performers have used the raised sidewalk and a stool to create a Place clearly for performance, with the humble tin in front for donations.

The seven people gathered in a close circle at the side of the road in Puducherry in Figure 13.4b have their own private seminar. An example of a third place that takes advantage of the climate and street availability in this part of India. The boy looking at the camera is ever alert to who is passing by, keen to protect the privacy of his group.

Figure 13.4 Street scenes in (a) Heidelberg, Germany, (b) Puducherry, India *(Continued)*

Figure 13.4 (*Continued*)

Rules of place

The opportunities which the street provides for many forms of entertainment go beyond the buskers in Figure 13.4. If the movement of people is enough, and the space allows for it, streets can become circuses and engaging places of entertainment (Figure 13.5).

Here there are even seats to enjoy the show from. A box in which the performer carries his equipment becomes a stage. The rules of Place are as clear as in any theatre. People keep an appropriate distance. That allows for a large audience and a respectful distance from the performer. He is definitely in charge of the proceedings. The watchers are subdued and attentive. This is not a performance where heckling is typically appropriate.

Beyond pedestrians following the mores expected in a theatre, when watching a street performance, there are many other examples of how Places on the street illustrate the power of rules that relate to specific locations, guided by the roles special to those locations. As considered in Chapter 1, an early discovery of these rules was elaborated by Whyte[18] in the 1940s when he referred to street choreography. This is the way in which people are able to move around without ever bumping into each other or indicating their breaking of the rules of movement by apologising if they do accidentally knock into someone else.

As a colleague of Whyte, Jane Jacobs developed his notion of a choreography into the broader term of a *place ballet*. These are the dynamic, informal dance-like transactions that characterise activities in public spaces, emphasising how they contribute to the

Figure 13.5 An escapologist draws the crowds on London's South Bank

vitality and character of urban life. They also clearly help to define the nature of where you are, carrying implications for what happens there. This became an important aspect of Seamon's phenomenology of places.[19] He argues that these "individual bodily routines rooted in a specific environment" point "to the possibility that everyday habitual routines regularly happening in material space can transform that space into a living place".[20]

In other words, streets come alive when a recognisable pattern of activities emerge. These activities follow rules understood by participants. They enshrine role relationships relevant to that particular setting. Whether it is buskers playing music, an escapologists entertaining a crowd, or just a homeless person designating a location for his private residence.

What's in a name

One detail of Places that carries consequence for many people is what the Place is called. The names of places often capture their history and culture. This can be especially important when the background enshrined in the name is felt to be pejorative or symbolic of a worldview that the residents wish to distance themselves from. This is directly revealed when a decision is made to change the names of streets. This is very rarely a response to a purely practical or functional requirement, or just to facilitate wayfinding. Street names are often a statement of identity and ideology. "They are active participants in the construction and perception of social reality".[21] This was notable in the wholesale renaming of 60 streets in East Berlin in the early 1990s after the reunification of Germany.[22] The new names changed the way the streets are conceptualised. Eradicating references to Russian Communist supporters was part of the process of claiming these streets as places within the unified Germany.

A rather more mundane example reveals how names of urban places are used to indicate their nature. From a local newspaper:

> If a recommendation by Hambledon Rural Council 's housing committee is approved, both sections of Peckhams Estate will be renamed. The Housing Officer felt the renaming would "help to overcome the discord between the County Council and District tenant and foster better relations between the two sectors". The need for Peckham to be given a new name arose from complaints made during the past few years by tenants living in Hambiedon Rural Council houses about unsocial behaviour by the Surrey County Council tenants, which had given the estate a bad name, they said.
>
> (Surrey Daily Advertiser *20.11.73, p. 11)*

The significance of such small details, similar to Proust's crack in the pavement, or, as with the residents of Peckham's Estate, the name assigned to a Place, is marked because Places frequently provide the greatest range of long-lasting associations. The crack in the pavement brought back to Proust a great variety of memories which could not be recalled so vividly any other way. The *Rural* Council tenants felt that the name of their estate implied a way of life, associated with *County* Council tenants, with which they did not wish to be linked. In other words, even a seemingly minor aspect of our physical surroundings may be imbued, like a child's blanket, with a variety of meanings because of the mixture of memories, habits and expectations with which it is linked. True as this is for something as seemingly trifling as a crack in the pavement, it is even more the case for larger units of publicly available Places, such as streets.

One recent example of the importance of changing the identity of a Place by changing the names of streets has been brought about by the Russian invasion of Ukraine. The popular desire to distance themselves from any implication of Russian identity has given rise to the renaming of many streets that have Russian references, even to internationally known heroes such as Yuri Gagarin.[23] These changes are seen by many as throwing off the yoke of Communist imperialism, revealing how something often taken for granted, seen every day, such as a street name, can embody layers of meaning.

Imposing identity

The changing of the names of streets is one example of the processes of consciously changing the meaning of Places so that they accord more closely with how residents want their places, and by association, themselves to be thought of. They are one aspect

Figure 13.6 17,000-year-old handprints from Lascaux Caves

of imposing an identity on a public Place. Putting your mark on a Place has a venerable history going back millennia to the prehistoric handprints on cave walls. The oldest known handprints date back around 200,000 years, to those of two children in what is now Quesang, Tibet.[24] But what looks like the residue of a street party of more recent, but still prehistoric, handprints exist in the French Lascaux caves (Figure 13.7). These marks demonstrate the desire to impose an identity, to record a personal presence, in what is otherwise a public context. That seems always to have been part of being human.

Urban walls

The contested meaning of Places in cities is revealed, literally graphically, by what is put on their walls.[25] Walls "hold a light to the complex and protean alternative history of urban life".[26] In other words, the marks on walls reflect the variety of different Places that any street location may contain when viewed from different perspectives. These include issues of social habits and personal identity, history and politics.

> on those surfaces, which are open to many different contemporary interventions ranging from posters to slogans, and messages with sexual content to serious newspaper clippings, we can discern the pulse of history.[27]

Some aspects of street art, which sit under the derogatory term of graffiti, draw attention to the way in which streets are Places in which forms of ownership can be contested. As with all art, new technologies change the form and content of graffiti. The

Figure 13.7 Example of street art as part of the urban renewal project in Milan

ready availability of permanent spray paint in the 1970s saw an epidemic of 'tagging'. The marking of territory, the designation of Places with special, personal significance. This erupted on the underground transport system of New York.[28] That demonstrated these transport 'streets' were being declared as the graffitists' domain.

Subversive indications of identity on city walls are an illustration of the different relationships people have to the street. Their roles as outsiders claiming a presence, or gang members declaring ownership, both in conflict with bureaucrats and city planners. They demonstrate what Berman[29] drew attention to, as characteristic of the city. "Vast forces clashing uncontrollably".[30]

Street art

In contrast to rebellious graffiti, there is a growing official use of street art.[31] The meanings of Places are deliberately enriched by facilitating the marking of buildings, as a form of art, as often a positive way of shaping the identity of a Place. This is an influence on the meaning of its physical form, rather than a focus on what goes on there.

A Milan suburb introduced a street-art-based renewal project (Figure 13.8). Changes to the image of the area and attachment to it, five years apart, from before the art was introduced until later showed significant differences.[32] Ratings of the image of the locality revealed increased dynamism, sociability, innovation, and creativity. The street art appeared to promote a contemporary vision of the neighbourhood that complemented its established history and culture. However, this only held for residents of the area. Visitors passing through did not show any differences between before and after the art was introduced.

Figure 13.8 Street art in Orgosolo, Sardinia (*Continued*)

Figure 13.8 (*Continued*)

The example from Milan is one of many that show how street art helps to inform the meaning of Places. This has been found notably in those Italian villages and small towns that have encouraged street art. Studies of these have demonstrated that:

> As an essential part of creative place-making, street art projects contribute to the revitalisation and regeneration of villages, attracting visitors and new inhabitants, preserving their local identity, and developing place collectivity as a cooperation between local stakeholders, inhabitants, local businesses, and street art artists. Furthermore, street art projects contribute to place visibility, a sense of belonging, and economic and social development, improving quality of life.[33]

A striking example of this use of street art is the more than 150 murals that cover walls of Orgoloso an apparently quiet town in the mountains of central-eastern Sardinia (Figure 13.9). The town has a violent history of bloody feuds, extortions, and kidnappings. That image of the Place was holding back development.

These murals first began to emerge in the late 1960s during economic turmoil in Italy. The murals became a medium for expressing collective dissatisfaction. Although

Figure 13.9a Ben Wilson's artwork

Figure 13.9b Easily missed underfoot on the bridge from St Paul's Cathedral to Tate Modern art gallery

the earliest works were created by a self-declared anarchist theatre company from Milan, a local art teacher, Francesco Del Casino, worked with his students to generate many further murals. Their creations were a form of political activism. They dealt with the local history of Nazi brutality, the battle for liberation, and social problems related to labour and education. They also referred to major styles of art, notably Picasso's portraits.

Changes in the artwork reflected economic recovery in Italy in the early 1980s. That included depiction of the daily lives of the town's residents. The global reach of the artwork subsequently developed, dealing with the Tiananmen Square protest of 1989, protests against the G8 summit in Genoa, and the destruction of the World Trade Centre in New York.

The consequences of all these creations were to convert the streets into art galleries. Places that both instantiate the views and opinions of the artists and inhabitants but also change the the town into a tourist attraction. These transformations of the nature of the town have fostered new identities and economic growth that has left the violence of the past behind. Orgosolo's inhabitants greatly appreciate the murals. They recognise them as reflecting the town's history, culture, and political sentiments. They preserve collective memory and identity, bringing pride and attracting visitors.[34]

Many other examples exist of changing the way Places are conceptualised by how the walls of their streets are modified. To take one more example, from Romania:

> ...graffiti and street art are positive, seen to some extent as a realignment of the city as a Place for people who live in it: e.g., a message on a wall in Bucharest says: "The city must be won back!".[35]

This means a further reappropriation of the city by the younger generation, who subject it to new challenges in its development and cultural identity. Such reappropriation illustrates the capacity of competing roles to find co-operation through street art. A younger generation connects with the city differently to their forebears. Places in the city mean different things to them when compared with those who created it. They can realign the city by acting on it.

One, literally, small example of street art that redefines the nature of a Place is the artworks created by Ben Wilson from the chewing gum left on the Millennium Bridge in London (Figure 13.10). The bridge becomes an art gallery commenting both on the possibilities of art from detritus and issues of concern. But only for those who notice them!

Third place

Some years ago, Raymond Oldenberg and his colleague Denniss Brissett suggested that it is useful to make a distinction between on the one hand the home and the workplace and on the other a 'third place'. These are:

> Places where people gather primarily to enjoy each other's company. They are not like businessmen clubs and singles bars which people inhabit in order to informally encourage the achievement of formal goals.[36]

Figure 13.10 A 'third place' in Sardinia? And in London

These are relevant to the consideration of the street because the most commonly cited examples are cafés, bars and pubs. To understand more fully what is implied by these locations Oldenberg and Brissett state:

> The tavern, or bar, is without doubt the dominant third Place in our society and we are not unique in this. Be it saloon, cocktail lounge, pub, or whatever - Place it among the golf links and call it a clubhouse, put it at the water's edge and call it a yacht club, or organize a fraternal order around it and call it a lodge - the bar is nonetheless at the core of the institution. But, neither the existence of the bar nor the dispensing of alcoholic beverages is essential to the establishment of third places. For old-timers in many communities, it was the local express office or the general store. For the young, increasingly, it is the "hamburger joint" as the malt shop has disappeared. In many European countries it is still the coffee house as it once was in London. In an earlier day in Germany, it was the *Gasthaus*; in the smaller cities and towns of America, it is frequently a favorite cafe or bakery, drug store, or hotel lunch counter.[37]

The locations that are not 'third places' are used to define what those third places are, as much as descriptions that help them to be identified. At the heart of this argument is a perspective on weaknesses in US life, but relevant throughout the developed and developing world. Failings that 'third places' are seen as remedying. Although writing half a century ago, this malaise in American society would be recognisable today, marked by dissatisfaction with quality of life, driving people to seek counselling and other forms of therapy in the hope it will lead to greater enjoyment of life. This is explained as a decline in personal responsibility, community participation, and social trust. The domination of the home and work is seen as limiting fulfilling social interactions.

Third places are proposed as providing opportunities, which workand home life do not. They are places that are accessible, everyday public settings. A natural part of daily life. They foster ordinary social connections and experiences. Vital opportunities for relationships and interactions not obtainable elsewhere, providing subtle yet significant roles in communal life.

In some senses this is an elaboration of Jane Jacob's much-cited 'eyes on the street'. The idea that informal settings in publicly accessible locations help to create a spirit of community.

The original essay by Oldenberg and Brissett makes clear that these Places were typical of small-town America. They claimed the need was particularly pressing in American suburbia, which had lost the types of Places presented in a nostalgic glow as:

> In the small towns of the Deep South one still finds card games and checker games going on under the shade trees in the town square. The younger men will be found congregating at the fishing camps and bait shops. In the larger cities some people casually drop in on friends at the lounging rooms of the indoor tennis or racquetball academies. In the north country, the humble one-man ice-fishing shacks often have given way to larger models, complete with carpeting, refrigerators, and poker tables where men spend less time fishing, perhaps, than simply getting away from their jobs and families.[38]

Figure 13.11 The statue of Edward Colston, a 17th-century slave trader, was removed during a Black Lives Matter protest in Bristol in 2020

The street corner of a town can be the locations where these Places are generated, as in Figure 13.13. Where, typically, a group of men gather in the shade for an informal get-together. Such gatherings are common across Southern Europe in the Summer, where the afternoon shade is a welcome relief from dark and uncomfortable spaces indoors. Illustrated in Figure 13.11 A stepped retaining wall provides the necessary affordance for locals to use.

It is by their very nature that third Places are created by locals. Their informal quality, with casual rules and limited, or no, formal role differences, provides the opportunity for meeting up with others whilst "getting away from their jobs and families". That all implies a spontaneous creation of these Places. Some may emerge unexpectedly (as in Figure 13.12) because the physical conditions, both for gathering and for seeing and being seen, are present. Others emerge in locations that might not have originally been intended for social gatherings. Such was the US 'drugstore' so popular in the novels of John Steinbeck, specifically *Cannery Row*. This was the relaxed hub of social activity. It provided a setting for portraying the humour and intensities of community life.

For those not familiar with the traditional US drugstore, the idea that a setting which sells 'drugs' is appropriate meeting place is based on a misunderstanding. They were typically pharmacies. They prepared prescriptions for legal medication. But many had soda fountains and provided sandwiches at a lunch counter; out of this, their roles as third places emerged. However, they have mainly disappeared from providing that role now, fading back into focusing on their role as pharmacies and more general healthcare providers, including vaccinations.

Figure 13.12 Sarah Everard vigil around the bandstand on Clapham Common

The informality and spontaneous emergence of third places means that they are naturally likely to change and eventually disappear over time. They are therefore the prime example of the dynamic nature of Places. They may consequently be regarded as at the heart of the shifting facets of the street.

Iconoclasm

An even more direct way of modifying the nature of public Places is by destroying monuments that contribute to the identity of those settings. The active engagement with the meaning given by statues and memorials has a long history.[39] It can be regarded as the antithesis of graffiti and street art, which are the addition of markers to streets and other public places. It is a further stage beyond changing the names of streets. The tearing down of civic sculpture demonstrates that the imagery and meaning of the culture, defined by those tributes to the past, is being radically reassessed. From the perspective of an understanding of Places, the removal of monuments is an active encounter with what is signified by that area of a city.

Contesting, transforming and/or removing a monument from an urban space operates as a means of political struggle and as a form of political engagement in urban contexts. Recent examples of this have been campaigns, and in some cases direct actions to remove statues of historically prominent citizens who were slave traders. A powerful illustration was the removal of the statue of Edward Colston, a 17th-century slave trader (Figure 13.12). The statue had pride of place in a central square in Bristol. By dominating that location, it was seen as giving that public space a meaning antithetical to the mission of the Black Lives Matter movement.

Recognising that it is inappropriate to try to alter history, many countries keep the remnants of historic monuments. The Edward Colston statue is an illustration to this, now held in a public museum in Bristol. Its presence there is a reminder of how Bristol became the city it is today.[40]

Social conflict

The tearing down of monuments, which influence the identity of Places, is an aspect of crowds using public settings as a basis for exerting their reactions in relation to authority. As noted, streets and the areas they connect are frequently the context for conflict between different roles, whether it be traders and motorists, pedestrians and cyclists, or people with different purposes for being there. Each of these groups operates with different rules, relating to their objectives and perspectives of what is possible. In open, democratic societies one potential clash of roles and rules is that between public gatherings and the police.

In such clashes the nature and understanding of what is expected of being in a particular public area comes to the fore. This is illustrated in the examination of the vigil for the murdered Sarah Everard.[41] Hundreds gathered around the bandstand on Clapham Common, in South London, to pay tribute to her and indicate their disquiet about how the murder happened and was investigated (Figure 13.13). The location is related to where she was killed. The focus given there by the bandstand, helped to give the people present a feeling of being part of a group that shared common feelings and norms.

Drawing on many years of study of crowds, the detailed examination of how events unfolded demonstrated the potential for role conflict between those who were operating with different norms. In this case, the people present and the police. This illustrates the social psychological processes that can energise action. Actions are given meaning from their context and behaviour associated with it.

Changing places

The dynamic features of streets, generated by the mixture of roles and purposes, ownerships and activities are changing their nature and the related kinds of Places they support.

Around the world traditional high street shops are being replaced by shopping centres and out of town shopping malls. The rapid growth of online shopping is also taking its toll on what streets can support. The change, illustrated in Figure 13.14, by two of very many examples which litter our cities, shows that the physical features, social interaction, sensory stimulation, security and comfort are rapidly being brought into private, commercial ownership.[42] The street is being denuded of the vibrancy that was once its distinguishing feature.

These changes are limiting the opportunities, or desires, to create third places as well as the many other aspects that brought people together and supported the variety of roles and purposes that Places on the streets enjoyed. As Ghel and his colleagues have pointed out:

> Many urban functions [have] moved indoors, and shops, institutions and organisations have grown larger. In the process, urban buildings have become bigger and correspondingly introspective and self-sufficient.[43]

Figure 13.13 (a) Shopping mall, Hong Kong; (b) market area, Rajasthan

Figure 13.14 Phones, not eyes, on the street

Informal gatherings of the sort that create third places are discouraged. Anyone who has visited a MacDonald's will be aware the seats are rarely comfortable enough for a lengthy stay.

Although it is worth noting that Starbucks coffee houses have recognised the value of reintroducing the opportunities so lauded by Oldenberg. There is evidence that the presence of outlets that facilitate informal social interaction has increased entrepreneurship through the development of networks.[44]

Zombie streets

A second challenge to the existence of vibrant streets, which were supported by many third places, is another development not really foreseen by Oldenberg in the 1980s. This is the advent of cell phones, the internet and social media. Against the background of the reduction of people participating in what may be regarded as traditional third places, it has been suggested that similar socialisation has moved to social network sites, such as Facebook[45] and the plethora of other social media that now exist. More recent internet-based applications for social interaction, such as WhatsApp, Snapchat and Telegram, may also be offering a vehicle for the type of informal sharing of interests and ideas redolent of the bars and drugstores of yesteryear.

As positive as the freedom offered by social media may be, its impact, as well as many other developments in technology, is clear to see on the streets of cities. Indeed, there is perhaps now, what is regarded as an old-world charm about the idea of casual observation of what is going on, stimulating the emergence of sociable communities. A further development is the glut of surveillance cameras in modern cities, over half a million in London for example. One for about every dozen people. They are very different types of 'eyes on the street'. They are dissociated from any human interaction, except by law enforcement. Yet their very existence demonstrates that Jane Jacobs' ideas were at best utopian. The image of people locked onto their mobile phones (Figure 13.15), stepping away from drug addicts and avoiding eye contact with

Figure 13.15 An emerging trend?

homeless people finding shelter, is a further degradation of the image of a friendly community, where collaboration with each other is a natural part of being on the street together.

In her book *Extinction of Experience*, Christine Rosen explores how technology impacts our sense of self and experiences. Of special relevance to consideration of Places on the street is her in-depth critique of the technology that undermines the experience of the here and now in public. Her analyses reflect an ongoing correspondence I have had with my colleague Reid Bishop. He has expressed grave concern that the informal contact that streets have so often encouraged, creating the lifeblood of social interaction in the city, is being extensively constricted by people being always 'on their phone' rather than being open to others around them.

This includes the prevalence of earpods, which hook people into voices or music in some other virtual reality, as well as studying maps on their phones – instead of asking the way, or even watching videos that transport them far beyond where they currently are. There is evidence that pedestrians are more prone to accidents when using their phones.[46] "Walking and talking or texting can be dangerous".[47]

Beyond the dangers, at a more subtle level, simple exchanges with strangers play a vital role in enhancing our overall sense of well-being.[48] It is, after all, at the heart of Jane Jacobs' advocacy of 'eyes on the street'. As Rosen points out, even "those who aren't wearing earbuds, or are buried in their phones ... effectively penalise those who do not".[49] If people use earbuds or phones frequently, physical proximity will no longer imply social expectations of shared experience.[50] This dystopian view leads to the prediction that streets and the public Places they link together will become "full of people ignoring one another, doing their best to be nowhere".[51]

I tested this hypothesis recently when I was sitting next to another lone man, who I did not know, in a crowded restaurant. We were both engaged with our phone whilst eating. In the spirit of empirical research, I boldly said to him "excuse me but it has been suggested that if we were not immersed in our phones, we would have an interesting conversation". He immediately put his phone down, smiled, and asked me why I was there. We then had a fascinating chat. It was a memorable part of my evening. A case study example of the possibilities in the absence of engagement with the internet.

Awareness of this issue has led to a small but growing move to reduce the prevalence of internet links in those settings where social contacts may be fruitfully encouraged (Figure 13.15). This is another illustration of how an apparently small change in the rules of a Place can have a significant impact of the nature of that place. It signals and facilitates a change in what activities are expected in there. That modifies the meaning of the Place, setting in a motion a productive cycle. Of course, it can also have commercial implications by discouraging customers from settling down for a morning with their laptop, buying only one latte. Although as some fast-food outlets and even railway stations have discovered a more austere way of keeping people from staying too long is by having narrow seats that quickly become uncomfortable.

There is, however, some evidence that mobile phone use in public is not entirely destructive of fruitful social interaction. An extensive observational study[52] claimed that rates of mobile phone use in public are lower than often presumed. Most mobile phone users were individuals without co-located companions, ranging from just 3% to 10% of people observed. Although there were gender-specific trends. Solitary women were more likely to be using their phones than men. Although that study happened a decade ago, it accords with my own more informal observations in places as varied as Verona and London.

Importantly, "mobile phones users appear less often in spaces where there are more groups, and most often in spaces where people might otherwise be walking alone. Mobile phone use may support gender equity in public space".[53] Some sociologists have even taken this aspect of being in public with a mobile phone as supporting "the ability of the individual to participate simultaneously in multiple spheres of action and communication. This state of affairs creates what we have called a *portable private-personal territory*".[54] That opens up the creation of public areas as palimpsests, layers of different Places on top of each other or at least coinciding. That, as mentioned earlier, has always been the nature of streets.

Public, civic Places, supported by conventions of interactions with strangers, have always also included private, personal exchanges, fuelled by existing relationships. The prevalence of electronic devices across most streets has led them to being anointed with the term 'hybrid spaces', that exist within 'cyber-physical environments'.[55] No longer is it the world of cyborgs, half human half robots, that needs to be understood, but Places that exist at the same time in both physical and virtual reality. The rules and meanings of these different contexts and how they cooperate or compete with each other have become a 21st-century issue of some magnitude.

Conclusions

Urban streets have always been a cornucopia of Places in which the personal and the public intermingle. As such, they teach us a lot about the nature of our interactions with the world around us. They reveal how the interplay between meanings, forms and anticipated activities produce an energetic mix of ever-changing Places. Their significance may be influenced by unexpected details that carry personal, social or historical importance. They are also likely to be maintained by the rituals that those present implicitly understand and the related rules that they follow. Streets are especially good at generating 'third places' which provide opportunities for informal get-togethers not available in the home or workplace.

Above all, Places on the street are the lifeblood of urban spaces. Especially the High Street (in the US often called Main Street). They capture the essence of a city, town or village. For residents, they enshrine their history and culture. For visitors they are the gateway to their experiences.

The swift advancement of communication technologies is significantly altering the nature of urban high streets. People's experiences of them are becoming multifaceted. Being here in the physical Place as well as being in some other cyber-location. Although some may see this as dystopian, others may recognise it as the inevitable evolution of streets. There are increasingly overlaps between shopping online and feeling and touching products in shops. The online world is influencing what it means to be here. In addition to direct contact with products, streets still offer opportunities for social interaction that cannot be obtained in the same way over the internet. Signing a petition online is not the same as taking part in a public demonstration. Sitting with a friend in a café can never be replaced by a conversation via computer screens.

References and endnotes

1 From Karssenberg, H., Laven, J., Glaser, M., & Van't Hoff, M. (2016) The city at eye level, in *The city at eye level: Lessons for street plinths* (Vol. 2), Delft: Eburon Academic Publishers, pp. 14–25, p. 8

2 Gehl, J., Kaefer, L. J., & Reigstad, S. (2006) Close encounters with buildings. *Urban Design International*, 13, 29–47.

3 Based on diagram on page 15 of Karssenberg, H., Laven, J., Glaser, M., & Van't Hoff, M. (2016) The city at eye level, in *The city at eye level: Lessons for street plinths* (Vol. 2), Delft: Eburon Academic Publishers, pp. 14–25.

4 Jacobs, J. (1961) *The death and life of Great American cities*, New York: Vintage Books.

5 Gray, A. (2024) The bookshop, the draper, the candlestick maker, London: Profile.

6 The Paris Review – No Walk Is Ever Wasted – The Paris Review.

7 One of many such studies of the impact of context on reinstating memories is Chun, M. M., & Nakayama, K. (2000) On the functional role of implicit visual memory for the adaptive deployment of attention across scenes. *Visual Cognition*, 7(1–3), 65–81.

8 Araya, A., Naoi, T., & Iijima, S. (2016) The effects of westerners' presence on Japanese evaluations of a historic district: The case of Takayama city. *Journal of Travel & Tourism Marketing*, 33(5), 628–644.

9 This term is often mentioned in an elision as 外人 (giajin) which is a mild insult because of its use on the phrase 変な外人 (hen na gaijin – that translates as weird foreigner. I mention this because it helps to understand the influence of the presence of 'Westerners' at tourist sites.

10 Rickly-Boyd, J. M., & Metro-Roland, M. M. (2010) Background to the fore: The prosaic in tourist places. *Annals of Tourism Research*, 37(4), 1164–1180.

11 Rickly-Boyd, & Metro-Roland (2010) Background to the fore, 1164–1180

12 Bierhoff, H. W. (2012) *Person perception and attribution*, Springer Science & Business Media.

13 Probably because the studies are carried out by geographers and students of tourism, ignorant of the relevant social psychology research.

14 Chapuis, A. (2017) Touring the immoral. Affective geographies of visitors to the Amsterdam Red-Light district. *Urban Studies*, 54(3), 616–632.

15 https://www.bing.com/ck/a?!&&p=bf848513ae37a11ba3d6f88d4d6ffc6d697ab0285a78b8604e406df5c3fb6584JmltdHM9MTc0MTgyNDAwMA&ptn=3&ver=2&hsh=4&fclid=350e143f-20d9-6442-2bad-1a3d213565b6&psq=Proposal+for+Amsterdam%27s+%27erotic+center%40.&u=a1aHR0cHM6Ly93d3cuYW1zdGVyZGFtLm5sL2VuL2xlaXN1cmUvbmV3LWVyb3RpYy1jZW50cmUv&ntb=1.

16 Although it has to be mentioned that the telephone boxes pictured in Figure 11.3 do also function as pencil sharpners!

17 Rickly-Boyd, J. M., & Metro-Roland, M. M. (2010) Background to the fore: The prosaic in tourist places. *Annals of Tourism Research*, 37(4), 1164–1180 p. 1170.

18 Whyte, W. F. (2012) *Street corner society: The social structure of an Italian slum*, University of Chicago press.

19 Seamon, D. (2015) Body-subject, time-space routines, and place-ballets. In *The human experience of space and place*, Routledge, pp. 148–165.

20 Seamon,D. (2018) *Life Takes Place*. New York: Routledge, p. 15.

21 Azaryahu, M. (1997) German reunification and the politics of street names: the case of East Berlin. *Political Geography*, 16(6), 479–493, 481.

22 Azaryahu (1997) German reunification and the politics of street names.

23 Pidkuimukha, L. (2025) Toponymic decommunisation in Ukraine: Renaming Gagarin Streets and reclaiming the symbolic landscape. Confruntarea Cu Simbolurile Sovietice. Conflicte Privind Interpretarea = Поводження з Радянськими Символами. Конфлікти Щодо Інтерпретації Минулогою.

24 Kids' fossilized handprints may be some of the world's oldest art | Live Science accessed 03/03/2025
25 The exploration by an artist/photographer is ravishing in the book Dogançay, A., Temel, B., & Dogançay, B. (2012) *Burhan Dogançay: fifty years of urban walls*, Munich: Prestel Verlag.
26 The exploration by an artist/photographer is ravishing in the book Dogançay, Temel, & Dogançay (2012) *Burhan Dogançay*, p. 15.
27 The exploration by an artist/photographer is ravishing in the book Dogançay, Temel, & Dogançay (2012) *Burhan Dogançay*, p. 15.
28 The history of graffiti from ancient times to modern days | The Vintage News (accessed March 2025).
29 Berman, M. (1987) *All that is solid melts into air: The experience of modernity*, London: Verso
30 Berman (1987) *All that is solid melts into air*, p. 18.
31 Boffi, M., Rainisio, N., & Inghilleri, P. (2023) Nurturing cultural heritages and Place attachment through street art—a longitudinal psycho-social analysis of a neighbourhood renewal process. *Sustainability*, 15(13), 10437.
32 Boffi, M., Rainisio, N., & Inghilleri, P. (2023) Nurturing cultural heritages and Place attachment through street art—a longitudinal psycho-social analysis of a neighborhood renewal process. *Sustainability*, 15(13), 10437.
33 Bruni, R., & Rauhut Kompaniets, O. (2024). Street art and place-making of villages: Examples of Italian painted villages. *Journal of Place Management and Development*, 17(4), 527–557.
34 Valentino, M., & Cicalò, E. (2020) Shaping identities through Street Art. Iconography of social claims in Orgosolo's Murales. *Disegnarecon*, 13(24), 25–1.
35 Cercleux, A.-L. (2022) Graffiti and Street art between ephemerality and making visible the culture and heritage in cities: Insight at international level and in Bucharest. *Societies*, 12(5), 129, https://doi.org/10.3390/soc12050129
36 Oldenburg, R., & Brissett, D. (1982) The third place. *Qualitative Sociology*, 5(4), 265–284, p. 269.
37 Oldenburg, R., & Brissett, D. (1982) The third place. *Qualitative Sociology*, 5(4), 265–284, p. 269.
38 Oldenburg, R., & Brissett, D. (1982) The third place. *Qualitative Sociology*, 5(4), 265–284, p. 270.
39 Frank, S., & Ristic, M. (2020) Urban fallism: Monuments, iconoclasm and activism. *City*, 24(3–4), 552–564.
40 A remarkable collection of Soviet-era statues and artefacts that recreates some of the feelings of being in Lithuania during those times is Grūtas Park. This is an open-air museum near Druskininkai.
41 Stott, C., Radburn, M., Pearson, G., Kyprianides, A., Harrison, M., & Rowlands, D. (2022) Police powers and public assemblies: Learning from the Clapham Common 'Vigil' during the Covid-19 pandemic. *Policing: A Journal of Policy and Practice*, 16(1), 73–94.
42 Ng, C. F. (2003) Satisfying shoppers' psychological needs: From public market to cyber-mall. *Journal of Environmental Psychology*, 23(4), 439–455.
43 Gehl, J., Kaefer, L. J., & Reigstad, S. (2006) Close encounters with buildings. *Urban Design International*, 13, 29–47p. 29.
44 Choi, J., Guzman, J., & Small, M. L. (2024) *Third places and neighborhood entrepreneurship: Evidence from Starbucks Cafés* (No. w32604). National Bureau of Economic Research.
45 Foster, J. W. (2013) *Oldenburg's great good places online: Assessing the potential for social network sites to serve as third places* (Doctoral dissertation) Tex tach University. Oldenburg's great good places online: assessing the potential for social network sites to serve as third places accessed March 2025.
46 Pešić, D., Antić, B., Glavić, D., & Milenković, M. (2016) The effects of mobile phone use on pedestrian crossing behaviour at unsignalized intersections–Models for predicting unsafe pedestrians behaviour. *Safety Science*, 82, 1–8.
47 Nasar, J. L., & Troyer, D. (2013) Pedestrian injuries due to mobile phone use in public places. *Accident Analysis & Prevention*, 57, 91–95.

48 Ascigil, E., Gunaydin, G., Selcuk, E., Sandstrom, G.M., & Aydin, E. (2023) Minimal social interactions and life satisfaction: The role of greeting, thanking, and conversing. *Social Psychological and Personality Science,* https://doi.org/10.1177/19485506231209793
49 Rosen, C. (2024). *The extinction of experience: Being human in a disembodied world*, New York: WW Norton & Company, p. 201.
50 Austin, D. (2019) Always In – *Real Life* June.
51 Rosen (2024). *The extinction of experience*, p. 201.
52 Hampton, K. N., Goulet, L. S., & Albanesius, G. (2015) Change in the social life of urban public spaces: The rise of mobile phones and women, and the decline of aloneness over 30 years. *Urban Studies*, 52(8), 1489–1504.
53 Hampton, Goulet, & Albanesius (2015) Change in the social life of urban public spaces.
54 Hatuka, T., & Toch, E. (2016) The emergence of portable private-personal territory: Smartphones, social conduct and public spaces. *Urban Studies*, 53(10), 2192–2208.
55 Heinrich, A. J., Heitmayer, M., Smith, E., & Zhang, Y. (2024) Experiencing hybrid spaces: A scoping literature review of empirical studies on human experiences in cyber-physical environments. *Computers in Human Behavior*, 108502.

CHAPTER 14

Maps in minds

Maps are never innocent

In the previous chapters I explored the ways in which our interactions with Places change the way we see ourselves and those Places. In order for these interactions to happen, we need to develop some understanding of what exists where and what is possible in those locations. One intriguing way of exploring these understandings is to examine the mental representations people have of what is where. These are often called 'mental maps'[1]. The term 'map' is not a very accurate description of our mental representations. They embrace many aspects of our experiences and emotions that are not embodied in the drawings that cartographic maps usually consist of.

This weakness of official cartography was captured elegantly by poet (and doctor) Dannie Abse[2] in his poem *Looking at a map.* He evokes many of the deficiencies of maps:

> False! False! Boring lines squiggle,
> meaning empty roads, hedges and wet tyres,
> or desolation of damp railway lines
> where no-one encounters a red lamp danger.
> But there's menace of a kind.
> Why else do official cartographers
> condemn the whole land behind
> a strict cage emptied of noughts and crosses
> Where no happy latitude is given?
> And this, too, another lie:
> this measurement of a lifetime's journey
> in inches, these little, exact circles
> for names of places where untamed people
> privately hide and love and cry

DOI: 10.4324/9780367808655-18

Abse's poem throws light on how even 'objective' maps incorporate selections and metaphors in the form of symbols. As Götz and Holmén put it[3] "all maps, from those on classroom walls, to foldouts of city streets and subways, to GPS on smartphones and aircraft screens are 'mental maps', whose design rests on the decisions of mapmakers" (p. 157). The recognition of the inevitable arbitrariness, and subjectivity, of what is put into a map by a professional cartographer has made the study of maps of all kinds a lively topic. Often, they are considered in terms of what they put in and leave out, their distortions and emphases. In an excoriating exposé of the power of maps, Wood[4] illustrates the many different ways in which they shape our understanding of Place. This in turn influences what people believe and how they act.

All maps are selective, inevitable distortions of reality. As Wood[5] elaborates in great detail, the aspects of maps that are chosen to be represented, or left out, always have a purpose. Maps are never innocent. They have power and significance. Wood argues that maps reflect "The ceaseless reproduction of the culture that brings them into being" (p. 1). He summarises a map as being "the product of a spectrum of codes that materialise in visual representations, orient these in space and time, and bind them together in some acceptable form" (p. 117).

Although Wood is mainly exploring 'official', formal maps his descriptions are also relevant for our own personal mental representations of the world we engage with. What we remember and represent in any account of the Places we interact with serves a purpose. The salient features of our 'mental maps', the landmarks and named locations, and the links between them, reflect, and provide the basis for, our transaction with the Places captured in those images. As a consequence, the study of representations people create of the world in which they live helps to elaborate an understanding of Places, their significance and meaning.

The taxi meter in our heads

The proposal that we have some internal representation of the world about us as an image of Places goes back a long way. It emerged with some clarity at the dawn of present-day cognitive neuroscience. The rather aptly named, Sir Henry Head, a neurologist, was concerned with how we are able to take into account changes in bodily posture and movement in order to carry out effective motor actions. How do we know where our limbs are? That this is not a trivial question is clear if you ask someone who is very drunk to touch his nose. To explain our abilities, Head proposed that we must carry in our brains a model of our body which is being continuously modified on the basis of information received about each action. He drew on an analogy of a taximeter, relevant to the early twentieth century when he was writing. Such a meter accumulates the distance travelled and presents it to us "already transformed into shillings and pence"[6].

In many ways, Head's concerns are close to those of present-day environmental cognition. His ideas can now be seen to contain the seeds of the psychology of Place as it emerged in the following half-century:

> The sensory cortex is a storehouse of past impressions. They may rise into consciousness as images but more often, as in the case of spatial impressions, remain outside central consciousness. Here, they form organised models of ourselves which

> may be called schemata. Such schemata modify the impressions produced by incoming sensory impulses in such a way that the final sensations of position or of locality rise into consciousness charged with a relation to something that has gone before.
>
> *(Head, 1920[7], pp. 605–606)*

Two aspects of this quotation stand out. One is that he recognises that the mental representations are 'models of ourselves'. Although Head was probably referring to a model of our body it is a small step, as noted in previous chapters, to see this as including our notions of who we think we are. The other term he drew on was that of the 'image'. A set of related ideas of what is where. These schemata are an internal representation of the world. Each schema is an organisation of concepts and actions that can be revised by new experiences and information.

One crucial aspect of this is that it is fundamentally active. Just as we are monitoring all the time where our fingers, hands, arms and legs are in relation to each other, so we are constantly structuring and reorganising our models of the Places with which we interact. Subsequent psychologists built on this process of actively reconstruing to emphasise its relevance to a wide range of psychological processes. In particular, one of the few psychologists to be knighted, Sir Frederick Bartlett,[8] set the emergence of cognitive psychology in motion (in contrast to the dominant behavioural tradition) by his arguments that all thought processes are constantly being developed and changed. Most notably he made a very clear point of this by calling his book on the psychology of memory *Remembering.*[9] This showed it was an active process he was studying. Memory is not a store of old-fashioned photographs that fade over time. It is dynamic, constantly rebuilding and reassessing the information available. Another telling aspect of Bartlett's title to his book is that he positions his studies of memory as part of social psychology. Remembering occurs within the context of contacts with others and as part of a larger society. The imaginative experiments he carried out, reported in detail in his book, have become the bases of a wide range of subsequent research of relevance to topics as diverse as false memories,[10] and computer-generated neural networks.[11]

The idea that we have schema that encompass an active set of ideas about ourselves and the locations, people and things we interact with was generalised by a number of authors to emphasise the power of the 'image' as a central explanation for much of what we think and do.[12] It is usual today to recognise that much of what we deal with and react it is an image rather than substance. A school of social psychology, sometimes referred to as microsociology, called symbolic interactionism,[13] has emerged to explore the ways in which human transactions draw on the subjective meanings and symbols that pervade a culture. What people do is shaped by the meaning that situations and their components have for them.

As discussed in previous chapters, any Place carries with it a range of different meanings and emotions, expectations and actions. These are part of the image of that Place. The room in which I am writing this cannot be experienced as a cuboid box stacked with printed matter. It is my study, referred to in the house as "David's room", with all the appurtenances that I have brought to give it the qualities I want. Similarly, my images of London, or Loch Ness, or Mars are shaped by all I have experienced, directly or indirectly about those Places. These images are constantly changing as I learn more about them and interact with them.

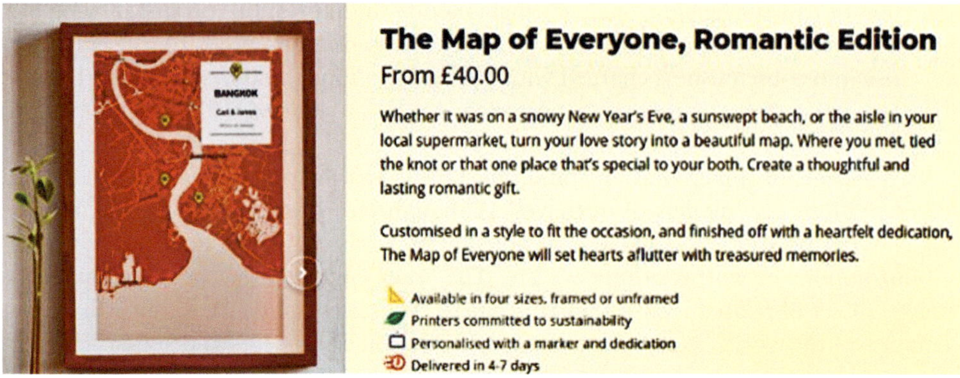

Figure 14.1 Commercialisation of maps that enshrine memories

The implication of the images and symbolic aspects of Places is that there can never be one definitive account of a person's conceptualisation of a Place. Whether someone is asked to describe it in words, draw a sketch of it, mark it on a map or identify it from a photograph, it is always a limited aspect of their image of it which is being explored. An important consequence of this is that any of these representations of the mental model someone has of a Place will be distorted to a greater or lesser degree. They will only capture a limited aspect of that person's understanding and experience.

The difficulty of capturing the image of a Place is one reason why travel writing is such a great art, and why there are so many literary works by poets and novelists with titles that attempt to describe Places.[14] Just put the term 'books about places ' into a search engine and see what an exciting range of possibilities emerge. When I did this, one option that emerged was an organisation cashing in on the fact that maps can embrace memories,[15] Figure 14.1.

Environmental roles and mental maps

The selections and distortions in the accounts people give, when compared with any attempt at a more 'objective' account, are therefore of value in understanding what a Place means to a person and how that is shaped by their interaction with it. For many years psychologists, geographers and other social scientists have been exploring the internal representations that people form of Places.[16] These representations that a person produces help to reveal what is particularly salient to that individual and how their world is shaped by their mental images. Asking people to draw a sketch map of a particular area has proved to be one fruitful way of exploring aspects of Place experience.

A starting point for these explorations was Kevin Lynch's *The Image of the City*.[17] He used sketch maps as a focus of interviews with residents of Los Angeles, Boston and Jersey City to explore what the form of a city means to the people who live there. His objective was to find out what a city planner can do to make the city's image more memorable and vivid. Lynch was not concerned with the distortions or idiosyncrasies of any individual's conceptualisation of a city. Rather, his focus was on general mental representation that a city evoked. From this he proposed various components that those images contained, giving rise to a vocabulary of Paths,

Edges, Districts, Nodes, and Landmarks that has found its way into many city planning discussions.

As a city planner, Lynch did not explore in any detail the basis of variations between individuals in the sketch maps they produced. Nonetheless, he does make very clear that there were indeed many differences not only in what maps people drew, but also in the process they went through in producing the maps. He gives one example, which speaks psychological volumes:

> ...the case of the taxicab dispatcher' s knowledge of a city street, which related house numbers to uses along block after block yet could not describe those buildings in any concrete sense.
>
> *(p. 88)*

Maps tell us where places are. The relationships and distances between them tell us how they relate in space to one another. However, the mental representations we have of what is where are usually not based on the objective assessments that are used by mapmakers.[18] Therefore, the differences between our internal representations of Places and what is regarded as actual reality does help to elaborate how our transactions with Places changes us and how we understand our world.

The role the taxicab dispatcher had in relation to the city (his 'environmental role') influenced what he knew about what was where, but not what those Places looked like. This introduces the interesting prospect of the various ways in which people's relationships to Places shape their image of them. As we shall see, this has implications for how that image influences their actions.

Many examples of the variations between people in their mental maps of the same location were brought together by Downs and Stea.[19] Influenced by Lynch's work, they edited an interesting collection of studies of such sketch maps. Of particular relevance to my argument here is what these studies reveal about those differences between groups in their conceptualisations of Places. For example, in one study residents of Rome and Milan[20] were asked to draw a map of their city 'so that a visitor could find his way', as well as answer other questions about their city. It was found that middle-class groups drew more detailed and extensive maps than those that the researchers called their 'lower-class counterparts' (p. 141). The ability to explore and make use of the city clearly related to the resources available to respondents and a person's occupation.

It is often a surprise to many professionals who have the ability to explore a city at their leisure, who may be required to visit various parts of it as part of their job, that there are other citizens who have only a very limited understanding of their city. They are constrained to the area in which they live and ply their trade. In US cities this is sometimes referred to as being on 'the other side of the track' because of the divisions in social status introduced by the railway line. In her books set in Naples written by Elena Ferrante,[21] the young girl, who is her central protagonist, is amazed by her first experience of the city centre and her first sight of the sea, because her whole life is so limited by growing up in Rione Luzzatti, the poor area of Naples in which she had spent all her life. Similarly, in discussions I've had with young people in North London, I discovered that none of them had been South of the River Thames.

More recently Edlund[22] reviewed the ways in which the maps people draw provide insights into their relationships with Places. He cites an early study by Carpenter[23] of the Aivilik Inuit. This revealed distinctly different emphases between the maps drawn by men and women. Edlund summarises the differences as:

> For Aivilik women, the most important features on their mental maps are the many trading posts and the paths that link them to their home base, as well as the distances to other villages. For men, however, landmarks are located with reference to the coastline, and boundaries generally play a greater role in their mental maps.
>
> *(p. 278)*

When a person lives and works in one area throughout a long life, they build up a detailed image with many associations that reflect their understanding of that Place. In some cases, they can pass this on to other's who are close to them. A particularly charming example of this is the map Edlund[24] (p. 275) recreated of the one his grandfather drew, of where he lived and worked, shown in Figure 14.2.

Edlund points out that this sketch illustrates his grandfather's activities as a farmer, forestry worker, fisherman, hunter and berry picker. Edlund also insists that the map contained the collective knowledge of his grandfather's village. "The abundant amount of information on the map was the result of 80 years of experience and incorporated the stories of many previous generations" (p. 277). It is not clear quite how these earlier narratives were incorporated into his grandfather's map, but the small drawings in the map are not that dissimilar from what might be put on a tourist map of a city to highlight its attractions.

Edlund does make clear that the map was "drawn in a manner designed to ignite the imagination" (p. 279). That opens up the possibility, following Wood's analysis of the power of maps,[25] that this detailed map was drawn with a distinct purpose in mind. Presumably to capture the mood of earlier, halcyon days, when all the activities illustrated were carried out. The cartographic details of the contours, used to indicate the hills in the Northeast of the map, and the careful drawing of the outline of the larger and smaller lakes show that this was no casual sketch map. It was an instrument with a distinct purpose. Although this particular personal map was carefully drawn to capture an era, all maps have some purposive quality, however mundane.

Map complexity

The mental representations of Places are inevitably more complex as time moves on. I was particularly struck by this when I returned to Liverpool thirty years after I had left it. I had grown up and been educated up to my early twenties in a small area, little more than a mile square, not far from the city centre. I therefore had a very detailed mental map of the part of the city I had lived in and moved around. On my return, this provided a kind of underlay to the new city I was experiencing, almost like a hidden archaeological stratum. The corner of the street, which I remember painfully as being the location where I had my pocket money stolen from me, when I was ten years old, was now a tidy pavement with a modern office block. When I asked a bus conductor for

Figure 14.2 Edlund worked with the graphic artist Maria Sundström to reconstruct from memory a map originally drawn by his grandfather of his home village of Berg in the parish of Björna, Ångermanland, Northern Sweden (reproduced with permission)

a ticket that would take me as far as a particular department store, he told me that shop has not been there for a dozen years. As my new use and experience of Liverpool grew a new cognitive representation of the city emerged. It really felt as if this new image was superimposed on the old one, which had so many associations and memories for me. Eventually the two 'maps' merged and a current, enriched set of ideas of what was where, and how to get there, took over.

Italo Calvino[26] captures this complex mixture of qualities and association of cities in his 55 prose poems. On the face of it, each of these is a description of a different city, each reflecting a different aspect of life (and death). To take just two contrasting examples, the city he calls Zora "is like a honeycomb in whose cells each of us can place the things he wants to remember". This contrasts with Perinthia, which was established following astrological principles to "reflect the harmony of the firmament" but now "guttural sounds are heard from cellars and lofts, where families hide children with three heads or with six legs". Within Calvino's narrative it becomes clear that there are all different perspectives on Venice. Each of his essays could therefore be regarded as a different facet of his mental representation of that eternal city.

Environmental roles and place meanings

Calvino's different facets of Venice and the layers of my memories of Liverpool, like Lynch's taxicab dispatcher image of his city, all reflect the purposes the person has for being in there. A fascinating example of such environmental roles is a paper delivery round, common in many cities in the mid-twentieth century, but rare although not entirely stopped these days. Daily and weekly newspapers were delivered to individual households, typically by teenage boys and sometimes girls. As Colin Ward[27] pointed out in his exploration of children's resilience and resourcefulness across the world, when children have an economic role, it changes their relationship to society in general. The paper delivery round is an interesting example of this because it also has a profound influence on their relationships to Place, the roles they play in relation to their environment.

The power of these roles in shaping a relationship to Places is enjoyably illustrated by Denis Wood[28] through explorations of maps he and his fellow delivery boys drew in adulthood from memory of their paper rounds. Some of these maps list who lived at each address, but they are dominated by routes, with only a rare indication of landmarks, such as the basketball court they were keen to get to as soon as they finished their work for the day, or where they would find what they called 'buckeyes', better known in the United Kingdom as conkers (horse chestnuts). These memories of Places also contain crucial details, notably access to the blocks of apartments, so important to ensure delivery:

> I didn't just know where these buildings where, I knew *in my feet* the number of steps in each flight of stairs, the handholds, where I'd have to stand to toss the paper onto a door mat without leaving the stairs, the smells of the hallways, how to get a locked lobby door to open by yanking hard on the outer door and getting across the lobby fast enough to grab the inner door before it clicked shut again after it popped.
> *(p. 19)*

The regular interaction with the roads and apartment blocks shaped what they were as Places to young Denis. Also, as he puts it, the series of maps he drew when trying to recall the development of his understanding of the area showed how his image "was getting deeper and deeper". For example, his impression of the Overlook area, shaped by his paper round as shown in Figure 14.3, reveals the depth of his knowledge.

Discussing all this in later years and requesting sketches of their paper routes from his brother and others who had been 'paper boys', the significance of each of their particular approaches to the delivery tasks is illustrated in their different maps. Their individual maps often reflect contradictions in what each remembers. These differences are a product of the variations between them in how they deal with the world. Those who think in terms of the focused task are content to mark a route on an old (now inaccurate) map. This contrasts with Denis' own fascination with maps.

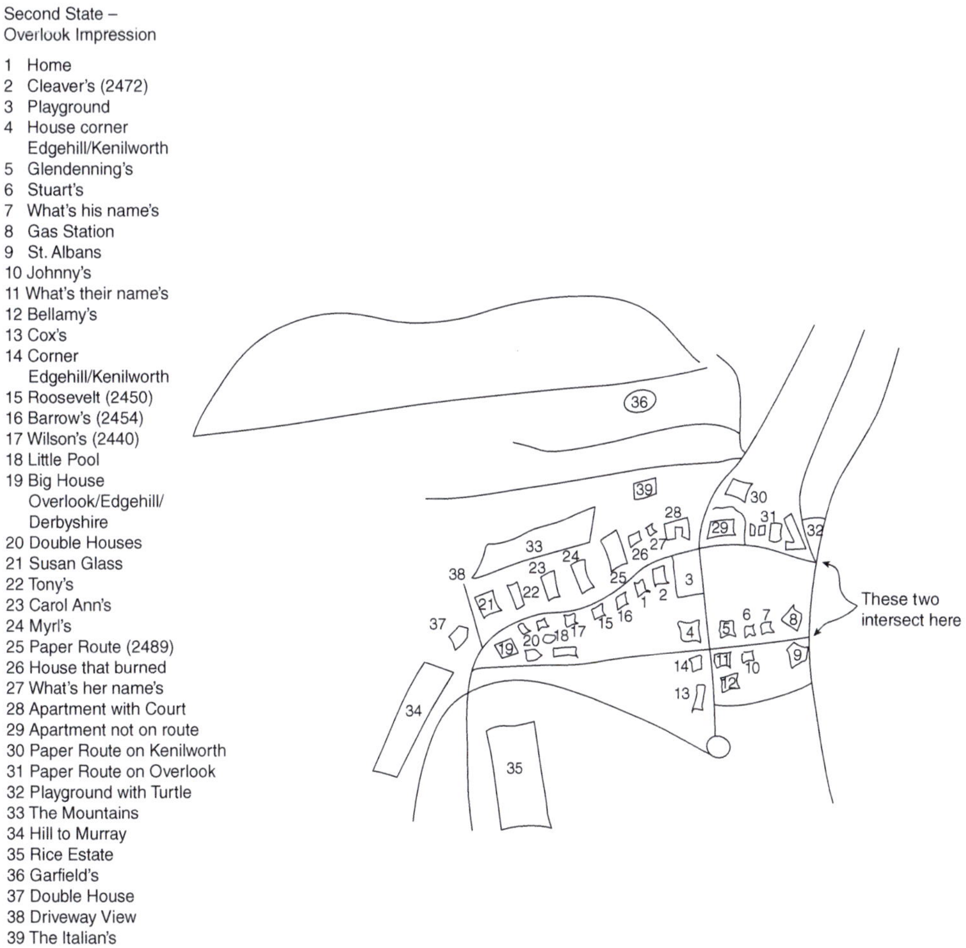

Figure 14.3 Denis Wood's paper round

As Wood put it in his Master's thesis, a person's "mapping strategies are integrated within the entire individual personality structure of a person". I would take this a step further and propose that mapping strategies reflect a person's being in the world. Who they are.

This is illustrated in a unique, fascinating study carried out by Wood and Beck.[29] In 1971 they monitored a group of American teenagers on their first trip to Europe. Where they sat on the tour buses was recorded and their personality as tourists (an interesting perspective on their environmental roles), as well as asking them to draw sketch maps of London, Rome and Paris, all gave a rich insight into the relationships between their spatial actions, characters and mental representations of Places.

Amongst the many complex findings of the study, of particular note is the identification of three broad ways in which these young men and women related to the process of the trip. One group explored little and indicated a general anxiety about engaging with the new surroundings as they became available on their travels. There was tendency for them to remain rather fixed in their base in any city. Perhaps a little mischievously,

Wood and Beck called them 'fixers'. They contrasted with the more extravert individuals who set off to explore as best they could, keen to embrace the adventure of travel, given the label 'rangers'. For a third group, travel was a fundamentally social process. They explored in groups of friends as 'mixers'.

The way in which these three types, in general, created distinct area of the tour buses has to be one of the most novel findings in environmental psychology. The fixers tend to sit near the front, the mixers in the middle and the rangers at the back. Anyone who has experience of a school bus will recognise this pattern. This is not dissimilar to how pupils will freely arrange themselves in a classroom, with the adventurous trouble-makers at the back and the quiet, studious students at the front.

The sketch maps the different groups drew also help to demonstrate how the environmentally related aspects of their personality are reflected in how they conceptualise the world. That also supports how they participate within it. As might be hypothesised, the rangers usually had the most accurate and detailed maps compared with the other groups. The fixers tended to map smaller areas around where they were staying, with the mixers mapping larger areas but with less detail and accuracy than the rangers.

The integration of seat choice, social interactions and mapping quality all support the perspective that environmental role reflects the characteristics of how a person typically connects with their surroundings. This is embedded in their cognitive processes. Their engagement with a Place is part of their being.

Domocentricity

Despite the complexities of mental images of Places, those mental maps do derive from direct and indirect experience of being in those locations. These usually develop from the base a person has, typically their home. This was intriguingly illustrated when I asked a prolific burglar to draw a map of the area in which he had carried out his burglaries.

The sketch he drew, shown in Figure 14.4, is a revealing approximation of his cognitive representation of where he burgled. Its clarity and (in)accuracy fruitfully reveal his knowledge of the area. Its variations from cartographical similitude give insights into how his mental representation helps to shape his criminal actions.

The crosses in Figure 14.4 show where this energetic chap carried out burglaries! There are a great many. But they are positioned very precisely. He told me he knew what sorts of alarm systems and security devices each of the buildings he burgled had. Other locations he specifically marked are also revealing: the police station at the top left and across the road from that the DHSS (this is where he collected his social security payment). The betting office and the local pub also are selected for particular notification. These landmarks do help to show us his world.

Of further interest is what the map reveals about the limitations of his activities. The police station provides one implicit boundary point on the map. Although he had the temerity to burgle near there, he would not go beyond it. That limitation of where he would burgle were presumably because of the increased risk of moving past the police station after committing a crime, when he would be carrying stolen goods. Similarly, the canal to the right of his sketch map acts as a limitation on his actions. His criminality also seems to stop at a road roundabout at the bottom of his sketch. In other words, the Place of his crimes is very constrained within a mentally distinct area.

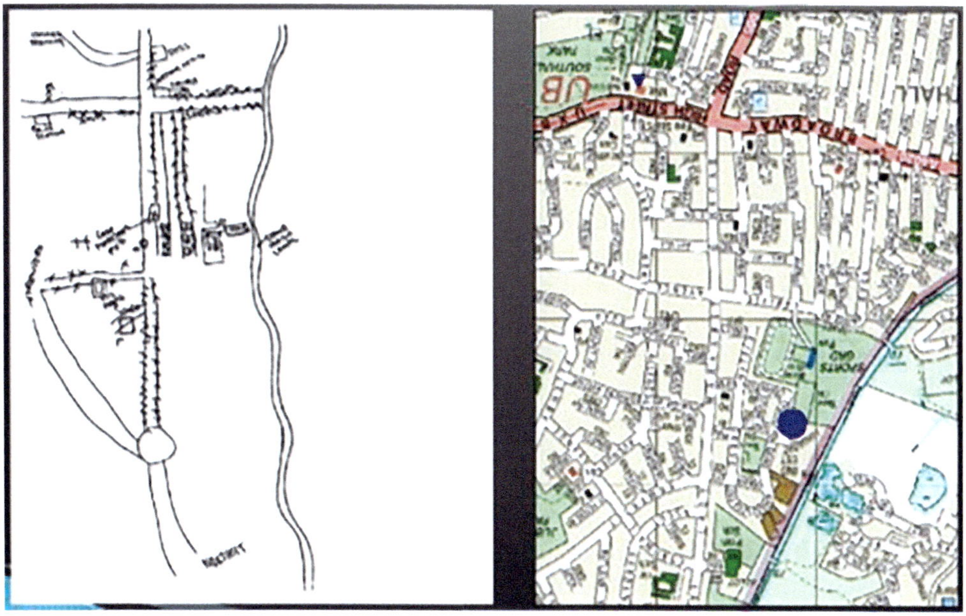

Figure 14.4 Sketch map drawn by a prolific burglar (the crosses indicate the Places he stole from) compared with an actual map of the area

There are two other crucial locations on this map: 'old house' and 'home'. These operated as the basis of his activities. It can be seen one set of crimes occurred where he used to live, along the roads around his 'old house'. The other set of crimes fanned out from his 'home'.

When his sketch map is compared with an 'actual' map in Figure 14.4, the way he defines an area around his home as a tightly familiar zone becomes even more apparent. The canal and the main road are drawn as parallel in the sketch map. In fact, they diverge considerably. This distortion and other similar ones are a natural aspect of sketch mapmaking because of how we store and construct spatial images in memory.[30]

One consequence of this is to make his mental area seem more constrained and conceptually compact than is geographically the case. It is also apparent that the land use on the right of his sketch map, beyond the canal, is very different with open spaces. Although it does not indicate the many bridges across the canal, the lack of any burglaries on the side opposite to his home indicates that this area is less attractive for the sorts of access to housing and pickings he wants.

An emerging map of London

The burglar's map indicated some development in the location of his crimes with the move from his 'old house' to his 'home'. This illustrates the dynamic nature of our cognitive cartography. Moving home is a powerful process for creating these developments. But the way in which we build up a map of a Place we are unfamiliar with is not always related to our home or base. Transport hubs and our actual exploration of an area enable us to build up a mental picture that serves as a framework for further exploration.

We also develop images in our minds of locations that we've never visited. These conceptions come from many secondary sources, representations in the media, accounts in books, discussions with people who have been there, even maps we may have looked at. It seems very unlikely, for example, that Edlund's grandfather has never seen a formal cartographic representation of the village of Berg.

I had an unusual opportunity in the early 1970s, to explore this development when Nick came to stay with me where I was living an hour's train journey, South of London. Nick was an American, living in Hawaii, with little knowledge of London. He was based with me for a short time whilst he found somewhere to live in London for a few months. Fortunately, I was able to pick him up at the airport and get him to draw a sketch map of London before he had ever visited it. Then after he had been there for a day's visit. After he had been living there for a week and then three weeks later. The sequence of sketches he produced is illustrated in Figure 14.5(a–d).

The first sketch Figure 14.5(a) drawn before his first visit to London reflects the landmarks he had heard of, as well as his awareness that the airport into which he had flown, Heathrow, was at some distance (12 miles) North of London. This sketch is therefore a fascinating list of the well-known locations that, for Nick, characterise London; Parliament, Big Ben, Westminster Abbey, the Tower of London and a

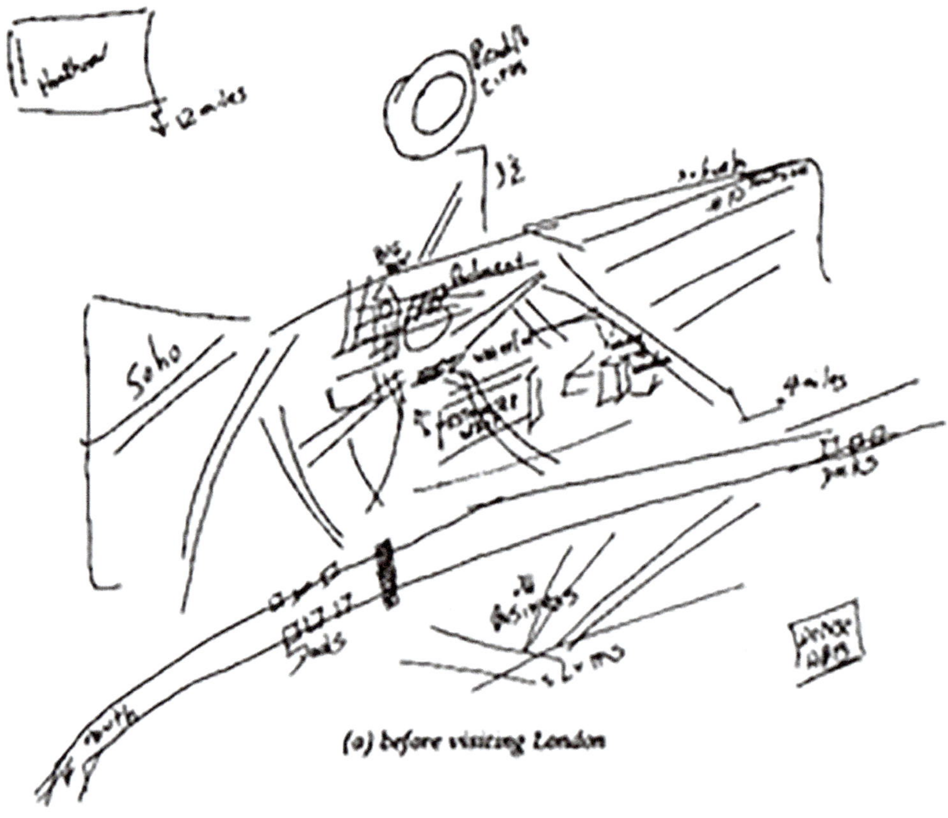

Figure 14.5a Nick's map of London before visiting London

(b) after one day in London

Figure 14.5b Nick's map of London after one day in London

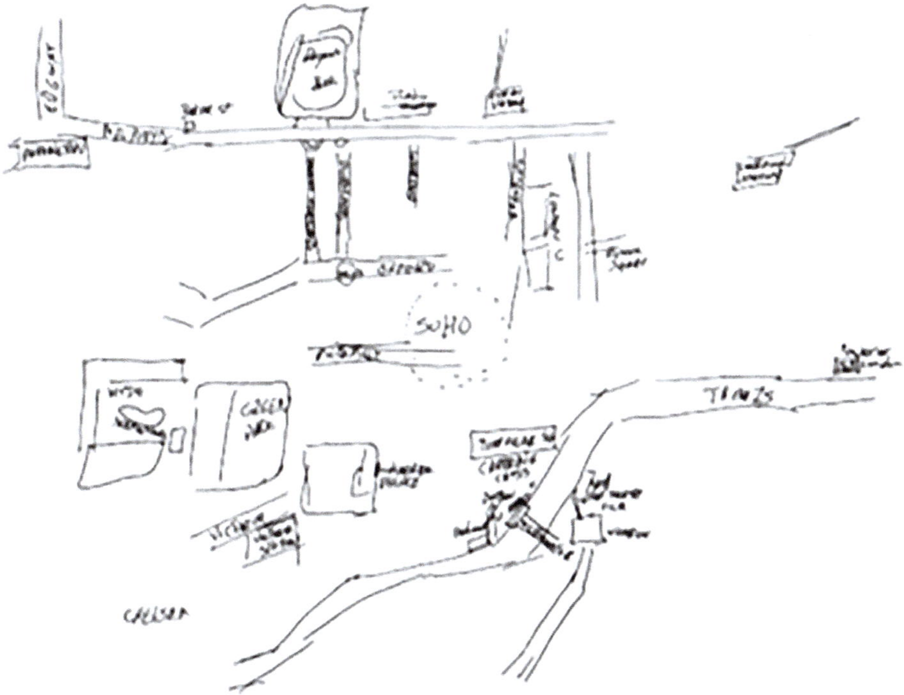

(c) after nine days in London

Figure 14.5c Nick's map of London after being there for nine days

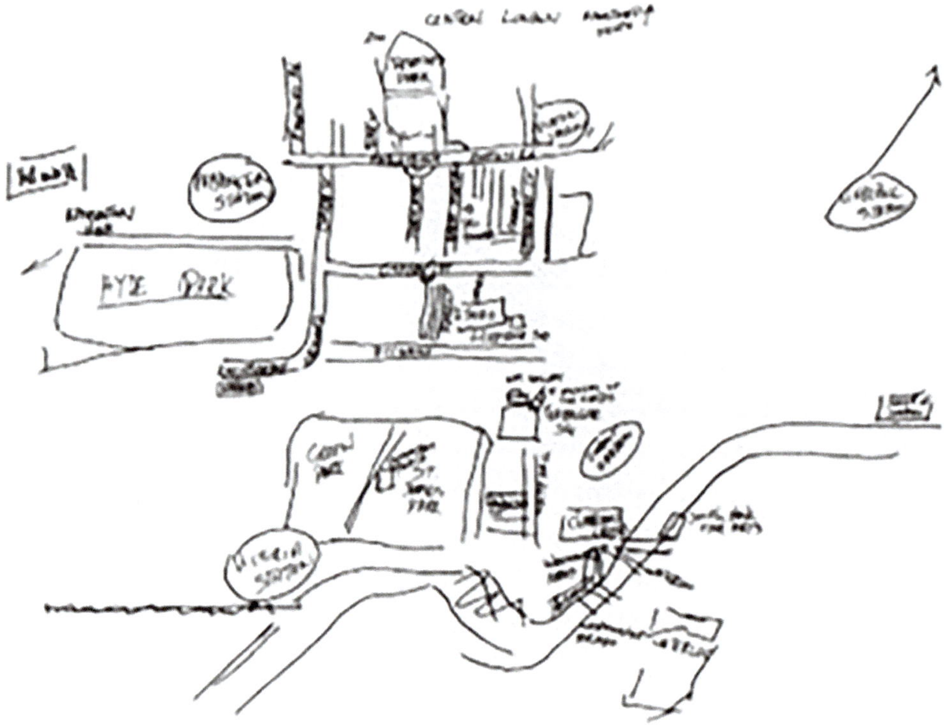

(d) after twenty-three days in London

Figure 14.5d Nick's map of London after being there for 23 days

'waterfront'. He is aware of a circular area called Piccadilly Circus as well as the River Thames, which he is careful to put a bridge over, with the river's wrongly to the East. The docks associated with the river are noted, as is an 'old business district' South of the river with associated 'slums' and nearby 'dense apartments'. The entertainment centre of London (still rather seedy in the 1970s with strip joints and sex shops), Soho, takes up a big area of his sketch. For someone from the United States, with the grid layout typical of cities, the almost random criss-crossing of roads in the centre of the map indicates Nick's apprehension that this may be a difficult city to find his way around.

Nick's initial sketch map can therefore be seen as a demonstration of what he knows about. He is offering his second-hand version of London, keen to demonstrate what he knows of, but also trying to be honest about the ambiguity and confusion of his image of London.. It makes very clear, though, that for Nick, London is a Place of famous Landmarks, a complex network of streets just north of the Thames. Beyond that focus there are outer regions of slums and docks, apartment buildings and the distant 'suburbs'.

Figure 14.5(b) shows the sketch Nick drew after his first direct contact with London. His train journey from where I lived took him into Waterloo Station, so that becomes the starting point for him at the bottom. The Place that London is for him has changed considerably because of this direct contact and exploration of it. The Place is still focused around the same area as in his imagined map. It seems to be rather more constrained. He is now aware that Piccadilly Circus does not have clowns, acrobats and performing animals, as he thought originally, but is one of a number of road intersections in London called a circus because a circular layout emerges when a number of roads meet there. He now records the parks that surprise first-time visitors to the metropolis, notably Regents Park which was the outer limit of his one-day explorations. He found somewhere to stay near there, interestingly providing the Northern limit of his map.

Just opposite Regents Park is a fascinating detail. A very small semi-circle is drawn with a dot within it. This clearly links to what Nick identifies as a road. The road is perceived as a main road because it is drawn with two straight lines. This detail refers to the impressive Park Crescent of Georgian terrace houses, in which there is also an underground-train station, from which he doubtless emerged. Clearly this sweeping row of houses in a neoclassical style attracted Nick's attention.

This second map no longer exhibits a confused set of landmarks. It is beginning to reflect the experience of being in a Place. It is likely that the related image has also been influenced by at least a cursory study of a map. The Thames now has a shape to it. It is not a straight line as in the first sketch. A number of bridges have also been indicated. A further elaboration is the straight line drawn upwards from Waterloo. This is the tube, underground-railway line, that is a common way of getting into the city centre from that station. London has apparently changed as a Place for Nick. Its river and railway system are becoming a shaping device. Soho is no longer a broad area in imagination, but a small, distinct locality just South of the Piccadilly crossroads. Although this and Oxford Circus are still drawn as circles.

Having established himself in London, I met up with Nick nine days after his arrival at Heathrow. The map he drew then has distinct roads on it but is still limited by Regent's Park at the top (and the carefully drawn park Crescent is now even more clearly a distinct street). The entrance to central London through Waterloo Station is still at the bottom of the map, but now the area around it including Charing Cross and Trafalgar Square, as well as the National Theatre, indicates some explorations in the immediate environs of Charinf Cross station.

The transport hubs take on special defining significance with Victoria Station to the bottom left, connecting with the area of Chelsea. To the top left is Paddington (Station) with Euston Station to the right of that. To the far right of it is Liverpool (Street) Station. London has become a Place defined by these major sources of public transport at its four corners. These provide Nick with ways into and out of London whilst still defining its reach. Some main roads are drawn with confidence, but the centre of London is still a bit of a mystery, except for the appearance of Buckingham Palace. The sketch map is more readily defined in terms of what Lynch would call 'districts' rather than the 'landmarks' that defined Nick's initial image of London. This is particularly clearly indicated by Soho becoming a central idea indicated by a dotted circle.

After twenty-three days London has become a network of streets. Nick is now aware that he is only dealing with 'central London' labelled at the top of his map. But this area is still defined by the railway stations at its four corners. The parks now also provide dominant districts, with even an arrow at the top pointing to the wide-open space of Hampstead Heath. Arts venues emerge in this map with the 'South Bank Fine Arts' being noted, and the Nat(ional) Gallery. This is still a tourist's map, but shows the particular ways of relating to the city that are special for Nick. It is an area of central London commonly known as the West End, now defined for Nick by the grid of main roads and the River Thames. It would appear that he is finding a network of streets that he can relate to the classic Manhattan structure of parallel avenues and streets at right angles to them.

Looking back on the three maps, drawn since his first visit to London, the elaboration of the street network does emerge as a dominant development from one to the next. This indicates a person whose contact with the city is walking around it, exploring its parks and art galleries. The maps act as both a record of his interaction with the city as well as an indication of the sort of Place it is to him. Like many foreign tourists, whose knowledge is based on photographs and hackneyed accounts of the London of history, his initial image was a ragbag of famous landmarks of well-known buildings, such as Westminster Abbey and the Tower of London. As he wandered the streets, this imagined Place dissolved into a criss-crossing of main thoroughfares. Buckingham Palace now forms the core of this, with the earlier feature of Soho reduced to a small rectangle hidden amongst the street network.

Nick's maps were drawn over fifty years ago, yet I've been able to make sense of his developing conceptualisation of central London when writing this chapter. That sense-making has drawn heavily on my own mental representation of London. I have not consulted any formal maps to interpret Nick's drawings; rather, I have tried to relate what they mean to me as a frequent visitor, but never a resident of London. His steady elaboration of what London means to him powerfully illustrates the significance of the interaction between mental maps and actions in Places. Places attractive to many tourists that he has avoided, such as Madame Tussauds, tell us something about his interests, especially as the very expensive department store, Harrods, has emerged after his 23rd day. Baker Street, made famous as the invented residence of fictional Sherlock Holmes, also makes an appearance, again telling us something about Nick's interests, all these years later.

By considering how Nick's mental maps relate to mine, I am engaging in a social transaction with him, even though I lost contact with him not long after he returned home. Our mental maps are part of us. We engage them whenever we connect with each other.

Inferring a criminal's mental map development

The consideration of how a person's experience of Place shapes their mental representations of them provides the opportunity for some fruitful inferences. If what a person is familiar with (as cherished in their mental map) influences where they go, it is possible to form a view of what they are familiar with by establishing where they go. Furthermore, any development in their location choices is likely to reveal the way their familiarity is evolving.

I applied this elementary principle to a major police investigation to which I was asked to contribute. Between 1981 and 1986 a number of rapes and three murders occurred in and around London. In 1985 the police determined that these were all committed by the same offender. In some rape cases the victims said two people were involved, but the details of what happened in the offences as well as forensic evidence drawn from blood and fibres, pointed to at least one of these two being involved in all the cases. As I describe in my book[31] once the police had linked all these crimes to the same offender, they were looking for help to locate that individual. Because of my work studying behaviour in buildings on fire, which involved studying witness statements collected by the police, those investigating the linked crimes found their way to me. I was asked if I "could help catch this man before he kills again". My readiness to take up this challenge changed my professional (and consequently personal) life.

It was a curious request to me to help a major police investigation, having had no involvement in such a project before. I therefore approached the task as I would any other research project. I took the information the investigation had available as data for analysis. But my approach to the analysis was shaped by my views on the significance of Places in people's lives and how the mental representations they develop of them reveals something about the person and their experience of those locations. An important aspect of this was my awareness that people develop and change in relation to their experiences of Places. Therefore, one analysis I carried out was to look closely at the geographical pattern of crime locations. Figure 14.6(a) shows where the first three linked rapes occurred, in 1982/3. The path of the River Thames, as it runs through central London, is indicated in the figure to give some idea of where these crimes were committed. Essentially, they all happened in an area of Northwest London, known as Kilburn. I wondered if this area had particular significance for the offender(s).

The police reported no related cases in 1984, but in 1985 there were at least seven rapes that were linked to the same offenders, as shown in Figure 14.6(b). These seemed to show a broader dispersion of locations away from those earlier assaults. As well as more frequent activity.

Was this a demonstration of a growing pattern of location selection? To test this hypothesis, the rapes that occurred in 1986 were considered, as shown in Figure 14.6(c).

Again, the frequency of the crimes was increasing as well as a wider dispersion of them. Examination of the actions in the assaults also showed an increased determination and planning of the crimes. They started to happen during the working week, when the earlier crimes had happened at the weekend. Was this an indication of more commitment to carrying out the crimes? A moving away from an almost casual seeking of opportunities where it was convenient to do so, to thinking through where the crimes could be committed without being caught? Where the offenders preparing to search out where there were vulnerable victims, with limited risk of detection? Were the offences changing from being opportunistic criminal to ones to being offences that were becoming a way of life?

Many of these crimes were committed near railway stations, with victims being forced along the station platform for the sexual attack, where there was no-one to witness it. For this reason, the offender was given the alliterative label by the media of 'The Railway Rapist'.

The determination of the offender to get away with the crimes came to a disquieting peak when in 1985 and early 1986 three murders were linked to the series of rapes. The locations of these fitted the developing pattern for the rapes. In Figure 14.6(d), they can be seen to be at the extremes of the area covered by these crimes.

The picture emerges from this pattern of an expanding area of activity emanating out from those first three linked crimes. When this is taken together with the emerging

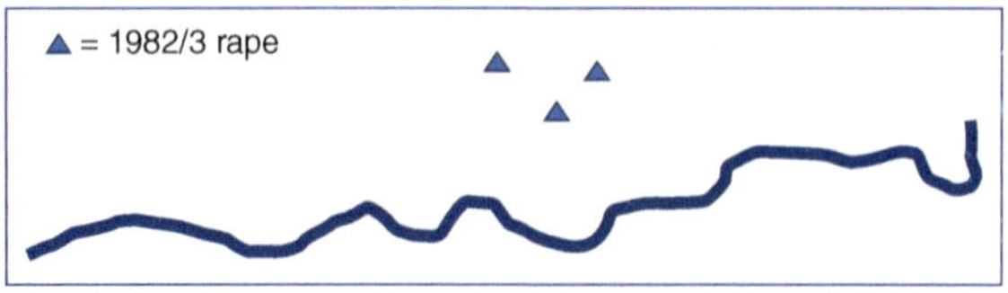

Figure 14.6a 1983/3 linked rapes relative to the River Thames

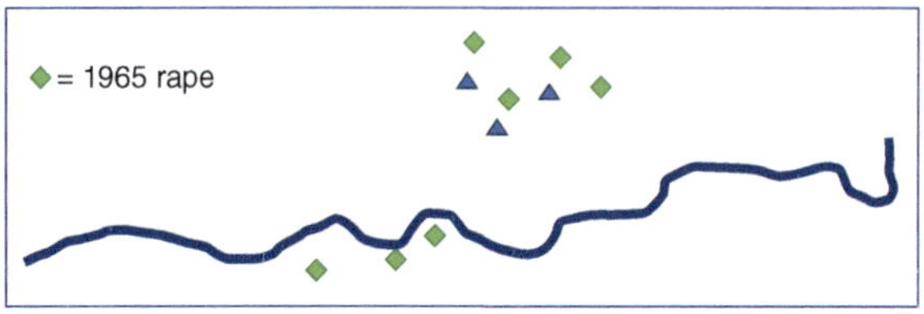

Figure 14.6b Addition of 1985 instances

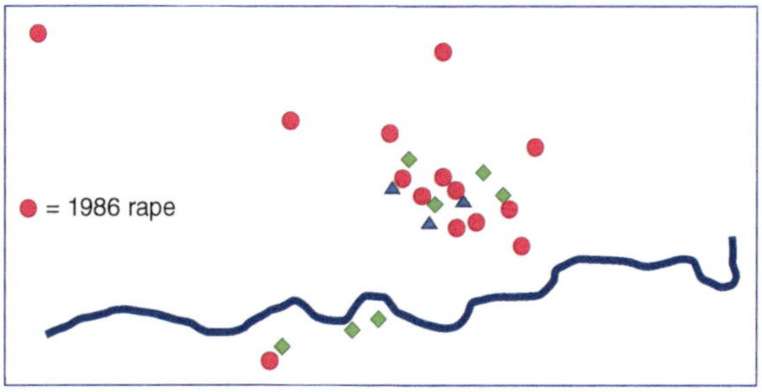

Figure 14.6c Further addition of 1986 instances

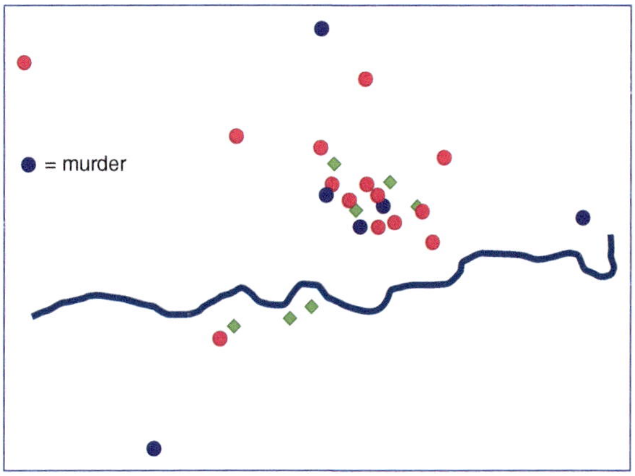

Figure 14.6d Original plotting of linked rapes with addition of 1985/6 murders

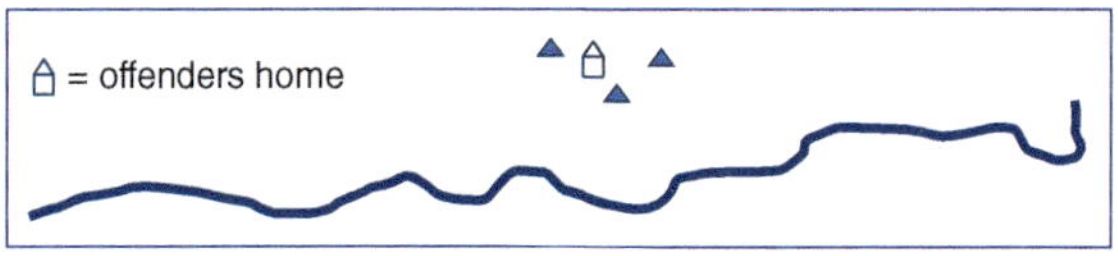

Figure 14.6e Prediction of where the offender's home was

planning and commitment to the crimes, which was evident in the actions of the criminal, it seemed obvious to me that those early crimes harboured a Place of particular significance for the offender. As argued in Chapter 6, the home is usually a person's most important Place. I therefore suggested to those investigating the crimes that the offender's home was as indicated in Figure 14.6(e) within the area circumscribed by the first three crimes.

There were a handful of suspects that the investigation had identified through trawling through police records for people convicted of sexual assaults and violence against women. But only one of them, John Francis Duffy, lived in that Kilburn area of London. This gave the police the basis for putting intense covert surveillance on Duffy. That enabled them to obtain enough evidence to get a conviction, with a life sentence of 30 years.

Although the contribution to this investigation was heralded as a breakthrough in police procedures in the United Kingdom, its importance in enabling us to understand the significance of home for many offenders was possibly of equal value. This understanding opened the way to considering many aspects of criminal, Place-related activity. The term 'geographical offender profiling'[32] emerged to describe the application of these ideas, leading to the development of a number of software applications[33] for helping to calculate the likely location of an offender's home. The key to the success of this approach, and related software developments, is twofold. One is the way an offender's mental map of a Place is shaped by transactions with it. The other is the power of the home as a base from which to venture out to commit crimes.

The influence of the home comes from many different aspects of it. Central to all these are the feelings of security it offers together with the possibility of privately preparing for criminal activity. People who have nowhere to live and sleep on the streets (recorded in the old legal term – no fixed abode) find it more difficult to carry out carefully planned crimes. They may be responsible for casual, opportunistic thefts, or assaults, but their helplessness on the streets, especially at their most vulnerable time – when they are asleep – reduces their possibility for sustained, determined offending. The chances are therefore very great of them being recognised and apprehended.

Geographical offender profiling

Both Duffy, the prolific burglar and my colleague Nick, exhibited an important aspect of their interactions with their surroundings. These developed as they explored further afield. You will remember the often-quoted aphorism from Churchill, "we shape our buildings and after that they shape us". That can be generalised to make the point that we interact with our surroundings and that influences how we think about and conceptualise them. Our 'mental maps' are constantly evolving as we make use of Places for many different activities.

In order to have a way of labelling the many criminals who move out from their homes to commit crimes, returning to hide from detection, then moving out again from the same base to commit their next crime, like John Duffy, I called them 'marauders'.[34] These contrast with those who move to an area to carry a series of crimes in that area before returning to their base. I thought such criminals were like a person going to work then returning home, so I initially called them 'commuters'. But this is rather misleading. The term does not reflect those criminals who travel extensively to commit their crimes. Travelling offenders is a better way of describing these.

It would be a mistake, though, to assume that travelling offenders have no form of 'home' to act as a base for their crimes. They typically have a vehicle that provides a moving location from which they can act. A particularly disturbing example of such a travelling killer is Robert Black. Robert Black was a Scottish serial killer and paedophile who was convicted of the kidnap, rape, sexual assault and murder of four girls aged between 5 and 11 in a series of killings committed between 1981 and 1986 in the United Kingdom.

The simple idea of 'commuting' and 'marauding' offenders has found its way into the crime psychology literature. This is probably because it is a simple notion that can be turned into multiple-choice examination questions! Like most simple notions that simplify a scientific theory, it is very limited and ignores many of the subtleties of criminal behaviour. One crucial oversimplification is the proposal that a marauding criminal's crimes will usually occur in an area around the home. It is postulated that this area can be usefully defined by a circle drawn using a diameter drawn between the furthest two crimes in the series. That proposal[35] was always just a limited, very simplified first approximation to defining the area of activity of a criminal. Many subsequent studies[36] have demonstrated that offenders operate both in relation to where they know crimes are possible and also to their patterns of routine activity.[37]

Design implications

The awareness that any person's image of a Place relates to their experiences and purposes in being in there has important implications for any processes of design that wish to take account of the perspectives of the users of those designs. This is not a trivial matter because by their very occupation as producers of Places, planners, architects and other members of the design professions have distinct role in relation to Places they are helping to create. It has been established[38] that part of their educational process is to give them a different understanding and way of looking at buildings and other design products.

A number of design teams have taken on board the consequence of the inherent differences between designers and users by setting in motion participatory design processes. A notable example is the consultancy practice set up by Goltsman and Iacofano[39] once they had completed the course I set up in Environmental Psychology at the University of Surrey. Their organisation specialises in a design process that engages users and potential users. This enables them to incorporate the conceptualisation of Places, into what people are trying to achieve with the help of the proposed designs. This contrasts with an architectural approach which assumes that designers know and understand what needs to be done.

A remarkable example of the Goltsman and Iacofano approach was the design of The Edelman Children's Court.[40] This is a unique courthouse in Los Angeles, dedicated solely to cases of child abuse and neglect. The legal processes there protect children from dangerous or imminently dangerous situations. This is a potentially extremely traumatic Place for all those involved in using it, but especially the children and their parents. Consequently, the design process as Goltsman put it:

> was to view the building through the eyes of the children who are brought to the facility and the parents who need help from the system. It was assumed that if the building accommodates those with the least 'power', everyone else would also be accommodated. People who work in the facility are there because it's their job. The families are there because they are in serious trouble.
>
> *(p. 38)*

The design team conducted focus groups, interviews, surveys and field observations to take account of the differing experiences and perspectives involved. With the children, special procedures were used to enable them to express what they thought the building was about and how it would best suit their purposes. A particularly innovative aspect was the modification of a focus group so that children could express their views, as shown in Figure 14.7.

This approach enabled the designers to change the nature of the Place. As Goltsman puts it:

> The physical environment of the building became the container for change. It locked in the management changes through new spaces that housed services- no one could use the old organizational systems in the new building. It became a place where new behaviors could be learned and old ones discouraged. It became a place where new life could begin for children and their families.
>
> *(pp. 56–57)*

This was achieved by dealing with all aspects of the design. For example, the entrance through a metal detector is part of an elaborate archway, moving into a lobby

Figure 14.7 A focus group where children work with graphic shapes to help indicate who should sit where in a courtroom

that is light and welcoming, with friendly artwork and natural construction materials. Groups that are best kept separate; judges, prisoners and children in protective custody, each have their own 'elevators' to keep them away from each other and the remainder of the users. The layouts of the courtrooms also convey dignity without being intimidating. All of these, and many other physical attributes, draw on meanings and associations whilst making clear how it is expected the Places will be used. From the large-scale building that is the Edelman Children's Court to the more local scale of the arrangement of furniture in the courtroom, the conceptualisations of the nature of these Places have been the dominant influence of what has been produced.

Conclusions

The exploration of how people sketch maps of various Places has been used as a route into their cognitive representations of them, their 'mental maps'. This has revealed how personal those maps are and indicated the purposes they serve in providing a matrix for actions. These purposes are part of how and why a person engages with the environment, what I have designated as their 'environmental role'. Different reasons for interacting with our surroundings give rise to different internal representations of them. These in turn influence our interactions. Mental maps are therefore always developing and changing to a greater or lesser degree as transactions with Places change and evolve.

The focus of any individual's activity will typically have a base, most often their home or at least where they usually sleep. This domestic location will therefore have a dominant influence on their mental maps. That influence will be increased by the distortions that occur in how we remember Places and what we remember about them.

It has been possible to demonstrate that because the transactions with Places reflect personal perspectives.. These transactions can be the basis of inferences about a person. In some criminal investigations this can be used to indicate where an offender may have a base or live. An area of investigative psychology has developed, known as 'geographic(al) offender profiling', specifically to take advantage of the relationship between criminal actions and a given individual's knowledge of locations.

The impressive work of Iacofano and Goltsman draws on the fact that Places are not only in the head. By manipulating physical forms to reflect users' anticipated experiences in Places, activities can be encouraged that are best suited to the aims and desires of the users of those Places.

References and endnotes

1 For a thorough review of what mental maps are and their research utility, see Kitchin, R.M. (1994) Cognitive maps: What are they and why study them? *Journal of Environmental Psychology*, *14*, 1–19.

2 Abse, D. (1970) *Selected poems* "Looking at a Map", London: Hutchinson. Reprinted with permission of the Estate of Dannie Abse through his agent, United Agents. *s*,

3 Götz, N. & Holmén, J. (2018) Introduction to the theme issue: "Mental maps: geographical and historical perspectives", *Journal of Cultural Geography*, 35(2), 157–161, https://doi.org/10.1080/08873631.2018.1426953

4 Wood, D. (1992) *The power of maps*, New York: The Guilford Press.

5 Wood, D. (1992) *The power of maps*, New York: The Guilford Press.

6 Head, H., Rivers, W. H. R., Sherren, J., Holmes, G., Thompson, T., & Riddoch, G. (1920) *Studies in neurology*, in two volumes, Vol. 2. Oxford University Press; Hodder and Stoughton, https://doi.org/10.1037/14209-000
7 Head, H., Rivers, W. H. R., Sherren, J., Holmes, G., Thompson, T., & Riddoch, G. (1920) Studies in neurology, in two volumes, Vol. 2. Oxford University Press; Hodder and Stoughton, https://doi.org/10.1037/14209-000
8 Bartlett was knighted in 1948 for his use of applied psychology to help the Royal Air Force during the Second World War, showing the real significance in saving lives of his seemingly abstract ideas.
9 Bartlett, F. C. (1932) *Remembering: A study in experimental and social psychology*, Cambridge University Press.
10 Newman, E. J. & Lindsay, D. S. (2009) False memories: What the hell are they for? *Applied Cognitive Psychology*, 23, 1105–1121, https://doi.org/10.1002/acp.1613
11 Abbott, L. F. (1990) Learning in neural network memories, *Network: Computation in Neural Systems*, 1(1), 105–122, https://doi.org/10.1088/0954-898X_1_1_008
12 Boorstin, D. J. (1963) *The image*, Harmondsworth: Penguin Books. Boulding, K.E. (1956) *The image: Knowledge in life and society*, Ann Arbor, Michigan: University of Michigan.
13 Carter, M. J. & Fuller, C. (2015) Symbolic interactionism, Sociopedia.isa, https://doi.org/10.1177/205684601561
14 To take one of many possible examples, the delightful anthology chosen by Ronald Blythe (1981) *Places : An anthology of Britain*, Oxford: Oxford University Press.
15 Here's a study waiting to be done! What do people actually choose to buy from this organisation? This would reveal what types of Places do have this significance.
16 A Google Scholar search for the term "Mental Maps" generated nearly 50,000 results. There is no possibility of summarising all that work here. I am therefore focussing on the particular insights that can be drawn from this approach about how Places have such power.
17 Lynch, K. (1960) The image of the city, Cambridge, Massachusetts: MIT Press.
18 Although distance estimations, for example, typically have a very close correlation with actual distances.
19 Downs, R. M. & Stea, D. (eds.) (1973) Image and environment: Cognitive mapping and spatial behaviour, Chicago: Aldine Publishing.
20 Francescato, D. & Mebane, W. (1973) How citizens view two great cities: Milan and Rome in Downs and Stea, pp. 130–152.
21 Ferranti, E. (2014) *My brilliant friend*, Europa Editions.
22 Edlund, L.-E. (2018) Some reflections on mental maps, *Journal of Cultural Geography*, 35(2), 274–285, https://doi.org/10.1080/08873631.2017.1362934
23 Carpenter, E. S. (1955) Space concepts of the Aivilik Eskimos, *Explorations*, 5, 131–145.
24 Edlund, L.-E. (2018) Some reflections on mental maps, *Journal of Cultural Geography*, 35(2), 274–285, https://doi.org/10.1080/08873631.2017.1362934
25 Wood, D. (1992) *The power of maps*, New York: The Guilford Press.
26 Calvino, I. (1974) *Invisible cities*, London: Secker & Warburg.
27 Ward, C. (1979) *The child in the city*. London: Architectural Press.
28 Wood, D. (2013). The paper route empire, in *Where you are: A collection of maps that will leave you feeling completely lost*.
29 Wood, D. & Beck, R. (1990) Tour personality: The interdependence of environmental orientation and interpersonal behavior, *Journal of Environmental Psychology*, 10, pp. 177–207.
30 One study of these distortions is given in Pocock, D. C. D. (1973) Urban environmental perception and behaviour: A review, *Tudsschrift voor Economish en Social Geographi*, 64, 251–257, illustrated with other examples in *The Psychology of Place*, pp. 53–57.
31 Canter, D. (1994) *Criminal shadows: Inside the mind of the serial killer*, London: Harper Collins (now available as an eBook and audiobook).
32 Canter, D. (2007) *Mapping murder: The secret of geographical profiling*, London: Virgin Books (also available as an eBook and an audiobook).
33 Technical explorations of the mathematics of geographical offender profiling are given in academic journal articles such as:

Canter, D., Hammond, L., & Youngs, D. (2012) The efficacy of ideographic models for geographical offender profiling, *Journal of Quantitative Criminology*.

Canter, D. & Hammond, L. (2007) Prioritizing burglars: Comparing the effectiveness of geographical profiling methods, *Police Practice and Research*, 8(4), 371–384, https://doi.org/10.1080/15614260701615086

Meaney, R. (2004) Commuters and marauders: An examination of the spatial behaviour of serial criminals, *Australia: Journal of Investigative Psychology and Offender Profiling*, 121–137.

A popular account of these ideas are given in Canter, D. *Mapping murder: The secrets of geographical profiling*, London: Virgin Books. Now available both as an eBook and an audiobook. This derived from a six-part documentary series which is available as a DVD boxset.

34 Canter, D. & Larkin, P. (1993) The environmental range of serial rapists, *Journal of Environmental Psychology*, 13(1), 63–69, https://doi.org/10.1016/S0272-4944(05)80215-4

35 Canter, D. & Larkin, P. (1993) The environmental range of serial rapists, *Journal of Environmental Psychology*, 13(1), 63–69, https://doi.org/10.1016/S0272-4944(05)80215-4

36 For example: Kocsis, R. N., Cooksey, R. W., Irwin, H. J., & Allen, G. (2002) A further assessment of "Circle Theory" for geographic psychological profiling, *Australian & New Zealand Journal of Criminology*, 35(1), 43–62, https://doi.org/10.1375/acri.35.1.43

37 The proposal that crimes occur where criminals are usually active for non-criminal activities was first outlined over half a century ago, as discussed by Felson, M. (2008) Routine activity approach, *Environmental criminology and crime analysis*, pp. 70–77.

38 As considered in Chapter 7 and illustrated in a number of studies including:

Wilson, M. A. (1996) *The socialization of architectural preference*, *Journal of Environmental Psychology*, 16(1), 33–44.

Wilson, M. A. & Canter, D. V. (1990) The development of central concepts during professional education: An example of a multivariate model of the concept of architectural style, *Applied Psychology*, https://doi.org/10.1111/j.1464-0597.1990.tb01065.x

Erdogan, E., Akalin, A., Yildirim, K., & Erdogan, H. A. (2010) Aesthetic differences between freshmen and pre-architects, *Gazi University Journal of Science*, 23(4), 501–509.

39 Goltsman, S. & Iacofano, D. (Eds.) (2007) *The inclusive city: Design solutions for buildings, neighborhood's and urban spaces*, Berkeley: MIG Communications.

40 Goltsman, S. (2007) *Helping children heal*, in S. Goltsman & D. Iacofano, pp. 35–59.

CHAPTER 15

Place attachment and involvement

Written on my heart

On 19 January 2021, President-elect Joe Biden said, in an emotional speech on leaving Delaware, his home state, for Washington[1]: "In our family, the values we share, the character we strive for, the way we view the world – it all comes from home, from Delaware. I am proud, proud, proud to be a son of Delaware. When I die, Delaware will be written on my heart". He choked up when he said: "I am proud, proud, proud to be a son of Delaware".

There could not be a clearer indication of attachment to a Place, in this case the State of Delaware, with the direct implications that aspects of his identity, and of his family, were intrinsically associated with what he took Delaware to be – its values, character and 'view of the world'. President-elect Biden's statement reveals how intricately related can be the attachment to a Place and the view of self. The identity of the person who is attached.

When such a distinguished person makes this claim, it may lead to the belief that Delaware was some sort of paragon state. In fact it has a crime rate typical of the United States as a whole, with murders, rapes and other crimes not being unusual. It has a high level of poverty, although its state laws encourage corporate headquarters, leading to a large discrepancy between rich and poor. Biden was born in Pennsylvania but moved to Delaware when he was 10 years old, living there in Wilmington that has some of the richest residents but also a higher crime rate than most other cities in the state. This indicates that Biden's reference to Delaware is to a symbolic Place, and specific aspects of his experience of it, rather than some summary of an identifiable way of life. Even his claim that he is proud to be a 'son of Delaware' is a rhetorical claim as he was not born there. Nonetheless, his emotional comments serve to emphasise the power of associating one's identity with a particular Place.

The symbolic qualities of Places enable any given location to encapsulate a set of meanings, assumed activities and views of the people who inhabit it. This enables many aspects of life in a house, neighbourhood, city, state, or country to be distilled into the meanings of a Place. Part of these conceptions can contribute to a person's view of who

DOI: 10.4324/9780367808655-19

they are, their identity. Biden's experience of family tragedies in Delaware, with local support from his church and others, doubtless framed his experiences of the state. These memories and personal history, including his role as a senator for the state over many years, are what Delaware means to him to the extent that it is "written on his heart".

What is place attachment?

The graphic claim of "When I die, Delaware will be written on my heart" has poetic rhetoric about it, but what does it really mean? Isn't being proud to come from a Place rather different from being attached to it? Is Biden really claiming that some aspect of who he is, and who his family are, has been shaped by their experiences when growing up in Delaware? Such questions reveal some of the complexities of exploring attachment to Places.

When the scale of Places to which people claim attachment is considered a further complication emerges. Does it mean the same to be attached to a favourite chair, or even a side of a bed, a room, a house, a neighbourhood, a town, state or country? Does environmental concern reflect a form of attachment to planet earth?

These complexities have provided the basis for the emergence of a vast domain of research, discussion, poetry and literature. In writing the original 1977 *Psychology of Place,* there did not seem to be any need or research basis for considering place attachment. Nor is it mentioned in Relph's widely cited book published the year before, *Place and Placelessness.* Intriguingly though, a decade ago Lewicka[2] carried out an extensive review of Place attachment research. This was based on the dramatic increase in related studies over the previous forty years. Her review has over 250 references. Although these are not all totally focused on place attachment, they do reveal how much research there was ten years ago. Without doubt the growth has continued beyond even the levels Lewicka monitored.

Place meaning and attachment

The ways in which Places incorporate feelings have been highlighted by Manzo.[3] Through intensive interviews with people in New York, she was able to elaborate the great variety of emotions people have about Places. These can be seen as one starting point for the development, or otherwise, of attachment. Many of her participants described deep love for some Places in New York. Others described fear, dread or even hatred of Places. Interestingly, the great majority of her participants indicated that Places that were meaningful to them were those that they felt ambivalent about. This makes clear that for a Place to have significant meaning it is not necessary for it to be liked, or for people to be attached to it. One corollary of this is that satisfaction or delight in a Place is not the same as it having meaning or significance. Even feeling attached to a Place does not inevitably reflect satisfaction with it.

Indeed, dislike may be a common aspect of Place meaning, at least for those interviewed by Manzo who were living in New York. Other Places whilst still "important" and "meaningful", were characterised in less emphatic ways with such comments as, "I come here regularly. I really like it; it is a nice place to be". This all adds up to the rather unsurprising mixture of reactions that can be found in any conversation about Places. The important point is that there is an assortment of feelings that people express when considering where they live, work and carry out the range of activities. Therefore, as a basis for attachment, such as President Biden's feelings about Delaware, it has to be assumed that there will be many different ways to be 'attached', or not.

A further caution needs to be repeated. One of the remarkable weaknesses of studies of Places and related experiences is, rather ironically, that they only rarely take account of *where* the study occurs. Practical considerations, especially in qualitative research that requires intensive interviews usually with a few people, generally dictate that the data is collected in one location. Manzo's study was conducted in New York; other interesting studies have been conducted in small towns. Yet no attempt is made to consider whether there is something about those Places which biases the results obtained. This is such a fundamental problem that there will be a need to return to it later.

Facets of 'attachment'

It is essential to be aware that the concept of 'attachment' when linked to the notion of place is inherently a metaphor. It draws on such analogies as a limpet being attached to a rock, or in a somewhat more psychological sense, children being attached to their parents. There are certainly situations in which these parallels are relevant. A person refusing to leave their home, which is to be demolished in order to build a major road, is a literal form of attachment. Or a colleague of mine, who finds himself unable ever to leave the ancient city in which he lives, is another example.

However, if the metaphor is relaxed and Place attachment is taken to mean "the cognitive-emotional bonds between individuals or groups and their important places" (p. 45)[4] then it has productive similarities to interpersonal attachment, like that between a mother and her child.[5] Yet, it has to be distinguished from other overlapping concepts.

Perhaps the most basic aspect of attachment is 'rootedness'. This is another metaphor, or perhaps more accurately an analogy, referring to the process by which a plant literally embeds itself in the ground. A process which enables it to gain nutrients from the soil and to withstand the wind and other environmental forces, which would pull it away from that which supports it. As with all metaphors, there are implicit connotations that give added power to its meanings. When a person feels 'uprooted' they are also indicating that they have been separated from their sources of sustenance. That this is most likely to be an involuntary move challenging their history of having 'put their roots down'.

Another, less specific aspect of attachment is what Feldman[6], more than 30 years ago, called this 'Settlement Identity'. The idea that people, who have some choice in where they live, have a commitment to a particular kind of Place. Examples would be those who want to live in the excitement of the city, or in a suburban enclave, a small town, or a rural retreat. When such people have mobility options, they will seek to reside in their chosen type of location. Bailey et al[7] cite examples of relocation decisions being reminiscent of their former homes, giving rise to consistent patterns of residence across the life course.

However, caution is needed when considering 'settlement identity'. It makes two fundamental assumptions, both of which are open to serious challenge. One is that an individual, or family, has some choice in where they live. A refugee who moves from one internment camp to another may show settlement identity without that ever being what they want or feel attached to. The second is that any consistency in where a person, who has opportunity for mobility, lives does not have to relate to their former home.

It is probably one of the limitations of the study by Bailey et al[8] that their respondents were living in a small town. It seems likely that those who had grown up there but no longer wished to, or were able to live in that community had moved away.

Most of my life has been spent living in rural settings, but I grew up in the very different environment of a major city. The move from cities to the suburbs, that started in the United Kingdom with the development of public transport, notably the railways, and the current exodus to small towns and the countryside, generated by the awareness of cities as breeding grounds for disease and the opportunity for online working from home, are powerful illustrations that the nature of the place in which a person was born is not necessarily any basis for where they want to live now.

A further aspect of attachment that has been surprisingly little explored, but strongly emphasised by Devine-Wright[9] is his critique of the approaches most human geographers take to place attachment. Besides the limitations imposed by lack if choice, there are pulls of family and amenities. Many people are attached to a particular location because of the social, economic and broader structural opportunities it provides. Where a family, for instance, has some choice of where to live, they may well attempt to live in the catchment area of a local school that is highly regarded or close to a golf course in which they can indulge their passion. House prices have been known to increase in an area around a school when a new, more effective Head Teacher is appointed to it.

Beyond the possibilities of rootedness, settlement identity and social aspects of attachment, there is the interest a person can have in a Place, which is characterised by their active involvement and discovery of what happens and is possible in that location. Lewicka in a number of publications based on impressively large surveys of people in a number of Eastern European countries[10] calls this a form of 'place discovered' attachment. She contrasts this with traditional forms of place attachment, which she labels (perhaps a little overzealously) 'place inherited'. Helpfully, she links this distinction to studies of dominant themes in personal narratives[11] in which people can be distinguished by whether they seek 'communion' with others – a desire for contact and friendship, or 'agency' which relates to being significant and powerful. Agency, she finds correlates with the 'place discovered' attachment, whilst 'communion' is more likely to be reflected in those with a traditional embedded attachment. It has to be said, though, that whilst the relationships Lewick reports are statistically significant in a meaningful way in her large samples, the actual size of the correlations – often referred to as their 'power', is rather limited, indicating that many other issues contribute to the forms of attachment a person exhibits.

Traditional and active attachments do not cover a rather broader concept of 'belonging'. This is captured in an explicitly sentimental way in the songs of the early 20th-century singer Al Johnson (1885–1950). Quite inappropriately this Jewish singer was blacked up to sing, almost as if he was a Southern States African American, but his heartfelt yearning carries a universal message, for example in his song *Mammy*:

> Here's what you'll keep saying
> When you're far from home:
> Mammy,
> Mammy,
> The sun shines east, the sun shines west,
> I know where the sun shines best–

Mammy,
My little mammy,
My heartstrings are tangled around Alabammy.

The yearning in *Swanee* is also intense:

Swanee, how I love you, how I love you
My dear old Swanee.
I give the world to be
Among the folks in D-I-X-I-E
Even though my mammy's
Waiting for me,
Praying for me
Down by the Swanee.
The folks up north will see me no more
When I get to that Swanee shore.

A close reading of many of Al Johnson's songs captures this mood of yearning for a lost home. My theory is that the power of these songs can be gleaned from the fact that Johnson was a Jew who came to the United States at a young age. He was an integrated part of an intense religious community, having started singing in public in the synagogue. I suggest that the idea of belonging to some rose-coloured image of a past place was an integral part of the identity of his family and community. After all, Alabama, Dixie and the Swanee River were the locations of many horrific abuses of African Americans, hardly reflecting a golden age of residence for the people his blacked-up, make-up was supposed to represent. The reason they joined 'the folks up North' was to get away from the depredations of the South.

Although these songs capture a feeling of belonging to a Place where the singer is no longer resident, they belong to the idea of that Place and all the concept of it encapsulates. As such, a myriad of examples can be found in daily conversation and throughout literature and music of this type of place attachment. The longing at the heart of this is typically associated with a person who symbolises a way of life, 'mammy'. The attachment is to the concept of what the Place represents. The synthesis of a set of values and culture. Yet another example of how Places are bundles of concepts associated with memories, people and activities.

How places and identity interact

Jo Biden's declaration of attachment and identification with Delaware implies a complex mixture of conceptualisations about the State, ideas about himself and his family and wider values that he strives to reflect in his actions. Crucially, it illustrates the transactional nature of relationships to a Place. The state of Delaware takes on a particular significance for President Biden, a set of meanings he ascribes to it as a Place. At the same time, he sees his identity as influenced by what he takes that State to mean. The sense he makes of Delaware is part of the character he sees himself and his family as having. It is an interactive process between the conceptions of Place and of self.

In one of the earliest psychological commentaries on individuals' relationships to place Harold Proshansky (1920–1970) and his colleagues[12] drew attention to person-place relationships being part of a person's identity. It is perhaps no coincidence that Proshansky and his colleagues were New Yorkers, embedded within the social and cultural life of that distinguished city.

They defined place identity as:

> To begin with, it is a substructure of the self-identity of a person consisting of, broadly conceived, cognitions about the physical world in which the individual lives. These cognitions represent memories, ideas, feelings, attitudes, values, preferences, meanings, and conceptions of behaviour and experience which relate to the variety and complexity of physical settings that define the day-to-day existence of every human being. At the core of such physical environment-related cognitions is the environmental past of the person; a past consisting of places, spaces, and their properties which have served instrumentally in the satisfaction of the person's biological, psychological, social and cultural needs.
>
> *(p. 59)*

It is therefore inevitable that most studies of place attachment[13] involve some notion of how a person's identity may relate to a Place. They explore the cognitive and emotional processes that develop and sustain both place-related self-concepts and their links to place attachment. This requires the exploration of three further issues.

One is the extent to which any Place has a distinct identity. It is difficult to see how a Place can be incorporated into a person's sense of who they are if it has no distinctive qualities. This takes us into the confusing world of 'placeless' places, anonymous locations that have no 'genius loci' (sense of place), discussed in earlier chapters. These considerations are confusing not least because of the interactive aspect of recognising the significance of a Place. If a person regards anywhere as relevant to their own self-image, then they are likely to regard it as having a distinct identity even though others may consider it as 'placeless'.

The second aspect of place-related self-concepts is the challenge of unpacking the meaning of a person's identity. This is assisted by considering the psychological nature of personal identity and how it emerges, is maintained and developed. I will explore that next, but for clarity, the third aspect to be considered is the nature of 'attachment' with regard to places. That will be considered later.

A psychological approach to identity

To quote one of the most profound psychological thinkers on identity, Erik Erickson (1902–1994):

> Ego-Identity, then, in its subjective aspect, is the awareness of the fact that there is a self-sameness and continuity to the ego's synthesizing methods and that these methods are effective in safeguarding the sameness and continuity of one's meaning for others.[14]
>
> *(p. 362)*

Erikson uses the term 'ego-identity' to draw attention to that aspect of a person's awareness of themselves which has stability and continuity. This is not just an individual's answer to the question "Who am I?" but behind that is the process that gives a person the sense that they are the same person now as they were in the past. Although Erikson, as a psychotherapist, embraces the understanding that this continuity of the ego is nonetheless an evolving changing experience of identity. The power and significance of where a person is, the places they use and inhabit emerges from the ways in which those places safeguard an individual's sameness and continuity.

Erikson also indicates many other considerations of identity in his mention of 'one's meaning for others'. He elaborates this by saying:

> The conscious feeling of having a personal identity is based on two simultaneous observations: the immediate perception of one's selfsameness and continuity in time; and the simultaneous perception of the fact that others recognize one's sameness and continuity.

Many social scientists have drawn attention to the distinction Erikson describes. An earlier social scientist George Herbert Mead[15] (1863–1931) characterised it as the difference between the 'I' as experienced in a person's own view of who they are and the 'me' as they think people with whom they interact see them. The 'me' is a form of 'social identity', which has become a central concept in social psychology. The recognition that identity is as much a social construction as a personal one opens the way to a theory that is starting to dominate social psychology in many different guises. Known as *Social Identity Theory*[16] (SIT). It has its origins in the work of Henri Tajfel[17] (1919-1982). His central postulate is that a person's sense of who they are is based on their group membership. Out of this, their own sense of self emerges.

Crucial to this perspective is that the social group, whom the person references as relevant to formulating a view of their identity, is seen as influencing their actions and attitudes. The 'me' is claimed to be dominant over the 'I'. The identity of being black or gay, for example, or a professional, or Arsenal supporter, is characterised by how the individual understands the characteristics of that section of society. Within this 'Social Identity Theory' framework a person's view of who they are is explained by reference to the group with which they identify. Two stages to social identity are specified. The first is an individual's recognition of differences between groups. The subsequent identification with a particular group is claimed to shape that person's view of themselves with consequent attitudes and actions. Importantly, the psychological search for self-esteem supports the process of seeing positive qualities in the group identified with.

However, many SIT studies are laboratory-based or deal with the attitudes and membership of groups in general. Yet, the presence of identity within a social context points to the crucial aspect of the role a person has in that situation. As emphasised in earlier chapters, people in actual places (rather than as 'subjects' in laboratories) are there for a particular purpose. That purpose is part of their membership of a group or organisation – even if they are on their own with implicit membership. They have a role that is relevant to why they are in that place. This can be the role of lone tourist taking in the sights, or of the leader of a protesting crowd. It can be the manager of a factory or a pupil in a school. In all these cases there is a purpose for being there that is explicitly or implicitly defined by their role in that situation. This has implications for the interpretation of a person's social identity. It consequently also has significance for how a Place has relevance for who they think they are.

Curiously, I have yet to see the influence of environmental role on social identity explored widely in the research literature. To repeat, the role a person has in any location has direct implications for experience of that as a Place. It is part of their place-related identity. If you are given an office on the top floor, as considered in Chapter 3, that helps you to identify with the senior management you are part of. The location itself, with all the related rules, activities and meanings, contributes to the identification of those who are there as being different from others on the lower floors. The initial stage of social identity – the recognition of differences between groups – is greatly enhanced by the Places they are associated with or inhabit.

If your role in the executive suite is as a receptionist, filtering access to your boss, although you will bask in the thick carpets and quiet ambience, so symbolic of the higher echelons of the company, your role does echo different aspects of that experience. Your privileged position takes on a rather different meaning to that of the Chief Executive Officer who defines the power of the location as much as it defines his position. Similarly, the leader of a public protest march needs to consider how the hordes will be guided through the streets. So, her experience of those streets and her identification with the protestors take on a different emphasis to those following her. Place-related identity can therefore be seen to be shaped by why a person is there and how their role interacts with the significance of the Place for them.

The place-related development of identity

Breaking with the Freudian tradition, which saw personal development as derived from a series of psychosexual stages in childhood, Erikson[18] expounded the view that identity emerged through stages of social interaction throughout a person's life. These social interactions are a series of dialectic crises the individual goes through; by resolving each, the next stage in maturity is reached. Very briefly they are:

- Trust versus mistrust
- Autonomy versus shame
- Initiative versus guilt
- Industry versus inferiority
- Identity versus role confusion
- Intimacy versus isolation
- Generativity versus stagnation
- Integrity versus despair

Whilst there is some debate about the ambiguity of these eight stages, whether they are distinct and inevitably proceed in a distinct order, there is still a great deal of current interest in their central social psychological implications.[19] Crucially, this is an active way of thinking about identity. It is a changing, evolving process. Each person is always in the throes of grappling with some inherent individual challenge out of which a further aspect of their identity emerges.

At the heart of these ideas about the development of identity is the way that emerges out of interactions with others. For example, in the earliest stage, the responsiveness and sensitivity of those who take care of the child facilitate the development of a person who trusts others and consequently is optimistic of future possibilities. At the crucial stage of adolescence, the challenge is to clarify "who am I". If successfully faced, this gives a sense of self-continuity and a strengthened ability to relate to others.

The power of the adolescent stage is reflected in the number of autobiographies that focus on the impact of this period of life. In terms of Place experience the significance of the family home in many later relationships to dwellings[20] illustrates the influence which that early Place of development has on subsequent experiences. Where the interactions with others and the development of self-understanding occurs plays an indirect role in contributing to the emergence and evolution of a person's identity.

The possibilities Places make available, and the meanings attached to them carry implications for who you are. It is not so much that a garden, for example, allows a child to play there, and thereby encourages certain aspects of autonomy and initiative, but that it is the particular garden, which is associated with those activities, building memories that become part of the person's awareness of what they are capable of. Thus, although there is little evidence that the general qualities of particular Places directly influence the emergence of a person's identity, there are many aspects of their meanings and the patterns of activity they make possible that contribute to who a person thinks they are.

To consider a very personal example, I grew up as an only child in a Victorian terrace that housed a dozen different, mainly one-room flats ('apartments' would be too grand a term for these). They all shared one bathroom and toilet, although I never considered that at all unusual or problematic. My parents and I lived mainly in one room with a table by the window, their double bed against one wall, with a curtain that could shield it off, and my single bed against another wall. Although it has been over 65 years since I was anywhere near that house, I can recall very many details of it and things that happened there. At the age of 11 my father bought a house a few doors further up the road, which we fully owned. I stayed there throughout my education at school and university but left in my early 20s never to return.

Looking at pictures for the first time ever of the buildings where I lived,, on Google Street View, there is not a rush of memories and emotions that come flooding in. Nor do I feel any attachment to these as Places, but I have to admit there is a powerful sense in which they are part of my identity. Of course, growing up as an only child,[21] the nurture of my parents and my comfortable relationship with them, my friends and schools, as well as my own potential and abilities for what they were, are all crucial to how I dealt with the identity crises Erikson elaborated. Nonetheless, these houses, the grand house across the road where my family doctor lived, the public park next to that, where I spent so much time, the small shop round the corner where I could buy liquorice sticks, as well as other parts of Liverpool that I explored, was educated in and enjoyed, were all doubtless an important backdrop to my unfolding identity.

Yet, being clear of what all these experiences of Liverpool contribute to my identity is not easy. The move from a one-room flat to ownership of a whole house doubtless strengthened my feeling of autonomy – I had my own bedroom. The particular nature of that large house with my enormous bedroom, decorated with hand-painted angels on the ceiling, provided opportunities for industry and intimacy that would not have been possible in my earlier dwelling.

These considerations reflect the ability of Places to condense many aspects of events, meanings and actions, to be symbols of unfolding experiences, assisting the awareness of who I was then. Given the age I was at the time, notions of myself as an autonomous person, developing, if only hesitantly, an awareness of my capabilities and industriousness are supported by what I remember of those Places in which I grew up. As I got older and moved to other cities and Places of work, married and had children, where they occurred reflected other features of Erikson's life struggles. Certainly, the ability to buy a Place to live and to be provided with an office in which to work, the freedom to travel with all the locations with which I engaged, now with a wife, then children, contributed to the development of satisfying intimacy and the eventual feeling that I was doing something worthwhile. The Places did not create or initiate these aspects of maturation, but they certainly capture significant features of who I was, and am.

It is perhaps not surprising that the house in which I grew up and even the Liverpool of my youth have only moderate relevance to my current identity, and for which I feel fond nostalgia, but not attachment. I left it, never to return, over half a century ago, losing all personal connections with it when the house where I had lived was sold and I no longer had any close relatives living there. For others, like Joe Biden, who had lived in the same city, enjoyed the delights and endured the tragedies of family life, and developed his political career there, it is understandable that Delaware has special meaning for him. He says Delaware is "written on my heart". That indicates he sees it as part of his identity. This is doubtless because his sense of his initiative, industry and generativity was all fostered in that context, forming the foundation for his sense of identity with, and attachment to, Delaware.

A closer association between identity and Place occurs when people invest time and resources in creating Places that help to demonstrate their identity and integrity. It is not uncommon for those buying a new house to declare that they want to impose their own individuality on it. In other words, to use the Place as a way of shaping and demonstrating who they are. This is a recursive process. Once a location has been modified to reflect what many homebuyers call 'putting our mark on' a Place, the process of modification itself, with all its challenges and successes becomes embedded in the experience of that location. They become part of the memories associated with a location that contribute to its meaning. Many people are reluctant to move from a home because it enshrines so many important memories. What is remembered is part of who they are. Their identity and Places experienced are an integral part of each other.

Places provide sources that contribute to identity through the meaning and significance of the social symbols they embody.[22] Such sources derive from the personal memories which actions in places have generated. They also enshrine their personal histories, captured by the symbolic qualities of Places. Beyond these personal memories are the shared histories that Places represent. These can be regarded as a form of social memory that a group, city or nation associates with particular Places. These can be created for that social purpose, as in the war memorials set up in most towns and cities in the world. Or emerge out of events that have happened there, such as the fields where major pop festivals occurred, such as Woodstock or Glastonbury. These Places are part of a social memory that has significance for people even if they never attended the events there. Identity is very much more than 'being where', the rich symbolic meanings of Places help to elaborate notions of 'being who'.

Place attachment and identity

Although thinking about Devonshire Road in Liverpool does generate memories of who I was and what happened there. I feel no particular attachment to that place. When the opportunity arose to take up a professorship in Liverpool, thirty years after I'd left the city as a student, I had no desperate desire to visit the road where I'd lived during my formative years. When on journeys that took me along that road, there was a shallow wave of nostalgia, but no intense need to knock on the door of number 62 to see if it was still divided into many flats, or to ask the residents of number 70 if they had kept the hand-painted ceiling. Having an emotional bond with a Place, being attached to it, would seem to be rather different from it contributing to a sense of self, personal identity, even if the two are entwined. It is possible to be attached to a Place without regarding it as part of your identity, and vice versa. It is possible to regard a Place as an aspect of your identity without having any emotional bond to it. Although these two psychological processes inevitably interact, it is necessary to consider a further psychological perspective to help clarify how people become attached to Places. This is to consider their purposes for being there. What is it about those places which contribute to what are often thought of as 'needs'?

A very influential theory that elaborates the objectives people have, couched in the language of motivation and 'needs' is Abraham Maslow's (1908–1970) 'need hierarchy'.[23] He proposed a rather elegant ladder of motivations which had physiological needs at the bottom and self-actualisation at the top. Originally Maslow proposed 8 needs, but usually they are presented in a distilled version of five, (Table 15.1).

Self-actualisation
Esteem–recognition
Belongingness–affection
Security safety
Physiological food–drink

These have often been simplified even further as:

- Basic needs – physiological and security
- Psychological needs – belongingness and esteem
- Self-fulfilment needs

Table 15.1 Maslow's needs hierarchy

Maslow's hierarchy of needs
Self-actualisation Esteem – recognition Belongingness – affection Security safety Physiological food – drink

Table 15.1 *Maslow's hierarchy of needs*

This provides an interesting list of what people seek, fundamental to their daily lives. I am putting 'needs' in inverted commas to indicate that Maslow's list is not an account of the necessities for survival, as the need for food, water and air to breathe, clearly are. Rather, they indicate what people seek to achieve their well-being and self-esteem.

It is usually illustrated as a pyramid, the proposal being that each 'need' builds on the success in achieving the one below. The argument is, for example, that you cannot satisfy your appreciation of beauty unless you are reasonably well-fed. Or you cannot develop affection and belonging until you have satisfied your need for security. However, common experience and much research[24] have shown that there is little evidence for these needs operating as a hierarchy. Neither is there any indication that all unsatisfied needs within the hierarchy lead to a search to satisfy them. Furthermore, there any evidence that once a person has satisfied a need lower in the hierarchy, they will naturally move on to satisfying the next one up. A person could be floating adrift in the sea, close to dying of starvation, but still appreciate the beauty of a starlit night. Many have suffered torture in wartime rather than reveal the identities of their associates. The central idea of needs being motivations falls foul of the big differences between people in how motivated they are, or indeed what particularly motivates them. Nonetheless, the list of 'needs' provides a useful template for considering how places can support or 'satisfy' the objectives people have in their daily lives. By examining such processes of satisfying, the bases for place attachment become more apparent. These are summarised in Table 15.2.

Table 15.2 Some benefits of place attachment linked to Maslow's needs

The ways in which Places provide security, and support esteem and self-fulfilment are revealed through many daily experiences and systematic studies. For example, the security potential of Places can be important for use as a retreat from threats, or to gain emotional relief. Children have been recorded as retreating to favourite Places to regulate their emotions.[25] For adults, Places that are important to them typically are regarded as safe and secure.[26] There is also an indication that Places to which people are attached contribute to their self-esteem.[27]

The contribution of Places to a sense of self-fulfilment is illustrated by the way dictators throughout history have sought to demonstrate their achievements by creating Places that they think symbolise their importance. Curiously, despite the apparent desire to indicate individual significance, a particular style of building is common in these ostentatious palaces.[28] There are physical features that those who wield total power turn to, usually reflective of flamboyant styles of the past, most notably Louis XIV's Versailles (Figure 15.1). They also draw in the ways in which buildings mean, explored in Chapter 11, notably scale, height, space and ornamentation.

Table 15.2 Some benefits of place attachment linked to Maslow's needs

Maslow's 'needs'	Attachment Benefits
Self-actualisation	Personal growth, feeling in control, freedom
Esteem – recognition	Enhancement of identity
Belongingness – affection	Memories, positive emotions
Security	Privacy, feeling sage
Physiological	Practical facilitation, relaxation

Figure 15.1 The palace of Versailles

With the demise of these potentates, their creations take on symbols for the nation, both of what they have overcome, but also the stylistic achievements of the past. Nadine Gordimer in her brilliant novel *A Sport of Nature* elegantly characterises the means by which cultures reinvent Places that were once symbols of oppression:

> With enough time, foreign occupations become part of a treasured history which is threatened by the latest foreign power: asserting national heritage in stone restored everywhere.[29]
>
> *(p. 265)*

For emerging nations, the parliament buildings are an important way of enhancing the self-image of a nation and to bolster its sense of accomplishment.

> These are the seats of national assemblies ...that host individual legislatures and which countries pride themselves in both architectural and symbolical grandeur. Usually located at the heart of capital cities, these (usually) forbidding and intimidatingly large structures can be spotted from a wide area within the central business district and while reservedly open to the public, they are mostly heavily secured and restricted.[30]

At the heart of Erickson's view on the emergence of identity is the search for self-worth. The self-evaluation, aspect of self-esteem, is seen by most psychologists working in a clinical or counselling role, as crucial to a person's effectiveness. Low self-esteem is proposed as the source of many psychological and behavioural problems. These grand, opulent buildings are a way for a nation, and especially their leaders, to enhance their self-esteem.

There can be little doubt that the Places one inhabits and uses, or carry significance for the group to which a person belongs, can contribute to feelings of self-worth. But in revisiting Erikson's view of the significance of self-esteem a limitation is useful to emphasise. His ideas were rooted in the Freudian theories in which he was schooled, being a development of the central conflicts between the conscious and unconscious aspects of the psyche. This has led to criticisms that his framework undervalues social processes in identity formation. As already noted, how we regard ourselves is influenced by how others regard us. Or more accurately, by our perception of how others regard us. This inevitably raises the question, crucial for understanding place attachment, of whether we regard how others see us as an accurate reflection of how we see ourselves. Or whether we deliberately set out to create an impression of ourselves that may not be exactly what we think to be the truth. *Esse Quam Videri* derived from Cicero's essay on friendship, meaning 'to be, rather than to seem' recognises that people often set out to present themselves in particular ways.

My early work of the impact of setting on judgements of people[31] was extensively developed in Gosling's[32] work on what people reveal about themselves through the Places they choose and create. This provides intriguing examples of the interplay, within any location, between what people are and what they seem to be to others. Some of the aspects that any setting reveals about a person are fairly straightforward. For example, Gosling found that people who have a variety of books on their shelves are high on the psychological dimension of 'openness'. This means they are more willing to embrace new ideas and seek out new experiences. In this context there are aspects of a person's residence that *are* their identity.

The extent to which any individual or group has been able to manage how any Place they are associated with reflects how they want others to see them influences their attachment to it. The corollary of this is a finding that surprised me when, as young academic, I studied house-buying behaviour. To my surprise I discovered that the people who took longest to move to a house more appropriate for their current circumstances, were those elderly residents who lived in large houses much bigger than they currently needed. It became apparent that their homes enshrined (sometimes literally) a lifetime of memories and a pattern of activities they were reluctant to accept they would no longer participate in. Now that my own longevity has undermined that earlier naiveté, I empathise much more fully with those long-ago participants in my research.

The essence of place attachment

The ways in which a person's experience of Places is part of their identity also contribute to their feelings of some sort of bond with them. But the interactions between personal identity and attachment to one or more Places are far from straightforward.

This parallel is most noteworthy when considering the first study to draw attention to the significance of place attachment. Fried's 1963 study, with the powerful title "Grieving for a lost home",[33] introduced the graphic impact of forced removal from Places to which people were attached. From interviews with those experiencing this removal, he claimed their loss was a powerful bereavement, a form of grief, similar to that when losing a loved one. In subsequent studies with much larger samples Fried[34] makes clear that what he calls 'commitment to local spaces' is particularly prevalent where people have few independent resources, being poor and lower status, such as those he designates as 'working-class' or immigrants.

Fried's argument about the basis of place attachment links closely to ideas of identity, especially social identity, as well as the role-rule relationships that Places enable:

> places come to symbolise those community socio-cultural patterns implicit in group identity only in relatively limited conditions. Such symbolization, for example, is facilitated by the organization of roles within the community social structure and the establishment of role places for local interaction. It is these role places, the regularized settings for activities and interactions, that dominate the sense of community identity rather than the purely physical quality of the places themselves.[35]
>
> *(p. 195)*

Although Fried was a psychologist[36] he introduced some important aspects of place attachment that are overlooked in many subsequent studies:

(1) Social class and associated resources are a crucial aspect of how commitment to a Place operates. President-elect Biden may have Delaware written on his heart, but his attachment to that State, as he sets off for Washington, is very different from someone eking out an existence, living in a trailer park. Fried makes clear that although the level of satisfaction people have with where they live may be very low, nonetheless it is influenced by their commitment or otherwise to where they live.
(2) There is considerable overlap between community identity and attachment to where that community resides. The Taos Pueblo's desire to own the Blue Lake is a strong example of how the identity which those people had of their community was a crucial aspect of their attachment to that Place.
(3) Community identity supports place attachment because every community develops some degree of functional specialisation. These different functions are carried out by people with different roles which have their own symbolic or actual Places associated with those roles. These can be a seat in a bar, a basketball court, the corner of a street, an apartment or even a window box. This is illustrated in Figure 15.2, for example. That concrete slab outside the barber's house is a fixed location well-known to the local community. People wait in line for their haircut, as they would in a city salon. Figure 15.3 reveals an even more elusive location that is created as a Place to which the street vendor is committed, at least whilst he is selling his wares. He has not chosen an arbitrary location. That corner provides enough space, general visibility and opportunity for a quick getaway if the authorities should want to move him on, or worse. Here Places are designated for particular roles and their associated activities, even though the physical definition of those places may not immediately indicate their significance to the casual passer-by.

These aspects of place attachment can be seen to have a natural development. During the process of living a variety of psychological developments unfold; memories of what happens where, symbols and images associated with particular Places, the extent to

Figure 15.2 A hair salon in Afghanistan (circa 1970)

Figure 15.3 Street corner shop, Hong Kong

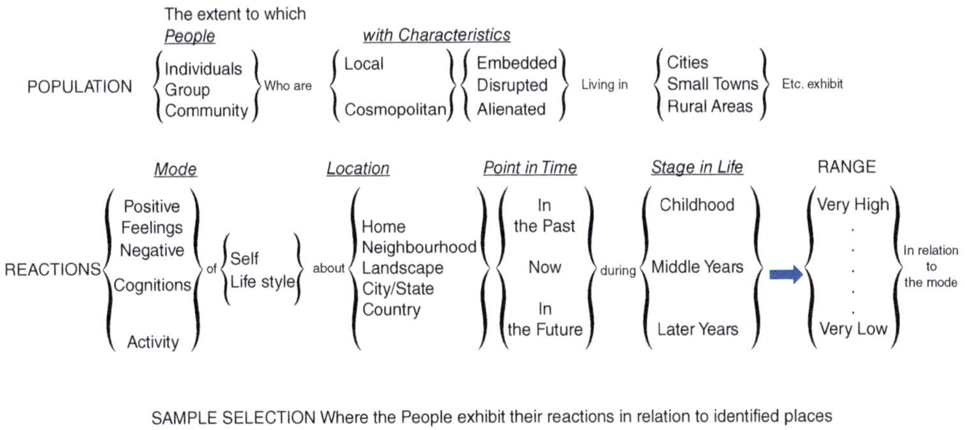

Figure 15.4 A mapping sentence for place attachment

which a person has been able to shape a Place to accord with the self they want to present, and current locations that make possible particular roles and their associated activities. As explored earlier, all of these are part of a person's identity. Threats to the Places to which a person is attached are a threat to their identity.

Dynamic aspects of identity and attachment

How I thought of myself when I lived in Devonshire Road, Liverpool in the decades after the Second World War is very different from how I think of myself now as I write this in an isolated old farmhouse in North Wales. Identities change, evolve, mature. The dynamic nature of identity, and the related changes that people may experience in where they live, raises questions about how variations in that experience might be associated with place attachment. In an interesting and unusual study, Bailey and his colleagues[37] asked 25 people to describe the Places where they had lived and their thoughts feelings and experiences there. Although this was a very small sample, it provided a useful illustration of concepts and hypotheses about the relationship between place attachment and aspects of residential 'life-place trajectories', as they call them, meaning residential histories.

Building on the extensive studies of Lewicka[38] Bailey et al identified three underlying aspects of residential experience that had relevance for forms of attachment to where they were currently living.

(a) Length of residence in the current place – long, moderate, or short. In essence, the longer the residence, the more committed to a Place a person would be; the more attached.
(b) Variety of residence – similar, moderate, or different. The implication is that when people have lived in similar Places to their current residence the more committed to that Place a person would be; the more attached.
(c) Amount of mobility – little, moderate. or much. This hypothesis is that the less mobility a person has had in where they have lived, the more attached they would be to where they are now.

Table 15.3 Relationships between aspects of life-place trajectories and attachment (derived from Bailey et al.[56])

Residence	*Mobility*	*Variety*	*Trajectory*	*Attachment*
Long	Low	Similar	Traditional	Strong Positive
Moderate	Moderate	Similar	Traditional-Active	Positive
Long	Moderate	Moderate	Continuity	Positive
Long	Moderate	Low	Estrangement	Strong Negative
Short	High	Low	High Mobility	Indifference

With this perspective there are theoretically 27 (3×3×3) combinations of these three facets of residential histories. However, some combinations are not practically viable. For example, it is unlikely that a person who has been very mobile, living in a number of different Places over their life, and also in rather different Places, will have lived a very long time in their current residence. It is therefore possible to identify a smaller logical subset of combinations of 'life-place trajectories; Bailey et al.[29] only report five of all possible life-trajectory profiles as shown in Table 15.3.

Table 15.3 Relationships between aspects of life-place trajectories and attachment (derived from Bailey et al.[39])

- Traditional attachment – Long-term residence in a single place ('score' of 6). These are people who may be regarded as what Gustafson (2001)[40] refers to as 'rooted' in the place. It connects with humanistic geographers' (such as in the early writings of Dovey, 1985,[41] and Tuan, 1980[42]) proposal of a place, for some, people being the embodiment of safety and familiar security.
- Traditional but mobile – These are individuals who have moved away from the current location, where they grew up, but returned to take advantage of the social support offered by their origins there. Such 'returnees' bring a rather distinct perspective to their attachment. In some senses they have decided to stay attached to a place, as distinct from those who have always lived there and may to some extent take it for granted.
- Continuity in settlement type – Mobility is associated with similar types of places. These are people who seem to seek out similar sorts of places in which to live. An idea which has been labelled 'place-congruity'.[43] Such residences have a generalised attachment to their current places, but one which is somewhat 'promiscuous' as it can be transferred with a subsequent move. An important aspect of this is that there is some essential quality of a place that they are drawing on when they move to similar places. The idea that a place can have a particular, recognisable quality to which they are drawn.
- Discontinuity in settlement type – When there is increased mobility over a life course with different sorts of places being involved in any given residence, there is likely to be ambivalence or even a feeling of estrangement to current residence. As Lewicka[44] points out, these are people for whom identity has very little place-related components. This accords with the idea of people being 'cosmopolitans' rather than 'locals'. People who identify with social and professional networks that are spatially distributed rather than being involved in a particular location.
- High residential mobility – Numerous relocations across the lifespan. For these people their current location is irrelevant. For them the concept of 'attachment' has little meaning. They may even feel alienated from where they are based.

Although the generation of five kinds of life-place trajectories from 25 people is supported by previous studies, they have to be regarded as an interesting hypothesis about forms of relationships to Places. It is to be expected, as Bailey and his colleagues report, that these are not hard and fast distinctions between types. Indeed, the three facets presented allow for other possible combinations than the five found in their respondents. For example, my own experience of growing up in Liverpool, living in a variety of different Places before returning to Liverpool, after a 30 year absence, for 15 years, is a mix not quite captured in any of the five types. It would suggest some identification with the city, as discussed earlier but relatively weak attachment to it.

Perhaps of most interest from the explorations carried by Bailey and his colleagues is the indication of the relative impact of their three different facets. Although it needs further testing with more precise measurements, it would appear that the most powerful influence on place attachment is, as might be expected, the overall length of residence in a location. If the residence length is less than total amount of time living there, then the degree of mobility comes into play. Once there is some mobility, then its variety, especially in relation to the current residence, has an impact.

This hierarchical set of influences can be seen to connect with the unfolding personal narrative associated with the Place or Places a person has experienced. The idea is supported of a broadening narrative in which the current location loses its power over who a person thinks they are as the range of other place experiences can be drawn on. The way social features of a Place can increase their influence on place attachment is inherent in these processes.

Lewicka[45] elaborates the role of social processes in place bonding by drawing attention to the value of considering the different dimensions of 'localism' and 'activity'. Those who were traditionally attached tended to be embedded in their local community drawing on local social and family contacts. By contrast, those whose attachment was more active, having been more mobile, whilst making a conscious commitment to a particular Place, had a much wider range of social and cultural contacts and were more open to experience.

In a subsequent study, Leicka[46] developed this distinction by relating it to two widely considered aspects of personality. One is that in which personal narratives are seen as emphasising interaction with others 'communion'. The other is 'agency' where the person focuses on individuality and achievements. Traditional place attachment reflects a communion orientation. The more active aspect of bonding to where a person is tends to relate to agency. In other words, the personal narrative that integrates an individual's identity carries implications for how that person bonds with any particular Place. Place attachment is not simply an aspect of what a person's identity is. It also reflects the mode of bonding the individual has with a Place.

Studying place attachment

The complexities of place attachment and its overlap with aspects of personal identity create a challenge for systematic research. As many scholars have pointed out[47] place attachment is given many different meanings by different researchers. Therefore, one way of gaining a further insight into what it is may, perhaps, best be achieved by considering the sorts of questions using questionnaire surveys that are used by researchers who study the topic. A sample of these are:

(1) This place is part of me
(2) I don't feel integrated in the neighbourhood
(3) I feel I belong in this neighbourhood
(4) This is the ideal neighbourhood for me
(5) It would be very hard for me to leave this neighbourhood
(6) I miss the place when I'm not here
(7) I feel safe here
(8) This is a good place to live
(9) I like living in this neighbourhood
(10) Even if there are better places, I'm not going to move out of this city
(11) No place can compare to where I live
(12) This is the best place for what I like to do
(13) I know this place well
(14) This place is special
(15) I like to wander around this city and discover new places

These questions cover many different issues. Some of them relate to who is answering the question, whether the personal 'I' or the more general 'This'. Others are about feelings, 'like' or thoughts 'know'. Yet others deal with interactions with places, or stages in the consideration of those interactions. To make sense of these disparate issues, a device known as a *mapping sentence* has great heuristic value,[48] given in Figure 15.3. This provides a form of summary of the issues considered in the present chapter.

Four aspects of place attachment are captured in the mapping sentence. One is who it is that is indicating their reactions – the *population*. A second is the nature of their *reactions*. The third is the *range* of responses that those reactions can take. The fourth is the description of how the *sample is selected* that is used in any study.

This is a 'mapping' because it identifies a range of aspects of the area of study in a way that allows them to all be related to some common range of possible answers. In intelligence tests, for example, this range would be whether the answer was right or wrong. In behaviours it could be how frequently they occur. In the present case we are thinking about the extent of the presence of feelings, thoughts and actions. Consequently, the common range is their intensity in relation to the mode of reaction. This may vary from very positive or negative feelings, a great deal to a little knowledge, a lot to a little activity.

This called a 'sentence' because the constituents of the topic being studied are given a framework with connecting words that allows them to be read as sentences. The mapping sentence therefore summarises a large number of possible issues that can be explored. For example, 'To what extent do individuals who are locals, embedded in an area now have negative feelings about their neighbourhoods when they were children?'. Another example would be 'To what extent does a community of alienated people plan to make use of their city in the future when they are older?'.

The mapping sentence as summarised here therefore indicates a potential for 3×2×3×4×5×3×3 research questions. That is rather a lot. Any particular study would take a subset of these to explore. Those aspects that are not included are kept constant. The mapping sentence helps to focus the selection of topics because the 'Population' components are the selection of respondents that will be studied, and often compared. For example, people who are part of local communities compared with those who are more cosmopolitan. In the language of experimental science these are the 'independent variables'.

The 'dependent variables' are those that are formulated from the reactions. For example, Question 2 in Table 8.1 "I don't feel integrated in the neighbourhood" is an individual with negative feelings towards a neighbourhood, presumably in the present. The mapping sentences serve to indicate what is left unclear in this statement. Another example is question 13 in Table 8.1 "I know this place well" is made up of the 'cognitions', knowledge mode, and an ambiguous location mode. Probably 'neighbourhood', with the other components being unspecified.

The mapping sentence brings together the various components that are explored in the many studies of place attachment.[49] These components are summarised, for example, in Scannell and Gifford.[50] Their three components relate directly to aspects of the mapping sentence. Their 'Person' is the *Person*, their 'Place' is the *Location* and their 'Process' is the *Mode*. However, in most discussions of the components, they operate as little more than lists of the issues to be considered. The mapping sentence takes this a stage further. It is actually a set of hypotheses about the components of place attachment and how they relate to each other. Those hypotheses are firstly, that the elements in each Facet (e.g. in the mode Facet - feelings knowledge, actions) operate differently from each other. That they are empirically distinct elements of the mode Facet. Secondly there are hypotheses about how the different Facets interact with each other. For instance, does the impact of feelings, knowledge or actions vary depending on whether the respondent is a local or a cosmopolitan? As can be seen the mapping sentence in Figure 15.4 offers a life-time of research activity!

Consequences of place (un)attachment

Studies of place attachment have typically drawn attention to its benefits. They reflect aspects of what it is that people wish to achieve in any place. As discussed earlier, summarised in Table 15.3. These objectives may be linked to the 'needs' proposed by Maslow. However, there are aspects of place attachment that are not necessarily all positive.

'Sedentarism'

One of the consequences of pandemic lockdowns was the increasing amount of time people spent just sitting around, being sedentary. This was recognised as a medical problem, though, long before COVID-19. In the medical tradition of labelling, the problem was called Sedentarism.[51] Many illnesses have been related to it. Although this is an aspect of a very localised attachment to a dwelling, it perhaps is also an allegory for the sclerotic commitment to an area despite the benefits of cutting ties with it.

Alienation

Once a resident becomes aware of changes in a neighbourhood the dissonance from a history of attachment can become extreme. The process of gentrification,[52] for example, can lead to a feeling of alienation from an earlier identity with that Place. The cognitive battle to deal with this either through campaigns to avoid the changes, or a disturbed alienation characterised by a need to avoid the Place as soon as possible.

The well-researched phenomenon of NIMBYism (not in my backyard) is an aspect of the determination to keep the Place to which a person is attached within the rule systems and meanings that create its identity for them. This is notable in relation, for instance, to the increase in homelessness in an area.[53] The attachment to an area is seen as having special meaning, which is part of the identity of residents. Homelessness is seen as changing key features that were part of the reasons for being so attached to that Place.

The introduction of wind farms into rural landscapes is another illustration of how attachment to Place plays an important part in people's reactions to them.[54] Their feelings about the nature of the area, an acceptance of the values the landscape embodies, provide the bedrock on which opposition is typically based. This is despite any guarantees of the reduction and containment of any actual environmental impacts.

The degradation of the nature of a home to which a person is deeply attached is often brought about by the feelings of violation produced by a burglary. That can lead to a desperate need to leave the home. What existed as a Place of security and comfort can feel destroyed. The feelings of attachment are severed.

Jingoism

One of the greatest forms of place attachment, which can be positive, but also can generate negative consequences, is the attachment to country. At its most extreme an intense nationalism can be dangerous. The term coined to describe belligerent patriotism was *Jingoism*. Interestingly, it derived from a music hall song in the 1870s that extolled the virtues of keeping Russian forces away from Constantinople.

> We don't want to fight, but by Jingo if we do,
>
> We've got the ships, we've got the men, we've got the money too!

An illustration of how leaders, in the past and today, have drawn on popular sentiment and concepts of the nature of a country to extol actions that might otherwise be unthinkable. Such place attachment is often enshrined in nationalist songs. In the United Kingdom, the anthem *Land of Hope and Glory,* composed in 1902, set out a definition of Britain with the implicit mission to stand up against any enemy with the words *Mother of the Free*. In the United States, a similar commitment to attachment to Place is the US folk song, written by Woody Guthrie in 1940, *This Land is My Land, from California to the New York Island*. Although the extensive verses of that do comment on issues of inequality and private property, raising questions about whose the land is.

Even the Israeli National Anthem makes clear the significance of Place attachment. It contains, in Hebrew, the words *to be a free nation in our land*. The anthem was written many years before the establishment of The State of Israel, given the title *Hope*, being a song of yearning for a future homeland.

These examples illustrate how place attachment, at the level of a home or as an idealised yearning for a future nationhood, can both enhance morale and focus commitment, or seed xenophobia and militaristic aggression.

Conclusions

What started as an apparently straightforward idea of emotional attachment to a Place has been shown to be more subtle and complex than first appeared. Understanding this process draws on many of the issues explored in earlier chapters. This includes the development of meanings of Places, the patterns of use and the personal identifications they personify.

This complexity of psychological processes underlies the mixture of different ways of considering place attachment. Many studies, for instance, confuse the exploration of what 'place attachment' *is* with the characteristics of those who exhibit it. An intriguing example of this is Lewicka's exploration of the relationships between place attachment and social/cultural capital. Is a person's investment in their local culture an aspect of place attachment or more appropriately regarded as a facet of the person who is being studied? Similarly, is residential rootedness, as may be indicated from the longevity of local residence, an aspect of attachment to a Place or a feature of the resident? In this chapter an attempt has been made to distinguish the nature of place attachments from the features of the people who are resident in any particular location.

A further complication in understanding the nature of place attachment is that, whilst it connects with feelings of the value of being in a Place, it also relates to a person's view of who they are, their identity. Psychological theories of identity are therefore helpful in clarifying how Places have their significance. This in turn influences the extent to which a Place has a distinct identity for any given individual.

The argument here is that whilst what is commonly called a *sense of place* is a location that has a recognisable set of characteristics, those are not necessarily objective features. They derive from the interpretations of individuals. Consequently, they reflect how people see themselves; their own identity is mirrored in the distinguishing characteristics they assign to where they exist.

A crucial characteristic that contributes to the attachment to a Place is the personal investment of time and/or energy into that Place it. Such an involvement varies for different roles within that context revealing different forms of place attachment for people whose engagement with where they are is different from each other. A system of interrelationships emerges which also has a dynamic quality because people's view of themselves and the nature of Places undergo changes over time. A summary of these many different facets of place attachment is provided by the mapping sentence in Figure 15.4. This provides the basis on which to explore the consequences of place attachment and involvement.

Lewicka proposed two fundamentally different ways that a person may be attached to a Place.[55] That is a dichotomy between people whose attachment is based on extended local involvement as distinct from those for whom places of interest are revealed and shaped through their active use of those places. This has an intriguing link to a distinction that emerges in literary discussions of landscape. That is between regarding the landscape as a resource, something 'out there' to be utilised, as contrasted with it being part of an identity and personal experience. The former is what Wordsworth called 'inmates' of places. In relation to a landscape, they regard themselves as being part of it. The latter may wish to cherish nature but as a resource that they exploit. This is the theme of Chapter 16.

References and endnotes

1 President-elect Joe Biden delivers emotional remarks before departing Delaware - YouTube.
2 Lewicka, M. (2011) Place attachment: How far have we come in the last 40 years? *Journal of Environmental Psychology*, *31*, pp. 207–230.
3 Manzo, L. C. (2005) For better or worse: Exploring multiple dimensions of place meaning, *Journal of Environmental Psychology*, *25*, 67–86.
4 Scannell, L., Williams, E., Gifford, R, & Sarich, C. (2021) Parallels between interpersonal and place attachment: An update, in Manzo, L. C. & Devine-Wright, P. (Eds.) *Place attachment: Advances in theory, methods and applications* (2nd ed.), London: Routledge.
5 Scannell, L., Williams, E., Gifford, R, & Sarich, C. (2021) Parallels between interpersonal and place attachment: An update, in Manzo, L. C. & Devine-Wright, P. (Eds.) *Place attachment: Advances in theory, methods and applications* (2nd ed.), London: Routledge..
6 Feldman, R. (1990) Settlement identity: Psychological bonds with home places in mobile society *Environment and Behaviour*, 43(5), 676–709.
7 Bailey, E., Devine-Wright, P., & Batel, S. (2016) Using a narrative approach to understand place attachments and responses to power line proposals: The importance of life-place trajectories. *Journal of Environmental Psychology,* 48, 200–211.
8 Bailey, E., Devine-Wright, P., & Batel, S. (2016) Using a narrative approach to understand place attachments and responses to power line proposals: The importance of life-place trajectories. *Journal of Environmental Psychology,* 48,
9 Devine-Wright, P. (2015) Local attachments and identities: A theoretical and empirical project across disciplinary boundaries. *Progress in Human Geography*, 39(4), 527–530.
10 Lewicka, M. (2013) Place inherited or place discovered? Agency and communion in people-place bonding. *Estudios de Psicología*, 34(23), 261–274.
11 McAdams, D. P. (1993) *The stories we live by*, New York: The Guilford Press.
12 Proshansky, H. M., Fabian, A. K., & Karminoff, R. (1983), Place identity: Physical world socialization of the self. *Journal of Environmental Psychology*, 3, 57–84.
13 Most recently overviewed in Manzo, L. C. & Devine-Wright, P. (Eds.) (2021) *Place attachment: Advances in theory, methods and applications* (2nd ed.), London: Routledge.
14 Erik Homburger Erikson (1946) Ego development and historical change. *The Psychoanalytic Study of the Child*, 2(1), 359–396, https://doi.org/10.1080/00797308.1946.11823553
15 Mead, G. H. (1934) *Mind, self and society*, Chicago: University of Chicago Press.
16 Reicher, S & Spears, R.. (2012)The Social Identity Approach in Social Psychology In M. S. Wetherell & C. T. Mohanty (Eds.) *Sage Identities Handbook*. London: Sage.
17 Tajfel, H., Turner, J. C., Austin, W. G., & Worchel, S. (1979). An integrative theory of intergroup conflict, in *Organizational identity: A reader*, pp. 56–65.
18 Erikson, E. H. (1950) *Childhood and society*, New York: Norton. Erikson, E. H. (1968) *Identity: Youth and crisis*, New York: Norton.
19 Dunkel, C. S. & Harbke, C. (2017). A review of measures of Erikson's stages of psychosocial development: Evidence for a general factor. *Journal of Adult Development*, 24, 58–76, https://doi.org/10.1007/s10804-016-9247-4
20 Marcus, C. C. *The house as mirror of the self.*
21 I did have two half-brothers from my parents' previous marriages but you'll have to wait for the full autobiography to get those details!
22 Twigger-Ross, C., Bonaiuto, M., & Breakwell, G. (2016) Identity theories and environmental psychology, in M. Bonnes, T. Lee, & M. Bonaiuto (Eds.) *Psychological theories for environmental issues,* New York: Routledge, pp. 203–233.
23 Maslow, A. H. (1943) A theory of human motivation. *Psychological Review*, 50, 370–396.

24 Lester, D. (2013) Measuring Maslow's hierarchy of needs. *Psychological Reports*, 113(1), 15–17, https://doi.org/10.2466/02.20.PR0.113x16z1
25 Korpela, K., Kyttä, M., & Hartig, T. (2002) Restorative experience, self-regulation, and children's place preferences. *Journal of Environmental Psychology*, 22(4), 387–398, https://doi.org/10.1006/jevp.2002.0277.
26 Scannell, L. & Gifford, R. (2017) The experienced psychological benefits of place attachment, *Journal of Environmental Psychology*, 51, 256–269, https://doi.org/10.1016/j.jenvp.2017.04.001
27 Scannell, L. & Gifford, R. (2017) Place attachment enhances psychological need satisfaction. *Environment and Behavior*, 49(4), 359–389, https://doi.org/10.1177/0013916516637648
28 An interesting brief review of this is *Through the palace keyhole* by Edwin Heathcote in *The I Paper*, Monday 8th February 2021, pp. 32 and 33.
29 Gordimet, N. (1987) *A sport of nature*, London: Penguin Books.
30 https://natekev.wordpress.com/2011/09/05/africa-and-its-parliaments/#comment
31 Canter, D., West, S., & Wools, R. (1974) Judgements of people and their rooms. *British Journal of Social and Clinical Psychology*, 113–118, https://doi.org/10.1111/j.2044-8260.1974.tb00097.x
32 Gosling, S. (2008) *Snoop: What your stuff says about you*, London: Profile Books.
33 Fried, M. (1963) Grieving for a lost home, in L. J. Duhl (Ed.), *The urban condition*, New York: Basic Books, pp. 151–171.
34 Reviewed in Fried, M. (2000) Continuities and discontinuities of place. *Journal of Environmental Psychology*, 20, 193–205, https://doi.org/10.1006/jevp.1999.0154
35 Fried, M. (1963) Grieving for a lost home, in L. J. Duhl (Ed.), *The urban condition*, New York: Basic Books, pp. 151–171.
36 Sadly, he died in 2008 at the age of 85.
37 Bailey, E., Devine-Wright, P., & Batel, S. (2016) Using a narrative approach to understand place attachments and responses to power line proposals: The importance of life-place trajectories. *Journal of Environmental Psychology*, 48, 200–211.
38 Lewicka, M. (2013) Localism and activity as two dimensions of people-place bonding: The role of cultural capital. *Journal of Environmental Psychology*, 36, 43–53.
39 Bailey, E., Devine-Wright, P., & Batel, S. (2016) Using a narrative approach to understand place attachments and responses to power line proposals: The importance of life-place trajectories. *Journal of Environmental Psychology*, 48, 200–211.
40 Gustafson, P. (2001). Roots and routes: Exploring the relationship between place attachment and mobility. *Environment & Behavior*, 33, 667–686.
41 Dovey, K. (1985). Home and homelessness, in I. Altman & C. M. Werner (Eds.) *Home environments*, New York: Plenum Press, pp. 33–64.
42 Tuan, Yi-Fu (1980) Rootedness versus sense of place. *Landscape*, 24, 3–8. UK Census Data (Mid-2011). Nailsea population statistics. Available online: http://www.ons.gov.uk/ons/rel/pop-estimate/population-estimates-for-uk–england-andwales–scotland-and-northern-ireland/mid-2010-population-estimates/index.html
43 Twigger-Ross, C. & Uzzell, D. (1996) Place and identity processes. *Journal of Environmental Psychology*, 16, 205–220.
44 Lewicka, M. (2011) On the varieties of people's relationships with places: Hummon's typology revisited. *Environment and Behavior*, 3, 676–709.
45 Lewicka, M. (2011) On the varieties of people's relationships with places: Hummon's typology revisited. *Environment and Behavior*, 3, 676–709.
46 Lewicka, M. (2013) Place inherited or place discovered? Agency and communion in people-place bonding. *Estudia de Psicologia*, 34, 261–274.
47 Williams, D. R. & Miller, B. A. (2021) Metatheoretical moments in place attachment research: Seeking clarity and diversity, in L. C. Manzo & P. Devine-Wright (Eds.) *Place attachment: Advances in theory, methods and applications* (2nd ed.), London: Routledge, pp. 13–28.
48 Borg, I. (2005) Facet theory, in B. S. Everitt & D. C. Howell (Eds.) *Encyclopedia of statistics in behavioral science*, https://doi.org/10.1002/0470013192.bsa216
49 Scannell, L. & Gifford, R. (2017) Place attachment enhances psychological need satisfaction. *Environment and Behavior*, 49(4), 359–389, https://doi.org/10.1177/0013916516637648.

50 Scannell, L. & Gifford, R. (2010) Defining place attachment: A tripartite organizing framework, *Journal of Environmental Psychology*, 30(1), 1–10, https://doi.org/10.1016/j.jenvp.2009.09.006
51 Goyal, J., & Rakhra, G. (2024). Sedentarism and chronic health problems. *Korean Journal of Family Medicine*, *45*(5), 239.
52 Tuttle, S. (2022). Place attachment and alienation from place: Cultural displacement in gentrifying ethnic enclaves. *Critical Sociology*, 48(3), 517–531.
53 Webb, J. & Dej, E. (2025). Citizenship and NIMBYism: Identities at the juncture of homelessness, place, and ideology. *International Journal on Homelessness*, 5(1), 152–169.
54 Dugstad, A., Grimsrud, K., Kipperberg, G., Lindhjem, H., & Navrud, S. (2023). Place attachment and preferences for wind energy – A value-based approach. *Energy Research & Social Science*, 100, 103094.
55 Lewicka, M. (2013) Place inherited or place discovered? Agency and communion in people-place bonding. *Estudia de Psicologia,* 34, 261–274.
56 Bailey, E., Devine-Wright, P., & Batel, S. (2016) Using a narrative approach to understand place attachments and responses to power line proposals: The importance of life-place trajectories. *Journal of Environmental Psychology*, 48, 200–211.

SECTION IV

Landscape

Out there with nature I was freer than I had ever been.

Edna O'Brien[1]

DOI: 10.4324/9780367808655-20

CHAPTER 16

Approaches to landscape

To use or to dwell

The significance of landscape's sense is best clarified when we know the different ways it can be revealed.[2]

Landscapes as special kinds of places

The meanings and significances of places take on particularly rich qualities when considering landscape. Of all the diverse places that can be considered, landscapes probably have the largest variety of psychological powers. An examination of the meanings and reactions to landscapes therefore provides further insight into the roles that Places play for individuals and society. Such an investigation also highlights the complexity of the human processes which are shaping the ways in which climate change and environmental degradation are being dealt with. An understanding of the emotional processes that relate to the natural world helps to reveal why mere knowledge of the impact of greenhouse gases and reductions in biodiversity does not influence human activities on the scale that the objective, doom-laden forecasts would predict.

A lengthy quote from a recent book on *Spirit of Place*, by Susam Owens, the British art historian and curator, serves to summarise the complexity of human transactions with landscapes.[3]

> Men and women have experienced the landscape in different ways at different times. Great physical changes have of course been made to the land over the centuries, as methods of farming have developed. Patterns of land ownership have altered the shapes and sizes of fields and urban sprawl have covered much of what was once countryside. But cultural shifts in aesthetic appreciation of landscape have played at least as important a role. There have been times when the countryside has been a place to lift the heart, and others when it has been regarded as better suited for melancholy reflection; times when it could offer

DOI: 10.4324/9780367808655-21

> spiritual enlightenment and time when people shut their door against it with a shudder of relief.
>
> *(p. 8)*

Changing attitudes to mountains are a particularly powerful illustration of the various ways in which landscape has and does take on meanings.

> Before the late eighteenth century, mountains were [generally] considered ugly and offensive...decades later tourists and artists alike could hardly tear themselves away.[4]

Words for landscape

The richness and complexity surrounding notions of landscape is further revealed by considering the mixture of words that are used in connection with the environment. Landscape, Countryside, Nature, the Land, Rural, and even Environment itself and other related terms are not exactly synonymous. Each term carries different baggage, revealing the nuances of meaning around our multifarious relationships to what is usually thought of as the 'natural world'. Although the term 'Landscape' had its origins indicating the shape of the land, it was taken up many centuries ago to mean an extensive view of natural scenery. In the last century this took on an even more distinctive notion of being a form, through landscape painting, of representation of outdoor places.. The 'scape' component becomes transferable, by analogy, to any visual impression, as in cityscape, townscape, or even moonscape or seascape. These all emphasise what the place looks like rather than what happens there or what it feels like to be there. From this perspective the natural environment is something out there to be looked at.

The 'Countryside' by comparison is more objectively a designation of an area of the country, but particularly a tract of land. It implies traditions and habitation in a way that Landscape does not. Often shortened to 'country', as in 'country music', it has taken on the nuance of being the opposite of the city, or urban existence. Inherent in both the terms 'landscape' and 'countryside' is the idea that somehow, they are 'natural', with the connotations of being untrammelled, not sullied by human actions. This is rather simplistic because there is hardly anywhere in the world where the land has not been modified by human activity. The desecration of the Amazonian rainforest is just a current example that is repeating the kind of overuse that is believed to have contributed, for example to the creation of the Sahara Desert.[5]

More generally, 'nature' has taken on an almost mystical quality. It carries fundamental, virgin associations. Having origins in the Latin *natus*, meaning *born*, and reflected in such words as 'innate', 'neonate', and of course 'natural', it encapsulates the idea of being untouched, unmodified, and even primeval. But the ramifications of its meanings can introduce ambiguities, as amusingly represented in this quote from Strunk and White's influential writing guides on the English language:

> *Nature* should be avoided in such vague expressions as "a lover of nature", "poems about nature". Unless more specific statements follow, the reader cannot

> tell whether the poems have to do with natural scenery, rural life, the sunset, the untouched wilderness, or the habits of squirrels.[6]

These very brief forays into the language of 'natural places' also draws attention to the psychological implications of 'landscape', 'nature', the 'countryside' and the 'environment'. The connotated meanings of these terms draw attention to the 'otherness' they each embody. They individually carry aspects of not being built up, not being within us, and not being spoiled. They contrast with the city, man-made objects, the artificial. That provides important features of the way landscape/nature has meaning and is experienced.

Given the network of terms that overlap with landscape, it is not surprising that what people mean by landscape is itself a topic for study by social scientists. These studies reveal that particular conceptions of landscape are often strongly tied to national identities. For example, the bucolic, tree-filled paintings of John Constable are often cited as illustrating a uniquely English identity. In Finnish, by contrast, identity[7] is indicated in pictures of vast forests, serene lakes, and rolling fields. Intriguingly, these refer to a bygone age when the great majority of the populations of these countries mainly lived in the countryside.

To use or to dwell

This imagery of natural settings, as capturing special kinds of Places and related experiences is everywhere. Pick up any literary book about Places, and the dominant topics will be on aspects of the non-urban, 'natural' landscape. To return to the Romantic poets, most notably, of course, William Wordsworth and his notorious 1807

> *A host, of golden daffodils.*
> *Beside the lake, beneath the trees,*
> *Fluttering and dancing in the breeze.*

Which, in my schooldays, every English child was required to memorise. The poet draws attention to the connotations the vision of the flowers has

> *For oft, when on my couch I lie*
> *In vacant or in pensive mood,*
> *They flash upon that inward eye*
> *Which is the bliss of solitude;*
> *And then my heart with pleasure fills,*
> *And dances with the daffodils.*

Although Wordsworth and other Romantic poets drew on a long tradition, which saw the power of nature coming in part from the value of solitude, these poets introduced a new perspective on the countryside. Up until the late 18th century, the countryside was regarded as the foundation of sustenance and wealth. But increasingly, as the industrial revolution brought people to find work in cities, the countryside was seen as a place of poverty and feudal ownership. With the influx into rapidly growing urban areas came desperate circumstances. The poverty and even feudalism were seen as innocent. That contrasted with the evil of the new metropolitan areas. It is no accident that Fritz Lang's powerful 1927 film heralding a dystopian future of downtrodden workers and arrogant, abusive employers is called *Metropolis*.

Surveys of attitudes to the environment

Beyond the literary and poetic explorations of the meaning of landscapes and human relationships to them, there are many more academically oriented explorations of attitudes to landscapes and the environment more generally. The meanings of words relating to the 'environment', as well as the plethora of accounts of landscapes and the experiences they elicit, raise questions about what is actually being explored in those empirical studies of attitudes towards the environment and nature that have flourished in recent years. The confusions over what is meant by landscape or environment indicate the need for caution when making sense of questionnaire surveys about attitudes to 'landscape' or 'nature'. The range of nuances that these and related words have must mean that these surveys are explorations of the stereotypical meaning of these terms, for any particular subgroup, rather than a reflection of their direct experience of these outdoor places.

The term 'environment' is probably the most slippery. Although it literally means that which surrounds, or more specifically "the aggregate of conditions in which a person or thing exists", it has come to mean the natural world, or even the Earth. This becomes especially significant when people are asked to answer how much they agree with statements drawn from 'The Environmental Attitudes Inventory' [8] such as:

> I think spending time in nature is boring.
>
> Humans were meant to rule over the rest of nature.
>
> Humans are severely abusing the environment.
>
> I would like to support an environmental organization.

I do want to make clear that I am not criticising these questionnaire surveys. My intention is to indicate something of the cultural background inherent in the terms used in order to clarify what is being studied. It is the meaning of these terms to the respondents, with all their associated connotations that are being explored in such surveys.

There are very many questionnaire surveys that produce results which complement literary and other artistic explorations of nature. One of the most comprehensive, by Milfont and Duckitt,[9] had 455 undergraduates completing a 99-item questionnaire made up of questions used in many other studies of environmental attitudes. Although this was published over a decade ago and attitudes have doubtless changed as the impact of climate change has become ever more apparent, their framework still covers a helpful range of environmental attitudes.

Interestingly, many of the questions in the survey exploring 'environmental' attitudes ask directly about Nature. In this context, the 'environment' tends to be equated with natural settings. This ignores attitudes towards the iniquities of many aspects of the *built* environment. This undervalues those environmental campaigns protesting about pollution in cities. Recently, for example, traffic has been stopped in crucial locations around London by people drawing attention to the need to insulate British homes from the noise the traffic causes. Yet the dominant focus of 'environmental' surveys is not about the appalling conditions still present in many cities, identified well over a century ago in the 'Dark satanic mills' of William Blake and the novels of Dickens. Nor do they consider the horrors of internment and refugee camps. Such depredations do not feature in academic studies of environmental impacts. It is the damage to the 'Blue Planet' on which studies of environmental attitudes focus.

The Milfont and Duckitt questionnaire illustrates the range of issues that can be considered in relation to environmental attitudes. Their questions were structured to ask respondents to indicate how strongly they agreed (from 1 to 7) with statements such as:

- I think spending time in nature is boring
- I would like to support an environmental organisation
- Humans are severely abusing the environment
- Humans are no more important than any other species
- Nature is valuable for its own sake
- I could not be bothered to save water or other natural resources

As discussed in Chapter 3, there are many weaknesses in using a questionnaire to explore such crucial and complex issues. For example, some of the questions are about the respondent 'I'; others are about 'humans', and some others are about 'nature'. Yet other questions deal with what an industry should do, or governments, involvement or otherwise, in environmental organisations, and so on. This questionnaire therefore illustrates the great range of issues that are encapsulated in the idea of 'environmental attitudes' across many different studies. Interestingly, in their 2004 study, Milfont and Duckitt do not ask questions directly about global warming or climate change as such. They focus on aspects of nature and more generally 'the environment'.[10]

Therefore, although the factor analysis[11] produced from student responses enables Milfont and Duckitt to identify 10 'primary factors', the subtle differences between each Factor relies heavily on issues identified in the questions and the way they are worded. This is not to castigate their very thorough and detailed analysis. It is extremely helpful in pointing to the complexity of the issues involved. For example, they are able to draw a distinction between 'the belief that nature is primarily for human use' (their factor IX) and 'support for conservation policies regarding industry and the use of raw materials' (their factor II). These are different again from questions that reveal a belief that 'human ingenuity and science will solve environmental problems' (factor V).

In other words, their study provides a useful list of the issues that can be identified under the very broad umbrella of 'environmental attitudes'. My summary of that list is given in Table 16.1. I have organised that list into two sections. These sections are based on the further analysis of the relationships between the 10 factors, known as 'higher-order factor analysis'. Milfont and Duckitt label their two overarching factors 'Preservation' and 'Utilisation'.

The Factors are ordered in terms of their degree of relationship to the underlying higher-order factors. The highest possible value is 1.0, and the lowest is 0.0.

Table 16.1 The environmental attitudes issues identified by Milfont and Duckitt (2004) as they relate to preservation and utilisation

PRESERVATION:	
Factor	
III Readiness to get involved in environmental protection	0.94
I Enjoyment of nature	0.73
VIII Personal conservation activity	0.65
II Support for conservation policies	0.40
UTILISATION:	
X Economic growth should have priority	0.69
IV Human welfare requires conservation	0.62
IX Nature exists for human use	0.50
V Science and technology will solve environmental problems	0.48
VI The environment is fragile	0.41
VII Humans have the right to change nature	0.33

The numbers in Table 16.1 provide a more detailed insight into the two major aspects of environmental attitudes revealed by Milfont and Duckitt. The clearest component is the willingness to participate in actions to protect the environment. With a value of 0.94, this virtually defines what is at the heart of the questions dealing with preservation. Not surprisingly, factor VIII, which asks about personal involvement in day-to-day conservation activities, also has a relatively high loading in Preservation, 0.65. That the 'enjoyment of nature' should be a strong component of this, 0.73, broadens our understanding of the personal interests that underlie this commitment to Preservation. Interestingly, Milfont and Duckitt refer to the research by Wiseman and Berger,[12] which found a relationship between preservation and the personality trait of 'neuroticism', which includes aspects of anxiety and emotionality.

It is worth noting that factor II 'support for conservation policies' only has a limited relationship to preservation. It actually has the same degree of relationship to the other second-order factor. That is in accord with factor IV that shows recognition of the benefits for human welfare of conservation. In other words, there is an aspect of concern for conservation that is based on its benefits to people, rather than the idea that preserving the planet is good in its own right.

The Preservation dimension can therefore be seen as reflecting a feeling of involvement in supporting nature, both at the personal level and at the institutional level, as well as enjoying the countryside. This indicates an environmentally committed role which is part of a person's identity. Is it too big a stretch to suggest this implies a feeling of being part of nature? 'Dwelling' in the environment, being an inmate.

The other second-order factor is not as clear as the first. The association values are much lower.[13] However, the combination of factors does indicate a view of the environment as a resource which exists for human use economic growth should have priority over protecting the environment [14]. Even, as mentioned, the support for conservation is because of its value for human welfare. Nature is an entity to use. An elaboration of the environmental role of using the environment, contrasting with dwelling within it.

It is important to emphasise that the results from surveys, such as those discussed here, are presented as *dimensions* not as distinct *types*. People are not assigned to one or other factor. They do not either 'use' or 'dwell'. Everyone has a position on both dimensions. Some may give more emphasis in their attitudes towards one dimension or the other. Some may have a balance between the two. As with any aspect of commitment, the roles implied by these attitudes can be more or less strongly motivated. Gradations in determination to help preserve the natural environment are everywhere to be seen. Some people may sign online petitions, whilst others superglue themselves outside the headquarters of international oil companies. Some throw red powder on art objects in galleries sponsored by organisations known to be degrading the environment. All of these illustrate different emphases of the environmental role that sees us all part of a great ecosystem.

This can be seen in other distinctions that have been made about ways of relating to environmentally significant activities[15]. One approach has been called *egoistic*. This implies that "individuals are entitled to use and extract natural resources to enhance their own lives and those of other members of society".[16] The dominant perspective is of the utilisation of the environment. Regarding it as a resource is very similar to the values expressed under the label of egoistic.

The focus on human use contrasts with the values summarised as *biospheric* or *ecocentric*. These present attitudes of being an integral part of an ecosystem. Assessing any actions in terms of their significance for the biosphere as whole. Dwelling in the environment is the key process here. 'Preservation' in Milfont and Duckitt's vocabulary.

As noted, though, pure types are not being offered here. These terms for how people relate to their surroundings are the extremes of variations along a continuum. This does allow for a more nuanced combination of what might seem like the extremes of egocentrism and ecocentrism. A perspective that puts emphasis on weighting the costs and benefits for people of interventions relating to the environment. They are concerned for the environment but also for how people may live. Groot and Steg[17] give this emphasis the, perhaps unhelpful, label of *social-altruism*. Many people will have this emphasis in their consideration of environmental issues. Put more generally, people may be placed along a continuum which has ecocentrism at one end and egocentrism at the other, with social-altruism inbetween.

Identifying social-altruism further shows that environmental attitudes are part of broader value systems. They are ways of relating to the world more generally. In terms of environmental roles, they demonstrate that the parts people play in daily life, what they regard as important, leading to how they act, are fundamental in understanding their attitudes to the environment.

Environmental roles in context

Milfont and Duckitt's survey was published over a decade ago. Attitudes are altering as the impact of climate change is becoming ever more apparent.[18] Studies of the conditions under which these modifications of attitudes occur further clarify the variations in attitudes and their implications for environmental roles.

Recently, Hoffmann and his colleagues[19] made a careful comparison of the relationships between experience of temperature anomalies, heat episodes and dry spells, and environmental concern, as well as voting for Green parties. This is a noteworthy move away from reliance solely on responses to a questionnaire. The results showed that as people experienced more examples of climate change, they did indeed show more eccentric attitudes and actions.

However, the relationships were stronger in regions with a cooler Continental or temperate Atlantic climate. The impact of climate experiences were weaker in regions with a warmer Mediterranean climate. They were also moderated by regional income levels. Public support for Green parties was more likely to be influenced by climate experiences in countries with favourable economic conditions. These results at a national level have also been found in studies focused on individuals.[20] Broadly speaking, the poorer people are the less willing they are to support or be involved in climate preservation.

The influence of prosperity is not the same as being committed to material wealth. Contrasting studies have demonstrated that an overarching general value, *materialism*,[21] those for whom wealth and ownership are important values, has a negative relationship to caring for or wanting to protect the environment. However, relying on generalised concepts, such as poverty or materialism, as in so many questionnaire surveys, ignores consideration of the specific environmental context of the people being studied. It does not consider the reasons people have for being in any particular place, the roles they play there, which interact with the significance the environment has for them.

Studies, for example, of the conflicts between seaside users illustrate the nuances of environmental roles. This is well illustrated in Japan, where the extensive coastline is a resource for swimming, leisure boat use and a large fishing industry.[22] The participants in these different ventures have quite different reasons for being there. They consequently vary in their views of what aspects of the environment should be preserved. Their purposive interactions in those coastal locations shape their attitudes to their environments. These conflicts in Japan are only one of many examples that play out around the world, illustrating the influence of a person's relationship to their environment, their environmental role, on their attitudes, and actions towards the environment.

There have been attempts to deal with this problem by creating sustainably developed tourism,[23] so that local populations change their relationship to where they live. A case study in Mwiba Wildlife Ranch, Meatu, Tanzani[24] (Figure 16.1) examined the consequences when those who live there were given ownership of the area and assisted in developing tourism that would enjoy the abundant wildlife there. This changes their relationship to their surroundings. They have an economic investment in maintaining their environment. However, this and many other examples are not without their challenges, having proven difficult, in many cases, to achieve in practice.[25] One dominant reason for these difficulties is that just giving local people another physical setting does not change their understanding of their relationship to the environment. The way they see themselves and their role. Centuries of being animal hunters takes a generation or more to become animal guardians.

Landscapes' significance

The variety of attitudes towards the environment reveals the complexity of associations with landscape. That mixture of associations has existed throughout human history. Consequently, some consideration of landscape in literature and art helps to elaborate the richness of meanings of natural settings. Turning to a less overtly scientific exploration of landscape helps to broaden ways of thinking about this crucial topic. Writings and visual explorations enable us to break out from the constraints of 'objective'

Figure 16.1 Mwiba Wildlife Ranch, Meatu, Tanzania

measurements. They facilitate insights into the experience of the environment. As discussed in Chapter 4, these insights are able to go beyond what can be collected in major questionnaire surveys or laboratory-based monitoring of reactions to photographs.

The distinction apparent in literary considerations of nature between 'dwelling' and 'using' complements the, essentially similar, two underlying dimensions identified in Milfont and Duckitt's large-scale survey of 455 undergraduates. This also supports the proposal that this distinction reflects widespread ways of relating to the environment. As argued, from the study of place attachment in Chapter 15, this distinction can also be seen between those for whom a place is where they are – usually over an extended period – and those for whom the attachment is derived from their active use of it.

There is not a perfect matching between the place attachment dichotomy and the underlying dimensions of environmental attitudes. Environmental attitudes are best regarded as a specific subset of the much broader, life course considerations inherent in the meanings of place attachment. Nonetheless, the literary tradition that distinguishes between the picturesque and dwelling in nature teaches a lot about the different approaches individuals and society have to natural places and the landscape.

Art and nature

That artistic and poetic tradition provides important insights into the psychological processes that make nature so special. They support the Psychology of Place principles that emphasise the social concomitants of place experience, notably the purposive relationship to places and the associated Environmental Roles and Place rules. A recognition of these psychological processes provides a basis for developing ways of changing people's activities in response to climate change as considered in the Chapter 19.

> Psalm 23: *The Lord is my shepherd; I shall not want.*
> *He maketh me to lie down in green pastures:*
> *He leadeth me beside the still waters.*
> *He restoreth my soul.*

I never thought I would be quoting from the psalms when considering the meaning of Places, but when I heard Psalm 23 at a funeral recently, it struck me that it makes a direct reference to a commonly expressed belief that nature is restorative. 'Green pastures' and 'still waters' are recognised as being able to 'restoreth my soul'.

In the Judeo-Christian tradition, with its origins in the Middle East and the temperate climates of the Northern Hemisphere, the power of the natural landscape is deeply embedded in its mythology. The Garden of Eden (delightfully captured in Henri Rousseau's depiction – Figure 16.2) does deserve the rather over-used term 'iconic', in representing a strong and clear image of innocent paradise. Google translates paradise into Hebrew as עדן גן (*gan ayden* – Eden Garden) although the word 'paradise' has its origins in various early Semitic languages such as Aramaic, probably drawing on

Figure 16.2 Henri Rousseau's *Eve in the Garden of Eden* (1910)

Old Persian, in which it usually means a garden, orchard, or park, often associated with relaxation and pleasure. The ruination of the soul created by quotidian concerns, especially work and involvement in metropolitan activities, contrasts with the pleasant untrammelled existence provided by a fecund garden. The profane city is distinct from sacred nature.

Being forced out of the free innocence of Eden is a 'fall' that heralded the guilt of human existence. Not long after, the fratricide of Cain killing Abel set in motion the violence endemic in subsequent generations. This Biblical mythology captures the social conflicts associated with the use of the land. Cain a farmer and Abel a shepherd. For although the murder is presented as an illustration of Cain's jealousy of Abel's good relations with God, it is symptomatic of the roles associated with land use that emerge once turfed out of the paradise of Eden.

I cannot resist mentioning that the conflict between Cain and Abel is also implicit in the wonderful song at the heart of the musical *Oklahoma* "Oh, the farmer and the cowman should be friends". The conflict that is being resolved there comes from the difference in role relationships to the land. For the cattle rancher, the prairies are an expansive Place in which they lived, drawing on the nomadic traditions of cattle herding, needing open ranges to drive cattle freely. This is challenged by farmers who want to fence off their land to protect crops. For those early settlers, specific sections of land were a resource to be controlled and used. In a very broad sense, this is the distinction between being part of the countryside as cowmen live and dwelling in it, or seeing it to be manipulated and used like a farmer. Although inevitably, in practice, these roles overlap, they are both distinct from the pure experience of the Garden of Eden.

As noted, somewhat naïvely being part of the countryside is often positioned as innocent and restorative in contrast to the wickedness and destructiveness of The City. This has origins in many religious invocations but swelled to particular significance in Western nations, with the emergence of the Romantic poets in the late 18th and early 19th centuries. Wordsworth notably espoused an approach to wild natural countryside that challenged the earlier proposals of merely looking at nature as a work of art, the *picturesque*. He foreshadowed the phenomenological approach initiated by Husserl and others, and more recently given impetus by Seamon, in which the experience of the natural world grows out of being part of it; 'dwelling' rather than only 'looking'. This is a radical change in the psychology and meaning of the landscape.

Places in general, and those in the countryside in particular, had been noted for what had happened there, or who was associated with any given location. For centuries, going back to Biblical examples, where miracles, or other major events happened, or significant individuals lived or died, gave Places their importance. These could be a lonely outcrop, such as Gethsemane Garden in Jerusalem, or a whole town (do you know where Shakespeare was born?).

The immersive contemplation of landscapes heralded by 19th-century poets and novelists, in which, for example, in Hardy's novels, the countryside and even the weather famously become characters that influence the plot, is a distinctly different way of contemplating and experiencing Places. This presaged the ecological perspective inherent in Darwinism, with the recognition of human ancestry having similar origins to other primates. That sees humanity as an integral part of the natural world. It also laid the groundwork for the emerging Environmental movement, which has as its essence that we are all part of nature.

These considerations, drawn from the historical and poetic literature, are usually ignored in empirical psychological studies of landscape. Aesthetic preference studies often owe more to an earlier notion of the Picturesque. Speculative evolutionary interpretations are presented of findings based upon inherently artificial laboratory studies. Explanations for the therapeutic and restorative power of the natural environment, ranging from a view of trees from a hospital bed to the experience of the Sierra Nevada, are also typically limited by ignoring the insights from that vast literary tradition which involves ways of being in the landscape. The benefits of being in nature are such a major topics of research and consideration that Chapter 18 is devoted to them.

Perhaps paradoxically, the ways of utilising and exploring landscapes in fiction support the relevance of the social aspects of being in non-built places. Overcoming the challenges of The Wild is a common trope in adventure literature. The isolated setting in which terrible things can happen is as much part of *Babes in the* Wood, as in many of Agatha Chrisie's murder mysteries. The social roles and associated different sets of rules in those contexts, allow a different form of being. These may be the contemplative roles of being absorbed in a dramatic view, or the adventure of surmounting the challenges of climbing a mountain, which of course are not mutually exclusive. Or the many other ways of relating to Places that are not so formally or societally structured as is the built environment, in which the great majority of the world's population now lives.

Landscapes in literature

As Bates[26] points out in his detailed exploration of the roles of landscape in literature, the most popular novels tend to be those that are either set in an imagined 'better life... where there is no place for the motor car', often as part of a supposed clash between culture and technology, on the one hand, and rural simplicity, on the other. This conflict may be encapsulated in the love interest central to many plots in fiction. This is most obvious in how Thomas Hardy's Bathsheba in *Far from the Madding Crowd* is propositioned both by the stalwart Gabriel Oak, the epitome of rural simplicity, and Mr Boldwood, who is a sophisticated, educated landowner. That she initially falls for a flashy, somewhat exotic soldier, Frank Troy, serves to emphasise the vulnerability of the rustic woman[27] to the attractions of a different world, external to the bucolic existence of her daily life.

This very brief literary consideration demonstrates the depth of meanings that the contrast between the city and the countryside has in many cultures. That contrast is typically between the natural, the earth, providing a pastoral life, and the artificial, pressurised built environment. Although a landscape may be shaped by human endeavour, as in a 'pleasure garden', it is its separation from public affairs that often leads to it being considered virtuous and unhindered by worldly concerns. This gives Places in the landscape special significance and layers of meaning. It reflects a common dichotomy, already mentioned, found across all cultures, distinguishing between the sacred and the profane. The innocent landscape is sacred the built environment, with its sin, is profane.

The attractions of the opportunities of cities led to an emptying and, in some cases, the death of villages. This was made worse by the opening of America and an exodus to that new 'promised land'. The rural depopulation was also accelerated by changes in ownership, fuelled by rich industrialists controlling and making use of vast areas of land with little concern for those who worked the fields. This is all exquisitely decried in the 1770 poem by Oliver Goldsmith 'The Deserted Village'.

Sweet Auburn, loveliest village of the plain,
Where health and plenty cheered the labouring swain,
Where smiling spring its earliest visit paid,
And parting summer's lingering blooms delayed,
Dear lovely bowers of innocence and ease,
Seats of my youth, when every sport could please,
How often have I loitered o'er thy green,
Where humble happiness endeared each scene!
How often have I paused on every charm,
The sheltered cot, the cultivated farm,
The never-failing brook, the busy mill,
The decent church that topt the neighbouring hill,
The hawthorn bush, with seats beneath the shade,
For talking age and whispering lovers made!

Goldsmith paints an idyllic image of a village full of innocent joy; 'humble happiness endeared each scene'. It was an everlasting place of 'health and plenty', with a 'never-failing brook' and a cultivated farm and busy mill. The characters in the village are sage and content, such as the schoolmaster and the local parson. But the changes in society brought about by industrialisation and the changing economics that enabled monopolistic land ownership produce devastation:

And desolation saddens all thy green:
One only master grasps the whole domain,
....
Far, far away, thy children leave the land.
Ill fares the land, to hastening ills a prey,
Where wealth accumulates, and men decay:
Princes and lords may flourish, or may fade;
A breath can make them, as a breath has made;
But a bold peasantry, their country's pride,
When once destroyed, can never be supplied.

However, intriguingly, Goldsmith never returned to the village where he was born. For him, it was what we would now recognise as rabid capitalism that had destroyed the country idyll. This linking of the change in the nature of rural places to 'one only master' *grasping* 'the land' laid the groundwork for a belief in a notional, previous golden age of happy, healthy peasantry who reflected the delights of the countryside. Such views support the common image today of rural places being the essence of a quiet virtue.

Landscapes of fear and spirituality

Yet, the countryside has not always been regarded as reflecting 'humble happiness'. At one stage, wild, untamed landscape was considered frightening, especially great mountains. There is a long tradition of woodland, and forest, in particular, being dangerous and uncivilised. There is hardly a Western fairy story in which something nasty does not happen in a forest, from Little Red Riding Hood, to Snow White and Babes in the Wood. The 'wilderness' still holds a special fascination as a strange and dangerous place. Even today, that fear of nature is prevalent. So much so that it has been given an academic name 'biophobia'[28]

The otherness of Wilderness has been found to enhance what many academics are happy to call 'spiritual' experiences in wild nature. It is worth pointing out that studies of wilderness experiences are limited to those countries in which real, unrestricted wildernesses still exist. This is typically the United States[29] and Australia,[30,31] which have the sorts of wide, open spaces that can be recognised as wilderness. They are notably rare in Europe and limited in the United Kingdom to parts of Scotland. However, it has to be admitted that the wildness of many of these open spaces is in part due to the wholesale forced movement, often associated with mass murder, of the indigenous populations.[32]

The contrast of the Wild with the paradise of Eden helps to elucidate the rich sets of associations that landscapes have. The same countryside can be a mystical wilderness for one person who wishes to 'commune with nature',[33] or (like a colleague from London who I went for a walk with in Scotland, when we were there for a conference) a biophobic person scared out of his wits when he is somewhere without street lights and can only hear the distant sound of unrecognisable animals. These contrasts in meanings and significance are relevant to how landscape has psychological consequences.

Taming the countryside

The distaste for wild nature was reflected in earlier times by, where possible, taming the landscape. The owners of large houses and estates, especially royalty and nobility, created formal gardens, such as Henry VIII's garden at Hampton Court Palace (Figure 16.3). It was the orderly control of nature that was seen as most pleasing.[34]

Carefully selected components were artfully placed to create a particular visual impression. This was greatly influenced by the Classical French Garden design, illustrated in Figure 16.4, itself derived from Italian formal gardens. These were laid out in geometric patterns structured to be seen from the main dwelling. In essence, they are an abstraction, with carefully trimmed evergreen shrubs and few flowering plants that would not disturb the decorous order (Figures 16.3 and 16.4). These are classical in the sense that they aim to reflect an abstract, Platonic, idea of beauty. They contrast with the Romantic idea of beauty being in the everyday, natural environment. In this way, nature supplies the opportunity for creating a particular aesthetic. It is not something organic to be immersed in. A stark contrast to the current emphasis on 'rewilding'.[35]

Otherwise, the landscape was a resource. Ownership of land was the basis of wealth. Far from Oliver Goldsmith's tranquil, happy village, those who possessed land had a means of controlling and exploiting others. It is of value to repeat that they would often use the power this gave them without any concern for those who lived there. This could be the clearance of people in the Scottish Highlands to make way for sheep farming,

Figure 16.3 The garden at Hampton Court Palace

Figure 16.4 A formal French garden design

or the supplanting of America's First Nations, to create massive cattle ranches. Or the present-day devastation of Amazon Forests and displacement of aboriginal inhabitants to farm livestock or grow cash crops.

Music and narratives of landscapes?

Further insights into the meaning of landscapes and the many different responses to them can be gleaned from considering how some composers have taken landscapes or types of landscape as the inspiration for their music.[36] How they explore this inspiration in their work offers an interesting, and perhaps unusual, perspective on how landscape enshrines aspects of meaning. The range of such musical interpretations is legion. Music as different as Beethoven's 1808, *Pastoral Symphony*,[37] Mussorgsky's (1867) *Night on a Bare Mountain*, Richard Straus's (1919) *An Alpine Symphony* (1908), Varèse's (1952) *Déserts*, Peter Maxwell Davies' (2001) *Antarctic Symphony*, to list just a few that come to mind.

Many composers have taken particular landscapes or types of landscape as the inspiration for their music.[38] How they explore this inspiration in their work offers an interesting, and perhaps unusual for a psychology text, perspective on how landscape enshrines aspects of meaning. The range of such musical interpretation is legion. One example draws attention to a crucial way that a landscape may gain its significance. This is Modest Mussorgsky's *Night on a Bare Mountain* composed in 1867. The mountain in question is associated with the legend of a Witches' Sabbath that occurs there on St. John's Eve. The mountain is given special meaning because of the sinister myth associated with it. As with many places, it is the actions that are known there which enrich their meaning. Even or perhaps especially when those actions are embedded in folklore.

A different conceptualisation of landscape is Beethoven's Symphony No. 6, known as the 'Pastoral', composed in early 1808. This is thought of as a sublime portrayal of gentle countryside, complete with a storm and birdsong. The very many other compositions across many genres that are inspired by landscapes demonstrate how varied are the sources of these inspirations. They also reveal the huge mixture of reactions that composers and others have to landscapes.

Probably the most well known of musical landscapes is Mendelson's *Hebridean Overture*, usually referred to by the name of the specific place that inspired the recurrent theme in the music, *Fingal's Cave*. For although Mendelson is reputed to have sketched a brief note of his theme shortly after visiting the cave, it apparently took him many months to digest the experience and complete the piece, similar to Wordsworth's later reflection in solitude.

The well-known rising and falling motif (Figure 16.5) developed throughout the piece, reflects the shape of waves. In doing so it provides both a graphic and emotional analogy for a very particular Place experience.

But it, and the piece overall, is much more than that. Most importantly for our consideration of Place, inevitably for music, it has a flow over time and explores many aspects of

Figure 16.5 The theme from Mendelsohn's Fingal's cave

Figure 16.6 Fingal's Cave Staffa, Scotland

the Place. This includes travelling from calm waters through to stormy sea, capturing not only the waves but also the rugged landscape of that part of the Hebrides (Figure 16.6).

Although it may seem obvious, composers draw our attention to the many moods that a landscape evokes. Unlike a tower block or supermarket, landscapes are constantly changing. What might be serene and inviting at one moment can quickly become frightening and alien. That is part of the awe that landscapes generate. They are, after all, living organic entities.

This aspect also contributes to the abstract imagery that different landscapes can arouse. This is illustrated in music very different from Mendelsohn's. Edgard Varèse composed *Déserts* in 1953. He made clear that his music dealt "Not only physical deserts of sand, sea, mountains and snow, outer space, deserted city streets...but also distant inner space...where man is alone in a world of mystery and essential solitude".[39] Here the type of landscape being imagined has its power from what it symbolises. Once again it is taking us back to Wordsworth's reflections in solitude.

Many pieces of musicdraw attention to both the ways in which landscapes are alive, changing, unfolding, and organic, and to the importance of the activities associated with those places. The static view of a landscape as a picture is only one of the many ways in which it can be experienced. Composers teach us how to be a part of the landscape/To be within it rather than just admire it. They also lead us into the possibility of experiencing landscape as if being part of a story.

Scarfo[40] takes the narrative aspect of landscape experience as a basis for guiding the design of landscape gardens. He argues that the analogy with storytelling is a powerful basis for designing gardens. He goes so far as to suggest that there are aspects of landscapes that can be thought of as words, sentences, and paragraphs, which can be combined to create stories. This has direct parallels to the insights that emerge from music that references landscapes. A composition epitomised by Beethoven's *Pastoral symphony* takes us on a journey in a similar way to a walk through the countryside. It makes being in the countryside an activity that engages with where we are, interacting with the landscape, being part of its story.

Instrument or experience

Composers approach to landscape contrasts with the 'taming' of nature in formal gardens. That consideration of the landscape as something to look at as in a picture, or as a resource to be exploited, deals with the countryside as something 'our there', an object external to the person observing or using it. For musicians, it is what it means to be in the landscape, experiencing it directly. This is the phenomenological approach in which the individual is inevitably part of any Place. An approach explored in numerous publications by Seamon, having philosophical origins in the work of Husserl and later Merleau-Ponty,as detailed in Chapter 1, Wordsworth heralded this philosophical perspective in his challenge to the instrumental attitude to nature. He contrasts this with being 'nature's inmate', the humility of *dwelling*.

As Bate[41] explores in some detail, the instrumental, objective viewpoint of Nature owes much to the dualist tradition of Locke and Descartes. The separation of subjective from objective – the mind distinct from the body. The world out there is a distinct entity that is quite separate from the experience of it. A framework in the positivist, philosophical tradition that the phenomenologists and their associates struggle so hard to escape from.

The psychological theory of Place helps to bridge the divide between these two orientations, what might be thought of as the objective (nature out there) versus the subjective (our being is part of nature). This is achieved by recognising the social aspects of being human. We are always, explicitly or implicitly, actors within a social context. These roles assume a presence in a Place, which also helps to define and facilitate those roles. Environmental roles therefore embrace both a subjective experience that the person has in a particular situation and the objective qualities of what that role implies in a social world, enhanced by its physical context.

Conclusions

The natural environment, countryside and more generally, 'nature', has a very special place in the public and poetic imagination. With all the challenges of climate change, there is an increasing focus on it and how it should be managed. The depredations of city life combined with the COVID pandemic pushed towards 'working from home' drew attention to the different roles that natural settings can have in our lives. This encouraged more people to seek out the countryside for recreation and as a place to live.

Whilst the ecological and functional implications of a move to engage with nature are widely explored, the consideration of the psychological processes that make landscapes such significant and special Places tends to have been limited to questionnaire surveys and other restrictive approaches. This contrasts with the long literary history that explores the meaning and emotional importance of nature. Go into any art gallery and you will find rooms filled with paintings of landscapes, whether the gallery houses mediaeval and renaissance paintings or the brave attempts of the local watercolour club.

By combining the results for questionnaire surveys of attitudes towards 'nature' with the insights that can be gleaned from explorations in the subjective traditions of the humanities, it is possible to discern two traditional approaches to landscape. One sees it as a resource that can be used, tamed, and exploited. In the past, this provided the roots of power and influence. Today it is a perspective incorporated into major international commercialisation of nature. The contrast is what Wordsworth drew attention to as 'dwelling'. Recognising the significance of our roles being in the environment.

References and endnotes

1 *Blue Road: The Edna O'Brien Story* Documentary www.player.tfi.org.uk. Quote by Edna O'Brien from Blue Road: The Edna O'Brien Story reprinted by permission of Peters Fraser & Dunlop on behalf of the Estate of Edna O'Brien.

2 Paraphrased from Charles Rosen's (2010) *Music and sentiment*, London: Yale University Press, where he refers to music rather than landscape.

3 Owens S. (2020) *Spirit of place: Artists, writers & the British landscape*, London: Thames & Hudson.

4 Owens (2020) *Spirit of place.*

5 Wright, D. (2017) Humans as agents in the termination of the African humid period, *Frontiers in Earth Science*, 26 January, https://doi.org/10.3389/feart.2017.00004

6 Strunk & White (1979) *The elements of style* (3rd ed.).

7 Maunu Hayrynen (2000) The kaleidoscopic view: The Finnish national landscape imagery. *National Identities*, 2(1), 5–19, https://doi.org/10.1080/146089400113418

8 Taken from Taciano L. Milfont & John Duckitt (2010) The environmental attitudes inventory: A valid and reliable measure to assess the structure of environmental attitudes, *Journal of Environmental Psychology*, 30(1), 80–94, ISSN 0272–4944, https://doi.org/10.1016/j.jenvp.2009.09.001.

9 Taciano L. Milfont & John Duckitt (2010) The environmental attitudes inventory: A valid and reliable measure to assess the structure of environmental attitudes. *Journal of Environmental Psychology*, 30(1), 80–94, ISSN 0272–4944, https://doi.org/10.1016/j.jenvp.2009.09.001

10 It is worth noting that this is a perennial problem of psychology and other social science research on issues of general significance. Research can take so long to conduct, analyse, and publish that it often is behind the curve of what is of public significance.

11 Factor Analysis is one of a number of statistical procedures that reveal the underlying components in a set of associations. It was originally, and most famously used to determine the make up of the intelligence measured in intelligence tests, i.e. verbal, numerical and spatial intelligence. There are many clear accounts of it and related procedures available on the World Wide Web.

12 Wiseman, M. & Berger, F. X. (2003) A higher-order model of ecological values and its relationship to personality. *Personality and Individual Differences*, 34, 783–794.

13 Although it is not clear in Milfont and Duckitt's paper I am assuming the numerical values in their Table 4 are a form of product-moment correlation. These only indicate the square-root of the force of the value. In other words, whilst a correlation of 0.9 accounts for 81% of the common variance, 0.6 only accounts for 36%.

14 This sentence was written before Donald Trump declared that any concern about environmental degradation is all its forms should not be believed. All though he expressed this view rather more succinctly.

15 De Groot, J. I. & Steg, L. (2008) Value orientations to explain beliefs related to environmental significant behavior: How to measure egoistic, altruistic, and biospheric value orientations. *Environment and Behavior*, 40(3), 330–354.

16 De Groot, & Steg (2008) Value orientations to explain beliefs related to environmental significant behavior, 33.

17 De Groot, & Steg (2008) Value orientations to explain beliefs related to environmental significant behavior, 333.

18 A clear indication of increasing environmental concern over the past decade is show from a detailed study across the United States, but intriguingly is related to liberal politics and is not widely reflected in actions from policy makers. Marlon, J. R., Wang, X., Bergquist, P., Howe, P. D., Leiserowitz, A., Maibach, E.,. & Rosenthal, S. (2022). Change in US state-level public opinion about climate change: 2008–2020. *Environmental Research Letters*, 17(12), 124046.
19 Hoffmann, R., Muttarak, R., Peisker, J. et al. (2022) Climate change experiences raise environmental concerns and promote Green voting. *Nature Climate Change*, 12, 148–155, https://doi.org/10.1038/s41558-021-01263-8
20 Uram, P., Skalski, S., & Kwiatkowska, A. (2021). Values and materialism as predictors of pro-environmental attitudes, https://doi.org/10.33910/herzenpsyconf-2021–4–87
21 Hurst, M., Dittmar, H., Bond, R., & Kasser, T. (2013) The relationship between materialistic values and environmental attitudes and behaviors: A meta-analysis. *Journal of Environmental Psychology*, 36, 257–269.
22 Funck, C. (2006) Conflicts over space for marine leisure: A case study of recreational boating in Japan. *Current Issues in Tourism*, 9(4–5), 459–480.
23 There is even a *Journal of Sustainable Development*.
24 Ngilangwa, B., Meney, R., & Msafiri, C. (2018). Exploration of a future scene for Community Based Tourism in the southern part of Serengeti ecosystem: A case study of Mwiba Wildlife Ranch, Meatu, Tanzania. *International Journal of Conservation Science*, 9(4), 733.
25 Sharpley, R. (2020). Tourism, sustainable development and the theoretical divide: 20 years on. *Journal of Sustainable Tourism*, 28(11), 1932–1946.
26 Bates, J. (2000) *The song of the earth*, London: Picador.
27 I will quickly pass over the misogyny inherent in much of hardy's writing.
28 Pauano, A. (2020) Biophobia and urban restorativeness Sustainability, 12, 4312, https://doi.org/10.3390/su12104312
29 Laura M. Fredrickson & Dorothy H. Anderson (1999) A qualitative exploration of the wilderness experience as a source of spiritual inspiration. *Journal of Environmental Psychology*, 19(1), 21–39, ISSN 0272–4944, https://doi.org/10.1006/jevp.1998.0110
30 Matthew G. McDonald, Stephen Wearing, & Jess Ponting (2009) The nature of peak experience in wilderness. *The Humanistic Psychologist*, 37(4), 370–385, https://doi.org/10.1080/08873260701828912
31 Kathryn Williams & David Harvey (2001) Transcendent experience in forest environments. *Journal of Environmental Psychology*, 21(3), 249–260, ISSN 0272–4944, https://doi.org/10.1006/jevp.2001.0204
32 Paul, D. N. (2008) presents harrowing evidence of the disastrous effects of various forms of colonisation, notably on the First Nations of North America in his book *First Nations history: We were not savages* (3rd ed.), Halifax: Fernwood Publishing.
33 The importance of this will be considered later. Jacquelyn H. Flaskerud (2014) Communing with nature. *Issues in Mental Health Nursing*, 35(12), 975–978, https://doi.org/10.3109/01612840.2014.919621
34 The management of gardens over time is such a huge and fascinating topic that you will have to forgive me only giving it the briefest mention. There is actually at least one major academic journal devoted to the topic *Studies in the History of Gardens and Designed Landscaped* (in its 42nd volume as I write).
35 Position-Statement-8_71.pdf (thesovereigner.net).
36 David Knight (2006), a timpanist and geographer explore this aspect of music in his *Landscapes in music, space, place and time in the world's great music*, Rowan and Littlefield.
37 Kumbier, W. (2010). Beethoven's birdstrokes: Figuration, subjectivity, and the force of the score in the pastoral symphony and copying Beethoven. *Literature Compass*, 7(8), 639–650.
38 David Knight, a timpanist and geographer, explores this aspect of music in his 2006 book *Landscapes in music, space, place and time in the world's great music*, Rowan and Littlefield.
39 Quoted from Samuel Andreyev, https://www.youtube.com/watch?v=ctYsn8p3P90
40 Scarfo B. (2023) *Landscape architecture as storytelling: Learning design through analogy*, London: Routledge.
41 Scarfo (2023) *Landscape architecture as storytelling*.

CHAPTER 17

Preferences for landscapes

Much the beauty, spirit, and effect of landscape, real or imitated, depend upon a just degree of variety and intricacy, on a due mixture of rough and smooth in the surface, and of warm and cool in the tints.

Uvedale Price (1842)[1] (p. 29)

The importance of landscape preferences

Over the past half-century, there has been an increasing recognition that developments in the countryside should take account of the visual effects of those developments. UK governments have had policies on the onshore and offshore location of wind farms that are influenced by their visual impact. The problem of such developments has been called 'visual pollution' and has even been shown to reduce house prices by 3%.[2] The term 'visual pollution' has its origins in city settings, notably due to hoardings and advertising displays.[3] It reflects a growing awareness of the importance, for well-being and environmental satisfaction, of what Places look like.

Political and more general policy concerns about what landscapes should look like, has spurred on a plethora of studies of landscape preferences. A simple search on Google Scholar for "Landscape Preferences" brings up about 10,000 publications. If you put "Landscape Preferences" into a general Google search engine, over 12 million examples are available. This is a vast area of research, now so large that no-one can comprehend or distil it all. This chapter therefore draws out some of the themes in these studies that help us to gain further insights into the Psychology of Place.

Studying landscape preferences

There are many practical difficulties to be overcome if people's landscape preferences are to be studied actually in natural settings. There are challenges to getting people to the locations, taking account of the weather and other variations that are brought

DOI: 10.4324/9780367808655-22

about by seasonal changes or human interventions. Even when people are present, there are the angles of view and other variations that can make comparisons difficult to make between different people and different views of the same area.

The task of recording landscape preferences is made somewhat artificial by regarding the view of a landscape as a 'stimulus', as in a classic psychology laboratory experiment. You are never only looking at a view without any other context, whether it is from a seated picnic, to paint it, or when determining the walking route you are about to take. The passive enjoyment of a view of the countryside is a rare moment that is a rather special way of being there.

Various surrogates for direct questioning of people about their preference when being in the landscape have been explored. As already mentioned, house prices that take account of various locations are one possibility.[4] Searches of the countryside views that are put up on social media[5] are another possibility. But these are always indirect substitutes for the exploration of the direct, experiential preference for a view of landscape.

Because of the challenges and effort of obtaining respondents' preferences *in situ*, it is not common in studies of landscape preferences to engage directly with people actively involved in the countryside. Social scientists, especially psychologists, have usually taken the easy way out of showing people pictures projected onto screens in lecture theatres and asking them to react,[6] or even measuring their physiological responses whilst looking at pictures. Other research uses the age-old methodology of getting people to complete questionnaires asking about their reactions to the landscape. The advent of readily available online surveys has further increased the abstraction from the direct experience of a place. Whilst these methodologies are not without merit, as we shall see, they tend to undervalue the Environmental Roles that are so important in understanding personal reactions in any location.

A study by Schirpke and her colleagues is typical of this academic process. They showed people photographs of a variety of places and asked them "to evaluate the pictures according to their own appraisal from 1 (I do not like it at all) to 10 (I like it very much)".[7] From this an overall evaluation of the different pictures is produced. Respondents assigned very high values to subalpine and alpine pictures with a diversity of landscape elements. The findings from this study were typical of those from very many other similar pieces of research. Those landscapes that included settlements, infrastructure or intensive agriculture were liked less. Overall, inclusions of urban structures, roads and forests had a negative influence, whereas water in the landscape increased preferences.

One study that illustrates the almost inevitable results of these rather artificial explorations of preferences is that by McMahan and his colleagues.[8] They showed the pictures in Figure 17.1 to both students and 'non-student adults'. The study was exploring the contribution of 'naturalness' to preferences for landscapes. In this context landscapes were conceived of as less 'natural' if they had more obvious human intervention.

Using an online survey:

> Participants were presented with two photographs of mountain landscapes and a short descriptive vignette. The vignette described two ostensibly real locations, labelled Site A and Site B, which were explicitly stated to be similar in most

Figure 17.1 Stimulus materials used in the current research. In both studies, approximately half of the participants viewed the top photograph pair, and the remaining participants viewed the bottom photograph pair

Source: McMahan (2016), reproduced with permission.

> ways yet differing in their degree of human-induced alteration. Site A was specified as the non-altered environment. Site B was specified as the human-altered environment.
>
> *(p. 8)*

Although the term 'natural' was carefully avoided, the instructions clarified the human intervention by declaring:

> …the sites differ in one important way. The stream in Site A is fed by a large spring located several miles up in the mountains. The stream in Site B was created approximately 75 years ago when a large dam was constructed, many miles outside of Site B, and construction of the dam redirected waterflow into this mountain valley.
>
> *(p. 9)*

McMahan and his colleagues can therefore be seen to have carried out this study with all the elegance and precision required of a psychological experimental in order for it to be acceptable to a distinguished journal, in this case *Ecopsychology.*

Their results support their hypothesis that awareness of human intervention reduces preferences for views of landscapes. This shows that the careful manipulation, in terms of human intervention, of how to consider the pictures shown, produced statistically significant average differences between pictures in ratings of naturalness and being aesthetically pleasing. However, the differences are not huge. The average rating for naturalness of the non-intervention scene was 94. For the conceptually altered scene it was 73. The instructions had an effect on average for which scenes people preferred but did not totally sway them. The differences were even more marginal for how 'aesthetically pleasing' the scenes were; for the 'unaltered' 91, for the altered 87. Remarkably, these small differences are used to suggest "that a preference for non-altered natural environments was selected over the course of human evolutionary history because such environments offered greater benefits and/or entailed fewer costs (on average) than human-altered natural environments" (p. 16). Beyond the extrapolation to thousands of years of human evolution from such marginal variations, further weaknesses in this claim are considered later in this chapter.

An explanation of the results that does not rely on reference to humanoid evolution can be drawn from the seminal work of Orne[9] who articulated the concept of 'demand characteristics' in experiments, mentioned in Chapter 3. In essence, these are the explicit or implicit indications the experimenter gives to participants of the sort of responses that might be expected. Machan's study is helpful in showing that people, on average, can make sense of the implications of human interventions in a mountainous landscape. The instructions to the study draw attention to those implications by clearly stating that *the sites differ in one important way.* Not that they differ, but the difference is 'important'. The results show that respondents, on average, are able to take accept the implications that such interventions make pictures of the landscape less appealing.

Beyond laboratory studies

I have devoted space to McMahan's study because it was so carefully crafted and analysed. It can be seen as typical of many of the experiments into landscape preferences. Treating the landscape as a stimulus that may elicit different responses under various conditions. The participants in these studies are passive observers, offering opinions about what they are looking at. How they look can be adjusted by indicating the role they are to take when looking. For example, responding to 'important differences'. Any particular viewpoint may be explicit within the instructions they are given or implicit in the mixture of images they are asked to look at.

The influence of the context and instructions on respondents is clear even when they are taken to a scene and asked to look at it whilst the direction of their gaze is being monitored.[10] The findings from such a study shows that people do look for interesting objects and do focus on them, which may be graffiti or, when nothing else is in the visual field or, for instance a flowing river. However, even here the implications arise of what can be seen, in terms of human activity.,.

When researchers move beyond the controls of requiring respondents to look at particular scenes andseek out the locations that people themselves choose to photograph, results emerge that are rather different from those typical of laboratory studies. In an innovative study, Tieskins and his colleagues examined the landscape pictures that people put on social media.[11] Their results show that visual attractiveness is not the only aspect that encourages people to photograph a location and post it online. Many landscape photographs uploaded onto social media emphasise monuments. People are, in effect, recording their presence in a Place of some significance. They are documenting their reasons (or role) for being there. This was also shown by the increased number of photographs that related to hiking trails, especially during winter and spring. Cycling paths featured more during the summer months. This evidence for the significance of agency in the photographs selected, nonetheless, was balanced by the finding in many other studies that the presence of water, forest and grass was also an influence on which photographs were submitted to social media.

The availability of photographs uploaded by people online has led to a spate of studies of the features of the photographs themselves.[12] Rather than considering what this reveals about landscape and related preferences, the research explores the photographs as indicators of the qualities of what people seek to record. The results do highlight the influences on what it is that is photographed. Unlike the results from asking people to judge landscapes, instead the objective analysis of photographs reveals that colour is a powerful factor.[13] This difference does, once again, raise important questions about what is being studied when people are asked to rate their preferences of pictures of landscapes.

Stereotypical findings

Studies of pictures of landscapes do reveal similar overall preferences for landscapes containing particular components. Forests, for example, are an important contribution to the landscapes people like.[14] Most people also select open landscapes.[15] Appreciation of landscapes is increased with long vistas.[16] Pictures without urban settlements and road infrastructures tend to be favoured.[17] The trend is to seek views that seem natural.[18] Unrestrained construction of settlements and roads has a negative impact on landscape preferences.

This preference for places of 'natural beauty' has led to the study of what it means for people to regard a landscape as 'natural',[19] given that it is rare to find anywhere in the world that has not suffered human influence. This has become legally significant because of the designation, for example in the UK, of areas being of 'outstanding natural beauty'. Such designation introduces controls over what is allowed to happen and be built or modified in those places. When people are asked to say what natural beauty is, many people "sought criteria that were primarily visual, reflecting the essential aesthetic and perceptual qualities of beauty; authenticity was similarly mentioned. This view was closely related to emergent properties such as tranquillity, relative lack of pollution, wildness, relative naturalness, integrity and associations".[20] This captures the mixture of idyllic visual characteristics and an understanding of the roles that can acted out within those Places, being free from the impact of industry and other intrusions that could undermine a relaxing experience.

The enduring picturesque

These general findings on landscape preferences are delightfully illustrated in the paintings which Bob Ross so skilfully produced in his very popular[21] television series, giving guidance on how to paint a landscape, as illustrated in Figure 17.2. The remarkable

Figure 17.2 Bob Ross at his easel with a typical one of his paintings

thing about Bob Ross' paintings is that they are totally in accord with the guidance given in 1792 by William Gilpin[22] in his delightful book on what it is that makes landscapes picturesque. Figure 17.3 is a quotation from that book.

Simplicity and variety are the cornerstones of the picturesque. Gilpin does go on to declare that simplicity and variety are not the whole answer to what makes a landscape

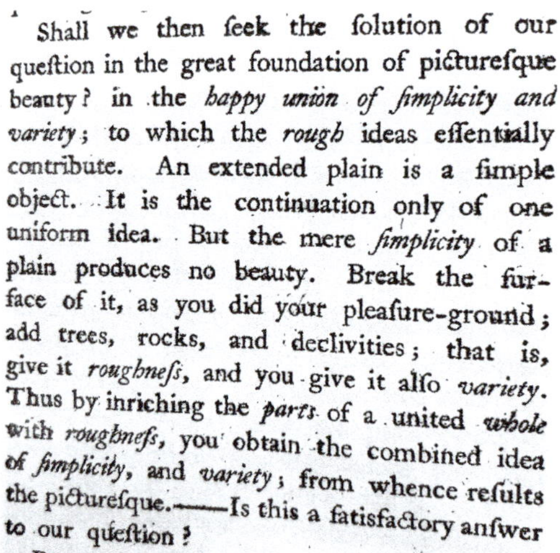

Shall we then ſeek the ſolution of our queſtion in the great foundation of picturesque beauty? in the *happy union of ſimplicity and variety*; to which the *rough* ideas eſſentially contribute. An extended plain is a ſimple object. It is the continuation only of one uniform idea. But the mere *ſimplicity* of a plain produces no beauty. Break the ſurface of it, as you did your pleaſure-ground; add trees, rocks, and declivities; that is, give it *roughneſs*, and you give it alſo *variety*. Thus by inriching the *parts* of a united *whole* with *roughneſs*, you obtain the combined idea of *ſimplicity*, and *variety*; from whence reſults the picturesque.——Is this a ſatisfactory anſwer to our queſtion?

Figure 17.3 Quotation from Gilpin (1792, p. 28)

Figure 17.4 Title page of Price's (1842) book about the picturesque

picturesque, but it nonetheless is an important component of what makes a landscape like a *picture*. That is the point. The formula of trees and water and distant views, especially of mountains, is relevant to what a landscape looks like. That is either in a painting or in a photograph shown to people when they are asked which they prefer.

Despite Gilpin's honest declaration that there are no fixed rules that make a picture or landscape beautiful, subsequent commentators still drew attention to the characteristics of the picturesque which Gilpin had highlighted. Followed up almost word for word by Uvedale Price, quoted at the start of this chapter. Figure 17.4 is the title page of his book, published in 1842. It has an illustration that Bob Ross would not be unhappy to have produced.

Picture or place

One argument against any idea of a ubiquitous theory of landscape preference emerges when pictures are compared with direct experience of Places.[23] When people were asked to indicate their conceptions of countryside locations they knew by looking at pictures of them, they tended to organise their thoughts as is common to many studies of landscape pictures. They commented on the content of the pictures, dealing with landform and the presence of water. When they were then asked to comment on them in relation to their *knowledge* of the Places, it was memories and their sensations when being there that came to the fore.

Subsequent studies[24] have demonstrated that the multi-sensory experience of being in a Place generates quite different preferences from looking at pictures of those locations. An extensive study[25] found that overall, there were similarities in preference judgements of landscapes between being there and looking at photographs. Although these similarities were weaker for some scenes than for others. The judgements being made also generated different degrees of similarity between being in a Place and looking at a photograph of it. Notably, 'quiet and silent', 'beautiful', 'attractive vegetation', 'vast', 'unspoiled', and 'human-influenced' generated variations between scenes that were actually experienced or photographs.

However, a fundamental weakness in the studies that have explored the relationships between being present and judging photographs is that the tasks respondents are set when they are in the landscape are not that different from William Gilpin's guidance on how to seek out and enjoy the picturesque in the countryside. Participants in these studies are asked to look at the scene (rather as if they were looking at a picture) and indicate their opinion about it. In such a situation it should be no surprise that the results from being *in situ* are, on average, very similar to those from looking at photographs.

Role variations in aesthetic judgements

Although the criteria for being *picturesque* dominate average preferences when looking at photographs, many studies reveal differences in landscape preferences between different subgroups. The passive taking in of a view reduces the agency at the heart of being there. The reasons for being there. When these influences on landscape preferences are taken into account, the general, average findings are shown to hide a great variety of different perspectives. Many studies show that there are significant differences between people in their landscape preferences when their purposes for being in a Place are not only to assess the view, but to live, enjoy or work there. Average, summarised preference values provide only limited information. Consequently, findings for overall preferences are questionable.

The most obvious differences are found between tourists and locals. The tourists, after all, are closest to those who come to look, rather than to consider the conditions of living in a locality. For example, in one study in Girona, Spain,[26] tourists most preferred grasslands. By contrast, it was orchards for residents. Perhaps not surprisingly, for farmers it was irrigated fields of herbaceous crops. Once again, revealing that the environmental roles people played, their relationship to the landscape, is a dominant influence on their visual preferences. A study in Norway demonstrated that whilst students preferred images portraying diverse and heterogeneous landscapes, neither diversity nor heterogeneity was correlated with the preference scores of the locals.[27]

In another study, in the mountain area of the Alpujarras (south-eastern Spain), exploring the role people play in the environment, respondents were asked to indicate which photographs of landscapes[28] they would prefer to see from their hotel room. Those people with a connection with farming were less likely to express the opinion that they were willing to pay for such a view than those without a farming background. Those without a farming background were also found to prefer having farm buildings within the Alpujarran landscape. The most valued landscape view is of irrigated farming on an intermediate slope where a village is visible in the landscape. The least-valued landscape in the area involves abandoned farmlands on steep slopes with no views of villages. This accords with the vernacular architecture of the small villages spread out over the slopes above deep gorges.[29] Visitors relate to these views in terms of their history and culture rather than merely what they look like.

In Ireland, the results from a survey of 420 respondents[30] reported that, overall, the general public has the strongest preference for landscapes with water-related features as their dominant attribute. Nonetheless, within this average, there was a significant heterogeneity in landscape preferences. Both personal characteristics and environmental value orientations strongly influenced preferences. Those who were agricultural producers had preferences for mixed farming landscapes but not for wild nature scenes.

A study in Japan[31] that took account of the long history of human–nature interactions mediated by agriculture explored the significance for landscape preferences of high biodiversity in Japanese rural landscapes. This study investigated the differences in perceptions of rural landscapes in the Arai-Keinan region, Niigata, Japan. Farmers and naturalists, people with very different relationships to the landscape, rated both rice paddy and woodland landscapes. For farmers, perceptions of stewardship and openness were significantly more important in determining preferences for rice paddy landscapes. Naturalness and biodiversity were significantly more important for naturalists. These differences between respondents were not found for woodland landscapes.

In a study on landscape preferences conducted by Schirpke and her colleagues,[32] participants were presented with photographs depicting various environments and asked to rate them on a scale from strong dislike to strong preference, based on their personal appraisal. These ratings were then compiled to generate an overall evaluation of the different images. Results indicated that subalpine and alpine landscapes with diverse natural features received the highest ratings. In contrast, images containing settlements, infrastructure, or intensive agricultural areas were rated lower. Additionally, urban elements like buildings, roads, and dense forests had a negative impact on perception, whereas the presence of water in the landscape contributed positively to its appeal.

Importantly, differences between respondents were also detected. Indeed, the researchers make clear that their sophisticated statistical analysis shows considerable variation between people in their landscape preferences. Of particular note are the differences between tourists and locals. Overall, their results suggest that gender, cultural background, and where people live, have an influence on landscape preferences. Once again this points to the importance of considering the reasons why people may be in a particular location, that is, the roles they have in relation to that environment. They are likely to be evaluating the landscape with regard to what they want to achieve in that setting.

There are also many examples of the embedded cultural significance of what a landscape is and how it should look. This generates quite different assumptions about the nature of landscape and related preferences. Particular conceptions of landscape are often strongly tied to national identities.[33] The paintings of John Constable, for instance, are cited as illustrating a uniquely English identity. Or a particular visual configuration is seen as supporting Finnish identity.[34]

Landscape preference and the *picturesque*

None of the studies that I can identify,[35] which present landscape pictures to people and ask them to appraise them, seem aware of the history of such appraisals.

Following the restoration of the English Monarchy in 1660, accompanied by the demise of Oliver Cromwell's puritan prohibitions, there was a flowering of the arts and literature. This was reflected in the expansion of grand country houses, for which the excess wealth meant that not all land had to be put to pasture or for growing crops. This was combined with the emergence of a rich, educated leisure class. A romantic attitude towards the countryside was fostered. That gave rise to the delight in a carefully constructed 'naturalness'. This was epitomised by the so-called 'ha ha' (Figure 17.5a) introduced into large estates. It is a device that hides a ditch so that from the house the garden seems continuous with the countryside (17.6b). The ditch keeps animals out of the garden and provides an uninterrupted view of the estate. That is the crucial point. It is structured to enhance a view from particular directions. Its purpose is to support a particular way of thinking about and looking at the landscape.

The emphasis on ways of looking at the countryside, rather than using it, or obviously taming it, became known in the 18th century as featuring the 'picturesque'. This was greatly influenced by the paintings of Claude Lorrain and as noted, the later the writing of William Gilpin (1724–1804), 'that peculiar kind of beauty which is agreeable

Figure 17.5a A 'ha ha'

Figure 17.5b The view across the 'ha ha' (the wall in this picture was added later when the ground became open to visitors, as a safety precaution. Historically it was not there so that the landscape looked continuous without a break.)

in a picture'. The essence of this perspective was that nature should imitate art, rather than the later Romantic view that art should reflect nature. Tourists in the 18th century even went so far as use what was known as a Claude Glass (or Lorrain Mirror) to look at a landscape (Figure 17.6), so that the landscape could be viewed through it 'as if in a painting'. These devices are readily for sale even today.

Gilpin provided detailed descriptions of what made a view attractive, together with drawings and indications of the locations of views from which these natural pictures could be enjoyed. This coincided with the emergence of vast schemes of 'landscape gardening' (Figure 17.7), most notably those designed by Lancelot 'Capability' Brown (1716–1783).

He reshaped large swathes of country estates as apparently natural settings, to be seen from particular views that had a pictorial aesthetic to them. There were those, then and now, who decried this meddling with nature to impose a particular perspective on it. Nonetheless, this tradition is still prevalent. Quite recently I have come across what might be regarded as current examples of the Claude Glass way of looking at nature. Figure 17.8 illustrates a few I have encountered in which a frame is actually provided for visitors. They are encouraged to see the landscape as a picture. A distancing from being in the landscape is offered so that its picture-like qualities can be enjoyed. Rather than being part of it.

Figure 17.6 Gurney Journey: Lorrain Mirrors

Figure 17.7 A typical Lancelot Capability Brown landscaped garden

Figure 17.8 Framing the landscape enacting the picturesque: (left) Petworth House, Sussex; (right) RSPB Nature Reserve Conwy, North Wales

Evolutionary[36] explanations of landscape preferences

Having looked at the variety of results of studies of landscape preferences, the question arises of what explains them? A frequently cited explanation draws on evolutionary theory. This theory was elucidated by Appleton,[37] being called 'prospect-refuge theory'. The idea here is that being able to see without being seen, having a prospect from a refuge, was the basis of landscape preferences. This approach was taken up by Kaplan,[38] who identified the following characteristics of scenes that were preferred:

> "understanding" (comprehending or making sense of a scene) and "exploration" (being held by the setting, being attracted by or pulled towards sources of additional information).[39]
>
> *(p. 10)*

There has been some elaboration of this framework[40] and richer labelling. Notably, understanding is elaborated as 'coherence' and 'legibility'. Exploration is developed as 'complexity' and 'mystery'. Yet, the emphasis is similar to the original Appleton 'prospect-refuge' idea, although within a stronger cognitive framework. For the Kaplans it is the comprehensibility that makes the 'prospect' so important. The possibility for exploration may be seen as the advantage of a 'refuge'. As already noted, the general findings of many studies support these components of preferences. For instance, a recent study, using many pictures of landscapes, offered similar dimensions of landscape preference, staying with 'coherence', but using the term 'fascination' rather than 'mystery'.[41]

Kaplan[42] makes clear he shares Appleton's evolutionary point of view that such environmental preferences enhanced the potential for survival of early humans:

> From an evolutionary perspective there may be great advantages in making a quick, automatic prediction about the informational possibilities of a place one is approaching.

The argument goes that it became innate to *Homo sapiens* to prefer landscapes that were similar to those in which that species of primate first emerged and thrived. As with many such claims, which Tallis[43] amusingly calls 'Darwinitis', there is no genetic evidence for this apparently innate characteristic. Furthermore, as noted in Chapter 16, the landscapes that are preferred today are different from those preferred in the past.

Further evidence for the weakness of the apparent unanimity of landscape preferences can be found looking at landscape paintings in any art gallery, especially those painted in the last 100 years. There are, of course, popular artists, notably Bob Ross already mentioned, whose landscape paintings reflect the stereotypical findings from the psychological research based on judgements of photographs, with distant hills, expanses of water and no hint of human intrusion, as in Figure 17.2. But look at any landscape painting, for instance by Vincent Van Gogh, Wassily Kandinsky, or John Piper, to see totally different ways of seeing natural places. Or consider the photographs of US landscapes taken by Ansel Adams.

The dominant themes that are used to support the evolutionary argument, of 'coherence' and 'mystery', are directly related to the 18th-century requirement for a view being picturesque: Price's "a just degree of variety and intricacy", or Gilpin's 'simplicity' and 'variety'. Are these features embedded in particular cultural traditions that emerged with the development of the Romantic movement in the arts? Or were these 18th-century commentators intuitively picking up innate forces? A more detailed examination of the evidence is given in the Appendix to this book on reductionism.

However, a persuasive argument against 'prospect-refuge' theory is that before the expositions of Price and Gilpin, wild landscape was associated with fear and lack of control. With urbanisation, wilderness was linked with freedom and the absence of a civilised context, although still potentially fearful, as so well illustrated in the 1972 film *Deliverance*. In that film people from a metropolitan existence seek the freedom and delight of the wilderness only to be defeated for their inability to control and cope with their experience of it and its inhabitants.

Beyond these challenges to an evolutionary explanation are the many findings that reveal large variations between people in their landscape preferences. How could some biological aspect of a person, of value in contributing to the survival of the species, be so patchy in its expression? By what mechanisms could landscape preferences have been generated through evolutionary processes of enhanced survival or mate selection? In essence, the speculative evolutionary interpretations of landscape preferences are derived from average findings based upon inherently artificial laboratory studies.

The aesthetic gaze

The results of studies of landscape preferences can be more readily interpreted as deriving from ways of looking. This emphasises the active making sense of surroundings. Evaluating them in terms of current purposes and aspirations, not some notional ancient benefit to survival. This includes the aesthetic gaze, looking on a landscape as a particular type of picture. This can inspire associations and evaluations embedded in historical and cultural experiences.

Conclusions

The examination of landscape preferences has contributed to a further understanding of how Places gain their significance. It has been demonstrated that the findings, on average, of the importance of water, forest, and distant views as components that make landscape views preferred hide many variations between people in their preferences. These general findings can be understood as a result of an 'aesthetic gaze', looking at landscapes as pictures. Such a process is encouraged by studies relying on judgements of photographs for their results. As a consequence, it has been proposed that the relationship of these results to late-18th-century definitions of the picturesque indicates a cultural context out of which landscape preferences emerge.

The interpretation of landscape preferences in terms of coherence and mystery was foreshadowed in the writings of Gilpin and Price two centuries ago. This leads to questioning of the, often repeated, evolutionary interpretation of these properties of landscape preferences. An alternative perspective is derived from the growing number of studies that reveal important differences between respondents' preferences for views of landscapes. These findings are especially clear when people are commenting in the presence of being in those Places.

The argument is put forward that people have many different ways of relating to the landscape, a variety of reasons for being there, and a mixture of purposes. This emphasis on human agency proposes that preferences relate to the possibilities and opportunities a landscape provides. That includes the enjoyment of viewing it as picturesque, but also includes personal and cultural associations. These involve related activities and experiences. The health-giving benefits are part of those processes to which Chapter 18 is devoted.

References and endnotes

1 Price, U. (1842). *On the picturesque*. Caldwell: Lloyd.

2 Jensen, C. U., Panduro, T. E., & Lundhede, T. H. (2014) The vindication of Don Quixote: The impact of noise and visual pollution from wind turbines. *Land Economics*, 90(4), 668–682.

3 Chmielewski, S., Lee, D. J., Tompalski, P., Chmielewski, T. J., & Wężyk, P. (2016) Measuring visual pollution by outdoor advertisements in an urban street using intervisibility analysis and public surveys. *International Journal of Geographical Information Science*, *30*(4), 801–818.

4 Jensen, C. U., Panduro, T. E., & Lundhede, T. H. (2014) The vindication of Don Quixote: The impact of noise and visual pollution from wind turbines. *Land Economics*, 90(4), 668–682.

5 Pastorella, F., Giacovelli, G., De Meo, I., & Paletto, A. (2017) People's preferences for Alpine forest landscapes: Results of an internet-based survey. *Journal of Forest Research*, 22(1), 36–43.

6 The study I carried out many years ago demonstrated how different reactions are to familiar places compared with reactions to pictures of place: Scott, M. & Canter, D. (1997) Picture or place? A multiple sorting study of landscape. *Journal of Environmental Psychology*, 17(4), 263–281, https://doi.org/10.1006/jevp.1997.0068

7 Schirpke, U., Tappeiner, G., Tasser, E., & Tappeiner, U.(2019) Using conjoint analysis to gain deeper insights into aesthetic landscape preferences. *Ecological Indicators*, 96(1), 202–212, ISSN 1470-160X.

8 McMahan, E. A., Cloud, J. M., Josh, P., & Scott, M. (2016) Nature with a human touch: Human-induced alteration negatively impacts perceived naturalness and preferences for natural environments. *Ecopsychology*, 8(1), 54–63.

9 Orne, M. T. (2017) On the social psychology of the psychological experiment: With particular reference to demand characteristics and their implications, in Denzin, N. K. (2017) (ed.) *Sociological methods: A sourcebook*. London: Routledge, pp. 279–299.

10 Cottet, M., Vaudor, L., Tronchère, H., Roux-Michollet, D., Augendre, M.,& Brault, V. (2018) Using gaze behavior to gain insights into the impacts of naturalness on city dwellers' perceptions and valuation of a landscape. *Journal of Environmental Psychology*, 60, 9–20.
11 Tieskens, K. F., Van Zanten, B. T., Schulp, C. J. E., & Verburg, P. H. (2018) Aesthetic appreciation of the cultural landscape through social media: An analysis of revealed preference in the Dutch river landscape. *Landscape and Urban Planning*, 177, 128–137, https://doi.org/10.1016/j.landurbplan.2018.05.002
12 Zhang, X., Xu, D., & Zhang, N. (2022) Research on landscape perception and visual attributes based on social media data—A case study on Wuhan University. *Applied Sciences*, 12(16), 8346, https://doi.org/10.3390/app12168346
13 Zhang, X., Xu, D., & Zhang, N. (2022) Research on landscape perception and visual attributes based on social media data—A case study on Wuhan University. *Applied Sciences*, 12(16), 8346, https://doi.org/10.3390/app12168346
14 Pastorella, F., Giacovelli, G., De Meo, I., & Paletto, A. (2017) People's preferences for Alpine forest landscapes: Results of an internet-based survey. *Journal of Forest Research*, 22(1), 36–43.
15 Tveit, M. S. (2009) Indicators of visual scale as predictors of landscape preference: A comparison between groups. *Journal of Environmental Management*, 90(9), 2882–2888.
16 Germino, M. J., Reiners, W. A., Blasko, B. J., McLeod, D., & Bastian, C. T. (2001) Estimating visual properties of Rocky Mountain landscapes using GIS. *Landscape and Urban Planning, 53*(1–4), 71–83.
17 Grêt-Regamey, A., Bishop, I. D., & Bebi, P. (2007) Predicting the scenic beauty value of mapped landscape changes in a mountainous region through the use of GIS. *Environment and Planning B: Planning and Design*, 34(1), 50–67.
18 Ode, Å., Fry, G., Tveit, M. S., Messager, P., & Miller, D. (2009) Indicators of perceived naturalness as drivers of landscape preference. *Journal of Environmental Management*, 90(1), 375–383.
19 Selman, P. & Swanwick, C. (2010) On the meaning of natural beauty in landscape legislation. *Landscape Research*, 35(1), 3–26.
20 Selman, P. & Swanwick, C. (2010) On the meaning of natural beauty in landscape legislation. *Landscape Research*, 35(1), 3–26.
21 My 9-year-old grandson was so impressed with the guidance that Bob Ross gave that he requested a painting kit for Christmas!
22 Gilpin, W. (1798) *Essay L. on picturesque beauty*, London: R. Blamire.
23 Scott, M. J. & Canter, D. V. (1997) Picture or place? A multiple sorting study of landscape. *Journal of Environmental Psychology, 17*(4), 263–281.
24 Kroh, D. P. & Gimblett, R. H. (1992) Comparing live experience with pictures in articulating landscape preference. *Landscape Research*, 17(2), 58–69.
25 Sevenant, M. & Antrop, M. (2011) Landscape representation validity: A comparison between on-site observations and photographs with different angles of view. *Landscape Research*, 36(3), 363–385.
26 Massoni, E. S., Varga, D., Sáez, M., & Pintó, J. (2016) Exploring aesthetic preferences in rural landscapes and the relationship with spatial pattern indices. *Journal of Landscape Ecology*, 9(1), 5–21.
27 Dramstad, W. E., Tveit, M. S., Fjellstad, W. J., & Fry, G. L. A. (2006) Relationships between visual landscape preferences and map-based indicators of landscape structure. *Landscape and Urban Planning*, 78(4), 465–474.
28 Sayadi, S., González-Roa, M. C., & Calatrava-Requena, J. (2009) Public preferences for landscape features: The case of agricultural landscape in mountainous Mediterranean areas. *Land Use Policy*, 26(2), 334–344, https://doi.org/10.1016/j.landusepol.2008.04.003
29 Sayadi, S., González-Roa, M. C., & Calatrava-Requena, J. (2009) Public preferences for landscape features: The case of agricultural landscape in mountainous Mediterranean areas. *Land Use Policy*, 26(2), 334–344, https://doi.org/10.1016/j.landusepol.2008.04.003
30 Howley, P. (2011) Landscape aesthetics: Assessing the general publics' preferences towards rural landscapes. *Ecological Economics*, 72, 161–169.
31 Yoji Natori, Y. & Chenoweth, R. (2008) Differences in rural landscape perceptions and preferences between farmers and naturalists. *Journal of Environmental Psychology*, 28(3), 250–267.

32 Schirpke, U., Tappeiner, G., Tasser, E., & Tappeiner, U. (2019) Using conjoint analysis to gain deeper insights into aesthetic landscape preferences. *Ecological Indicators*, 96(1), 202–212.

33 Olwig, K. R. (2016) Natural landscapes in the representation of national identity, in *Ashgate research companion to heritage and identity*, London, New York: Routledge, pp. 73–88.

34 Maunu Hayrynen (2000) The kaleidoscopic view: The Finnish national landscape imagery. *National Identities*, 2(1), 5–19, https://doi.org/10.1080/146089400113418

35 Laura Menatti, Mikel Subiza-Pérez, Arturo Villalpando-Flores, Laura Vozmediano, & César San Juan (2019) Place attachment and identification as predictors of expected landscape restorativeness. *Journal of Environmental Psychology*, 63, 36–43, ISSN 0272–4944, https://doi.org/10.1016/j.jenvp.2019.03.005

36 An excellent, wide-ranging set of critiques of the application of Darwinian theory to many areas of psychology is H. Rose and D. Rose (Eds.) (2000) *Alas, poor Darwin: Arguments against evolutionary psychology*.

37 Appleton, J. (1984) Prospects and refuges re-visited. *Landscape Journal*, 3(2), 91–103.

38 Kaplan, S. (1987) Aesthetics, affect, and cognition: Environmental preference from an evolutionary perspective. *Environment and Behavior*, 19(1), 3–32.

39 Kaplan, S. (1987) Aesthetics, affect, and cognition: Environmental preference from an evolutionary perspective. *Environment and Behavior*, 19(1), 3–32.

40 Kaplan, R. & Kaplan, S. (1989) *The experience of nature: A psychological perspective*. Cambridge: Cambridge University Press.

41 Weinberger, A. B., Christensen, A. P., Coburn, A., & Chatterjee, A. (2021) Psychological responses to buildings and natural landscapes. *Journal of Environmental Psychology*, 77, 101676.

42 Kaplan, S. (1987) Aesthetics, affect, and cognition: Environmental preference from an evolutionary perspective. *Environment and Behavior*, 19(1), p. 23.

43 Tallis, R. (2016) *Aping mankind*. United Kingdom: Taylor & Francis.

CHAPTER 18

The enigma of restoration

To sit in the shade on a fine day and look upon verdure is the most perfect refreshment.
Jane Austin, *Mansfield Park*, Chapter IX

The benefits of experiencing nature

Some years ago, after I'd been briefly in intensive care, following a relatively routine operation, I was wheeled back to a hospital ward. As I looked up from my bed there, I could see trees out of the window. Winter trees, starkly devoid of leaves. The emotions this sight evoked were out of all proportion to that simple experience of seeing even desolate nature after the buzzing busyness of the intensive care unit. Something about connecting again with t a hint of nature, beyond the somewhat parlous state I had been in, brought a huge wave of relief. Little tears of joy caused the nurse who was with me to comment on how good it was to be back in the world. Clearly a reaction she had often witnessed.

The sight of something other than the quasi-industrial features of the hospital made me aware again that I was not only a patient. I was a person who had other roles in society than the passive one imposed on me by being in a clinical setting. I was feeling my autonomy again. The view of nature reminded me of other ways of being. An aspect of surviving that connected me with something other than the administrations of doctors and nurses.

What is it about nature, even, or perhaps especially, gnarled barren trees that can evoke such reactions?

There is considerable evidence that I was far from unique in my reaction. The widely cited study by Ulrich[1] found that patients who had had gall bladder surgery took fewer strong analgesics and left hospital more quickly when they had views from their windows of a natural setting dominated by trees than those whose views were of brick walls. Another exploration of the benefits of a view of nature was reported by Lindemuth.[2] She found a reduction in prisoners' indicators of stress when they have

DOI: 10.4324/9780367808655-23

some view of gardens and natural settings. Even in less stressful settings, views of the natural surroundings have been found to be more beneficial than views of a built environment. Kaplan,[3] for example, reported that those office workers with a view of nature, when compared with those who did not:

> Felt less frustrated and more patient, found their job more challenging, expressed greater enthusiasm for it, and reported higher life satisfaction as well as overall health.
>
> *(p. 199)*

In addition, those with a view of nature reported fewer ailments in the previous six months (2.45 from a list of 11) compared with those who did not have a view of nature (3.02). A small but statistically significant result.

The claim that this result is a direct consequence of the view of nature may, however, be an oversimplification of a more complex process than a biological causation. Curiously though, but perhaps not surprisingly for a cognitive scientist like Kaplan, there is no report of the details of the jobs these respondents carried out. They are simply described as being participants with "relatively similar jobs (i.e., desk jobs)". But any consideration of organisational cultures draws attention to the explicit hierarchy that is at play. In Chapter 9, the space syntax analysis made clear that the more senior a person is, the more likely they are to have an office on the periphery of a building (presumably with a higher probability of a view outside). In addition, the more senior the person, the more able they are to choose the location of their desk.

There is no doubt that having a view out is preferred to a windowless office. There is not really any need to cite empirical research to back this up, but there are a growing number of studies to support this claim.[4] It is therefore quite a strong hypothesis that the more senior a person is, the pleasanter the view she will have from her office window. Consequently, it is possible that Kaplan's findings relate as much to the seniority, or at least the ability to control the outlook, of respondents as to the view itself.

The view of nature can symbolise the particular position a person has in the organisational hierarchy. That can carry implications for the status of the occupant of an office. The consequences for well-being may thus relate to position in an organisation, not the direct benefits of the view out. The symbolic qualities of the view contribute to the status, but the status can influence what view the person has.

The question of why a view of nature carries symbolic associations with status is raised by these results. There can be little doubt that a view of trees is pleasanter than a blank brick wall. As we have seen in previous chapters, the natural world is more varied and intricate than most human creations. The symbolic qualities of nature offer associations and meanings that are typically enjoyable.

However, the symbolic qualities of a view of nature do not provide a fully convincing explanation of why landscape, especially 'natural' landscape, plays such a powerful role in poetry and mythology as well as being regarded as being a primary locations for 'restorative' experiences. Certainly, the studies by Ulrich and by Lindemuth imply that there is something more of benefit from the experience of nature than merely offering some abstract association.

My reactions to a view of nature, and the similar responses documented by many others, are taken a step further when consideration is given to actual contact with natural settings. There is a growing literature on the many different benefits, not just of looking at nature but of being in nature. In the late 1960s, when I lived in Glasgow, a major city that allows remarkably ready access to wild countryside, I remember people saying they went out into the landscape "to recharge their batteries". This idea has become institutionalised in references to the 'restorative' qualities of being in nature.[5]

The notion of 'restoration' refers to the idea that an earlier state was not present and has now been reinstated. This is exemplified[6] by findings that show people have improvements in how they feel and are more able to concentrate after a nature experience. There is even an aspect of 'restoration' that includes the ability to be less impulsive and more considered.

Such qualities are now recognised in popular culture, even being given a more elaborated engineering analogy. A recent *Lifestyle* section of the renowned British newspaper *The Guardian*[7] called the contact with the natural world a way of generating 'Positive Energy'. Ten 'active retreats' are listed there that enable people to engage with the countryside in a variety of different ways. These are as varied as 'Poetry, yoga and forest bathing in Monmouthshire', 'Women's sailing on the Norfolk Broads' and 'Mindful hill walking in the Peaks'. Even a local newspaper reports on a "Wellbeing Garden to boost health",[8] stating, "We'd like to encourage all visitors to the leisure centre to enjoy this green space, allowing them to gain the many associated physical and mental health benefits". A review of 50 studies[9] of nature-based interventions that covered gardening, green exercise, and nature-based therapy showed that they improved mental health outcomes in adults, including those with pre-existing mental health problems. In some countries doctors are even prescribing nature contact for people with mental health issues.

The countryside companion

The benefits of interacting with natural surroundings have long been apparent. For instance, the history of giving special meaning and significance to the 'Countryside' is illustrated, somewhat nostalgically, in the collection of essays published soon after the Second World War under the title *The Countryside Companion*. The opening page (Figure 18.1) makes clear a number of issues that emerge throughout the present chapter, linking also to central themes in The Psychology of Place. The countryside is set as distinct from the towns and cities. Urban living is conceived as separating people "from their natural surroundings". This is linked to the industrial revolution, in ignorance, of course, that people have gathered together in cities around the world for well over ten millennia. They came together thousands of years ago, in large conurbations in South America, China and the Indus because of the advantages that come with a density of people to work with and the support and facilities that were available.

Stephenson writes of people being 'uprooted' from the land, a powerful implicit metaphor that also regards the countryside as a natural place. The countryside as a resource is also emphasised in it, allowing 'flight from the ugliness we have created to the beauty we have not yet marred'. The distinction between the profane, marred city

INTRODUCTION

by TOM STEPHENSON

FROM the early days of the industrial revolution there has been an increasing tendency to separate great masses of mankind farther and farther from their natural surroundings, to congregate them in towns and cities where, for the greater part of their lives, they are deprived of the simple yet most satisfying pleasures of the countryside.

In recent years, however, there has arisen a widespread recognition of the need for contact with the land from which many of us have been too long uprooted. Never have there been so many people taking every opportunity to escape from town to seek recreation (re-creation we might say) in places where rural peace still endures.

Much of this flight from the ugliness we have created to the beauty we have not yet marred is, no doubt, to be explained by shorter working hours and increased facilities for travel. Yet the driving force behind it all is probably a growing realization of the need for closer touch with Nature for the full enjoyment of a healthy and happy life.

Professor G. M. Trevelyan has said: "Without vision the people perish and without sight of the beauty of nature the spiritual power of the British people will be atrophied. The longing, too often a thwarted longing, for natural beauty and the great unspoilt spaces, is a most touching and a most hopeful thing in the modern city population. The condition of any real value in modern city life is holidays spent in the country. How our people long for them and save up to get them!"

Thus we are discovering that the sights, and sounds, and scents of the countryside meet some elemental longing, and give greater delight than any artificial pleasures can provide. Even the man born in town, and bred of several generations of townsfolk, may find that a field of rippling corn, or grass ready for mowing, is a thing of joy, and that the spread of meadow and pasture, the rise of a hill, or the long, sleek flowing lines of the downs and the quiet peace and beauty of the valleys, stir in him a feeling of satisfaction and of being at one with the land.

The tuneful song of thrush or blackbird, the gay piping of the lark, or the less melodious, but still attractive, cry of the plover, or the peculiar wail of the curlew across a lonely moor or marsh, leaves none of us entirely unmoved.

MARKET DAY

Many a sleepy little town comes to life on market day when the people come in from the surrounding countryside. A scene in Richmond, Yorks.

Figure 18.1 Opening page of *The Countryside Companion*[10]

and the sanctity of nature is emphasised by it supporting 'the spiritual power of the British people'.

This distinction between the 'sacred', apparently untouched, countryside and profane, blighted, metropolitan urbanisation has been noted in Chapter 16. There the exile from the paradise of The Garden of Eden was shown to be engrained in the Western cultural notion that nature is sacred. The built environment, typified by Blake's "dark Satanic mills", is evil.

There is also a long history of autobiographical accounts of the value of being in nature. Henry David Thoreau's autobiographical 1854 book, *Walden* or *Life in the Woods* is a well-known forerunner of the arguments for the benefits of escaping from the pressures of the built environment to live simply in nature. He went there, in part, to explore whether he could, or at least how he could, survive without the support of what he called 'over-civilisation'. This was a quest to understand himself better, as well as seek out a different way of living in the world, a different environmental role. But his seclusion also kept him away from the demands of city life long enough to have the opportunity to write two books. Further, it gave him deeper insight into the workings of nature. He writes of how this knowledge encouraged him to feel a deeper connection with the natural world.

Thoreau reflects the view of Stephenson but takes the value of being away from 'over-civilisation' a step further. He grasps the benefits of understanding himself better when isolated from the demands of being with others.

> I went to the woods because I wished to live deliberately, to front only the essential facts of life, and see if I could not learn what it had to teach, and not, when I came to die, discover that I had not lived.[11]

This tells us about the different ways of being in a Place. By stripping away the distractions of his metropolitan life, he could see himself more clearly. Understand what was needed to survive and how well he coped with those challenges. He had time to contemplate on what he was as a person. Being in nature provided the service of testing himself and exploring what his competences were.

The personal growth that comes from overcoming the trials of isolated immersion in wild, inhospitable Places is epitomised in Western culture by the accounts in The Gospels of Jesus spending 40 days fasting in the desert. Overcoming battles there with the devil can be understood as using the demands of survival to create a new way of dealing with the world. This is going beyond 'restoration' to a new creation of the self.

Shinrin-Yoku (森林浴)

A somewhat different perspective on the values of immersion in the natural landscape is the Japanese activity, usually translated as 'Forest Bathing'. The process of being quiet and calm in a natural setting, much as Thoreau would have advocated. No contact with society is allowed, notably no electronic/technological devices that could be a disruption to quiet meditation. There is no requirement to expend great energy by strenuous activity. Strolling and listening to the sounds you and the surrounding nature are making. You are encouraged to stroke the bark of trees (or even hug them) or lie down and absorb the uninterrupted experience of being in nature. As shown in Figure 18.2. The participant there is sitting in silence, connecting to Nature through her senses – listening to sounds, feeling sensations of the air on her bare skin, the texture of the tree stump against her body, and smelling the air as she slowly breathes in and out.

Studies of the consequences of this activity have shown that, at the very least, it can reduce anxiety.[13] That is part of a groundswell of evidence of the influence of a direct experience of the countryside on well-being. Of particular note is a recent, extensive report on 'Valuing the Mental Health Benefits of Woodlands'.[14] Admittedly this was commissioned by the UK government department responsible for woodlands. It therefore has a vested interest in supporting the value of woodlands. Nonetheless, the study is remarkably thorough and systematic, being part of an extensive research programme focusing on the benefits of woodlands and trees.

As is not unusual for reports seeking to influence government financial decisions, this Forest Research study attempts to assign economic benefits to woodlands and trees. These are derived from estimating the money saved by the NHS due to reduction in mental health problems brought about by people utilising woodlands and enjoying treescapes. Saraev[15] and his colleagues examine the literature on mental health benefits to determine the apparent effects of people visiting woodlands or even just having trees on their streets.

Figure 18.2 A woman 'Forest Bathing'; the picture was taken in Croxteth Park, Liverpool[12]

These studies range from identifying very specific values, such as having a pleasant view, to consideration of wider health benefits, including reductions in mental illness and increased feelings of well-being.

What are the processes that generate the effects of nature?

Despite the growing academic and considerable anecdotal, personal evidence for the benefits of connecting with and directly experiencing nature, it is not at all clear why that might be. I have called this the 'enigma of restoration' because there are many questions about how being in natural settings can have such frequently found benefits. After all, as already noted, human beings have lived in cities for well over ten millennia. Most of the breakthroughs in technology, relating to such matters as health care and longevity, have emerged within cities. Although Thoreau described great benefit from his woodland isolation, he still returned to the city to benefit from the social and cultural (as well as financial) benefits he could accrue there.

The image of the idyllic rural existence was, and still is, different from the calm, peaceful, healthy setting that myth and legend would have us believe. The challenges of existing in nature, or even exploring it briefly, can be very great indeed. Mountain Rescue England and Wales dealt with 2,775 incidents in 2024, most of which included accidents in rural areas. They include falls, exposure to extreme weather, drowning, and incidents involving wildlife or livestock. In previous centuries, the challenges of the countryside were even more severe.

This has not prevented the promulgation of a widely cited and explored theory that claims nature supports the recovery from stress:

> because resource rich and safe natural environments were conducive to human survival, natural selection has equipped our species with an adaptive readiness for psychophysical stress reduction in such settings and a shift towards positively toned moods.[16]

This theory was labelled by its originator, Ulrich,[17] Stress Recovery Theory (SRT), developing ideas from his initial study, already mentioned, of hospital patients' recovery. Drawing on landscape preference studies, discussed in Chapter 17, the proposal is that those outdoor places, which have moderate complexity, some mystery, and a surface that is even, would have the most impact on reducing stress.

Yannick Joye and his colleagues[18] have published a masterly, extremely scholarly critique of this proposal. I would add to that critique the question of how to explain the recognised stress recovery effects that cause millions of human beings throughout the world to crowd beaches in the Summer? Those Places do not fit the description of stress recovery locations promulgated by Ulrich or those who delight in spending time in deserts? These locations are devoid of the apparent cues that, it is claimed, are innately attractive. There are also plenty of accounts, as well as empirical studies, that show the stress recovery benefits of visiting museums,[19] of listening to music, and of enjoying a night out with friends. Is some contortion of the evolutionary benefits necessary to explain these processes? Or are quite different explanations needed for these other benefits? Explanations grounded in education, socialisation, and culture. But why should stress recovery in one context need such a different explanation in another?

Furthermore, the studies that support stress reduction explanations only find moderate support for these claims, although the statistical results may be declared 'significant'.[20] A much stronger effect would be expected for a trait that contributed to survival. Even if the evolutionary adaptations were initially small, for them to have an impact, they would be expected to leave a clear result in humans today, as do all the biological benefits, such as opposable thumbs and large brains.

The detailed challenges which Joye and his team make demonstrate the lack of evidence for evolutionary explanations in SRT. The claim in that theory is that the restorative, emotional benefits emerged to deal with danger and the challenge of limited resources. This leads, apparently, to the proposal that savannah landscapes, from which *Homo sapiens emerged*, would be the most beneficial. But "positive affect and stress reductions have also been observed for nature that seemingly lacks life-sustaining elements and/or safety".[21]

Attention restorativeness?

Besides the unhelpful evolutionary attempts at explaining the value of being in nature,[22] the most obvious,[23] is that any sort of physical exercise has health benefits. Besides looking at the landscape, getting out into the countryside requires some sort of active effort. Broadly speaking, this activity is likely to be more beneficial if it is away from the fumes and dangers of metropolitan settings. The evidence for this, as in so many such studies, is less than clear.[24] Part of the problem is that what counts as a natural setting mixes so many different types of places, reasons for using that space for exercise, and what type of exercise, that drawing one generic, overall conclusion is problematic.

The varieties of who and what are being studied add complexity to making sense of psychological studies of the benefits of natural environments. As considered in Chapters 16 and 17, too often overviews of research combine studies based on looking at pictures with those that examine direct experiences of being in green spaces. However, beyond the direct health benefits of activity in the countryside, further possibilities for how nature 'recharges our batteries' have been offered. By being in a situation that does not require dealing with the demands of urban life, or even being reminded of that setting by looking at pictures, it would be expected that daily cares would be reduced. With that difference would surely come a more relaxed state. Plenty of studies[25] show that after experiencing natural settings people feel more relaxed and 'restored' in various ways.

A cognitive approach to explaining the value of nature is for it to contribute to 'recovery from attentional fatigue', given the neat acronym ART (Attention Restoration Theory).[26] This is based on the view that human beings only have a limited capacity for attending to a scene or object that does not naturally attract their attention, causing a reduction in the ability to attend to what is available. This is elaborated by arguing that if a scene is 'fascinating', has a lot going on, is away from daily hassles, and is compatible with an individual's proclivities, then it will contribute to restoring attention. Reviews of research seeking to determine if this sort of exposure to nature restores the ability to attend find some limited support for this claim.[27]

There are insightful critiques of this theory,[28] but some comprehension of its weaknesses can be seen by direct examination of the procedure used to test for the impact of natural settings. This is the Perceived Restorative Scale[29] (PRS). The full set of questions in the PRS is given in Table 18.1.

Rather than being purely cognitive questions that relate a person's limited capacity to attend, these questions are about ways of being in a Place. 'Doing things you like' implies that you are acting in a way that is different from other situations. 'Being distracted' indicates that you want to get on with something else. 'Wanting to explore' suggests a different role in the place. That is not being an observer but a participant.

None of these aspects deal directly with attention or the notion of a deficit that is restored. Instead, they are different ways of being in that place. They indicate much more than dealing with attention deficits. They are interesting examples of being able to take on a different role and follow different rules in that place. These include having the freedom to carry out actions that contribute to self-identity: "I can do things I like here". Or taking on a more powerful agency: "I want to explore the area".

Once again, the actual indices of the benefits of being in nature do not point to a mechanical-like topping up of a person's reserves of attention. They point to the opportunities the activities and experiences give for engaging with the surroundings. They do assume a person having agency not just being a reactive organism. People, as is worth repeating, take advantage of escape from the hurly-burly of metropolitan life for many reasons. The benefits of those escapes are therefore likely to differ depending on who the person is and why they are there.

Table 18.1 The Perceived Restorative Scale (PRS). Items are grouped according to their intended subscale designation

Being Away
It is an escape experience.
Spending time here gives me a good break from my day-to-day routine.
Fascination
The setting has fascinating qualities.
My attention is drawn to many interesting things.
I would like to get to know this place better.
I want to explore the area.
There is much to explore and discover here.
I would like to spend more time looking at the surroundings.
Coherence (Extent)
There is too much going on.
It is a confusing place.
There is a great deal of distraction.
It is chaotic here.
Compatibility
I can do things I like here.
I have a sense that I belong here.
I have a sense of oneness with this setting.
Being here suits my personality.
I could find ways to enjoy myself in a place like this.[30]

Artificial experiments

It is helpful to understand how the proposals from ART and SRT have been supported so widely across a vast set of studies over more than 30 years. It is because they have generated tidy research paradigms that are readily replicable. Research feeds on itself. Once a process is in place, which a PhD student can tweak and replicate, the machinery takes over. There is no need for the student to question the basic assumptions from which the paradigm is derived. Indeed, the conservatism of academic institutions, as well as the power hierarchy that supported the paradigm, will oppose any attempt to replace it.

The implications of why, when, and where people have contact with nature for their well-being benefits are nicely illustrated by those who choose to run long distances in challenging landscapes, as illustrated in Figure 18.3. Most people would find even walking up Yr Wyddfa (Mount Snowdon, in North Wales) too great and daunting a challenge. They would not regard being on top of the highest peak in Wales, particularly uplifting or promoting of their well-being. The biphobia of unforeseen dangers and the required exertions would be a dominant reaction. Yet Lily Canter,[31] who is committed to running 'ultramarathons', was totally enthralled by the experience. As she said[32]:

> I am pretty scared of heights, always have been. So, climbing up Snowdon TWICE in one day (I'm going to keep saying that because it took me by surprise!) gave me the heebie jeebies big time. But I'm very proud that I did it and just cracked on. Running with an amazing bunch of ultra runners was super inspirational, and I never would have done this on my own. What an incredible day out!

Figure 18.3 Dr. Lily Canter 'running' up Yr Wyddfa in Wales

Lily's is one of a great many women[33] and men, young and old, taking on aspects of the natural world. They contrast with the relaxed, otherworldly experience of *Shinrin-Yoku*. But, like that 'forest bathing', it is what people are doing in those settings that helps us to understand the many ways in which natural settings can support well-being.

Well-being

To develop an understanding of the role of human agency, which is manifest in the purpose for being in a Place, and its relationship to well-being in natural settings, it is helpful to unpack the idea of 'well-being', which is commonly cited as the impact of being in nature. Well-being was characterised by the ancient Greeks as either hedonic or eudemonic. The hedonic perspective, derived from the ancient Greek word for pleasure, ἡδονή, emphasises the search for pleasure and the avoidance of pain. It is a relatively simple, almost mechanical seeking for what has become known as a 'dopamine hit'. This contrasts with a *eudemonic* view of well-being. Derived from the Greek εὐδαιμονία that has a meaning closer to happiness or living well.

The components of well-being have been elaborated by Ryff and Keyes and widely cited.[34] They include having goals in life and feelings of continued development, which may be characterised as having commitment and aspirations. Another aspect is feeling independent, being autonomous. A third aspect is feeling positive about oneself and competence in what one does. This often includes warm and satisfying relationships with others.

There are many features during a person's daily experiences and unfolding personal narrative that support these different aspects of well-being. How do they relate to being in nature? Does activity in the countryside have the possibility of contributing to well-being as elaborated by these different facets of it.

To answer these questions, it is helpful to know that Ryff and Keyes' account of well-being owes a lot to those psychologists concerned with a sense of self, notably Carl Rogers and Abraham Maslow. Their therapeutic goals are for the person, in essence, to feel good about themselves. This includes a feeling of achievement and self-worth.

Table 18.2 A nature connectedness scale[37]

1.	I am an integral part of nature.
2.	My relationship to nature is an important part of who I am.
3.	I feel a sense of oneness with the natural world around me.
4.	I feel spiritually bound with nature.
5.	I think of the natural world as a community to which I belong.
6.	I feel joy just being in nature.
7.	I feel a deep love for nature.
8.	I feel emotionally connected to nature.
9.	I feel happy and at home when I am in the midst of nature.
10.	Contact with nature gives me a feeling of peace and tranquillity.
11.	I often go out to the countryside or nature.
12.	When I am in the midst of nature, I merge with it.
13.	I take care of nature as if it were a part of myself.
14.	I often listen and watch nature.
15.	I take care of animals as if they were human beings.

That is a positive way of being. The indications are that, whilst the experience of natural environments is not the only way to do this, there are facets of being in nature that support particular aspects of this.

Intriguing evidence for the claim that being in nature facilitates being positively different can be found in those studies that have demonstrated a link between being 'connected to nature' and well-being. Those who are more connected to nature have higher levels of self-growth.[35] What is going on here becomes clearer if a commonly used questionnaire of connectedness to nature is examined, as indicated in Table 18.2.

The psychological assumptions on which it is based are clear from an examination of the questions. They are about selfhood. Who the person thinks they are: "nature is part of who I am"; "I am emotionally connected to nature"; "I merge with it". These are strong expressions of oneness with nature. Is it taking this too far to say that people who strongly agree with these statements believe they are different people in nature? Their relationship to themselves and others, changes when they are in the countryside.[36] That being in nature supports feelings of autonomy, whilst also being aware that it is possible to sense being a presence in something that is much bigger than oneself.

Environmental roles and rules

Two well-established theories, Stress Recovery Theory (SRT) and Attention Restoration Theory (ART), have already been mentioned with some comments on the weaknesses of these proposals. Yet they are commonly cited as explanations of the restorative benefits of being in or looking at nature. However, despite their popularity, as already noted, both theories face important challenges, as Joye and his colleagues make clear in an excellent, recent review of them.[38]

The central challenge to both SRT and ART is that they both suffer from being embedded in a passive, positivistic view of human beings and their interactions with their environments. People are thought of as receiving stimuli from their surroundings which modify their emotions and cognitions. This is the age-old determinism that has dogged environmental psychology since its earliest studies. It reduces considerations of human agency. Why people are present in a given location. What they are trying to do there.

A crucial problem with such a view of people being fundamentally passive leads to experiments that only allow respondents to operate as responding to stimuli. The typical test of ART or SRT proposals is to expose some respondents to stress or some cognitive limiting experience and others to act as a 'control' without that. Both groups are then exposed to pictures of nature or to nature *in situ*. There is then a subsequent test of their emotions or cognitions. This experimental paradigm is relatively straightforward to carry out, allowing many different studies to be conducted with little need to carry out a detailed examination of what is actually going on with participants.

Given the confidence and self-assurance of these theories, it is surprising how minimal and contradictory many of the results are. To take just one of many possible examples,[39] of research into these theories, student participants were shown "forest-related videos" for either 5, 20, or 30 minutes after they had been exposed to a stressful situation. That consisted of being presented with 49 sequential numbers, randomly scattered in a 7 × 7 grid, being instructed to complete the connections between them, as well as identify repetitions and missing values. Before that test and after watching the video, three measures were made of the effects of exposure to scenes of nature, stress reduction, attention increase and relaxation increase. Only the stress reduction, and the correlated increase in relaxation measures, showed any statistically 'significant' difference for the longest time period exposure. But even those differences were less than 10% of the total value achieved on the measure. It is therefore more likely that any limited results that are found in support of the theories are a result of respondents' expectations about what the researcher is looking for. These are the 'demand characteristics',[40] and related 'experimenter effects'[41] described in Chapter 3. An even more direct explanation of any results is that the tasks themselves are rather boring, so looking at nature gives them something pleasant to look at. This was demonstrated in a simple but clever experiment.[42] When respondents were told the tasks were a game, any influence of experiencing nature disappeared.

These studies ignore human agency. People have purposes, goals, ambitions, and reasons for being in a Place or deciding to go to one. Imagination allows us to consider what it would be like in a place from descriptions or photographs, or even to suspend that type of relationship by treating a picture as an art object to be admired in its own terms, which can of course include associations and experiences of the Places pictured.

Looking closely at systematic studies of the relationships to experience of the natural landscape helps to elucidate the processes involved. One helpful, thorough meta-analysis of the relationship between environmental contact and positive emotions by McMahan and Estes[43] drew the conclusion that there are differences in the size of that relationship depending on the measure of positive emotions. Of particular note is that when the PANAS[44] (Positive And Negative Affect Scale) questionnaire is used, a reasonably respectable correlation, typically of 0.41, is found between exposure to the natural environment and positive emotion. However, when the ZIPERS[45] (situation-specific trait-state test for the prediction and measurement of affective responses) measure was used, the much lower correlation of 0.20 was achieved.

It is important to be aware that correlations indicate the square root of the common variance explained. In other words, a correlation of 0.41 can be regarded as accounting for nearly 17% of the relationship between environmental contact and positive emotions, whereas a correlation of 0.20 only accounts for 4%. Although technically both may be declared 'statistically significant', this is a consequence of the large sample size. Such 'significance' should not be thought of as 'importantly meaningful'. Rather, the results are an indication of some process at play against a background of many other influences.

Nonetheless, the difference between the sizes of the relationships of these two measures is worthy of closer examination. This helps to indicate the psychological mechanisms at play. The differences in the two measures reveal rather different ways of assessing the benefits, or otherwise, of being in a natural setting. The PANAS questionnaire has a focus on the extent to which a person feels enthusiastic, active, and alert or has a negative effect of general distress and unpleasurable engagement. In other words, it explores how the person feels about their possible actions there. Whether they feel animated and have potential for engaging with the Place being considered, or the experience is one of not wanting to carry out further actions in that location.

ZIPER is rather different. It asks about (a) awareness of internal physiological arousal, such as "my heart is beating faster"; (b) labelling of the internal state in affective terms, such as "I feel fearful"; and (c) an overt response tendency such as "I want to avoid or get out of the situation.". This addresses personal emotional states, with little attention to what it might mean for actions in the there, in any positive sense. A somewhat more passive view of emotional reactions in nature than the PANAS emphases. In a nutshell, PANAS is hinting at the purpose a person has for being in a Place, whereas the ZIPER measures just considering being there.

Another extensive, carefully conducted study also helps to highlight the weaknesses in the different ways in which the impact of being in a natural setting are studied. A wide-ranging review[46] of 215 studies that compared the mental health benefits of different 'green spaces' concluded that:

> Green space can foster mental health, but exposure to their different types and components induces different effects and it is not yet clear which green space types or characteristics are most beneficial (Section 4).

Their term 'green space' covered a multitude of settings that included, parks, forests, trees and vegetation, urban green space, gardens, grassland, and meadows. The authors were aware that people are likely to be in these locations for very different reasons. Some are just visiting; others live in the area being studied. There are those who exercise there or have health care reasons for being there. Some of the green spaces studied are part of school environments. However, amidst their rich and complex explorations of many different studies the authors give no indication of whether there is any evidence that different sorts of natural settings have different sorts of benefits when people are there for different reasons.

The static way of thinking about the effects of natural, green environments is generated by the practical limitations of most environmental psychology research. Pictures can be shown to people, or their responses can be gathered in a particular setting. Understanding the roles of settings in the lives of respondents requires a more intensive exploration of who the respondents are and how and why they are in a particular Place at one time or another.

Another debilitating influence on the research is the acceptance of the measures that have become standard. These are derived from the prevailing theories. ART, with its focus on cognitive processes, especially the idea of 'recovering' from attention deficits, leads to studies that only consider these possible changes in cognitive performance. By contrast, for SRT stress reduction is given primacy. This gives rise to studies that examine broad emotional consequences of natural environment experiences. In other words, the measures used drive the research rather than a consideration of the wide and various panoply of experiences that being in natural Places can and do generate. The measurement tail is wagging the theory dog.[47]

Fortunately, a multinational team of researchers has become aware of the weaknesses in ART and SRT as theoretical paradigms. They have begun to offer a perspective that takes account of human agency, what it is people are trying to achieve, for which being in nature offers some assistance. They[48] propose what they call 'goal-discrepancy' explanations of the processes ART and SRT use to explain the benefits of nature-based practices. In essence, their idea is that people have goals in any situation which may be thwarted in various ways, and "nature helps individuals to reduce discrepancies between their current situation and their goals".[49]

They propose that "Nature can facilitate this discrepancy reduction process through three pathways: (a) by modifying goals, (b) by modifying interpretations of the situation, or (c) by affording actions that can fulfil thwarted goals".[50]

This framework is developed by listing what they call 'services' which nature provides as a way of fulfilling thwarted goals, particularly from the third pathway of allowing actions that can fulfil the thwarted goals. Such a listing of the different opportunities that nature provides is a large step forward from the passive reactions in theories about stress reduction or attention restoration. They are therefore worth considering in a little more detail.

- *Visual enjoyment* (which Joye and his colleagues grace with the label 'Hedonic Value') is a common benefit of nature, relating to the consideration of the *picturesque* discussed in Chapter 16. This is a way of relating to nature as a distant object to be admired and appreciated.
- *Tranquility.* The peace and quiet of the countryside (if they are not ruined by the sound of tractors, motorbike scramblers, or summer raves) are widely recognised as an experience to seek out. Not everyone welcomes this, notably those who flock to crowded beaches. Joye characterises this as an example of dealing with goal discrepancy. That is wanting quiet after the busyness of daily life. Is it not possible that on some occasions some people enjoy tranquility, but on other occasions welcome the bustle of metropolitan existence?
- *Autonomy.* Interestingly, this is couched as being in natural places "enabling individuals to act in self-determined ways and to be their authentic selves".[51] This can be seen as another aspect of a person. Another way of being in the setting. A different environmental role that has different place-related rules.
- *Social Connectedness.* Often people are in natural settings with other people. But invariably their relationships with each other are different in those settings. For

example, the value of outdoor team-building activities is widely recognised.[52] By putting people in a different context, with tasks rather different from what they have to carry out when working together, their relationships change. That allows the development of new social bonds.

- *Competence.* As Joye puts it, "natural environments...[offer] opportunities for learning or exploration".[53] Many examples come to mind, from abseiling to camping, from mountaineering to skiing. They all facilitate feelings of self-efficacy and empower a feeling of mastery.

These 'services' available from the countryside are, of course, not provided in isolation from one another. The feeling of personal achievement from reaching the summit of a mountain is enhanced by the awesome view, whilst at the same time supporting the experience of being truly oneself. The tranquillity in a wood can be enriched by sitting quietly there with a loved one. Furthermore, none of the opportunities that are provided by the countryside and landscapes are unique to those settings. A game of tennis on an indoor court, for instance, may offer feelings of connectedness, autonomy, and competence. A masterful tennis service, for instance, can be very beautiful, even art-like. Even a feeling of tranquillity as attention is focused on the game rather than the travails of daily life. That is everything except perhaps the distancing perspective of admiring beauty. Going to a theatre or visiting a museum, even a walk around an old city, can offer many of the 'services' so clearly provided by a trip into natural settings. I suppose, though, that few offer all of them, possibly at the same time.

It is also important not to forget the direct physical benefits of being away from the pollution, noise, distressing sights, and inherent dangers of being in many cities. Many green spaces, whether urban parks, private gardens or the open countryside, tend to avoid these unhealthy aspects. The crucial requirement of walking or cycling in the countryside,[54] as a basic mode of getting around, also has direct health benefits that can enhance feelings of well-being.

Autonomy as the essence of nature's benefits

When considering the evaluation of Places, I wrote over 35 years ago:

> Expressed satisfaction with, or pleasure in, a given place is a consequence of the possibilities for achieving the role-related purposes for being there".[55]
>
> *(Canter, 1988, p. 1)*

Struggling with ways in which to elaborate 'role-related purposes' in relation to the benefits of being in nature, I took myself off for a walk in the Welsh countryside from the cottage where I live. On that walk I introspected about what it was when moving along that uninhabited track which gave me its benefits. Thinking of this whilst musing over the five 'services' of being in the landscape, it becomes clear that all those 'services', as noted earlier, are available in many other settings, whether tranquillity, a feeling of competence, or visual delight.

Wandering along a path, through a farm and into some woods that I know so well, probably allows the possibility of experiencing those active experiences more readily than would be the case if I had been walking along a city street. But there was something that was typical of my walk that is more difficult to achieve in other contexts, especially as I was walking alone. An awareness that I was free from any obvious quotidian pressures. I had to get back in time for tea, and the physical exertion involved would limit how far, or fast, I would walk, but beyond those sorts of demands, I had *autonomy*. For the period of my walk, I was independent.

Someone doing exercises on a lawn as part of an outdoor gymnastic class would not have that much autonomy, but they would have the physical benefits of being outdoors, which could be enhanced by some freedom to move their body. Many people find a sense of freedom in a bath, but the mechanical restrictions on movement may make that experience feel less autonomous. Overall, many experiences can be thought of that do not, in their essence, remove the possibility of autonomy but are likely to limit its availability. It is just that in nature the possibilities are more reliably present and can be more strongly felt. They also, typically, do not cost very much!

The possibility that autonomy is at the heart of the experience of natural settings opens up the prospect that other aspects of landscape experience can be ways of expressing that autonomy. Turning again to Joye et al.'s list of services, consider *competence*. Doing carpentry, solving a mathematical equation, and learning to play an instrument are all activities in which it is possible to gain and feel increased competence. However, if any of those activities are enhanced by the autonomy possible in nature, they take on a differently enriching role. In addition, being in the countryside offers special opportunities for being competent. Getting to the top of the hill, where I usually turn round to return home, is a particular way of exerting my autonomy.

Contemplative use of *tranquillity* is another facet of autonomy. The repose and reflexion that are supported by the lack of offensive noises and the calming chatter of birds found in many forests, the unfolding emptiness of a desert, or the serene presence of a lake in the mountains allow you to experience yourself in a different way. This lets you be a different self from the office worker, caterer, plumber, or architect, or even husband or mother, that you are in other settings. For those for whom the landscape is their place of work, whether farmer or tree surgeon, it is possible to have moments to enjoy such tranquillity, but the countryside does not offer the same opportunity for a different environmental role or them that it does for other people.

The opportunity that being in nature offers for inhabiting a different, more autonomous role is provided by the *Visual enjoyment* of natural scenes. When just looking at nature, we are free to focus on the details, as in a field of dandelion 'clocks' (Figure 18.4), or the broader track of my walk (Figure 18.5a). This is an often-underrated aspect of autonomy, available when looking at art objects, but with much greater variety of perspectives in the landscape. This variety changes all the time, as illustrated in Figure 18.5b. Variations that are hardly ever considered in studies that show people photographs or videos of locations to evaluate.

A further benefit, frequently identified, of being in nature is its potential for different relationships to others, aspects of *sociality*. This, again, is possible and common in many other settings, but typically it requires people to take on rather different roles from those in other situations, as illustrated in the examples listed in The Guardian mentioned earlier. The freedom of choosing those roles is a particularly attractive aspect made available by being in the countryside.

Figure 18.4 A local focus of nature in mid-summer

All of these considerations are ways of being in the landscape. Roles that are especially readily available when out and about in nature. There is the offer of different relationships to who you are and different environmental roles, facilitated by the outdoors. This is the proposal that actions in natural settings provide positive opportunities to experience different ways of being. That is a challenge to the idea that nature 'restores' or provides some replacement of a deficit.

The application of Goal Directed Theory to explanations of nature's benefits relies on the idea that those benefits derive from resolving discrepancies between actual and desired states. Such resolutions fit well with the proposal that the main discrepancy, which being in the countryside can help to resolve, is reaching the desired state of autonomy. That can be difficult to achieve in built, urban, and metropolitan environments. The physical and mental health benefits doubtless provide people with many different sources of well-being. To assume that they are all replenishing aspects missing in other settings is to put people in a limited, somewhat restrictive box. It sees people reacting to losses rather than seeking out new possibilities. It also undervalues the opportunities that nature offers of adding to resources before they are depleted.[56]

I suggest, though, that being in nature has a positive capacity that goes beyond dealing with discrepancies. Seeking out pleasurable and self-enhancing experiences may, on occasion, go beyond dealing with some deficit. The experience of living a different role, even if momentarily, may produce many other benefits.[57]

Figure 18.5a Distant view of the same place as in Figure 18.4

It also must be kept in mind that the 'great outdoors', landscape, the countryside, and many other terms for 'nature' cover a vast array of situations and contexts. Curiously, hardly any published research deals, for example, with the weather, season, and time of year when 'being in nature' is studied. Those carrying out research in California may benefit from pleasant climates the whole year round (except when they experience horrific forest fires, of course), but in North Wales, for instance, where I live, the variation in what the outdoors has to offer changes enormously from season to season, from day to day, and even from hour to hour. The number of daylight hours has a huge impact on what can be done in the countryside, as well as the temperature and weather conditions. All of these variations have an impact on the day-to-day culture of Places outdoors, with the consequent opportunities, or lack of them, for the roles that people can enjoy, or must suffer, in different climates. Monolithic studies of 'the benefits of nature' or its 'restorative' capabilities can be seen as extremely limited when they do not take these great climatic and latitudinal contrasts into account.

One further oversimplification in the study of nature and its benefits that makes many studies of little value was briefly considered in Chapters 16 and 17. This is the treating of any consideration of natural settings as if they are representative of them all. This reduction of the complexity and variety of natural settings is a consequence of the experimental paradigm so favoured by university-based psychologists. Many hundreds, possibly thousands, of experiments have been published that consist of showing

Figure 18.5b Misty path as Figure 18.5a in mid-winter

people a few pictures of landscapes or taking them to one or a few settings as the basis for determining if the benefits of 'nature' can be determined from those experiences. This may be after exposing the participants to some stressful or other stimulus in order to establish if the nature experience has any benefits. Sadly such simple 'experiments' are endemic across science because they support career development.[58]

The ludicrousness of the universalist claims from such studies is hidden by the academic patois that occludes what is being explored. It could be likened to determining the quality of restaurants in a city by tasting a dish in a Chinese restaurant and a fish and chip shop. Part of the problem with this approach is that there is no conceptual framework for classifying types of natural settings or even types of activity that typically occur there. As a consequence, there is no straightforward way of establishing what type or class of Place is relevant to any particular study. A step towards this framework is proposed that draws on the roles people can take in natural Places, as considered next.

A psychology of place model of the benefits of nature

An alternative to looking for 'restoration' or other cognitive, stress-relieving benefits derived directly from the influence of nature is to consider active interactions with the natural surroundings. The agency that draws on and creates the meaning of Places implies an active transaction between the person and the context. The many ways in which people engage with the meanings and physical components of that context each cohere as a set of appropriate actions – rules of Place. Sitting quietly to enjoy the tranquillity of nature is one such 'rule'. Observing an awe-inspiring view implies another way of being in the countryside. Climbing a hill involves other actions. The rules of friendship and support come into play when being outdoors with other people. Each of these sets of actions can be regarded as creating an implicit or explicit role particular to that Place. An environmental role which summarises the pattern of activities that people associate with a Place.

The values of being in natural settings are the different roles that such a presence enables. As has been elaborated earlier, it is the way nature allows us to be a different aspect of ourselves, at least for the moments we are there, that is at the core of the contributions to well-being that are derived from being outdoors. That freedom, facilitated by being outdoors, is the underlying aspect of 'autonomy' explored earlier. That can be expressed in many different ways.

Two broad facets of autonomy in nature are proposed. One is the distinction between being passively engaged with the setting. The other is to actively participate in some opportunities nature provides. This has parallels to the externally engaging places (front stage) in the house, discussed in Chapter 6 as well as the more external aspects of building types explored in Chapter 7. The second facet relates to whether the role being experienced is essentially part of the individual's own repertoire as opposed to opening up other possibilities facilitated by aspects of the environmental experience. This two-fold system gives rise to the four elements of autonomy hypothesised as a model, illustrated in Figure 18.6.

The model encapsulates a number of hypotheses. For example, the passive individualistic role of being tranquil is opposite the active connectiveness roles, summarised as 'social'. The passive role of enjoying the physical and aesthetic aspects of the landscape contrasts with the active personal roles of mastering opportunities that being

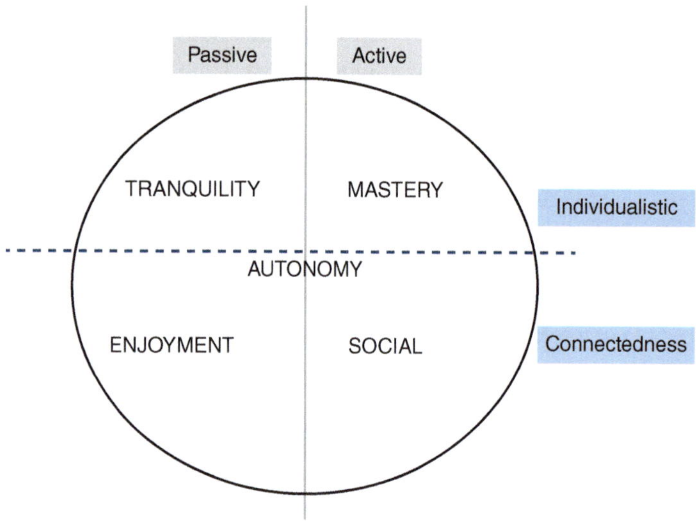

Figure 18.6 Hypothesised model of the benefits of being in nature

in the countryside provides. The circle implies that there are overlaps possible between the different elements. They are not totally distinct roles. Quietly painting a landscape combines being tranquil with developing a particular skill. Other skills will often be enhanced by contact with others, such as trekking or climbing. Sitting with others admiring the view can enhance that enjoyment. As can the peace and quiet be a feature of that enjoyment. Importantly, the circle also encapsulates the idea that all of these aspects of freedom in nature are always present. Different emphases dominate at various points in time, but none is ever entirely absent.

There is no single process that generates the benefits of green places. Physical, psychological, and social features may be generated within the person, such as the search for scenic beauty or the desire to increase stamina. They may also be initiated by pressures from outside the person, most obviously being invited to go for a walk or the intrigue of what is over the next hill. All of these can be understood as being fundamental to being human. As a consequence, it is the opportunities for benefits that the outdoors provide, which reveal why and how those places can so enhance well-being.

This structure draws, to some extent, on the much broader self-determination theory – a psychological framework that explains human motivation and personality. Developed by Deci and Ryan[59] in the 1980s but recently elaborated and tested with a major empirical study,[60] it suggests that people are most motivated when key 'psychological needs' are met:

- **Autonomy** – The need to feel in control of one's actions and choices.
- **Competence** – The need to feel capable and effective in one's activities.
- **Relatedness** – The need to feel connected to others and experience meaningful relationships.

As discussed in Chapter One, there has long been a debate about what are 'basic needs'.[61] However, the idea that people find benefits in being able to exert autonomy, demonstrate competence, and feel related to others is not really open to challenge.

I was thinking about this when I was carrying out a mundane, not overtly pleasant, task in my garden, sorting out the compost heap. I enjoyed doing this on my own, not needing any advice or guidance from others, hence taking pleasure in my autonomy. A few aspects of the task required some innovation, such as providing a ready way of getting access to it so that it could be excavated for use on plants. Thereby feeling some delight in my own competence. Further, although I was doing this on my own, I was aware that others in my family would see it and benefit from the much tidier structure I had created – relatedness.

Surely, an illustration of how being outdoors offers many opportunities for aspects of self-fulfilment? There are many other contexts that can provide similar experiences, but there is something about natural settings that readily provide these even in the most mundane contexts. One particularly noteworthy example of all this was the introduction of farming and gardening into prisons[62]. The many benefits of prisoners taking an active role in the countryside can be summed up as offering the sorts of feeling of autonomy and competence, as well as developing effective, productive relationships with others that are usually destroyed in the institutionalisation of prison regimes. It also turned out to be financially profitable.

Conclusions

There is one very important implication of how the benefits of green experiences are understood. If they are regarded as determined by biologically based responses to stimuli from natural settings, then the manipulation of those influences can be assigned to experts who know about these things. The stimuli proposed are likely to be thought of as of universal benefit because they are based on 'hard-wired' aspects of being human. By contrast, if human agency is a crucial aspect of how nature generates its magic, then design decisions should involve people in generating environmental possibilities.

The discussion in this chapter and the model suggested here propose a variety of advantages to being in nature. There will also be differences between people in the benefits they are seeking and obtain when in the countryside. Nor will those benefits necessarily always be the same for each person at different points in time. The implications for environmental planning and design are to encourage a much richer range of opportunities and possibilities.

References and endnotes

1 Ulrich, R. S. (1984) View from a window may influence recovery from surgery. *Science*, 224, 420–421.
2 Lindemuth, A. L. (2007) Designing therapeutic environments for inmates and prison staff in the United States: Precedents and contemporary applications. *Journal of Mediterranean Ecology*, 8(1), 87–97.
3 Kaplan, R. (1993) The role of nature in the context of the workplace. *Landscape and Urban Planning*, 26, 193–201.
4 For example, Heerwagen, J. H. & Orians, G. H. (1986) Adaptation to windowlessness: A study of the use of visual décor in windowed and windowless offices. *Environment and Behavior*, 18, 623–639. This study even shows that in windowless offices people are more likely to put up pictures of the sort of view out they would have preferred, notably of natural settings.
5 For example, Hartig, T., Korpela, K., Evans, G. W., & Gärling, T. (1997) A measure of restorative quality in environments. *Scandinavian Housing and Planning Research*, 14(4), 175–194.
6 For example, in the excellent review by Collado, S., Staats, H., Corraliza, J. A., & Hartig, T. (2017) Restorative environments and health, in G. Fleury-Bahi, E. Pol, & O. Navarro (Eds.) *Handbook of environmental psychology and quality of life research. International handbooks of quality-of-life*. Cham: Springer, https://doi.org/10.1007/978-3-319-31416-7_7
7 *The Guardian*, Saturday 10 February 2024.
8 *Harborough Mail*, 18 April 2024, p. 7.
9 Coventry, P. A., Brown, J. E., Pervin, J., Brabyn, S., Pateman, R., Breedvelt, J., ... & White, P. L. (2021) Nature-based outdoor activities for mental and physical health: Systematic review and meta-analysis. *SSM-Population Health*, 16, 100934.
10 Stephenson, T. (1947) *The countryside companion*, London: Odhams Press.
11 Examine the role of nature in Henry David Thoreau's *Walden*; accessed May 2025.
12 Permission from Claire Deeney, http://www.journeysinnature.com
13 Kotera, Y., Richardson, M., & Sheffield, D. (2022) Effects of shinrin-yoku (forest bathing) and nature therapy on mental health: A systematic review and meta-analysis. *International Journal of Mental Health and Addiction*, 20(1), 337–361.
14 Saraev, V, O'Brien, L., Valatin, G., & Bursnell, M. (2021) *Valuing the mental health benefits of woodlands*, Edinburgh: Forest Research.
15 Saraev, O'Brien, Valatin, & Bursnell (2021) *Valuing the mental health benefits of woodlands*.
16 This summary is taken from Joye, Y. & Dewitte, S. (2018) Nature's broken path to restoration. A critical look at Attention Restoration Theory. *Journal of Environmental Psychology*, 59, 1–8, 2.
17 Ulrich, R. S. (1993) Biophilia, biophobia, and natural landscapes, in S. E. Kellert and E. Wilson (Eds.) *The biophilia hypothesis*, Washington, D.C.: Island Press, pp. 73–137.

18 Joye, Y. & Van den Berg, A. (2011) Is love for green in our genes? A critical analysis of evolutionary assumptions in restorative environments research. *Urban Forestry & Urban Greening*, 10(4), 261–268.
19 Kaplan, S., Bardwell, L. V., & Slakter, D. B. (1993) The museum as a restorative environment. *Environment and Behavior*, 25(6), 725–742.
20 For a detailed, very important criticism of the ways statistical analysis is abused, see Guttman, L. (1977) What is not what in statistics. *Journal of the Royal Statistical Society. Series D (The Statistician)*, 26(2), 81–107.
21 Guttman (1977) What is not what in statistics, 4.
22 A different perspective from mine but supporting my contention is Joye, Y. & Dewitte, S. (2018) Nature's broken path to restoration. A critical look at Attention Restoration Theory. *Journal of Environmental Psychology*, 59, 1–8.
23 But if you want a review of reviews, see Warburton, D. E. & Bredin, S. S. (2017) Health benefits of physical activity: A systematic review of current systematic reviews. *Current Opinion in Cardiology*, 32(5), 541–556.
24 Marini, S., Mauro, M., Grigoletto, A., Toselli, S., & Maietta Latessa, P. (2022) The effect of physical activity interventions carried out in outdoor natural blue and green spaces on health outcomes: A systematic review. *International Journal of Environmental Research and Public Health*, 19(19), 12482.
25 An interesting review of three such studies can be found at 533 (arkitekturforskning.net) accessed 2 April 2024.
26 Recently developed by Basu, A., Duvall, J., & Kaplan, R. (2019) Attention restoration theory: Exploring the role of soft fascination and mental bandwidth. *Environment and Behavior*, 51(9–10), 1055–1081. But having its origins in the widely quoted: Kaplan, S. (1995) The restorative benefits of nature: Toward an integrative framework. *Journal of Environmental Psychology*, 15(3), 169–182.
27 Ohly, H., White, M. P., Wheeler, B. W., Bethel, A., Ukoumunne, O. C., Nikolaou, V., & Garside, R. (2016) Attention Restoration Theory: A systematic review of the attention restoration potential of exposure to natural environments. *Journal of Toxicology and Environmental Health, Part B*, 19(7), 305–343.
28 Joye, Y. & Dewitte, S. (2018) Nature's broken path to restoration. A critical look at Attention Restoration Theory. *Journal of Environmental Psychology*, 59, 1–8.
29 Hartig, T., Korpela, K., Evans, G. W., & Gärling, T. (1997) A measure of restorative quality in environments. *Scandinavian Housing and Planning Research*, 14(4), 175–194.
30 Hartig, Korpela, Evans, & Gärling (1997) A measure of restorative quality in environments, 182.
31 My daughter, if you're curious.
32 Lily Canter (@lilycanter) • Instagram photos and videos.
33 Wilkinson, E., & Canter, L. (2025). *Ultra women: the trailblazers defying sexism in sport.* Canbury Press.
34 Ryff, C. D., & Keyes, C. L. M. (1995). The structure of psychological well-being revisited. *Journal of personality and social psychology*, 69(4), 719..
35 Pritchard, A., Richardson, M., Sheffield, D., & McEwan, K. (2020) The relationship between nature connectedness and eudaimonic well-being: A meta-analysis. *Journal of Happiness Studies*, 21, 1145–1167.
36 Menatti,L., Subiza-Pérez,M., Villalpando-Flores,A., Vozmediano,L., & San Juan,C. (2019) Place attachment and identification as predictors of expected landscape restorativeness. *Journal of Environmental Psychology*, 63, 36–43, https://doi.org/10.1016/j.jenvp.2019.03.005
37 Cuadrado, E., Macias-Zambrano, L., Carpio, A. J., & Tabernero, C. (2023) The ABC connectedness to nature scale: Development and validation of a scale with an approach to affective, behavioural, and cognitive aspects. *Environmental Education Research*, 29(2), 308–329.
38 Joye, Y., Köster, M., Lange, F., Fischer, M., & Moors, A. (2024) A goal-discrepancy account of restorative nature experiences. *Journal of Environmental Psychology*, 93, 102–192.
39 Janeczko, E., Bielinis, E., Wójcik, R., Łukowski, A., & Szymanowska, A. (2024). The Impact of Forest Video Exposure on Stress Recovery: A Randomized Controlled Trial. *Forests*, 15(1), 123. https://doi.org/10.3390/f15010123

40 Orne, M. T. (2017) On the social psychology of the psychological experiment: With particular reference to demand characteristics and their implications, in *Sociological methods*, London: Routledge, (pp. 279–299), https://doi.org/10.4324/9781315129945-26
41 Rosenthal, R. (1966) *Experimenter effects in behavioral research,* Appleton-Century-Crofts.
42 Joye, Y., Lange, F., Lisauskienė, A. *et al.* (2024) Watching (natural) beauty boosts task performance: Testing the nature-as-reward hypothesis. *Psychological Research*, 88, 1045–1059, https://doi.org/10.1007/s00426-023-01922-9
43 McMahan, E. A. & Estes, D. (2015) The effect of contact with natural environments on positive and negative affect: A meta-analysis. *The Journal of Positive Psychology*, 10(6), 507–519.
44 Watson, D., Clark, L. A., & Tellegen, A. (1988) Development and validation of brief measures of positive and negative affect: The PANAS scales. *Journal of Personality and Social Psychology*, 54(6), 1063.
45 Zuckerman, M. (1977) Development of a situation-specific trait-state test for the prediction and measurement of affective responses. *Journal of Consulting and Clinical Psychology*, 45(4), 513.
46 Beute, F., Marselle, M. R., Olszewska-Guizzo, A., Andreucci, M. B., Lammel, A., Davies, Z. G., … & de Vries, S. (2023) How do different types and characteristics of green space impact mental health? A scoping review. *People and Nature*, 5(6), 1839–1876.
47 Joye et al. (2024) also supports the claim that changing the measurement process produces rather different results from those expected by ART and SRT.
48 Joye et al. (2024).
49 Joye et al. (2024, p. 4).
50 Joye et al. (2024, p. 6).
51 Joye et al. (2024, p. 9).
52 Ginting, H., Mahiranissa, A., Bekti, R., & Febriansyah, H. (2020) The effect of outing Team Building training on soft skills among MBA students. *The International Journal of Management Education*, 18(3), 100423.
53 Joye et al. (2024, p. 9).
54 It is worth noting that not everyone treats the countryside as a place to be active in. The perhaps especially English tradition of driving to a car park in the countryside, taking out chairs to sit and watch next to the car is a remarkably passive way of enjoying being outdoors.
55 Canter, D. (1983) The purposive evaluation of places: A facet approach. *Environment and Behavior*, 15(6), 659–698.
56 Joye et al. (2024).
57 Apparently there is some attempt to recognise the benefits of nature beyond the notion of 'replenishing' something missing enshrined in the concept of 'Restoration'. The term 'instoration' is used seemingly to indicate adding something further beyond 'restoration'. However, in a recent study that set out to measure 'instoration potential', it is stated, "Perceived instorative potential was measured with the 16-item Perceived Restorativeness Scale" (Korpela, K. M. & Ratcliffe, E. (2021) Which is primary: Preference or perceived instoration?. *Journal of Environmental Psychology*, 75, 101617).
That neologism seems to have escaped questioning by reviewers. A dictionary search reveals that "Instoration" appears to be a variant or misspelling of the archaic term "instauration", which used to mean "Restoration or renewal, especially after decay or neglect." It therefore seems to mean the same as restoration. Perhaps something has got lost in translation?
58 A recent claim that Artificially Intelligent systems were studying vast arrays of medical data to predict likely *illness* outcomes is drawing on the data available, even though a much more powerful study would draw in lifestyle and other difficult-to-obtain data that would predict *wellness*!
59 Summarised in Ryan, R. M., & Deci, E. L. (2000) Self-determination theory and the facilitation of intrinsic motivation, social development, and well-being. *American Psychologist*, 55(1), 68.
60 Lee, E. S., Maillet, M. A., & Grouzet, F. M. (2022) Why do individuals engage with the natural world? A self-determination theory perspective on the effect of nature engagement and well-being. *Applied Research in Quality of Life*, 17(3), 1501–1532.
61 Streeten, P. (1984) Basic needs: Some unsettled questions. *World Development*, 12(9), 973–978.
62 Wright, H. (2017) *Outside Time* Devon: Placewise Press.

Conclusions

Place is where our history, our stories, are held but set free, where layered, in collaboration with the world around us, evolve to live a different life, overgrown with atmosphere.
Alice Maddicott[1]

Lake Udaipur, India, 2017
Copyright David Canter

DOI: 10.4324/9780367808655-24

CHAPTER 19

A psychology of places

Introduction

This book is a paean to the significance of Places in our lives. The experience of being here in time and space is one important distinction from being a computer or robot. Machines, no matter how artificially intelligent they are, never truly experience growing up in a location full of meanings and significance that shapes their identity. Their essence is placeless. For us, human beings' actual presence, in any given Place, is part of who we are.

There is no doubt that there are enormous benefits from what the digital revolution has to offer. But what is sacrificed is being here. Direct engagement with a Place. That can be the corner of a room, a building, a city, a country, and importantly a feeling of presence on the Earth. Digital, virtual realities are generated by software engines and their myriad algorithms. They play with each other in an electronic limbo.

Although they feed on accounts, descriptions and pictures of actual locations the computers that generate these online experiences have never walked in a wood when Autumn leaves are falling. They have never tripped over a dog sleeping by the fire. They have never grown up in a one-bedroom apartment and then moved to a detached four-bedroom house. They have never had arguments about what colour to paint the walls or remember the private Place behind the school bike sheds where they had their first kiss. Even the rapidly developing, much-vaunted, machine learning and related large language models have never had to decide to accept a job offer that required moving the whole family to a new city, far away.

At the core of this argument is the proposal that Places are dynamic assemblages created by and creating those who know, experience, shape, or enjoy them. They have a physical existence. That interacts with the meanings assigned to their form to generate a wholistic experience. That combination of physical environment and significance provides the basis for a virtuous cycle in which expectations, habits, assumptions, and actions all interact to generate the Places that encapsulate our lives.

DOI: 10.4324/9780367808655-25

The prevalence of social media and internet access is frequently mentioned as disconnecting people from actual reality. Focus on electronic screens, especially the ubiquitous mobile phone, is a detachment from the physical surroundings, making people less engaged with the world around them. This happens on the street, in bedrooms, and at dining tables, in restaurants and museums, in schools and colleges, out in the countryside and wherever people can gain access to the World Wide Web.

This final chapter summarises some key features of Places that have been explored throughout *Revisiting the Psychology of Place*. These are illustrated by examining particular cases, each illustrative of one of the three scales of Place, Buildings, The City, and Landscapes: each a section of the book.

The importance of understanding place

When we look at or experience Places at a distance, or in imagination and memory, they embody meaning. They are never merely the kind of numerical or abstract symbolic entities that computer algorithms manipulate. The more we understand what Places entail, the more we will be able to survive as fully human against the multipronged onslaught of climate change, environmental degradation, and the technologies that are stealing what it means to be a person who is actively engaged with other people in a world that can be touched, tasted, smelt, and even seen in all its actual three-dimensional glory.

It is worth remembering that Places exist at every scale from the desk at which I am writing to the concept of the Cosmos. It could be argued that "The 'Blue Marble' photograph of Earth taken on the Apollo mission on the way to the moon, December 7th 1972" (Figure 19.1) was the strongest representation of the Earth as a distinct Place, making people extremely aware, possibly for the first time, that it had clear significance and meaning which required particular actions to maintain its status as 'Mother Earth'.

This picture could be regarded as an important moment for the change in humanity's relationship to places. It occurred with press interest, but with little awareness of its psychological importance. Figure 19.1 shows the first detailed photograph of our complete planet – Mother Earth's first selfie. This 'blue marble' picture was taken by the crew on the Apollo 17 spacecraft. In fact, it was made up of a great many different photographs, but it epitomised the age of ubiquitous camera-generated self-portraits. The earth becomes a more clearly conscious entity, a distinct Place, when we can see it as a picture of itself in space.

Psychologically, Places are not nested entities. They do not get their relevance from where they are in any notional hierarchy. As explored in the introductory section of this book, the concept of Place is generated from a combination of perspectives. These include such behaviourally oriented theories as Behavior Setting theory, as well as cognitive perspectives. The cognitive approach draws on the constructive nature of thought. It fills in the gaps and generates memories as well as direct perceptions. This constructive process gives rise to structures in our cognitive systems. They shape our actions and are shaped by them. When Churchill so famously declaimed, "we shape our buildings and after that they shape us", he may more fundamentally have said "we are in constant interplay with where we are. Shaping

Figure 19.1 Mother Earth's first selfie[2]

our experiences of places as they shape our understanding of who we are". But that would not have been so elegant.

The dynamic aspect of Places, whereby meanings, influenced by physical form, support actions, and the consequent interactions with Places, is the basis for the emergence of environmental roles and the related rules of place. They are the motor that drives forward any understanding of how Places signify.

The home as the archetypal place

When considering the contribution of the actual form of buildings to the experience of Places, the home, the first Place that is experienced, provides a model that helps to elucidate the meanings of all other buildings. Domestic settings personify most of the Places that emerge in other building forms. They highlight how the reasons for being in a location, the purposes that Place serves, contribute to important aspects of its meaning. The assemblage of Places in the home creates the home as much as their being in that home gives them their meanings.

A dramaturgical framework, following the idea of environmental roles, indicates major differentiation in Places in the home. There are those 'frontstage' Places where people may feel they are on show. Or at least these are the Places where they are most likely to present themselves as if for others to see. The mantlepiece, or even fridge magnets, reflect this process. Then there are the areas of preparation and other locations once thought of as 'backstage', such as the kitchen or bedroom. This distinction has been eroded with changes in family life. The use of open, plan kitchen and dining areas and the bedrooms as meeting Places, especially in crowded homes, mirrors broader changes in society and relationships between family members.

The distinctions between Places in the home, driven by the identification of Places for separate purposes, parallel the emergence of different types of building. The idea of a building type is that it summarises a combination of physical forms that reflect the functions of the different sorts of Places that may be housed. These may be public, frontstage buildings like Town Halls and art galleries, or they may be associated with private domestic activities. However, even that simplistic distinction was broadly ignored by the Modern Movement in architecture. That generated buildings that tended to disregard the different types of Places being created.

Buildings – a place for optimism

Thinking of buildings as contributions to the experiences of Places is at variance with the central idea of architectural modernism. The slogan of modern architecture was 'form follows function', which was interpreted in a somewhat mechanical way. The 'function' was typically interpreted in terms of the size of spaces. The world was subsequently filled with identikit, high-rise tower blocks. They tended to look the same anywhere in the world, despite varying climate, social, and cultural differences.

Reactions against these monoliths recognised that the functions of architecture go beyond providing space for the activities to be housed and appropriate relationships between those spaces. There are important aspects of what the building filters. The sounds and weather it keeps out and the heat and acoustics it keeps in. This function has become even more significant with the growing awareness of the impact of the energy it takes to create a building and maintain a comfortable internal environment. Another component of a building's function is the meanings it reflects. What it signifies. How it contributes to the understanding and experiences of Places that it facilitates.

The design of buildings in the last half century has moved away from the rectangular blocks of modernism. This has been driven in part by criticisms of those edifices constructed in the early part of the 19th century. That critique is epitomised in Heatherwick's[3] clarion call to *Humanise* architecture. He pours scorn on many of the architectural innovations of the 20th century. In essence, he calls for more interesting looking buildings. This is couched as insisting that buildings should prioritise human emotion over soulless buildings driven by the profit motive. Yet, as Chapters 6–12 have elaborated, when considering Places, there is so much more to what buildings contribute than looking interesting and generating pleasant feelings. Major architectural designs have certainly shaken off the limitations of 'modernism' and the idiosyncrasies of 'post-modernism' (Chapter 12), giving some cause for optimism that an understanding of the Psychology of Place, even if only implicitly, is now pervading many areas of building design.

An example of building and assemblage of Places

One example of this new imagining of built Places is the innovative, award-winning building – the LSE Saw Swee Hock Student Centre. When I set out to find it, following a map, I wandered down some narrow streets and reached a small open square. I was puzzled to think where the building could be. Then I looked up. There it was (Figure 19.2).

The sightlines required to avoid overshadowing its neighbours had been used by the architects both to fit the building neatly into its metropolitan space and to generate a unique, distinct building form.[4] The building immediately presents itself as a lively Place. What else could it be but somewhere for students to meet, use various facilities,

Figure 19.2 A first glimpse of the LSE Saw Swee Hock Student Centre

Figure 19.3 LSE Saw Swee Hock Student Centre, London, designed by O'Donnell and Tuomey architects

such as a gym, a restaurant, and a performance space, and for offices where their Union can be organised?

As I got closer to the building, its stark geometry became more evident. The building opens out to reveal its mathematical complexity (Figure 19.3). That striking form possibly implies something scientific, or at least academic, because it evokes associations of abstract forms and thinking. The brick it is built out of gives it a comfortable presence, neighbourly with the more day-to-day London buildings around it. The glass-covered entrance, allowing direct visibility into the building, beckons visitors. In addition, the clever use of leaving out alternate bricks in areas of the façade adds interest to the texture of the building but also provides special forms of daylighting within key parts of the building.

For me, as an interested tourist, it offers an intriguing sight. It provides a distinct location for visiting groups to experience a vision of contemporary London (Figure 19.3). Various signs on the building are made possible from the street-level glass. They invitingly offer more insights into what the building is and what it houses.[5]

The inside of the building also deals with the challenge of making sense of it's the inevitable complexity of housing so many different types of Place. It has a readily comprehensible overall structure reminiscent[6] of Wright's Guggenheim Museum (Chapter 9). One spiral path unfurls throughout the building. That is not just an architectural conceit; it is a recognition of the way students engage with the space. It demonstrates that it is all available to them. The student predilection for searching through such a Place to see if there is anyone there they know, is therefore also accounted for.

The idea of an assemblage of Places that give the building meaning but which in their combination also give significance to each of them is also captured by this innovative design. Off the central, spiral path are a number of distinct Places. Rather than a set of boxes that can be harnessed for different uses, each of the major activities for which a Place was identified is given its own distinctiveness. This includes Places as contrasting as a quiet corner for respite or a small meeting and bigger places for groups and even a roof terrace (Figure 19.4). Different types of gym each have their own mood (Figure 19.5). Even the cafeteria area is divided up (Figure 19.6), which avoids the incessant hubbub such spaces usually engender.

The brickwork clearly seen in Figure 19.6 is not some odd aberration, but is reminiscent of the use of brick in Italian hill towns to mitigate the effect of bright sunshine. But it is also a clever use as a screening device that allows some view out but virtually no view in.

Only a few of the Places in the building are noted and illustrated here. All sorts of special facilities, as well as a large performance area, are elegantly incorporated into it. Together they can be regarded as an 'assemblage' of Places. As discussed in Chapter 1, Dovey[7] draws attention to how Place operates as a whole whose properties emerge from the interactions between parts. One crucial aspect of this is the recognition that it is the interaction between Places that contributes to the meaning and experience of Places at every scale form the small corner for a quiet to chat to the building as a whole.

Detailed attention to this building has elaborated on the abstract exploration of the meaning of Place in relation to a building built a decade ago. It shows how a pioneering design team can embrace the challenges of the site and the requirements of what is to be housed to create a clear identity for the LSE Student Union building. The brick-and-glass façade has a coherence that, nonetheless, provides different variations of its form in different places, as can be seen in Figures 19.4, 19.5, and 19.6. Thus, whilst each space has its own character, it both draws on and contributes to the overall sense of Place that the building provides.

Personal development from being present

More than a building, the experience of a city illustrates the need to develop mental representations of Places. Making sense of a city requires extended moving through it. An understanding of a city and the creation of a mental image of it emerge from the various contacts that a person has with it. That conceptual system with its associated

Figure 19.4 Quiet corners of the LSE Student's Union building

Figure 19.5 Part of the gym

Figure 19.6 Part of the cafeteria area

meanings in turn influences what a person does where. As illustrated in Chapter 14, that is a two-way process. The mental model that a person holds of a city provides an indication of the locations that they may want to visit. Any search of the city, for example *en route* to desired locations, will in turn contribute to the understanding of that area of the city the person is formulating. The consequence of this is that our ways of thinking about a city are constantly changing. They are also sensitive to what we use a city for. The related purposes we have for being, or going to, anywhere in the city.

This conceptualisation of the city is particularly significant when considering city streets (Chapter 13). They often embrace the essence of a city. Through the many Places that make up the street experience, the history, culture, and social life of a city.

The great reductions in the number and variety of Places on many city streets have been brought about by the demise of shopping opportunities and the encroachment of commercial ownership of parts of the street that were once public places. A move towards reinvigorating The Plinth, 'the city at eye-level', explored in Chapter 13 consists of creating Places that will attract people, notably those 'third places' where people will gather and meet.

Distancing from being here

A further significant influence on the nature and experience of cities is being produced by the radical retreat into an existence within an online world. A momentous process that is moving people further away from being part of actual Places. Giving significance to our virtual presence in various places is rapidly being taken a step further to an existence in a virtual reality. The particular location and its significance are being eroded by technological manipulations. Some authorities are already writing about the iPhone as a Place.[8] Even a 'transportal' home. The Place within which we live. This viewpoint accepts the idea that smartphones have become integral parts of our lives, serving as Places where we live and express our personalities.

Such a conclusion has been derived from an extensive study in which 11 anthropologists each spent 16 months living in communities in Africa, Asia, Europe, and South America, focusing on the take-up of smartphones by older people. Their research reveals that smartphones are technology for everyone, not just for the young. They found that smartphones have become as much a Place within which people live as a device we use. As a result, it quickly assimilates personal and cultural values. This is revealed through a range of "national and cultural nuances, such as visual communication in China and Japan, mobile money in Cameroon and Uganda, and access to health information in Chile and Ireland – all alongside diverse trajectories of ageing in Al Quds, Brazil and Italy".[9]

The report of that research does not for one moment decry the move away from direct experience to existence in an online, virtual reality. Many benefits from that are identifiable perhaps notably in developing countries. There, mobile connectivity leapfrogs earlier modes of communication. Yet, a lot is lost by this move into a placeless reality.

Ever since the advent of electronic media, there have been those who have pointed out what is missing when these media dominate. Writing in the 1980s, Meyrowitz[10] suggested that the media taking over then, notably television, had eroded the "sense of place". He points out that being in an actual place structured social roles and expectations. Engaging wholeheartedly in electronic media admittedly "liberated individuals from rigid, place-bound identities—but also introduced new tensions as norms are renegotiated in a fluid, media-saturated world".[11]

Three decades on, Rosen's *The Extinction of Experience: Being Human in a Disembodied World*[12] provides a critique of how digital technologies are eroding the richness of embodied human life. She argues that the increasing reliance on screens, apps, and virtual interactions has led to the decline of essential experiences—like face-to-face communication, authentic emotion, a sense of place, and even boredom.

She emphasises the deleterious effects of people avoiding direct interactions with others and the Places where they are because of their often seemingly addictive engagement with their screens. This is especially notable and important with the use of mobile phones on many city streets. As she puts it:

> ...our unmooring from physical space has had a gradual but noticeable impact on civic life...The appeal of online pseudo-communities is understandable. They require only limited commitment whilst still providing a sense of belonging, and participants can opt out and disappear at any time, something not always possible in real communities. However, they are neither a substitute for nor an improvement on traditional community.
>
> *(p. 194)*

She puts this even more directly with regard to public places:

> We compromise experience in public space by using technology to remove ourselves temporarily from it.
>
> *(p. 195)*

My erstwhile PhD student and long-time friend, Reid Bishop,[13] has railed particularly against the ever-present use of mobile phones that he has observed on streets everywhere. He put his views very strongly in messages to me as:

> The potential of *any* geographic location to become a genuine PLACE with its attendant qualities, can only happen if people genuinely believe that what is on their screen can never (or very rarely) be more important than what's happening around them.

These insightful commentators have drawn attention to the way all-pervasive technology is undermining quite different attempts to bring people back into direct connection with each other. From the perspective of the psychology of places, the ability to feel you are present somewhere else, whilst still having a physical presence you are ignoring, undermines the development of a rich understanding of Places. If you are looking at your phone to find your way, you are limiting the opportunity to develop a mental map of where you are. That cognitive structure emerges from engagement with actual locations.

Actual engagement

The way in which the understanding of a city is shaped by direct, actual engagement with it was revealed in Chapter 14 by examining personal sketch maps. When asking people to draw a sketch map of a Place, the emphases and distortions in those drawings do themselves indicate a lot about what that Place means to them, and how their reasons for being there influence what they are aware of.

This was illustrated in Chapter 14 by examining Nick's sketch maps of London, especially how they changed as he spent increasing amounts of time there. Those maps are a rich illustration of the emergence of conceptualisations of Places. I therefore thought it would be fascinating to ask him to produce a similar sketch map nearly half a century later. By the wonders of the internet I was able to contact him. He gladly took up the task (Figure 19.7). This shows a very different conceptualisation of London, but the same processes are revealed of involvement and elaboration, shaped by his being there with particular goals in mind.

His role in London in 1975, as a young tourist, was very different from the experienced adult on a mission in 2019. As a tourist, he was exploring the sights, but although now well established as a productive Associate Professor and psychologist in Australia, his visit to London was to further a quite different string to his bow. He was seeking an opportunity to stage the musical he had written about the Death of Captain Cook[14]! This changed his relationship to London, as shown in a distinctly different sketch map (Figure 19.7).

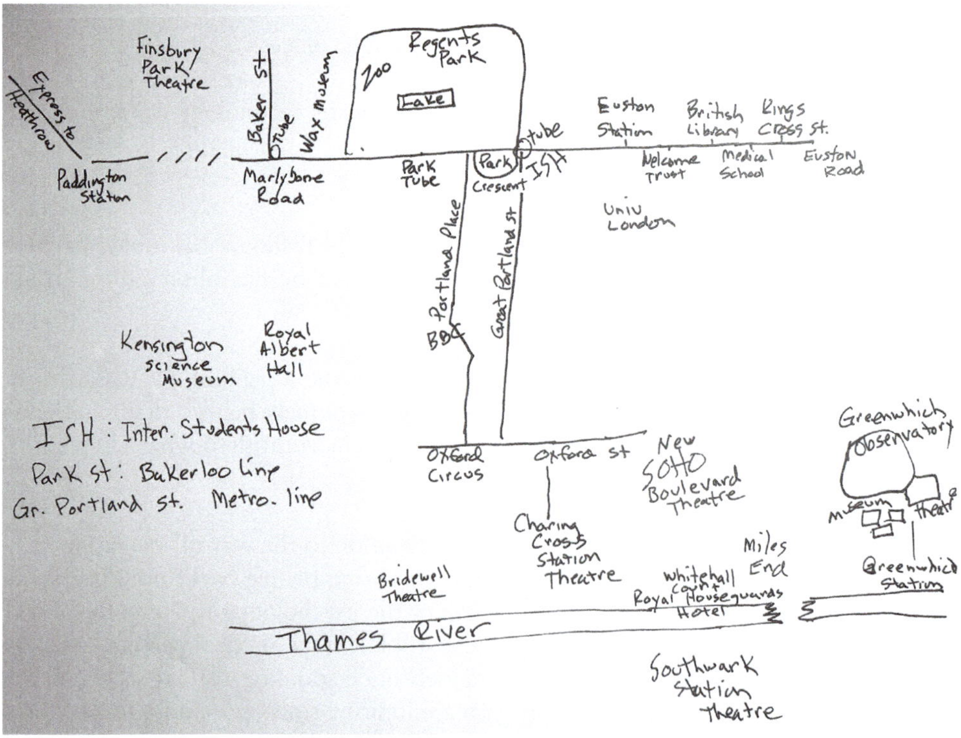

Figure 19.7 Nick's 2019 'mental map' of London

As in his earlier maps, his starting point, the International Students' Hostel, still dominated, revealing a 'domocentricity'. In this case where he was staying for the duration of his visit. As he says:

> I walked down Great Portland Street nearly every day, visiting lots of shops and figuring out where they were in relation to each other. I bought groceries, premade sandwiches, coffees, whipped up fruit drinks, in different shops and needed a stationary store to photocopy my script to give the theatre managers.

The distortions in the map, with the small area indicated for Regent's Park but the considerable detail given to Great Portland Street, directly reflect his activities on the focused journey that was the purpose of his time in London and also reveal his changed way of engaging with London:

> Portland Place, running into Park Crescent, is a really exciting avenue of stately Georgian homes and offices, including various professional societies and embassies, such as the Chinese Consular Embassy, which had a small protest station out front (Falun Gong). I loved gazing at the impressive Langham Hotel across from the BBC. I often walked down Portland Place late at night to relax and deal with jet lag, and several times used it to reach Oxford Circus tube.

There is then a significant distortion in his sketch with the jump from Oxford Street to Charring cross. This shows how layered are conceptualisations of cities. As he said:

> I joined or left the tube at Oxford circus several times. I mostly used the Bakerloo Line at Regent's Park tube (Marylebone Rd/Park Crescent). My end points going south were Charing Cross station theatre (half dozen visits), and then to Southwark Playhouse (3 visits including a performance). To reach Greenwich, I got Great Portland St tube Metropolitan line then transferred to the DLR. I went under Piccadilly Circus a bunch of times with Bakerloo Line but obviously the memory trace was not that strong when I sat down cold to do the map.

This account also reveals how mental constructions of Places can readily incorporate virtual information. In this case, a memory of the underground and light railway routes he needed to get to the theatres that were his main interest. Intriguingly, he says nothing of bus routes, the knowledge of which is a true indicator of being at home in London.

Nick also mentioned in passing one distortion that can be built into the methodology of sketch maps. Unless respondents are experienced cartographers, there is a tendency to start drawing the map with only a loose idea of how it will be developed. As a consequence, the map drawer could run out of space and constrain the sketch to what will fit on the sheet of paper used. In Nick's case, the crucial link to Paddington Station and the train to Heathrow Airport for his flight home.

In microcosm, Nick's reengagement with central London is a delightful illustration of the role of 'the city at eye level' (Chapter 13) in shaping the experience of a city. It demonstrates the significance of personal purposes in shaping what a Place means and how conceptualisations of it unfold at many different levels of understanding by being actively involved with what it has to offer.

The attachment to Places (Chapter 15) is most clearly revealed when considering cities, although, of course, attachment to a home or a part of a city commonly occurs. In Nick's case, the International Students Hostel that had been his first base in London, one in which he met people who became lifelong friends, provided an anchor for his itinerant role. His early memories of that, and continued connections with it and those he could meet there, illustrate a form of Place attachment that assisted his enjoyment of the return to London.

The question Rosen and Bishop both raise is whether seeking the possibilities that Nick did, by travelling many thousands of miles to London, would have been as valuable if he had sat at home and tried to contact over the internet the people he needed to?

Placemaking – the 15-minute city

There is a notable aspect of sketch maps of cities, well-illustrated in Nick's drawings. They tend to focus on a limited area of the city. The conceptual structure formed of a city tends to be a series of elemental units. This is often referred to as treating a city as a number of linked villages. It is an indication of the tendency to recognise the distinctiveness of an area that leads to it being thought of as a distinct Place. The model of the home, examined in Chapter 6, with all the different activities it supports, provides a framework for understanding this. Their relationship to the schematic model of building types in Chapter 7 also provides a prospect of this offering a framework for local aspects of an urban setting. When an area of a city supports most of these activities, its strength as a discrete Place is enhanced.

Different Places in a city will give prominence to different features. For example, the entertainment area will still have cafes and hotels. Residential areas are most successful if they house shops, schools, and other leisure activities. The drive to create areas of a city to encompass a comprehensible and accessible range of important and meaningful Places has given rise to the worldwide development of "15-minute cities". The psychology of Place enables these developments to be seen as providing a bridge between two interrelated processes. One is the understanding of how buildings contribute to the meaning and experience of Places (explored in Section II). The other is how the development of urban form can facilitate enjoyment and attachment to Place (discussed in Section III).

15-minute cities are approaches to urban planning that focus on local living.[15] They implicitly accept that people typically make sense of their urban context in relation to where they are living. As a consequence, the model of the major Places that are assembled to support human life is proving very powerful. In effect, the 15-minute city extols the benefits of bringing all the required Places to within walking or cycling distance of each other, but especially of the home. To some extent, this is based,, on the belief that the persistent challenges of urban life are generated by the need to use motor cars. By promoting lifestyles largely independent of motorised travel modes, it is possible to promote active mobility, encouraged by the proximity to essential facilities (Figure 19.8).

However, Figure 19.8, with the home at the centre of the opportunities for ready access to all the Places that make up daily life, is curiously naïve. It represents the perspective of one person from their own home. But except for a few homes located next to

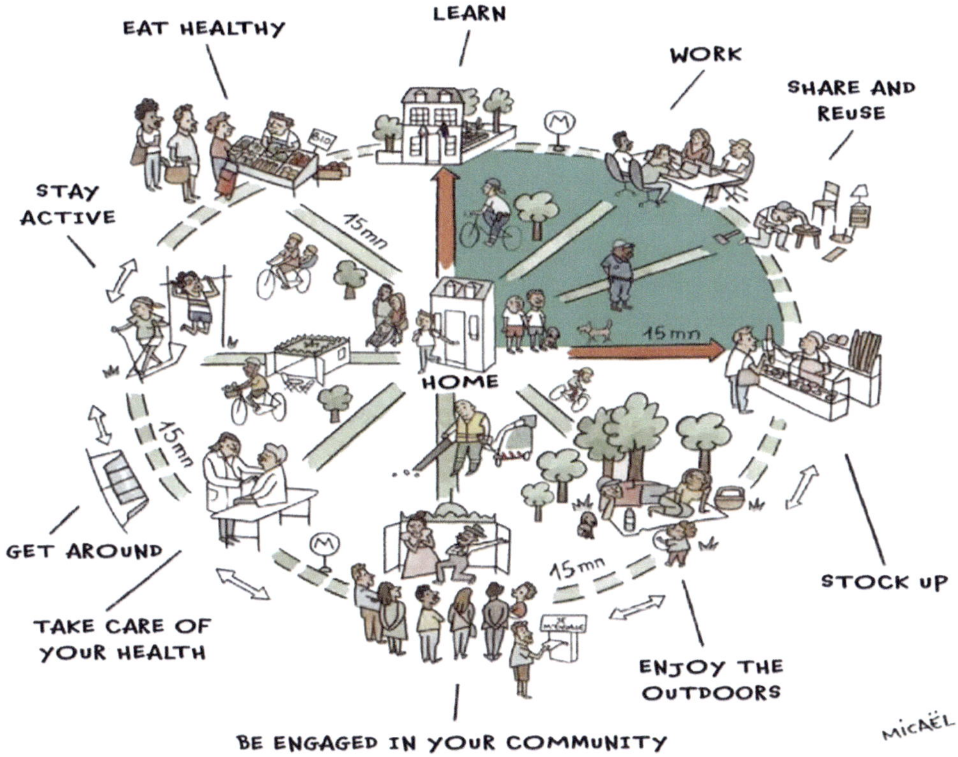

Figure 19.8 The concept of the 15-minute city

each other, homes are inevitably distributed throughout a city. As a consequence, there have been many different approaches to achieving the general objective of enabling people to get access, without using a vehicle, to all the Places that support a full and healthy life. These have highlighted different facets, depending on the practical possibilities for enhancing the qualities of the Places available. Redesigning urban pathways so that walking or even cycling is the preferred choice is one example. Cities in The Netherlands, notably Amsterdam, have done that almost by default, partly because of the impact of the existing network of canals.

In other cases, the focus has been on reallocating car space so that automobiles are not the focus of the urban experience. This was embedded into the planning of the new city of Milton Keynes with its network of pedestrian pathways, known as Redways, separated from the main roads. Whilst they had many attractions, they did suffer safety concerns. The secluded nature of some Redways raised fears about personal safety, particularly at night, because their separation from main roads reduces surveillance from passersby.

A further development is the careful consideration of the location for the provision of essential amenities. Whether this is schools, a swimming bath, shopping opportunities, or citizen support facilities. Doing this struggles against commercial considerations and pressures from online activities. Out-of-town shopping precincts have attractions for retail chain stores. Online contacts can reduce the uptake of meeting Places (as described in Chapter 6).

From the perspective of the psychology of Place, all of the changes under the broad umbrella label of 15-minute cities are attempts to change the nature and experience of Places. Removing cars and facilitating local access to amenities, are attempts to create distinct neighbourhoods, perhaps not that dissimilar from the image of medieval villages. Those who enjoy contemporary city life with its dense traffic have, consequently, led challenges to the proposed developments.

Those challenges help to show how, for some people, the presence of cars and the need to use them to gain access to amenities are part of the identity of those Places for them. Controlling the movement of vehicles around an area, which is a key objective of 15-minute cities, therefore changes, for some people, their view of the whole nature of their neighbourhood. They read into that, ideas about being controlled, limited, and watched. Once again, as considered throughout this book, different ways of being in a Place can give rise to quite different perspectives on what the Place is.

Section IV investigates the psychology of Places in the landscape. One case used to illustrate some of the main aspects discussed in that section is my walk in the local forest. This demonstrates it is possible to emphasise that, even in such a benign context, environmental roles and changes over time emerge as dominant ways of understanding a Place.

In a nutshell, considering conceptualisations of cities and related aspects of Place experience influenced by the purposes for being in a Place elucidates the psychological processes which should be utilised for placemaking. This forefronts the significance of human agency in interacting with Places. Appreciation of the importance of being able to form effective conceptualisations of Places in a city is part of the mission to encourage the creation of '15-minute cities'.

Landscape – a walk in the woods

In Section IV, attention was turned to Places that are usually regarded as the antithesis of the city and built environment. That enabled further features of Places to be explored. It also threw light on the fundamental dynamics of Place experience as well as illustrated that no Place is an island (not even islands).

In the time-honoured tradition of many writers, in order to try and organise my thoughts for this final, tidying-up chapter, I went for a walk in the woods near where I live. These woods, or possibly more accurately Forests, are extensive. They are far from any large conurbations and thus always free from traffic and other people. Yet, the first thing that strikes me on this walk is that this countryside is also a resource used by the local Forestry Commission when the trees are harvested (Figure 19.9). Although for me as someone in the environmental role is of enjoying the quiet and freedom of a stroll from my house, uninterrupted by other demands, for the forestry workers, it is a Place of employment. In this case, the two roles only conflict when they overlap in time and location.

The richness of the experience of this Forest is enhanced by the melodious singing of the blackbirds, the busy chatter of chiffchaffs, and even the urgent whistle of blackcaps. I am no ornithologists, though. These birds are invisible in the trees. It is the sound pattern recognition app on my smartphone that tells me who are my neighbours around me. Like most of the Earth, this forest is not separated from the World Wide Web. This

Figure 19.9 Trees, along the path, having been logged

Place, therefore, inevitably takes aspects of its significance from guidance I can glean through my handheld device.

The birdsong also highlights another aspect of the woods as a Place. Some time ago when I was last here, there was no discernible birdsong. The changing, unusually warm season, but perhaps more importantly the opening up of space between the trees through logging, has created a more attractive habitat for our avian friends. A further illustration that landscape and countryside are ever-changing. These changes are brought about by changes in climate as well as by human intervention when used as a resource. Indeed, these pine forests themselves are a product of War. They were created after the First World War to provide for the timber shortage, created to a large extent by the need for pit props in the trenches of that devastating conflict.

Taken together, the experience of this rural setting has profound layers of meaning. The changes that build those meanings are typically slower than those that happen on a high street or to areas of a city. They nonetheless demonstrate the richness Places in the landscape have. That range of ways of being, offered by the countryside contributes to the health benefits of being away from the city (Chapter 18).

Landscapes also have a particular power from being portrayed (Chapter 17). When these portrayals reflect notions of the *picturesque*, with a forest-surrounded lake and distant hills, they encapsulate many different meanings. At the same time, they offer enough complexity to attract a purely aesthetic response.

Broadening ways for understanding and making of places

I have been at pains to draw on many different sources for perspectives on Places, experiences of them, actions in them, and their meaning. Any process by which a particular Place is understood will generate biases and distortions. The people involved in collecting and providing insights into places will each have their own comprehension, environmentally relevant roles, and expectations of the rules that influence what happens there. This is particularly significant when modifying, creating, or conceptualising what Places will become. That includes a family deciding where to live as much as the planning of a new city. All the procedures for revealing what places are, are also relevant to generating ideas about new places. Talking, walking, looking, drawing, and reading with others or alone, are all pathways to unpacking the possibilities for future Places, including modifications of those that already exist.

Crucial to these explorations of future possibilities is the recognition that there are two significantly different sets of environmental roles in relation to the actual production of Places. One are the roles of producing the Place – those who design, plan, or build the Place. The others are those who experience or are responsible for the place in some way. This may be as residents, financiers, managers, and so on. The difference in what they bring to thinking about Places has been revealed by many studies of design participation going back over half a century.[16]

As a consequence of the challenge of communication between, to put it simply, architects and users, a great mix of design participation methodologies have been explored. Some of these design participation methods consist of surveys of potential users, other as considered in Chapter 2, are organised around physical objects that can be manoeuvred on a table. These often run into difficulties illustrated by Kaplan:

> A group of us landscape architects were to work with a small community on a small playground project. So, we went to them and said, "what do you want?" and they said, "well, what have you got?" so we went back and worked up some drawings of what we thought they should do. When we showed them the drawings they said "Oh, no, that's not it at all." so we said, "well what do you want?" and they said "well, what have you got?"[17]

As Simon illustrates[18] in a project to assist the Burwash Native Peoples in planning a new settlement, the Psychology of Place framework gives a productive approach to design participation beyond asking people 'what do you want?". The challenges of working with people from a culture different from that of the architects and planners wishing to help were given particular significance because "Burwash was conceived of as a community where those who have had troubles with alcohol, drugs or the penal system could be healed by a program that stresses their cultural traditions".[19]

The focus on cultural issues led to the 'meaning' aspect of Place being explored through "the cultural development of the group, focusing on information about their way of life", including "historical and mythological information". Comprehending the interaction of this with implied physical forms required collecting information on "activities, as well as the physical attributes of the spaces they lived in and incorporated into their myths".[20] Anthropological accounts, as well as cognitive maps, sketches of an ideal community, or modelling with coloured plasticine, and interviews with volunteers from the Burwash Native peoples, all provided input into the design process. These volunteers formed the client group, who were actively involved in the data collection. Consequently, "an important role reversal occurred the clients were the experts". Their views took precedence. The planner merely offered technical advice about their planning issues. This process resulted in a radically different plan for the community than that originally envisaged by the local planners. This included an emphasis on traditional concerns for the location of the core settlement, proximity to water, as well as contemporary requirements of access to the highway.

This participatory planning process was an early example of what has become known as 'Indigenous Planning', an activity that now has very many examples around the world.[21]

However, there is growing recognition that such participatory design processes are not only relevant for indigenous communities. The acceptance that potential users of Places have much to contribute to the design or modification of those Places is relevant to all other design and planning contexts, whether for built settlements or landscape development.

The emergence of a variety of approaches to participation in design has opened up awareness of the many issues that such activities generate.[22] The different roles that people have in relation to what is being designed bring different perspectives, understanding, and vocabularies to the tasks involved. These differences become part of a social process that requires negotiation. Yet aspects of power and authority can undermine any objective of generating coherent design solutions. The power struggles can weaken any attempts to reflect the qualities and contents that those using and experiencing the proposed Places deem necessary.

Why do we leave it so late?

Understanding these different environmental roles and the inevitable struggle between them, as well as the power of Places in our lives, contributes to answering the central question that is challenging human existence. Why, with all the information that is available about climate change and environmental degradation, has humanity not grasped the nettle and made real efforts to reverse the coming apocalypse? Place psychology helps to explain why there is such inertia in reacting to climate change.

Understanding the challenge of responding to what is required for creating appropriate Places helps to answer the question of why there is such a slow response to environmental threats. Given what is known about global warming and all the environmental changes that are so obviously going on, why are people not reacting to them much more effectively and quickly? Why do people stay where it is the vulnerability to environmental threats is clear, Or return to them, even when other places to live are available? By contrast, the United States has responded more effectively to the threat of terrorism than to climate change.

Physical scientists think that politicians and everyone else just need more information to be convinced of the necessity to modify their actions. This explanation is profoundly ignorant of social psychology and how much of each person's identity is embedded in where they are., Places enshrine social interactions and behaviour. The day-to-day norms and expectations of what is appropriate where, the 'rules of place', are strongly rooted in an understanding of where we are.

I became aware of the power of these place-related processes some years ago. I was asked by a major British industry,[23] which made use of a variety of potentially dangerous manufacturing activities in a large factory with many different departments, to advise on how the industry could reduce accidents. The request was loosely couched as wanting an indication of what posters it could put up that would make the workforce follow safety procedures. These posters were part of factory-wide campaigns every month or so. Each campaign focused on a different safety topic. This might be keeping the workplace clean one month, and checking fire extinguishers the next.

Instead of responding to this request, I carried out a survey of attitudes to safety across the whole factory. From this, I prepared safety attitude profiles for each department. Each of these departments was in a different art of the large complex factory. They carried out different activities relating to the overall process that went on across the factory with related rules of conduct. Some were mere storage and distribution centres. Others were engaged in the central, potentially highly dangerous process. Each had its own distinct physical form developed to support the actions that went on there.

I proposed that each department set up a safety committee to address the weaknesses revealed in that department's safety attitude profile revealed by answers to the survey. In other words, each committee was to generate rules of activity that were specifically relevant to their Place of work. With this proposal was the recommendation that they aim to reduce accidents by 20% each year – a five-year plan to reduce all accidents. To my amazement, the most dangerous department in the factory reduced all accidents within the first year.

This was a powerful illustration of the process, well known in social psychology, of the power of group membership. By making each department responsible for its own safety objectives and giving them the organisational and informational tools on which to plan this, the people in different Places demonstrated that their patterns of behaviour, Place rules, can be changed by the interactions between people and the common norms they embody.

That study illustrated how any location carries powerful meanings that help to inform what goes on there. That strengthens the expectations of how a place is to be used and what one is required to do there. These meanings are not independent of the person and the view that individual holds of his/her characteristics. This makes the cycle of action and expectation, the rules of Place remarkably difficult to break.

Those socially acceptable ways of acting typically also inhibit attitude and behaviour change. People tend to continue to do what is the convention for where they are, too often generating the sort of inertia that leads to emergencies becoming disasters. There are many examples at scales from the level of building evacuations when a threat is discovered to the actions of nations, such as the deadly inertia that gave rise to genocide in Rwanda and similar actions in Gaza and Ukraine as I write. These are all situations in which governments and individuals continue with their quotidian activities despite the growing evidence of how extremely destructive it is to do so.

All these examples illustrate what might be thought of as a law of human activity that parallels Newton's first law of motion. People carry on with their existing Place-related activities unless some external force leads them to recognise that different rules are now relevant to their behaviour in a particular location. This can be summarised by common misestimates of the development of danger, illustrated in Figure 19.9.

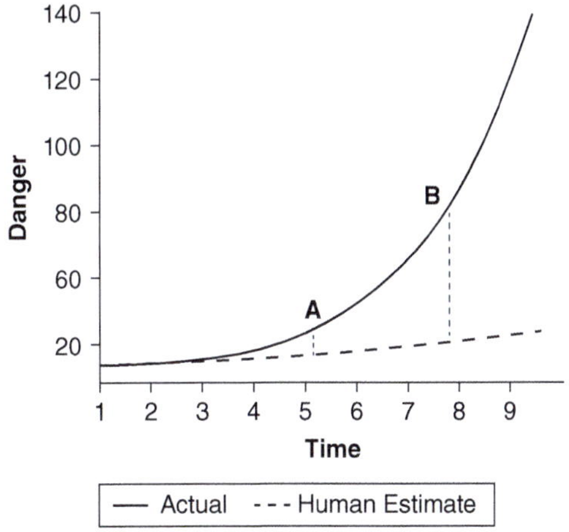

Figure 19.10 A conceptual graph comparing estimates, over time, of the growth of danger compared with the actual growth. It shows that underestimates increase rapidly over time

Although derived from the study of estimates of the growth of a fire and case studies of actions in emergencies,[24] it could just as readily be applied to how most people and governments anticipate that climate crises unfold.

Figure 19.10 shows to lines. One is the typical actual growth on an emergency if it is not dealt with early on. The other are people's general estimates of how it will grow. The difference between these two lines reveals the growing misestimation of the emerging disaster as the emergency changes over time. That variation in how people think danger increases over time compared with how it typically really does grow increases until the emergency gets out of control. At that point new rules of Place become clear. Broadly speaking, people think that danger grows in a simple linear fashion. This means that in the early stages, the estimate of change is broadly in line with actual change, indicated by letter A in Figure 19.10. However, early stages contribute to later stages, so there is an increase not just in the amount of change but in the rate of change. This is an exponential or geometric increase in danger. In the early stages, therefore, the estimates of growth are reasonably accurate. This lulls people into thinking that they understand what is happening, but their estimates become ever more inaccurate over time.

These misinterpretations support inertia in reacting because the existing patterns of behaviour, and understanding what is expected of our interactions with each other, and with the places that we know, act as anchors to keep us in our usual routines. It takes a major jolt to get us to re-evaluate what we think is happening and to change how we think of ourselves and our activities. We have to recognise that the Place we are at has changed. Different rules apply. Until we understand and act on that understanding that this is now an altered Place, we are reluctant to change what we do.

It is worth emphasising this central point. Emergencies become disasters because initial warnings are ignored. They are not ignored out of obstinacy or ignorance, but because of the psychological processes that underlie habitual patterns of activity, informed and guided by social norms and Place rules. They are embedded in our culture through the environmental roles that Places encapsulate.

These habitual patterns are there not just for ordinary citizens but, even more importantly, for governments and leaders of major international companies. Until they change their attitude to nature as a resource to use, and seek to support the emergence of new rules of place relevant to the changing circumstances, then the impacts of the delay in dealing with environmental degradation and climate change will increase in severity. The resources needed to combat these changes and deal with their consequences will increase at ever-growing rates.

Conclusions

In highlighting the themes of *Revisiting the Psychology of Place*, this chapter has provided examples that illustrate particular aspects of each of the topics that are dealt with in each of the main sections. The complexity of *Landscape* as a Place is demonstrated. That shows its roles as a resource and as a Place to be. An awareness of its culture and history contributes to its influence on personal identity. But as with all Places today, its role is always influenced by its physical and virtual contexts.

The rich meanings of any *City* as well as the challenges of making sense of it are examined through mental sketch maps that reveal crucial foci of the experience of Places in the city. The practical implications of this are demonstrated with reference to the worldwide move to reduce reliance on cars. This is often summarised as the idea of 'the 15-minute city'. In effect, these are attempts to change the nature of Places so that they serve more clearly as distinct neighbourhoods. This is not without its problems, because for many people, their way of life and identity in any given location are greatly affected by their notion of the sort of Place in which they live.

A consideration of a recent prize-winning *Building* demonstrates how an innovative design can contribute powerfully to the use and experience of a Place. It also illustrates how Places always consist of an assemblage of Places, which in their turn give meaning to the building as a whole. That these qualities have emerged from the challenges of fitting the building into an awkward site in Central London is an illustration of the imagination of the architects and designers. It also reveals the insights of the official clients' consideration of the students' Place requirements, leading to an understanding the nature of the Place they wanted to build.

The participation of all those responsible for creating a building does demand the use of creative ways to express the sorts of Places to be produced. Those can draw on *methods* used for studying interactions with Places, as shaped by the purposes people have for being there. Those factors are at the heart of procedures for use in design participation. Although this has been an activity particularly harnessed for minority groups and First Nation communities, they are clearly relevant to all design processes that aim to produce effective and satisfying Places.

Moving forward, the recognition that we are so bound by our ways of being in Places helps to explain how climate and environment emergencies become disasters. When early warnings are ignored, because such disregard supports ingrained habits and social norms, counteracting the looming catastrophes demands exponentially growing resources. Without shifting attitudes toward nature and meaningful places, the Earth as a Place becomes less appropriate for human existence.

References and endnotes

1 Maddicott, A. (2023) *Tender Maps: travels in search of the emotions of Place*. September Publishing. Page 124. Reprinted by permission of the publisher.
2 I am grateful to my old friend and colleague Bob Duffield for this insight.
3 Heatherwick, T. (2023) *Humanise: A maker's guide to building our world*, Random House.
4 There are excellent videos on YouTube describing the origins and concepts that gave rise to this building. For example, Bing Videos.
5 Although I'm not sure if the architects welcome such 'defacing' of their pristine geometry?
6 I've found no quotes that show this reference is intentional, but it is so much part of architectural history it must be embedded in the mindset of many architects.
7 Dovey, K. (2020) Place as assemblage, in *The Routledge handbook of place*, Routledge, pp. 21–31.
8 Miller, D., Abed Rabho, L., Awondo, P., de Vries, M., Duque, M., Garvey, P., ... Wang, X. (2021) *The global smartphone: Beyond a youth technology*, UCL Press, p. 123, https://doi.org/10.14324/111.9781787359611
9 Miller, Abed Rabho, Awondo, de Vries, Duque, Garvey, ... Wang (2021) *The global smartphone*
10 Meyrowitz, J. (1986) *No sense of place: The impact of electronic media on social behavior*, Oxford University Press.
11 Meyrowitz (1986) *No sense of place*.
12 Rosen, C. (2024) *The extinction of experience: Being human in a disembodied world*, WW Norton & Company.
13 The same Reid Bishop whose fascinating PhD on time in place was discussed in Chapter 11.
14 A 'sizzle' of the show is at https://www.youtube.com/watch?v=EsNGzTUkc5g&feature=youtu.be
15 Teixeira, J. F., Silva, C., Seisenberger, S., Büttner, B., McCormick, B., Papa, E., & Cao, M. (2024) Classifying 15-minute cities: A review of worldwide practices, *Transportation Research Part A: Policy and Practice*, 189, 104234.
16 Brought together in a prescient set of papers in Canter, D., Krampen, M., & Stea, D. (Eds.) (2024) *New directions in environmental participation*, Taylor & Francis, first published in 1988.
17 Kaplan, S. (1977) Participation in the design process: A cognitive approach, in D. Stokols (Ed.) *Perspectives on environment and behavior: Theory, research, and applications*, Boston: Springer, pp. 221–233.
18 Simon, J. (2024) Participation and community: Transcultural perspectives, in D. Canter et al. (Eds.) *New directions in environmental participation*, Routledge, pp. 36–49.
19 Simon (2024) Participation and community, p. 38.
20 Simon (2024) Participation and community, pp. 40, 41.
21 Porter, L., Matunga, H., Viswanathan, L., Patrick, L., Walker, R., Sandercock, L., ... Jojola, T. (2017) Indigenous planning: From principles to practice/a revolutionary pedagogy of/for indigenous planning/settler-indigenous relationships as liminal spaces in planning education and practice/indigenist planning/what is the work of non-indigenous people in the service of a decolonizing agenda?/supporting indigenous planning in the city/film as a catalyst for indigenous community development/being ourselves and seeing ourselves in the city: Enabling the conceptual space for indigenous urban planning, *Planning Theory & Practice*, 18(4), 639–666.
22 Mosleh, W. S. & Larsen, H. (2021) Exploring the complexity of participation. *CoDesign*, 17(4), 454–472.
23 Canter, David V. (1996) Changing safety culture in a steel works, in D. Canter (Ed.) *Psychology in action*. Dartmouth Benchmark Series, Hampshire, UK: Dartmouth Publishing Company, pp. 231–238.
24 Canter, D. (2024) An overview of human behaviour in fires, in D. Canter (Ed.) *Fires and human behaviour*, pp. 205–234.

Epilogue

Although I've written this before,[1] I think it is worth repeating. Books all whisper to each other. They agree and disagree, comment on, and draw from their bedfellows. That conversation has moved onto the internet. There are less clear indications available of origins, sources, and the naming of compatriots. Old-fashioned, cellulose-based libraries (as opposed to the silicon foundations of electronic sources), like the one that fills the walls of the room in which I write, has the advantage of its historical and indeed archaeological, characteristics. The deeper in the pile, the older was my last access to it. These aspects tend to be lost in the instantaneity of the online world. One particular quality of books, which internet sources do not share, is that they have a present physical existence. They are always experienced in a place, even if it is the carriage of a train, the side of a mountain, or in bed.

Books, copies of journal articles and newspaper reports, acquired some time ago, buried under more recent ones, may be regarded by some as only of historical interest, suffering from the common belief that only the latest science is valid. However, like objects archaeologists dig up, it is notable in studies of Places that many publications from years ago still have a lot to teach us. I have therefore made a point of drawing on material from half a century ago as readily as something published yesterday. In truth, often recent publications are unwittingly, recycling what was known many years ago. Although typically discussed with a somewhat different vocabulary.

Escaping my background

Aware of the value of digging up the past to better understand the present and possible futures, the present volume consciously seeks to elaborate the central arguments, presented over the half-century ago, in my 1977 book *The Psychology of Place*. Since that was written the world has changed enormously in many ways; physically, politically, emotionally, and technically, to list only those changes that come immediately to mind. These carry huge implications for how we experience, use, and think about places. As a consequence, there are aspects of my earlier formulation of the psychology of place that may no longer be relevant. But there are also enduring features that are perhaps even more significant today than when that young, 30-year-old set about writing.

In revisiting my 1977 book I have become aware of the confident, but rather insular, academic I was all those years ago. I suppose that was due to my university upbringing. I was schooled in psychology at the University of Liverpool in what was then known broadly as 'Experimental Psychology'. There was a declared ideology that psychology was a science like any hard science, notably physics, in which controlled experimentation was the only sure basis for doing 'real' research. Hypotheses had to formulated from predetermined theories and concepts, then 'rigorously' tested in psychological laboratories.

Although such scientistic ideologies still thrive in many areas of psychology, it did dawn on me quite early in my academic career that this limited perspective could not even be applied to the noble sciences. For example, astronomy has no double-blind controlled experiments. Even support for Einstein's theory of relativity depends on particular cases, such as the bending of light by massive objects. Many discoveries in medicine also depend on particular correlations, such as the crucial discovery that milkmaids who had cowpox did not get smallpox. This was then tested in a one-off case study that opened up the whole area of immunisation.

A further crucial aspect of scientism and the deference paid to experimental methods is that it just does not make sense for studying any psychological aspects of the environment. The idea of 'controlling' for unwanted influences on the 'dependent' variable is based on the idea that there will indeed be other possible influences. If that is a chemistry experiment in which impurities would confound the results, trying to avoid such impurities makes sense. But if a new building is being studied, or an area of countryside being visited treating those locations as independent variables raises questions about the impurities that must be controlled for The reactions people have to those Places are an embedded part of being there. Isolating out a particular view, for instance, or shape of a room, totally ignores why a person would be there or the relationship they have to that actual Place. As David Seamon states clearly in his seminal exploration of the phenomenology of Place "Neither can parts of place be ranked higher or lower or be claimed as independent or dependent variables".[2]

I became aware of another feature, ignored by the emphasis on a limited view of what science is, when providing consultancy to organisations that wish to act on the basis of my advice. I found that as much as they admired statistics and some background number crunching, what caused them to take notice of what I was advocating was a well-presented case study illustrating the process. For example, no matter how sophisticated the model I developed of human actions when caught in a building on fire,[3] backed by examination of many incidents, what made policy makers take notice was a graphic account of one particular event that illustrated the model. Even better if the people I was advising could relate that example directly to their own experience.

Journalists are very aware of this phenomenon. When the new COVID-19 vaccinations were set in motion, the newspaper reports did not highlight figures of how many people were being jabbed, or the research results that had given rise to this breakthrough. They had a photograph of the first person to be vaccinated with an account of who they were and their experience.

Of course, the argument by the illustration of a particular case has the risk that the case is not typical. In these circumstances spurious arguments can be supported by inappropriate or irrelevant cases. I have found this when explaining to police investigators that the majority of burglars do not travel far from their homes. I know this to be the case from many statistical studies. But this is often challenged by a police officer who cites one offender he knew who travelled great distances to commit his crimes. This illustrates that case studies on their own can never provide all the evidence to support an argument, but they can be a crucial part of that evidence, and essential in getting across the message that the statistics reveal.

My disquiet with the constraints of the rigid experimental approach and its current association with neuroscientific measurements requires careful argument in its own right. The appendix to this book therefore examines that directly. In addition, it provides the opportunity to critically examine the current popularity of Darwinian explanations of human actions and experiences. These issues have been touched on in earlier chapters but bringing them together in an appendix enables a more thorough summary of the crucial critiques of this reductionist approach.

An alternative perspective

The criticism of the limited theories and methodologies for studying Places, does not mean that such research is doomed to failure, as I hope I have made clear. Elaborated throughout this book is a coherent framework, backed by an extensive academic literature, as well a day-to-day experience, that provides a rich alternative to the determinist, reductionist perspective. This is founded on the assumption that people are active agents. They bring their experiences, personal and social history, as well as their cultural context to participate in and make use of their surroundings.

Fundamental to this is a psychological model of what makes us human. People have purposes, goals, expectations, and desires. These overlap and change with maturation, education, social interactions, knowledge, understanding, and of course direct experience. All of that influences what Places mean to people, the sense they make of them and how they take part in them.

As I have been at pains to elaborate throughout this book although engagement with Places is part of what makes us and we make, there are many pressures undermining this fundamental aspect of being human. As Matt Haig writes in his time-hoping novel:

> Places don't matter to people anymore. Places aren't the point. People are only ever half present where they are these days. They always have at least one foot in the great digital nowhere.[4]

This somewhat dystopian view rather undermines many of the aspects of Place experience that I have been explored. Although it is a salutary warning of one possible view of the present domination of the 'digital nowhere', it ignores the embodied nature of human agency within a particular physical *context*.

The processes that support this agency can be best elaborated and appreciated by exploring actions and experiences *in situ*. That requires direct encounters with people in actual Places. Or drawing on accounts from such encounters. That will inevitably overlap with sociological, anthropological, and even on occasion, political methodologies and perspectives. It will always need to reflect on why people are there, their roles in the broadest sense and the related rules which guide their expectations and actions. All of that is embedded in the history and experiences of Places.

Terry Pratchett explores this in his plaintive novel *Nation,* when he writes:

> *It was a sacred place, and not because of some god or other. It was just ...sacred, because it existed, because pain and blood and joy and death had echoed in time and made it so.*
>
> *(Terry Pratchett (2008)* Nation, *p. 209)*

Psychological facets of the process of engagement with places are revealed through the way we structure our understanding of where we are. Those studies of aspects of cognition that dominated the 1977 *The Psychology of Place,* are subsumed under the many explorations of Place significance and meaning in the present volume. A person, not a brain or bundle of neurons, exists in a Place. That is the vital component of any understanding of the Psychology of Place.

This complexity is captured richly in the discussion between Marco Polo and Kublai Khan in Italo Calvino's mesmerizing book:

> Marco Polo describes a bridge, stone by stone.
>
> "But which is the stone that supports the bridge?" Kublai Khan asks:
>
> "The bridge is not supported by one stone or another," Marco Polo answers,
>
> "but by the line of the arch that they form."
>
> Kublai Khan remains silent, reflecting. Then he adds:
>
> "Why do you speak to me of the stones? It is only the arch that matters to me."
>
> Polo answers: "without stones there is no arch."
>
> *(Italo Calvino (1974),* Invisible Cities, *translated by William Weaver Vintage Classics, p. 82)*

References and endnotes

1 An opportunity to mention my award-winning 1995 book *Criminal Shadows*.
2 Seamon, D. (2018) *Life takes place: Phenomenology, lifeworlds, and place making*, London: Routledge, p. 25.
3 Canter, D. (Ed.) (2024) *Fires and human behaviour*, Taylor & Francis.
4 Haig, M. (2018) *How to stop time: A novel*, Harmondsworth: Penguin, p. 109.

A counterproductive approach

No theory can exclude everything that is wrong, poor or even detestable, or include everything that is right, good or beautiful.

(Schoenberg,[1] p. xvi)

Introduction

Popular interest in science tends to seek out exciting, unexpected or even seemingly magical explanations for observable phenomena. As a consequence, many psychological researchers readily accept explanations that appear to provide insights that go beyond what might be regarded as obvious. In addition, obeisance is paid to the use of technologies that require special expertise and equipment. A search for exciting counterintuitive results also propels research methodologies that are hijacked from the hard science where they are often (but not always) relevant, even though they are far from being appropriate when studying the Psychology of Place.

This aping of the 'hard' sciences with laboratory experiments, apparently evolutionary biology-based theories and medico-physiological measuring instruments generates publishable studies. It attracts research funding and with that promotion and other career accolades. The experimental, biomeasuring approach also allows relatively quick and easy projects instead of the much more challenging and time-consuming requirement of field research and intensive interactions with people. Happily, one of the few advantages of retirement from paid university employment and healthy longevity is that I no longer need to be concerned with these career-related demands. I can take the role of pointing out that often the emperor has no clothes.

I have therefore taken the opportunity throughout this book both to propose positive ways of understanding the psychology of place and critically comment on those theories and methods that I see as fatally flawed. In order to avoid bogging down chapter after chapter with these criticisms this appendix brings those critical comments together in more detail. It reviews weaknesses in the types if explanation that are given for our interactions with places. It considers the limits in the laboratory experiment paradigm. The uncritical use of biometric measurements is also decried.

The central reason for these negative evaluations is that the approach they all embrace is fundamentally insulting to human beings. It treats them as passive organisms. It leads to the belief that people are manipulated by mechanistic processes. That, in turn, supports the idea that such processes can be harnessed to engineer our experiences and actions. That is the essence of totalitarianism. My criticisms, summarised in this Appendix may therefore be seen as a concern that these approaches carry implicit political implications.

Unsubstantiated 'explanations'

Professor of Medicine and neuroscientist, Raymond Tallis, called his exceptionally erudite and thoroughly researched 2016 book, *Aping Mankind: Neuromania, Darwinitis and the Misrepresentation of Humanity.*[2] In it Tallis recognises the great leaps that neuroscience has contributed to the understanding of the workings of the brain, with tremendous benefits for medicine. However, he provides detailed evidence for why so many attempts to explain human behaviour, consciousness, and culture, using ideas from neuroscience and evolutionary theory are not only illogical but also totally lack any empirical basis.

Prime examples explored throughout *Rethinking the Psychology of Place* of such attempts to use pseudo-evolutionary theory (which Tallis[3] amusingly calls 'Darwinitis'), are speculative explanations of Place preferences, notably in relation to landscapes. These are the claim that there are evolutionary bases for what people find beautiful in scenic views. The general argument revolves around these preferences being reflections of aspects that enhanced the potential for survival of early humans. The argument goes that it became innate to *homo sapiens* to prefer landscapes which were similar to those in which that species of primate first emerged and thrived. As with many similar claims of evolutionary processes, often given the electronic analogy of being 'hard-wired', there is no genetic evidence for these apparently innate characteristics.

This theory has its roots in broader considerations of aesthetic judgements in the 1930s when John Dewey,[4] enamoured with the then fashionable Darwinian interpretations, argued that assessments of beauty were a product of the experiences of early humans, remaining as instincts to the present day. His proposal was that just as animals have an instinct to seek optimal environmental conditions, so in humans, environments that, in neolithic times and earlier, were helpful for survival, would be those that were found today to be aesthetically pleasing.

Biophilia

In the 1970s this theory about the innate tendency to delight in nature was elaborated into a rather broadly ranging notion. It was given the label *biophilia,* from the Latin *bio* (life) and *philia* (love of). That neologism was originally coined by Erich Fromm, best known as a psychoanalyst, who claimed that human beings had a:

> ...passionate love of life and of all that is alive: it is the wish to further growth, whether it is in a person, a plant an idea or a social group.[5]

The term was taken up by Edward O. Wilson, an evolutionary biologist who had carried out intensive studies of ants. He popularised the term in his book called *Biophilia* (1984),[6] proposing that human affinity for nature has a genetic basis. Like the game of 'pass the message', that term was taken up in an even more limited way by those studying people's reactions to their surroundings. The most widespread of these evolutionary elaborations of Biophilia are Kaplan's Attention Restoration Theory (ART) and Ulrich's Stress Recovery Theory (SRT), discussed in Chapter 18. The promulgaters of these speculations assert that the benefits of nature, for attention restoration, and stress recovery, derive from the millennia of human evolution that have given survival benefits to these relationships to the natural world.

The evolutionary argument falls on several counts. But perhaps the greatest challenge comes from the question of how the evolutionary benefit of preference for, or influence of particular types of landscape would be achieved? There are two essential mechanisms that increase the likelihood that a species will survive. One is that the benefit achieved by a particular mutation enables the individual to live long enough to reproduce, with the offspring preserving that mutation. The other is that sexual selection is biased towards individuals with a particular mutation.

There are a limited number of examples in humans of environmental factors directly influencing the development of genetic variation. The most notable is that the Bajau, or 'Sea Nomads', who have engaged in breath-hold diving for thousands of years. They now have spleens larger than other humans, enabling them to hold their breath for longer.[7] The mechanism here is readily understandable. Their culture requires deep diving. Individuals who could not hold their breath long enough would die out, leaving the Bajau with those who could.

What could the mechanism be for people who liked open vistas with trees and water to enable them to survive and reproduce? Would women prefer men with that special aesthetic outlook? How could such a complex, cognitive process be incorporated into the human genome? Is it not more likely that the aesthetic preference grows out of cultural traditions best expressed in pictures? Traditions that come to the fore when people are shown photographs and asked which they prefer. Furthermore, the landscapes that are preferred today are very different from those preferred in the past. How does genetics generate such a change?

Ignoring of what it means to be human, as opposed to what it means to be an evolved primate, can be found in many more examples of 'evolutionary' explanations of behaviour. They are rather like Kipling's 'just-so' stories. They seek to frame every aspect of human propensities in pseudo-Darwinian accounts of the likely evolutionary benefits of those aspects. These explanations, whether it be of kindness, rape, arson, music, or a host of other features of human activities, are claimed as having roots in the distant past of early hominids. That they exist in what people do is taken as *prima facie* evidence that they have evolutionary benefit and therefore origins deep in humanity's past. These speculations are given the status of scientific theories without any possibility of demonstrating their validity, or even an elementary indication of some genetic support for the claims.

A further challenge to these 'theories' are recent discoveries that show early hominids, possibly as long ago as 50,000 years, had much the same propensities and imagination as *homo sapiens* today. This indicates that there is something about being human which distinguishes us from animals. Changes in how we deal with and experience the world derive from social and cultural processes that cannot be reduced to coping with the challenges of surviving on the Serengeti. The vulnerability of very young hominids leading to the requirement of family arrangement, with the associated emergence of language and self-consciousness, all point to ways of dealing with the environment very different from even the most intelligent ape.

The idea that hominids grew up in particular types of natural settings, therefore adaptations occurred that caused such settings to be attractive, and be places where people are at ease, is an oversimplified view of early human's interactions with their surroundings. The hypothesis that the benefits of being in nature have origins in neolithic adaptations, do not survive even mild scrutiny, like most speculative, evolutionary explanations of human actions and experiences,. Any understanding of how early hominids survived reveals that they were typically much cleverer than chasing after game for food. They herded them over cliffs, so that the animals died from the falls. Or used other communal approaches that enabled them to trap meat.[8] It is difficult to see how this accords with the notion of an innate desire for an idyllic image of being in nature. Indeed, it would seem that the difference nature provides from current metropolitan existence may be more important than harking back to an era long before cities, or even large communities, existed.

One more issue opens further the consideration of the benefits of seeing, or being in, natural settings. There is little in the natural environment that is truly natural. Few places in the world can be genuinely called wildernesses, untouched by human intervention. Most countryside has been shaped over millennia by the activities of people. Even primordial forests were modified by early humans. Going back as far as 80,000 years ago, many indigenous peoples in different places, set fire to forests. This was to turn dense woodlands into open areas that would encourage the growth of certain plants and increase the opportunities for hunting and gathering. The gathering of nuts and fruits also changed the distribution of plants.[9] It is therefore not to the inherently 'natural' aspects of views, and direct experience of landscapes, to which we should look for explanations of their 'restorative' qualities.

The modification of the environment for human purposes from the earliest stages of hominid existence, indicates that there was no innate, or evolutionary benefit, for being in natural environments. What ecologists call 'niche construction theory'[10] proposes that many organisms need to re-build, and/or re-organise their natural environment in order to thrive and survive. This emphasises an inherent agency when interacting with the surroundings. It makes clear that human beings from their earliest origins have not inherited a passive shaping of their needs and desires by their experience of nature. Rather, they have always acted on their surroundings to make them compatible with their understanding of the world around them.[11]

One aspect of environmental modification is illustrated by humans leaving 'nature', building large settlements and increasingly large cities. That questions why, if the desire for contact with nature was such an innate part of human biology, did human do that? If anything, that might indicate that the love of nature was not that strong. The view of nature as a resource, which is such a dominant perspective, as discussed in Chapter 16, also indicates that it is what nature provides that is welcomed, not some innate love of it. There are also so many obvious examples of people deliberately going into settings that are not characterised by the qualities the evolutionary theories suggest.

Those endeavours that seek out obviously inhospitable locations challenge the idea that people are hard-wired to seek analogies to African savannahs.

Inappropriate research designs

Evolutionary theories point to studies of the direct impact of the environment on behaviour. They are determinist in the sense that such research seeks to find the influence of certain causes within the environment that gives rise to reactions within in people. The challenges that generates for researchers are the practical difficulties of actually studying people in actual locations. Because of the effort of doing so, it is not very common in studies of the significance of landscape, for example, to engage directly with people actively involved in the countryside. Many studies consist of showing people pictures and asking them to react.[12] Whilst these research designs are not without merit, they remove the essential aspect of place experience – the reason for being there. They ignore the Environmental Roles and related Place Rules that are so important in understanding personal reactions in any location.

Another major problem, that I became aware of in the early 1970s, described in Chapter 3, was that experimental methodology, which require relatively few conditions each to be studied independently, is extremely limited. Once I tried to add further facets to studies, not relying on just two or at most three building components, it all became too complicated to run as an experiment and the interactions between independent variables became too difficult to make sense of. Further, running the study again in other contexts gave totally different results.

Such experiments involve 'controlling' for unwanted variables that might distort the results, making it difficult to establish *causality*. It is claimed that without such experiments it is not possible to be sure what was influencing what. That, in turn, requires identifying what the 'independent' variables are – those that are being manipulated by the experimenter – and what the 'dependent' variables are – those that are being measured as the outcome produced by the independent variables introduced. This is regarded as allowing causes to be established. The researcher could claim with confidence that the variations in the independent variable are indeed what gave rise to the differences in the dependent variables. This is often considered to be the yellow brick road to the support for theories from carefully argued postulates.

The approach implies that key concepts be defined before any data is collected. These concepts are to be brought together in a theory, which generated hypotheses that the study was specifically designed to test. This way of doing research is given the grand name of 'The hypothetico-deductive system'. That way of doing research is not without its critics[13] but is still defended by many as the gold standard for scientific methodology.[14]

A particular problem with the experimental, hypothetico-deductive approach is that the paraphernalia required to do it turns it into a set of rituals that students have to master. This includes the designation of the 'significance' of a result from calculations of the probability that the result could have happened by chance. An approach roundly criticised by many statisticians for many years[15,16]as being inappropriately used. Some have even identified this approach as a form of religion or ideology that they have called 'scientism'.[17]

There is also difficulty with heralding the testing of hypotheses under controlled laboratory conditions as the epitome of good science. This is that, although some forms of survey research and metaphorically named 'field' experiments are acceptable, they are all regarded as less 'scientific' than a double-blind, laboratory-controlled experiment. Case studies are dismissed as merely 'anecdotal', although possibly of use in generating hypotheses for careful testing in experiments. Reviewers of research proposals in psychology have even been known to dismiss out-of-hand anything that included questionnaire surveys, rather than laboratory studies.

One consequence of this rigid perspective is that whole disciplines are dismissed as being of no value to psychologists because they are 'unscientific'. This notably includes anthropology and large chunks of sociology and related social sciences. 'Cross-cultural psychology' often used to ignore the details of cultures. For instance, instead of exploring the mechanisms by which cultures might interact with personality or cognitive process, there was a preference for testing whether people from different contexts were differentially susceptible to optical illusions.[18] This also meant that many studies in areas of psychology and a range of social science disciplines were dismissed as merely 'descriptive'. That is, they did not indicate any causal processes. Furthermore, if it were not possible to convert everything being studied into numbers then that was not being properly scientific.

There is a heavily reductionist quality to all of this. Not only must psychologists put numbers on everything they study, but people are regarded as so vague an assembly of components that the more they can be reduced to their biochemistry, physiology, and neurology the better. Consequently, currently many psychologists would rather call themselves neuroscientists. A term which covers many areas of research that were once seen as 'experimental psychology', or more recently 'cognitive psychology', such as studies of memory, learning, personality, and perception.

Neuroscientists interpret psychological processes in terms of the parts of the brain that 'light up' when those processes are in action. For medical concerns, to do with disorders of the brain, such analyses can be of great significance, but in terms of human thought and feelings, spurious distinctions, for example, between 'left-brain' and 'right-brain' oversimplify complex processes.[19] Many other explanations of psychological experiences by reference to brain processes add only a little to our understanding of those. The illusory patina of being 'scientific' in these considerations nonetheless attracts funding and accolades.

A typical example

The weaknesses of such apparently, sophisticated experimental studies are revealed in l, technically and statistically thorough studies of reactions to components of architecture. One typical study explored the effect of difference between linear and curved 'transitional' spaces.[20] The examples of the actual images used, in virtual reality headsets are given in the Appendix figure.

The study consisted of getting 40 people to experience the mild stress of giving a short talk and doing some arithmetic for ten minutes, then to experience the conditions indicated in the Appendix figure, seen in virtual reality headsets, for five minutes. Throughout their biomedical markers were recorded.

The results reported that there were small but statistically significant differences in the psychophysiological measures. These were taken to indicate reduced stress for those in the 'curved' transitional spaces compared with those in the linear spaces. However, the psychological questions used to measure experience of stress showed no difference. The researchers speculated that "that this is possibly due to the short duration of the

Appendix Figure The layout of the four virtual reality transitional spaces (from Huang and Whyte, 2022): (a and b) a plaza, linear and curved, respectively; (c and d) a café space, linear and curved, respectively

experiment. The questionnaires do not provide as much immediate feedback as physiological responses".

The results of this experiment are then used to claim that it "provided some evidence that the geometry of the environment in transitional spaces can reduce human stress to achieve human wellbeing". They go even further to state that:

> "a transitional space could potentially become an urban shelter that is revitalizing, alleviating the stressful impact of increasing crowding. With that in mind, we could envision the near future with optimism that designers, developers and government officials could acknowledge the unique features of the curved architectural elements and therefore facilitate more stress-recovery friendly transitional spaces for the wellbeing of the broader community".

This particular study is one of many possible illustrations that exist of the increasingly sophisticated technology of readily available biomedical markers and virtual reality stimuli. This is encouraging the sort of determinist advocacy of design principles that were the objective of architectural psychologists in the late 1960s and 1970s using more primitive procedures[21]. But the results of that research nonetheless revealed that the atomistic exploration of small variations in physical form, presented as visual stimuli for short periods of time was a dead-end for research.

Buildings are not dealt with as Places in experimental studies. These are not treated as whole entities that are reacted to in relation to their meanings and why a person might be there. Testing the impact of the components of a Place, such as the curvature of a wall, proportions or degree of enclosure, in isolation of the nature of the Place they are part of can be very misleading.

There are further technical problems with studies such as the one described in detail here. The studies typically have very short exposure. Does any form of adaptation to the stimulus need to be considered when commenting on long-term effects? Places are experienced over time, used in a variety of different ways. Claiming that particular design features will reduce stress ignores that process. The small physiological responses found in studies such as the one illustrated could be due to people reacting to subtle differences in the nature of the Places presented on their VR headsets. Did they expect slightly different things to happen there, or that different people would be met there? Without that information it is difficult to know what is giving rise to the marginal differences found in biomarkers.

One final nail in the coffin of the claims of such experimental studies are the demand characteristics described in Chapter 3. Participants in experimental studies are typically asked to react to stimuli that have clearly distinct characteristics. It may therefore be expected that they will have some awareness of what the researcher is seeking. The relatively small differences between different conditions may therefore be explained by some respondents wishing to give the expected answers. That tendency would not be overridden by physiological measures. They reflect the reactions of the participants.

Misleading measurements

The use of biomarkers is a further drive towards treating human beings as organisms that are inevitably influenced by their environment, biology, and genetics. This is a determination to reduce all understanding of human experience to biological processes, embedded within Darwinian theory. Of course, it cannot be denied that what we feel, think, and do must be reflected in brain activity and that many of our innate habits and characteristics must have evolutionary origins. However, as many scholars have argued, both the baby and the bathwater are thrown away when all human experience is reduced to biological explanations.[22] They ignore the fact that human beings can talk and interact with each other, generating cultures and societies that have an existence that cannot be reduced to their mere organic components.

There is no surprise that every aspect of being human is reflected in something going on in bodily, especially brain, activity. Discovering what those neurophysiological processes are does without doubt contribute insights into people's make up. What does it add to comprehending personal experiences? How does it actually help to augment the clarification of being in places? Although it clearly is of enormous value in many areas of medicine and related disciplines, how do they help us to make sense of what it means to be human?

Neuromania

When considering measurements of reactions in Places neuromania[23] prioritises a search for neurological indications of what is being experienced over accounts people may give or direct observations of their actions. That includes physiological and hormonal measurements as well as explanations based on which part of the brain is found to be active when people do or feel something. This reference to aspects of the human organism is usually based on the belief that it is more 'scientific', or even 'objective' than asking or observing.

There are crucial differences between psychological exploration of Places and the rapidly developing trend that sits under the umbrella term 'neuroarchitecture'. The hasty growth of techniques for determining activity in different parts of the brain have unleashed a flood of studies indicating which areas of the brain are active when a person experiences particular sensations or carries out particular actions. These findings have given rise to new perspectives in many disciplines. These include, amongst a plethora of others, 'neurolaw', 'neurocriminology' amd 'neurogeography'. In essence, these disciplines reflect on which parts of the human brain are active when actions relevant to those disciplines are carried out.

Although such neuro studies may help to clarify and distinguish between different human functions, by showing how they relate to different brain activity, there are two challenging paradoxes to the utilisation of their findings. One is that the validation and clarification of what the technology is picking up, depends on accounts from human subjects.[24] To take just one of many possible examples, neuroarchitecture studies have shown that "noise causes feelings of stress". Or that "spaces with scented plants were preferred". Showing what neurophysiological activation is associated with these sensations and preference is certainly of interest, but it does not enhance the understanding of the experiences. To be clear, the way in which the neurophysiological measurements are validated is by relating them to subjective accounts from participants. Without those accounts the biometric measures would lack substance. Furthermore, in those studies that show neuro activity which is not related to declared human reactions, the question has to be asked of whether the human reactions were being sensitively recorded by the bio-markers. In all the examples it is the human reactions that are important to understand in the unpacking the psychology of those experiences.

The second paradox derives from the brain operating as a complex integrated system. Thoughts and emotions, even though they are mirrored in neurology, are well established as being part of social, cultural, and even historical contexts. Yet studies in 'neuroarchitecture' hark back to the days of phrenology. That was an 18th-century pseudoscience claiming to study the shape and size of the skull to infer personality traits, intelligence, and mental capacities.

Although current neuroscience is more firmly based in scientific observations, in some ways it is less sophisticated than phrenology. Rather than exploring the broad features of a person, neuroarchitecture studies tend to deal with very specific aspects of the built environment, specific colours, ceiling height, natural lighting, and so on. How these combine and take their significance from traditions, expectations, and the rich qualities of context, to mention just a few aspects that give physical form their meaning, are ignored when people are put in an fMRI scanner and subjected to other biomedical measurements.

The case being made for 'neuro' everything is that it is 'objective'. Obtaining people's opinions is dismissed as 'subjective'. This is despite the fact that there is well over a century of social science, including psychological research, that has demonstrated that these so-called subjective measures can achieve very high standards of reliability and validity. In other words, they can have very good, some would insist, objective, qualities as measurements.

The ease of measuring such aspects as blood pressure, heart and breathing rates, galvanic skin response, as well as biochemicals in saliva such as cortisol, means that these are now regularly used to assess a person's reactions into the environment. These studies do demonstrate that there are measurable physiological correlates of regularly reported emotional reactions to being in actual, but usually simulated locations. There is the problem though that virtually all physiological and many neurological measures do not indicate the meaning or significance of the 'objective' recording. That requires an understanding of the context. Usually, it also needs some clarification from the person experiencing the phenomenon.

The question is why anyone should be surprised that human physiology and neurology reflect subjective experience? Or why these measures are given more value than what people say or do? Of course, if there is a discrepancy between the 'subjective' experience and the 'objective' measure that would be very interesting. Would it mean that people were hiding their feelings are the physiological measures were misleading. The weaknesses of these biomedical assessments can be summarised as follows:

(1) Psychophysiological responses generally indicate energising, or 'arousal', of the nervous system. This can be exciting or frightening, pleasurable or disconcerting. Context is necessary, and preferably 'subjective' responses are important to clarify which reaction is being experienced.

> *Although surges in heart rate and the clamminess of palms can certainly indicate when a person is becoming aroused, such measures do not differentiate between euphoric highs and plummeting feelings of anxiety and doom.*
>
> *Colin Ellard (p. 83)*[25]

(2) The extrapolation from focused, highly controlled measures to more general claims are often made without any caveats. For example, the argument that clinical biosensors are indicators of stress is generalised to suggest that the forms of architecture considered in studies using these measures could carry significance for the long-term health of building occupants. But typically, there are no indication of the power of the results, or even the statistical 'significance' levels of the effects claimed.[26]

(3) The studies typically have very short exposure. Does any form of adaptation to the stimulus need to be considered when commenting on long-term effects?

These neuroscience emphases lead to the bizarre claims that the physiological measurements validate the subjective experiences. Such a focus ignores the fact that every aspect of human activity and experience inevitably has some neurophysiological correlates. However, the meanings of such 'objective' measures require an understanding of the setting. That, in turn, has to draw on the particular understanding of that context by the person being measured. Increased heart rate can be generated by fear or excitement, or physical exercise. The person's account of their experience is no less valid than a neurological measurement. It is certainly likely to be more revealing of what is actually being experienced.

In a recent clear review of such studies, the claim is that 'bioethics' are being investigated that have ethical implications.[27] The strong claims for this research, also published in a shorter review in the highly regarded *British Medical Journal*[28] raise concerns. There can be no doubt that dilapidated housing conditions, with insanitary facilities, mould and overcrowding can cause distress and related medical problems. It is also therefore important to draw attention to the responsibilities of those who produce these building. Indeed, throughout developed countries building regulations exist to outlaw the creation of such conditions.

However, the claims are being made, from neuroarchitecture studies that clinical biomarkers responses to details of building form have to be considered in the same way.

A cause for concern

The criticisms of the theoretical, methodological, and measurement emphases that characterise a growing number of studies of the psychology of place are not merely an academic squabble.

They are dangerous for a number of reasons. The reduction of human beings to mere organisms ignores the great mixture of social, political, and psychological process that are part of the experiences of Places. That is the way to a totalitarian belief in the management of people.

The claim of being highly 'objective' by using biomedical assessments in highly controlled experimental conditions can mislead architects and others, who do not understand the profound weaknesses and fatal flaws in this research. Without that understanding the results can be utilised in ignorance. It will be believed that local, social, or personal reactions to proposed developments are unnecessary. The results of these scientific experiments are enough to influence what should be produced. The profound consequence of this will be lost. The real ways in which the Psychology of Place operates, with all its nuances, sensitivity to individual differences, cultural and social influences will be ignored.

Most crucially the absolutely fundamental basis of democracy and the rule of law is being sidelined by these determinist studies. That is people making their own decisions by drawing on all their information and experiences – their subjectivity.

References and endnotes

1 Schoenberg, A. (1983) *Theory of harmony*. Oakland, CA: University of California Press.
2 Tallis, R. (2016) *Aping mankind: Neuromania, Darwinitis and the misrepresentation of humanity*, London: Routledge.
3 Tallis, R. (2016) *Aping mankind*, United Kingdom: Taylor & Francis.
4 Dewey, J, (1931) *Philosophy and civilisation*, New Rochelle: Knickerbocker Press.
5 Fromm, E. (1973) *The anatomy of human destructiveness*, London: Random House, p. 366.
6 Wilson, E. O. (1986) *Biophilia*. Cambridge, MA: Harvard University Press.
7 Ilardo, M. A., Moltke, I., Korneliussen, T. S., Cheng, J., Stern, A. J., Racimo, F., ... & Willerslev, E. (2018) Physiological and genetic adaptations to diving in sea nomads. *Cell*, 173(3), 569–580.
8 Roebroeks, W. (2001) Hominid behaviour and the earliest occupation of Europe: An exploration. *Journal of Human Evolution*, 41(5), 437–461.
9 Cooper, C. F. (1961). The ecology of fire. *Scientific American*, *204*(4), 150–163.
10 Laland, K., Matthews, B., & Feldman, M. W. (2016). An introduction to niche construction theory. *Evolutionary Ecology*, *30*, 191–202.

11 A recent critique of Biophilia is given in Joye, Y. & De Block, A. (2025). Our not-so-natural connection to nature. *Trends in Ecology & Evolution*, 320–322.
12 The study I carried out many years ago, demonstrated how different reactions are to familiar places compared with reactions to pictures of place: Scott, M. & Canter, D. (1997) Picture or place? A multiple sorting study of landscape. *Journal of Environmental Psychology*, 17(4), 263–281, https://doi.org/10.1006/jevp.1997.0068.
13 Rozeboom, W. W. (2016) Good science is abductive, not hypothetico-deductive, in *L.L. Harlow, A.Stanley, Mulaik &, J. H. Steiger (eds.)What if there were no significance tests?* New York: Routledge, pp. 349–400. *https://doi.org/10.4324/9781315629049.*
14 Sprenger, J. (2011) Hypothetico-deductive confirmation. *Philosophy Compass*, 6(7), 497–508.
15 Cowger, C. D. (1984) Statistical significance tests: Scientific ritualism or scientific method?. *Social Service Review*, 58(3), 358–372.
16 Guttman, L. (1977) What is not what in statistics. *Journal of the Royal Statistical Society. Series D (The Statistician)*, 26(2), 81–107.
17 Haack, S. (2012) Six signs of scientism. *Logos & Episteme*, 3(1), 75–95.
18 A typical example is this study that tells us virtually nothing about the culture of Himba semi-nomadic children being studied published by Bremner, A. J., Doherty, M. J., Caparos, S., De Fockert, J., Linnell, K. J., & Davidoff, J. (2016) Effects of culture and the urban environment on the development of the Ebbinghaus illusion. *Child Development*, 87(3), 962–981. I can find no comment on the children's reactions to being asked, via an interpreter, to respond to questions about the size of circles on a laptop screen in a shaded tent.
19 Corballis, M. C. (2014) Left brain, right brain: Facts and fantasies. *PLoS Biology*, 12(1), e1001767.
20 Li, Z., Huang, X., & White, M. (2022) Effects of the visual character of transitional spaces on human stress recovery in a virtual reality environment. *International Journal of Environmental Research and Public Health*, 19(20), 13143, https://doi.org/10.3390/ijerph192013143
21 The weaknesses of this determinist approach were already being expounded in the first Architectural Psychology conference outside of the U.S. as brought together in Canter, D. (1970) *Architectural psychology: Proceedings of the Dalandhui Conference March 1969.* Re-issued 2026, available from dvcanter@btinternet.com
22 My introduction to a special issue on 'Biologising the Social Sciences' which brings together a range of critiques is Canter, D. (2014) Contemporary social science also in D. Canter and D. Turner (Eds.) published as a book *Biologising the social sciences: Challenging Darwinian and neuroscience explanations*, London: Routledge.
23 Another appropriate neologism offered by Tallis, R. (2016) *Aping mankind*, United Kingdom: Taylor & Francis.
24 I was struck by an example of this when I used my new smart watch to measure my stress level. Although it was measuring variations in my heart rate it still asked me ten questions about how I was dealing with daily challenges. I guess the answer to these were used more than the physiological measures to say my stress level was 'normal'.
25 Ellard, C. (2015) *Places of the Heart: The psychogeography of everyday life*, New York: Belleview Literary Press.
26 A typical such study is Kim, J. & Kim, N. (2022) Quantifying emotions in architectural environments using biometrics. *Applied Sciences*, 12(19), 9998.
27 Valentine, C. & Mitcheltree, H. (2024) Architecture and bioethics: Investigating the ethical implications of recent advances in the field of neuroarchitecture. *Intelligent Buildings International*, 1–7, https://doi.org/10.1080/17508975.2024.2407319
28 Valentine. (2024) Architecture and public health: From harmful designs to healthy built environments. *British Medical Journal*, 387 (December), q2773, https://doi.org/10.1136/bmj.q2773

Selected bibliography of books relevant to the psychology of place

There are a great many books relevant to The Psychology of Place, as well as thousands of publications in journals. I've only been able to draw on a fraction of them for the present volume, leaving out many of great value, for lack of space and to reduce the complexity of my arguments,. This bibliography therefore provides a selected list for further study.

Copies of most of these books are available in *Professor Canter's Environmental Psychology Collection* within The Historical Repository for Environmental Psychology at Vancouver Island University, Nanaimo, BC, Canada. At the University of Huddersfield, UK, there is also a Personal Archive and Library of Professor David Canter. The Library section of the collection contains works on the discipline of environmental and investigative psychology, collected by Professor David Canter and deposited with the University in 2011.

Exploring concepts and meanings of Place are a number of books drawing on many different disciplines and writing traditions. The following are engaging reading as well as full of insights.

- Augé, M. (2008) *Non-places: An introduction to Supermodernity.* Verso.
- Blythe, R. (1981) *Places: An anthology of Britain,* Oxford University Press.
- Casey, E. S. (2009) *Getting back into place: Toward a renewed understanding of the place-world* (2nd ed.), Indiana University Press.
- Castello, L. (2016) *Rethinking the meaning of place: Conceiving place in architecture-urbanism*, Routledge.
- Cresswell, T. (2015) *Place: An introduction* (2nd ed.), Wiley Blackwell.
- Dovey, K. (2009) *Becoming places: Urbanism/Architecture/Identity/Power,* Routledge.
- Ellard, C. (2015) *Places of the heart: The psychogeography of everyday life,* Belleview Literary Press.
- Edensor, T., Kalandides, A., & Kothari, U. (Eds.). (2020) *The Routledge handbook of place*, Routledge.

- Freestone, R. & Liu, E. (Eds.). (2016) *Place and placelessness revisited*, New York: Routledge.
- Hunt, J. D. (2022) *Genius loci: An essay on the meaning of place*, Reaktion Books.
- Lindstrom, R. S. (2024) *An architecture of place: Topology in practice*, Routledge.
- Malpas, J. (2018) *Place and experience: A philosophical topology*, Routledge.
- Owens, S. (2020) *Spirit of place: Artists, writers & the British landscape*, Thames and Hudson.
- Raymond, C. M., Manzo, L. C., Williams, D. R., Di Masso, A., & von Wirth, T. (Eds.) (2021) *Changing senses of place: Navigating global challenges*, Cambridge University Press.
- Steele, F. (1981) *The sense of place*, Boston: CBI Publishing Company.

Phenomenological ways of exploring places exist in many different guises. These are some key sources.

- Bachelard, G. (2014) *The poetics of space*, Penguin.
- Coverley, M. (2018) *Psychogeography*, Oldcastle Books.
- Kunstler, J. H. (2003) *The city in mind: Notes on the urban condition*, Simon and Schuster.
- Seamon, D. (2018) *Life takes place: Phenomenology, lifeworlds, and place making*, Routledge.
- The *Environmental and Architectural Phenomenology* newsletter is freely available at
  - https://ksu.academia.edu/DavidSeamon
  - http://newprairiepress.org/eap/
  - http://krex.k-state.edu/dspace/handle/2097/1522 (archive copies)

These edited volumes bringing together publications on **Place Attachment**, are all a very useful source of research. The newer ones add to previous studies rather than replacing them.

- Altman, I. & Low, S. M. (1992) *Place attachment*, New York: Plenum Press.
- Manzo, L. C. & Devine-Wright, P. (Eds.) (2014) *Place attachment: Advances in theory, methods and applications*, London: Routledge.
- Smith, J. (2018) *Explorations in place attachment*, London: Routledge.
- Kopec, D. & Bliss, A. (Eds.) (2020) *Place meaning and attachment: Authenticity, heritage and preservation*, London: Routledge.
- Manzo, L. C. & Devine-Wright, P. (Eds.) (2021) *Place attachment: Advances in theory, methods and applications* (2nd ed.), London: Routledge.

General Books that Review **Environmental Psychology** often with an uncritical determinist perspective.

- Bernheimer, L. (2017) *The shaping of us*, Little, Brown.
- Donald, I. (2022) *Environmental and architectural psychology: The basics*, Routledge.

- Gallagher, W. (1993) *The power of place: How our surroundings shape our thoughts, emotions and actions*, Poseidon Press.
- Gifford, R. (2007) *Environmental psychology: Principles and practice*, Allyn and Bacon.
- Goldhagen, S. W. (2017) *Welcome to your world*, HarperCollins.

Methodologies for Studying Places and experience of them are covered in a number of books.

- Gifford, R. (Ed.) (2016) *Research methods for environmental psychology*, Wiley Blackwell.
- Groat, L. N. & Wang, D. (2013) *Architectural research methods*, John Wiley & Sons.
- Michelson, W. (Ed.) (1975) *Behavioral research methods in environmental design*, Dowden, Hutchinson & Ross.

The popular literature on aspect of nature and the environment is legion. Here are some I have found well worth reading.

- Bate, J. (2000) *The song of the earth*, Picador.
- Blythe, R. (Ed.) (1981) *Places, an anthology of Britain*, Oxford University Press.
- Louv, R. (2010) *The last child in the woods: Saving out children from nature-deficit disorder*, Atlantic Books.
- Maddicott, A. (2024) *Tender maps: Travels in search of the emotions of place*, September Publishing.
- Speight, E. (n.d.) *Practising place: Creative and critical reflections on place*, Art Editions North. ISBN 978190683233

Acknowledgements

The writing of much of this book was started during the COVID pandemic, when people were stuck in place. For academics and other scholars, as well as many businesspeople, this meant their home became their place of work. Their keyboard and computer screen were a major mode of access to colleagues and libraries, meetings and discussions. Despite the tragedies of the pandemic and the struggles to cope with it, one consequence of the retreat to the domestic desk was that for many of us it felt as if we were all in one big international workplace. My writing this book benefitted enormously from that. Colleagues past and present, all over the world, responded quickly to any requests for help or comments on what I was writing. That continued long after the pandemic had waned. I am deeply grateful for all their assistance. Of course, any confusions, mistakes, or wrongheadedness is entirely my fault.

I've tried to remember the names of everyone who helped me over the few years it took me to write this book. My deepest apologies to anyone who may have inadvertently been left off the following indications of my gratitude.

I am grateful for the through and patient way Mary Rose MacLachlan took on the task of finding usable photographs and dealing with the permissions so essential in the current copyright environment.

It was fun to make contact again with Nick Higginbotham after half a century. His willingness to engage with me again is greatly appreciated.

I am indebted for general support, guidance, and helpful comments (in no particular order) to Marie Houghton, David Rowlands, Donna Youngs, Ann Hewitt, Cleo Valentine, Lauren Griffen, David Seamon, Marta Saniewska, Rhona Byrne, Clare Cooper Marcus, Kaeko Yokota, Patrick Devine-Wright, Denis Wood, and Simon Ungar. They have all unflinchingly given their time and insights. The book would have been much less worthy without their assistance.

It is misleading to mention others, whose help possibly has been more focused on particular chapters or tasks, if that is taken to imply their assistance is more or less significant than those listed above.

However, I would like to mention David Stea for his friendship and guidance over many years. John Peponis, a gifted architect and promulgater of space syntax, has provided detailed commentary on a number of crucial aspects of the book. In contrast to David, and John, who both qualify as old-timers, Yannick Joye is a young blood making important waves in his scholarly contributions. He has provided invaluable in-depth guidance on fascinating aspects of the study of landscapes.

Reid Bishop is one of my students who became a friend and colleague in recent years. He has been a masterly commentator on everything from this book he has read.

Rosie Jacobs, who I am proud to identify as my granddaughter, did a Stirling job of sorting out many of the technicalities inherent in creating a book overflowing with illustrations.

This book is dedicated to my wife Sandra Canter, her comments on draft chapters were always helpful. More importantly, over the more than 60 years that we have been together she has made the world a better Place to live in, for me, our family, and many others.

Acknowledgement is due to the following for permission to reproduce photographs and illustrations:

Chapter 1: Figure 1.4 Courtesy of Het Arresthuis. Photo by David Canter; Figure 1.5 © Pix569 | Dreamstime.com

Chapter 2: Figure 2.1 NASA; Figure 2.4 Lee Earle/Shutterstock

Section 2: Drawn by Mikko

Chapter 6: Figure 6.3 Courtesy of David Canter by permission of the photographer; Figure 6.9 By 663highland – Own work, CC BY 2.5, https://commons.wikimedia.org/w/index.php?curid=4436506; Figure 6.10 BScar23625 – Flickr/CC0 1.0; Figure 6.12 richard sowersby/Alamy Stock Photo; Figure 6.13 Architect: Sou Fujimoto. Photo by Forgemind ArchiMedia/CC BY 2.0./https://creativecommons.org/licenses/by/2.0/

Chapter 7: Figure 7.1 GillyBerlin via Wikimedia, CC BY 2.0; Figure 7.2 Tognopop via Wikimedia Commons; Figure 7.3 Carol M. Highsmith/Library of Congress; Figure 7.4 Francisco Anzola, Wikimedia, CC BY 3.0; Figure 7.6 Courtesy of Reid Bishop; Figure 7.7 © Olegmit | Dreamstime.com

Chapter 9: Figure 9.4 and Figure 9.6 Peponis, J. & Hedin, J. (1982) *The layout of theories in the natural history museum*, 9H, 3, pp. 12–25. By permission of Peonis and Hedin; Figure 9.9 National Park Service, U.S. Department of the Interior; Figure 9.10 © Hassocks5489/CC0; Figure 9.11 Tom Fisk/Pexels; Figure 9.12b © Studioclever | Dreamstime.com; Figure 9.13 Contains Parliamentary information licensed under the Open Parliament Licence v3.0.; Figure 9.14 David Henry/Pexels; Figure 9.15 © Evgeny Kosharsky | Dreamstime.com; Figure 9.16 © Isabel Poulin | Dreamstime.com; Figure 9.17 Michael D Beckwith, this file is made available under the Creative Commons CC0 1.0 Universal Public Domain Dedication

Chapter 10: Figure 10.1 Robert Levine/Wikimedia CC0; Figure 10.2 Lance Cpl. Quinn Hurt/U.S. Department of War; Figure 10.3 Photo from Marta Saniewska; Figure 10.4 ideabug/iStock; Figure 10.5 With permission from Caral and Ben and the photographer Kate Swerdlow kate@kateswerdlowphotography.com; Figure 10.6 Des Green/iStock; Figure 10.7 Photo by Toohool. Bicycle Wheel, by Marcel Duchamp. Reproduction created in 1951, displayed at the Philadelphia Museum of Art.; Figure 10.8 © York Archaeology; Figure 10.9 and Figure 10.10 Rhona Byrne; Figure 10.11 Cairn (Andy Goldworthy 1997) Photo by Gail Leenstra,

CC BY-SA 3.0; Figure 10.12 The Nature Box, CC BY 4.0; Figure 10.13a Released into the public domain by author Ceoil; Figure 10.13b Patraick A. Mackie

Chapter 11: Figure 11.1 MiNe/Wikimedia/CC BY 2.0; Figure 11.2 Deni Williams/ Shutterstock; Figure 11.4 Tom Bastin via Flickr/CC BY 2.0; Figure 11.5 Tim Sheerman-Chase via Flickr, http://www.sheerman-chase.org.uk//CC BY 2.0; Figure 11.6a Amjad Sheikh/Wikimedia/CC BY-SA 4.0; Figure 11.6b © Santiago Calatrava, Study for the sculpture Turning Torso, 1995. Pencil on paper

Chapter 12: Figure 12.2 U.S. Department of Housing and Urban Development Office of Policy Development and Research; Figure 12.3 Matgrt, Wikimedia, CC BY 4.0; Figure 12.4 David Kasparek, via Flickr/CC BY 2.0; Figure 12.5 Courtesy of Wiliam Wood; Figure 12.6 Photography Robert Lemermeyer, Courtesy of the Art Gallery of Alberta; Figure 12.7 Photographer unknown, Courtesy of the Art Gallery of Alberta; Figure 12.8a Paste. This work has been released into the public domain by its author; Figure 12.8b Marc Cluet/Wikimedia Commons/CC BY 2.0; Figure 12.8c Colin/Wikimedia Commons/CC BY-SA-4.0; Figure 12.9 PookieFugglestein/ Wikimedia/CC0; Figure 12.11 From Palliser's New Cottage Homes and Details from the 1880s, published by Dap Capo Press (1975)

Chapter 13: Figure 13.2 Dierdre Boys/Unsplash; Figure 13.6 Servalenthusiast/ Wikimedia/CC BY-SA 4.0, Figure 13.7 © 2025 My Guide. All rights reserved; Figure 13.9a and 13.9b Art by Ben Wilson. Photo by David Canter; Figure 13.11 PA Images/Alamy Stock Photo; Figure 13.12 Guy Bell/Alamy Live News; Figure 13.14 Stockete/Shutterstock; Figure 13.15 Courtesy of Le Mirador Resort & Spa

Chapter 14: Figure 14.1, Figure 14.2, Figure 14.3 Courtesy of David Canter with permission; Figure 14.7 Photo by Wayne Thom

Chapter 15: Figure 15.1 King of Hearts/Wikimedia/CC BY-SA 4.0

Chapter 16: Figure 16.2 Henri Rousseau (1844–1910), Eve in the Garden of Eden, oil on canvas, Pola Museum of Art. Public domain; Figure 16.3 Memory Catcher/Pixabay; Figure 16.4 Jean Aernoudts via Wikimedia/CC BY-SA 3.0, https://commons.wikimedia.org/w/index.php?curid=1165380; Figure 16.6 Luk/Wikimedia/CC BY 4.0

Chapter 17: Figure 17.1 McMahan, E. A., Cloud, J. M., Josh, P., & Scott, M. (2016). Nature with a human touch: Human-induced alteration negatively impacts perceived naturalness and preferences for natural environments. *Ecopsychology*, 8(1), 54–63. Reproduced with permission; Figure 17.2 Everett Collection Inc/Alamy Stock Photo; Figure 17.7 Rott70/iStockphoto

Chapter 18: Figure 18.2 © Photo by Claire Deeney, Journeys in Nature, 2022; Figure 18.3 Permission granted by photographer

Chapter 19: Figure 19.1 Image courtesy NASA Johnson Space Center Gateway to Astronaut Photography of Earth; Figure 19.2, Figure 19.3, Figure 19.4, Figure 19.5, Figure 19.6 Dennis Gilbert; Figure 19.8 From The surprising stickiness of the "15-minute city", World Economic Forum, March 15, 2022

Appendix: Figure 21.1 Li, Z., Huang, X., & White, M. (2022) Effects of the visual character of transitional spaces on human stress recovery in a virtual reality environment. *International Journal of Environmental Research and Public Health*, 19(20), 13143, https://doi.org/10.3390/ijerph192013143.

All other figures photographed by, created by, or courtesy of the author.

Index

Note: *Italicized* and **bold** pages refer to figures and tables, respectively; and page numbers followed by "n" refer to notes.

For Product Safety Concerns and Information please contact our EU representative GPSR@taylorandfrancis.com Taylor & Francis Verlag GmbH, Kaufingerstraße 24, 80331 München, Germany